DATE DUE

JUN 17 '81	APR 21 '89		
OCT 21 '81	MAR 15 '90		
APR 18 1975	MAR 29 '90		
FEB 7 1985	APR 9 '91		
MAR 12 1985	MAR 2 1994		
	APR 14 1994		
APR 12 1985			
APR 27 1985	DEC 22 1994		
OCT 24 1985	APR 24 1995		
	OCT 17 1995		
FEB 5 1986			
OCT 3 1 1986			
NOV 24 1986			
MAY 22 1987			
JAN 4 1988			
MAR 17 1988			
MAY 10 1988			
NOV 13 1988			

DEMCO 38-297

Interviewing
*strategy, techniques,
and tactics*

THE DORSEY SERIES IN SOCIOLOGY
Editor   ROBIN M. WILLIAMS, JR.
Cornell University

Interviewing

Strategy, techniques, and tactics

RAYMOND L. GORDEN, Ph.D.

Professor in Cross-Cultural Research
Department of Sociology-Anthropology
Antioch College

1975

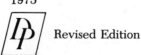 Revised Edition

The Dorsey Press *Homewood, Illinois 60430*

Irwin-Dorsey Limited   Georgetown, Ontario   L7G 4B3

Revised Edition

First Printing, January 1975
Second Printing, June 1975
Third Printing, January 1976
Fourth Printing, August 1977

ISBN 0-256-01511-2
Library of Congress Catalog Card No. 74–18712
Printed in the United States of America

To Charlotte, Gregory, and Karen

Preface

The treatment of interviewing in this Revised Edition should be helpful to research directors, to supervisors and trainers of interviewers, and to a wide variety of interviewers. I consider as an interviewer any person who uses conversation as a means of obtaining information from another person. Often great skill is needed by people who do not carry the title of interviewer because interviewing is the means rather than the end of their function. These *auxiliary interviewers* include teachers, nurses, doctors, clergymen, lawyers, social workers, law enforcement officers, and management personnel in business, industry, and government. The ideas presented here should assist this group as well as the more *specialized interviewers* engaged in research projects, community studies, and opinion polling or the more applied areas of social work and counseling insofar as the emphasis is upon information-gathering rather than therapy.

The first three chapters of Part I present an overview of interviewing in terms of who uses interviewing, how it is related to other basic methods of information gathering, and how the basic styles of interviewing are related to different general objectives. The four chapters in Part II present a frame of reference viewing the interview as a communication dyad in the context of the larger society. The inhibitors and facilitators of the flow of relevant information in the interview depend upon the triadic relationship between the respondent, the interviewer, and the information sought. These relationships are not hermetically sealed within the interview situation, but take their meaning from the larger social context.

The tools of interviewing are viewed as ways of minimizing the inhibitors and maximizing the facilitators of communication. The tools are divided into *strategies,* dealt with in the six chapters of Part III, *techniques,* elaborated in the two chapters of Part IV, and *tactics,* described in the three chapters of Part V. The final Part VI presents the method of developing the basic skills needed in the performance of an interview.

To put philosophy into practice this book provides a series of 14 laboratory problems providing the experiential component at strategic points in the book. Laboratory Problem 1 immediately launches the learner into a rather complex critique of the interaction in the transcription of a real interview in order to sensitize him to some of the basic problems in interviewing. The next 12 laboratory problems begin by breaking down the problems and tools of interviewing into simpler components, then become progressively more complex. The final laboratory problem is actually a field assignment to plan, do, and analyze three tape-recorded interviews on the same topic. This final assignment provides a learning paradigm for the student to follow independently in the future to become an excellent interviewer, supervisor, or trainer of interviewers.

I gratefully acknowledge the inspiration, help and encouragement given along the way by John W. Bennet, Everett C. Hughes, David Riesman, Everett Wilson, and Stephen A. Richardson who influenced the basic framework laid down in the first edition. Also, Lawrence Atherton has my thanks for his help with the visual conceptualizers and the concepts they communicate in the second edition. I am particularly indebted to my wife, Charlotte Gilson Gorden who untangled some of the stylistic peculiarities, read proof, and supervised the production of the final draft of the manuscript for both editions.

Among the groups of persons who have had a vital place in my experiences leading to the writing and revision of this book should be mentioned the Disaster Study Team at the National Opinion Research Center; the interviewers on the Youth Study Project and the Social Cohesion Study in Dayton, Ohio; the Colombian interviewers on the Cross-Cultural Communication Project in Bogota, financed by the U.S. Office of Education; the management interviewers of the Illinois Bell Telephone Company and the Toledo Edison Company, the trainees of the Michigan State Nursing Association; and the interviewing crews on several opinion and attitude surveys. Most important have been the students at Antioch College, who over a period of years showed keen interest in learning to interview and in applying their skills in their work-study program jobs. They have helped to develop materials and to demonstrate the effectiveness of a broad systematic approach to interviewer training.

December 1974   R. L. G.

Contents

part one
An overview

1. The uses of interviewing   3

Trends in interviewing. Reliability and validity: *Reliability. Validity.* Illustrative interviewing problems.

Laboratory problem 1: Critique of telephone company interview, 22

2. Interviewing in perspective   32

Interviewing related to other methods: *Personal documents. Participant-observation. Unobtrusive measures. Relative value of methods. Triangulation. Empathy.* Interviewing compared with ordinary conversation: *Expression. Persuasion. Therapy. Ritual. Information.*

3. Styles and objectives of interviewing   58

Dimensions of interviewing style: *Scheduled and nonscheduled interviews. Topic control.* Basic objectives of interviewing: *Discovery objectives. Measurement objectives. Use of an interview guide.* Interview versus questionnaire: *Advantages of the interview. Advantages of the questionnaire. Combined use of the interview and questionnaire.* Summary.

part two
The interview as communication
in society

4. The social context of the interview   85

A contextual model. Implications of the model. Objectives, tasks, and problems of communication: *Objectives of the interviewer. Tasks of the interviewer.* Problems of communication.

Laboratory problem 2: Universe of discourse in White County, Arkansas, 102

5. Inhibitors of communication   104

Linking theory and practice. Recognizing effects of inhibitors. Inhibitors: *Competing demands for time. Ego threat. Etiquette. Trauma. Forgetting. Chronological confusion. Inferential confusion. Unconscious behavior.*

Laboratory problem 3: Detecting potential inhibitors, 121

6. Facilitators of communication   123

The facilitators: *Fulfilling expectations. Recognition. Altruistic appeals. Sympathetic understanding. New experience. Catharsis. The need for meaning. Extrinsic rewards.*

Laboratory problem 4: Detecting potential facilitators, 136

7. Ethics of interviewing   138

What is ethics? Interviewer ethics as conflicting loyalties. Responsibilities to the larger society: *Suppression of findings. Intentional bias in data collection. Intentional bias in interpretation.* Responsibilities to the research organization: *Always follow the sampling instructions. Do not fictionalize responses. Probe fully where needed. Do not bias responses. Report possible invalidities in the interview schedule.* Responsibilities to the respondent: *Gaining access to the respondent. Voluntary participation. Do not harm the respondent. Anonymity and confidentiality. Help the respondent, if possible. Do not deceive the respondents. Share the results with the respondents.* Ethics and hypocrisy.

part three
Strategy of interviewing

8. General strategy   177

Assumptions underlying the treatment of strategy. Contrasting types of field situations: *Friendly versus hostile territory. Open versus closed communities. Single versus multiple contacts.* General types of respondents: *Key informants. Special respondents. Representative respondents. Uses of kinds of respondents.* Steps in field strategy: *Locating and contacting representative and special respondents. Securing the cooperation of key informants.*

9. Selecting appropriate respondents   196

Who has the relevant information? *High-low status. Active-passive types. Insider-outsider types. Mobile-stable types. Who is accessible? Who is willing to give relevant information? Who is most able to give the information?*

Laboratory problem 5: Selecting appropriate respondent, 211

10. **Selecting appropriate interviewers**   213

Selecting the person: *Overt characteristics of the interviewer. Basic personality traits of the interviewer. Attitudes of the interviewer. Special knowledge possessed by the interviewer.* Selecting the appropriate interviewer role: *The nature of role-taking. Functions of the auxiliary role. Dimensions of role relationships. The central role of the interviewer.*

Laboratory problem 6: Selecting appropriate interviewer, 246

11. **Time and place of the interview**   248

Some effects of place: *Minimizing inhibitors. Maximizing facilitators.* Some effects of time.

Laboratory problem 7: Strategy problems of time and place, 261

12. **Structuring the interview situation**   263

Defining the interview situation: *Interviewer's introduction. Sponsorship. Explaining the purpose of the interview. Explaining the selection of the respondent. Providing anonymity.* Recording the interview: *Note-taking on informal interviews. Note-taking on structured interviews. Tape-recording the interview. Transcribing tape-recorded information.* Planning the opening question.

Laboratory problem 8: Field strategy in hostile territory, 283

13. **Sample surveys**   291

Basic types of sample surveys: *Sampling element. Cross-sectional versus longitudinal surveys. Approximating longitudinal surveys.* Basic sampling strategies: *Simple random sampling. Systematic sampling. Multistage sampling. Stratified sampling.* Survey mode: *The mailed questionnaire. The personally administered questionnaire. Telephone or face-to-face.* Gaining access to the respondent. Format of the interview schedule or questionnaire: *Body of the interview schedule. Some suggestions for good format for interview schedules.*

part four
Techniques in interviewing

14. **Verbal forms used by the interviewer**   333

Contexts aimed at communicating the question. Contexts aimed at motivating the respondent. Selecting appropriate vocabulary. Delimiting the scope of the question: *Dimensions of scope. Values of broad questions. Values of narrow questions. Structuring the answer.* Using leading questions: *Forms of leading. Effects of leading questions.*

Laboratory problem 9: Verbal techniques in studying parent-child conflicts, 367

15. Nonverbal techniques   370

Modes of nonverbal communication: *Prozemics. Chronemics. Kinesics. Paralinguistics.* Foci of nonverbal techniques: *Silence as a technique. Attitudes as foci of nonverbal communication. Attitudes toward the interviewing task. Attitudes toward the information received. Attitudes toward the respondent as a person.*

Laboratory problem 10: Recognizing techniques (vocational choice interview), 394

part five
Tactics of interviewing

16. Advance planning of tactics   401

Arranging topics and subtopics within an interview: *Chronological order of topics and subtopics. Introducing each topic. Preparing an interview guide.* General patterns of questions for developing a topic: *The funnel sequence. The inverted funnel sequence.*

17. Probing to meet informational objectives   422

Probing versus other tactics. Topic control: *Types of topic control. Using topic control.* Taking probe notes.

Laboratory problem 11: Recognizing forms of probing (vocational choice), 443

18. Dealing with symptoms of resistance   445

Specific countertactics: *"I'm too busy now!" "I don't know anything about that!" "I don't want to be on tape!" "Why are you taking notes?" "I don't remember, I don't know!" "What do you think about that?" "What do you mean by that?" Dealing with falsification.* The informal post-interview.

part six
Developing skills in interviewing

19. Focal skills in interviewing   463

Interviewing performance cycle. The focal skills: *Accurately receiving information. Critically evaluating the information. Appropriately regu-*

lating the interviewer's behavior. A procedure for improving interviewing skills: *Preparing for the interview. Doing the interview for self-improvement. Analysis of the interview for self-improvement.*

Laboratory problem 12: An interview critique (car-buyer motivation study), 487

20. Two data-gathering problems   **498**

Laboratory problem 13: The layman's conception of science, 499
Laboratory problem 14: Images and feelings on the American way of life, 508

Epilogue   **516**

Aims and assumptions. Review of concepts and tools: *Interviewing as maximizing communication. Strategies of interviewing. Techniques in interviewing. Interviewing tactics. Developing skills in interviewing.* Subjective aspects of learning to interview.

Appendix A. Sharing the consultants' experiences   **531**

Appendix B. One strategy account   **551**

Appendix C. Highlights of information collected   **558**

Bibliography   **560**

Index   **581**

part one

An overview

1

The uses
of interviewing

The demand for scientific approaches to human problems is growing rapidly. This demand results from the accelerating rate of social change coupled with the growing acceptance and success of applying the basic canons of scientific method to studies of human behavior.

This growing demand is reflected in more rigorous methodology. The cry "How do you know?" frequently enters discussions of both pure and applied studies of human behavior. In many studies this question is so central to the purpose and so uppermost in the consciousness of the investigators that no one need utter it aloud.

TRENDS IN INTERVIEWING

Accompanying this increasing consciousness of the need for greater validity and reliability in methodology is an increase in the methodological difficulty intrinsic to the types of problems being posed. For example, social anthropology has seen a shift from the description of external environment, artifacts, and behavioral patterns to analysis of the subjective meaning of these for the members of the culture. Thus there has been increasing emphasis on values, worldview, beliefs, expectations, and socialization of the child.

In social psychology there has been a gradual shift in empirical studies from observation of external forms of behavior, where high reliability is relatively easy to obtain, to more theoretically meaningful categories of human phenomena that tend to have greater predictive value but which present more difficult problems of data gathering.[1]

---

[1] For example see Roger W. Heyns and Ronald Lippitt, "Systematic Observation Techniques," in *Handbook of Social Psychology*, vol. 1, ed. Gardner Lindzey (Cambridge, Mass.: Addison-Wesley Publishing Co., 1954).

In sociology there has been an increasing shift of emphasis from the use of easily observable facts such as sex, race, and residential location to more meaningful but less obvious categories such as social distance, expectations, cognitive dissonance, attitude, definition of the situation, latent and operative values, channels of influence and decision making. There has also been a historical shift in emphasis from static descriptions of public opinion or social class, for example, to the more dynamic problems of the formation and function of public opinion and social stratification systems. There has also been a historical shift away from reliance on the use of data already collected for some official or practical purpose toward the collection of information more directly relevant to the theoretical or practical requirements of the specific problem at hand. These general trends in the basic behavioral sciences of social anthropology, social psychology, and sociology are reflected in trends which follow in applied areas such as industrial relations, race relations, family relations, mental health, and education.

This increasing demand for methodological sophistication has two complementary facets. First is the data-analysis aspect which includes research design, theoretical models, sampling, statistical methods and electronic data processing. Although this phase of the answer to "How do you know?" is vital, it cannot be emphasized to the exclusion of the second aspect which concerns data-gathering methodology.

It is clear that no amount of refinement in data analysis can counteract the effects of faulty data-collection methods that provide raw information which is false, distorted, or incomplete. Nevertheless, there is still a tendency for the advances in data-gathering methodology to lag behind those in data analysis. This can be seen in the content of contemporary examinations on methodology for the doctorate degree in anthropology, sociology, and psychology; these are mainly devoted to methods of analysis rather than collection of data. This same imbalance is seen in the title of the papers presented in the methodology section of professional meetings of social scientists.

Considerable effort has been made over the past two decades to improve data-gathering methods. There have been substantial advances in knowledge about interviewing based upon experimental studies. However, much of this has not yet been integrated into a general theoretical framework, nor has it been put into a form to be translated into applied skills in interviewing. Thus, along with the steady growth in the use of interviewing and the increased knowledge about the interviewing process, there appears to be a widening gap between what is known and what is applied in interviewing.

The writer's experience in consulting on data-gathering problems and in training interviewers has suggested several obstacles to closing this gap. First, there is an unfortunate tendency to consider data gathering as a lower status activity than data analysis or theorizing about the data. Second, large research organizations or consultants often discover that there is a demand for pseudoscientific "findings" that a client needs either to justify decisions already made or to transfer the blame for a decision to the "independent research organization." In either case, there is no need for data-gathering methods which probe deeply into social reality.

Another barrier to the actual application of the best data-gathering methods is the fact that it often costs more in time or money to collect valid data than it does to collect invalid data. Of course, this is a false economy if any real decisions are to be based on the data. This conflict between the realities of collecting valid information and the demands of economy can result in irrational behavior by otherwise intelligent people. For example, the writer was asked to design a study of certain aspects of a community to help decide future directions of the local public school system. An interesting dilemma developed when the consultant was told that the valid but more time-consuming methods could not be used because "the information must be in the hands of the Citizens' Committee on Curriculum and Physical Plant before February 15 so they can use it to make some important decisions before the meeting of the Finance Committee in March." In essence, the argument was that since the information was so vitally important, they had no time to be concerned with its accuracy.

A third and perhaps the most significant factor contributing to this lag between what is known and what is applied in interviewing is the shortage of qualified interviewers. Often a research organization or project is aware that the methods they are using are not the most desirable, but they are the best second choice in view of the short supply of well-trained interviewers. If an organization were to devote its energies to convincing the client of the values of high quality interviewing, they might then only be embarrassed by not being able to find qualified personnel to do the interviewing or to train others to do it well.

This shortage of skilled interviewers is felt not only by research organizations hiring specialized interviewers, but also by institutions whose employees need interviewing as an auxiliary skill. It is impossible to estimate the social cost of ineffective interviewing when important decisions in practically all types of institutions depend at some point upon one human being obtaining valid information from another.

RELIABILITY AND VALIDITY

The central aim of any data-gathering methodology is to improve both the reliability and validity of the information obtained. Method becomes scientific method when evidences of unreliability and invalidity are actively sought to discover their sources and to develop strategies, techniques and tactics to minimize the effects of bias.

Reliability

Reliability of any measure or observation refers to the probability that an observation if repeated at a different time by the same person, or at the same time by another competent observer, will give the same result. Of course this assumes that conditions are such that the nature of the object or property of the object being observed has not changed with repeated observation.

The reliability of observations is occasionally mentioned in reports of empirical studies, while questions of validity are almost completely ignored. Validity is a concept which has more varied definitions and also requires more complicated and costly methods to measure than is the case with reliability.

It has been experimentally shown that under certain circumstances the reliability of a set of observations can be perfect yet the observations may be wrong. For example, if two different interviewers ask a random sample of 25 employees in the White House whether they were involved in any illegal activities in the Watergate case, and if the interviewer were representing the FBI, there is a high probability that the two interviewers would consistently get a "no" answer from all 25 in the sample. The second questioning might produce the same result. This would represent 100 percent reliability. Whether some of the answers might be false is a question of validity.

Validity

Validity then refers to the extent to which the data conform to the fact. In this case the data consists of the 25 "no" answers and the facts consist of the actual activities of the respondents with respect to the Watergate case. The problem of validity becomes clear when we realize that most observations are indirect. The actual sensory stimuli used as evidence of the existence of the object or property we want to observe are merely indicators or indices of that object or property. For example, if we want to know the temperature, we look at a thermometer and say that it is 75 degrees. We do not see the temperature, only the length of a mercury column. To prove the validity of the thermometer, we must show that the mercury varies in length in a way that correlates with temperature, which is actually the speed of molecular movement! Similarly, in the social sciences we cannot directly see another person's attitude, but we use that person's response to questions, to projective tests, or his body movements as indirect indicators of the attitude hidden inside.

It is clear that for observations to be valid they must be reliable, but the fact that observations are reliable is no guarantee that they will be valid. So we can say that reliability is a necessary but not sufficient condition for validity.

Tests of validity. There are at least six different validation procedures used by social scientists. All have their appropriate applications and limitations.

1. Selection validity. As applied to interviewing there are two kinds of selection validity. In one type the information sought is some *subjective orientation* (feeling, attitude, belief, or expectation) which everyone in the target population has to some degree. In this case selection validity is obtained by taking a *random sample* large enough to adequately represent the total population to which we want to generalize.

The second type of selection validity is applied to situations where the information sought is some *objective fact* which lies outside the minds of most of the population but which is known by someone. In this case validity is obtained not by taking a random sample but by finding those in the community who have the knowledge and who are willing to give it. In this case a sample of one person might be enough to validly obtain the information. We cannot settle a question of objective fact by taking a reading of the democratic majority of the respondents in a random sample. The majority's belief may or may not be a valid indicator of the objective fact.

2. Face validity. Face validity refers to the *assumption* that the index actually directly represents the reality we are trying to measure. There are occasions when this is the only type of validation possible. For example, if we want to determine the effect of morale on people's walking speed in the city during a time of racial tension, we cannot directly measure speed; we need to measure the length of time it takes pedestrians to walk the length of the block at a certain time of the day. In this case we accept the validity of the watch as a measure of time and the tape measure as a measure of distance, and we conclude "on the face of it" that we are indeed measuring speed.

3. Concurrence validity. The assumption underlying concurrence validity is that we are using a true indicator of some property if it correlates (has concomitant variation) with some other indicator. For example, if we want to know whether the answers to a set of questions will validly diagnose whether or not the respondent is schizophrenic, we might correlate the diagnoses made by the questionnaire with those made by a psychiatrist. Of course this form of validation assumes that the psychiatrist's judgments are valid and that any disagreement between the psychiatrist and the questionnaire shows that the questionnaire is wrong. This is probably correct if the psychiatrist has had considerable opportunity to talk with and observe the person. It is even more likely to be correct if the particular people in the criterion group of schizophrenics and nonschizophrenics include only those people who were reliably classified by several psychiatrists.

Many experimental studies have been done to measure the validity of information obtained by interviewing. Most of them seem to use the concurrence validity test. For example, De Fleur[2] tests the validity of interview information against the results of the lie detector. Another concurrence test is the comparison of the information obtained by one form of interview, like a highly structured one, with another form, like the unstructured depth interview. The comparison of the results obtained by an inexperienced interviewer with those obtained by a highly experienced one is another kind of concurrence test. Bailar[3] used this test and points out that her results indicate that this type of re-interview test of validity is best when (a) the second interview of the same respondent is done relatively close in time to the original interview, and (b) the second interviewer has not seen the results obtained by the first interviewer. If condition (b) is not observed there is a danger that an invalid concurrence is obtained by the second interviewer who assumes the first interviewer's information is correct and therefore does not probe deeply when the respondent's initial reply is as expected.

Another specific test of concurrence validity of the interview is obtained by comparing the respondents' statements in the interview with official records. Weiss,[4] in a study of response error among mothers receiving public assistance in New York, checked the mothers' statements against the official records of the Welfare Department. Similarly, Steinkamp[5] compared the statements of his respondents regarding the size of their bank account with the actual bank records. He used this measure of validity to study the differences between those interviewers who obtained the accurate information from those who did not. Another experiment by Berry[6] measured the validity of news stories in three daily newspapers in the San Francisco area by checking the facts as reported in the papers with those gained by careful crosschecking at the source of the information.

---

[2] Lois B. DeFleur, "On Polygraph and Interview Validation," *American Sociological Review,* vol. 32 (1967), pp. 114–15.

[3] Barbara A. Bailar, "Recent Research in Re-interview Procedures," *Journal of the American Statistical Association,* vol. 63 (1968), p. 321.

[4] Carol H. Weiss, "Validity of Welfare Mothers' Interview Responses," *Public Opinion Quarterly,* vol. 32 (1968–69), pp. 622–33.

[5] Stanley Steinkamp, "Some Characteristics of Effective Interviewers," *Journal of Applied Psychology,* vol. 50 (1966), pp. 487–92.

[6] Fred C. Berry, Jr., "A Study of the Accuracy in Local News Stories of Three Dailies," *Journalism Quarterly,* vol. 44 (1967), pp. 482–90.

There is a danger of over-generalizing the conclusions in studies of validity of interviewing. Sometimes a particular method of data gathering is rejected as being generally invalid because it was clearly unsuccessful under particular circumstances. For example, Schwab[7] in his review of the employment interview concludes that the preponderance of evidence is against the validity of interviewing as a satisfactory technique for the selection of employees. Actually, it may not be interviewing per se that is at fault, but the lack of knowledge and training of the interviewer used in the experiment, the particular circumstances in which the interviewing was done, or the fact that the respondent perceived the interviewer as a person representing management, and who could deny him the job if the "wrong" answers were given in the interview.

4. Predictive validity. In predictive validation it is assumed that the type of observation used can allow the observer to predict the differences in *future* behavior on the basis of current observations. For example, if the scores on the College Entrance Exam Board's tests correlate highly with success in college, then we can say that the test is a valid one in that it successfully predicts what it intends to predict.

5. Construct validity. Construct validation is usually used in a situation where the researcher has no direct criterion measure, no concomitant measure with which to compare it, and no future events which are legitimate dependent variables to be predicted. To a great extent this type of validation consists of examining the internal logical relationships in a set of propositions making up a definition and their relationship to other variables of theoretical or empirical interest. The process by which a set of questions and their responses can be demonstrated to be unidimensional by Guttman scaling technique is an example of construct validity. Only if the combination of responses made by each person fits into a logically scalable pattern can we say that the items in the questionnaire constitute an attitude scale.[8]

6. Convergent-discriminant validation. Social scientists have frequently used convergent validation alone. That is, they have only asked, "do these measures correlate, correspond, or *converge* with some other index of the quality we are trying to measure?" However, there is an additional test of equal importance which raises the question, "do these measures discriminate between the variable we are trying to measure and some other related variable which might easily be mistaken for it?" If we wanted to construct a questionnaire or interview which would measure men's attitudes toward equal rights for women, we would

---

[7] P. P. Schwab, "Why Interview? A Critique," *Personnel Journal*, vol. 48 (1969), pp. 126–29.

[8] Louis Guttman, "A Theory of Intergroup Beliefs and Action," *American Sociological Review*, vol. 24 (June 1959), pp. 318–28.

want it to discriminate between this attitude and an attitude toward women in general, or an attitude toward human rights in general. This two-fold test of validity is described in detail by Campbell and Fiske.[9]

Experiments to measure the validity of interviewing under particular circumstances are crucial to the improvement of interviewing. The validity of the information is the criterion *par excellence* for comparing the effectiveness of different data-gathering methods, of different interviewing strategies, of different tactics and techniques, and of different interviewers. Also the effectiveness of a particular method of training or selecting interviewers can be evaluated by the validity of the information the interviewers obtain.

There is considerable evidence that validity can be measured, the sources of invalidity detected, and remedies applied to reduce bias at its source. This is being done at an accelerating rate as shown by the increase in such studies over the past 20 years. We can safely assume that the next two decades will see further improvements. We have not yet achieved perfect validity of response, so what should we do in the meantime? Do we abandon studies using interviewing except for those aimed at solving the validity problem? The answer is an emphatic "no"!

We must avoid both extremes—naïve optimism and stubborn pessimism—regarding the interview. There is no way that interviewing can be eliminated; people will always try to obtain information from other people whether they think of the act as "interviewing" or not. We can try to reduce the amount of bias, to detect the existence of bias so that we will not accept biased information as truth, and to learn how to use information more intelligently when we recognize its weaknesses.

While we are waiting upon improvements in the validity of interviewing, we should recognize that it is possible to use partially biased data to arrive at unbiased conclusions by using methods of analysis and interpretation that take the bias into account.

Drawing valid conclusions from biased information. On the surface it would seem safe to assume that no valid conclusions could be based upon biased information. Yet it can be clearly demonstrated that valid conclusions *can* be drawn from invalid or biased information. The reason for this apparent contradiction is that information is not necessarily either biased or unbiased as a whole. Instead, it can be biased in one dimension and not in another. Since this is the case, we can devise methods of analysis and interpretation that counteract the bias or exclude its effect. Although research design is not the central focus of this

---

[9] Donald T. Campbell and D. W. Fiske, "Convergent and Discriminant Validation by the Multitrait-Multimethod Matrix," *Psychological Bulletin*, vol. 56 (1959), pp. 81–105.

book, it is worthwhile to demonstrate that all is not lost if we cannot always obtain perfectly valid and unbiased data.

Suppose that a survey was done to determine the voters' feelings regarding the impeachment of a federal judge. Some respondents, because of their respect for the office, would minimize their expressed desire to have the judge impeached. Others might over-express their desire for impeachment because they are generally hostile personalities who welcome any target. Thus, the measurement of the opinion toward impeachment of the judge would be biased by two other variables which we had not intended to measure. If we knew that the one tendency would quantitatively balance out the other in a random sample of the U.S. population, then we could say that the results validly represented the amount of support of impeachment. Since this is probably not the case, how can we use the data to draw valid conclusions? We could repeat the random survey in a month. Then, if the second survey showed a great difference in public sentiment we could validly say that there had been a change in sentiment about impeachment, and that the change had been either more pro or more anti impeachment. This would be true because the other two variables, the attitude toward the office of a federal judge and the personality trait of hostility, would be relatively constant in comparison with the variable the surveys were trying to measure.

To give another example, suppose that a detective were trying to discover the whereabouts of a nine-year-old girl who had been reported missing by her best friend. He interviewed the parents and they claimed not to know. Then he interviewed 15 more adults and 5 children in the neighborhood. All but one child claimed to know nothing of the girl's whereabouts. All of the adults who said they did not know were lying to protect the child from a kidnapping threat. When the one child, however, gave the address of the aunt with whom the girl was staying, the detective was able to check the story and get the police to provide protection until they apprehended the would-be kidnappers. In this case the correct conclusion was found despite the fact that the majority of the respondents gave invalid information, because the information sought was an objective fact that could be verified. Even interviewing a set of respondents in situations where most of the information is invalid will get us to the truth faster than if we do not interview anyone for fear they might lie.

These two examples could be multiplied, but they are sufficient to point out that information can be fruitfully used despite the fact that it is not all correct.

This whole book is an attempt to share experience, insight, and ideas on increasing the validity and reliability of information gathered through interviewing. We will begin by showing the similarities and differences between interviewing and ordinary conversation so that the reader may retain some of the basic skills while discarding some of the limiting habits built up in his conversational experience. Then we relate basic styles of interviewing to the basic objectives of discovery and measurement. The conceptual heart of the book is a theoretical frame of reference defining eight major facilitators and eight major inhibitors of valid communication in the interview. The major portion of the book presents a variety of strategies, techniques, and tactics as tools at the interviewer's disposal to minimize the inhibitors and to maximize the facilitators of the flow of relevant and accurate information in the interview. Since we do not merely intend to discuss interviewing but also want to help improve interviewing, we have presented a procedure for developing the skills necessary to put the concepts into practice.

ILLUSTRATIVE INTERVIEWING PROBLEMS

Rather than rush on anxiously to the concepts and tools of interviewing, let us pause for a moment to observe some concrete examples of typical errors made in different interviewing situations.

These cases show that success in many different fields may depend upon one's ability to obtain complete and accurate information from another person. Much of the art of human relations lies in the skills of creative, sympathetic listening and artful probing beneath the usual superficial level of communication. To help break down the stereotype of the interviewer as a housewife who knocks on a random sample of doors to obtain responses on public opinion or buyer motivation, we offer the following examples of range of interviewing situations in which the person asking the questions may or may not think of himself as an interviewer.

In each of these seven cases consider the purpose of the interview, its setting, the nature of the interviewer and the respondent, and then try to empathize with the respondent to determine when he might be unwilling or unable to give the information sought by the interviewer in view of the methods used. The discussions which follow each case are intentionally short and nontechnical since they are aimed at illustrating some of the typical problems in interviewing which transcend particular interviewing purposes and settings.

Situation 1. A settlement house social worker in the Puerto Rican area of New York City is collecting life histories of delinquents and pre-delinquents to determine how peer groups, parents, and cultural conflict influence attitudes in the teenager, leading him to perform illegal acts. In the portion of the interview reported here the interviewer is probing the respondent's attitudes toward the New York police. The social worker is a 40-year-old man and the respondent is a 15-year-old Puerto Rican boy. The respondent can speak Spanish more fluently than English, but insists upon being interviewed in English although the social worker is fluent in Spanish.[10]

I: Manuel, you know I have been working here at Washington Center for years and I am interested in how so many in this area get in trouble with the law. I'm not interested in blaming anyone, but want to know how these situations develop, from your point of view. Could you tell me how you first got into trouble with the police?

R: The first time was when we were fighting the gang on 129th street. The cops came and grabbed three of us and all the others got away.

I: What was the fight about?

R: This gang, the Eagles, were rumbling about us coming in on their territory, but it wasn't true. They said they were going to beat us up the next time they saw us. That was about two weeks before the big fight.

I: I see, and what were you doing in the meantime?

R: What else? We started packing some weapons to defend ourselves. I had a blackjack and a knife. I heard that one of the Eagles had a gun he made.

I: Why didn't you call the police instead of trying to protect yourselves with knives?

R: The police would not believe us. They would just tell you to go along and peddle your papers. They are just a big bunch of crooks looking for an easy buck, besides how could they protect us, even if they were interested?

I: You don't feel that the police are interested in protecting you?

R: No!

I: Where did you get that idea?

R: I knew that all the time.

I: Did your pals in the gang tell you this?

R: I have always hated the cops for good reason.

I: Do your parents feel the same way about the police?

R: I don't know how they feel.

I: How long have you been in New York?

R: We left Puerto Rico in June, 1965, and came here.

I: You say that you have always disliked the police?

R: Yes, always!

I: Then you didn't get this idea about the police from your friends or from your family?

R: No.

I: I see. Whose idea was it to start carrying knives?

At this point the interviewer shifts the discussion to how the gang member decides what kind of weapon to carry. The interview lasted over two hours and the above portion of the interview involves a basic communication problem which the interviewer seems to have no tactics for solving. This same problem recurred throughout the interview.

---

[10] The interviewer is designated by *"I"* and the respondent by *"R."*

Discussion. If we remember that this interview is trying to determine the effect of peer groups, parents, and cultural conflicts in forming attitudes leading to delinquency, it is clear that the interview was not successful. One of the basic attitudes often found in the delinquent is that the police are "crooks." There is hostility toward the police which is often reciprocated. Yet according to the delinquent's testimony, he had not obtained this attitude from anybody. To him it seemed to be a self-evident truth.

One basic problem here is that the interviewer assumes that the respondent will be conscious of the source of his attitudes; therefore, he asks for a direct report by the respondent. But the source of a person's attitudes is often unknown to the person himself. To obtain this information accurately it would be necessary for the interviewer to ask the respondent to begin with a detailed account of his attitude toward police in Puerto Rico. If "the Puerto Rican police were different," the interviewer could begin unraveling the respondent's experiences before his arrival in New York. He might discover when the delinquent had first heard about the New York police. To insure validity, the information should be a natural part of an account of the respondent's total ego-involved experience pattern. Thus, by encouraging the respondent to verbally relive his first contacts with the New York police, relevant information might be obtained so that the interviewer, rather than the respondent, could judge the source of the attitude. Sometimes in such an interview the respondent himself becomes aware of the sources of his attitudes for the first time.

Situation 2. A social scientist has been hired as a consultant to study what effects a profit-sharing plan in a manufacturing company has upon morale in the plant. Some of the employees do not own stock, others own one share which was deducted from their first month's pay check, and others have purchased additional shares in response to company drives. Those with only one share have purchased it after they had indicated in their job application that they would like to participate in the profit-sharing plan to the extent of one share. Interviewers were assigned to interview a random sample of the 1600 workers in the plant. The interviewers were to discover how long each respondent had been employed at the plant and how much stock he owned. Then they asked him a series of questions to measure his morale level.

I: How long have you worked for Morris Johnson Co.?
R: It's been almost three years now.
I: Has it been nearer to three than two years?
R: Yes.
I: Have you purchased stock in the company to participate in the profit-sharing plan?
R: No.

I: Now, I have a series of questions here asking for your opinion of Morris Johnson Co. as a place to work.

R: Okay, let's hear them!

I: We assume that you will feel free to give your frank opinion on these questions. That is why the interviewing is being done by someone from the outside rather than by management or other plant personnel who might know you and have some axe to grind.

R: I don't care, I'd tell the boss how I feel. But I know what you mean. Some people are timid.

I: Right. . . .

The interviewer goes on to ask the ten morale questions which takes approximately a half hour since this respondent seems willing to volunteer full information. However, after the first 25 of 100 interviews were completed it was discovered that a basic communication barrier was operating and seriously distorting a portion of the information.

Discussion. Amazing as it seems, employees are often unable to report accurately whether or not they own stock in the company where they are employed. If the respondent owns only one share, deducted from his first paycheck three years ago, he may not recall the fact, particularly if the method of paying dividends is such that he is not clearly reminded of his stock ownership. A study by Moore, for example, showed that only 50 percent of the employees in a British company could accurately report whether or not they owned stock in the company.[11]

Situation 3. A high school teacher is interviewing the students of her home room class to obtain a health record. Since this is the freshman class, the school does not have any previous record. The state law requires vaccination for smallpox before entering elementary school. In addition, the health record must indicate when the child had any communicable diseases as well as when he had been immunized. The teacher interviews each student privately.

I: We must get a medical record of each student when he comes to Bryan High School. There are a few questions we need to ask. Have you missed any school in the last year because of illness?

R: No, except for a cough one time; I missed two days.

I: Uh huh. Have you ever been vaccinated for smallpox?

R: Yes, I guess everybody has!

I: Have you ever had chicken pox?

R: No.

I: Have you ever had whooping cough?

R: No.

I: Measles?

---

[11] B. V. Moore, "The Interview in Industrial Research," *Social Forces*, vol. 7 (1929), pp. 445–52.

R: No.

I: Did you have a chest x-ray in the last year?

R: Yes!

I: Did you have a tuberculin test in the last year? That's where they put a little scratch on your arm and a little patch over it for a few days.

R: No.

I: Did you have all three of your polio shots?

R: Yes.

I: Has any of your family been in the mental hospital?

R: No.

I: Will you usually bring your lunch, eat in the school cafeteria, or go home for lunch?

R: I'll bring my lunch.

I: That's all, thank you.

In view of the techniques and tactics used for obtaining the medical history in this case, it is highly doubtful that the information is accurate enough to warrant the time expenditure.

Discussion. It is doubtful that the student's memory would be accurate enough to make such a superficial interview worthwhile. A more reliable respondent would be the child's mother. Additional information could be obtained from the family physician's records.

Situation 4. State police investigators found that the defendant's auto skidded a considerable distance before it crashed into a car entering the highway from a side road. The defendant is being sued and his lawyer is interviewing him to determine the exact nature of the accident and the legal and moral liability.

I: In order to prepare a defense, I must know exactly what happened in the accident! Were you exceeding the speed limit when it happened?

R: No.

I: Did you see the other car before it had entered the highway?

R: It came out very suddenly from this little side road, and there were trees along the shoulder of the road. He was a fool to pull out like that!

I: Did you hit the other car near the front or the rear?

R: Near the rear.

Although the client might be telling the truth, the whole truth and nothing but the truth, thus far the lawyer has unknowingly left the door open for falsification by the client.

Discussion. The lawyer should depend upon the State Police reports for an estimate of the car's speed. If it is clear that his client was exceeding the speed limit, the lawyer should indicate this to the respondent by saying:

The report by the State Police, based on the measurement of your skid marks, clearly indicates that you were exceeding the legal speed limit. Did you realize that at the time?

Or if the lawyer has not yet had an opportunity to see the police report, he might say:

> I haven't seen the police report yet, but as you probably know, it is part of their routine investigation to measure the skid marks and determine quite accurately the speed of your car. How much were you exceeding the speed limit? It is quite important that I know this before talking to the police.

Once the client is allowed to make a defensive false statement, *rapport* may be damaged if the lawyer points out the client's falsification. Therefore, tactics should be used to *prevent* falsification.

Situation 5. A personnel manager in a large corporation with over 15,000 employees is doing an exit interview to determine why an employee is leaving the company after five years of service. Management wants to obtain information to reduce the turnover of employees.

I: As you know, we always talk to employees who are leaving because we are interested in knowing if there is anything in particular they dislike about the company policy or anything we could have done to make the employee more satisfied with her work here.

R: I see.

I: I believe you are going to work for Pacific Electric, is that right?

R: That's right.

I: I see that it is closer to where you live, isn't it?

R: Yes, it is about six miles closer.

I: Is there any particular reason why you are leaving Johnson Electric?

R: No, nothing in particular.

I: Is there anything which we could have done differently to make you more satisfied with the work here?

R: No, there's nothing you could have done. I have nothing against Johnson Electric.

I: What kind of work will you be doing with Pacific Electric?

R: I'll be wiring panels almost the same as those I do here.

I: Then you're not getting a promotion.

R: Oh, no!

I: What would you say is your main reason for leaving Johnson Electric?

R: Well, like I said, it is easier to work closer to home and Pacific Electric is six miles closer . . . so I will drive 12 miles less each day.

I: I see. Thank you very much, Mrs. Robin. Good luck to you and I hope you enjoy working for Pacific Electric.

Discussion. In this type of exit interview, the respondent tends to show deference to the interviewer who represents management. He may be inclined to withhold his gripes about Johnson Electric, rationalizing that it is "too late to do any good with my complaints." The interviewer then unwittingly assists the respondent in evading his complaints and in rationalizing his move by pointing out that Pacific Electric is six miles closer to the respondent's home. Note that four questions later the interviewer obtains the answer which he had suggested earlier.

One possible solution to this problem is to have a person who does not represent the company conduct the exit interview. If this is impossible several techniques and tactics can help in overcoming this etiquette barrier. We will discuss these later.

Situation 6. The dermatologist for the Student Health Service at a large university is interviewing a graduate student. He wants to obtain a medical history which might explain the causes of a rash on the patient's right hand. The dermatologist suspects an allergy and is trying to narrow down the field of possible causal agents.

I: How long have you been at the university?
R: Five years. I'm working on my dissertation now.
I: Do you spend time in dusty stacks in the library?
R: Yes, I spend some time there each week.
I: Are you worried about taking the Ph.D. exams?
R: No . . . I couldn't be worried about that because I have passed them all and have only my thesis to finish.
I: When did you first notice the rash?
R: When I first arrived in Chicago six years ago. Before I enrolled here I was a group worker at a settlement house.
I: Did you have any medical treatment at that time?
R: No, it just seemed to disappear for no reason that I was aware of.
I: When did it disappear?
R: I remember I had it in June just before I went to spend the summer in a small village in Mexico. After I was in the village for about two days it disappeared. When I went to Mexico City it returned. I came back to Chicago and still had it until I went on a field trip to rural Arkansas and it disappeared in a day or two. Then I returned to Chicago and the rash reappeared. That was last fall, in October, and I have had it in varying degrees since that time.
I: I see. Every time you came back to Chicago the rash appeared. Now let's see how you write. Here is a pencil and paper, just show me how you hold the pencil when you write. (The patient writes something on the paper.) That's just as I suspected. See, the sides of your fingers constantly rub on the paper. If the paper is dusty you can work the dust into the epidermis and set up an irritation . . . it might even be the paper fibers rather than the dust. I'll give you a prescription to apply each morning. . . .

The above interview contains a problem typical in situations where the interviewer has high status. It was later discovered that the tentative diagnosis was wrong and could have been avoided if the physician had been a more skilled interviewer.

Discussion. The dermatologist seems to initially suspect that the rash results from some type of nervous tension. Then he relinquishes this hypothesis in favor of the possibility that it is an allergy to the dust found in libraries or on paper. After leaving the physician's office the patient reported, "That dermatologist is a poor diagnostician. He either didn't hear what I said, or he didn't believe me, or he can't think logically. This rash reappeared *not only* when I returned to my studies in Chicago, but also when I was on vacation in Mexico City. The one consistent pattern is that in rural areas it goes away and when I am back in a big city it returns."

Note that the patient did not point out the apparent diagnostic error to the dermatologist. People who enjoy high status must be particularly careful not to depend on correction from the respondent.

Situation 7. A guest's room in a large hotel in Detroit has been burglarized and the house detective is interviewing the cleaning maid in order to establish the time of the robbery.

I: Did you clean room 819 this morning?

R: Yes, I did.

I: Did you notice anything out of order when you went in?

R: No, sir, I don't think so. It looked just like it has the last three days since the same man has been there.

I: What time did you clean the room?

R: I don't know exactly.

I: Was it the first thing when you came on shift?

R: Oh, no! I came on at 6:30. It was later than that.

I: Was it as late as 10 A.M.?

R: I don't think so.

I: About 9?

R: That's about right. Yes, it was about 9 A.M.

I: Thank you—that's all.

In this case the detective has committed a common error in interviewing, making the accuracy of the information doubtful.

Discussion. In view of the probable difficulty in remembering the exact time she cleaned the room, the maid would be susceptible to the detective's loaded question "About 9 A.M.?" Also the higher social status of the interviewer tends to make the maid susceptible to the detective's suggestion. In a situation like this it would be particularly important to take time to stimulate the respondent's memory. A series of questions could lead up to the time the room was cleaned and help the maid find clues which would narrow down the time segment in which the burglary took place.

The seven episodes above contain typical examples of errors made in interviewing. The errors are not all obvious and the interviewer in each case is not particularly inept. In fact, there are many good points in each interview showing insight into the information-gathering process. In each of these cases, however, the interviewer is unaware that the situation contains social-psychological dimensions which tend to make the respondent either unable or unwilling to give accurate information.

These episodes illustrate only a few applications of interviewing; they are mainly situations in which the interviewer does not consider himself a specialist in interviewing. These examples do not begin to cover the variety of situations in which interviewing is the basic tool. To expand our panorama a bit without taking time to illustrate with dialogue from each, let us consider some purposes and settings of intentional interviewing in which the interviewer specialist encounters different kinds of respondents.

In journalism and oral history studies there have been some interesting accounts of the interviewing process. For example, Milford[12] describes the difficulties of interviewing associates of those who have become in any way legendary. Jacobson[13] gives an example of the field problem involved in eliciting information from delegates who are attending international assemblies, a problem which is complicated by cross-cultural communication problems. Even the Supreme Court[14] has been invaded by interviewers. Urban ministers[15] recently have been the focus of interviews to determine their relationship to the changing problems on the urban scene. The aged[16] have been a target of study for many years. The effects of environmental factors such as noise and pollution[17] have been the subjects of more recent probes through interviewing. Children's psychosocial development has long been the subject of probing by psychologists, sociologists and anthropologists, as illustrated by Piaget's[18] study of the spontaneous development of religious concepts in children. It has been shown that delinquency can be discovered directly from the confidential confessions of teenagers,[19] rather than relying on only the delinquencies that have been detected

---

[12] Nancy Milford, "The Golden Dreams of Zelda Fitzgerald," *Harper's Magazine*, January 1969, pp. 46–53.

[13] Harold K. Jacobson, "Deriving Data from Delegates to International Assemblies: A Research Note," *International Organization*, vol. 21 (1967), pp. 592–613.

[14] David Grey, "Interviewing at the (Supreme) Court," *Public Opinion Quarterly*, vol. 31 (1967), pp. 285–89.

[15] W. C. Kloetzle et al., "Guide for Interviewing the Minister and Selected Key Members of the Congregation of the Urban Church Effectiveness Study," *Social Compass*, vol. 9 (1962), pp. 387–402.

[16] J. Zelan, "Interviewing the Aged," *Public Opinion Quarterly*, vol. 33 (1969), pp. 420–24.

[17] Erland Jonsson, "On the Formulation of Questions in Medico-hygienic Interview Investigations," *Acta Sociologica*, vol. 7 (1963), pp. 193–202.

[18] David Elkind, "Piaget's Semi-Clinical Interview and the Study of Spontaneous Religion," *Journal for the Scientific Study of Religion*, vol. 4 (1965), pp. 40–47.

[19] Martin Gold, "Undetected Delinquency Behavior," *Journal of Research on Crime and Delinquency*, vol. 3 (1966), pp. 27–46.

and entered in the court records. Bersoff[20] developed an interviewing strategy to uncover the psychosituational factors that elicit, reinforce, and perpetuate certain patterns of behavior. In short, all types of people, from the children to the aged, from criminals to supreme court judges, from delinquents to ministers, have been the respondents in interviews.

Once we begin to explore the use of interviewing, we increasingly realize that it would be impossible to write a special book on interviewing designed for use on a particular problem, or with a particular type of respondent, or for a particular category of interviewer, or for each possible combination of these three. This explosive growth in the variety of uses of the interview as a tool in the study of groups, organizations, or institutions makes it necessary to seek some basic underlying principles and sensitizing concepts that can be applied to a range of specific interviewing situations. The following chapters attempt to provide a perspective, some guiding principles, and a kit of tools—called strategies, techniques, and tactics, all designed to help the interviewer plan and perform more valid interviews under varying conditions and purposes.

The next chapter will show how interviewing is related to other basic methods of information gathering, so that interviewing can be seen in perspective as one of a set of basic methods, each of which has its own strengths and weaknesses.

Before you go on to the next chapter, however, you should think about the discussion questions and do the first laboratory problem. It is essential that you do some problem solving now, lest you receive the impression that learning to interview is a spectator sport!

DISCUSSION QUESTIONS

1. What changes are taking place in the kinds of studies being done in the social sciences that increase the use of interviewing?
2. Criticize the statement that reliability is more important than validity.
3. Think of one example in which you would use each of the six types of validity.
4. Think of some situations in which people are using interviewing to obtain information but do not define themselves as interviewers.

---

[20] Donald Bersoff and Russell Grieger, "An Interview Model for the Psychosituational Assessment of Children's Behavior," *American Journal of Orthopsychiatry*, vol. 41 (1971), pp. 483–93.

Laboratory problem 1

Critique of telephone company interview

This first laboratory problem gives you the opportunity to critically analyze the performance of another interviewer. Your success in this will depend to some extent upon the degree to which you can imaginatively put yourself in the role of the interviewer and clearly understand both his objectives and the setting in which he is operating. Of course playing the role of the interviewer also involves being sensitive to the respondent's probable reaction to what the interviewer does or fails to do. To get the most out of this experience carefully follow the procedure below.

Procedure

Preparation. Before writing your critique (which can probably be done in two or three typewritten pages) you must carefully prepare with the following steps.

1. Note the nature of parts A and B of the written critique as described below.
2. Carefully read the description of the telephone company's study from which the interview script was taken. Note the setting of the study, the general purposes, and the specific information objectives of the interview.
3. Read the script of the interview up to the interviewer's fifth question (*I–5*) then write Part A of your critique (described below).
4. Now read the entire script only once, writing the critique of each of the 20 specified questions as you go along. This is Part B of your critique (described below).

Nature of the critique

A. *Strategy errors.* By strategy errors we mean errors in the way the interview situation is set up: the time, place, selection of the respondent, selection of the interviewer, how the interviewer approaches the respondent, how the interviewer explains the situation, or any aspect of the interview setting which might help or hinder the flow of relevant and valid information.

This part of your critique should be written after you read up to *I–5* in the script and before you go on to read the remainder of the interview. Simply say what was wrong, if anything, with what was done or with what was not done up to this point. This part of your report should be only a few succinct statements.

B. *Errors in tactics and techniques.* This category includes everything the interviewer says or does not say which affects the relevance, completeness, and validity of the information given by the respondent. What the interviewer says and how he says it should be viewed in terms of its probable effect upon the respondent.

Twenty only. You are to comment on only 20 of the interviewer's questions. These are indicated by the numbers 1 through 20 in the margin. This sample of the interviewer's behavior was selected to avoid unnecessary repetition in your critique and yet provide a representative portion of this interviewer's behavior.

Context. Comment on each of the questions before going on to the next. When judging the adequacy of the question, keep in mind the context in which it appears. The context in this case includes everything that precedes the question, including the silence, but *not* what follows that particular question.

Diagnosis and treatment. Each of the 20 critiques should include the number of the question you are analyzing followed by (*a*) your diagnosis of what was wrong with it, and (*b*) your suggested treatment in the form of a concrete example of what the interviewer should have done instead. If no improvement is needed, say so, and go on to the next question. Here is a sample of one of the 20 critiques.

I-49   *a.* The interviewer should have probed instead of accepting the superficial answer.

        b. "That's very interesting. Could you explain that a little more?"

The number *I–49* in the above example is furnished in the script. Note that the silences of one second or longer are indicated in parentheses. The silence immediately preceding each question is considered to be part of the interviewer's behavior connected to the question, since the interviewer determines the length of the silence before he breaks it with his question.

Now that you can visualize the form of the critique you are to do, carefully read and think about the study as described below. You must understand the setting of the study, its general purposes, and the specific information objectives of the interviews in order to do a valid critique of each of the 20 points.

Description of the study

The company's purposes. The central purpose of the study from which this interview has been taken was to evaluate management's efforts to influence the employee's attitudes and beliefs. A telephone company decided to launch an employee information program in which management would explain to the 40,000 employees the company's need for an increase in the telephone rates. Management felt that the first task was to sell the employees on the need for the rate increase and hope that the employees would carry the campaign to the public through contacts with their families, friends, and telephone subscribers. It was considered important to influence general public opinion because the company expected the main opposition to the rate increase to come from the lawyers for many of the larger cities in the state at the request of politicians, who then could point to their "record" of opposition to the "big monopolies" for its vote-getting appeal.

Information was gathered and summarized in attractive pamphlets containing tables, charts, and graphs; a movie was produced using employees as actors; all the employees met with management in small discussion groups where the materials were presented and discussed. There was considerable variation in the way in which the discussion was handled and the way in which the materials were used from one meeting to another, depending upon the particular manager leading the group.

The basic ideas in the company's rate-information program included the following:

a. Telephone services, in order to be efficient, must constitute a monopoly in any one geographical area.

b. To protect the consumer against the company's taking unfair advantage of its monopoly position, the government grants the company a charter to operate only as long as it charges a "fair and reasonable" price for its services.

c. The state commerce commission is the governmental agency set up to protect the consumer and must determine whether the company is in fact charging a "fair and reasonable" price.

d. The calculation of a reasonable price should take into consideration not only the percent return on the investment, but also the need to pay greater dividends to stockholders during prosperity in order to compete with more prosperous industries for the investor's money.

e. The telephone company is more vulnerable to financial recessions than other utilities because people are more likely to give up telephone service than gas, water, or electricity. Therefore, during times of prosperity it must accumulate an emergency fund to protect it against such times.

f. The increased efficiency of service due to the accelerating trend in installation of dial phones and other automation is offset by the fact that phone service, unlike other utilities, becomes more costly as a larger number of subscribers is included in any local-call area. This is due to the fact that a potential electrical connection must be made between each phone and every other one in the system. The cost would be much higher if it were not for efficiency.

g. The cost of telephone service has not risen nearly as much as prices in general since World War II. Therefore, a rate increase would not be unfair to the consumer. The company, too, is a victim of inflation since it must now pay more for materials and labor.

Specific information objectives of the interview. In order to evaluate the effectiveness of the rate-information program the company set up the following criteria of effectiveness:

a. The amount of relevant *information* the employee retains. (Here relevant is defined as being related to points (*a*) through (*g*) above.)

b. The general *attitude* of the employee toward the way in which the materials were presented in the *group* meeting.

c. The degree of *conviction* or faith the employee has in the correctness of the company's arguments.

d. The willingness of the employee to *influence* others to see the company's point of view.

Strategy used in the study. A random sample of employees to be interviewed was selected from the payroll lists. The interviews were done by management people about three months after the small group meetings had been held. In no case did a manager interview any of his own subordinates or anyone in his own department. All interviewers introduced themselves as working for the Employee Information Department and explained that this was a staff department which has no supervisory jurisdiction over employees. The interviews were done on company time in any office or conference room where complete privacy was available.

The interviews were all tape-recorded so that the interviewer could devote his full attention to the respondent. Later the information was transcribed by the interviewer who selected out relevant verbatim excerpts and organized them into a report under the four main headings shown above. Neither the respondent's name nor that of his supervisor was known by the interviewer. Therefore, all reports were anonymous. Most of the summary report consisted of statistical tables and verbatim excerpts to illustrate the meaning of the categories used in the tables.

In each case the employee was sent to the interview room by his immediate supervisor who was supposed to explain the nature of the interview. All of the supervisors had been told that the interview would take from one to three hours. Since the aim of the study was to detect any *lasting* effect of the information program, the employee was intentionally not notified until the day of the interviewing so that he would not be tempted to refresh his memory by rereading some of the materials he had forgotten.

The interview script

The following is a detailed report of the events from the time the employee arrived at the interviewing room. The employee enters the room with a questioning look on her face and the interviewer rises to greet her. He does not know how much she has been told about the interview by her supervisor. He begins . . .

I–1: How do you do! I'm Mr. Anderson, but you do not need to tell me your name since everything you tell me is supposed to be anonymous. (1)[21] We want you to feel free to say anything you have on your mind.

R–1: That's okay with me! (Smiling) (2)

1 I–2: How much have you already been told about this interview? (1)

R–2: Not much . . . (3) just that someone wanted to talk to me about the meetings we had a couple of months ago. They didn't say who it was or why. (2)

I–3: I see. Well, I'm working for the Employee Information Department which is interested in what the employees think about the rate-information meetings and how they were handled. (1)

R–3: Gee, that was a long time ago. I can't remember a thing about how well the meeting went! (1)

2 I–4: Won't you just try? I'm sure you must remember something about it . . . (2) . . . there are things you probably remember much longer than that. (1)

Read only to this point before writing Part A of your critique.

R–4: Well, of course I remember something but nothing of any great importance. (2)

I–5: Just tell me in your own words what happened at the meeting. (2)

R–5: Uh . . .

I–6: You know just how it started and all that. (3)

---

[21] The numbers in parentheses represent the number of seconds of silence.

R–6: We just went to the conference room and there was some man I had not seen before. He just gave us the facts about the situation. (1)

3   I–7: He just gave the facts? (2)

R–7: Yes, he didn't preach at us or anything. He asked if there were any questions . . . (1) . . . just listened. I don't think there was anything very complicated. (2)

I–8: You felt that it was not very complicated. (1)

R–8: Yes . . . there were a few questions asked about the proposed suburban rates but outside that nothing was said. (1)

4   I–9: Do you feel that the leader was well-informed? (2)

R–9: Yes, he knew what he was talking about. He had all the facts. (1)

I–10: Did he hand out any materials to read? (3)

R–10: Oh yes, we had pamphlets with very nice charts and pictures. They were very well done and must have cost quite a bit of money.

I–11: You feel they cost quite a bit of money.

R–11: That's right. (3)

I–12: Did they show you a movie?

R–12: Yes. (1)

5   I–13: Did you think it was a good movie considering it was made by amateurs? (1)

R–13: Yes, it was very interesting. It was good to see a movie for a change with amateur actors. They were people just like me and my own friends in real life. It was sort of matter-of-fact. People were bored and not too brilliant or beautiful. I got a bang out of that . . . (5) . . . I guess we're all amateurs at heart and we like to know that others are too. I understand that all the actors are employees. I can believe that even if I didn't recognize any of them. After all there are over 40,000 employees and I know only about 20 of them. I guess there are some disadvantages to working for such a large outfit. A girlfriend of mine works in the bookkeeping department. This was not her first job. She had worked in an office before where she had her own desk and a private room and could bring in a few flowers now and then to brighten up the place. It was her own room. She almost quit the first day when she saw that her desk was one of about 40 in a large room and they all looked exactly alike. She felt like one of a herd. (1)

6   I–14: How did you feel about the meeting in general?

R–14: Oh, it was fine. (1)

I–15: Does that mean that you liked it? (2)

R–15: Sure (giggling), if I hadn't been in the meeting I would have been at the switchboard. (3) It was good to take a break and get away from it all. The meeting lasted, I guess, a couple of hours. (1)

7   I–16: But outside of that, was there anything good about the meeting?

R–16: Of course. Like I said, it was very informative. (2) I learned a lot of facts. It was packed with facts and figures. Most of them I had never heard before. (2)

8   I–17: Were you with the company the last time they asked for a rate increase?

R–17:   No.

9   *I–18:*   Why do you suppose we gave all this information to the employees this time before we file for a rate increase? (4)

R–18:   I can't understand why they want to know how people think unless it is just for their own satisfaction or to see how people will take it. I guess they think, this is my humble opinion, that if the people are accepting it maybe the Commerce Commission would accept it too. (2) They want to see if it holds water. (2)

10   *I–19:*   Do you feel you learned something new at the meeting or in reading the pamphlets? (1)

R–19:   Like I said, I learned a lot of facts and figures.

I–20:   For example . . .

R–20:   Well, they said that there was inflation which made everything cost more and that the company was in a pretty bad way. They also showed how if the rates were increased they would also give additional service and also put in more dial phones. (1)

I–21:   Anything else you can remember?

R–21:   That's about all (2) it was a long time ago.

11   *I–22:*   Some say that since we are now making 6.7 percent profit on our investment we should not ask for a rate increase now. Do you agree with this? (3)

R–22:   I think that they should be allowed to make more than 6 percent but assuming that what they said in the book (pamphlet) is true, that they look in pretty bad shape. (2) But you wonder how could a business like this that is so well established (2) and almost as valuable as your public utilities like water, gas, electric, (1) how could they be in such a tough spot. (4) Their operating expenses can't cost that much compared to the business they do. I think that more people have phones today than they ever had before and the communities are building up so rapidly, I can't see where they are in such poor shape financially. (2)

12   *I–23:*   Would you say the company is government regulated? (2)

R–23:   That means that the government has the power to freeze your job, or make the company comply with their rules of secrecy and stuff like that. They have the power with the telephone company, which is very vital in the national defense, to do things or come in and suggest doing things in their way. There is no other way the government can regulate the company. (1)

13   *I–24:*   Would you say that the company is a monopoly? (1) If it were, how could the subscriber be protected against having to pay unfair rates for telephone service? (3)

R–24:   Well, it is true like Western Electric or AT&T. But it has to be that way. Something that is a utility has to be *one* as far as I can see. It would be impossible for bookkeeping purposes too. And how about the poles? Who would use them, or would there be two sets? It's just like any other utility . . . you can't get your gas or water somewhere else. (2) I think the people benefit by the monopoly because it is cheaper. (1)

I–25: You feel that a monopoly is good for the people.

R–25: Yes! Don't you think so too? (1)

I–26: (Smiling) I guess I would logically have to say 'yes.' What stops us from raising the telephone rates higher and higher if we have a monopoly?

R–26: They might raise the rates but they lose a lot of business in doing so. People can only take so much and they'll see through it. Coffee is a good example. The price went up so high that people quit drinking it and drank other things like tea instead. In the case of the telephone, when you have a choice between eating or having a telephone, you'll eat and get rid of the telephone. That's the way . . .

I–27: So the only thing that stops the rates from going up is the threat of the subscribers getting ride of the phone.

R–27: That's the only thing I can see.

14   *I–28:* Do you think it is a good thing that we have to obtain the permission of the Commerce Commission before getting a rate increase? (3)

R–28: Yes, that is a good thing. (2) I think that is the way it should be.

I–29: Is it true that the more subscribers the company has the more profit it can make? (2)

R–29: Maybe they don't always make more money at the time when they are expanding and getting more subscribers, but later on that equipment pays for itself and I would think that they would make more profit in time, (2) Isn't that true?

15   *I–30:* I suppose you might be right, but doesn't the company claim that growing doesn't increase its profits?

R–30: To me that's silly because . . . well, in the first place just let a lot of people pull out their phones and they'd be complaining that business is falling off. They'd naturally have to get rid of some of their help and then they would probably complain that business wasn't what it used to be and they'd be contradicting what they said. I mean in any business when you grow that is your benefit. Don't you agree with this? (2)

I–31: You would like to know if I agree with you.

R–31: That's right. (1)

16   *I–32:* I don't really know the answer to that question. It sounds like it would make sense to most people. (1) Do you feel that the telephone company needs to make higher profits than other utilities like gas and water? Should we make more or less than the Edison Electric is making at the present time? (3) What factors determine this, such as the effects of inflation, deflation, the rate of dividends paid by competitive business or anything like that? (2)

R–32: I don't see any reason why the telephone company should make any higher profits than any public utility (2) but this depends on what you mean by *profit.* You have to figure in the higher cost of living, (3) the cost of putting new equipment where the old stuff wears out, convenient and efficient, to improve the service. The telephone company has to give service, it isn't just like putting in the water mains and letting the individual pay for connecting to it and for all the plumbing in the house. The telephone company supplies *all* of the equipment and on top of that they need all the operators and all the bookkeeping to put the calls through and keep track of the charges that have to be made. I think the telephone company has more expenses to pay. (2) It should make higher profits than the gas or electric company.

I–33: Does the company need to pay higher dividends to stockholders in good times than in a depression? (2)

R–33: It should because it makes more money in good times than in bad so it should pass along the profit to the shareholders. That's only right . . .

I–34: But is it *really* necessary for the company to pay higher dividends.

R–34: Higher than what?

I–35: Higher than during a depression.

R–35: Well, I'd say that it was necessary, yes.

I–36: Why is that? (2)

R–36: It's just the nature of economics—if you don't pay the people, there is less buying power and the situation would just be worse.

17 *I–37:* Pay who, the stockholders? Does a monopoly have to compete for stockholders? Or can they just pay any dividend they want? (2)

R–37: I guess they would have to pay the stockholders good dividends or they would put their money in some other company. So I guess you could say that even a monpoly has to compete for stockholders. (2)

I–38: When all things are considered, do you actually feel that the company needs a raise in rates? (2)

R–38: I don't really know. Since I have a 50 percent concession on my phone bill it would be easy for me to say the rates should be raised but what about the other people who have to pay the full rate because they are not employees of the company. You should maybe ask them what they think.

I–39: That would be a good idea, but right now I am interested in what you think. (3)

R–39: What bothers me is this whole program. They have been putting out pamphlets and everything. What good does it do? (2) It wouldn't make any difference whether people said they weren't for it. That wouldn't stop them from getting a raise, would it? Because no one wants to pay more, let's face it. And all this stuff about asking your opinion . . . (1) but when it comes down to it they may ask 50 people what they think and if they need this raise, I mean if they really need it, they will still raise the prices even if 50 people say "no."

I–40: Then you feel that this whole thing is sort of a fake.

R–40: Well, I . . .

I–41: I mean you don't really believe the information that has been given out on the rate increase.

R–41: I wouldn't say that exactly. They have all the facts so what can you say. There it is in the book complete with charts and pictures. But the poor working man could put his facts before them and say, "I pay so much for this and so much for that and I'm not getting a raise, I can't afford it." (3)

18   I–42: Has anyone ever asked you about the rate increase? I mean anyone outside the company, (2) family, friends, neighbors or people you see on the way to and from work? (3)

R–42: When it comes out in the papers and people know you are working for the telephone company, they always blame it on you because you're getting a raise. Or they think, well . . . not that you are to blame but it kind of aggravates them. (2)

I–43: Did anyone ever talk to you about it or did you ever bring up the subject yourself with anyone at all? (2)

R–43: I really don't talk to people about it much.

I–44: Did you talk to your family about it? (1)

R–44: I don't know if I brought the pamphlet on inflation home or not because we covered everything in it and it wouldn't make very interesting reading to anyone at home. When I explained to others what was told to us, they thought that it didn't hold much water because people today are using their phones more than ever and the equipment and telephones are built to last a lot longer. But they say in the pamphlet that every four years a phone is put in a house, but all the people I have talked to have had their phones for years.

19   I–45: Then how many people would you say you have talked to about the rate increase? (3)

R–45: I guess when it comes right down to it. I only mentioned it to my mother. (2)

I–46: Is there anything else you would like to say about the rate information program to round out the picture?

R–46: I don't think so. (3)

20   I–47: Well, thank you for your help.

2

Interviewing in perspective

To the uninitiated, interviewing is "just talking to people!" Perhaps this deceptively simple appearance accounts for the historically recent advent of systematic attempts to analyze and experiment with the interaction between interviewer and respondent. Since the dawn of civilization, man's survival in organized groups has depended upon his ability to ask a question and get an answer. Even though a certain amount of confusion, distortion, incompleteness, and outright lying has always occurred in this communication dyad, there was always enough success to keep society functioning. Even ancient civilizations did systematic interviewing to obtain a crude census, but it is likely that more systematic analysis of the communication process has been done in the last 30 years than in the preceding centuries.

This advance in knowledge about information gathering is not a luxury but a necessity for the survival of civilization. As the tempo of social change speeds up, populations grow, and complexities of the world urban industrial societies increase, it becomes necessary to obtain more reliable and valid information on social-psychological factors operating in individuals, groups, organizations, communities, and nations. We must press forward on the social science front to provide reliable and valid information if the quality of the content of communication media is to justify the rapid dissemination made possible by advances in the communication technologies.

To place interviewing in the broad perspective of human activity, we will first show how interviewing, participant-observation, the use of personal documents, and the use of unobtrusive measures are all based on three elementary human capacities: *empathy, participation,* and *observation*. From these basic forms many different information-gathering methods, techniques, and procedures can be devised to fit the nature of the phenomenon under scrutiny and the conditions under which the information must be obtained.

Second, we will devote some discussion to empathy which is the only one of the three human capacities used uniquely in the social sciences, where it provides special advantages under certain conditions yet acts as a pitfall under others.

Third, we will show how interviewing is related to ordinary conversational purposes and skills. Successful interviewing consists of using all of the functions of ordinary sociable conversation in a disciplined way at the appropriate times.

INTERVIEWING RELATED TO OTHER METHODS

There are many methods used to collect information about human behavior used by anthropologists, sociologists, and psychologists and anyone trying to understand human behavior. Regardless of the form of the data collected, how it is recorded, or the purpose for which it is used, it is collected by three elementary forms of human activity: *empathy, participation,* and *observation.*

In this context empathy refers to feeling with another person or understanding how he *feels* about something. By participation we mean *doing* something with people in order to observe something about them. By observation we mean any *sensory perception,* not only visual, of external cues which help us to understand human behavior. Observation of the phenomenon under study is common to all branches of science from astronomy to nuclear physics.

From these three activities all of the methods for studying human behavior such as the interview, questionnaire, pure observation, participant-observation, and nonreactive methods are derived. Within this framework interviewing is seen as one specific form of empathizing, participating, and observing which takes place between two people. The interviewer's participation takes the form of determining the setting or social context in which the interview takes place and asking questions or presenting other stimuli to elicit information from the respondent. The observation consists of not only noting the content of the verbal message but also noting the tone of voice, facial expressions, and body movements. Empathy is involved in anticipating probable reactions to questions and sensing how the respondent felt about events he is relating. In this context the questionnaire is seen not so much as a unique data-gathering method, but simply as a technique for extending the interview in which the researcher participates by constructing the questionnaire. His observation is restricted to noting the written responses on the questionnaire unless he is present while the respondent is filling it out. Then he can participate more fully by clarifying questions, motivating the respondent to complete the questionnaire, encouraging him to be full in his answers. Also if the researcher is present, his observation function can be expanded to include noting the nonverbal behavior of the respondent as he fills out the questionnaire.

Personal documents

The use of personal documents such as diaries or letters involves the observation of verbal behavior elicited by someone other than the researcher himself. The use of such spontaneous documents has both advantages and disadvantages over direct eliciting of information via the interview; however it is not our task to compare the relative merits of these different sources of information but to show how they involve the same or different basic activities. Two classical treatments of the use of personal documents have been done by Allport[1] and by Gottschalk.[2]

One of the most monumental uses of personal letters was in the classic work by William I. Thomas and Florian Znaniecki in their study of *The Polish Peasant in Europe and America*. Personal documents were used to demonstrate processes of acculturation and assimilation of the Polish immigrants to the U.S.A. Although the study came under severe criticism as a case of proof by example in which there was no evidence that either a representative sample or negative cases were sought, it is still clearly an excellent exploratory study giving insights, discovering new relationships, and suggesting hypotheses to be tested by more logically rigorous methods.

It is sometimes suggested that many types of spontaneous documents such as diaries[3] and confessions[4] should be suspect because of the possible bias introduced by the fact that very few people, and therefore

---

[1] Gordon W. Allport, *The Use of Personal Documents in Psychological Science* (New York: Social Science Research Council, 1942).

[2] Louis Gottschalk, Clyde Kluckhohn, and Robert Angell, *The Use Of Personal Documents in History, Anthropology and Sociology* (New York: Social Science Research Council, 1947).

[3] For example, *A Young Girl's Diary* (translated in 1921 by E. and C. Paul from the German version which Hug-Helmuth claimed to be the unedited diary of a young girl, demonstrating her psychosexual development) was referred to by Freud as a "gem," but was later discovered to be a fraud.

[4] St. Augustine, in his *Confessions, Book X,* even gives his reason for writing the confessions, "As to what I now am while I am writing my Confessions, there are many who desire to know—both people who know me personally, and people who do not, but have heard from me or about me. Yet they have not their ear to my heart, where I am, what I am. They wish, therefore, to hear from my own confession what I am inwardly where they cannot pierce with eye or ear or mind."

unusual people, write such things. They may either have unique experiences to write about or they may have special motivations leading them to deceive rather than enlighten the researcher. This problem of possible falsification is not unique to spontaneous personal documents; it is also a problem in the use of the interview and the questionnaire.

Personal documents may be completely spontaneous, as in the case of some diaries or the same type of information elicited by the life-history interview; the latter has some advantages of historical perspective but some disadvantages in loss of detail over time. A classic example of this is Sutherland's[5] interviewing of a professional thief to learn how professional thieves operated in relationship to each other, to lawyers, judges, police, their family, and society in general. Sutherland obtained the information by having the thief write on certain topics, and then having 7 hours of discussion per week for 12 weeks. The thief was paid a small weekly wage for his work from funds provided by the Social Science Research Committee of the University of Chicago. Much of the information was of the type a professional in any field might write in his diary, but it was guided and stimulated by the researcher's participation.

A more recent study in the same life-history category produced an autobiography of a drug addict.[6] Howard Becker, a sociologist with an interest in playing jazz piano got acquainted with Janet and her husband who played in the band. Janet came to the Becker's house frequently to talk about mutual acquaintances of the jazz world with the Beckers. She was persuaded to tell her life story and make a series of tape recordings. She was paid a small amount for these sessions. She needed the money but also hoped to have an opportunity to become an author. Her attendance at the appointed sessions was sometimes irregular because of the need to steal and evade police to raise the price of a "fix." The result is a case study of a personality being molded by a series of forces in a large American city, a rare personal account from the addict's point of view on how she got "hooked."

Becker's role was at times that of an interviewer engaging in an unstructured give-and-take, but the interviewer had other roles in the jazz world giving him a special link to the respondent. His role was a combination of interviewer and participant-observer.

Although the informal series of interviews or discussions can blend into the participant-observer role, it is helpful to think of the pure type of participant-observation as something clearly different from the pure-type interview.

---

[5] Edwin H. Sutherland, *The Professional Thief* (Chicago: University of Chicago Press, 1937).

[6] Helen McGill Hughes, (ed.), *The Fantastic Lodge: The Autobiography of a Drug Addict* (Greenwich, Conn.: Fawcett Publications, 1971).

Participant-observation

Participant-observation differs from the interview in that the research situation involves more than two interacting participants, and the researcher participates in some role other than interviewer. One of the major problems of the participant-observation method is to find some role in the group, community, or organization which the researcher can successfully play and which will provide access to those people and situations he must observe to reach the objectives of the study.

This problem of getting a role inside the group has been solved in many distinctly different situations. Respectable suburbia was studied by Gans[7] by simply deciding to study the community in which he lived. His participant roles as property owner, taxpayer, parent, and neighbor were readily accessible, but there were still problems of maneuvering into the right position at the right time to observe and hear what was relevant to his study of Levittown.

In contrast to this setting is Liebow's[8] study of lives in the black ghetto in Washington, D.C., in which he focused on the family, friendship, and worklives of the black underemployed men. Liebow, being a white stranger in a black ghetto, was met with suspicion at first, but after helping with the legal defense of a man accused of killing his wife, he became accepted as someone who wanted to help.

In another study of the black ghetto, Hannerz[9] gives a fascinating account of the challenges and problems in explaining who he is and what he wants to black residents of a Washington, D.C., ghetto.

In some instances participant-observer methods have given rise to controversy concerning ethics, particularly in the study of secret societies or any groups hostile to outsiders. Many political sects, religious sects, and social movements have the attitude that "if you are not for us, you are against us," and only the true believers are allowed access to the group. In these cases the researchers must either quit trying to understand these groups, or they must enter in some acceptable role such as a "believer" or at least a "potential recruit." This ethical problem of simulating a role is seen in the controversy over the study by Festinger et al.[10] of a group predicting the destruction of the world on a certain date in the near future. The research team posed as travelling

---

[7] Herbert Gans, *The Levittowners* (New York: Pantheon, 1967).

[8] Elliot Liebow, *Tally's Corner* (Boston: Little, Brown & Co., 1967).

[9] Ulf Hannerz, *Soulside: Inquiries into Ghetto Culture and Community* (New York: Columbia University Press, 1969).

[10] Leon Festinger, Henry Riecken, and Stanley Schachter, *When Prophecy Fails* (New York: Harper & Row, 1956).

business men who had learned of the group's activities and were interested in learning more. Their description of the group's reaction to the failure of their prophecy is interesting and useful to the understanding of human behavior, and the participation of the research team did no harm to the members of the group studied, but the ethics of playing a false role is still controversial.

The fact that it is possible for a participant-observer to study deviant groups' behavior without playing an false undercover role is demonstrated by Humphreys' study of homosexuals, including their sexual activities in restrooms known as "tearooms."[11] His roles in the homosexual community included being a "lookout" at the "tearooms" to warn of any possible intrusion upon their privacy and being an "advocate" in organizing homosexuals to protect themselves against police harrassment, blackmail, and discrimination.

One of the apparent dilemmas of participant-observation is that, if the researcher does not succeed in getting into the group in an acceptable role, he cannot get the opportunity to observe; but if he is fully accepted as an equal member of the group, he is in danger of losing the objectivity needed to carry out valid observations and interpretations. This problem is dramatically illustrated in the account by Reiss[12] of a large-scale study of the police in several cities. The researchers were so thoroughly assimilated into the police that observers playing the role of plain-clothesmen threatened suspects with nightsticks. Another on duty in the police lockup adopted a measure police officers used to humiliate the prisoners. Others gave vent to race hatred that shocked even the officers they were supposed to be studying. According to Reiss the majority of the participant-observers became pro-police.

This problem of finding an intermediate position between being an objective outsider with no opportunity to observe and being an insider whose participation has rendered him incapable of objective observation is central to the method of participant-observation. It has been solved in several ways. The observer may assume *marginal* roles which provide the opportunity to observe but do not require the types of participation liable to totally assimilate the observer. Such roles are those of "potential recruit," "consultant," or "friend of the cause." Another solution is to train the researcher to observe carefully and report his own feelings, attitudes, and beliefs as they change during the time that he is being assimilated into the group. Another strategy ap-

---

[11] Laud Humphreys, *The Tearoom Trade* (Chicago: Aldine Publishing Co., 1970).

[12] Albert J. Reiss, Jr., "Stuff and Nonsense About Social Surveys and Observations," in *Institutions and the Person*, eds. Howard S. Becker et al. (Chicago: Aldine Publishing Co., 1968).

propriate in some cases is the substitution of pure observation or non-participant observation. In this case, of course, there is no opportunity to ask questions, to stimulate discussion, or to manipulate the situation experimentally.

Pure observation has little relationship to interviewing in that it does not provide a context for either formal or informal interviewing, which participant-observation does provide. For this reason it will not be dealt with separately. However, we would like to point out how certain unobtrusive measures can combine the values of pure observation with the values of participation without requiring the researcher's direct participation.

Unobtrusive measures

The term *unobtrusive measure* has developed in reference to types of observation which remove the observer from any direct interaction with the people involved in the behavior he is studying. Webb[13] has given an overview with examples of unobtrusive measures. Such methods include *hidden observation* or photography; *trace examination* that deals with examining the physical effects of human behavior, such as wearing down of the stone steps in a Mayan pyramid; or examination of *documents* such as marriage licenses, auto-registrations, and newspapers; or *contrived observations.* It is this last category which is of particular interest here because it combines the advantage of not being observed (a disadvantage of pure observation) with the advantage of being able to participate by providing certain stimuli to those in the situation being observed.

The researcher participates *indirectly* by contriving the situation to include certain stimuli designed to elicit action toward some object. Instead of having to directly ask someone, for example, his attitude toward certain organizations like the American Legion and the Communist Party, the observer contrives to have the person demonstrate his attitude by action. One way of doing this is by the "lost letter technique" described by Milgram.[14] In this study, stamped letters addressed to different organizations were dropped about the city. Then an observer recorded whether the "lost letter" was left on the sidewalk, picked up and destroyed, or picked up and mailed. It was assumed that the differences in behavior reflect differences in attitude toward the organizations to whom the letters are addressed.

---

[13] Eugene J. Webb, Donald T. Campbell, Richard D. Swartz, and Lee Sechrest, *Unobtrusive Measures: Nonreactive Research in the Social Sciences* (Chicago: Rand McNally, 1966).

[14] Stanley Milgram, "The Lost Letter Technique," *Psychology Today,* vol. 3 (1969), pp. 30–33.

With imagination, researchers can contrive other situations requiring a choice of alternative actions by those to be observed.

Relative value of methods

There is much literature devoted to studies and experiments on the relative value of interview, questionnaire, pure observation, empathy, and participant-observation. Some studies show that one method was more valid and other studies show that another method was more valid. Gradually, the question has shifted from "Which method is most valid?" to "Which method is best for what purpose under what circumstances?"

Interviewing is most valuable when we are interested in knowing people's beliefs, attitudes, values, knowledge, or any other subjective orientations or mental content. Whether the interview is more valuable than the questionnaire depends upon the degree to which we know exactly what we want to know and what the possible range of answers might be. The exploratory values of the unstructured interview are impossible to attain in a questionnaire where there is no opportunity to formulate new questions or probe for clarifications.

Observation is often superior to the interview in situations where we are asking the respondent to report his own overt actions in the past but where his memory may be faulty or he may want to hide the real nature of his actions from the interviewer. In this case an observer who is either unseen or not defined as such by the observer can get more reliable information. On the other hand, observation of isolated physical actions is often very difficult to interpret unless we know the person's intent or motivation. If our purpose is to predict what a person will do in the future, we need to know not only what he did in the past, but also why he did it. Then, too, many situations, for example those involving private sexual behavior, are not accessible to observation, yet people are willing to discuss them under the proper circumstances.

Participant-observation has many of the advantages of pure observation while allowing the researcher to intervene in a meaningful way in the ongoing action under observation. It has the one disadvantage in comparison with pure observation of the researcher, as participant, possibly having unintended effects upon the behavior of the observed.

Personal documents present an advantage since they often have already been accumulated, and they cannot be biased by the researcher because he was not involved in eliciting the information. However, since the researcher was not present to guide the response, to ask additional questions, or to probe for further elaboration or clarification, much of the information in a diary, letter, or confession will be irrelevant to the problem being studied, and much of the relevant information the person could have furnished is missing. The historian must often wish that he could interview a certain historical figure to find out what really happened or why he did what he did in a particular situation.

One strong recommendation made more and more often in studies of comparative method is that we cease quibbling over which method is the best, use methods to fit the purposes or conditions of the study, and use multiple methods whenever possible. This use of multiple methods, each to cross-check or supplement the others, is often referred to as *triangulation.*

Triangulation

Often the nature of the problem under investigation demands a multimethod approach because the various methods give totally different kinds of information that can supplement each other, because we do not know how to interpret some of the information unless we can couple it with other information, or because we need a cross-check to verify the validity of our observations.

For instance, we may want to supplement our analysis of certain public speeches made by a Congressman with interviews with him. The interviews may be supplemented (and prepared for) by reading about him in a standard biographical source. By using all these sources, we would be better able to predict how he will vote on a specific issue in Congress than by using any one source alone.

Community studies must triangulate information from public records, personal documents, newspapers, direct interviews with the focal persons, interviews with others about the focal persons, participant-observation and pure observations merely to obtain the many types of information needed to cover the complex phenomenon we call a community. Experimental studies, naturalistic communities studies, and statistical surveys can be fruitfully combined in many instances. The general topic of triangulation is clarified by detailed examples of comparative studies by Denzin.[15]

All of these methods of gathering information in the social sciences are influenced by the profound fact that empathy enters into not only the way we participate or observe as part of the information-gathering activity, but also into the way we interpret and analyze the information and in the application of the results to future situations. Only the scientist studying man is a part of the phenomenon he is studying. In a sense he is studying himself and therefore can empathize with his subject

---

[15] Norman K. Denzin, "Triangulation: A Case for Methodological Evaluation and Combination," pt. 12 in *Sociological Methods: A Sourcebook,* ed. Denzin (Chicago: Aldine Publishing Co., 1970).

matter. This unique relationship between the observer and the observed in the social sciences has both its advantages and disadvantages, which we will now try to describe.

Empathy

The concept of empathy, under various names, is found in the literature of philosophy, anthropology, sociology and psychology. George Herbert Mead used the phrase "taking the role of the other," and Max Weber discussed what he called the "verstehende" method. Charles H. Cooley used the term "sympathetic introspection," while Freud and others speak of "empathy," "identification," and "rapport." Anthropologists have often dealt with the problem of understanding the meaning behind overt acts of people in a culture foreign to the observer. They might use the term "rapport," "insight," or "understanding." All of these concepts overlap in their meaning and involve to some extent what we mean by empathy. We define empathy as the process by which one person is able to imaginatively place himself in another's role and situation in order to understand the other's feelings, point of view, attitudes, and tendencies to act in a given situation. In essence, empathy is the ability to correctly answer the question, "How would I feel or act in the situation if I were in his place?"

Some reject this method as being too subjective. They argue that it is useless because it is based upon an *if* proposition which may be untrue. Others have too much faith in empathy and rely upon it in situations where it is not dependable. We prefer to turn away from the question, "Is it or is it not reliable?" to the more fruitful question, "Under what conditions is it valid or invalid?"

In general terms we can say that a person's ability to successfully empathize with another person in a situation depends upon:

a. the degree to which this person's knowledge of the other's situation is complete and accurate;

b. the extent to which this person has experienced the same situation, or the degree to which he can imaginatively construct such a situation from elements of several similar situations;

c. the degree to which this person accurately observes and remembers his own experiences.

Let us assume that one person's observation and inferences regarding the other's situation are complete and accurate. Then we can ask how the probable validity of empathic prediction varies with the probability that the observer has had an experience similar to the one observed. This probability generally corresponds to the degree of universality of the behavior to be predicted. We can think of all forms of behavior and experience as ranging on a continuum from the most to the least universal.

$$MOST \longleftarrow \hspace{4cm} \longrightarrow LEAST$$
$$UNIVERSAL \hspace{6cm} UNIVERSAL$$

Biological	Human	Cultural	Role	Personal
behavior	behavior	behavior	behavior	behavior

Biological behavior includes those biological attributes which *all* members of the *homo sapiens* species share. For example, all people are born, must eat, and must eliminate waste material from the body. All people have sexual impulses, are startled by loud, unexpected noises, become fatigued, and must finally die. These are all necessary aspects of man's biological nature, regardless of the amount or type of interaction with other human beings.

Human behavior signifies those characteristics of behavior which all human beings share as a result of interaction with other human beings. In contrast to biological behavior, which is inherited, human nature must be learned in social interaction. Therefore, characteristics of behavior such as the use of language, self-consciousness, conscience, and sentiments (such as love, hate, embarrassment, or the desire for recognition) are acquired, but are universal to mankind.

Cultural behavior encompasses those aspects of behavior which are common to a particular group of people, but which distinguish them from another group. This would include such aspects as the particular *content* of the conscience rather than the mere possession of a conscience. Similarly, culture determines the *particular* language spoken by a group as distinguished from the more general characteristic of having a language. It includes all the folkways, mores, values, ideologies, and attitudes which distinguish one group from another and which all members of each group normally hold in common.

Role behavior includes those actions which depend upon a particular *role* played with a culture group. Therefore, this aspect of behavior varies *within* a culture group, depending upon the role or combination of roles played by a person. A corollary to this is that the range of role behavior within a culture group depends upon the complexity of the social organization (role structure) in that group. The differences between the behavior of a father and a mother toward their child are essentially differences in role.

Personal behavior indicates those characteristics of behavior which may vary from person to person while playing the same role in the same culture. Here we are intentionally avoiding the concept of personality as the "total behavior pattern of an individual," sometimes used in anthropology, sociology, and psychology, because our scheme is intended to bring into sharp focus the varying degrees of universality of behavior forms. Our definition includes such things as individual tastes, preferences, basic personality traits such as optimism or pessimism, and feelings of security or insecurity.

This scheme suggests that one person cannot empathize with all people in all situations with equal success. He can be limited by the degree of universality of the situation and by his own experience. Thus, if the behavior to be understood is at the biological or the human behavior level, the empathizer need not be from the same culture or have the same role in society as the person with whom he is empathizing. However, if the behavior is at the cultural or role level, the person attempting to empathize may fail miserably in the attempt unless he has participated in the same culture or the same role.

This is not to suggest that anyone can empathize with others at the biological or human behavior level. That has been proved untrue. But if the person attempting to empathize at this level is not successful, it is not for lack of common experience, but rather because he does not perceive the other person as being human in the same sense as himself. In other words, he does not appreciate the other's circumstances, or he is unaware of what his own reactions would be in the same circumstances.

Not only would we expect a person with a wider fund of experiences to empathize more successfully, but we would also expect a person who accurately observes and remembers his own behavior to have more success. We have all encountered individuals who have difficulty understanding or predicting the behavior of others mainly because they miscalculate how they themselves would behave under the same conditions.

Often, this type of person has difficulty empathizing because he tends to preserve his feeling of security by hiding, even from himself, any discrepancy between what he feels *should be* and what actually *is*. He may repress any memory of his own behavior unflattering to his self-image. Differences in this ability to see oneself objectively were dramatically demonstrated by respondents in studies of disaster-stricken communities. For example, one respondent would readily admit that he did not act in a heroic fashion but thought of his own physical safety first. Another person would feel compelled to explain the behavior of others as well as his own behavior in terms of heroism. In the eyes of such a person, the community emerged from chaos through a series of miracles. Frequently, upon closer examination, this type of respondent was found to have acted in a singularly self-centered fashion even after he was removed from physical danger. Thus, he was often genuinely disturbed and puzzled by the less than ideal forms of behavior brought to his attention.

A person's ability to empathize may be distorted by his tendency to see only the "good" aspect of reality. All human beings tend to do this to some extent, but there are wide variations in people's ability to see themselves or others objectively when what they see does not correspond with what they would like to see.

The following situations illustrate some of the values and limitations of empathy. Agreement will vary greatly, but the situations will demonstrate some of the strengths and weaknesses of the method.

Situation 1. Samu lived in the crescent-shaped clearing in the palm grove. His thatched hut was near the coral reef on the island of Baikta. Although he was only ten years old, he proudly assisted his father who, like most of the inhabitants of the island, was a fisherman. These pre-literate people had never seen a movie nor heard a radio. The island was a battleground between the Americans and the Japanese for about three days in 1945. These soldiers were the last foreigners on the island. The fastest transportation on the island was the dugout canoe with outrigger pontoons and no sails. Samu's father was proud of his skill in launching and paddling a canoe in the heavy surf when they went fishing each day. None of the islanders had been farther than Choru Island about 60 miles away.

Samu had never seen a white man until a boat arrived in the lagoon with the technical staff of the movie "Coral Sands." In Samu's words, "My father told me that they were not a war party like the last white men he had seen, but that they wanted to make a story which the white man called a 'movie.' They talked to my father and asked whether they could take me with them for several weeks to an island about 285 miles east of Baikta. No one lives on the island because no fruit trees grow there. They said that I was just the right size for the movie. One of them spoke our language, but it was difficult to understand his words. He told my father that if I would stay for six weeks or more he would give my father a new fishing net. That is something my father would like very much. They had no room for any of my relatives on their boat and they needed a boy just my size."

In this case what would the father's reaction be?

Discussion. If we look at this situation more abstractly, we see a father being asked to let his ten-year-old son leave home with strangers. They would be taking the boy to an uninhabited island almost five times as far away as any of his acquaintances had traveled in their lives. Furthermore, all but one would speak only a foreign language, and that one person showed only a crude knowledge of the native language and was difficult to understand. In effect, the father was being asked to entrust his son to strangers with no more compensation than the *promise* of a fishing net. The boy would be among strangers who spoke a foreign language and ate strange food. None of his relatives would be with him.

In the primitive culture, where kinship ties are extremely strong, a ten-year-old boy is an important asset in helping his father, and his absence would upset the family's usual division of labor. Samu's people had never heard a radio, seen a movie, or read any books which might have given them knowledge beyond the traditional folklore of the tribe. Therefore, little motivation could be attached to appearing in a movie. Furthermore, it is improbable that the earlier battle between the Americans and Japanese would make the father remember Americans as kind, predictable people.

Considering these factors, we are almost certain that the father would refuse the offer. The ten anthropologists and sociologists who were consulted agreed unanimously.

Untrained interviewers gave various reasons for believing that Samu's father would accept the offer: "The father is proud of his son and would like to have him in a movie." "The father realized that these men were different from the other white men he had seen." "The father knew that the white men would not harm Samu." "The islanders would be honored that Samu was chosen." "The father would want to give Samu an opportunity that he himself had never had." "There's not enough information." "There's no information about this particular culture telling how they react to strangers."

The "reasons" above reflect two general types of errors: first, the failure to realize that there are certain conditions which, when viewed abstractly, become *universal* tendencies or forces; second, the tendency of an observer to *project* the values of his own culture and to assume that people in another culture have knowledge which they could not possibly have.

Situation 2. It seemed like any other Saturday afternoon when a typical farm family had one of its most unforgettable experiences. Mrs. Boswell, the farmer's wife, was in the country visiting a friend while her husband and seven-year-old daughter went to Judsonia, Arkansas, about five miles away. The husband dropped his daughter off at Aunt Emma's house as had been planned and then went to a friend's garage to help him repair a tractor. Aunt Emma lived three blocks north of the main highway, and the garage was an equal distance south of the highway on the same cross street. Later that afternoon, Mrs. Boswell heard a newscast reporting that a tornado had struck Judsonia, demolishing all its buildings. Unable to believe it, she asked her friend to drive her to Judsonia in the pickup truck. As they approached the town on the main highway, from almost a mile away they could see that the steel water tower had been crushed like a piece of tin foil. Mrs. Boswell became distraught and screamed, "Almighty God, what has happened?"

Assuming that they are equally accessible, would you expect Mrs. Boswell to go to her husband or her daughter first in this situation?

Discussion. One basic question here is, which dominates Mrs. Boswell, her role as a mother or as a wife? Another question is, how will she define the situation regarding the relative threat to two members of her family?

We will assume that (*a*) the mother believes that both her husband and daughter are in mortal danger, (*b*) that both are equally accessible, and (*c*) that the equal access to each calls for a *choice* between the two alternatives.

Any general knowledge about the relationships in a rural family, in contrast to those in a suburban professional family would be relevant. Certainly, the mother would be more emotionally attached to a seven-year-old daughter than the father would be. Also, she is considered more directly responsible for the daughter than is the father. The usual assumption is that children are helpless and that "big strong men" can care for themselves. The rural community would consider it natural for the "mother instinct" to be manifested during an emergency.

The validity of this rationale has been affirmed in empirical studies of disasters. There is little evidence to compare the rural family's reaction in a disaster to that of an urban or suburban family. However, most of the studies done by the National Opinion Research Center of disasters in rural areas revealed a pattern of interaction during the crisis where the mother was first concerned for her children, particularly if they were young and female, and second for her husband. In contrast to this, the husband was usually concerned first with the welfare of his wife and later with that of the children, although this pattern is not so clear as the first.

Of course we must remember that the tendency to conform to such a pattern is only one social-psychological force and that there are other forces in the situation.

Disagreements with this pattern follow such lines of reasoning as: "It depends on the particular mother." "The mother would be more concerned with her husband because she is dependent, at least financially, upon him." "She has been attached to her husband longer than to her daughter." "It depends on Mrs. Boswell's previous experiences in disasters." "The daughter is in the care of relatives so there is nothing to worry about."

The solution to this problem depends mainly upon understanding the mother's position in the structure of the rural farm family considered as a subculture pattern. It might be argued that all American families as a common culture would share this pattern or that it would be universal to *homo sapiens* as a biological instinct or universal trait. Without evaluating either of these points of view, we say that their truth or falsity is logically irrelevant to the stated problem, because with either or both true, the answer to the problem would be the same. There is reason to suspect, however, that such a pattern is *not* universal to all families in disaster situations.

Situation 3.   A friend has offered Bob, a student at college X, free transportation and lodging for a weekend of skiing. If they go, it will be impossible for Bob to return to campus in time to attend his Monday morning philosophy class. Although college regulations do not require obtaining permission to miss classes, Bob feels that he should find out from the professor how to make up anything he might miss in the Monday session. He goes to the professor's office and says:

Bob: Hello, Dr. Belden! Could I speak to you for a minute?
Dr. Belden: Surely.
Bob: I was just wondering if anything important will be going on in class on Monday?
Dr. Belden: Why do you ask?
Bob: (Enthusiastically) Well, to be frank, I have a chance to take a skiing trip this weekend, and I wanted to find out if I would be missing anything.

What is likely to be Dr. Belden's reaction in this situation?

Discussion.   This situation is a matter of two points of view associated with two complementary roles in an institutional setting. In general, professors feel that they work hard to transform the raw material they find in freshmen into a more educated version of man. They usually do not enter a field unless they think it is important, and their egos are intimately involved with that field. Under these conditions, the student, who has been wondering if "anything important" would go on in class Monday, implies with his choice of words that there have been days when nothing important occurred.

Even though the professor responds with a civil "Why do you ask?" he certainly has not been flattered by the student's question. Nor is the student's answer gratifying. Instead of asking how he can make up what he will miss, he asks whether he will miss anything.

For these reasons, it seems that the professor would react with a negative feeling. This hypothesis has been substantiated by the responses of a small sample of college professors teaching where class attendance is not required. None of them reacted favorably. Two said they would have no special reaction, and the remaining 19 said they would react unfavorably.

Several typical reasons were offered by untrained observers who thought the professor would react positively: "The professor will probably be impressed by the student's interest in making up the work." "The student didn't have to make any excuses since permission to miss class is not required." "The professor would admire the student's honesty. After all he could have used the 'sick aunt' excuse."

These types of replies simply show an inability to empathize with the professor's role in the student-teacher relationship, and their complete identification with the student causes them to marvel at Bob's honesty.

Situation 4. Bob Cains and Roger Holden, 20 and 24 years old, were hiking in the Sierra Nevada mountains. They had driven as far up as the side road would take them and after packing their food and camping equipment into knapsacks, headed for the top of Donner Pass. They reached their objective the morning of the second day's hike. They decided to return by another trail in order to enjoy a variety of scenery, and they thought it would be worthwhile to take their time and explore interesting side trails. However, they took a wrong turn and became hopelessly lost. They had wandered for three days without food and had hiked about 35 miles when they accidentally stumbled upon a good trail. They followed it downhill for about seven miles, and came to a fork which was clearly marked. A sign pointing to the right said, "Kyber Creek—5 miles" and a sign to the left said "Camino Ranger Station—4 miles." (A ranger station is a place where U.S. Forest Rangers or Forest Guards live the year around.)

"We've gone around in a circle!" Bob observed. "Our car would be about one mile upstream from where this trail hits Kyber Creek, or about three miles by the highway downstream from the Ranger Station which is also on Kyber Creek."

"That's right," said Roger, scratching his head. "That means it is about six miles to our car if we take the trail to the right and about seven miles if we go by way of the Ranger Station. It's cold now but it won't be dark for three more hours."

"Okay, Roger," Bob replied. "Since it is downhill either way, and the trails are both good, we had better head for . . . ."

Assuming that Bob and Roger's assessment of the situation when making the decision is correct, which way would they go?

Discussion. This problem is a clear-cut example of behavior which would be universal to man, primarily because of the simple biological urges of hunger and fatigue. The crux of the problem is to determine which alternative would be chosen by a man who has been without food and has hiked 35 miles in three days. Will he hike four miles to the ranger station where he can obtain food and shelter? Or will he walk six miles to the car which he can drive to get food?

For anyone who has had a similar experience, there is little doubt of what they would do under the circumstances. The basic error made by people who predicted the wrong decision in this case was an overemphasis on the importance of getting to the car rather than to food. They failed to appreciate the significance of two miles under such conditions.

The ability to empathize is an integral part of the interviewing process. An interviewer who is incapable of empathizing with the respondent has little success. Differences between individual interviewers' abilities to empathize are more striking when the general style of interviewing is less structured and when the topic of the interview contains more ego-involved material for the respondent. This is true because the nonscheduled interview gives more freedom to the interviewer to select the content, form, and sequence of questions. He is freer either to make more errors or to take advantage of opportunities not open to him if he were restricted by a highly scheduled interview.

It is the interviewer's ability to empathize which allows him to select techniques and tactics most appropriate to the circumstances. Without this basic skill, the interviewer who has learned several specific techniques cannot use them effectively when faced with the respondent. He can only proceed in either a mechanical fashion or a way that satisfies his own ego. Neither course will produce best results.

Although empathic predictions are sometimes incorrect, the interviewer must constantly *try* to empathize in order to utilize his observations of himself and the respondent as a guide to effectively modifying his own behavior during the interview.

This possibility of error makes it necessary for him to treat his prediction of the respondent's behavior as a tentative hypothesis to be modified by subsequent observations. Thus, the interviewer, through the use of empathy and observation, is constantly revising his predictions of the respondent's behavior and adjusting his own behavior accordingly.

An interviewer also should be aware of his strengths and limitations in empathic observation in order to judge which types of interviews he can handle effectively. For example, a social worker whose background was anti-Catholic might have great difficulty empathizing with a Catholic's feeling on the socialist state or on contraception. Or a young sociology student doing a community study might find that his Protestant background interferes with his appreciation of an older Jewish woman's feelings about anti-Semitism in the community. A personnel interviewer in a large industry might not be able to empathize with the employee's untrusting attitude toward the company's in-service education program.

The individual researcher who will do most of his own interviewing must recognize his own limitations and either select his problem accordingly or, when necessary for a particular problem, use another interviewer. From the point of view of a director or supervisor of any large-scale research project, it is often more efficient to *select* interviewers with the best background experiences and personality characteristics for a project rather than to try to train people for increased empathic ability.

INTERVIEWING COMPARED WITH ORDINARY CONVERSATION

Just as interviewing cannot be divorced from other methods of gaining understanding of human behavior, neither can it be separated from the basic skills of ordinary conversation. Any two-way conversation involves many of the same skills and insights needed for successful interviewing. The main difference is in the *central purpose* of interviewing as opposed to other forms of conversation.

There is a tendency for those faced with the problems of obtaining information on human behavior to vacillate between two views: that interviewing is just talking to people in a spontaneous sociable way or that it is a magical and mysterious formula which allows the interviewer to put away all of his common-sense knowledge, insight, and intuition. People with the latter view tend to follow a single "technique" with a slavish rigidity. During the process of training interviewers in industrial, governmental, and educational settings, it is common to hear that "here, we use the _____ technique of interviewing." This blank is filled in with such words as "permissive," "nondirective," "focused," "understanding-listening," "supportive," "depth," "structured," "unstructured," "free-wheeling," "subjective," "expressive," "spontaneous," "projective," "phenomenological," "indirect," "transactional," or "psychiatric." The remarkable thing is that the same technique is often used for divergent types of interviewing situations and at all points within a particular interview.

Experience in interviewing, training others to interview, and doing research on interviewing methods, shows that no single approach, style, or technique of interviewing is adequate except within narrow limits. The interviewer should strive to increase his range of techniques and his ability to adapt flexibly to the purposes of the interview and the requirements of the specific situation.

The interviewer should realize the wide range of functions of ordinary conversation and how they relate to interviewing. If this is not done in a self-conscious way, the interviewer may be limited by habits acquired in previous forms of conversation, or be reluctant to use insights or skills learned previously, for fear that they are not "techniques" but merely "common sense."

Whenever two or more human beings are conversing, several social-psychological types of communication may prevail, one at a time or in combination. These types may be delineated according to their purpose.

Expression

One of the most common functions of conversation is the joy of self-expression. One or both of the conversationalists may be fulfilling the need to express ideas, feelings, attitudes, or moods. One person may assume that the other is listening in fascination when in reality his expression is in response to his own thoughts, which he is organizing for the next assault. This illusion of an audience is important to the person expressing himself. Such a conversation may be quite satisfying to both participants even though neither has the slightest idea of what the other has said. Of course there are times when one person's eagerness to express himself interferes with the other's opportunity to do the same.

This urge for spontaneous expression can be a vital asset in interviewing, provided that once it has been encouraged in the respondent, it can (a) then be directed by the interviewer toward the information-gathering objectives of the interview, and (b) the interviewer himself does not give way to the urge for self-expression.

One of the common errors made by the novice interviewer is to yield to the temptation to impress the respondent with his own knowledge of the subject of the interview. This form of expression runs the risk of threatening the respondent, who will then tend to guard his responses rather than expressing his thoughts and feelings frankly. It should not be inferred from this that it is always undesirable for the respondent to express ideas not directly relevant. On the contrary, it is often vital to the respondent's morale. Neither should it be assumed that any spontaneous expression of feeling by the interviewer is detrimental to the success of the interview. However, the interviewer must keep both his own and the respondent's urge to express himself within bounds by constantly asking himself, "How will this effect the completeness and accuracy of the information I seek?" This self-discipline distinguishes the interviewer from the conversationalist.

Persuasion

To a certain extent, the concepts of expression and of persuasion overlap in that both involve the expression of feelings and ideas. Expression includes only those cases where the speaker is not concerned with convincing the other person. He merely wants an opportunity to express his own ideas and feelings spontaneously. Persuasion is behavior which may or may not be spontaneous but which is essentially aimed at convincing the other person.

There are times when persuasive conversation is an integral part of the information-gathering process. In certain types of survey work one of the chief problems is to "sell" the potential respondent on the importance of the study, to persuade him that he is of vital interest, or that the information will be kept anonymous.

There are many situations in which an interviewer's urge to persuade the respondent may endanger the interview. In extreme cases, yielding to this urge has sent the interviewer to jail. For example, the sociology department in a graduate school was studying racial tensions in an area between an all-black and an all-white residential area. One of the graduate student interviewers felt strongly about the injustices of the violence against blacks who moved into the white residential area. During interviews, he could not resist the temptation of admonishing the respondents for their social values and for their superstitions about race. Respondents began to react defensively and aggressively, and a rumor began to circulate that a "bunch of Communists" were going from house to house "stirring up trouble." One respondent then called the police, informing them that a Communist was molesting his wife, and the police took the interviewer to jail. This dramatically illustrates a situation in which the role of the information-gatherer and the role of reformer could not be mixed.

More frequently, the interviewer's urge to persuade results in gathering distorted information. Tape-recorded interviews have provided the following examples: a minister could not resist the opportunity to "convert" disaster victims during the interview; a social worker could not separate her therapeutic function from giving the client advice; and an opinion pollster unconsciously and subtly influenced the respondent by the context and wording of the questions used. Only by the systematic analysis of tape-recorded interviews can these subtle manifestations of the persuasive urge be demonstrated.

Therapy

In ordinary conversation with a friend, a person often expresses ideas and feelings to release emotional tension. This release is called catharsis and is encouraged by the psychiatrist or clinical psychologist in therapeutic interviews.

The permissive atmosphere and spontaneous give-and-take involved in certain types of social science interviews may also have a therapeutic effect on the respondent by fulfilling his need for catharsis. However, the interviewer should not delve into the respondent's inner conflicts if these conflicts are not connected to the information he seeks. In some cases, the respondent will feel resentful later if the interviewer has "allowed" him to talk of irrelevant matters in seeking catharsis. This is a particular danger when the attempt is unsuccessful and when the interviewer needs to establish a continuing relationship with the respondent or with some of his acquaintances.

There are many times when the information sought is closely related to the respondent's inner conflicts and tensions. This was frequently the case in interviews with disaster victims. Many times it was obvious to the interviewer that the respondent was suffering from guilt feelings about his behavior in the disaster. For example, a mayor of a small town felt guilty because he had been unable to direct the rescue operations and had become confused "just like anyone else." A mother felt guilty because she had let the tornado jerk her baby from her arms while her husband had kept the other child safely. And a husband felt guilty because, when the storm struck his house, he was talking with a waitress rather than eating supper at home with his wife.

In a study of industrial personnel, the interviewer might detect an employee's guilt feelings about stealing certain supplies from his employer. He might note that a management person feels guilty that he teaches honesty in his Sunday School class, but keeps two sets of records on production efficiency, sending the "fixed" set of records to the central office. He feels forced into dishonesty because an accurate record would compare him unfavorably with heads of other departments whose efficiency records are also "fixed." He cannot expose their deceit because he is also guilty.

The social scientist, primarily concerned with collecting valid information, sometimes finds it necessary to play a therapeutic role temporarily to get the desired information. Other times he feels a moral obligation to do what he can therapeutically if he is qualified to do so. More often, however, the interviewer finds that some therapy results without any special effort.

Often the sensitive interviewer is concerned with the ethics of dabbling in therapy while obtaining information. This cannot altogether be avoided. Anyone who speaks to another person giving sympathetic understanding or creating a permissive nonjudgmental atmosphere is likely to encourage cathartic release in the other person. This is true whether the two people involved in the conversation are just good friends or whether the conversation takes place in the confessional or on the psychoanalyst's couch. In trying to obtain valid information it is often necessary for the person studying human behavior to offer just such an atmosphere.

Ritual

Another common form of conversation might be called ritualistic. It is merely a form of verbal behavior which has no real significance other than to provide the security in interpersonal relations which comes with having certain forms of verbal behavior acceptable in all instances of a certain type of occasion. These empty forms may provide little real information. When a person says "Good morning!" he is not trying to persuade, nor does he give information which characterizes the particular morning. Occasionally, situations are confusing because a question is asked but the responding person does not know whether the question calls for objective information or for a ritualistic answer. For example, in the hospital when the nurse says, "How are you this morning?" the patient doesn't know whether to say, "I have a bad headache," or to say, "Fine, thanks, and how are you?"

In interviewing, we must learn to detect ritualistic answers by the respondent and also learn to avoid giving them ourselves. For example, a common error appears when the respondent says, "You know what I mean!" and the unwary interviewer unthinkingly responds as he would in an ordinary conversation with, "Uh huh," when he does not actually understand what the respondent has in mind. To obtain more accurate information, it would be much better to say, "I'm not sure I know exactly what you mean. Could you tell me a little more about it?"

In general, this ritualistic function of conversation has little use in gathering information. The interviewer must merely be aware of the danger of engaging in such rituialistic conversation and then confusing the results with valid information.

Information

A fifth function of conversation is to exchange information. Although the previous four functions have a peripheral place in the type of interview we are dealing with, the exchange of information is the *central* purpose of the interview. The word "exchange" reminds us that in the interview the flow of information must be two-way. Too frequently, an interviewer becomes so concerned with the information he wishes to obtain, and with interpreting what the respondent says, that he forgets to be equally concerned with communicating to the respondent the type of information he needs. He must also communicate the appropriate attitude toward the respondent and toward the information to motivate the respondent to continue to give relevant information.

The exchange of information is not found only in interviews. Two excavators discussing possible ways to avoid a cave-in, two scientists engaged in a discussion of a common problem, a teacher leading a discussion, or two criminals planning a bank robbery—all are participating in an exchange of information. Two characteristics often distinguish an interview from the other situations just mentioned. Often the problem about which the interviewer is seeking information is not equally important to the respondent; hence there might be certain motivational problems. Also interviewers often deal with a wide variety of types of people in obtaining a wide variety of types of information;

because of this diversity there may be an initial communication barrier between interviewer and respondent which does not exist between two people whose activities bring them into regular contact.

This lack of an equal stake in the problem and of a habitual channel of communication between the interviewer and respondent puts the burden of overcoming these barriers on the interviewer. He must translate the problem to a level of concreteness clearly understood by the respondent and learn the vocabulary familiar to the respondent. The interviewer must be sensitive to the important difference between the information he needs in conceptual terms and the concrete questions he asks in order to obtain the information. For example, it is hopeless for an anthropologist to try to explain to a tribesman that he would like his help in a structural-functional analysis of the kinship system of the tribe. It is equally difficult to explain to a disaster victim that you are interested in the process of progressive redefinition of the situation in the first few minutes of the crisis period and its relationship to adaptive behavior and psychosomatic illness during and after the crisis. Less obviously, it is expecting far too much to ask a college freshman, "Why did you come to this college rather than to some other one?"

In studies where the investigator will have many contacts with the respondent, it becomes more possible to build up a rational sharing relationship, even where the cultural backgrounds of the interviewer and the respondent may be quite different. For example, Whyte[16] found that his informants were becoming sophisticated in their observations and in the way they thought about them as a result of a process of progressive sharing and mutual education. However, in studies involving only one contact between the interviewer and respondent, rarely do we find a respondent with whom we can discuss the problem directly in common theoretical terms.

Many interviews may involve the functions of expression, persuasion, therapy, and even a minimum of ritual; but the interviewer must keep in mind that these four functions (whether they are found in the behavior of the interviewer or the respondent) must be subordinated to the main function of exchanging information. This does not mean that the interviewer should hesitate to use any mode or type of communication that aids in the free flow of relevant information.

Thus far we have shown some of the relationships between interviewing and other general methods of obtaining information about human behavior such as empathy, participation, and observation. Also, we focused more closely on the relationship between various functions of conversation and the central function of the information-gathering

---

[16] William F. Whyte, *Street Corner Society: The Social Structure of an Italian Slum* (Chicago: University of Chicago Press, 1943).

interview. Now we will be concerned only with the information-gathering interview, looking at it from the point of view of its various styles and objectives.

DISCUSSION QUESTIONS

1. Think of situations in which empathy, participation, and observation would be useful in an interview.
2. What are the advantages and disadvantages of using personal documents in research? Think of a situation in which you might use personal documents profitably.
3. What are some of the difficulties in using participant-observation? What are some of the advantages? Think of a situation in which you might choose this method.
4. How would you answer the question "Which method is most valid?"
5. How would you predict a person's ability to empathize successfully in a given situation? Illustrate with specific examples.
6. Give an example of situations in which each of the functions of ordinary conversation might be used in interviewing.

SELECTED READINGS

Allport, Gordon W.   *The Use of Personal Documents in Psychological Science.* New York: Social Science Research Council, 1942.

Deals with diaries, letters, case studies, and other documents in the scientific study of human behavior and makes a basic plea to the psychologist to avoid dealing in abstractions not connected to everyday behavior.

Denzin, Norman K. (ed.)   *Sociological Methods: A Sourcebook.* Chicago: Aldine Publishing Co., 1970, pt. 12—"Triangulation: A Case for Methodological Evaluation and Combination," pp. 471–525.

Shows the need for both methodological and theoretical "triangulation" as a means for achieving greater validity in conclusions about human behavior.

Festinger, Leon, et al.   *When Prophecy Fails.* New York: Harper & Row, 1956.

A fascinating example of the use of team participant observation of a religious sect awaiting the end of the world on a specific date in the near future. Raises both methodological and ethical issues.

Gottschalk, Louis, et al.   *The Use of Personal Documents in History, Anthropology and Sociology.* New York: Social Science Research Council, 1947.

The methods of utilizing personal documents are treated separately for each of the fields. The contexts of these fields are preserved as they give many illustrations of research using personal documents. This is a classic in the field.

Hughes, Helen M. (ed.)   *The Fantastic Lodge: The Autobiography of a Drug Addict.* Greenwich, Conn.: Fawcett Publications, 1971.

An example of a "personal document" in the form of an autobiography stimulated by the writer's interaction with a sociologist. The young woman came to the Beckers' house to tell her story, which was recorded on tape.

Webb, Eugene J., et al.   *Unobtrusive Measures: Nonreactive Research in the Social Sciences.* Chicago: Rand McNally, 1966.

Nonreactive methods are those that do not involve direct interaction between the researcher and the people being studied. This includes the measurement of physical erosion and accretion, governmental and other records, and simple observation.

3

Styles and objectives of interviewing

A review of the growing number of books on interviewing shows that some are written for specific use and others for general use. Both types have their legitimate place in methodology. The reader, however, must avoid the tendency to overgeneralize. Often the book clearly warns the reader that any generalizations made in the form of "do's or don'ts" should be kept within the context of the specific purpose and setting which is assumed. Sometimes the title clearly specifies that the book is written for interviewers connected with a particular organization's functions. For example, a handbook of one polling organization[1] makes it clear that the suggestions hold only on the assumption that most interviews are done to obtain information on opinions, beliefs, and attitudes rather than on objective verifiable facts. Also, the polling function assumes that the respondents will be a random sample of some population, usually interviewed in the home, and that the interviewer will use a highly structured interview schedule (guide or questionnaire).

Sometimes the title of the book may not give warning that it deals with a highly specialized type of interview. For example, Polansky's excellent book[2] deals mainly with the therapeutic interview. Instead of dealing with a random sample of the U.S. population at their own residences, the respondents were usually those who found their way into the office of a social worker, psychiatrist, or clinical psychologist. In this case a more helpful subtitle might be "Theory for the *Psychotherapeutic* Interview" rather than "Theory for *the* Interview." The

---

[1] National Opinion Research Center, *Interviewing for NORC* (Denver, Colo.: National Opinion Research Center, 1947).

[2] Norman A. Polansky, *Ego Psychology and Communication: Theory for the Interview* (New York: Atherton Press, 1971).

point to remember is that we must be careful not to generalize from what is effective in one specific interview setting to all interviewing.

Specialized treatments of interviewing can be classified into three kinds: those which put the focus upon the type of *respondent,* the type of *interviewer,* and the *function* of the interview. The respondent-specialized books tend to deal with groups such as children,[3] adolescents, the aged,[4] the elite,[5] parents,[6] or prospective employees.[7]

The interviewer-specialized treatments usually focus upon a particular profession or role of the interviewer such as supervisor,[8] pollster,[9] social worker,[10] nurse,[11] psychiatrist,[12] journalist,[13] or physician.[14] Some of these professionals, such as the social worker, pollster, psychiatrist, and news reporter, may consider interviewing as one of their most important activities; others such as the supervisor, nurse, policeman, teacher, or lawyer may not think of the interview as one of the main tools of their trade.

The function-specialized treatments focus upon some basic function of interviewing such as the focused interview,[15] the assessment interview,[16] the depth interview,[17] the problem-solving interview,[18] or the helping interview.[19] Usually, such function-specialized treatments view the purpose as something other than, or in addition to, information

---

[3] J. Rich, *Interviewing Children and Adolescents* (New York: Macmillan Co., 1968).

[4] R. Kastenbaum and S. Sherwood, *VIRO: A New Scale for Assessing the Interview Behavior of Elderly People,* Proceedings of the 20th Annual Meeting of the Gerontological Society, 1967.

[5] Lewis Dexter, *Elite and Specialized Interviewing* (Evanston, Illinois: Northwestern University Press, 1970).

[6] Grace Langdon, *Teacher-Parent Interviews* (Englewood Cliffs, N.J.: Prentice-Hall, 1954).

[7] David Turner, *Employment Interviewer* (New York: Arco Publishing Co., 1968).

[8] L. L. Steinmetz, *Interviewing Skills for Supervisory Personnel* (Reading, Mass.: Addison-Wesley Publishers, 1971).

[9] J. S. Adams, *Interviewing Procedures: A Manual for Survey Interviews* (Chapel Hill: University of North Carolina Press, 1958).

[10] Anne Fenlason et al., *Essentials of Interviewing* (New York: Harper & Row, 1962).

[11] Loretta L. Bermosk and Mary J. Mordan, *Interviewing in Nursing* (New York: Macmillan Co., 1964).

[12] John D. Davis, *The Interview as Arena* (Stanford, Calif.: Stanford University Press, 1971).

[13] Hugh C. Sherwood, *The Journalistic Interview* (New York: Harper & Row, 1969).

[14] Robert Froelich and F. M. Bishop. *Medical Interviewing* (St. Louis: Mosby, 1969).

[15] Robert K. Merton, *The Focused Interview: A Manual of Problems and Procedures* (New York: The Free Press, 1956).

[16] G. Shoulksmith, *Assessment through Interviewing* (Oxford: Pergamon Press, 1968).

[17] William H. Banaka, *Training in Depth Interview* (New York: Harper & Row, 1971).

[18] Wilbert E. Beveridge, *Problem-Solving Interviews* (London: Allen & Unwin, 1968).

[19] Alfred Benjamin, *The Helping Interview* (New York: Houghton Mifflin, 1969).

gathering. The gaining of information is seen as a means to some end in relationship to the respondent himself. The purpose might be to educate the respondent, to help him make a decision, to change his attitude, to give him therapy, to help him solve a problem, or to arrive at some agreement for future action. In any case, the success of the interview depends upon obtaining valid information from the respondent.

A more general treatment of interviewing focuses on the information-gathering function which is involved in all interviews regardless of a specialized purpose. During this information gathering, the interviewer's behavior is aimed at facilitating the flow of relevant and valid information.

One such general treatment was done by Kahn and Cannell[20] who lay down a psychological theory for the basic information-gathering function but apply this theory to specific settings such as medicine, surveying, personnel work, and social work. Another broad approach is taken by Richardson[21] who draws upon studies and experiments with a variety of interview types to arrive at some generally applicable ideas about the relationship between basic forms of the interview and its information-gathering function.

DIMENSIONS OF INTERVIEWING STYLE

One aspect of interviewing style[22] is the dichotomy between standardized and nonstandardized interviews. The standardized interview is designed to collect precisely the same categories of information from a number of respondents; and the answers of all respondents must be comparable and classifiable. Thus, we can be sure that any differences in the answers are due to differences among the respondents rather than in the questions asked. Subtle differences in the form or content of a question may in some instances elicit distinctly different answers. For example, the question "Do you agree that premarital sex is permissible?" the question "Do you feel that premarital sex is permissible, or not?" or the question "Do you agree with psychologists who say that premarital sex is permissible?" may get very different answers. In contrast the question "What do you think should be done about the energy shortage?" might get precisely the same response as "What do most

---

[20] Robert L. Kahn and Charles F. Cannell, *The Dynamics of Interviewing: Theory, Techniques and Cases* (New York: John Wiley & Sons, 1957).

[21] Stephen A. Richardson et al., *Interviewing: Its Forms and Function* (New York: Basic Books, 1965).

[22] In this chapter when we deal with styles of interviewing, we will use an adaptation of Richardson's "forms" (ibid., p. 34). We prefer styles because one of the "forms" is essentially formless, but all can be clearly thought of as styles.

people think should be done about the energy shortage?" Strange as it may seem at first glance, under certain conditions it may be necessary to use different wordings to convey the same meaning to two respondents of different social backgrounds. Obviously, if we are to make any quantitative statements regarding the aggregate, we must convey the same meaning to all respondents regardless of whether we use the same or different words. In either case the interview could be considered as standardized.

There are two sub-types of the *standardized* interview, the scheduled and the nonscheduled. The *scheduled* interview not only specifies the questions in advance but also uses the questions in the same order with each respondent. The *nonscheduled* interview gives the interviewer some choice as to the order of the questions, freedom to attempt alternative wordings of the same question, and freedom to use neutral probes if the first response to a question is not clear, complete, or relevant. To keep within the requirements of a standardized interview, however, the nonscheduled interviewer must either initially record the responses on a standardized form, or reduce the free flow of information to a standard form, later, by the process of content analysis. Otherwise there is no way individuals can be clearly compared, or the aggregate response of the group summarized statistically.

The *nonstandardized* interview does not pose all of the same questions to all respondents, and there is no way the information can be statistically summarized to reflect the aggregate response of the group or to compare one individual's response with another's. Since the nonstandardized interview is essentially formless, the sub-types are according to purpose rather than form. We can refer to these sub-types as preparatory and independent.

The *preparatory nonstandardized* interview is done in order to prepare a more standardized interview. The preparatory interview is free to explore such things as the vocabulary used by different respondents discussing the topic or to determine the qualitative or quantitative range of answers to establish reliable and valid answer categories. Contexts which respondents use to interpret the meaning of questions may be discovered, or qualified respondents can be located.

The preparatory interview can investigate the appropriate time and place for the interview, the types of resistances the respondents might have to giving certain information, and anything else needed to construct a standardized, scheduled interview which then may be field-tested.

The *independent nonstandardized* interview is not preparatory to any standardized interview but has an independent function of its own. It is used in situations where there is no need either to compare one set of responses with another or to summarize the responses of a sample of respondents. For example, if we want to retrace the channels through which some rumor or other report has traveled, we might conduct a chain of interviews in which the approach in each subsequent interview would depend on what we have learned in all of the previous interviews. Or if we want to discover the structure of some organization and how it functions, we would have to ask different kinds of questions of people in each position in the organization.

Neither type of nonstandardized interview is ever used in public-opinion polling or any other study where we need to measure some attribute of each individual in a sample. Strangely, very little has been done systematically to study the strategy, tactics, or techniques of the nonstandardized interview. Richardson[23] speculates that this is because its methodology is more varied, more complex, more difficult to make explicit, and more difficult to develop into a set of routine practices.

This book will be concerned mainly with the standardized interview in both its scheduled and nonscheduled forms. The nonstandardized interview may enter tangentially as it affects the early stages of a field study. Let us now examine the important dimensions of the standardized interview.

The first dimension deals with the degree to which communication between the interviewer and respondent is specified and controlled by a prepared schedule.[24] The second deals with the amount of freedom which the interviewer allows the respondent in selecting topics and sequences of topics related to the objective of the interview. As will be shown, an interviewer can purposefully vary his behavior both in the dimension of *scheduling* and the dimension of *topic control.*

Scheduled and nonscheduled interviews

The completely nonscheduled interview is one in which the interviewer is guided only by a central purpose and must decide for himself the means. In contrast to this, the completely scheduled interview spells out the objectives in terms of specific questions which must be asked in a fixed sequence, using specific words. It may also restrict the respondent by providing answer categories from which he is allowed to select. The schedule to a great extent restricts the techniques used by the interviewer and the form of information given by the respondent.

---

[23] Richardson et al., *Interviewing*, p. 36.

[24] In most interviewing literature, "schedule" refers to a list of questions used by the interviewer, but not used directly by the respondent, in which case the schedule becomes a questionnaire. Interview schedules may vary considerably in the degree to which they specify details of context, question wording, sequence of topics, and forms of answers needed.

An interview may be scheduled in varying degrees depending on how many aspects are specified. A schedule may specify (*a*) the content of questions related to the central problem, (*b*) the exact wording of the question, (*c*) any context to be supplied with each question, (*d*) the sequence in which the questions are asked, and (*e*) the answer categories, if any, which are to be used. In the case of the completely scheduled interview, these decisions are made by the person who designs the interview schedule; in nonscheduled interviews, the interviewer himself makes these decisions. To illustrate control of interview style by a schedule, let us look at a completely nonscheduled interview, a moderately scheduled interview, and a highly scheduled interview, all concerned with the same interview topic.

Assume that we wish to discover types of conflict between parents and children and their relationship to juvenile crime. We interview a sample of children who are known to have committed no crimes and a group who have been known to commit several typical juvenile crimes.

THE NONSCHEDULED INTERVIEW

Instructions to the interviewer: Discover the kinds of conflicts that the child has had with the parents. Conflicts should include disagreements, tensions due to past, present, or potential disagreements, outright arguments and physcical conflicts. Be alert for as many categories and examples of conflicts and tensions as possible.

THE MODERATELY SCHEDULED INTERVIEW

Instructions to the interviewer: Your task is to discover as many specific kinds of conflicts and tensions between child and parent as possible. The more *concrete* and detailed the account of each type of conflict the better. Although there are 12 areas of possible conflict which we want to explore (listed in question 3 below), you should not mention any area until after you have asked the first two questions in the order indicated. The first question takes an indirect approach, giving you time to build up rapport with the respondent and to demonstrate a nonjudgmental attitude toward teenagers who have conflicts with their parents.

1. What sorts of problems do teenagers you know have in getting along with their parents?
   (Possible probes: Do they always agree with their parents? Do any of your friends have "problem parents"? What other kinds of disagreements do they have?)

2. What sorts of disagreements do you have with your parents?
   (Possible probes: Do they cause you any problems? In what ways do they try to restrict you? Do you always agree with them on everything? Do they like the same things you do? Do they try to get you

to do some things you don't like? Do they ever bore you? Make you mad? Do they understand you? etc.)

3. Have you ever had any disagreements with either of your parents over:
   a. Using the family car
   b. Friends of the same sex
   c. Dating
   d. School (homework, grades, activities)
   e. Religion (church, beliefs, etc.)
   f. Political views
   g. Working for pay outside the home
   h. Allowances
   i. Smoking
   j. Drinking
   k. Eating habits
   l. Household chores

THE HIGHLY SCHEDULED INTERVIEW

Interviewer's explanation to the teenage respondent: We are interested in the kinds of problems teenagers have with their parents. We need to know how many teenagers have which kinds of conflicts with their parents and whether they are just mild disagreements or serious fights. We have a checklist here of some of the kinds of things that happen. Would you think about your own situation and put a check to show which conflicts you, personally, have had and about how often they have happened. Be sure to put a check in every row. If you have never had such a conflict then put the check in the first column where it says "never."
(*Hand him the first card dealing with conflicts over the use of the automobile, saying,* "If you don't understand any of those things listed or have some other things you would like to mention about how you disagree with your parents over the automobile let me know and we'll talk about it.")
(*When the respondent finishes checking all rows, hand him card number 2, saying,* "Here is a list of types of conflicts teenagers have with their parents over their friends of the same sex. Do the same with this as you did with the last list.")

The first of the three interview examples given does not provide any specific questions to be asked, but merely states the problem for the interviewer, leaving him with the choice of techniques. In the second kind of interview, specific questions related to the central problem are provided. The order of the three basic questions is indicated and for questions 1 and 2 some possible probes are suggested but not mandatory. Question 3 is followed by a list of various areas of possible conflict which should be covered by the interviewer, but neither the actual wording of the questions nor the answer categories are supplied. The

AUTOMOBILE	Never	Only Once	More than Once	Many Times
1. Wanting to learn to drive				
2. Getting a driver's license				
3. Wanting to use the family car				
4. What you use the car for				
5. The way you drive it				
6. Using it too much				
7. Keeping the car clean				
8. Putting gas or oil in the car				
9. Repairing the car				
10. Driving someone else's car				
11. Wanting to own a car				
12. The way you drive your own car				
13. What you use your car for				
14. Other				

third interview example shows how the information designated by question 3a in the second example is obtained by completely scheduled interviewing, in which not only the exact wording of the questions and their sequence is given but the answers are also structured qualitatively and quantitatively.

As is implied in the examples above, an interview may be scheduled to a consistent degree throughout its total length, or certain portions of it may be more completely scheduled than others. The degree of scheduling of any portion of an interview depends upon the purpose to be achieved. This will be discussed in detail later. At the moment we will proceed to define the second dimension of style and relate both dimensions to the two basic objectives of information gathering.

Topic control

Just as the first dimension dealt with the degree to which the interviewer's behavior is determined by an outside source, the schedule, the second dimension deals with the degree to which the interviewer allows his behavior to be controlled by another outside source, the respondent.

Topic control is the extent to which the interviewer controls the topic of discussion and so takes the initiative in directing the course of the interview. It is helpful to think of the area of discussion as having (a) a central focus and (b) a certain scope with the boundaries more or less defined. Thus, the amount of topic control exercised by the interviewer depends upon the extent to which he takes the initiative in either shifting the central focus of the discussion or changing the scope of the topic. At one extreme, the respondent leads while the interviewer merely listens and shows interest in anything he wishes to say, and at the other, the interviewer abruptly changes the central focus and scope of the discussion, even if he has to interrupt the respondent's trend of thought to do so.

With the two basic dimensions of interviewing style defined, let us now describe the two basic objectives of interviewing—discovery and measurement—in order to relate them to the dimensions of style.

BASIC OBJECTIVES OF INTERVIEWING

Discovery objectives

Discovery indicates gaining new consciousness of certain qualitative aspects of the problem. The problem is viewed broadly to include both substantive and methodological aspects of the interview. This will become clearer as the specific discovery functions are described.

Locating special informants. In many types of surveys and community studies where the informants are not all selected by random sampling, a rough-and-ready pilot study is done to locate a certain type of informant. Often there is no need to interview all informants of this class, but several must be located because they have had certain relevant experiences. In this case, the only reason for interviewing more than one is to obtain a more detailed account of the event and to cross-check the accuracy of the informant's observations.

In this type of situation, the interviewer, often a stranger in the community, does not know whether the person he first contacts is one or several steps removed from the type of person he needs to interview. The first informant may be the type of person he is trying to locate, know someone who is, or know someone who knows someone who is. He may or may not wish to help the interviewer find the type of person he seeks. An interviewer studying the conditions which contribute toward peaceful integration of public schools would probably have to do a long series of interviews leading him to the persons involved in bomb-ing the local school board office.

Focusing of the problem. It is helpful to think of any study as involv-ing four interrelated levels: first, focusing the problem; second, decid-ing upon definite types of information relevant to the problem; third, formulating specific questions to be asked in order to obtain relevant information; and fourth, deciding upon the strategy, techniques, and tactics to be used in obtaining answers to the questions. Often it becomes apparent in the early exploratory field work that the problem must be focused more clearly on some specific manifestation of the more general problem being studied.

For example, in a study of intergenerational conflict a few explora-tory interviews indicated that most of the conflict which either adults or children could report was within their own family. Therefore, the investigator decided to focus on parent-child conflict. Further non-scheduled interviews with college students indicated that there was a sudden reduction in parent-child conflict when the children went away to college. This narrowed the focus to high school students living at home. Deeper nonscheduled interviewing showed that it was very difficult to obtain accurate information about conflicts which occurred more than a year in the past. Earlier conflicts were either forgotten or so vaguely remembered that the teenager was unable to give complete information, or he tended to dismiss the whole thing as "just kid stuff" not worthy of discussion. So the quest was further restricted to an analysis of conflicts occurring within the past year. Thus, in this study the nonscheduled interview was used to focus the problem.

Discovering, defining, and testing categories. Often the researcher begins a study with certain general ideas of the questions we want to ask, but with little knowledge of categories appropriate for the answers. For example, in a study of the layman's misconceptions of science we first needed to discover the layman's images of science. This neces-sitated a set of categories within which the images could be arranged. Since the problem called for classifying the images into two dimensions, we devised a tentative *a priori* set of categories which were to be tested in exploratory interviews. The first *a priori* dimension was called "areas of science" and included the physical, biological, and social sciences. The second dimension was called "aspects of science" and included the purposes, methods, and results of science. Although this system of cross-categorization was relevant to the problem, it was not clear that all the images or misconceptions people could have would fit into this system.

Therefore, using the categories in the exploratory interviewing was avoided by using a very broad open-ended question followed by a series of neutral probes.[25] The opening question was, "What comes to your mind when you think of science?" This would be followed by such neutral probes as, "That's interesting!" "Tell me a little more about that." "I see, now why do you feel that way?" etc. The respondent was allowed to follow his own free association as much as possible and very little topic control was used by the interviewer. These interviews were tape-recorded and the content of the responses was analyzed to determine whether the *a priori* categories were sufficient or whether they would need some modification. Certain types of statements made by the respondents were considered very relevant to the problem but did not fall into the *a priori* categories. In the dimension of "areas of science" we found that we needed a fourth category, and in the dimension of "aspects of science" we found we needed two additional categories. Thus, in this case, the nonscheduled interview was used to determine the clarity and adequacy of a set of categories.

Once a system of categories is worked out, it sometimes appears to be "obvious" and therefore possible to have been decided in an *a priori* fashion. In some cases, the system appears to be unnecessarily complex or the definitions seem either too loose or too detailed. The only criteria by which to judge any set of categories arrived at by any method are (*a*) how relevant the categories are to the problem at hand, (*b*) whether the categories include the full-range of relevant responses, and (*c*) how reliably the information can be classified by using the system.

Determining range of response. "Range" refers to quantitative variations in response, in contrast to qualitative categories. To illustrate, in a community study of a village in an underdeveloped area, the interviewer wanted an interview schedule in which he could check the appropriate class interval representing a family's cash income per year. As an American, he would have very little idea of the range needed. Should the item on income run from $25 to $200 per year, $100 to $1,000 per year, or $500 to $5,000 per year? In some cases, studies of income have already been done so that exploratory interviewing is not necessary. However, sometimes nothing is published on the problem, or only mean or median figures are given, with no range. Here the nonscheduled interview can determine the range of responses.

Determining best sequence of questions. In many interviews there is a natural order in which the various subtopics seem to flow. In some studies the natural flow will follow the same sequence for nearly all respondents. In other cases, it will vary depending upon the type of

---

[25] A "neutral" probe is one which indicates that the interviewer would like more information on the topic about which the respondent has been speaking, but it does not restrict the scope of the topic because no specific information is requested (for example: "Tell me more about that." "That's very interesting. Could you say more about that?").

respondent. For example, Schatzman and Strauss[26] found that this pattern varied with social class. In some cases, the order of the topics will be different for each individual. The best way to discover the natural order of topics and the degree to which a given order is either general or individualized is to interview a small sample, exerting *minimal topic control*. Each respondent is thus allowed to follow his own inclinations. If a given sequence of topics is found to be general, it is then feasible to use a more scheduled interview. The more individualized the pattern appears, the freer should be the topic sequence in the interview schedule.

Exploratory interviews sometimes show that information obtained early in the interview is not valid because a "warm up" period is needed. This gives the respondent time for unhurried reflection and free association. In the interview it is often best to begin by discussing related events which occurred prior to whose which are of central interest to the interviewer. For example, in the study of the effectiveness of an employee information program referred to in laboratory problem 1, the main point was to discover (*a*) the amount of factual information absorbed by the employee, (*b*) his general attitude toward the information meetings, (*c*) the degree to which he believed the information he was given, and (*d*) the degree to which the employee passed the information on to other people.

Since the interview took place many days after the meetings, it was necessary to start with a question which was in itself irrelevant; but since it focused on a time immediately before the events in which the interviewer was interested, it stimulated the respondent's memory and initiated a trend of thought leading to the central focus of the interview. The interview was opened with the question, "How did you first hear about the information meeting?" This was followed by, "What happened at the meeting?" These two questions usually laid a good foundation for obtaining information regarding the respondent's attitudes toward the meeting. The information obtained was probably more valid than it would have been if the first question had been, "How did you like the information meeting you attended last week?" This question asked abruptly before the respondent had an opportunity to "relive" his experience would tend to elicit a response like, "Oh, it was nice," or "I don't really remember much about it."

Similarly, in a study to determine why people bought "Brand X" automobiles, it was found that the respondent could talk more spontaneously about his first purchase of a "Brand X" if a thoughful, permissive atmosphere was established. The interviewer started with "When

---

[26] Leonard Schatzman and Anselm Strauss, "Social Class and Mode of Communication," *American Journal of Sociology*, vol. 60, no. 4 (1955), pp. 329–38.

did you first drive a car?" and later, "When did you first own a car?"
This helped establish a reminiscent mood, sometimes quite nostalgic,
which always led smoothly into more recent car-buying episodes. By
the time the more recent events were reached, the respondent was
becoming aware of changes in his own tastes and motivations in car
buying as well as certain consistent patterns. All this provided not only
a stimulus to the memory, but also a general *context*, enabling the
interviewer to make inferences and pose more searching questions.

Discovering special vocabularies. Every social group has its own special vocabulary, or "universe of discourse," which is often not clearly
intelligible to outsiders. We are seldom aware of this universe of discourse in our own group unless it is consciously learned as a defense
mechanism against the outsider, as is done by professional groups in
medicine, education, arts, crafts, and the underworld.

The plumber might complain about the philosophy professor using
a lot of "big words," while the plumber himself has a vocabulary equally
confusing for the professor. Often these jargons distinguish the initiated
from the uninitiated. A person not only has to have the "right ideas,"
but must also express them in a particular way to be recognized by the
group.

These universes of discourse are not always merely a protective
jargon, but often provide a type of shorthand or code which may be
more efficient and accurate than ordinary language. Special vocabularies are not only associated with professions and occupations but also
with certain social strata and geographical regions.

The nonscheduled interview with minimal topic control is needed
to discover these special vocabularies. By carefully listening to the
modes of expression the respondent uses to talk about certain topics,
the interviewer learns which words can be used in phrasing questions
for a more scheduled interview.

Detecting inhibitors and facilitators of communication. Later we will
deal in detail with a theoretical framework outlining certain types of
inhibitors and facilitators of communication in the interview situation.
Now we will merely illustrate the need for using nonscheduled interviewing as an aid in mapping out possible trouble spots in the interview,
as well as possible "spontaneity producers" which might be brought
into play. Experience shows us that attempts to empathize with an
imaginary respondent to predict his reactions to certain questions
sometimes fail completely. Our empathic hunches should be tested in
a few exploratory nonscheduled interviews.

As an example, a social worker was interviewing Puerto Ricans in
New York to determine the need for aid to dependent children. Three
items of information were necessary to estimate the future budget
requirements of certain social welfare agencies: whether the woman

of the house was married, how many children she had, and the ages of the children. The social worker assumed that the best order of questioning would be as follows:

a. Are you single, married, widowed, separated?
b. (If ever married) How many children do you have?
c. What are the ages of your children?

She had assumed that the first question should precede the second, because a woman would be embarrassed if she first answered she had three children and then was asked whether she was married. To avoid this embarrassment, it was assumed that the respondent with children would falsely report that she was married even if she were not. In this case, however, the interviewer's own cultural values prevented her from empathizing correctly with the respondent.

During a few exploratory interviews the interviewer discovered that there was a large percentage of couples with children who were not legally married. However, these couples did *not* have guilt feelings. If they lied about their marital state, it was usually to avoid embarrassing the interviewer. The longer the common-law couple had been in the United States, the more they were likely to lie about their marital state to those outside the Puerto Rican community. On the basis of this experience, the interviewer decided to reschedule the sequence and phrasing of questions as follows:

a. How old is your oldest child? The next? The next? etc.
b. Are you married, living common-law, or alone?

This order of questioning indicated to the respondent that the interviewer realized there was no necessary connection between having children and being legally married. If, in addition, the interviewer's attitude was not one of condemnation or shock, the respondent was assured that the interviewer "understood" the situation.

The nonscheduled interview frequently discovers unexpected inhibitors or shows that expected inhibitors are not actually present under the conditions of the interview.

In order to understand why people are willing to talk about some things and very reluctant to talk about others, we must be free to explore many avenues of information in addition to those immediately relevant to the subject of the interview. We need to know:

a. how the respondent interprets the interview situation;
b. how we can influence his definition of the interview situation;
c. what "meaning" the information signifies for the respondent in terms of his own ego or social status; and
d. what the respondent can gain by talking to the interviewer.

Sometimes this type of information is obtained through skillful non-scheduled interviewing and sometimes it is stumbled upon by accident. The use of the nonscheduled exploratory interview should considerably increase the probability of obtaining this needed information since, unlike the highly scheduled interview, it does not rule out accidental findings which might be relevant.

Measurement objectives

It is possible to combine the objectives of discovery and measurement in the same interview; but as more emphasis is placed upon one objective, the other must be subordinated. What style is best for the purpose of measurement? Generally, the scheduled interview, with high topic control, is more efficient and effective in obtaining uniform coverage, precision, and reliability of measurement. The measurement is likely to be valid if the interview schedule has been constructed on the basis of results from skillful nonscheduled interviews.

Although the scheduled interview where the measurement objective predominates is used more, there are several situations in which the nonscheduled interview would be capable of more valid measurements if done by a skilled interviewer. This would be true in several types of interview situations where communication barriers would arise if the strictly scheduled interview were used.

One of these situations would be where the *universe of discourse* varies so greatly from respondent to respondent that the interviewer must vary the wording of his questions and sequence of probes to fit the understanding of the particular respondent. This might be the case in dealing with topics like toilet training of children, sex behavior among teenagers and adults, and other topics dealing with private spheres of experience.

The nonscheduled interview is also needed where communication on the topic is inhibited by the respondent's *fading memory.* The interviewer must be free to exercise low topic control and to vary the sequence of questions, thus allowing the respondent to follow the natural paths of free association. To further stimulate the memory, the interviewer must be free to probe particular vague points in the story. Also, he must be free to create a mood of thoughtful reminiscence and to return to the same topic several times. In this case, a skilled interviewer can be more effective if he is free to devise his own tactics as the interview progresses.

There are other barriers to communication which can be surmounted best by a skilled interviewer unhindered by a schedule. The next chapter deals with eight inhibitors of communication, at least four of which can be handled better by skilled nonscheduled interviewing.

They are forgetting, chronological confusion, inferential confusion, and unconscious experience.

A basically different situation in which the nonscheduled interview might be more practical for measurement purposes occurs where the measurement is simple and the respondents so few that the construction of a schedule is not necessary or efficient to validly and reliably rank the respondents on the variable being measured.

In deciding whether a scheduled or nonscheduled interview should be used, one argument advanced is that the nonscheduled interview is dangerous because the interviewer is free to bias the responses. This is true if unskilled, careless, or dishonest interviewers are used. However, bias can also be built into the interview schedule itself, offering the doubtful virtue of uniformity to the bias. We must be careful not to simply trade one source of bias for another. Neither should neatness of the interview schedule, efficiency of coding, or reliability of response be confused with the more important criterion—validity of the information.

It is sometimes argued that the scheduled interview is usually more reliable and *therefore* more valid than the nonscheduled interview. This reasoning is not necessarily correct. It can be demonstrated that it is possible to have perfect reliability, in that the same or different interviewers obtain precisely the same answers from the same respondent on two different occasions, yet despite this reliability, the validity of the information may be very low.

In cases where the purpose of the interview is to obtain accounts of deviant behavior, but where the situation or the interviewing methods jeopardize the respondent if he reports the deviant behavior, we can expect the reliability to be high and the validity low. For example, if a manager of a department store used an interview or a questionnaire to ask, "Do you often steal from the company?" the answer would be a simple "no" even if the respondents were reinterviewed. Thus, we could reliably depend upon the falsehood being repeated.

This validity-reliability conflict would also be found when the interview seeks information considered by the respondent as a competitive secret. In this case, the most ironclad guarantee of anonymity for the respondent is of little value, since the object of the secrecy is to prevent the information from getting to a competitor. This situation is found, for example, in governmental secrecy where the object is to keep the information from a competing or hostile nation and in industrial secrecy where the purpose is to avoid leaks to competing corporations. It is interesting that in both of these situations a system develops in which each institution tries to obtain the secrets of its competitors. Thus, it is to be expected that the naïve interviewer who asked an employee of the automotive industry questions about the next year's model of his company's automobile, or who asked a member of the State Department what the next move was to be in disarmament negotiations, would not obtain valid information except for the occasional straightforward response, "That is a secret."

A third situation, much more frequently encountered by interviewers, is that in which the information sought has faded from the respondent's memory so that the images he can recall are confused, amorphous, or ambiguous. If the situation in which this interview takes place, or the methods used, tend to suggest a plausible or socially acceptable answer, the bias will be in that direction and will persist upon repeated interviewing under the same conditions.

These three examples do not exhaust the types of validity-reliability conflicts which can result from the inhibitors of communication described in detail later. Here, we merely wanted to point out that validity and reliability do not necessarily go hand in hand, nor are they necessarily related to whether a scheduled or nonscheduled interview is used.

Both the scheduled and the nonscheduled interview may be reliable or unreliable, valid or invalid, depending on the conditions and purposes. The nonscheduled interview may suffer from bias due to freedom permitted unskilled interviewers. Likewise, the scheduled interview may have a built-in bias which prevents the best interviewer from obtaining valid information. One type of error may be no better than the other.

Use of an interview guide

When using a nonscheduled interview for discovery or measurement, the interviewer is not engaging in a completely unplanned trial-and-error activity. The topics he is exploring or the dimensions he is measuring should be as clearly defined as possible. In addition, an *interview guide* should be prepared to help direct him toward the objectives of the interview.

The *interview guide,* in contrast to an *interview schedule,* provides only an outline or checklist of the topics and subtopics to be covered but does not specify a sequence. In some cases, it might also include several ways of wording questions or various probes which might be useful in pursuing the subject. The interviewer is not only free to vary the sequence of topics and subtopics to fit the particular situation but he may also return to a topic more than once. He is free to omit questions suggested by the guide if he feels that the information was already obtained indirectly. He is also free to add questions and reword others when this will help convey the meaning.

The *interview guide* can have two general functions. It may simply remind the interviewer of the areas to be covered in his investigation. It can also be a form for recording the answers under certain topical areas so that the interviewer can maintain an inventory of what has been covered and what has not. In a sense, the interviewer uses the interview guide as a motorist uses a road map. It reminds him of possible routes to many objectives and is a convenient way of recording where he has been and what he has missed. In some cases, the interview guide, once written, is memorized by the interviewer so that his questioning appears spontaneous.

In a series of exploratory interviews aimed at developing a structured interview schedule, the original tentative interview guide may go through several revisions in which the content of the questions, their wording, sequence and context, as well as the response categories, become more detailed, more structured, and clearly relevant to the objectives of the interview.

INTERVIEW VERSUS QUESTIONNAIRE

Earlier, when comparing interviewing with other basic methods of information gathering, we did not mention the questionnaire. The questionnaire is not a separate basic method; it is an *extension* of the interview.

The most essential difference between an interview and a questionnaire is that the interviewer asks the questions orally, while in a questionnaire the respondent reads the questions. There is nothing about the nature or form of the questions or answers which can reliably distinguish the interview from the questionnaire. Thus, according to this minimal definition, an interview can resemble a questionnaire to the point where the differences are insignificant. For example, the principal of a high school requeted each of the teachers to distribute 4 x 6 index cards to students at 10 A.M.; each student was to put his full name in the upper left-hand corner and write the numbers from 1 to 5 in the left-hand margin to designate the answers to five questions which were to be asked by the principal over the intercom system. In this way the answers were obtained from 1,000 students simultaneously without having to duplicate 1,000 copies of a questionnaire or to make up the answer sheets. Whether or not this should be called a "group interview" or an "oral questionnaire" is a fruitless controversy.

There are forms of questionnaires which have many of the attributes ordinarily associated with an interview. Typically, we may think of a questionnaire as being sent to the respondent through the mail, but this is not necessary. Instead, the researcher might give it to the respondent personally with an explanation of the purpose of the study and then leave. The respondent might be instructed to mail it back or to finish it by a certain time when the researcher will return and pick it up. Or, the researcher might distribute the questionnaire to a group of people and wait to collect the questionnaires as soon as they are completed. Or, even more similar to the interview situation, one researcher may personally administer a questionnaire to a single person with instructions that, if the respondent has any difficulty interpreting the questions, he should feel free to ask for help. These different ways of administering a questionnaire represent different degrees of opportunity for the researcher to help the respondent interpret the questions and to motivate him to respond to the questionnaire.

Despite the degree to which a questionnaire and an interview may resemble each other, there are certain general differences which must be taken into consideration in choosing between the two modes of gathering information.

Advantages of the interview

1. The interview provides more opportunity to motivate the respondent to supply *accurate and complete information immediately.* This motivation factor becomes more decisive as the amount of needed information increases, as the degree of answer-structuring decreases, and as the extrinsic rewards for supplying the information decrease. Thus, motivation supplied by an interviewer would not be needed in a case where the respondent merely has to give his name, address, and phone number in exchange for a free chance on a $100,000 lottery. Similarly, the respondent will promptly and accurately fill out an insurance claim form if it is short and simple and the amount to be collected is high. On the other hand, the probability is small that a member of a random sample receiving a form with 200 complex questions about his premarital sex life would supply the information through the mail.

2. The interview provides more opportunity to guide the respondent in his *interpretation* of the questions. This interpretation factor is more important when the questions are complex or abstract and when the literacy level of the respondents is lower. There are cases where the respondents may be completely illiterate or where the reading skill is so low that the probability of understanding the questionnaire accurately is very low. Also, the more varied the respondents in their understanding, interest, and universes of discourse, the more the interviewer is needed to interpret the general purpose of the interview and the meaning of specific questions.

3. The interview allows a greater *flexibility* in questioning the respondent. The more exploratory the purpose, the greater the need for flexibility in determining the wording of the question, the sequence of the questions, and the direction and amount of probing used. When the

emphasis is upon discovery as opposed to measurement, we must give serendipity a chance to operate and allow the interviewer to pursue hunches and clues he may get as the interview progresses.

4. The interview allows greater *control* over the interview situation. For example, it may be extremely important in some cases that the respondent deal with questions in a certain sequence, that he answers one question before seeing a subsequent question, or that he does not change the answer to a question in view of the context or clue furnished by a subsequent question. Or it may be necessary that the respondent not consult others in giving his answers. All of these factors can be more clearly controlled in the interview unless we use a personally administered questionnaire in which the researcher stays with the respondent while he answers the questions to one section of the questionnaire before he is given the questions for the next section.

5. The interview provides a greater opportunity to *evaluate* the validity of the information by observing the respondent's nonverbal manifestations of his attitude toward supplying the information. Although it is possible to supply certain cross-checks in questionnaires to detect the respondent who is not serious or who is deliberately lying, it is much simpler to detect, prevent, and rectify such attempts by the respondent in the interview. This type of evaluation is particularly important when the subject matter or the circumstances of the interview tend to be controversial or ego-threatening.

Advantages of the questionnaire

We have mentioned some of the major advantages of interviewing, but there are also several advantages in favor of the questionnaire.

1. The most obvious advantage of the questionnaire is in its *economy*. There are several possible dimensions to this economy. First, if we use mailed questionnaires, we avoid all of the expenses of training and paying interviewers. Also, it eliminates the cost of travel and travel time. This economy becomes more important as the ratio of travel time to interviewing time increases. Thus if we have to ask only two simple questions of a random sample of the United States population, the mailed questionnaire would be infinitely more efficient in getting the questions to the respondents. Another dimension of economy is in the possibility of administering questionnaires to a large group of people simultaneously as, for example, to an audience of a movie.

2. Under certain conditions, the questionnaire can provide a type of *anonymity* not provided by the interview. Occasionally we have circumstances in which the only persons qualified to interview on a topic know all or many of the potential respondents. This was the case when the university foreign student advisors were used to interview

Colombian professors regarding their experiences in teaching foreign students in their classes. Some of the questions dealt with the professors' philosophies and practices in teaching, which, if answered frankly, might be negatively evaluated by the Dean of their department or by the Rector of the university. These particular questions were omitted from the interview but included in a questionnaire which could be returned by mail in a self-addressed stamped envelope directly to the research center which had no connection with the university with which the professor was affiliated.

Combined use of the interview and questionnaire

When we design a research strategy, we must not assume that we need to choose between a mailed questionnaire or an interview. It is possible to collect part of the information in one way and part in the other. Even in those cases where a questionnaire is an appropriate data-gathering instrument and most of the respondents will provide required data, it may be necessary to interview those who would not respond to the questionnaire. In other cases, an interview may be needed to complete or clarify the answers, even though the person did respond to the questionnaire.

Another general way of combining the two is to intersperse a questionnaire with an interview at points where the question or the answer structure is so complex that the respondent could grasp it better in writing. This allows him to reread it as many times as he wishes and to proceed at his own speed. In some cases, the respondent is given only the answer choices in writing after the interviewer has asked the question orally.

Even in those cases where all of the data are gathered by questionnaire, it is usually necessary to do some interviewing to develop a valid questionnaire. Often, apparently simple and foolproof questionnaires can be improved by pretest interviews. It is dangerous to devise "swivel-chair" questionnaires without benefit of pretest interviewing for several reasons. First, only by trying a question and being able to probe for a full response can we discover whether the question is clear. The vocabulary may not be appropriate, the issue may not be a real one in the minds of the respondents, or there may be a need to provide more context for the question in order to standardize the interpretations. Second, in the cases where structured answers are used, we must actually derive answer choices which are meaningful to the respondent, which do not overlap, which include the full range of possible responses, which do not seem to the respondent to be unduly restricting, which do not suggest answers, and which are clearly relevant to the purposes of the questionnaire. This appropriate structuring of answers often requires exploratory interviewing. And third, while he is face to face with the respondent, the researcher can more easily detect those aspects of the questionnaire which make the respondent *unable* or *unwilling* to give a full, frank response. Exploratory interviewing can demonstrate any need to restructure the questionnaire to be more or less direct, to use more or fewer open-ended questions, to provide more complete or more face-saving prologues to the questions.

In spite of conscientious efforts to pretest, when the questionnaire results begin to come in, we sometimes discover a need to reevaluate the effectiveness of a particular question. Additional interviewing may show that a question or its answer structure is invalid and should not be included in the analysis.

Both the interview and the questionnaire have advantages under certain circumstances, but frequently they are used as complementary instruments. Both may be used to collect related data, or the interview may be used as an exploratory tool in building a valid questionnaire or as an evaluative tool after the data have been collected by questionnaire.

This comparison of the interview with the questionnaire is useful to help decide which is more appropriate for a specific purpose. But we will not deal again here with the quesionnaire as a separate entity because all of the basic diagnostic concepts regarding the inhibitors and facilitators of communication and most of the tools described under the headings of strategy, tactics, and techniques are applicable to the design and administration of a questionnaire as well as to interviewing.

SUMMARY

Interviewing can be seen in five different perspectives. First, it can be seen as one of the most basic modes of collecting data on human behavior along with the other basic modes of empathizing, participating, and observing. All of these basic modes are intertwined and are included to some extent in the nonscheduled interview which, therefore, provides an excellent focus for learning basic skills for studying human behavior.

Second, in comparing the interview with ordinary conversation we note that interviewing may include several possible functions of ordinary conversation, but these must be judiciously subordinated to the central purpose of gathering information. Habitual patterns of conversation must be modified in order to maximize the flow of relevant information in the interview.

Third, in viewing the different styles of interviewing we see that one of the most important distinctions is in the amount of freedom allowed in the interview. The interviewer's freedom is controlled by the degree to which the interview schedule is structured in all dimensions. The respondent's freedom is inversely related to the amount of topic control used by the interviewer within the bounds of the interview schedule. In the highly structured interview, topic control decisions by the interviewer are limited to probing for elaboration or clarification of the immediately preceding response, but in the nonscheduled interview the interviewer has considerable latitude in his use of topic control.

Fourth, interviewing has two basically different functions—discovery and measurement. Discovery must always precede measurement. The nonscheduled interview is more effective for discovery, and the scheduled interview for measurement. Both the scheduled and non-scheduled interview may be used reliably or unreliably, validly or invalidly, depending on the purposes and conditions.

Fifth, we assume that the questionnaire may fruitfully be viewed as an extension of the interview method. Both have advantages and disadvantages under different circumstances, but the same basic principles, strategies, techniques, and tactics can be applied to both.

To develop the skills and insights needed for good nonscheduled interviewing or for building good interview schedules to be used by less skillful interviewers, a person must be free to make his own decisions and then evaluate the results of his performance. Before he can use this freedom fruitfully, he must be guided by some diagnostic concepts regarding the problems of communication in the interview. He must be aware of a variety of interviewing strategies, techniques, and tactics available to solve or prevent these communication problems.

DISCUSSION QUESTIONS

1. There are specialized and generalized treatments of interviewing. What must the potential interviewer be aware of before he tries to use any of them?

2. How may the degree of scheduling control the interview style? Try to think of situations in which you might want to use the nonscheduled, the moderately scheduled, and the highly scheduled interview.

3. How could each of the seven discovery objectives be important to interviewing success? Try to think of situations in which each would be especially necessary.

4. What is an interview guide and what is its purpose?

5. Which is more valid, the scheduled or unscheduled interview? Which more reliable? Which would you use for discovery purposes? Which for measurement?

6. What are the differences between the interview and the questionnaire? What are the advantages of each?

SELECTED READINGS

Benjamin, Alfred. *The Helping Interview*. Boston: Houghton Mifflin, 1969.

Deals mainly with the counseling interview. One of the better books on the conditions, stages, and forms of interaction in the interview. Gives many examples of the helping interview.

Bermosk, Loretta L., and Mary J. Mordan. *Interviewing in Nursing*. New York: Macmillan Co., 1964.

An amalgamation of accepted principles from clinicians and survey researchers. Stresses the use of a scientific orientation to the intellectual, motor, and emotional dimensions of the interview. A good list of criteria for evaluation is given on pages 171–72.

Burdock, E. I., and A. S. Hardesty. *Structured Clinical Interview Manual*. New York: Springer-Verlag, 1969.

A carefully constructed, highly standardized interview, with a convenient recording format for the assessment of psychopathology. The manual includes both an interview transcription and an inventory of 179 verbal and nonverbal behavior items for the interviewer to observe in scoring six dimensions of psychopathology.

Cannell, C. F., and R. L. Kahn. "Interviewing," in *The Handbook of Social Psychology*, 2d ed., vol. 2, ed. G. Lindzey and E. Aronson. Reading, Mass.: Addison-Wesley, 1968, pp. 526–95.

A review of current opinions in the field and research on the use of the information-gathering interview for *opinion surveying* and other social-psychological research. Reviews empirical findings related to the conditions for successful interviewing, and for the selection and training of interviewers.

Dexter, Lewis A. *Elite and Specialized Interviewing*. Evanston, Ill.: Northwestern University Press, 1970.

Application of interviewing to the study of political elites in and out of office. Contains a 30-page bibliography on the topic.

Fenlason, Anne; G. Beals; and A. Abrahamson. *Essentials of Interviewing*. New York: Harper & Row, 1962.

An orientation to the *social casework* interview and related professional interviewing. Stresses the importance of knowing the client's culture, roles, and personality in the dynamics of the interview. Provides many interview excerpts as examples.

Hariton, Theodore. *Interview! The Executive Guide to Selecting the Right Personnel*. New York: Hastings House Publishers, 1971.

A simply written guide, without footnotes or bibliography, dealing with what to appraise, how to get the respondent talking, how to keep him talking, how to control and guide the interview, how to interpret and evaluate the information, and how to organize and report the findings.

Langdon, Grace, and I. W. Stout. *Teacher-Parent Interviews.* Englewood Cliffs, N.J.: Prentice-Hall, 1954.

A persuasive presentation of the vital need for teachers to interview parents and interview them well. Gives excellent practical guides for what to talk about, what situations call for an interview, what to expect and what information to try to get, what solutions the teacher may try, and what to do with special problems during the interview. Examples of content covered in actual interviews from kindergarten to high school are given.

Merton, Robert K. *The Focused Interview: A Manual of Problems and Procedures.* New York: The Free Press, 1956.

A classic on the assessment of people's reactions to mass media or any other stimulus situation where (*a*) the exact nature of the stimulus situation is known, (*b*) the interviewer has been able to analyze the stimulus situation and hypothesize the respondent's reaction, (*c*) the stimulus content of the situation provides the framework for the interview schedule, and (*d*) the interviewer focuses on the respondent's subjective experiences to ascertain his definition of the situation.

Sherwood, Hugh C. *The Journalistic Interview.* New York: Harper & Row, 1969.

Informally written, without footnotes or bibliography. Gives a good picture of some of the major objectives of journalistic interviewing and the conditions under which much of it is done. Deals with telephone interviews, face-to-face interviews, group interviews and the pros and cons of recording on tape or taking notes. Highly specialized and nontheoretical.

Steinmetz, Lawrence L. *Interviewing Skills for Supervisory Personnel.* Reading, Mass.: Addison-Wesley Publishing Co., 1971.

Elaborates on basic forms of interviewing and how they can be utilized by the operating supervisor. As a training technique it provides role-playing cases at the end of the book in which real case situations are described without any dialogue as background for improvised role-playing.

part two

The interview
as communication
in society

4

The social context
of the interview

This chapter deals with the interview in the larger social context and shows the implications of this context for potential communication problems in the interview and the very general tasks of the interviewer in dealing with these problems. This overview provides the foundation for a more detailed analysis of the social-psychological inhibitors and facilitators of the information flow, to be described later. It is important to establish this larger context of the interview situation lest we myopically focus on the techniques of the interaction and forget that the *relationship* between interviewer and respondent is determined to a great extent by how their roles fit into the larger society, and that this relationship tends to either inhibit or facilitate the flow of certain types of information.

The methods we can use to improve this relationship will be dealt with as *strategy* in Part III, as *techniques* in Part IV, and as *tactics* in Part V of this book.

A CONTEXTUAL MODEL

Figure 4–1 attempts visually to conceptualize the social context of the interview. Note that "C" in the center represents the communication process we are trying to facilitate.

This communication process depends upon the relationships among three factors in the interview situation: the *interviewer*, the *respondent*, and the *questions* asked. This relationship between interviewer, respondent and question can be manipulated by the interviewer's behavior to a limited extent after the interview has begun. Much of this

FIGURE 4–1
Social Context of the Interview

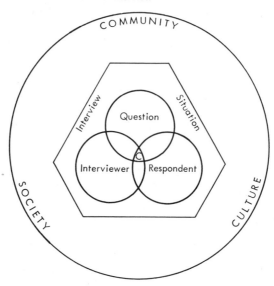

relationship is determined *before* the interaction between the interviewer and a particular respondent begins. These "predetermined" relationships include such things as the time and place of the interview, the sponsoring organization, the combinations of interviewer and respondent, the potential threat of failure to preserve the respondent's anonymity, or the respondent's ability to understand the potential value of the study for which the interview is being done.

All of these social psychological factors determine the *definition of the situation* by both the interviewer and the respondent. Although there is little the interviewer can do about many of these factors *after* the interview has begun, there is much that can be done in planning the interview situation in advance. This phase of planning is dealt with later under the heading of strategy and consists of such decisions as selecting respondents who are the most able and willing to giving relevant information, selecting interviewers with the best relationship to the respondent, choosing the most appropriate time and place for the interview, giving respondents the most acceptable explanation of the purpose and sponsorship of the interview, and promising the appropriate safeguards of anonymity when needed.

In making strategy decisions we must consider the probable effects on the meaning of the situation as viewed by the respondent. To know this we must know how the intra-situational factors in the interview (information, interviewer, respondent) are connected to the extra-situational factors relating the interview to the larger society, community, or culture.

IMPLICATIONS OF THE MODEL

There are several important practical considerations which can be derived from the social context model that can help in planning any study using interviewing. Here we will describe some of the most important.

1. Consider the problem as primary. Since we can assume there is a wide variety of possible strategies, techniques, and tactics to be used in data collection, we should make no final choices of method until *after* we have clearly specified the problem and the precise information relevant to it.

There is no rational way, for example, to decide whether to use white or black interviewers until we know what information the interviewer will be seeking and from whom. Even if the information sought could be obtained only from black respondents, this does not automatically tell us whether we should use white or black interviewers, because some information a black could give about himself would be as freely given to a white as to a black interviewer, while other information would not. An experiment done by Shuman,[1] for example, in a northern city after the urban riots of 1967 clearly showed that certain kinds of information on racial discrimination, blacks' living conditions, and personal background was given as freely to white as to black interviewers, but information on militant black protest and blacks' hostility toward whites was given less freely to white interviewers.

2. Consider the triadic relationship as fundamental. The interrelationships between the nature of the *information* sought, the nature of the *respondent,* and the nature of the *interviewer* is the fundamental *unit* of analysis in the interview process.

This model assumes that it is impossible to say how the relationship between a certain type of respondent and the interviewer would affect the information flow unless we know what kind of information we want to make flow. Similarly, we can not say that a particular respondent will or will not be willing to give certain types of information unless we know to whom he is expected to give that information. Also, we cannot predict whether a particular kind of interviewer is the right one to ask a particular question unless we know to whom he must pose that question. This triadic relationship is demonstrated in the Shuman study

---

[1] H. Shuman and J. M. Converse, "Effect of Black and White Interviewers on Black Responses in 1968," *Public Opinion Quarterly,* vol. 35 (1971), pp. 44–68.

where the white interviewers could get one type of information much better than another type. Thus, if the nature of the problem restricts us to one kind of respondent, we must select interviewers to fit the other elements in the triad. If the nature of the interview restricts us to one type of interviewer, then we must take care to select the type of respondent willing to give the required information to that type of interviewer. Clearly, we cannot consider these elements in isolation one at a time, but must view the interaction among the three elements as a unit.

3. Classify needed information. Do not assume that there is one best way to obtain all the items of information needed. Classify these needed items, considering for each the best interviewer, the best respondent, and the most appropriate method.

There is a tendency in planning a study to assume that a particular method (interview, questionnaire, or observation) will be used to collect all of the data needed. If the interview method is chosen, there is a tendency to assume that the same type of interviewer and respondent will be used for all of the interviews. Often this assumption of uniformity of strategy is unfounded because there is not a corresponding uniformity of information needed. Before accepting this assumption, we must examine specific questions carefully and regroup them according to who would be most willing and able to validly answer each question.

The temptation to be apparently efficient by having all of the needed questions on the same interview schedule so that they can all be collected at the same time by the same interviewer is often the source of invalid data. This spurious efficiency in collecting data is often reinforced by the additional desire for more efficient data analysis which is possible when all of the information is on the one interview schedule. Any "efficiencies" gained at the expense of validity is gross inefficiency; nevertheless these temptations exist!

4. Maximize flow of specific types of information. Once the needed information is divided into different types, you should plan the strategies, techniques, and tactics to maximize the flow of each particular type of information and then see where a common method may be used and where different methods must be used.

Sometimes information that is potentially ego-threatening, such as getting a person to report any delinquencies he or she has committed, can be obtained simply by using an appropriately structured questionnaire with safeguards of anonymity that are trusted by the respondent. This has been demonstrated by Clark and Tifft,[2] who used the questionnaire approach to elicit reports of delinquent acts and were able to

---

[2] John P. Clark and Larry L. Tifft, "Polygraph and Interview Validation of Self-Reported Deviant Behavior," *American Sociological Review,* vol. 31 (1966), pp. 516–23.

show by means of a later interview and polygraph analysis that the results were valid.

Sometimes the conditions of the community are such that no promise of anonymity will be trusted by the respondent. For example, a study on industrial conflict collapsed early in the data-collection phase because valid responses from respondents were conspicuously unobtainable. The study took place in a community where a Textile Workers Union of America (TWUA) strike was in progress. The textile workers were questioned as to their sentiments regarding the TWUA and asked to weight the importance of various sources for such sentiments. According to Roy[3] there were several reasons for the failure: the respondents did not trust the interviewers to keep the information anonymous; the potential consequences of information leakage to the management of the mill were perceived as very serious; and conflict in the organizing campaign was intensive. This points to the possibility that a strategy for collecting certain information might be perfectly valid at one point in time and useless later if a conflict situation develops, making a leak of the particular information dangerous to the respondent.

In a current study of the phenomenon of rape in a large city, a team of information gatherers is used in which each member obtains a different type of information. Later, all of the information is assembled to obtain a holistic picture. The strictly medical information is determined by a physician; a description of the rapist and certain facts such as the time, place, and circumstances of the attack are obtained by a policewoman. A female psychiatric social worker elicits details about the precise nature of the attack, how the victim responded, and how she feels about the experience and about reporting the attack. Other information is obtained to cross-check the story given to the police department. Gradually, this multi-interviewer strategy is being developed to improve the relevance, validity, and completeness of the data. All this is necessary because of a tendency for policemen to be unsympathetic to rape victims and for the victim to be reluctant to report being attacked for fear of damaging her reputation. The project is also developing other strategies to persuade victims to report attacks that previously would have been unreported.

Even the most potentially threatening information will be given to a skillful interviewer under the right circumstances. This is clearly demonstrated in a study by Ball.[4] In Puerto Rico he interviewed 59

---

[3] Donald F. Roy, "The Role of the Researchers in the Study of a Social Conflict," *Human Organization*, vol. 24 (1965), pp. 262–71.

[4] John C. Ball, "The Reliability and Validity of Interview Data Obtained from Fifty-Nine Narcotic Drug Addicts," *American Journal of Sociology*, vol. 72 (1967), pp. 650–54.

narcotic drug addicts who had been formerly incarcerated at the U.S. Public Health Service Hospital at Lexington, Kentucky. The respondent's report of the time and place of his first arrest was validated against FBI arrest records; his report of whether or not he was currently using the drug was validated by a urine analysis. According to Ball the information collected in the interview was highly valid because of the skill of the interviewer, the absence of the police function, and the use of a carefully structured interview.

5. Do not overgeneralize from experiments. Studies and experiments on different strategies, techniques, and tactics of interviewing may appear totally contradictory if we do not take the social context of the interview into consideration.

The contextual model is not only useful as a sensitizing framework in planning interviewing methods for a particular study; it is also useful for determining the applicability of studies and experiments of interviewing methods to a particular situation. Frequently, the apparently contradictory results among experiments testing the validity of the same strategy, technique, or tactic can be accounted for by differences in the triadic relationship within the interview, or by differences in the relationship of the interview situation to the local community and larger society.

All too frequently, researchers may select a method proven successful in a different setting, only to be disappointed by its failure in the situation where it is currently applied. There is a danger also that a particular approach, potentially effective in the current situation, is rejected because of studies showing its inadequacy in quite different circumstances. Both of these unfortunate errors can be reduced by applying the contextual framework when making comparisons of results of different studies of interviewing methods.

Now that we have given an overview of the interview in its social context, let us turn to the basic tasks of the interviewer in any interview situation and look at some of the problems that may arise in trying to carry out these tasks. Here we do not pretend to furnish any of the tools for dealing with these problems; that will be the subject matter of chapters 8 through 20. Here we simply want to show some of the general problematic dimensions of the interaction between interviewer and respondent.

OBJECTIVES, TASKS, AND PROBLEMS OF COMMUNICATION

There are basic *objectives* common to all interviews. These objectives, in turn, present the interviewer with very general *tasks* common to all interviews. These basic tasks generate certain general *problems* found in all interviewing situations. Now let us consider these objectives, tasks, and problems in a general way.

Objectives of the interviewer

The general objectives of the interviewer in any interview are three: *relevance, validity,* and *reliability.* Assuming that we already have clear informational objectives for a study and that we have already designed questions relevant to these objectives, then the interviewer is responsible for obtaining relevant, valid, and reliable responses to those questions. Once the respondent understands the question, he has at least four logical alternatives as a response. In rare cases he might say nothing, as may happen when a psychotherapist interviews a schizophrenic patient. However, a normal person can more gracefully avoid answering the question, if this is his wish, by saying something irrelevant or ambiguous. If the interviewer does not accept irrelevancies or ambiguities, the respondent may then do one of two things, he may simply fabricate an answer that is relevant to the question but untrue, or he can give an answer which is both relevant and true. If all respondents said nothing, responded with the truth, or said "I won't tell you!" the tasks of the interviewer would be much simpler! Unfortunately the respondent can avoid appearing uncooperative by responding voluminously with irrelevancies or misinformation, and this presents a challenge to the interviewer.

Tasks of the interviewer

In harmony with the distinction between relevance, validity, and reliability, we divide the interviewer's basic tasks into essentially two groups. The first deals with obtaining relevant information and the second with increasing the validity and reliability of the information given by the respondent.

The relevance-related tasks include (*a*) having a clear understanding of the purpose of the interview, (*b*) clearly communicating specific questions in accordance with the purpose, (*c*) detecting and correcting misunderstandings of the question by the respondent, (*d*) distinguishing between the irrelevant, the potentially relevant, and the clearly relevant, and (*e*) guiding the respondent to avoid the irrelevant and probing the potentially relevant to convert it into actually relevant information.

The validity-reliability related tasks depend upon maintaining generally good interpersonal relations with the respondent and include (*a*) being aware of the potential inhibitors which make the respondent unwilling or unable to give valid information, (*b*) using both verbal and nonverbal means to help the respondent become more willing and able to give valid information, (*c*) detecting symptoms of resistance in the respondent, and (*d*) refraining from pressuring the respondent for information before he is willing or able to give it.

The interviewer must be constantly alert and ready to modify his own behavior in a way that will maximize the flow of relevant and valid information. To do this he must clearly understand the objectives of the interview, observe the behavior of the respondent, and be aware of his own behavior as it influences the respondent.

Problems of communication

Both of the interviewer's tasks depend upon verbal and nonverbal modes of communication. Nonverbal communication includes the tone of voice, facial expression, gestures, posture, and pacing which accompany the words.

Verbal communication problems. Rarely is there lack of communication because either the interviewer or the respondent does not understand the dictionary definition of a word. More frequently the interviewer's problem is to become acquainted with special jargons currently used by subcultures associated with an occupational group, social class, age level, ethnic group, political party, religious group, or geographic region.

The successful interviewer must be willing to learn special universes of discourse. Without the interest and sincerity to master the knowledge needed to make the question meaningful to the respondent and to understand his answer, the interviewer has no right to the respondent's time. Interviewing auto mechanics about the problems of their business without a familiarity with their special, extensive vocabulary is insulting and fruitless. The interviewer cannot show a vital interest in what the respondent is saying if he does not understand what he is being told.

This need of an appropriate vocabulary is more obvious when interviewing someone with more education or higher social status or when the interview deals with a specialized problem. Nevertheless, the need is often just as urgent in interviewing a respondent of lower social status about a nonspecialized problem. For example, in preparing to interview scientists about recent cancer studies, it is apparent that the interviewer would have to learn a special vocabulary to be effective. It is not so obvious, but just as important, to learn a special vocabulary to interview an Arkansas farmer about his experiences in a tornado.

It is sometimes *more* important to know the correct vocabulary when interviewing a person of lower social status. The lower-status respondent feels less free to educate the interviewer, and the interviewer is less likely to perceive his own misunderstandings. Even though the interviewer assumes the role of the "ignorant but willing student," the respondent still is less inclined to assume the role of teacher than he would be if he had higher social status.

As an example of the necessity of special vocabularies, an interviewer planning to interview the personnel of a mental hospital about morale problems should not approach the first respondent without knowing the meaning of common abbreviations such as "EST," "BM," "IV," "GP," "GI," or "GU." Respectively, these usually stand for electroshock treatment, bowel movement, intravenous injection, general paresis, gastrointestinal, and genitourinary. In addition to the medical vocabulary, he would encounter the vocabulary of abnormal psychology and the highly specialized vocabulary dealing with the local physical and social structure of the hospital.

Similarly, if a study of employee morale is to be done in a large telephone company, the interviewer must understand terms such as "CO," "ACO," "PBX," "rate structure," "traffic department," "plant department," "ICC," "A.T.&T.," "employees' concession," and "key-pulse dialing." The same symbol can have entirely different meanings in different universes of discourse; for example, the first abbreviation, "CO," means carbon monoxide to the chemist, chief operator to the telephone employees, commanding officer in the army, and conscientious objector in a Mennonite community.

The examples above have perhaps been misleadingly obvious, since abbreviations are frequently used to express the most unique vocabulary in any occupational group. It is also quite easy to detect special meanings when they are conveyed by words or phrases which are *not common* to the universe of discourse of both the interviewer and the respondent. If a college girl from New York heard a farmer say, "We just built a new water closet"; or a carpenter say, "This ladder needs new dogs"; or a mechanic say, "Your worm-gear is growling"; or a farmer in a semitropical area say, "We use triple-deck farming here"; or one plumber say to another, "Give me the snake, Joe"; or a man on skid row say, "Pete is a snowbird"; she would probably be aware that she didn't understand some of these phrases.

However, the same student might hear an Arkansas farmer explaining his experiences in a tornado with, "I wasn't excited during the big blow, but I studied all night the first four nights afterward." She would probably *not* realize that she did not understand him since only common words are used and the context does not give a clue to the special regional meaning of two of the words.

Another type of universe of discourse is illustrated in the following example. It is more difficult to detect because it is associated with a particular person's life history.

A local women's political organization was studying academic freedom at three colleges in the area by interviewing all members of their social science facilities. One of the interviewers arrived for her appointment with a faculty member and felt that she should first build *rapport* with a friendly conversation before launching into the formal interview.

I: Good morning! I am Mrs. Kirk from the Politics Club.

R: Oh yes, how do you do! I have been expecting you.

I: It's nice of you to give me an appointment. You are helping us with such an important project. We feel that it is important to have academic freedom in our colleges.

R: I can certainly agree with you there. Won't you sit down?

I: Thank you. I am so glad to have a chance to interview someone in the sociology department. When I was young I used to enjoy reading about Eugene Debs and that sort of thing. I think everyone should know how the other half lives. . . . (Pause) Could you tell me how many social workers your department graduates each year?

In this dialogue, the interviewer has unintentionally damaged rapport with the professor. Let us consider the last line which, although not part of the formal interview, is the only question. In its denotative aspect, it is simply *asking* for a concrete number of social workers who are graduated in a year. The answer is "zero." However, the context of the question allowed the professor to induce several assumptions on her part that he felt needed correcting.

First, he was amazed by the question but recovered in time to explain the relationship between socialism, social reform, social work, and sociology. Since the interviewer knew she was talking to a member of a sociology department of an undergraduate school, yet expected them to be graduating social workers, the professor knew she did not understand the difference between sociology and social work. Furthermore, her remark about Eugene Debs implied that she saw a connection between socialism and sociology.

The professor's immediate response was to the *connotative statement,* rather than to the simple *denotative question.* He hastened to explain that sociology had not more in common with socialism than it did with capitalism, vegetarianism, or fascism, except for the first four letters.

The general effect upon the respondent was to make him distrust the interviewer because he doubted that anyone so grossly ignorant of his field could sympathize with the problems of academic freedom or be able to accurately record his opinions on the matter.

These confusions of universes of discourse can be prevented in most cases. Sometimes it is practical to recruit interviewers from the same cultural background as the respondents, interviewers already familiar with the particular universe of discourse. If a large number of interviewers are needed and it is not possible to recruit and train them, exploratory interviewing can be done by a few experienced interviewers. When special words and meanings are detected, they can be taken into account in modifying the wording of the questions and a special glossary can be included in the instructions to warn the interviewers of the special meanings which might appear.

Experimental studies of interviewing[5] show that different respondents sometimes read different meanings into the same questions and, therefore, they are actually answering different questions. These different interpretations are due to differences in the basic assumptions held. C. Wright Mills[6] points out that different sets of basic assumptions are expressed in different "vocabularies of motive" used from one historical period to another. Thus, an act that would have been explained in terms of the "battle between God and the devil" in the Middle Ages would be explained in Freudian terms of "the battle between the *id* and the *superego* in the arena of the *ego*" in a later era.

For example, a tornado took a diagonal path (from southwest to northeast) across White County, Arkansas, destroying four towns along the highway running in that direction. The disaster team which followed in its wake asked the following question (among many others), "Why do you think the tornado struck the way it did?" This question brought into play the "vocabulary of motives" of this local subculture. Most of the responses were based upon the assumption that God controlled the fate of men and that the tornado was an instrument of God's justice. Based upon this premise, then, the respondents were asked to explain how the inhabitants of one village had been more sinful than those of another and why certain people in their own stricken village were killed and others spared. Some typical responses were, "God does not have to explain his ways to man!" "The youngsters in this town have been going straight to the devil!" "Who am I to judge the ways of God?" In contrast, the members of the disaster study team thought the explanation was to be found in the statistical regularity with which tornados traveled from southwest to northeast through "tornado alley" and could be explained in terms of the rotation of the earth, prevailing winds in the northern hemisphere, local atmospheric conditions, and rapid changes in temperature.

The field team members were initially prepared for this question to elicit some pseudoscientific manifestations of anxiety such as: "They shouldn't seed those hurricanes in Florida because it just broke up one

---

[5] R. S. Crutchfield and D. A. Gordon, "Variations in Respondents' Interpretations of an Opinion-Poll Question," *International Journal of Opinion and Attitude Research*, vol. 1 (September 1947), pp. 1–12.

[6] C. Wright Mills, "Situated Action and the Vocabulary of Motives," *American Sociological Review*, vol. 6 (December 1940), pp. 904–13.

big hurricane which might have stayed out to sea into a lot of tornados which pop up all over the South!" Indeed, such explanations did come from some of the respondents.

With this wide gap between the interviewer's and respondent's silent assumptions, there was a danger of a breakdown in communication if the interviewer was not aware of the respondent's assumptions. The unaware interviewer might think that the respondent did not hear the question correctly, that the respondent was joking with him, or that the remark about the supernatural was merely a manner of speaking rather than a serious intellectual attempt by the respondent. Rapport would have been shattered if the interviewer had laughed, or even smiled, and said, "Really now, why do you think it struck the way it did?"

Garfinkel's study[7] shows how this "cognitive substructure" of silent assumptions is not only associated with the more stable values, beliefs, knowledge, and expectations of a subculture; but it is also being constantly reformed and shared in the interaction between members of a group such as the family. Thus, the understanding of the real meaning of today's conversation in the family depends upon having shared yesterday's experiences which provide the unspoken context.

Nonverbal communication problems. We now turn our attention to the interviewer's tasks which relate to nonverbal communication from respondent to interviewer. The interviewer must listen to *how* the respondent says what he does. Auditory clues include changes in pace, pitch, intensity, and volume level. In addition, there are visual clues such as facial expression, gestures, bodily position, and movements of hands, feet, and head.

Many respondents have learned to hide certain nonverbal clues to their feelings and attitudes. This control is usually exercised either by maintaining a neutral or noncommittal expression or by pretending an opposite feeling. In exercising such control most respondents manifest this inner conflict by inconsistencies. They are unable to control all of the symptoms of their attitude. For example, the respondent might display a calm facial expression and a casual tone of voice, yet betray anxiety by twisting his hands.

The interviewer can observe these inconsistencies if he develops the habit of watching the *total* bodily response rather than concentrating only on the tone of voice and facial expression. In ordinary conversation, most people look to facial expression more than to other bodily changes for clues to feelings and attitudes. Perhaps it is precisely for this reason that we learn to control the facial expressions more readily.

---

[7] Harold Garfinkel, "Studies of the Routine Grounds of Everyday Activities," *Social Problems,* vol. 11 (Winter 1964), pp. 225–50.

There is also a problem of accurately judging the meaning of various visual and auditory nonverbal clues. One reason is that respondents vary greatly in their normal range of expressive behavior; unusual tension for one person would be normal for another. The interviewer can deal with this by focusing his attention on *changes* in the level of these expressive symptoms.

Also, if the interviewer has more than one contact with the respondent or can observe him in another setting, it is easier to make more accurate judgments of the respondent's emotional state.

The nonverbal clues noted by the interviewer have little meaning if isolated from the verbal communication and the situational context of the interview. Only when the nonverbal clues and the denotative and connotative verbal messages make a consistent picture to the interviewer, can he feel sure that his interpretation of the respondent's message is correct. If there is some inconsistency, the interviewer should probe further until the matter is clarified for the objectives of the interview.

Thus, for maximal utilization of nonverbal respondent-to-interviewer communication, the interviewer's tasks are:

a.   to observe a broad range of nonverbal activity and be alert for inconsistencies;

b.   to be alert for *changes* in the respondent's nonverbal activity rather than being aware of only the general level which distinguishes one respondent from another; and

c.   to interpret the meaning of any inconsistencies and changes in nonverbal behavior in the broader context of the verbal communication and the situation in which the interview is taking place.

Now let us examine the interviewer's tasks related to nonverbal communication in the other direction, from interviewer to respondent. This aspect of communication will be studied extensively later under "Nonverbal Techniques." Here we will merely point out the nature of the task.

In general, the interviewer must strive to communicate certain positive attitudes toward the value of the interview itself, toward the respondent as a person, and toward his cooperation. This does not imply that an interviewer can turn his attitudes on and off as the chameleon changes his colors. However, several precautions can be taken to minimize negative attitudes which might damage interpersonal relations sufficiently to invalidate the information obtained.

First, the interviewer can be selected to fit the task. From the viewpoint of a field supervisor, this is a matter of selecting the right interviewer for a particular topic and respondent. From the point of view of the single independent investigator, it is a matter of being aware of his own limitations and avoiding interview situations where he cannot control his negative attitudes.

Second, the interviewer may deliberately seek the kinds of topics or respondents toward which he has a negative attitude in order to broaden his views, gain tolerance, and learn to control his expression of these negative attitudes. However, the same interview which is used for this educational purpose will be of little value as a source of valid and complete information.

Third, the interviewer must learn certain techniques to counteract his negative attitudes. Even with ordinary precautions to match the interviewer with the topic and respondent, or to retrain the interviewer's attitudes, there will be some degree of self-control necessary, since it is hardly possible to find any one person who agrees with everything another person believes or has done. Just as it is difficult for the respondent to hide his attitudes with a neutral expression, it is also difficult for the interviewer to hide his attitudes from the respondent.

The interviewer's task is to displace real negative attitudes with equally real positive attitudes. This way, he avoids the problems inherent in attempting to remain neutral or refusing to admit to himself that he has such an attitude. Thus, if the interviewer strongly disagrees with the attitudes and beliefs being expressed by the respondent, he must be so vitally concerned with the information-gathering task that he can show sincere appreciation for the respondent's frankness. Or he can manifest a strong interest in how the respondent arrived at these views, if this is an objective of the interview. In both of these cases, scientific objectivity rather than cold neutrality allows the interviewer to demonstrate positive attitudes of appreciation and interest rather than negative attitudes of disagreement and rejection.

In summary, the interviewer achieves his main goals—obtaining maximum relevant information and maintaining optimum interpersonal relations—by being sensitive to both verbal and nonverbal communication. The interviewer's tasks occur in the following cycle:

First phase. The interviewer must accurately receive information through both verbal and nonverbal modes of communication.

Second phase. The interviewer must then make valid inferences regarding the adequacy of the information and the condition of the interpersonal relations.

Third phase. He must then translate what is learned to modify his own behavior at the verbal and nonverbal levels to maximize the flow of relevant information and to maintain optimal interpersonal relations.

It will be noted that although the aim in the third phase is twofold, we have guarded against interviewer ambivalence or vacillation by not giving the two aims equal weight. The aim is *maximal* information with *optimal,* rather than maximal, interpersonal relations. Optimal interpersonal relations is whatever form and degree of relationship that will maximize the flow of information, or at least not interfere with the flow. Thus, the satisfaction of spontaneous interpersonal relations is viewed as a means to an end.

The precaution of using the word "optimal" is necessary, since there are situations where the best way to *maximize* the feeling of warm interpersonal relations is for the interviewer to "stop asking all those questions!" Often the neophyte thinks he has conducted an excellent interview because "rapport was perfect" and the respondent was "completely at ease, talked spontaneously, and commented that she had enjoyed the interview." Yet when the interview is analyzed for the amount and clarity of relevant data, it is found to be incomplete, superficial, and ambiguous.

Often there may be a conscious or unconscious desire on the part of the interviewer, respondent, or both to avoid any psychological strain in the interview. The interviewer may retreat into rapport-building chitchat or the ritualistic asking of required questions, while uncritically accepting irrelevant, evasive, incomplete, or ambiguous answers, instead of probing. The respondent may cooperate with the conspiracy by appearing cooperative while contributing a verbal smoke screen, obscuring the relevant material.

At times, a respondent may take the initiative in this disguised resistance, inundating the interviewer with meaningless verbiage, which he is unable to appraise systematically for its relevance in time to fulfill the objectives of the interview. The loquacious respondent who decides to sidestep the interviewer in this manner often presents a much more difficult problem than the taciturn respondent whose reluctance is more obvious.

Just as it is possible to overemphasize the importance of interpersonal relations, it is also possible for the interviewer to be so concerned with gathering the appropriate information that he neglects to lay even a minimal foundation of interpersonal relations. In this case, the interviewer gives the impression that the respondent is merely a means to an end. The respondent begins to feel like the patient whose medical specialist obviously loses interest upon discovering that the patient does not have a rare disease but merely a common but painful malady.

Thus the interviewer's task is to be approached as the acrobat approaches a balancing stunt. The interviewer must balance his information-gathering task with the rapport-building task. He should develop a sensitive awareness of moments when he should devote more attention to one or the other.

In this chapter we have tried to show in a general way how the flow of relevant, valid, and reliable information depends not only upon the interaction within the interview situation but also upon the relationship between that situation and the local community and larger society. Against the background of this contextual model we tried to show general objectives, tasks, and problems to be dealt with by the interviewer in all interviews.

We have been careful not to overcomplicate the exposition with any details on specific forces that tend to inhibit or facilitate the free flow of relevant information. To gain a more analytical and practical understanding of how to maximize the flow of relevant information, it is helpful to see the interview situation as a social-psychological field in which forces act as either facilitators or inhibitors of the information flow.

DISCUSSION QUESTIONS

1. What important factors help determine the respondent's ability or willingness to give the information he has other than the actions of the interviewer?
2. In planning an interview or series of interviews, which must be done first: selecting the respondent, choosing the interviewer, picking a time and place, or clearly defining what information is needed? Why?
3. Why do experiments on the use of certain interviewing techniques sometimes arrive at contradictory results even when the methodology is valid and reliable?
4. What are the central tasks of the interviewer?
5. What is a universe of discourse? How does it affect the interview? Give an example of some part of your own universe of discourse that would be unintelligible to outsiders.

SELECTED READINGS IN THE APPLICATION OF INTERVIEWING METHOD

The references below were selected because they are studies of social conduct where much of the information was collected by interviewing and where the type of information needed makes the importance of the *social context* of the interview evident. Most of the studies involve deviant or at least private behavior.

Bryan, James H. "Apprenticeship in Prostitution," *Social Problems,* vol. 12 (1965), pp. 287–97.

Gaylin, Willard. *In the Service of Their Country: War Resisters in Prison.* New York: Viking Press, 1970.

Hess, Robert D., and Handel Gerald. *Family Worlds.* Chicago: University of Chicago Press, 1959.

This deals with the attitudes and emotions involved in family interaction.

Humphreys, Laud. *Tearoom Trade.* Chicago: Aldine Publishing Co., 1970.
   This is a study of the relationships of homosexuals to each other and to the
   straight world.
Irwin, John. *The Felon.* Englewood Cliffs. N.J.: Prentice-Hall, 1970.
   An in-depth study of the felon.
Wiseman, Jacqueline P. *Stations of the Lost.* Englewood Cliffs, N.J.: Prentice-
   Hall, 1970.
   A sensitive study of the life of alcoholics.

Laboratory problem 2

Universe of discourse in White County, Arkansas

One way the local community intrudes into the interaction between interviewer and respondent is in the local universe of discourse used by the respondent. When interviewers leave their own subculture to interview members of a different region, social class, occupation, or ethnic group, they are often puzzled by strange words or strange usages of familiar words. Sometimes these differences are immediately detectable by the context in which the word or phrase appears and sometimes no clues are visible.

Below are excerpts from an interview in Judsonia, Arkansas, with a victim of a tornado that destroyed over 95 percent of all man-made objects in several towns along its path. Read it carefully to pick out any words or phrases that you suspect have a special meaning not generally understood in the United States as a whole.

1. Make a list of these words and phrases in the order they appear.
2. Identify each with the number of the line in which it appears.
3. Make a guess as to the possible meaning of each if you can.

The collective results can be summarized and used as a basis for class discussion if the instructor wishes.

Line
No.

1   I said to mother, "It's going to be a big blow . . . better shut
     all the windows." When I saw the big black funnel coming, I
     wasn't excited at all. The wind got stronger and stronger. While

I was trying to hold the door shut the window light went out. Then
5 it got so dark I couldn't see across the room, but just then the house
blew apart and I landed in the pecan orchard and was in the mud
beside the branch."

I must have got a lick on the head because I took a big headache.
As soon as I come to myself I was proud my sisters worked off but
10 I didn't know what happened to mother. I wasn't hurt bad so I
went back to where the remains of the house was and saw mother
pokin' through the rubble. She was taking on something awful.
Just running around in the rain looking for her daughter and her
belongings I guess. We had oodles of clothes but they was all wet.
15 I could see by her pale face that she was in bad shape, but she
wasn't hurt none.

At first I didn't realize that all of the town was wrecked, but
when I heard this I lit out for Judsonia on foot because my car was
all buggered up by the blow. In fact a tree was on top of it.
20 Anyway, on the way home . . . no I guess it was on the way to
town . . . I came across a cookie drummer from Bald Knob a few
miles from here. Then I knew Bald Knob was hit too. So I thought
maybe Searcy was hit too. So I began to worry about my sisters.
So instead of going on to town I went back home to tell mother
25 we'd better go to Searcy to look after Susan Mae and Mary Ellen.

I was surprised to see mother with a broken hand, she had said
nothing about it before. Then I wanted to get her to the hospital
in a hurry so I borrowed a truck from our neighbor but the roads
was all blocked with trees and telephone poles. I finally carried
30 her out across the fields to Searcy. She is fine now . . . but I studied
all night long for the first four or five nights after the storm. I didn't
get much sleep.

5

Inhibitors of communication

This chapter will deal with the *inhibitors* of communication in the interview and chapter 6 will deal with the *facilitators*. Each inhibitor is seen as a barrier or obstacle to communication that should be avoided, circumvented, or removed from the respondent's mind. Each facilitator, on the other hand, is not merely the absence of an inhibiting barrier but is a positive force motivating the respondent to communicate. Within this framework the interviewer's task of maximizing the flow of relevant information is transformed into the more specific objectives of *minimizing the inhibitors and maximizing the facilitators of communication.*

LINKING THEORY AND PRACTICE

The inhibitor and facilitator frame of reference (IF) does not claim to be a theory, nor do we feel that a single theory of interviewing is currently possible. Interviewing is a microcosm of many forces operating within the human personality, within the interaction situation we call the interview, and within the whole community, society, or culture. Separate theories would be needed to explain each different system. The lack of a single theory of interviewing does not mean that theory is not applicable. Interviewing is a practical art to which many types of theory apply. Concepts drawn from anthropology, sociology, social psychology and psychology all are involved in interviewing. For example, the concepts of culture and subculture, role and status, social structure, role theory, group dynamics, perception, memory, ego-psychology, trauma, competition, and definition-of-the-situation all are borrowed without apology from the social sciences and without pausing to develop the total theoretical schemes from which they come. If we tried to do this, we would be in danger of losing sight of the practical objective of learning to interview. Furthermore, we would become paralyzed by the realization that there are gaps and ambiguities in some of the theory.

The IF frame of reference has been developed as a sensitizing framework to connect the specific theories which often lay behind the experimental studies of interviewing and the practical problem of planning and performing an interview. To some, the eight inhibitors and the eight facilitators may appear to be an eclectic hodgepodge, lacking in symmetry and elegance. Yet analysis of hundreds of verbatim interviews shows that these *are* the types of things which from the point of view of the practitioner hinder and help the flow of relevant information.

The reader will note that all of the inhibitors and facilitators become more meaningful when viewed within the general framework of the *social context of communication* presented in the previous chapter. We are not concerned, for example, with generally inhibited personalities but in how a person is either unable or unwilling to give some particular type of information, to a certain type of interviewer, at a particular time and location for the interview which is defined by the respondent in a certain way. Thus, we see that the triadic relationship (involving the type of information sought, the type of respondent having the information, and the type of interviewer asking for the information) is brought into play within the interview situation which has certain characteristics because of its relationship to the larger society, community, or culture.

Even though the *science* of interviewing draws upon experimental studies and theoretical concepts, the practice of interviewing involves more. The additional element might be called the *art* of interviewing. In both the planning and execution of the interview, the art of interviewing consists of making judgments as to whether a particular inhibitor might be present and of making judgments as to which strategy, technique, or tactic might be most effective under the conditions at hand. In short, the application of theory in interviewing, as in any field, becomes an art.

In interviewing, the practical art accounting for success depends not only upon the interviewer's clear knowledge of the theoretical concepts and the informational objectives of the particular interview at hand, but also upon his *skill* in anticipating potential inhibitors and facilitators so that he can plan to minimize one and maximize the other. This anticipatory skill is based on experience, empathy, and commitment to the purposes of the interview. Another set of skills comes into play once the interviewer-respondent interaction begins. These skills include the ability to listen empathically while evaluating the relevance and completeness of the response, proficiency in quickly adopting tactics appropriate to the stage of the interview, and expertness in controlling one's own behavior to conform to the objectives of the interview.

There is no doubt that both the knowledge and skills, the science and the art, of interviewing can be learned. This has been proven by demonstrations of improvement in performance of interviewers after a period of training. That "interviewers are born not made" and its opposite, that "anyone can learn to be a successful interviewer," both have some truth. It is clear that the cognitive concepts of theory can be learned rather quickly but the basic human skills come more slowly. For this reason studies of improvement of interviewing through training show that even though the training improved everyone's interviewing performance, those who had the most effective performance before the training period tended to have the most effective performance at the end of the training period. The importance of the training is demonstrated by the fact that often the performance of the best interviewer on the pretest was not so good as the performance of the worst interviewer on the post-test.

All the evidence seems to show that such personal qualities of the interviewer as intelligence, empathic ability, listening habits, and observation skills take a long time to develop, but new concepts, strategies, techniques, and tactics can be learned relatively quickly and will pay increasing dividends as we gain skill in their application. In short, interviewers *can* be made.

RECOGNIZING EFFECTS OF INHIBITORS

Often the neophyte interviewer is deceived into thinking that the interview has been productive because the respondent has "talked on and on." He may accept this as evidence that no inhibitors were at work in the situation. Unfortunately, this is not necessarily true. If inhibitors always had the effect of making the respondent quiet, their presence would be easy to recognize. Often a respondent will talk animatedly without saying anything relevant to the question at hand. In this case the response is a smokescreen of words designed to hide his noncooperation.

It is also invalid to conclude that the respondent's failure to give relevant information is any indication of inhibitors at work in the interview situation. It may be that the respondent does not have any relevant information to give.

For these reasons we must keep in mind that for the purposes of interviewing we must define an *inhibitor* as any social-psychological barrier which impedes the flow of *relevant* information by making the respondent *unable* or *unwilling* to give it to the interviewer at the moment.

INHIBITORS

The eight categories listed under this heading operate more frequently to inhibit rather than to facilitate communication. The first four categories tend to make the respondent *unwilling* to give information, while the last four categories tend to make the respondent *unable* to give the information even though willing.

Competing demands for time

The respondent hesitates to begin an interview because of other ways he should or would like to be spending his time. He does not necessarily place a negative value on being interviewed, but must weigh the amount of time he is asked to devote to the interview against other activities competing for this segment of time. The interviewer must sell the idea of being interviewed to obtain the respondent's initial cooperation.

This inhibitor functions only in situations where the respondent is free to decide whether to participate in the interview. Sometimes the respondent is obligated to participate, even though he would rather be devoting his time to something else; here, competing time demand is not a factor. This would be the case if the personnel department of a company decided to interview all employees, or if a social worker decided to interview a mother to determine whether she were still eligible to receive certain welfare services, or if a clinical psychologist wished to interview a patient in a mental hospital. In these situations, the problem is not obtaining the respondent's time for the interview, but the sophisticated interviewer knows he must not assume the captive respondent to be *willing* or *able* to give the information needed.

In the free choice situation, the initial problem is to obtain the respondent's cooperation. Once this is accomplished there may be few obstacles to obtaining the information if the amount of time needed is small and if the nature of the interview was clear to the respondent before he gave his consent.

It is possible, however, for an interview to begin without interference from competing demands, but to continue into a block of time where other current or anticipated activities compete for the respondent's attention. In this case, his interest diminishes. For example, the housewife may begin a market research interview gladly, but begin to lose interest and feel apprehensive as it grows closer to the time for her husband to return for dinner.

Ego threat

The respondent tends to withhold information which may threaten his self-esteem. The effect of an ego threat can range from mild hesitancy in giving information to complete repression. The importance of ego-threat as a barrier to communication in the interview is emphasized by Polansky,[1] who devotes most of his book to the various ego-defense mechanisms used by different respondents in social work and therapeutic interviews. Unfortunately, he does not follow through with suggestions for any methods the interviewer can use to overcome these ego-defense mechanisms.

Three broad categories may be defined according to the strength of the effect of ego threat. The strongest effect is repression. The respondent not only refuses to admit the information to the interviewer, but also hides it from himself to preserve his self-esteem and avoid a guilty conscience. He is being honest when he answers that he does not know or that he has forgotten. This level of ego threat primarily occupies the psychiatrist, psychoanalyst, and clinical psychologist, but is sometimes a factor in the information-gathering interview.

Scott[2] found that in 1955 people were very worried about the possibility of an atomic attack upon the United States, yet it was threatening to admit fear. In many cases the person had repressed his anxiety to the point where he would not admit his anxiety to an interviewer or even to himself. When the respondents in a survey were asked "Are you worried about an atomic war?" there were many fewer admissions than when a projective picture test was used. The picture showed a woman standing in what might be a doorway scanning the sky in which some distant objects are seen only as formless specks. If the question about the picture was "What do *you* see?" there were many fewer admissions of anxiety than when the question was "What do you think *others* might see?" This tendency to project one's own feelings onto others and deny them in ourselves is a common mechanism for avoiding ego threat.

A less intense, but more common, effect of ego threat is found when the respondent, although he consciously possesses the information,

---

[1] Norman A. Polansky, *Ego Psychology and Communication: A Theory for the Interview* (New York: Atherton Press, 1971).

[2] William A. Scott, "The Avoidance of Threatening Material in Imaginative Behavior," *Journal of Abnormal and Social Psychology*, vol. 52 (1956), pp. 338–46.

hesitates to admit it because he anticipates that the interviewer may disapprove. Often the respondent is torn between withholding the information and his yearning for catharsis. Since he has not successfully repressed the memory which threatens his self-esteem, he may have guilt feelings. If he is made to feel confident that the interviewer will not condemn him, he may welcome the opportunity to divulge the information.

Sometimes the shrewd respondent indirectly interviews the interviewer to discover the latter's attitudes. For example, the respondent who would like to confess socially disapproved forms of sex behavior may first try to discover the interviewer's probable reaction. He may mention a case similar to his own and may even try to provoke the interviewer into condemning it. If the interviewer condemns the hypothetical case, the respondent will not tell about himself. Confession is usually easier if the interviewer is a stranger whom the respondent never expects to see again. In any case, a generally accepting and sympathetic attitude toward the respondent as a person goes far toward eliciting candid responses.

A lesser threat to the respondent's self-esteem exists if the respondent is willing to give information to the interviewer, but fears losing status if the information becomes public. This respondent must be assured that his anonymity will be respected. This is not always easy to do. The respondent may fear that the interviewer, even with the best of intentions, will be unable to conceal the source of the information. The higher the respondent's status, the more difficult it is to describe his actions in the community without revealing his identity.

This greater fear in higher status people of losing anonymity was demonstrated in the contrast between the attitudes of the officials in disaster-stricken towns and those of average citizens toward tape-recorded interviews. It was rare to find an ordinary citizen who, as an anonymous number of a random sample, objected to the tape recorder. However, objections from officials were quite common. Even though the official was willing to talk candidly to the interviewer, who was a stranger in the community, he felt that his anonymity would be sacrificed if the tape recording were heard by some member of the local community. He was aware that any of the small-town populace could identify the speaker's voice.

Not only must the interviewer assure the respondent of anonymity at the beginning of the interview, but he must also be sensitive to any need for further assurance as the interview progresses. Often the respondent is too shy at the beginning of the interview to show open concern about anonymity; but as he gathers confidence during the interview, he becomes more willing to show hesitancy. This delayed reaction may be more common when the respondent's cooperation is not voluntary. Bain[3] in his analysis of interaction between a research team and workers in a laundry plant, found that the workers' initial cooperation changed to hostility. The researchers did not need the workers' permission to gain access to the plant. Therefore, a thorough, systematic, and convincing explanation of the study had not been given to the workers. Latent doubt flowered into open suspicion when a temporary recession caused the layoff of a few workers. Rumors spread that the researchers were company spies hired to inform management of who should be laid off next. Several weeks were required to rectify this misperception so that the study could continue.

The numerous symptoms of ego threat can be seen as different effects upon the information flow. These effects may range from simply refusing to volunteer any information to fabricating information as a cover-up. A respondent might defend his ego in an interview in various ways. Assume that an interviewer is talking to a person whose home town was destroyed by a tornado. The interviewer asks, "How did you *feel* when your house took off over the pecan orchard?" Here are examples of answers by several respondents.

Evasion. "I looked out the window and could see the tops of the pecan trees below. The roof had blown clean off the house, but it was still holding together. I don't even remember a jolt when we landed in the trees!"

Simple, emphatic denial. "Well, to tell the truth I wasn't scared at all. There's no sense in getting excited 'cause there is nothing you can do. Of course, the women and children screamed, but there is no sense in a man getting scared at a thing like that."

Elaborate, subtle denial. "Ordinarily, anybody with good sense would be scared stiff but I think that it all happened so fast that I had no time to think about it. I couldn't really believe it. Could you believe it if you looked out the window and saw that you were sailing over the trees? I was just trying to hold the door shut and the next thing I knew was when we landed about 300 feet away from where the house left the foundation."

Depersonalization. "I imagine most people would be plain scared at a time like that. People were all scared and excited. Who wouldn't be at a time like that?"

Minimization. "I was nervous, of course, but not really scared like a lot of people were. I'd been through worse than this in the war, so it didn't seem so bad. I'm sort of the calm type, myself, so it didn't have too much effect on me."

---

[3] Robert K. Bain, "The Researcher's Role: A Case Study," *Human Organization* (Spring 1950), pp. 23–28.

Defense. "Of course I was scared! Anyone who had good sense would realize that there was no way to protect yourself. Planks flew right through brick walls and bricks bounced around like pingpong balls. Human flesh is no match for that kind of thing. The worst thing about it is that there is nothing you can do about it. You can't run, you can't hide, and you can't stay and fight it. It is a pure helpless feeling. You feel helpless because for the first time in your life you *are* completely helpless!"

Confession. "When I saw the porch blow off, I was scared to death. I was almost petrified, but I managed to run into the dining room and hold on to the door casing. When the house left the foundation, I was so weak that I could hardly hold on. I prayed out loud and begged God to save me. I'm ashamed, but what else could I do?"

Although, in general, the respondent's ego threat leads to omission, distortion, and fabrication of information, there are exceptional circumstances where it is even more ego threatening to withhold the information than to reveal it. For example, when a respondent who has certain information realizes that the interviewer knows he has it and will insist on having the truth, he may give the information even though it damages his self-image. This use of pressure to obtain information becomes more successful as the power and prestige of the interviewer increase and as the respondent has more assurance that giving the information will not result in any reprisals from the interviewer or others. We are all familiar with children confessing to an adult rather than to risk the disfavor of such a powerful figure.

When the interviewer is of a lower social status than the respondent, as would be a newspaper reporter who was interviewing a senator, it is usually impossible to pressure the respondent into giving ego-threatening information. There are even institutionalized responses for handling such a situation. The person of higher status and power merely says, "I don't care to comment on that at this time," or simply, "no comment," or "I'm sorry, but I am not free to give such information."

In general, ego threat is an inhibitor of the free flow of information from respondent to interviewer. Even in cases where pressure seems to succeed, it is unlikely that the response will be as detailed and candid as under conditions where no pressure is applied.

In some cases the purpose of a study is not to penetrate the ego-threat barrier, but to directly study the specific nature of the ego-defense system. We may want to know how people in a particular culture or subculture go about verbally defending their actions which have not measured up to the group or community's expectations. Often, the respondent feels that the interviewer will hold him morally accountable for some untoward behavior which he has admitted or about which the interviewer has previous knowledge. In this case, the respondent tries to bridge the discrepancy between his actual behavior and the ideal by giving an account designed to neutralize any negative feeling toward him. Whether or not this account is honored depends upon the underlying assumptions held by his community regarding the nature of human beings and society. Scott and Lyman[4] give many examples and a refined conceptualization of this process of giving "accounts" in the form of excuses and justifications.

Etiquette

The etiquette barrier operates when the answer to the interviewer's question contains information perceived by the respondent as inappropriate to give to the type of person doing the interview or inappropriate to the situation in which the interviewing is done. Answering candidly would be considered in poor taste or evidence of a lack of proper consciousness of one's status relationship to the other. The etiquette barrier inhibits the flow of certain types of information both up and down the status hierarchy.

To understand this phenomenon, society must be viewed as not only a web of communication between people in different roles and statuses, but also a pattern of conscious and unconscious barriers to the indiscriminate flow of information. All types of information do not flow equally well among all persons in society. There cannot be a pattern of communication unless there is also a complementary pattern of non-communication.

Etiquette is one of the inhibitors of communication which acts as a qualitatively selective filter, encouraging the passage of certain messages and obstructing the flow of others between two people with a certain relationship to each other. This selectivity may be governed by the nature of the situation as well as the relationship between the sender and receiver.

To a great extent, we learn these subtle patterns of noncommunication unconsciously, but we are painfully aware of them when they are violated. The five-year-old who repeats some bit of intimate family life to his kindergarten teacher learns from her reaction that he has done something wrong. The teenager who uses obscene language in front of the high school teacher knows that the topic is inappropriate for the teacher. However, he often has not yet learned that she does understand his vocabulary, even though she never uses these words in front of students. The teacher may be handicapped in meeting the situation if she is afraid to let the student know that she understands such words.

---

[4] Marvin B. Scott and Stanford M. Lyman, "Accounts," *American Sociological Review,* vol. 33, no. 1 (February 1968), pp. 46–62.

It is accepted that there are things which men do not discuss in front of women and vice versa, things that married couples do not discuss in front of unmarried people, things students do not tell teachers, things doctors do not tell patients, things parishioners do not tell the clergy, etc. These inhibiting effects of etiquette are often taken for granted as acceptable barriers as long as their inhibiting effect applies to someone else. The problem is that each person's ego, particularly in a democratically oriented society, tends to blind him to his own limitations as a receiver of communication due to the etiquette barrier.

This can be seen in the case of the American returning from a trip around the world who says, "I found nothing but love for Americans everywhere I went." Similarly, a manager of a large corporation may assure the consultant that it is perfectly all right for the middle management people to interview the employees regarding their attitudes toward management because, "We have spent years building up good relations between management and workers; we are just one big happy family." And then there is the parent whose child has been charged with a delinquency who tells the social worker, with all sincerity, "But I asked him if he did it and he said he is innocent. I believe him because he always tells me everything he does." Usually, under these circumstances the person involved can admit that the etiquette barrier would *ordinarily* be operant, but he wrongly assumes that in his case, his charm and desire to hear the truth make him an exception.

This desire to avoid embarrassing, shocking, or threatening the other person is quite distinct from the fear of exposing oneself, as in the case of an ego threat. The distinction becomes useful when it is demonstrated that the treatment of one barrier is quite different from the treatment of the other. The ego-threat barrier can be reduced by the interviewer's demonstrating a nonjudgmental attitude toward the respondent's information and by guaranteeing his anonymity. This would not facilitate communication if the respondent's information was harmless to his self-image but was felt to be inappropriate for the interviewer.

The effect of the etiquette barrier may go beyond simply withholding information to spare the interviewer's feelings and extend to the point where the respondent tries to please the interviewer by telling him what he wants to hear through selective reporting or fabrication. This desire to please may be particularly detrimental to the validity of the information when the interviewer consciously or unconsciously suggests the "appropriate" answer.

Often the negative effects of the etiquette barrier can be forestalled by selecting the appropriate interviewer and situational setting for the interview. Also, if there is a choice of respondents having the desired information, the respondent having the most appropriate relationship to the interviewer should be selected. Sometimes these precautions are not enough in themselves and special techniques and tactics described later can be used.

Trauma

"Trauma" is used to denote an acutely unpleasant feeling associated with crisis experiences. The unpleasant feeling is often brought to the conscious level when the respondent is reporting the experience. This is distinctly different from the fear of losing self-esteem, as in the case of an ego threat, or the fear of shocking the interviewer, as in the case of etiquette. Here, the unpleasantness of the topic results from forcing the respondent to relive the original emotions associated with the experience. In these circumstances, there is no tendency for the respondent to vacillate between evading a topic and talking about it in order to obtain a cathartic release from guilt feelings. He does not feel remiss for his acts, but has an unpleasant feeling regarding something which happened to him.

The marriage counselor talking to a recently divorced person, the physician obtaining a detailed case history of a person whose close relatives have had untimely deaths, the detective interviewing the widow of a recent murder victim, the social worker interviewing a mother regarding legal charges brought by neighbors against the father for beating his wife and children, the policeman or insurance investigator interviewing the survivor of an auto accident, the personnel counselor interviewing an applicant regarding the circumstances under which he was fired from his last position, the teacher talking to a student suddenly rejected by his peer group because of a rumor regarding the student's family—these and other interview situations are likely to involve some probing of traumatic experiences.

The four inhibitors above (competing time demands, ego threat, etiquette, and trauma) are similar in that they reduce the respondent's *willingness* to talk about a certain topic. The specific recognizable symptoms of unwillingness vary to some extent with the particular inhibitor.

There are four inhibitors which reduce the respondent's *ability*, rather than his willingness, to provide valid information. This inability has two general results. First, and least problematical, the respondent may simply admit that he cannot supply the information at the moment for some reason. Second, the respondent, in trying to cooperate, may supply "information" which is no more than a well-meant mixture of imagination, guesswork, and confusion. The second type of respondent poses a much greater problem for the interviewer. He must learn to anticipate, detect, and counteract this tendency in the respondent. In practice, the solution of the problem is not so difficult as it might seem because much of the respondent's feeling that he has to "say something" is due to a general atmosphere created by the interviewer.

Of the factors which make the respondent *unable* to report relevant information, the first is forgetting.

Forgetting

A frequent inhibitor is the respondent's inability to recall certain types of information. This is not a problem if the objectives of the interview deal only with *current* attitudes, beliefs, or expectations. However, the moment we move into the area of facts we are dealing largely with the past.

This natural fading of the memory (which may be hastened by selective psychological repression) makes it easier for the ego-defense system to reconstruct one's image of his own past by simple omission, addition, or distortion. This idea of the "reconstruction of biography" is a continual theme in the insightful writings of Alfred Schutz.[5]

The memory problem is a much more frequent obstacle than is generally expected by interviewers. Even some of the most seemingly simple and obvious facts cannot be obtained by superficial interviewing methods.

For example, a simple fact such as the date of starting work at a factory cannot be accurately determined in a superficial interview. This was demonstrated in an experiment by Moore[6] in which the respondents' replies to an interviewer were checked against the company records.

Historians have been aware of the "treachery of recollection" in trying to reconstruct even recent historical events.[7] More recent experiments have been done to determine the extent to which forgetting is a function of elapsed time versus the nature of the facts to be remembered. For example, Dakin and Tennant[8] found in a survey at different time intervals after the fact that, although the greater the time lapse the less accurate the memory, there were also great differences in accuracy of remembering one fact versus another at the same time

---

[5] Alfred Schutz, *Collected Papers*, vol. 1, ed. Maurice Natanson (The Hague, Netherlands: Martinus Nijhoff, 1962).

[6] B. V. Moore, "The Interview in Industrial Research," *Social Forces*, vol. 7 (1929), pp. 445–52.

[7] Daniel Aaron, "The Treachery of Recollection: The Inner and Outer History," in R. H. Bremner, *Essays on History and Literature* (Columbus: Ohio State University Press, 1966).

[8] Ralph E. Dakin and Donald Tennant, "Consistency of Response by Event-Recall Intervals and Characteristics of Respondents," *Sociological Quarterly*, vol. 9 (1968), pp. 73–84.

interval. One example, only 24 percent could remember their income while 98 percent could remember their former address.

Fortunately, the respondent's experience of a particular event is not simply either remembered or forgotten. His ability to remember depends, in general, upon three types of factors. First, the vividness of recall of the experience is related to various dimensions such as its original emotional impact, its meaningfulness to the person at the time, and the degree to which the person's ego was involved. Second is the simple problem of the amount of time elapsing between the event itself and the interview pertaining to it. Third is the nature of the interview situation, including the interviewer's techniques and tactics.

Knowledge of these factors as they are related to a particular respondent will help the interviewer to *predict* probable trouble in certain areas of subject matter. The second factor, time lapse, is sometimes controllable by the interviewer if he is free to select respondents whose experience is fresh. If he has no control over the amount of time lapse between event and interview, his knowledge of the length of this time span will at least warn him when special techniques and tactics are in order to refresh a respondent's memory. That a once-forgotten event can subsequently be recalled is frequently demonstrated in interviews when the respondent has given a spontaneous and sincere reply early in the interview, only to contradict himself later when his memory has been more adequately stimulated. There are many strategies, techniques, and tactics available to help the alert interviewer overcome the memory barrier.

Chronological confusion

This term refers to the respondent's tendency to confuse the chronological order of his experiences. This may occur in two ways: (*a*) Two or more events may be correctly recalled, but the respondent is unsure of the sequence of their occurrence; or (*b*) only one condition or event is recalled and is incorrectly assumed to have also been true at an earlier point in time.

The second type of confusion is more complicated and merits further explanation. It usually occurs when the interviewer is inquiring into a *developmental* sequence such as relations between people or the respondent's past attitudes, beliefs and expectations, and in his interpretations of past events. Often the original conditions are forgotten and subsequent conditions which are recalled more readily are assumed to have also been true in the prior situation. There is a strong tendency for the respondent to utilize hindsight in interpreting events of the past. Therefore, if we are interested in discovering what the respondent's original interpretation was at the time of the event, special techniques and tactics must be used.

For example, in a suburb of Rochester, New York, leaky gas lines exploded, damaging and the reducing valves which prevent natural gas from entering homes at an extremely high pressure. When the gas pressure suddenly increased 100 times, houses filled with gas and began to explode one at a time over a period of three hours until 45 houses had been completely demolished.

When respondents were asked why they ran from their homes when they first heard an explosion, some said that they wanted to get out of the house before it exploded. Actually, there was no way for people to suspect that the initial explosion was to be the first in a series; the causal connection between the first and succeeding blasts could not have been known immediately. But once the facts were known, running out of the house appeared the rational thing to have done. These respondents, because of chronological confusion, did not realize that they were explaining their behavior at one point in time as being motivated by an idea not gained until *after* they had acted.

This type of problem is commonly encountered in interviews seeking case history information. This would include studies of how people's attitudes and values change, how interpersonal relations in the family or any other group develop, how conflicts arise and are resolved, how people's interpretation of events change, or studies of any problem involving a chronological dimension.

Inferential confusion

This term designates confusion and inaccuracies resulting from errors of inference on the part of the respondent. These errors fall into two general categories: (*a*) due to faulty *induction,* when the respondent is asked to convert concrete experiences into a higher level of generalization; and (*b*) those due to faulty *deduction,* when the respondent is asked to give concrete examples of certain categories of experience supplied by the interviewer.

It is common for the respondent to make a misstep in either ascending or descending the ladder of abstraction. Even though the respondent's memory of his experience might be correct, the moment he begins to interpret, explain, or generalize from these experiences he can make an inferential error. There are two main sources of inferential error, regardless of whether it is the inductive or deductive type. The first is simple; the error may result from the respondent's failure in abstract logic ability. The second is a distortion of thinking which may be produced by strong attitudes and preconceptions.

Errors of the first type are often caused by the interviewer's providing categories of experience which are not clearly defined for the respondent. In this case, the respondent's attempt to provide concrete examples fitting the categories may fail. For example, the interviewer who is studying family conflicts, and who needs to categorize the specific examples of conflict into role conflict, value conflict, and lack of communication, would not be wise to ask, "What are some examples of role conflict in your family?" The probability of the respondent's giving an example which was totally or mainly a case of role conflict is very low, even if an attempt is made to define the term "role conflict" for the respondent. A request for such an example places too much of the burden of analysis upon the respondent.

In order to help the respondent up and down the ladder of abstraction, the interviewer must break the general question into steps which will accumulate relevant details, allowing an accurate analysis to determine which category is appropriate for a specific conflict episode. Often, the respondent is quite adept at giving examples which correctly fit into categories that are his *own*. However, the problem arises when these categories are irrelevant to the purpose of the interview and the respondent is forced to think in unfamiliar terms. The interviewer should use techniques and tactics which either avoid the necessity of the respondent's making inferences or that help him to make them accurately.

Errors of the second type, those involving distortions of inference due to strong attitudes and preconceptions, are common in many types of interviews. These errors usually occur when the objectives of the interview call for some generalized forms of information such as, "How do the black and the white people get along in this school?" "How were the rescue operations handled in the disaster?" "What philosophy of child rearing do you use with your child?" An accurate response to these questions would involve a thoughtful process of inductively reaching a generalization on the basis of a representative sample of observed, concrete events. All of these questions also involve value judgments which are liable to act as premises for a deductive process resulting in the unconscious line of reasoning which says, "This is the way things *should* happen and, in the absence of glaring evidence to the contrary, let's assume that is the way it *did* happen." Thus, the teacher reports that race relations are "tranquil" in her school, the disaster victim reports that the rescue operations were carried out in a "heroic fashion," and the parent reports that she handles the child in a very "permissive and democratic way." In each instance, the respondent may be simply expressing his desire, intent, or assumption. This must be checked by bringing the generalization down the ladder of abstraction to specific concrete events. Often the interviewer will discover that there is no concrete experience to back up the generality.

Unconscious behavior

Often the interview objectives call for information about a person's unconscious behavior. Behavior that is not consciously directed may be classified into three types. The most common is simply custom or habit. The degree to which this is unconscious is indicated by Sapir.[9] Into this category would fall those questions about repetitive behavior such as, "What is the difference between the way you speak to a male and a female on the phone?" "When do you use the prepositions 'of' and 'at' after a verb in the English language?" "Which sock do you usually put on first in the morning?"

Next, there is a type of unconscious behavior which Blumer[10] calls "circular reaction," or the immediate, unwitting response of one person to the subliminal, nonverbal cues furnished by another. This is not usually a repetitious form of behavior, but one which arises only under special circumstances. The following questions would be asking about this type of behavior, "What made you dislike him when you first saw him?" "How did you decide to join the lynch mob?" "How did you know that she loved you?"

The third type of unconscious behavior is found under conditions of acute emotional stress in crises where the behavior does not follow a habitual pattern and where it does not result from circular reaction with others. For example, in a disaster interview a respondent was unable to report how he traveled from his house to a cousin's house in the neighborhood. The evidence indicated that the behavior forgotten by respondent covered a five-minute interval. The interviewer thought the respondent could have been knocked unconscious and then either blown through the air to that point or carried by a rescue worker. Later, the interviewer discovered that both possibilities were incorrect because other witnesses had seen the respondent climbing frantically over the rubble on the way to his cousin's house and heard him shouting to his wife who had been at the cousin's house before the storm struck.

In general, this type of information is difficult to obtain by interviewing, but it is not uncommon for respondents to say that they had never been aware of certain aspects of their behavior until after the interview

---

[9] Edward Sapir, "The Unconscious Patterning of Behavior in Society," in *The Unconscious: A Symposium,* ed. E. S. Dummer (New York: A. A. Knopf, 1927), pp. 114–42.

[10] Herbert Blumer, "Collective Behavior," in *An Outline of the Principles of Sociology,* ed. Robert S. Park (New York: Barnes & Noble, 1946), p. 224.

had been in progress for some time. When interviewing methods fail, the information must be obtained through direct or indirect observation.

SUMMARY

Of the eight inhibitors we have named, four of them (competing time demands, ego threat, etiquette, and trauma) tend to make the respondent *unwilling* to give relevant information. The other four (forgetting, chronological confusion, inferential confusion, and unconscious behavior) tend to make the respondent *unable* to give relevant and valid information to the interviewer.

The effects of these inhibitors are not always obvious to the interviewer because the unwilling respondent may fill the air with irrelevancies, ambiguities, or pure fabrications to make a smokescreen concealing his lack of cooperation. If the respondent is willing but unable to give relevant and valid information, he may use these same tactics if the interviewer exerts too much pressure to cooperate without critically evaluating the relevance and validity of the information given.

Fortunately, the effect of inhibitors is not absolute. Inhibitors should be viewed as potentials to be avoided or counteracted. They can be avoided to some extent by methods aimed at minimizing their intrusion into the interview situation. Their effects can be counteracted by maximizing the facilitators which act as counter forces in the interview situation.

The next chapter will describe and illustrate eight facilitators which can be used as positive forces to counteract or displace inhibitors.

DISCUSSION QUESTIONS

1. What is an inhibitor of communication?
2. How is the inhibitor-facilitator model helpful to interviewers?
3. To what extent is interviewing seen as an art or a science?
4. What is the author's response to the idea that "interviewers are born not made"?
5. How many inhibitors are there? Under what two more general categories can they be grouped?
6. To predict whether a certain inhibitor will come into play in a particular interview, what do we have to know about that interview? Give an example of an interview situation in which you would expect a certain inhibitor to be present.

Laboratory problem 3

Detecting potential inhibitors

Below are examples from a variety of interview situations. Select the inhibitor most likely to intrude in each. Note that after some items there are letters in parentheses corresponding to one or more of the inhibitors to be omitted from your selection. This rules out the most obvious possibilities in those cases with multiple inhibitors. There is no absolutely correct answer since it depends on the assumptions you happen to make regarding any unspecified but relevant aspects of the interview. Write the answers on a sheet of paper after the problem numbers 1 through 10, using the following answer key.

a. competing time demands   *e.* forgetting
b. ego threat   *f.* chronological confusion
c. etiquette   *g.* inferential confusion
d. traumatic experience   *h.* unconscious behavior

1. The prosecuting lawyer in a murder trial asks a witness for the defense, "Has your lawyer coached you on what to say and what not to say?"

2. A mother in the Parent Teachers Association who has a spoiled child asks a teacher during a conversation at tea, "How is my son doing in your class?" (Not *b*)

3. One Vietnam veteran asks another, who is a close friend, "How did you feel when you came back from Vietnam last week and found Jane had broken your engagement and married an old high school friend?" (not *b*)

4. A psychology student, in obtaining a case history from a neurotic

121

teenager, asks, "Did you ever have any big fights with any of your brothers?" (Not *d, e,* or *g*)

5. A student asks his roommate, who has some difficulty keeping up with the reading assignments, "When you read, do you read words or groups of words; and do you 'back track' over a word or phrase very often as you read?" (Not *b*)

6. At 5:30 P.M. a public opinion interviewer knocks on the door of a dwelling unit falling in the random sample. He does not know the family's name, but he does know that the husband is a junior executive in a local firm, that there are three children in the family (ages one, three, and five), and that he must interview the wife. The wife answers the door and the interviewer explains that he is studying an important problem of improving the nursery school and kindergarten facilities in the area, and would appreciate cooperation in an interview which takes about an hour.

7. A public opinion interviewer who is studying the pre-election political situation says to the respondent near the middle of the interview, "You mentioned that you don't like the Democrats because they say so many foolish things . . . could you give me some examples of what you mean?" (Not *b, c,* or *e*)

8. One young businessman (about 25 years old) says to another of about the same age, "That's interesting—you know I am a Princeton man too . . . we must have been there at the same time. Which eating club did you belong to?" (Not *c*)

9. Two politicians who have been personal friends since childhood are discussing their political careers when one asks the other, "I remember how you correctly predicted the election of Senator Young even though his opponent, Bricker, was the forecasters' choice. How did you know that Bricker wasn't going to make it?" (Not *e* or *h*)

10. A detective is trying to discover how the victim (who is still alive) was poisoned. He asks the victim, "What did you eat for lunch five days ago?" (Not *f* or *h*)

6

Facilitators of communication

This chapter will emphasize the potential *facilitators* of communication in contrast to the inhibitors emphasized in the previous chapter. The two chapters together present the inhibitor-facilitator model of communication that views the interview situation as a field of social-psychological forces. These forces arise from the relationships between the information sought, the respondent, the interviewer, the interview situation, and the larger social context as described in chapter 4.

THE FACILITATORS

The facilitators will be approached from the point of view of the respondent as were the inhibitors. And like the inhibitors, these facilitators are also treated as social-psychological resultants of the relationship between the information and the situation in which it is communicated. Some of the situational stimuli for communication apply to any type of information and others only to more narrow categories of information. Although these facilitators occur in other forms of conversation and can be illustrated with examples from a wide variety of settings, the main concern here is with their value in the interview for both maximizing the flow of relevant information and for maintaining optimal interpersonal relations.

Fulfilling expectations

One of the important forces in social interaction is the tendency for one person to communicate, verbally and nonverbally, his expectations to another person. The second person then tends to respond, consciously or unconsciously, to those expectations. This may be viewed as one manifestation of the more general human tendency to conform to the group of peers and to the suggestion of higher status persons in the society. It is in this conformity to the group norms that security is sought and usually found. The theoretical and empirical treatments of this basic human tendency are so abundant that we will not attempt to review them here.

More specifically relevant to interviewing is the question of *how* the interviewer communicates *which* expectations to the respondent. In answer to the latter part of this question, we must be aware that the interviewer should communicate both a general expectation of cooperation as well as the more specific expectation of an answer to his specific questions. Although the respondent reacts to his own perception of these expectations, we cannot assume that the response will always mechanically (in a stimulus-response fashion) fulfill the expectation. Instead, by the steady and consistent communication of his general and specific expectations to the respondent, the interviewer will exert a steady, and often cumulative, force affecting the respondent's cooperation. This expectation may be communicated between persons of equal or unequal status, but cooperation requires a type of creative reciprocity that has been described as *dyadic creativity* by Murray.[1]

When we turn to *how* the interviewer communicates his expectations, we must clearly distinguish between *asking* for cooperation and *expecting* it. The former is mainly a verbal communication while the latter is mainly nonverbal. As pointed out by Rogers[2] there must be harmony between what one says and what one feels if the interviewer is to be "dependably real" to the respondent. The inexperienced interviewer who lacks confidence, or who fails to see the importance of his task, will often ask only verbally for the information. He dutifully poses the question, while his whole nonverbal manner communicates his doubt that he has any right to expect an answer. It is this neutralizing effect of the verbal and the nonverbal communication which often causes the novice to lose faith in the "power of positive expectations." He may say, "I told him it was all right to tell me anything that was on his mind, but I'm sure he was withholding important information." This problem persists where the interviewer is not aware that he is also communicating nonverbally with the respondent.

In some cases, the interviewer's negative expectations also interfere with his ability to observe the respondent accurately. His attitude so colors his interpretation of the respondent's behavior that he imagines

---

[1] Henry A. Murray, "Dyadic Creations" in Warren G. Bennis et al. *Interpersonal Dynamics* (Homewood, Ill.: The Dorsey Press, 1964), pp. 638–46.

[2] Carl R. Rogers, "The Characteristics of a Helping Relationship," *On Becoming a Person* (Boston: Houghton Mifflin, 1961), pp. 39–58.

resistance. This makes him more doubtful and the reinforced attitude is then communicated unwittingly to the respondent. Thus, a form of circular reaction is set up with one aspect reinforcing the other until the interviewer feels it almost unbearable to contact another respondent.

The following example shows how one interviewer projected his expectation of failure into his interpretation of the respondent's behavior:

I knocked on the door and explained what I wanted. She had a skeptical look on her face. Then a male voice mumbled something from behind her. Then she said that she couldn't do the interview at that time, but that I should come back the next day. I just knew that she was lying because you could see that she was afraid and she had a sort of weak, high-pitched voice. The man was probably trying to protect her so that gave her an excuse to offer.

I didn't expect to find her there the next day and was I ever surprised when she came to the door and invited me in! I could see that I had been wrong in my original judgment of her, because she was very willing to talk. That tone of voice I had heard the day before was natural for her, even when she was talking about something humorous.

Usually interviewers gain confidence with experience. However, the experience must be mostly successful. The wise novice accepts his limitations and begins with easier assignments and, with increasing confidence and skill, he progressed to more difficult ones. Confidence is not all that is needed, but it is one of the positive forces in the interview situation. When the interviewer gains a better understanding of the numerous factors which make an interview successful or unsuccessful, he is less likely to lose confidence through failures causes by forces beyond his control. Just as the physician, lawyer, and minister, in their roles, can expect and receive privileged communications, the interviewer learns his role and is able to communicate it in a subtle way to the respondent.

Recognition

All human beings need the recognition and the esteem (as distinct from affection) of others. Much of literature of social anthropology, social psychology and sociology is concerned with concepts which involve this element of recognition. Studies of such factors as competition, social status, prestige, or approval all involve this element. W. I. Thomas[3] was one of the early sociologists who consciously conceptual-

---

[3] Edmund H. Volkart (ed.), *Social Behavior and Personality*. (New York: Social Science Research Council, 1951), pp. 125–29. Thomas's "four wishes" are the desire for new experience, security, response, and recognition.

ized the idea as one of the "four wishes" basic to human motivation. The desire for recognition is fitted into a carefully developed theoretical framework of *social exchange* by Homans,[4] who shows that social interaction often depends upon an exchange of social goods such as esteem and admiration for certain activities. In short, people will "perform" in exchange for recognition and other social rewards. Parsons and Bales[5] use the words *approval* and *esteem* to cover what we refer to as recognition. In their scheme, approval refers to that positive attitude in response to *specific* performances by the other person, while esteem is reserved for the positive *overall* evaluation of that person. Sutherland[6] has demonstrated that even criminals find ways to gain esteem, approval, or recognition (and hence self-respect) by conforming to the norms of the underworld.

The need for recognition is fulfilled by attention from people outside the individual's intimate circle. Being appreciated and loved by one's wife is gratifying, but does not fulfill the need for recognition as we use the term. People may enjoy recognition even though it is based upon notoriety or upon a good reputation which is not deserved.

The skillful and insightful interviewer takes advantage of every opportunity to give the respondent *sincere* recognition. Experimental studies of interviewing have shown that praising the respondent's cooperation has a definite positive effect on the interview.[7]

In addition to direct, sincere praise, there are many sources of ego gratification for the respondent. For example, the respondent may be flattered that he was *selected* because he has some information that is *needed.* The same feeling may result because the respondent's town, his place of employment, his school, or any other group with which he identifies is being studied. It is no accident that there have been several magazine articles on the theme, "I was interviewed by Mr. Kinsey." People who have had such an experience are unique in the eyes of those around them.

Altruistic appeals

There seems to be a human need to identify with some high value or cause that is beyond immediate self-interest. This may be a form of identification with the objectives of some larger group. The group may

---

[4] George C. Homans, *Social Behavior: Its Elementary Forms* (New York: Harcourt, Brace and World, Inc. 1961), pp. 51–82.

[5] Talcott Parsons and Robert F. Bales, *Family, Socialization and Interaction Process* (New York: The Free Press, 1955), pp. 86–87.

[6] E. H. Sutherland, *The Professional Thief* (Chicago: University of Chicago Press, 1937).

[7] Joan B. Field, "The Effect of Praise in a Public Opinion Poll," *Public Opinion Quarterly*, Vol. 19, 1955, pp. 85–90.

be real or imaginary, contemporary or not. Altruistic deeds usually increase self-esteem whether or not the person's deeds have been public. This distinguishes altruism from recognition.

In every case, the individual is responding to some group value which he has internalized. In some cases, value may be *latent* in that the holder seldom acts upon it because more immediate practical values take precedence. Often the interviewer, if he understands the respondent's value system, can use strategy, techniques, and tactics to reactivate the latent value.

Altruism is of major importance in motivating many respondents in sociological, psychological, and anthropological studies. For example, the Martin brothers gave detailed case history material on their crimes, feeling that this might help other youths stay out of the underworld.[8] In some cases, respondents have volunteered information that was obviously painful to give because they felt it would be of value to others. In a study of marital adjustment, it was obvious that some of the husbands and wives volunteered information beyond what was asked and accepted the blame for an unsuccessful marriage because "it might help someone avoid the mistake I made." Also members of a disaster-stricken community willingly gave information with the hope that it might help future disaster victims.

Sympathetic understanding

Human beings need the sympathetic response of others. They like to share their joys, fears, successes, and failures. This need of understanding differs from the need for recognition which requires success and increased status in the eyes of people with whom one does not share an intimate relationship; in fact, a person can feel "famous" without knowing any of his "fans" personally. In contrast, sympathetic understanding may be obtained in connection with failures and shortcomings as well as successes, and it is usually extended by a member of the primary group, but it may also be extended by the therapist or interviewer.

This need for sympathetic understanding has been incorporated into many schemes of human needs and it has been given several names. Some of the concepts most closely synonymous with sympathetic understanding are: the "desire for *response,*" as used by W. I. Thomas,[9] and a combination of the desire for *acceptance* and for *approval,* as used by Parsons and Bales.[10]

This desire to be understood and to have someone offer a "sympa-

---

[8] Clifford R. Shaw, *Brothers in Crime* (Chicago: University of Chicago Press, 1938).

[9] Volkart, *Social Behavior,* p. 129.

[10] Ibid., p. 86.

thetic ear" is seen not only in the therapeutic interview but also in many information-gathering interviews. Teenagers often need someone who "really understands" them and who knows what they mean by "problem parents." Old people are often easy to interview, not only because they are retired and have more time, but also because they have problems which no one takes time to hear. Also, until recently their problems have received much less attention than the problems of youth in the American culture. Shut-ins, socially deviant persons, and other types of isolates often cause the public opinion pollster great difficulty because they want to chat about everything but the subject of the interview. In this case, the need for sympathetic understanding interferes with the efficiency of the interview, and the interviewer must decide to what extent he should allow the respondent to talk about his own problems in view of the effect upon interpersonal relations and the adequacy of the information.

People do not have to be obviously isolated to have a pent up need for a sympathetic ear. In their routine pattern of living, many people have few opportunities to meet a good listener. Ordinarily, when they begin to talk about their problems, the listener retaliates with a long list of his own grievances which tend to pale the first person's difficulties. Often, people refrain from expressing their feelings because "my husband hears that from me all the time," or "he hears people's gripes all day long at the office and doesn't want to hear more of the same thing when he comes home."

Interviewers who reflect a sympathetic attitude and who know how to direct it toward the objectives of the interview will find their percentage of successes much higher than those who cannot.

New experience

All human beings welcome some form of new experience.[11] Even though variety may not be the only spice of life, escape from the dreary routine is sought by everyone. In interviewing personnel in hospitals, industry, and schools, there have been many cases where the interview appeals to the respondent's need for new experience. For example, educators who were cosmopolitan by training and who found themselves temporary captives of a small, local community, found it stimulating to be interviewed on such subjects as academic freedom, foreign trade, or trends in the development and application of social science.

When interviewing industrial employees, it was often obvious that they welcomed a coffee break during which they could discuss anything. After the formal interviews were completed respondents com-

---

[11] Ibid., p. 121.

mented, "Do I have to go back to work now?" "That was very interesting. I had never thought about a lot of these things before." "I hope I didn't bore you with all this talk, but I found it very exciting." "I'm not much of a talker, but if we can talk on company time that's fine with me." "This is a lot more fun than what I do all day at the plant."

Similarly, as market research people know, the housewife has a *certain* pattern of activities, and although these may vary in detail from tenement house areas to suburbia, a break in this routine is often a welcome relief. In suburbia, many of the women rarely see a man in the neighborhood during the day, much less have the opportunity to be interviewed by one.

Sometimes the respondent is motivated by his curiosity regarding the interviewer, and the interviewer should consider this in deciding what to say about himself.

We must not assume, simply because an interview is a new experience for a particular respondent, that is will satisfy his need for new experience. There are some negative effects when certain aspects of the respondent's perception of the new situation are ego threatening. The respondent may be anxious about whether he will make a good impression on the interviewer or whether there may be some hidden purpose in the interview. This apprehensiveness can often be detected by the interviewer at the beginning of the contact. Once these fears are dispelled, the respondent frequently finds the interview a new and interesting experience.

Catharsis

By "catharsis" we mean the process by which one person obtains a release from unpleasant emotional tensions by talking about the source of these tensions and expressing his feelings. The psychotherapist is most often concerned with catharsis as a release from guilt feelings which may be repressed in the subconscious. Similarly, the religious confession usually involves an expression of guilt in an attempt to relieve the pangs of conscience. Although catharsis is often associated with deep personality disturbances, in its broadest concept it is found in the everyday experience of most people. We have mild guilt feelings over the way we have treated someone during the day, or we have pent up feelings of frustration and inhibited aggression against our associates. This tension may be released by kicking the cat or by pouring out our difficulties to another person.

Although we are all familiar with the frequent need for catharsis in ourselves, we do not always perceive the same need in others. Most people dealing in human relations know that this need to "air our gripes," to verbalize our feelings of hostility, guilt and frustration, is omnipresent. The sensitive field worker frequently recognizes his role as the itinerant "father confessor." For example, a college professor, whose colleague was fired during loyalty hearings, feels guilty for not having come to the defense of his friend. Although he knew his colleague had no communist connections, he was afraid he, too, might lose his job. A mother of a delinquent son might blame herself for his behavior. More commonly, a mother might feel frustrated because her three children keep her so exhausted that she cannot be a good companion for her husband or use her college training creatively. In any of these cases, the need for catharsis increases the spontaneity of the interview once an atmosphere of sympathetic understanding has been established.

The need for sympathetic understanding and the need for catharsis are related, but they are not the same thing. A person may satisfy his need for sympathetic understanding by sharing with the interviewer his joys, plans, and achievements that do not involve any past frustration, aggression, guilt, or repression. Since no moral connotations are involved, it is not so necessary for this respondent to feel assured that the interviewer will respect his confidence. He is mainly concerned with finding someone to talk to and does not consider whether the interviewer will divulge the information or not.

Frequently, motivation behind the conversation may move by imperceptible degrees from the simple need for a sympathetic listener to the need for catharsis. Although at some points in this process it is difficult to distinguish which motive is dominant, this does not make the distinction between the two motivations meaningless.

There can be a situation in which the need of sympathetic understanding is being fulfilled without catharsis. However, it is impossible to fulfill the need for catharsis without first establishing an atmosphere of sympathetic understanding. For this reason sympathetic understanding usually *precedes* catharsis. The interviewer who does not have time to listen to what he considers inconsequential egocentric talk will not find the respondent ready to share important confidences.

The need for catharsis is usually a positive factor, but once the proper atmosphere has been established, there is sometimes a detrimental delayed reaction, and the respondent begins to feel embarrassed or resentful toward the interviewer for "making" him talk about ego-threatening topics. Once his need for catharsis has been fulfilled, the respondent may become concerned about the possible results of having given the information. The respondent's doubts grow when the interviewer is no longer present to provide the constant reassurance of anonymity, and to display his own nonjudgmental attitude toward the respondent. As a result, any second contact with the respondent may begin with coolness or hostility. In cases where no second contact is needed, the respondent may still damage the study by negatively influencing other potential respondents. Ways of minimizing this possibility will be shown later.

The need for meaning

Another general human trait is the need for meaning. The desire for an answer to such questions as "Who am I?" "Where did I come from?" "Where am I going?" or "Why do events happen as they do?" often tempts a person in higher status to give a person in lower status an answer that he does not believe himself but which he thinks will satisfy his questioner. For example, a child may ask his mother, "What holds up the moon?" and in desperation she may reply, "It hangs on a string," or "It is full of gas like a balloon." Most primitive tribes have a myth which explains the origin of their tribe, if not of the whole universe, which fills the void between desired knowledge and available knowledge.

Every society has a set of assumptions, values, explanations, and myths lending order to the confusion of reality in which the members of that society live. Cantril[12] has spelled out in some detail the interrelationships between different parts of the system as they are internalized in one personality. Particularly relevant to the problem of interviewing is his general observation that under changing social conditions, the individual's system of meaning becomes inadequate to explain real events from which he cannot escape. When the social matrix is disturbed, the individual embarks upon a search for meaning which often makes him highly susceptible to suggestion and a likely candidate for some social movement.

This concept of the *need for meaning* has been dealt with experimentally by Festinger[13] and others as the need to resolve *cognitive dissonance.* They point out that there is a psychological tension set up in the individual when he becomes aware of any incongruence of facts, assumptions, or interpretations. This tension is painful and its reduction is rewarding to the individual.

As the interviewer with wide experience knows, these disturbances of an individual's belief system result from wars, depressions, catastrophes, and other large-scale crises. Disaster interviews often show that the crisis left the members of the disaster-stricken town groping for the meaning of what has happened. They would wonder, "Why did some people get killed while others were spared? Why was I spared?

---

[12] Hadley Cantril, *The Psychology of Social Movements* (New York: John Wiley & Sons, 1941), pp. 53–77.

[13] Leon Festinger, *A Theory of Cognitive Dissonance* (Row-Peterson, 1957), p. 13.

How could a just God allow this to happen to innocent children who are too young to be sinners? What would have happened if Robert had been late to the high school dance as he usually was . . . would he have been killed on his way?"

This need for meaning and the tendency to search for answers was noted in these people's increased attendance at several different local churches for some weeks after the disaster. Usually, each minister responded to his congregation's expectation of an explanation by showing how these events could be reconciled to the concept of a "just and loving God." The need for meaning was also shown in the respondents' reflections during the interview.

More common sources of insecurity accompanying loss of meaning are seen in the life cycle of individuals. In a dynamically changing society, the adolescent is beset by confusion as he tries to adjust to the process of becoming an adult. The examples set by his own parents no longer apply to conditions of life in the atomic age. Similarly, the graduate from a teachers college is shocked in his first teaching job when he finds a great discrepancy between his idealistic expectations and the actual operation of the school in which he teaches. He might wonder, "Is this what I went to school for? Do parents really want their children to be educated, or do they merely want them to be taught the same things they learned? Are teachers hired mainly to keep the kids off the streets, out of the labor market and away from their mother's bridge game? Is it really possible to teach, thinking of the individual needs of each child, while trying to prevent bedlam in a class of forty children? Why didn't anyone mention these things in our courses on teaching methods?" During this initial disillusionment he may seek someone to talk to as an aid to thinking through the problem and deciding on a future course of action. Likewise, it is found that people who never felt pressed by questions about things such as sickness, loneliness, and death, begin to face some new questions as they approach later maturity. Their philosophy of life sometimes needs to be reevaluated when it becomes apparent that they will not live forever.

In those cases where the interview topic deals directly with the sources disturbing a person's system of meaning, there is a strong motivation for the respondent to talk it through, once he is convinced of the interviewer's interest in his search for meaning. It is sometimes possible for the interviewer to elicit the respondent's interest by pointing out contradictions, inconsistencies, dilemmas, or facts that might stimulate the respondent's need for meaning. In other words, the interviewer may try to disturb the respondent's equilibrium by involving him in a problem. This is usually more difficult than dealing with a problem in which the respondent is already involved. Valid public-opinion polls on "controversial issues" are often difficult to do, because problems defined as public issues by the information collectors may not concern those who are answering the questions.

Once the interviewer has been sensitized to this omnipresent need for meaning, he can use skills, techniques, and tactics to maximize the stimulation and fulfillment of the need, thus utilizing another basic motivation to communicate.

Extrinsic rewards

This term refers to those rewards motivating the respondent other than those he gains directly from interaction within the interview itself. These extrinsic rewards are helpful insofar as the respondent sees the interview as a means to an end. Even though the objectives of the interview may not coincide with the respondent's objectives beyond the interview, the interviewer may skillfully utilize various extrinsic rewards in order to obtain the respondent's cooperation.

Many forms of extrinsic rewards have been used. Money may be given in exchange for the respondent's time, or the interviewer's study may help solve some problem in which the respondent is interested. A respondent may submit to an interview, or even seek it, as a means of obtaining a job. A recently divorced mother may agree to an interview with a social worker, hoping that she will be able to obtain financial aid and psychotherapy for her daughter. A businessman may cooperate in an interview because he is interested in reducing juvenile delinquency, particularly shop-lifting from his own store. A college professor may have an interest in being interviewed on the topic of academic freedom, hoping that the study might stir up public sentiment for the protection of this freedom.

Extrinsic rewards are usually not needed to obtain cooperation in studies involving human interest, but they become more necessary as intrinsic rewards decrease and as the amount of time and thought demanded from the respondent increase. For example, it is more necessary to pay people to submit to a psychological study of sensory perception or reaction time than to pay respondents to cooperate with an opinion poll on a current issue. Sometimes an extrinsic reward is desirable even though the respondents are members of a captive group who do not give their permission as individuals. This is true particularly if the reward is given by the agency sponsoring the interviewer rather than by the agency that allowed the interviewer access to the respondents. The extrinsic reward sometimes helps overcome initial resentment or allows a series of contacts without causing the respondent's increasing resentment of time spent.

There are circumstances in which any extrinsic reward, particularly money, is detrimental. If the offer of a reward has the effect of attracting one type of respondent and repelling others, this selectivity may bias the study. Offering money may damage the prestige of participating in the study or may encourage bargaining by people who are interested only in the money. The effective use of extrinsic rewards will be explored in the next chapter on field strategy.

Extrinsic rewards are rarely needed and then mainly for obtaining the initial contact. Once the interview begins, the interviewer must bring as many of the intrinsic rewards into play as possible.

SUMMARY

From the interviewer's point of view, there are two basic tasks to be accomplished. The main one is to *maximize* the flow of relevant and valid information. As a means to this end, he must maintain *optimal* interpersonal relations between himself and the respondent. Unlike a social conversation, the task of maintaining optimal interpersonal relations is subordinated as a means to the end of maximizing the flow of useful information.

It is helpful to view the interaction in the interview-respondent dyad in the broader theoretical framework of *social exchange* to which we have referred from time to time.[14] This framework helps us focus upon the essential fact that the interviewer must take stock of the social-psychological rewards he can offer in exchange for the information he seeks from the respondent. From the point of view of the respondent, we can see that the exchange in the interview involves both *costs* and *rewards.*

The *cost* to the respondent is represented by his effort to overcome the inhibitors classified as (1) competing time demands, (2) ego threat, (3) etiquette, (4) trauma, (5) forgetting, (6) chronological confusion, (7) inferential confusion, and (8) unconscious experience. The *rewards* to be offered by the interviewer to offset the costs consist of the facilitators classified as (1) fulfilling expectations, (2) giving recognition, (3) providing altruistic appeal, (4) supplying sympathetic understanding, (5) providing new experience, (6) facilitating catharsis, (7) fulfilling the need for meaning, and (8) supplying extrinsic rewards when the preceding seven intrinsic rewards are not sufficient.

Figure 6–1 summarizes the interviewer's tasks in terms of the social psychological forces over which he has some control in the interview situation. His task consists of *reducing the costs* to the respondent by minimizing the eight inhibitors and of *enhancing the rewards* by maximizing the eight facilitators of communication.

---

[14] Peter M. Blau, *Exchange and Power in Social Life* (New York: John Wiley & Sons, Inc., 1964). Contains one of the best formulations of social exchange theory.

FIGURE 6–1
Facilitators and Inhibitors of Communication

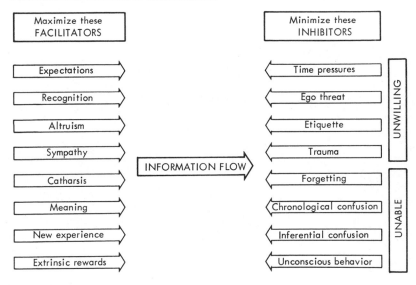

The remainder of this book provides a variety of strategies, techniques, and tactics to be used by the interviewer in performing the two basic functions in the dyadic social exchange we call the interview.

DISCUSSION QUESTIONS

1. What are the eight potential facilitators of communication in the interview?
2. What is the difference between asking for the respondent's cooperation and expecting it?
3. Would a woman be more able to give her husband recognition or sympathetic understanding? Why?
4. What is the difference between altruism and recognition as facilitators of communication in the interview?
5. Which two of the following three are most closely related and how: catharsis, recognition, or sympathetic understanding?
6. To predict whether a certain facilitator might come into play in a particular interview, what do we have to know about that interview? Give an example of an interview situation in which you would expect a certain facilitator to be present.

Laboratory problem 4

Detecting potential facilitators

Below are examples from a variety of interview situations. Select the facilitators most likely to be present in each. Note that after some of the examples there are letters in parentheses corresponding to one or more of the facilitators to be omitted from your selection. This rules out some of the most obvious possibilities in those cases with multiple facilitators. There is no absolutely correct answer since it depends on the assumptions you happen to make regarding any unspecified but relevant aspects of the interview. Write the answers on a sheet of paper after the problem numbers 1 through 10, using the following answer key.

a. fulfilling expectations
b. necessary recognition
c. altruistic appeal
d. sympathetic understanding

e. new experience
f. catharsis
g. need for meaning
h. extrinsic rewards

1. A physician asks a patient who is having his semiannual physical exam, "How frequently do you usually have bowel movements lately?"

2. A newspaper reporter asks a miner to explain how he rescued five of his fellow miners after an explosion a week earlier. (Not *a* or *e*)

3. A sociologist, studying the effects of the arrival of the first child upon the adjustment between the husband and wife, is interviewing a mother with a two-month-old girl and begins the interview in the respondent's home by saying, "I know from my wife's experience that the first few weeks after you return from the hospital can be very trying, so I have waited until Janet was two months old to do this third interview we had arranged. How do you feel now?" (Not *a* or *f*)

4. A juvenile-court social worker, in obtaining a case history of a twelve-year-old delinquent child, asks in a matter-of-fact one, "When did you first skip classes at school?" (Not *b*, *e*, or *f*)

5. Mr. Farnsworth, interviewing for the National Opinion Research Center, is studying a sample of students in a secluded girls college to obtain their views on U.S. foreign policy. (Not *a* or *c*)

6. A minister is talking to a mother about her child who has recently been sent to a juvenile detention home. "You mentioned a while ago that it is hard to know whether you have done the right thing with your children and that you had made some mistakes in raising yours. Would you like to tell me a little more about that?" (Not *a* or *c*)

7. A public opinion interviewer says to a farmer, "I understand that you have lived and farmed here in Boyd County for 27 years. With that much experience, what is your opinion of the present federal farm policy?" (Not *a* or *e*)

8. Two partners in a small business have been independently studying a new income tax law, reducing the amount of state tax on small business incomes, which just arrived in the mail. One partner asks the other, "Is there anything you don't understand about the new tax law?" (Not *a, f,* or *h*)

9. A market research interviewer promises a ticket for a free chance on a color television set to all those who give an interview on their movie attendance.

10. An interviewer, studying the social-psychological problems in disaster-struck communities, approaches a respondent in a random sample of the inhabitants of a town three miles from one which has been devastated by a tornado just two days before. He says, "I'm Mr. Gower. I am working on a study for the government of the problems arising in the rescue and relief activities in major disasters. We need to interview not only those people who were directly involved but also some the the lucky ones in nearby areas which the tornado missed." (Not *a, e,* or *g*)

7

Ethics of
interviewing

In our discussion of ethics in interviewing we will attempt to touch on some of the most vital ethical issues of data collection; we will emphasize the interviewer's rights, obligations, and ethical choices.

We are acutely aware of the fact that, when we take sides on a particular case, we are expressing our own ethical choices. Rather than pretending that these choices are obvious deductions from universally accepted principles, we see them as our efforts to find a resolution of the conflict between competing values.

WHAT IS ETHICS?

For the sake of brevity let us define ethics as the application of social values to concrete behavior. It is the practical application that distinguishes ethical problems from the problems of building a system of values or a set of ideals. In the abstract world of thought we can imagine a set of harmonious and mutually reinforcing values which never compete with one another. However, in the empirical world of deeds and actions, the most attractive set of ideals can be thrown into conflict.

Ethical choices are problematical at two levels. First, we must decide what value to assign to a particular action on the basis of its assumed or known result. This is necessary because most acts are not good or bad in themselves but are judged so according to their known or assumed probable effects. Only those who have no moral scruples, or who have never engaged in any intentional action to change society, can easily assume that there is no problem in doing the right thing as an actor in society. Second, once the results of each alternative act are evaluated in terms of different standards of competency, then the actor must choose among the possible actions by deciding how to weigh each of the competing standards.

To the uninitiated there can be no conflict among values if each one alone is considered good. It seems logical to say only good and evil conflict, not one good with another, but this is not true! For example, here are three statements which all sound "good" to many people but frequently are in direct conflict with each other:

a.   "Social science should help bring equality of human rights!"
b.   "Social scientists should never use deceit in any form!"
c.   "Social scientists should never be backed by physical force, to obtain what they need to carry out a scientific project!"

Merely to declare these three values is not an ethical act. But we are forced into ethical decision-making as social scientists if we start to act toward objective a. Under certain conditions the attempt to achieve the first value will conflict with the maintenance of the second two values.

To give a concrete instance, Pierre van den Berghe,[1] a Belgian, wanted to pursue objective a by doing an empirical study of *apartheid* in the Republic of South Africa. It was clear that he would not be admitted to the country for this purpose. Yet it was important to gain a detailed understanding of *apartheid*, which is perhaps the most extreme application of racial segregation and discrimination in the world today. In order to obtain a visa admitting him to the country he stated that he wanted to study the economic growth in that booming economy. Thus, to attain value a he violated value b, which was to "never use deceit." Some might argue that he then should have stayed out or worked for the liberation of the blacks through insurrection and revolution. If he did this of course he would be violating value c, which is that social scientists should never be backed by physical force.

To give another illustration of values in conflict, assume that you agree with the following three value statements:

a.   "Social scientists should use their skills to improve the system of justice!"
b.   "No one should intrude on the privacy of jury deliberations!"
c.   "Social scientists should not use deception in their pursuit of knowledge."

The first value is not the pure scientific value of the "right to know" or that "knowledge of any subject is always better than ignorance" but

---

[1] Pierre L. van den Berghe, "Research in South Africa: The Story of My Experiences with Tyranny," chap. 8 in *Ethics, Politics and Social Research*, ed. Gideon Sjoberg (Cambridge, Mass.: Schenkman Publishing Co., 1971).

is an amalgam of the pure scientific value and the general societal value of improving justice. The University of Chicago fielded a research team funded by the Ford Foundation in 1953 to study the jury system, to understand better its strengths and weaknesses in bringing about justice. As the study evolved, consultants in the legal profession suggested that the use of simulated trials, mock juries, and interviews with real judges and jurors after a trial would leave certain crucial aspects of the process in obscurity. It was suggested that the actual deliberations of real juries in noncriminal trials be tape-recorded so that their understanding of the facts of the trial, the judges' instructions on points of law, and the jurors' patterns of influence upon one another could be analyzed.

This was done with elaborate safeguards[2] to protect the jurors and the judicial system. The judges whose permission was needed initially suggested that the jurors would have to be informed in advance that their deliberations were being recorded. However, the judges were persuaded that this attempt to avoid the deception of the jurors, value c, would make them conscious of the recording and result in the interference with the free deliberations of the jurors, thus violating value b. The only way to resolve the conflict between b and c would be to give up the recording of the jury deliberations, thus relinquishing the original purpose: basing reform of the jury system upon solid knowledge of what actually happens in jury deliberations.

The fact that this attempt exploded into public controversy clearly illustrates the first principle that acts are usually judged as good or bad on the basis of the *assumed* probable outcomes under certain conditions. In this case the outcomes, as pointed out by Vaughn,[3] were very different from those anticipated. First, the attempt to keep recordings secret failed. Second, the lawyers and judges cooperating with the social scientists did not represent the same point of view on the value of a scientific investigation as that held by the members of the Internal

---

[2] For example, the recording device was locked so that the tape could not be removed except by the judge, who had the only key. No recordings would be made of criminal cases. After the trial the recording would be sealed and remain in the custody of the trial judge until final judgment had been entered and all appeals had been terminated. Then the research committee would produce a single transcription and destroy the original. The committee would then edit out all identifying information, such as the name of the court, the geographical locations, the dates, the names of all participants. This edited manuscript, along with the verbatim transcription, would be submitted to the court for any further editing and approval. The entire project of the recordings was to not receive any publicity until after the project was completed. All additional expenses incurred by the court in aiding in the process would be paid by the research project funds.

[3] Ted R. Vaughan, "Governmental Intervention in Social Research: Political and Ethical Dimensions in the Wichita Jury Recordings," chap. 3 in *Ethics, Politics and Social Research,* ed. Gideon Gjoberg (Cambridge, Mass.: Schenkman Publishing Co., 1971) pp. 50–75.

Security Subcommittee of the Senate Committee on the Judiciary, who carried on widely publicized hearings in which those on the research team were called as witnesses, ostensibly to "determine how and why the recordings were made." Actually, the Subcommittee chairman, in asking the questions, showed that he was not really interested in the *how*, the *why*, or the *ethical* issues involved. Instead, this Subcommittee, which in those years had been accustomed to looking for communists' subversive activities, saw this as an opportunity to discredit the University of Chicago and the Ford Foundation.

The inconsistency between the stated objectives and the hidden agenda of the Subcommittee was indicated in the fact that when witnesses tried to explain *how* they had done the recording, in terms of the safeguards taken, or *why* they had done it, in terms of the need to know and the need for secrecy to avoid affecting the deliberation process, they were cut short by the Chairman of the Subcommittee. Never was there any free discussion of the ethical problems of resolving the conflict between the different values involved. Another indicator of hypocrisy on the part of the government was that the same people who strongly supported legislation to prevent recording jury deliberations for any reason were supporting a bill to permit wiretapping under certain conditions for nonscientific reasons. Attorney-General Herbert Brownell scored the research project particularly, and the University of Chicago generally, for "spying on panels' deliberations in sociological study," yet his office sponsored the wiretapping bill.

One of the most lamented outcomes of this conflict from the point of view of the social scientists was that a law was passed in 1956 to prevent recording jury deliberations for any purpose and under any condition. This became another barrier to the free discussion of the ethical merits of any particular case and the possible values to be derived by social justice from such a study. The law, in effect, says that either we must never modify the jury system in the United States or we must do so without any adequate knowledge of how juries currently function.

These two studies, *apartheid* in the Republic of South Africa and the Wichita Jury Study, are mentioned merely to establish the fact that making ethical decisions in social science is not a facile exercise in the self-righteous recitation of ideals. Such decision-making is a series of knotty problems which force us not only to make choices among different values but also to make predictions regarding the probable results of any decisions we make. It becomes clear that values and ideals often rest on certain assumptions and knowledge regarding cause and effect in the real world. Perhaps as we can more accurately predict or control the results of our actions we will be able to become more ethically responsible.

INTERVIEWER ETHICS AS CONFLICTING LOYALTIES

The ethical problems of social science research could be viewed from the perspective of the larger society, the client organization for whom the study is done, the larger scientific community, the research organization doing the work for the client organization, the interviewer, or the respondent. For the purposes of a book on interviewing we will view the ethical problems from the point of view of the individual interviewer, for whom ethical problems often present themselves as conflicting demands from these different segments of society, or as a set of sometimes conflicting obligations to these different segments. Fortunately, in the majority of instances all of these possible conflicts of loyalty or obligations do not actually develop; many can be avoided by an appropriate delineation of the problem and by seeking an optimum field strategy.

In examining ethical conflicts from the point of view of the interviewer, we assume that he is a responsible ethical agent, that he cannot escape the ethical implications of his acts by merely saying he is "following orders." Interviewers are never forced to carry out their tasks; they can make decisions ranging from whether they will work on a particular project to how they shall carry out their specific responsibilities.

RESPONSIBILITIES TO THE LARGER SOCIETY

Analyses of the ethics of interviewing are relatively rare. In the few examples that do exist, there is a tendency to regard the ethical behavior of the interviewer only in relationship to the sponsoring organization, to scientific objectivity, and to the respondent, thus leaving out the larger society. The implication seems to be that there could be no conflict between the aims of the sponsor of the study and the values of the larger community. Actually there is often a direct conflict of interest, particularly in those cases where the sponsor of the study is interested in influencing or manipulating people as consumers, as workers, as taxpayers, or clients.

Suppression of findings

To give examples of the sponsor of surveys using information which helps exploit the public while withholding information which might be helpful to the public, I need only think back to my experiences with commercial motivation-research interviewing projects I was acquainted with while I was a graduate student. For example, in a survey for a whiskey company it was found that a majority of the men over 50 years of age had been advised by their doctors to quit drinking alcohol, but this information was suppressed and not reported in the findings. Another survey involved interviewing men who had at different times in their life used a straight razor, a safety razor, and an electric razor. At that time it was clear that those who had tried all three preferred the safety razor because it was quicker and easier on the face, yet they bought electric razors as gifts for others because "you can't buy a man a $1.59 safety razor for a gift and not look like a cheapskate." The electric razor company was not anxious to be seen as the most frequently unused man's product.

Not only commercial concerns but also public and private social agencies may try to hide the results of studies which they have commissioned. For example, when a team of three researchers representing a joint effort of a college, a private welfare council, and a city plan commission did a detailed study of the social problem rates in a metropolitan area, several attempts were made to suppress the findings which were relevant to all of the organizations and citizens in the area. The data indicated that Boy Scout troops were not located in lower-class areas and that there was a city-wide dropout rate from Boy Scouts which started at 12 years of age and rapidly accelerated until most had dropped out by the age of 14, the age at which the delinquency rate began to climb. This irritated the local Scout officials who were accustomed to making appeals during the United Fund Drive that implied that the Scouts were a strong character building force to prevent delinquency. In desperation they even tried to claim that the information they had given was false or inaccurate. The Council of Churches (Protestant) in the same city insisted that the County Juvenile Court routinely record the religious affiliation or non-affiliation of each delinquent so that they could show the positive effect of the church in the community, but when the resulting figures indicated that those who went to Protestant churches were *most* likely to be delinquent, Catholic next, then non-affiliated, while the lowest rate was among Jewish youth, the Church Council tried to suppress publication of the results.

The City Plan Commission and the Community Welfare Council, with some urging from the prominent citizens who were angling to win a City Beautiful Award, tried to suppress the publication of the whole package of data relating social organizations to the rates of social problems such as schizophrenia, school dropouts, adult crime, illegitimacy, juvenile delinquency, divorce, and separation. The report was organized so that all of the information on each of 95 census tracts appeared in a two-page format. Instead of publishing and widely using the whole report, the Plan Commission and the Welfare Council each wanted half of the information on each tract in its office and the other half in the other office with only one copy in existence. This, of course, would give these two organizations a monopoly on the information which should have been in the hands of every school, church, and social agency in the city. As the third partner on the team, the college insisted on full dissemination of the report in printed form, and a local publishing house did the printing free of charge.

In each of these cases it was one of the front-line field workers, viewed as "hired hands" by the sponsoring agencies, who had to press for full dissemination of the findings to the public at large. In the cases of the commercial firms the demand was ignored, but in the case of the public and private social agencies the attempt to prevent repression was successful. Even though much of the applied research by business, industry, and government is considered "in-house" evaluation and not for publication, there are still ways that the lasting results can be disseminated. One way is to lump together statistical data on several institutions or organizations of the same type so that not only are individuals not identified but also the organizations and the geographical locations are obscured. In some cases the researcher may have to agree to wait one to ten years before the results can be published. Whether or not such a prior agreement is ethical depends upon the nature of the study, which of the competing organizations or special interest groups might be harmed or benefited by the findings, and the significance for basic social science.

In some instances an individual researcher has initially accepted certain restrictions on dissemination of information, but upon discovering the nature of the information decides that his loyalty is to the larger society rather than to the special interest group. For example, Daniel Ellsberg, an economist on the staff of the Rand Corporation, went to Vietnam convinced that the defeat of the communist-led forces was essential and that social science could lend a strong helping hand.[4] At that time he saw no conflict of interest between the Pentagon and the American people. However, upon becoming acquainted with the contents of a massive 47-volume Pentagon-sponsored history of American involvement in Vietnam, classified as top-secret, he felt his duty was to let the American people know; and in June 1971, he turned documents over to the *New York Times.* Whether or not one agrees that this was an ethical decision, it is clear that it was a painful decision of conscience from which no personal gain was expected. It is clear that this exposé of the "Pentagon Papers" gave impetus to the anti–Vietnam War movement in the United States.

The moral conflict between the interests of any special interest group or organization and the larger society manifests itself in the use of secrecy. Any time the researcher is working for an interest group or

---

[4] Myron Glazer, *The Research Adventure: Promise and Problems of Field Work* (New York: Random House, 1972), pp. 173–78.

must get the permission of an interest group which acts as the gate-keeper controlling access to respondents, there is a chance that he will soon find himself in an ethical conflict. For example Gaylin,[5] a psycho-analyst, hoped to understand the young men who had refused induction into the U.S. Army in protest against the Vietnam War. To do this he needed regular access to the inmates of a federal prison. His approach was to use a nondirective (nonscheduled) interview with the draft resis-ters who were desperate for someone, particularly an intellectual, to talk to. He was able to collect insightful information on their reasons for refusing induction, their relations with their parents, with fellow resisters in prison, with other prisoners, their fears of homosexual at-tack, their sense of isolation, and the lack of any rehabilitating influ-ences in the prison.

Gaylin's preliminary manuscript of his book also included a general critique of prison life and the unpredictable nature of the parole sys-tem. The reaction of the prison officials was to exclude him from further contact with the men before his study was finished. His argument that this was government censorship was to no avail. Although he was never again given access to the prisoners, the government officials made no effort to suppress the book which was published in 1970.

To this point the examples of conflict between the interviewer's loyalty to a particular interest and to the larger society have been those in which a relatively powerful and conservative organization was pitted against the interests of a relatively weak segment of society. This is not always the case. Sometimes the social scientist is opposed and ham-pered by those who may be of a radical ideology and claiming to speak for the suppressed minority. This claim is sometimes true, in that they actually know how and are in fact helping a minority. In some cases they would like to do so but either do not have the necessary knowledge and skills or they are too constrained by a straitjacket of simplistic ideology to be of any help to anyone. In other cases they may be using idealistic rhetoric to hide the fact that they are engaged in a form of political manipulation of the downtrodden who have value as potential recruits to swell the ranks of the cause. In some of these circumstances some radicals interfere with studies which could be useful to the op-pressed and to anyone seriously interested in helping them.

For example, Lansberger, a sociologist with long experience in study-ing peasant movements in Latin America, decided to study the cooper-ative movement among black farmers in Southern United States. He wanted to bring his experience to bear on the struggle of southern blacks. When the Ford Foundation financially supported the develop-

---

[5] Williard Gaylin, *In the Service of Their Country: War Resisters in Prison* (New York: Viking Press, 1970).

ment of farm cooperatives among blacks in the South, Lansberger acted as a consultant to evaluate the effectiveness of the program. As a Ford Foundation consultant, he was cordially welcomed by the indigenous farm leaders who made up the Board of Directors of the Federation of Southern Cooperatives as well as by members of the individual black farmers' co-ops and their officers; but the organizers from outside the community were hostile.[6] According to Glazer, "Lansberger never received the cooperation of his youthful, often urban-born, more highly educated, and certainly more radical, critics."[7] These men wanted Ford Foundation support, but they did not want an independent evaluation of their efforts to help the rural blacks. According to Lansberger, the facts were perceived as a threat by middle-class radical leaders who were proposing to help the poor.

> To query the feasibility of a project for the poor or the black on any basis except that it is really "an establishment plot to avoid tackling the underlying problem," is to lay oneself open to charges of racism, insensitivity, and the like. But to query a project on such specific bases as the possible lack within the poor or black communities of technical or managerial skills; or to conclude that membership apathy is a fact of life among poor blacks (as it is among poor and rich whites) is to make certain that such accusations will be made. . . . [but] . . . I think well enough of my fellow man—both the humble in the co-ops, and the powerful in the foundations and in the government—to believe that they frequently, and increasingly, welcome the truth.[8]

Lansberger's position in this situation is a most difficult one for the educated person so often reluctant to be labeled a reactionary or a racist. Yet he held to the hard-nosed position that any successful attempt must be based upon objective, relevant information on the local situation rather than upon reactionary ritual or radical rhetoric.

Evaluative investigations have been opposed by both conservatives and radicals. The conservatives fear that such studies will show the establishment's foibles and methods of maintaining power. The radicals fear that the information will be used by the establishment to repress them, that it will show a gap between their ideology and their practice, or that their attempts at social change are ineffective. Both the conservative and the radical objector will try to clothe his objections in terms of freedom and ethics, when the real issue is often power.

All these examples are intended to illustrate the fact that there is a tendency to prevent studies of human behavior and to suppress the

---

[6] Henry A. Lansberger, "Southern Rural Cooperatives: A Provocative Preliminary Assessment of Their Past and Their Prospects," Unpublished paper.

[7] Glazer, *Research Adventure*, pp. 157–58.

[8] Ibid., p. 158.

findings of such studies if they are not to the liking of a particular individual or group. This tendency is found in all groups to some extent, whether they are weak or powerful, uneducated or educated. None makes an absolute value of truth for truth's sake. Not only do those agencies who pay for studies sometimes try to control them, but the research organization or individual hired by the sponsoring organization may also try to suppress the truth to some extent for fear that any findings unpopular with either the sponsor or the public in general may weaken future ability to attract research funds. This fear throws into gear all of the mechanisms of self-preservation in any organization.

Intentional bias in data collection

The conflict between the researcher's loyalties to the humanistic values of the larger society, the survival values of a particular organization, and the scientific values of pure truth may pose some agonizing dilemmas, resulting in disagreement on what is ethical. It is often easier to obtain consensus on the ethics in a situation where the researcher intentionally uses his skills to distort the truth to deceive the larger community. Although it may be difficult to establish that the deception was intentional, it makes little difference if the distortion was in fact the result of incompetence on the part of a person claiming to be a social scientist.

An infamous example of the biasing of the data-collection process or the misrepresentation of the representativeness of the data is given by Cain.[9] He points out that a study billed as a national sample of the aged and their attitudes regarding health, medical care, medical insurance and related topics was in fact a systematically biased sample. Even though respondents in many states were interviewed to get a geographical spread, the sample was powerfully biased in that it excluded all blacks, all persons receiving old-age assistance, and anyone in hospitals, homes for the aged, nursing homes, or other institutions; a large portion of those remaining were also excluded if they were in the lower economic class. Furthermore, 20 percent of those falling in this "sample" did not respond. It is possible that over 55 percent of the aged were excluded, and all of these were the less affluent.

This study became the center of a national controversy when the American Medical Association used the report to support their opposition to the Medicare Bill then before Congress. Press releases were issued and Congressmen quoted the study as showing that 90 percent

---

[9] Leonard D. Cain, Jr., "The AMA and the Gerontologists: Uses and Abuses of a Profile of the Aging: USA," chap. 4 in *Ethics, Politics and Social Research,* ed. Gideon Sjoberg (Cambridge, Mass.: Schenkman Publishing Co., 1967), pp. 78–114.

of the aged had no unfulfilled medical needs and that the remainder listed lack of money as one of the least important reasons for failure to relieve their needs. Several of the research associates complained about this interpretation and said that they had been uninformed about the overall nature of the national sample when they were doing their geographical portion of the interviewing. The study was discredited at the National Gerontological Congress and was later generally discredited, but the whole controversy indicated the lack of clearly ethical conduct on the part of some individuals within the social science profession as well as a lack of any developed means of enforcing ethical conduct within the profession.

Probably if those who worked on the study had known in advance how the findings were to be used, they would have raised serious objections to participating in the study.

Intentional bias in interpretation

It is not necessary to introduce bias into the data-gathering process to have a detrimental effect on the community at large. In some cases the valid results of a study can be used to the disadvantage of those studied. Even though those doing the study may be motivated by the desire either to improve the performance of the existing program or to design a better one, it is possible for any results showing shortcomings of the program to be used politically as an excuse to simply cut it out rather than build something better. This is a particular danger in program evaluation studies done to measure the effectiveness of any action program in the areas of health, education, and welfare. An example of this problem is provided by Pilisuk[10] from a case in which investigators working with a grant from the Office of Economic Opportunity produced findings which questioned the effectiveness of the Headstart Program, particularly in its ability to improve the preschool child's reading-readiness scores. These findings were successfully used by those arguing for a cutback in funds. Instead of benefiting more children and families with a higher quality program—the real need shown by the investigation—there was a lower quality or smaller program because of the resulting cut in funds. The researcher does not have to be willingly seeking to prostitute his craft in order to be taken advantage of, and therefore he must be constantly alert to the uses and misuses of his findings.

It may seem to some readers that this discussion of obligations to the larger society, which are sometimes in conflict with obligations to the

---

[10] Marc Pilisuk, "People's Park, Power and the Calling of the Social Sciences," in *Toward Social Change: A Handbook for Those Who Would,* ed. Robert Buckhaut et al. (New York: Harper & Row, 1971).

sponsoring organization, is not a legitimate responsibility of all interviewers on a project. These ethical decisions may apparently belong to only those who are charged with the responsibility of choosing the problem, finding a funding organization, designing the field strategy, analyzing and interpreting the data. To some extent this is true, but there is a better chance of achieving a high level of ethical behavior if everyone recognizes that he or she has certain choices of action.

Every interviewer has the opportunity to decide whether to work with a particular project. Everyone should know who the sponsor of the study is and to what purpose the findings are to be used. As some of the illustrations have shown, it is also wise to be alert for how the findings are used and to see that they are not misused. Once the interviewer is assured that the aims of the study are harmonious with the common welfare of the larger society and that the sponsoring organization will use it accordingly, it is easier for him to handle those ethical conflicts arising from his loyalty to the research organization, the research team, and the respondent.

RESPONSIBILITIES TO THE RESEARCH ORGANIZATION

There are some ideals regarding the interviewer's relationship to the research organization that are easily stated but under some conditions may be difficult to follow.

Always follow the sampling instructions

In studies where it is necessary to obtain responses from an accurate representative sample, it is extremely important either to make no substitutions or to have a predetermined system for making random substitutions. The temptation to make an unauthorized substitution of a more available and willing respondent may become strong near the end of a study when it is necessary to clean up the remainder of the random sample, but this can result in considerable bias in the results that cannot be compensated for by simply increasing the total number of interviews.

Do not fictionalize responses

Fictionalizing may occur in the most mild form when the interviewer is instructed to take *verbatim* notes but abbreviates words and phrases and then fills in the missing portions immediately after the interview is over. There is a temptation at this point for the interviewer to slightly pad the response with some concrete imagery to make up for a failure to probe more deeply during the interview. An intermediate form of fictionalizing sometimes occurs when the interviewer discovers after leaving the respondent that certain questions were omitted. Here the temptation to fill in the occasionally missing answer by guess may become strong. It is better to leave a blank so that later random answers may be substituted, a phone call may be made to the respondent, or the space simply left blank in the tabulation.

It makes research directors shudder to think of the most extreme form of fictionalizing in which the interviewer fills out the whole interview schedule or questionnaire for an imaginary respondent. This sometimes occurs when a study has been going for some time, the work load has been heavy, and the obstacles to contacting the respondents are many. The obstacles may be physical things like an above-90 or below-zero temperature, or social-psychological things like fear of being refused. It is more ethical for the interviewer to protest the work load, the working conditions, or the lack of a high morale-producing atmosphere rather than to avoid conflict by fictionalizing an interview now and then. Such fictionalizing subverts the whole purpose of the enterprise.

Descriptions of the conditions under which cheating arises and some telling case studies are given by Roth[11] under what he aptly calls "hired-hand research." He shows how interviewers who were supposed to probe for five reasons why parents had put their child in an institution, could rarely extract that many reasons from the same person. They would often fill in the blank with an imaginary reason, particularly after the director of the study had criticized some for not getting five reasons as others had done.

If pressures exist to encourage the falsification of information, it is more ethical to bring these to the attention of the study director *early* in the project rather than devoting more time to the collection of useless data. If one interviewer finds that others are cheating, it would be better to try to discuss with that person the pressures which cause the behavior and get the interviewers to agree jointly to bring the problems to the attention of the project director. If this is done early it is more likely to be appreciated.

Probe fully where needed

There is a tendency for interviewers to become less thorough in probing for complete, adequate, and valid responses as they become fatigued, bored, or simply lose their initially fresh curiosity. For example, the writer[12] discovered that a team interviewing disaster victims

---

[11] Julius Roth, "Hired Hand Research," *American Sociologist*, Vol. 1 (August 1966), pp. 190–96.

[12] Raymond L. Gorden, "An Interaction Analysis of the Depth Interview" (Ph.D. dissertation, University of Chicago, Department of Sociology, 1954).

over a ten-day period averaged about 2½ depth interviews per day. The interviews were long and there was considerable difficulty in finding the sample of respondents who had moved after their houses had been destroyed by a tornado. Over the ten-day period, the average length of each interviewer's first interview of the day dropped from about 35 to 28 pages of transcription. Analysis of the interview transcriptions revealed that the shortening of the interview was due somewhat to increased efficiency in obtaining relevant information. However, the main cause of the drop in interview length was the flagging curiosity of the interviewer who had heard so many respondents' accounts that he felt he knew what the respondent would say without having to probe to really find out.

The thoroughness of the probing becomes an ethical problem in those settings in which boredom, fatigue, and a lack of interest in the purposes of the study tempt the interviewer to take a short-cut. Any director of any project involving many repeated interviews, particularly when they are done on a full-time basis, must realize this danger of settling for the stereotyped response. In some cases this can be remedied by rotating functions such as locating respondents, monitoring tapes, editing interview schedules, transcribing tapes, public relations chores, and preliminary data analysis.

This principle of relieving boredom and increasing responsibility for completeness of the information was applied by the writer in developing a system for outreach workers in a local poverty program to collect data on each client. Instead of having an interviewer collect the information, another person punch the cards, and a third person do the statistical analysis, we developed a McBee Keysort Card on which the interviewer could record the information on the spot; then the same person would punch his own cards, and later do a statistical analysis of the accumulated cases every three months. In this way the interviewer became acutely aware of missing information, of faulty punching, of his own accumulated accomplishments and the meaning of the data in the aggregate. Training these interviewers, many of whom had not finished high school, to carry out a wider range of functions required considerable effort. This was a continuing operation to be carried out by the same people over several years, so it was well worth the trouble.

Do not bias responses

Interviewers can bias the responses by the tone of voice used in asking the question, by gestures, and by facial expression as well as by deviating from the required wording of the question or structuring of the answers. Sometimes consciously or unconsciously an interviewer will try to bias the responses, particularly if he or she has a strong emotional attachment to the issues involved and the use of the results.

In some cases an interviewer may frankly feel that his emotional bias is so strong and the problems of self-control so great that for the good of the scientific objectivity of the study he should not interview on the subject. Sometimes this is not discovered by the interviewer until after a few interviews have been done. In this case the problem should be discussed with the project director. In a later chapter we deal with this problem of manifesting nonbiasing attitudes.

Report possible invalidities in the interview schedule

Ethical problems may develop if the interviewer discovers that he, himself, has no difficulty in being unbiasing in his behavior but that the wording of a single question, a particular sequence of questions, or the structured answer choices of a particular question may be highly biasing in its effect. Under these circumstances it is the interviewer's ethical duty to report this opinion to the project director and give as clear evidence as possible for the opinion. In this case the interviewer should be prepared to discover that the bias is intentional because the results are intended to be used as propaganda or advertising to deceive "enemies, clients, constituents, or customers" to the benefit of the sponsoring organization. Here the interviewer must decide whether his loyalty is to the larger society or to the sponsoring organization. Also involved is the interviewer's loyalty to the respondent, whose opinion should not be distorted for someone's gain, and loyalty to one's own conscience. This ethical dilemma most frequently arises in studies involving conflicts over public issues or in commercial motivation research where product competition is strong.

It requires moral courage for an interviewer to approach the project director with the proposition that the interview schedule is biased. If the bias is intentional and the interviewer persistent, he may be fired. On the other hand the project director may be grateful for the help, particularly if the problem is dealt with early in the field work. Again, the joint opinions and experiences of all the interviewers would be more useful than just one. From the project director's point of view, assuming that he does not want to bias the responses, it is helpful to have the same interviewers do one or two field tests and revisions to make the questions more relevant or valid.

The interviewer has an ethical obligation not only to report possible bias in the wording of questions but also any possibility that certain very crucial questions are omitted. The interviewer might discover that some of the questions are in a form which misses the most relevant dimensions of the issue or that different kinds of respondents need different kinds or wordings of questions. These are all things which should be worked out in the development and field-testing of the interview schedule, but there is always the possibility that some serious errors remain.

Even if such problems are discovered and reported very late in the data-collection process, the report is still useful and will be welcomed by the truly scientific project director since it will be helpful in making interpretations of the responses. Obviously, for practical purposes, at least in a survey where the data are to be statistically summarized, it is impractical to keep changing the form of questions or adding and subtracting questions throughout the duration of the study, but it is never too late to weigh the relevance, validity, and reliability of the information.

The probability of an interviewer's reporting these problems grows with any increase in his understanding of the purpose and importance of the study, with any increase in his faith in the project director's integrity, and with any increase in his general allegiance to scientific standards.

The number and kind of ethical problems which arise seem to depend on the extent to which the purposes of the research organization and the problem under study are consonant with the values of the larger society and the values of the scientific community. In those happy situations where there is consonance, the interviewer's obligations to society in general, to the research organization, and to his own conscience are one and the same. However, this happily harmonious state is rare in situations where the purpose of the research is to evaluate existing organizations or to develop better patterns of human behavior. We can expect that, with the growing interest in applying social science to social change, ethical issues will be generated at an increasing rate.

RESPONSIBILITIES TO THE RESPONDENT

Again, in discussing ethical responsibilities to the respondent, we will present each value that should be ideally pursued in this relationship. Yet we must point out that often these values conflict with others, and therefore the interviewer has to make an ethical choice, whether or not this is a conscious decision.

Gaining access to the respondent

There are several possible ethical problems involved in gaining access to the respondents needed for a particular study. One problem might be called "getting past the gatekeepers." This is an obvious problem in the case where the potential respondents are in some closed institution as was true in the case cited earlier in which Dr. Gaylin needed to interview war resisters in prison. In that case the conflict arose between the scientific value of completing the study and the institutional value of the prison's protecting itself from criticism. Another type of gatekeeper problem arises when it might be physically possible to sidestep the gatekeeper but the gatekeepers could facilitate access to the respondent. He could orient the interviewer and tell him where certain people, things, or information could be found. In this case the gatekeeper is not in a position of absolute power but may attempt to drive a bargain for favors in exchange for his information. Under these conditions the researcher may be lured to promise more than he can produce as in the case of Berreman's[13] study of an Hindu village.

Berreman was tempted to exaggerate the possible values of his study of the village in "putting the village on the map." This appeal would fit into the villagers' feeling of having underdog status because they were on a mountain rather than on the plain. Berreman's experience also points out a danger in entering a community through the usual channels of the high status gatekeepers. This may make it difficult for the interviewer to assure respondents that no harm may come to them, or it may prevent the respondents from providing complete relevant and reliable information. For example, the gatekeepers of the Himalaya village were high-caste merchants who were viewed by the villagers as dishonest, cheating exploiters of the common people. This was a negative force in the early portion of the study.

Another example of the danger in going through instead of around a gatekeeper is given by Babbie who tells of a study of church women, in which the ministers of the churches were the gatekeepers:

> The ministers in a sample of churches were asked to distribute questionnaires to a specified sample of members, collect them, and return them to the research office. One of these ministers read through the questionnaires from his sample before returning them, and then proceeded to deliver a hell-fire and brimstone sermon to his congregation, saying that many of them were atheists and going to hell. Even though he could not know or identify the respondents who gave particular responses, it seems certain that many were personally harmed by the action.[14]

It becomes a field strategy problem to decide whether to use one gatekeeper or another or none at all. For example, in a study of employees of a large corporation, it would be convenient to interview them at work. A list of the employees and an opportunity to interview them at work might be sought by approaching either the union or the

---

[13] Gerald D. Berreman, *Hindus of the Himalayas*, (Berkeley, Calif.: University of California Press, 1963).

[14] Earl R. Babbie, *Survey Research Methods* (Belmont, Calif.: Wadsworth Publishing Co., 1973), p. 350.

management. Either could play a maximum role by furnishing a list of names and a time and place at the plant to interview and by expressing approval of the study. Either could play a minimum role by providing a list of employees' names and addresses; the researcher could then interview each employee at home. The former procedure would require less time and be more convenient; the latter procedure would reduce the interviewer's obligations to management or the union.

It becomes apparent that the ethical problem and the methodological one become intertwined. In some cases it is particularly difficult if the gatekeeper has absolute power to deny access to the respondent. In other cases he has relative power as a negative nuisance or a positive convenience for the researcher. In either case the interviewer must be careful not to sell his scientific soul, his obligations to the larger society, or the rights of the respondents in exchange for the gatekeeper's cooperation.

Voluntary participation

Voluntary participation is desirable but often impossible because of its conflict with other values. One of the most obvious conflicts is with the democratic ideal that everyone's opinion is important. Since all adult citizens can vote, any attempt to poll all voters cannot strictly adhere to the principle of voluntary participation. If we define a volunteer as anyone who would come to the interviewer to be interviewed, representative studies could not be done. If we mean that anyone who is "busy" or "doesn't know anything about that" on the first contact should not be interviewed, then accurately representative polls would be impossible.

Fortunately, our ethical dilemma dissolves to some extent when we make a distinction between the pure volunteer, the "persuaded," and the "coerced." Most "volunteers" are actually "persuaded" cooperators or at least nonresisters to gentle coercion. There are many legitimate claims which can be made to persuade the respondent to be interviewed. These have been described earlier as *facilitators* of communication. From an ethical point of view, to appeal to the respondent's altruism, and even to his need for recognition, is an appeal to the values and ideals of the larger society.

Often the respondent can be activated by evidence of selflessness on the part of the interviewer. For example, Babbie points out that certain interviewers are more persuasive than others in obtaining cooperation of respondents as he says, "experience has shown an eight-month-pregnant interviewer is more successful than the average in this regard."[15]

---

[15] Ibid., p. 348.

The writer has also found that the interviewers who understand most clearly the purposes of the interview and have the most respect for the respondents are most successful in obtaining cooperation.

The fact that social pressure and altruism can persuade volunteers to undergo extreme privation has been demonstrated by the experiments at the University of Minnesota during World War II, in which volunteer conscientious objectors were subjected to slow starvation of 500 calories per day for months at a time, reducing them to walking skeletons.[16] Undergoing this privation can probably be accounted for to a great extent by the conscientious objectors' feeling that they did owe something to their country and would like to make a sacrifice equal to that of many of the men in the armed forces without having to kill a fellow human being. Was he, then, a volunteer or was he coerced by the draft law and the fact that his country was at war? Regardless of the answer to this question, it is clear that he chose this more sacrificial route when others were legally available to him.

Once we discover the extent to which respondents can be persuaded to cooperate, we have solved a practical problem but are in danger of running aground on the ethical question of *how* we persuade them. There is a temptation to promise anything feasible to obtain cooperation: promising respondents a copy of the results of the study, promising to help them in some way, or promising to pass their name along to some other agency which can help them. Of course, these strategies and many more are ethical as long as you are prepared to actually follow through on the promise and as long as it does not injure anyone else.

The respondent's cooperation can be gained not only by giving some positive incentives but also by reducing the costs to the respondent. This cost-reduction approach includes choosing a time when there will be the fewest competing demands on his time, avoiding the use of unnecessary time in the interviewing, or offering to come a second time to finish. The problem of offering the respondent incentives is particularly important in gaining the initial contact. Once the interview begins we can usually rely on the *facilitators* to keep the motivation.

Do not harm the respondent

Rarely does anyone argue with the idea of avoiding harm to the respondent, yet the naïve interviewer can injure him in many ways. In some situations it may be harmful to the respondent to even be seen with the interviewer. This was the case when the writer was interviewing college professors about violations of academic freedom at colleges where the president had refused to allow the interviewers from Louis Harris Associates on the campus. To avoid possible retribution from the

---

[16] Ancel Keys, *Human Starvation* (Minneapolis: University of Minnesota Press, 1950).

presidents of such colleges, I interviewed the professors at their homes. This problem arises in many conflict situations in which "anyone who is not a known friend must be treated like an enemy." Even though someone might feel he is a captive of an in-group and want to contact a neutral outsider, he may be viewed as a traitor.

Harm can be done to the respondent by leaking information which could be used against him either by legitimate authorities such as the police, company management, or the dean of students—these might have power either to withhold rewards or to mete out punishment to the person on the basis of the information given. The protection of the respondent from any harm resulting from the interview becomes an ethical problem when the respondent has engaged in deviant behavior punishable according to the values of the larger society. This problem can arise when an interviewer discovers that a manager has falsified company records, that a worker has made personal long-distance phone calls on the employer's charge account, that a person has committed a felony for which he was never apprehended, or that he shoplifts regularly to pay for his heroine habit.

To give a concrete case, a field study was done in a Mexican-American neighborhood to evaluate the effectiveness of gangworkers and to formulate certain generalizations about the development of delinquency within the context of a lower-class urban ethnic group:

> In another instance a social worker was contacted late at night by one of his boys, who was a drug addict. The boy was scheduled to go on a voluntary commitment to the federal narcotics hospital, but his bus did not leave until the next morning. His supply of drugs had been raided and he had no money. If he was to get through the remaining 12 hours, he needed a "fix." In San Antonio at present, there is no way for an addict legally to get a fix. On the other hand, if he didn't get it the withdrawal symptoms would become "unendurable," at which point he might try to steal some money in order to get more drugs. This would place the boy in jeopardy, and if he were caught, it would lead to imprisonment, a criminal record, and possibly involuntary commitment to a hospital.
>
> The social worker was in an extremely delicate ethical position. . . . The worker's solution was to place the boy in a situation where he could get a fix, although the worker was not present when the boy bought and used the drug. The worker stayed with the boy part of the night and met him in the morning to get him on the bus and on the way to voluntary withdrawal from drugs. The boy stayed in the hospital until his release and has been off drugs ever since. Had these events led to some unfortunate consequences for the worker or for the boy, we might have had to view the ethical issues in a somewhat different light."[17]

---

[17] Richard A. Brymer and Buford Farris, "Ethical and Political Dilemmas in the Investigation of Deviance: A Study of Juvenile Delinquency," chap. 13 in *Ethics, Politics and Social Research*, ed. Gideon Sjoberg (Cambridge, Mass.: Schenkman Publishing Co., 1971), pp. 311–12.

Clearly this field worker was protecting his respondent from any harm resulting from the knowledge he had gained; yet this made the social worker an accessory to the crime of buying and using illegal drugs. At the same time the social worker was fulfilling the values of both the respondent and the larger society by making available a voluntary treatment to cure his addiction. As the author implies, the whole ethical decision-making process depended upon the social worker's correct prediction of the outcome which he helped to bring about. Thus, values in their application cannot be separated from knowledge about cause and effect, prediction and control. What would be ethical under one set of circumstances becomes unethical under another.

Precisely where to draw the line in protecting a respondent would depend upon the value to be served in the larger society, the potential value of the research project to society, and the effect on the scientific community, on the respondent and on the interviewer. Obviously, we are not going to propose a formula for doing this; but it is realistic to note that people must make ethical decisions involving both human values and assumptions or predictions about the probable effects of their decisions. Even inaction is a decision by default.

Anonymity and confidentiality

The major way of protecting the respondent from harm resulting from information he gives is to keep that information confidential or anonymous. Confidential means that no one except the interviewer knows from whom the information came. Anonymous means that not even the interviewer knows from whom the information came.

We will leave the discussion of methods of preserving anonymity or confidentiality to the next chapter and at this point emphasize the differences in the potential ethical issues in each. First, the social research interviewer (whether a professional sociologist, psychologist, anthropologist, social worker, manager, or a paraprofessional interviewer of any type) has no legal guarantee of privileged communication as does the lawyer, physician, or clergyman. If a court wants to subpoena a tape recording, interview transcription, or interview schedule, or if it calls the interviewer to the witness stand to report what he was told, there is no clear legal recourse. Therefore, if we promise confidentiality to our respondent, there may be certain circumstances in which the promise is hard to keep.

If the information is collected by an anonymous questionnaire and if there are enough cases so that no individual can be pinpointed by some combination of characteristics, then there is no possibility of the information being used against the respondent or interviewer. Often, the kind of information needed and the field methods required make the anonymous questionnaire impractical. In this case, if the interviewer has an ethical obligation to protect the respondent against the effects of the information, he may have to destroy the original form of the data and refuse to depend upon his faulty memory for testimony.

This precise issue arose when Humphreys[18] reported on his study of the behavior of male homosexuals in public toilets. The study was a Ph.D. dissertation financed by the National Institute of Mental Health. The university administration tried to have NIMH withhold a second grant pending an investigation of the methods used to obtain the information.

In order to be an observer, Humphreys had played the role of a lookout in the public toilets to warn the homosexuals of any possible intrusion by police or other unfriendly strangers during their brief intimate encounters. Then in order to see how their homosexuality fit into the rest of their lives, he traced automobile license numbers to locate the men's home addresses; allowed a year to lapse, changed his hair style, manner of dress, and car to avoid recognition and introduced himself as a researcher studying community health patterns. Most homosexuals were heads of families and this gave him an opportunity to see them prepare barbecues, have their evening drinks, and talk with their families. In addition he did an intensive study of a dozen of these men who were willing to talk freely with him about their homosexuality after knowing the purposes of his study. He did not secretly observe or interview anyone.

The study flared into public controversy when Nicholas von Hoffman,[19] writing in The *Washington Post,* accused Humphreys of the same invasion of privacy as police are often charged with. Others charged that no human being should be trusted with such incriminating evidence about another and that more clear ethical codes should be drafted to govern the conduct of social science investigators.

Humphreys himself says that he took each step in the study only after agonizing appraisal of the ethical pros and cons, the practical dangers to himself and his respondents, and the ultimate value to society of such a candid descriptive study. He totally rejects the analogy to the police violations of privacy. He made a large distinction between the violation of his own privacy by the police who arrested him and his intrusion into the private domain of his respondents:

> The real concern of the founders of our liberties was with protecting the citizen against the awful force of military and social control agencies, who

---

[18] Laud Humphreys, *Tearoom Trade* (Chicago: Aldine Publishing Co., 1970). Also, "Tearoom Trade: Impersonal Sex in Public Places," *Transaction,* January 1970, pp. 10–26.

[19] Nicholas von Hoffman, Irving L. Horowitz, and Lee Rainwater, "Sociological Snoopers and Journalistic Moralizers: An Exchange," *Transaction,* May 1970, pp. 4–8.

have the power to arrest, prosecute, imprison, and destroy those whose privacy they violate. As I wrote Nicholas von Hoffman shortly after my arrest: "You see, the real point is that the former (John Mitchell et al.) can and do arrest the latter." (Laud Humphreys et al.)[20]

There is general agreement among psychologists, sociologists, penologists, and administrators of social agencies often dealing with homosexuals that we need more unbiased description of the development of homosexuality itself and how it affects the lives of the homosexual, his family, and the community before we can reform current irrational practices. For example, those who would like to send boys to the army "to make a man out of them" must face the fact that homosexuality is more prevalent in the army, in prisons, and in other sexually segregated institutions than it is in the community at large. Perhaps it is the reluctance to face some of these apparent dilemmas that generates some hostility to the study of homosexuals.

Even though it is true that in this case the private information given to Humphreys was never used to blackmail or to legally prosecute any of his respondents, it must be admitted that in the hands of less careful and courageous researchers there could have been some backlash affecting the respondents. Even those social scientists who feel that Humphreys did the ethical thing recognize that this modus operandi is not possible for everyone:

> My conversations with Humphreys convince me of his extraordinary courage and ability to withstand condemnation and abuse. Yet these very characteristics make him a poor model for others to emulate without the most painful self-scrutiny. . . . While admiring Humphreys, I know that I could not pursue such research myself and would attempt to dissuade others from such a path.[21]

Fortunately, such painful dilemmas rarely arise in the attempts to keep private information anonymous or confidential, but the basic ethical point here is that any researcher who wants to study deviant behavior of any kind should take very seriously his responsibility to prepare for possible attempts to get the original data for use illegally in blackmail or legally in prosecution of either the respondents or the interviewer. Part of this preparation is a careful soul-searching of one's own motives, of the study's probable value to society, and of the dangers to the social science professions, and to individuals involved in the study.

Why do social scientists engage in the study of deviant behavior if the data cannot be used to reform the individual deviants? One answer is that any rational decision-making about the value of eliminating any

---

[20] Glazer, *Research Adventure*, p. 164.

[21] Ibid., p. 116.

form of deviant behavior requires seeing that behavior in a broader context of alternatives, and evaluating the possible effects of various methods available to reduce deviance. Second, evidence shows that most of society's attempts to reform or to cure individual deviants, whether we are thinking of drug addicts, criminals, schizophrenics, or alcoholics, are not successful. The major hope for success in reducing antisocial forms of deviant behavior lies in *prevention,* and any successful prevention program must be based upon a realistic knowledge of the process by which the individual becomes a deviant member of society. A third answer is that by studying deviant behavior we can further basic social science knowledge regarding the nature of generic processes such as socialization, personality development, social control, conformity and nonconformity to norms, and changes in social values and norms. Obviously, Humphreys probably believed more strongly in the value of his research to society in the long run than those who advised him that it was not worth the risks to all concerned. The relatively happy ending to the affair was due mainly to his foresight in destroying the evidence, including the list of respondents, *before* he was asked for it by authorities.

Help the respondent, if possible

Helping the respondent is both a means of attracting or maintaining his cooperation and of ethically reciprocating or showing appreciation for what he has contributed. Often the non-social-scientist interviewer is interviewing a person in order to obtain information which can be used to help him. In some cases the information may also be used to the person's detriment, particularly from the point of view of the respondent. In either case the non-social-scientist is obtaining the information in order to directly influence the respondent one way or another. Often this effect depends upon the nature of the information elicited.

This is the typical situation with the employment interviewer, the social work interviewer, the poverty outreach worker, and the college admissions interviewer. When the interview results in a person obtaining some needed social service, obtaining a job or a promotion, or in getting into the college he chooses, then we have certainly helped the respondent. However, when the result of the interview is not what the respondent wants, there is often little thought of how some secondary help might be given to the person on the basis of the same diagnostic information. Such help could be built into the interview as a fallback position to show the respondent that you are still interested in his welfare as a fellow human being. For example, a person who is found to lack the qualifications needed for a job could be informed of the probable nature of the future job market, what additional knowledge or skills they should develop, where they can obtain the appropriate schooling or on-the-job-training to make themselves more marketable. As a minimum the interviewer could refer the respondent to other agencies which could provide these types of information.

The situation of the social scientist interviewer is quite different with regard to his opportunities to help the respondent. Rarely does the study itself call for attempting to bring about some change in the respondent as a result of the information obtained. For this reason the rewards used, either to elicit the respondent's cooperation or to maintain his goodwill, must be less connected to the nature of the information sought.

In community studies social scientists have often undertaken some practical social service project which will keep them in contact with the respondents or generally make them more welcome in the community. When the writer was field supervisor of a disaster study team, he noted that the interviewers began increasingly to develop guilt feelings for taking up the time of the disaster victims with interviews which could help future disaster victims but not those being interviewed. Since the project was short-term (about one month in the field), the interviewers could not donate time or services, but they decided to make a cash contribution for a disaster relief fund to be administered by the local village council.

Berreman[22] in his longer-term study of the Hindu village developed some ad hoc forms of helping the village by letting villagers listen to his radio and by supplying simple medical remedies. Liebow[23] obtained cooperation by offering Tally a ride to the courthouse where he had been subpoenaed as a witness in the trial of his friend Lonny, accused of murdering his own wife. From this time on, Liebow was looked to for advice on a wide range of things. Lewis,[24] in his study of a Mexican village, Tepoztlan, found that the Mexican government was interested enough in the value of his study to attach to his project the services of two agronomists, two doctors, and two social workers to give direct practical help to the villagers.

All of these aids to the respondent might be classified as extrinsic rewards in our framework of facilitators and inhibitors. However, the rewards given in community studies may go to many people in addition to the respondents and may have little quantitative relationship to the amount of time or effort expended by a particular respondent.

There are several ethical problems which can arise in the attempt

---

[22] Berreman, *Hindus.*

[23] Reported in Glazer, *Research Adventure,* pp. 18–19.

[24] Oscar Lewis, *Life in a Mexican Village: Tepoztlan Restudied* (Urbana, Ill.: University of Illinois Press, 1951), p. xv.

to follow the rule of helping the respondent when possible. First, there is the temptation to promise more than can be produced as a result of the study. This typically occurs when the respondents have strong hopes that the study will help them in a particular way.

Another ethical problem arises when the interviewer, in order to get the respondent's cooperation, promises to give him the results of the study. Unless this has been included in the budget for the study, there is very little chance that it will be done. Also the respondent population may be so transient that with the lapse of time needed to complete the analysis, the problems of getting the results to individual respondents is overwhelming. Preparations must be made in advance to share results with the respondents. This can be done even in cases where the respondents are anonymous. For example, in a study of the racial attitudes of students, parents, and teachers in a public school system, one copy of the study was put in each school library, in the local neighborhood branches of the county library, and also given to all social agencies in the city.

A third problem arises when the field phase of the study is long and the needs of the respondents are great. In studying ethnic ghettos, rural villages, or any low status groups, there is the danger that the research staff in empathizing with the respondents or acceding to their expectations will gradually shift their activities from science to service to such an extent that science is lost. The writer has had experience with this problem in a field study trying to discover the obstacles to getting female-headed families out of poverty. Even though the evidence was strong that the organization had at least a 90 percent failure rate despite their large budget, the individual interviewers on the project could easily be diverted to such activities as finding a pair of shoes for a child or raising emergency funds to take care of some need when it was clear that such activities in the past had not solved the problem. In their more rational moments the interviewers would admit that this was not helping the poor out of poverty.

Do not deceive the respondents

Even though ideally it may be good to tell the truth, the whole truth, and nothing but the truth to the respondents, all this is not necessary to conform to the rule not to deceive the respondent. There are many circumstances in which telling the respondent too much can cause considerable problems. For example, Whyte, in his study of street corner society in an Italian slum, found that it was not possible to explain the purpose of his study to the slum dwellers. He had no reason or desire to deceive them but simply could not explain the theoretical purpose of his study in terms that people of a different background could grasp. Often what is done in such cases is to give a very general explanation that will include all of the researchers' activities. In community studies such an explanation as "doing as history of X community" is acceptable and broad enough to include the kinds of data collected.

We have already shown that in many cases to give a respondent a complete explanation may stop the study before it gets off the ground if that respondent is one of the gatekeepers of the organization or community to be studied. Having a legal or moral right to do the study may have no persuasive effect upon the gatekeeper if he feels threatened by the sponsorship of the study or its purpose. A precise explanation of the purpose or sponsorship not only has the possibility of preventing the study but also of biasing the responses if the respondents tend to want either to please or deceive the sponsoring organization. The researcher to be honest must be prepared for the possibility that certain types of studies simply cannot be done at certain times and places if we are to stay within the bounds of ethics. It is not always possible to convince oneself that the potential value of the study to the larger society or to the scientific community is great enough to justify the means to that end.

Often the question of deceiving the respondent is more personal than either the purposes of the sponsorship of the study. Since the interviewer is the instrument by which relevant information is elicited from respondents, it is often desirable or necessary to change the nature of the instrument to fit the social environment in which it must be used. This change may involve how he presents himself to the respondent. In some cases interviewers have merely chosen from among their various real roles the one that may have the most appeal to the particular respondent. That fact that the interviewer lives in California, that her grandfather was a Baptist minister, that she graduated from Berkeley, that she belongs to a woman's liberation group, that she wants to be a child psychologist, or that her mother speaks Spanish more fluently than English may all be true, but it is obvious that under certain circumstances one of these roles might have a different effect upon the respondent's willingness to trust and cooperate than would another one. Is this deceiving the respondent if the interviewer puts his best role forward?

This is a common tactic in everyday interactions between people, and I personally do not feel it is unethical as long as the study is beneficial to society and will do no harm to the respondent.

In other cases interviewers must decide whether to assume behavior that is not their own in order to conform to the demands and expectations of the people being studied. This was the problem Daniels[25] found

---

[25] Arlene Kaplan Daniels, "The Low-Caste Stranger in Social Research," chap. 12 in *Ethics, Politics, and Social Research*, ed. Gideon Sjoberg (Cambridge, Mass.: Schenkman, 1967), pp. 267–96.

in a study of the U.S. Army practices in the training of recruits. Her self-concept was of a competent professional, director of a research project with a mandate from Washington, and equal to the officers with whom she dealt. Her use of humor, her strong handshake, her steady gaze, and brisk competent manner was seen as inappropriate for a woman. The initial response to her was either to resist any spontaneous cooperation or to try to seduce her. She did not realize that in many situations according to the army subculture she appeared to invite seduction. In order to gain access to the needed interviews and observation situations, she had to change her manner to more "feminine" helplessness, less aggressive, less self-assured, waiting to be helped by the officers.

In this case the researcher was engaging in a type of deception as to the kind of person she was in order to conform to the expectations of the group she wanted to study. This was the price of her admission to the group. Is this an unethical form of deception or is this merely adjusting to the field situation and showing respect for another subculture? In this case the fact that the researcher was emotionally involved with the basic issue of women's rights in her own society made it more difficult to separate the value of fighting for a new status for women from the value of gathering valid, reliable, and complete information on the army training process. Clearly the pressure to assume a specific role came from the respondent.

In contrast, in Humphrey's study of homosexuals the pressure to assume the role of lookout did not come from the respondents but from the interviewer's desire for access under circumstances where an opportunity to observe and interview would not be assured without it.

It is interesting that researchers often have more conflict and feelings of hypocrisy when they adjust temporarily to subgroups in their own culture than when they go through the ritual of crossing an ocean to a foreign land or an exotic culture.

A more thorough deception of respondents is reported by Festinger,[26] who was a member of the team doing a study of an apocalyptic group lead by a woman who believed that through "automatic writing" she had received messages from beings living in outer space forecasting the destruction of the earth by flood on a certain date in the near future. Since the predicted date was close, it made possible a study of how the group behaved during the time before that date and how they would adjust to the failure of the prophecy. To gain access to the group the research team posed as a group of traveling businessmen; this provided an excuse in advance for the team to leave after the date of the

---

[26] Leon Festinger, H. W. Riecken, and Stanley Schacter, *When Prophecy Fails* (Minneapolis: University of Minnesota Press, 1956).

prophesied destruction. They posed as being interested citizens who merely happened to hear about the prophecy. This case of "misrepresentation of self" is different from the previous two in that it combines the masquerade of personalities with the misstatement of purpose of the study.

Another type of masquerade is that of showing sympathy for a cause in a way that may either contradict the neutral objectivity stance or exceed the amount of uncritical acceptance actually felt for the cause. This was the situation when Bonilla and Glazer[27] did a study of the professional and political attitudes of Chilean university students. Since it was a participant-observation study, they engaged in informal political discussions with students in which they were expected to share their own political views. In some situations they allowed their respondents to feel that they agreed more with the discussion than they actually did by either emphasizing points of agreement or refraining from expressing their disagreements. This raised the ethical question for the researcher: What right do I have to expect the respondents to give me their candid political views if I do not give an equally candid account of my own political position?

The above examples do not pretend to cover all possible forms of masquerade in the process of presentation of self to obtain information from others, but they should serve to illustrate the reality of the problem. If we were blindly to follow the formula of telling nothing but the whole truth to our potential respondents and their gatekeepers, it would be impossible to study many important controversial issues or to get an inside view of any group we do not already belong to.

Share the results with the respondents

The scientific value of sharing information with fellow human beings is obviously served by showing the results of any study to the respondents who furnished the information. It also serves the general humanistic value of reciprocity to the respondent, and it is frequently necessary to disseminate the results of a study if they are to be applied to any action toward larger societal goals. Superficially, it may seem rather difficult to generate an ethical problem through the sharing of the results of a study.

Yet problems do arise. For example, one of my former respondents in a study of miscommunication between North Americans and Latin Americans on reading the rough draft of the report said, "Yes, that is

---

[27] Frank Bonilla and Myron Glazer, "Note on Methodology. Field Work in a Hostile Environment: A Chapter in the Sociology of Social Research in Chile," Appendix A: in *Student Politics in Chile* (New York: Basic Books, 1970), pp. 313–33.

true, but I don't think you should say that; it makes Americans look like fools, and they were actually a much better than average bunch in their sensitivity to the host culture." True, they were better than average. Also, it should be noted that nothing in the text of the paper suggested that their behavior could be explained by their lack of concern for the Colombians; yet objectively reporting the results was perceived as a threat, even though the specific individuals were not identified.

A more dramatic example of this tendency to reject certain reflections of reality was encountered in this same study.[28] A group of Peace Corps Trainees, not yet accepted as Volunteers, had lived in a Colombian home for several weeks. They were then asked to "Describe how the Colombian home you now live in differs from North American homes as you know them," and they gave written responses. The remarks in these short essays were classified into general categories and quoted back to the Trainees as a group. A hot discussion ensued with some hostility toward the researcher because the Trainees recognized the statements as a series of complaints about the lack of physical comforts and conveniences in even the middle-class homes of Colombia. This image did not jibe with the official image of the Volunteer or with the Trainees' stated desires to get out into the villages with the Volunteers where the discomforts would be even greater. When the Trainees learned that this information was used in a course orienting other North Americans in Bogotá, they went on strike against attending classes in the training program.

They protested that they had been promised that the information would be confidential. This charge lost steam when it was pointed out that the preface to the questionnaire, which all respondents were required to read, stated that no individuals would be identified, but that the results would be used in training programs for other Peace Corps groups and for North American undergraduate students coming to Colombia. In resentment of the nonidealized image of themselves, they had forgotten their initial enthusiasm for providing information useful for orienting other arriving North Americans.

If such results are shared before a field study is completed, there is the danger that the backlash can prevent the study from going any further. On several occasions such sharing of information has put researchers in the position of having to compromise their scientific value of giving a full, uncensored report because some of the facts shown were threatening to one of the gatekeepers. For example, in studying the effects of a tornado on a small company town built of scrap lumber around a lumber mill in Arkansas, suddenly the complete 100 percent

[28] Raymond L. Gorden, *Living in Latin America: A Case Study in Cross-Cultural Communication* (Skokie, Ill., National Textbook Co., 1974).

cooperation of the respondents reversed to a 100 percent refusal rate. After consulting with the owner of the company town and the lumber mill, it became clear that we would not be allowed to continue the study unless we agreed to stop collecting information on the income of the mill workers which was less than 30 percent of the rate for similar work in other places in the same state. In this situation just the realization of how such information would look in print was highly threatening to the gatekeeper.

In general the ethical problem about sharing results arises when the potential findings will be perceived as a threat by individual respondents, by the organization or community studied, or by some other interest group. This immediately raises the question of the ethics of suppressing the facts or the interpretation of those facts by the people who collected them. In some cases the suppression is indirect; the research organization may exercise "prudence" in reporting to their client, for fear of angering them and risking the loss of future research grants. For this reason an individual researcher may resist censorship of findings more easily than can a research organization with a large investment in staff and equipment which they must protect.

In sharing results of a study there are ethical rules of thumb: (a) promise to share results unless there is some very unusual reason why this would be harmful; (b) when the promise is given, prepare and follow through on the promise; (c) give respondents a chance to correct any errors of fact or interpretation before the final draft is completed; (d) do not back down from the facts and your best interpretation merely because it would put someone in an unflattering light; (e) do not distort the findings to avoid embarrassing yourself or the research organization doing the study. Usually, all or most of these norms can be followed without great agonizing over conflicting values, but any researcher must be prepared to meet possible conflict courageously.

ETHICS AND HYPOCRISY

The information gatherer cannot hope to be ethical by being innocent or naïve about how society works. If he is timid, he may try to avoid ethical questions by studying only topics that are safe at the moment, but there is no necessary relationship between the ethics of one's action and the likelihood that it will stir up controversy. Often very noncontroversial information-collection activities—for example, gathering data in the area of motivation research—may be used to victimize the consumers, add to pollution problems, and channel human and other resources into nonproductive areas. The fact that this may be accepted as operating procedure does not mean that it is an ethical use of social science.

Earlier we gave the example of the senators who supported a bill in Congress to permit wiretapping but desperately fought the idea of studying the effectiveness of the jury system by tape-recording the deliberations. It is not usual for interest groups to deplore methods used by social scientists as unethical when they are commonly used by the same interest group making the complaint.

Often a controversy arises in which the social scientist's actions are likened to the police state's invasion of privacy. This completely obscures the importance of the fact that in one case the invasion of privacy may be backed by force, used to terrorize the weak and to punish the person whose privacy is violated, and used to maintain a form of illegitimate power; while in the other case every effort is made to avoid harm to the respondent and to resolve the types of conflicts in the larger society that lead to the use of terror, suppression, and force. Thus, in situations where there is the least congruence between the welfare of individuals and the aims of power elites, we can expect the most difficulty for the social scientist and the most hypocrisy in the double standard of ethics as applied to social scientists versus the practices of the power elite.

The banner of ethics is raised not only by powerful groups in an offensive battle to monopolize information, but also "ethics" can be a phony slogan sounded by the less powerful to defend themselves. For example, as a consultant, the writer designed an information system for a five-county anti-poverty program. There followed a long period of resistance by many in the organization to the recording of certain basic information about the clients they were supposed to help. Among those bits of information that workers resisted collecting and recording on a McBee data card were the following: full name, address, telephone number, age, race, sex, source of income, social security number, marital status, and draft status. Despite the fact that each of these items was needed to help the respondent obtain social services and income maintenance, some staff argued that "we have no right to that information," "it might be used to throw my client off welfare," "it takes too much time to get all that stuff," "to record the person's sex, race, or ethnic background engages in discrimination," "I don't think we should be interested in people in categories," or "it is not humanistic to try to reduce people to numbers and statistics."

Some arguments were conscientious, but others were inspired by fear of exposure. This was true when field workers had been making up fictitious clients to make their work load appear greater. In other cases they did not want the central office to discover that they were serving more non-poor than poor, that they were not serving as many blacks as they should, that they were dealing only with acquaintances in their local neighborhood, or that they were reporting more mileage than actually traveled in the line of duty. Thus each item of information could be perceived as a threat to different field workers, depending on which of their own activities or non-activities they were trying to hide. Yet the rhetoric was in terms defending the privacy of their clients.

These are all examples of interest groups trying to stop someone else from seeing or collecting certain information. There is another form of hypocrisy in which the interviewers raise the issue of the "ethics" of their activities only after they had gotten themselves into an embarrassing, boring, or dangerous situation. For example, a group of graduate students in sociology had begun a study of the city government in a steel-industry city. They discovered by accident that the city attorney was in collusion with a local group connected with a large underworld syndicate. They discussed the ethical and practical problems of bugging the city attorney's office to record possible conversations with those with whom he plotted, and they decided to do this.

In their enthusiasm for the intellectual super-sleuthing, they forgot to consider seriously the probabilities of getting caught in their amateur effort or the possible repercussions if the "bug" were discovered. One of the students who worked in the mayor's office arranged to have a microphone placed in the light fixture above the city attorney's desk. They were amazed at the content of the conversations which intimated bribery and plans to fleece the taxpayer and deceive the voters. Just about the time they began to discover the awesome power group involved and the full extent of the corruption of the city attorney, a most untimely accident occurred. The fluorescent bulb in the fixture above the City Attorney's desk burned out. The janitor came to replace it and found the planted microphone. By following the wire, he discovered that it led to the office of one of the graduate students. As soon as the student heard it had been discovered, he left for an early lunch, called the other members of the team, and they all left town without returning to work that afternoon.

After what they had already learned from monitoring the tapes, they realized that the organization might resort to violence against them. Perhaps one thing that saved them was the fact that the recorded tapes had been numbered and dated and left in the student's office only because he was afraid to return for them. But this made it possible for those who traced the wire to find the tapes and destroy them all. The point to note here is that *before* the bug had been discovered, the students seemed to have no pangs of conscience, and no doubts regarding their own ethics because they had no intention of giving the information to the mayor or to the police department; they were trying to discover some of the basic conditions under which such violations of trust by men in public office developed. All this could be used to design better city governments without necessarily exposing the individuals involved in this particular case.

It was not until *after* they had been seriously frightened by the discovery of the bug that some members of the team began to feel genuine remorse for having violated the city attorney's privacy. These members argued that the ends do not justify the means, that they should have gotten the mayor's permission, or that what they did was illegal. Those who still felt the bugging was not unethical argued that they should have not been so amateurish, they should have used a wireless bug, that it had proven impractical but not immoral, or that it certainly could not be called immoral to listen in on crooks out to victimize the citizenry.

Regardless of what the team would decide if they had an opportunity to study the same kind of situation in another city, it is clear that their ethical discussion would be more serious and would take into consideration a wider range of factors than before. Their amateurish enthusiasm would be more tempered by realism.

The important point in this episode is that we must have some way of sifting out the difference between right and might, between ethics and politics, between fear and reason, lest we become frightened into elevating pure expediency to a high moral principle. If we are unwilling to admit fear, we are in danger of taking the side of the corrupt in any situation where they are powerful enough to punish those who would disturb peace with the truth. We cannot realistically demand that all seekers of truth be beyond the reach of fear, but fear will have a less insidious effect if we recognize it for what it is.

It does not always require such a threat of violence to make the information gatherer doubt his own ethical position. More typically, any direct contact over a long period of time with members of any group under observation can become uncomfortable and lead the observer to look for escape under the banner of ethics. This occurred when four undergraduate students undertook, as their senior project, a participant-observation study of faith healing. They observed evening meetings at the Church of the Open Door which were held for the purpose of "revival of our faith in the Lord and to cure the sick with our faith."

After three weeks of observing three times each week, one of the students on the team wanted to drop out because he felt that it was "unethical" to attend the meetings as an observer. He felt he was "deceiving the people there into thinking that he was one of them." Yet he admitted that others came who were not yet "saved" and in fact the minister made it abundantly clear that all were welcome, "sinners and saved alike." In our discussion about his feeling, it developed that he was from a Protestant background and had been to Latin America where he had repeatedly attended a Catholic church without feeling hypocritical. We explored the differences between his experiences in this American lower-class Protestant church and the lower-class Catholic church and discovered some important facts: he could feel detached in the Catholic church because he did not have to interact with others in the congregation during mass, while in the Church of the Open Door he was immediately surprised and embarrassed by how warmly and personally the members of the Protestant sect had received him. He was immediately accepted as a unique individual and there was obvious concern for the fate of his soul. Genuine affection was displayed among the members; there was considerable body contact among the men and among the women; even though the students were considerably younger than the average male member this did not stand as a barrier as far as the members were concerned. Much of his complaint of embarrassment over the demonstration of affection resulted from the fact that he was obviously expected to participate, not simply to observe. Pure observation was easier at the Catholic Mass.

He seemed to feel a bit like my carpenter friend who accepted a job doing repair work on buildings in a nudist camp. His initial enthusiasm turned to retreat when it was explained upon his arrival that he would have to take off all his clothes while he worked to avoid embarrassing the members who were nude. He had gone to observe and not to participate and be observed.

Other sources of the student's discomfort at the healing meeting seem to be related to his vague fear that he might actually be converted to the church after seeing paralyzed people walk away from their wheelchairs. There was also an attractive feeling of security in the warmth and simplicity of the people's faith which he felt he should not yield to. He would have felt less uncomfortable if he were not required to make any systematic observations, yet he felt that it was precisely this requirement of disciplined observation which kept him from succumbing to the lure of the group. All of these cross-pressures exerted upon him could be escaped by finding a legitimate excuse for dropping out of the research team. Since he began to feel subjective strain, he interpreted this as guilt feeling resulting from his "unethical" behavior. This very understandable reaction should not be confused with ethics.

These examples illustrate the principle that under certain conditions the banner of ethics can be used to hide unethical practices in a struggle for profit or power or to disguise a retreat from battle as an ethical advance.

SUMMARY

We have tried to deal only with some of the most vital issues which directly affect the interviewer's ethical choices. Contrary to the naïve view that only good and evil conflict, any social action contains conflict or competition between propositions, each of which may be considered good in its own right. The process of making ethical choices involves two dimensions: the *valuation* of particular acts in terms of assumptions or knowledge regarding their probable effects, and the *weighing* of the relative importance of different values. Thus, ethics does not merely involve some fixed hierarchy of abstract ideals isolated from knowledge of cause and effect in the empirical world; ethics involves decision-making guided by both values and knowledge. Knowledge of the concrete situation and of the general principles of cause and effect in that situation is needed.

The ethics of interviewing is seen as the interviewer's choice of actions in which his moral obligations to the larger society, to science, to the research organization, and to the respondent must all be taken into consideration to find the best short-run and long-run effects. There is no way the interviewer can avoid making ethical choices, whether or not he is aware of them.

There is no escape through the claim that "I was only following orders," because any interviewer decides whether to work on a particular project, whether to work for a particular organization, and how to carry out a particular assignment. We cannot rest assured that we have made the best ethical choice merely because no one is complaining or no obvious conflict results. Nor can we escape responsibility for the information collected and the use to which it is put by saying that we just collect the facts which speak for themselves. This is unrealistic; facts are collected for some purpose and should be relevant to that purpose. To interpret them we must show how they are relevant. We cannot escape ethical decisions by avoiding the study of controversial areas or of social change; such avoidance is a decision. Once we accept the idea that we cannot escape making ethical judgments, we become more conscious of *how* we make them.

Heightened awareness of ethical decisions allows us to resolve some of the ethical dilemmas by creative data collection. The point in the data collection process at which the most ethical problems can be resolved or avoided is at the strategy phase when decisions are made on who should get what information from whom, where, when, and how. The next section of this book will deal with such strategy decisions.

DISCUSSION QUESTIONS

1. What is the difference between ethics and ideals?
2. In what way do knowledge and values interact in ethics?
3. Why is it often difficult to determine whether a person is acting ethically?
4. Give an example of social research that you feel is clearly unethical. Why is it unethical?
5. Give an example of social research which you feel offers the toughest ethical dilemma. What makes it so difficult?

6. Do you feel that the ethical obligations of the interviewer are clearest in relationship to the larger society, to the research organization, to the scientific community, or to the respondent? Why?

7. What conflict may be encountered when the interviewer tries to fulfill his obligations to the respondent?

8. What are some of the ways that the accusation of being unethical can be used by the unethical? What are usual motivations in these cases?

SELECTED READINGS

Glazer, Myron. *The Research Adventure: Promise and Problems of Field Work.* New York: Random House, 1972.

The book deals mainly with the field strategy problems encountered by social scientists in Chile, India, South Africa, and Vietnam, as well as in American subcultures such as the Indians in Alaska, the Italian American slum, the black ghetto, the military, the judicial, the homosexual, and the small town. Woven throughout the whole presentation are implicit and explicit ethical problems.

Orlans, Harold. *Contracting for Knowledge.* San Francisco: Jossey-Bass Publishers, 1973.

Orlans's purpose is to make an assessment of the value and limitations of government-sponsored research. He summarizes and evaluates evidence and expert opinion on such sensitive subjects as the politics and biases of social scientists, the politicization of social science associations, the evaluation of government social programs, the scholar's ethical responsibilities to government, and the kinds of research for which universities, nonprofit institutes, and other organizations are best suited.

Sjoberg, Gideon (ed.). *Ethics, Politics and Social Research.* Cambridge, Mass.: Schenkman Publishing Co., 1971.

This is an excellent collection of writings by 14 different authors all squarely focused on ethical issues in social research. Each case illustrates the pressures and counter pressures exerted by sponsors, by government, by professional associations, by political pressure groups, by the respondents, by colleagues. The conflicts among the values of science and politics are clearly shown.

part three

Strategy
of interviewing

8

General strategy

The central task of the interviewer is to minimize the eight inhibitors and to maximize the eight facilitators of communication to increase the flow of valid, relevant information. The tools for this task are of three general types: strategies, techniques, and tactics.

The first of these three, *strategy*, involves making those decisions which determine the general social-psychological setting of the interview. In dramatistic terms, we would say that strategy determines the *plot* (purpose or objectives), the *scene* (time, place, and definition of the situation), and the *cast* (who is to interview who). However, it does *not* include writing the *script* (the interview guide or schedule). The script, or who says what to whom, includes both techniques and tactics as will be defined here. Unlike the cast of a stage drama, the interview is usually limited to two persons and only one has a script.

In making strategy decisions we must specify the purpose of the interview as clearly as possible since the selection of the cast and scenes depends upon the plot. Even though the research director may seem free to determine the purpose of a study, he is never completely so because he may be limited by the availability of funds, by theoretical problems, and by methodological shortcomings in view of the particular field conditions in which the research must take place.

One of the most general of these field conditions is the subculture in which the study is to be carried out. Often we take for granted that the cross-cultural communication problem must be dealt with in the strategy of the anthropologist who travels afar to exotic cultures, but we are not prepared for some of the same problems in our own land. A subculture may be associated with an occupation (policeman, teacher, circus performer, etc.), an institution (college, prison, hospital, etc.), a geographical location (Southern U.S., Greenwich Village, inner city, etc.), an ethnic group (Jewish, Chicano, WASP, or French Canadian), or a race (Nisei, Afro-American, etc.)

Each subculture has its own characteristics, its way of distinguishing insiders from outsiders, its way of deciding who to trust, and its sensitive issues vis à vis other subcultures and the larger power structure. The potential strategy problems depend on how the topic of the interview, the sponsorship of the study, and the identification of the interviewer relate to that subculture's *current* sensitivities in relationship to the larger society.

For example, Gaylin's[1] experience interviewing prisoners indicated that only cooperation came from the inmates themselves who were resistors to the draft during the very unpopular Vietnam War. The only serious backlash came from the "gatekeeper" administrators. In contrast, Giallombardo,[2] who deals with the problems of interviewing more typical prisoners, shows that we can anticipate considerable resistance from the prisoner-respondents themselves, since the problem of establishing mutual trust is very different from winning the trust of war resistors who did not identify with the criminal underworld.

During the 1960s there was a growing hostility to surveys and community studies in the black ghettos of the United States. For example, Josephson[3] discusses the resistance to community surveys in Harlem in the late 1960s and concludes that it was extremely important to screen prospective interviewers in terms of race, accent, and attitudes. Also, he admits that there are times and places where it is difficult if not impossible to collect data on deviant behavior because of the suspicion toward outsiders, regardless of the personal characteristics of the interviewer.

There are two dimensions to the ghetto culture that affect communication between interviewer and respondent: the social characteristics associated with race and those associated with socioeconomic class. There are barriers to communication between lower and middle classes regardless of race. As pointed out by Fein,[4] experience in inner city interviewing shows a number of general barriers to cross-cultural com-

---

[1] Willard Gaylin, *In the Service of Their Country: War Resisters in Prison* (New York: Viking Press, 1970).

[2] Rose Giallombardo, "Interviewing in the Prison Community," *Journal of Criminal Law, Criminology and Police Science*, vol. 57 (1966), pp. 318–24.

[3] Eric Josephson, "Resistance to Community Surveys," *Social Problems*, vol. 18 (1970), pp. 117–29.

[4] Edith Fein, "Inner-City Interviewing: Some Perspectives," *Public Opinion Quarterly*, vol. 34 (1970–71), pp. 625–29.

munication. One of these is that the forms of verbal expression and the thought processes in the lower-class respondent is different. Furthermore the idea of research as an established institution, a way of examining social phenomenon, and the possible benefits seem unreal to the respondents. This is a type of general apathy underlying the hostility which may flame up on certain sensitive issues. She suggests that one way to convince the less-educated respondent that we are serious in saying that their participation is meaningful and valuable is to pay them for the interview time. Here we are in effect substituting a cash extrinsic reward for an appeal to the respondent's altruism. Others oppose the cash payment, saying that respondents might expect cash even when the U.S. Census taker comes around, or that it might only be interpreted by the respondent as an indication that the interviewer himself does not believe in the value of the study to the larger community. More research needs to be done on the conditions under which certain amounts of cash payment may be both effective and ethical.

Once we have a tentative formulation of the plot we can then choose the actors. In selecting potential respondents we must think about who has the needed information, who is most likely to give the information, and who is most accessible in terms of the efficiency of the project. In selecting the interviewer we must think of the types of persons who will have the best understanding of the purposes of the study and the best relationship to the people who have the needed information.

We cannot mechanically proceed from the consideration of the plot, to the selection of the cast, and then to the specification of the scene. Instead, realistic choices of scene, in view of the actual field conditions, must be taken into consideration in selecting interviewers or respondents and in revising or specifying the purpose of the research. The researcher, unlike the playwright, is not completely free to create the scene from his imagination, but must consider the actual field conditions in which he must operate. Nor can he proceed effectively without creative imagination to conceive of ways to exercise some control of the scene by the selection from among real possibilities of time and place, and by devising effective ways of influencing the interviewer's and respondent's definition of the situation in a way that will minimize the inhibitors and maximize the facilitators of communication.

The researcher does not have a choice of either making or not making strategy decisions. He uses a strategy whether he is aware of it or not, whether he consciously selects from among alternatives or not, whether it is guided by any theoretical rationale or not. The fact that a particular interviewer is not aware of these problems does not mean that the decisions have not been made by someone. In large-scale research projects these strategy decisions are rarely made by the corps of hired specialized interviewers. Instead, they may be made by a research director, a supervisor for the specific study, or a special consultant-interviewer. Regardless, the person making the strategy decisions should be someone intimately familiar with the purposes of study, with the types of potential respondents, and with various possible settings in which the interviewing might be done. Frequently it is necessary for the strategist to do some pilot interviewing and, usually, some of the early pretesting of the first drafts of the interview schedule, if it is to be used by a team of specialized interviewers. The larger the research organization and the greater the amount of data to be collected on a particular study, the smaller the proportion of the total personnel involved in the strategy decisions.

Whether it is a small-team effort or a large-scale survey, it is advisable to clearly specify all of the strategy decisions as part of the instructions to the interviewers. It is not uncommon for the instructions for a 10-page interview schedule to be as long as 40 to 50 pages. The neophyte is often unaware of the importance of this manual of instructions for a particular interview study. It is important to their performance and morale for the interviewers to understand what decisions have been made regarding strategy, techniques, and tactics, and why these are necessary.

ASSUMPTIONS UNDERLYING THE TREATMENT OF STRATEGY

It may be assumed that other sources of information such as personal documents, official records, census data, questionnaires, participation, and observation have been considered and that there has been a decision that some or all the information must be collected by interviewing.

A myriad of practical specific questions must be resolved to meet minimum requirements of any field operation. Specific problems such as how to select a random sample of respondents (if such a sample is needed), how to obtain a list of special respondents, how to locate respondents once they have been selected—will not be taken up here. This is not because they are considered unimportant, but because the concrete answers to these questions vary infinitely, owing to the variety of specific settings, and the questions themselves do not deal with the central problem of minimizing inhibitors and maximizing facilitators of relevant information.

It is useful to discuss *general* types of problems, and an array of problem-solving tools, without giving rules to cover the multitudinous specific situations which might arise. These general problems must be considered by the designer, field supervisor, or sophisticated interviewer so he can effectively select from among several possible strategies. The principles which we might illustrate in only one or two cases are often applicable to many different specific settings.

CONTRASTING TYPES OF FIELD SITUATIONS

It has already been pointed out that the researcher, unlike the playwright, cannot create the scene completely from his imagination, but must operate within the limitations of the realities of the field situation in which the study must be done.

The following classification of field situations sensitizes us to three vital dimensions of the broader context in which studies operate. Each dimension has important consequences in that it places different types of limitations and poses different types of problems calling for different types of strategies. These three dimensions are: friendly versus hostile, open versus closed, and single versus multiple contacts.

Friendly versus hostile territory

Logically, there might be three points on a continuum which indicate community attitude toward the interviewing. At one extreme would be the completely hostile situation with a minimum of cooperation expected. This would be approximated in the military interrogation of a prisoner of war or in the policeman's questioning of a suspect. Less extreme would be the case of the sociologist interviewing the president of a college to discover flagrant violations of academic freedom. Similarly, a social scientist studying the effects of the "sit in" against restaurant segregation would encounter hostility in interviews with leaders of a restaurant association formed to combat the "sit ins."

At the other extreme of the continuum would be a group inviting a social scientist to help them achieve some goal they have spontaneously agreed upon. This type of field situation, as long as it remained one of pure cooperation, would not pose any particular problems for the strategist. However, even though the interviewer had been invited to do the study, initial cooperation might change as the interviewing progressed and disturbed the social equilibrium. The good strategist is prepared for this possibility.

Between the two extremes of hostility and complete cooperation is a middle ground encountered more frequently. Three classes of intermediate types can be delineated. The first is simply a form of *limited cooperation* where the cooperation has certain implicit or explicit limits. These limits may consist of certain quantitative or qualitative conditions which are imposed. For example, the middle-management people in a large corporation might be happy to be interviewed by a consultant regarding problems of management training programs if a "reasonable limit" was placed upon the amount of time or the number of interviews involved. If this limit was exceeded, the initial cooperation might turn to mild hostility.

The implied limitation may be qualitative. A civic organization that invited a consultant to interview a sample of suburban residents later withdrew its support because he asked "personal questions" such as the source of the respondent's income, and his religion.

Another type of intermediate point might be called *ambivalence*. This is a more volatile circumstance in which individual respondents have the potential for both excellent cooperation and explosive hostility. The respondent's ambivalence may be due to either conflicting values and desires within himself or potentially opposite perceptions of the interview situation. This type of ambivalence was sometimes found in respondents recounting their marital difficulties; they would feel torn between confessing certain actions to obtain catharsis and cutting the interview short to avoid confessing such ego-threatening information.

A third type of middle ground might be called the *polarized* situation. Here, as in ambivalence, both ends of the hostility-cooperation continuum are actually or potentially present in the group. However, each individual is consistently cooperative or hostile depending upon his attitude toward some issue related to the interview topic. The split in the community or organization might occur between strata of power or prestige, between subcultural groups, or between occupational categories. The polarized situation would be probable in a study of labor-management conflicts. In this case, if the interviewer were perceived as partial to the union, he would also be perceived as unsympathetic or hostile to management, and vice versa.

Open versus closed communities

Here, "closed" refers to the degree to which persons of power or prestige can prevent the interviewer from contacting or gaining the cooperation of subordinates in the group. If a group is open, each individual respondent is free from any legal or other direct social pressure determining his decision to cooperate with the interviewer. The degree of closedness of a group, organization, or community depends upon the degree to which the power figure has absolute control over members, the degree to which the membership of the group overlaps with other groups, and the degree to which the members feel committed to the wishes of the power figure, even though they can be contacted through other groups or in the open residential community.

To illustrate these dimensions, assume that we wish to interview prison inmates. The prison warden has absolute control over the inmates in his institution; during their stay in prison they are not members of any group through which the interviewer might gain access to them as respondents. However, if the criminal were interviewed after his release from prison, he would not feel any obligation to the warden.

On the other hand, in doing a social-psychological study of certain monastic orders, we would find a different pattern of closedness. In some orders, the person in charge of the monastery may grant or deny permission to anyone who wishes to enter or leave, and each monk's total life pattern may take place within the monastery walls. In these characteristics, the organization is as closed as the prison, but if a brother were to leave the order and return to the outside world, he may have internalized the point of view of the church hierarchy and still be strongly under its influence. A different pattern of closedness prevails in a delinquent gang not in custody. No one's permission is needed to make contact with any members of the gang, since they all have homes and may even go to school regularly. Nevertheless, obtaining information about their illegal operations is very difficult unless the informal leader gives an affirmative nod.

The closed community is not always easy to recognize or to anticipate because of various possible complications. The community may be polarized between two nearly equal power groups, one favoring and the other opposing the interviewing. The opposition may be hidden from view, while the favoring group may be reluctant to acknowledge the opposing group's existence. The control over the respondents may be either legal or extralegal, while the sanctions for violation may be either positive punishment or withdrawal of certain privileges or status. The followers may perceive their leader's desires as external pressure or as "the right thing to do."

Strategy problems are not necessarily greater in the closed community than in the open, but the problems are different. Regardless of the quality or amount of closedness in a group, certain common strategy must be planned to obtain the goodwill of the power group which can allow contact with respondents and give some assurance of their cooperation. If this sanction is given by the leaders, plans must be made for maintaining their support throughout the study. If the community is not only closed but also polarized between power strata, an interesting dilemma arises. The support of the superordinate group, which must be obtained to gain access to the subordinate group, is double-edged; the interviewer may be suspected by the respondents *because* he has the approval of their superiors. Finally, if the power group does not give its support, plans must be made, if no other community can be substituted, to gain access to respondents without the leader's sanction. The extent to which this can be accomplished depends upon to what degree the respondents are completely controlled by the one closed group or community.

Single versus multiple contacts

Whether or not each respondent must be contacted more than once depends upon several conditions. For example, if the interview calls for a wide variety of special respondents, the first contact may be devoted to checking the respondent's qualifications in terms of the experiences he has had and his ability and willingness to report them. Or, if the type of information needed requires a more intimate relationship than can be established quickly, the first contact may be devoted mainly to building a suitable relationship. In other cases, multiple contacts are required simply because the amount of information to be obtained is too great to obtain in a single interview without encountering fatigue or competing time demands.

Another common type of information requiring multiple contacts is the panel study or any study where the objective is to trace changes in individuals over a period of time. Also, the study may be in the initial stages of exploration so that the interviewer does not know during the first interview all the questions which must be asked. There are times when the interviewer needs to return to the respondent to clarify or to verify some of the information obtained in the first contact. Finally, there is the strategy based on the interview followed by a questionnaire. Although it is often possible to do both the interview and the questionnaire in the same session, it may be valuable to use the multiple-contact strategy either because the combination would be too long for one session, or because it is desirable to allow more time for the respondent to mull over the issues stimulated in the interview before filling out the questionnaire.

In either case it has been shown by Alderfer[5] that, even though highly structured questions and answers are wanted, more relevant information can often be obtained from the questionnaire method when it has been preceded by an interview. In some cases the interview provides an equally important portion of substantive data; in other situations it may simply furnish qualitative verbatim quotations to give meaning to the statistical results of the questionnaire. The interview may furnish no data in itself but be used to stimulate the respondent's thinking in certain areas, to provide a context for interpreting the meaning of the questionnaire, or to build a more personal relationship between the respondent and the agency sponsoring the study.

---

[5] Clayton Alderfer, "Comparison of Questionnaire Responses with and without Preceding Interviews," *Journal of Applied Psychology,* vol. 52 (1968), pp. 335–40.

Regardless of whether the multiple-contact strategy is used for one of the foregoing reasons or whether the job can be done with a single contact, there are problems associated with either of the strategies. If only one contact is to be made, there may be a problem of building good rapport in the short time available. However, there are advantages to the single contact in that the interviewer is usually perceived as a stranger who will leave the local scene immediately and therefore not become involved in local matters.

In some circumstances the single contact seems to be advisable regardless of the large amount of information to be collected from each respondent. A very long interview makes it more difficult to find a sufficient block of time uninterrupted by competing demands. However, the efficiency of the interview might be improved by using auxiliary questionnaires or check lists, by pruning out all unnecessary questions, and by carefully selecting a time and place for the interview which will minimize competing time demands. Of course, the latter solution will often spread the same number of interviews over a longer period of elapsed time.

A danger to guard against in the long interview is simple fatigue or loss of interest by both the interviewer and respondent. Fatigue is not necessarily a result of the length of the interview; there is considerable evidence that fatigue is often more the result of the presence of the communication inhibitors and the absence of the facilitators. It has been demonstrated that it is possible to interview one person for eight hours at a time without fatigue seriously interfering with the flow of information.[6]

In making strategy plans involving the possible use of extremely long interviews, pilot interviews should be done to explore any negative effects of fatigue. It might be found necessary to abandon plans for a single contact and split the interview into two sessions.

When single contacts are to be made with a large number and variety of special respondents, a much larger proportion of the interviewer's time will be spent locating and contacting than would be the case where a series of contacts is made with the same person. This is an unavoidable consequence which must be recognized in planning the rate of progress of the field study.

Let us now examine some of the potential problems present when the interviewer makes multiple contacts and stays longer in the community. First, we must guard against the contamination effects of one respondent directly or indirectly influencing another. This influence may be negative. For example, a respondent might feel uneasy about

---

[6] N. Gross and W. Mason, "Some Methodological Problems of Eight-Hour Interviews," *American Journal of Sociology*, vol. 59, no. 3 (November 1953), pp. 197–204.

confidences given even though the interview had a pleasant cathartic effect at the time. His delayed reaction may cause him to warn others in the community about "that interviewer who makes you say things you don't mean." Often, this possiblility can be reduced by ending each interview with a short informal conversational period aimed at building the respondent's ego. In some cases, the respondent will use this ego-building period to rationalize or "explain" things he said but "didn't really mean." If the interviewer simply accepts these rationalizations without question and praises the respondent where he can do so conscientiously, there is less tendency for the respondent to try to retaliate after the interviewer leaves.

Another contamination effect is found where one respondent tries to explain to a potential respondent the purpose of the interview, the sponsorship, and so on. Although his intentions are good, his account may distort the facts so that the interview is seen as simply worthless or even ego-threatening. This difficulty can sometimes be forestalled by preparing a written explanation, combined with a note of appreciation, to be left with each respondent after completing the interview. This pamphlet or letter should contain clear information on the purpose, sponsorship, and anonymity of the interview. Perhaps more important, it should include the name, address, and phone number of some locally trusted person who endorses the project and who can quell any doubts. Another safeguard is to give news releases to local papers explaining the study, reporting its progress, and praising the community for its cooperation. Also, the possibility of contamination can be reduced by maintaining contact with key informants regarding any developments of rumors or opposition.

Another problem arising when the interviewer stays longer to make multiple contacts might be called "role confusion." On the first contact, the interviewer may be given confidential information because he is perceived as a stranger who will not remain long enough to carry confidential information to others in the community. When the same interviewer is in the community weeks later talking to neighbors, a respondent might temper his remarks in the next interview or show suspicion of the interviewer's purpose.

Much of this role confusion can be prevented by stating clearly at the start how long the interviewer intends to stay in the community, by reassuring respondents regarding the interviewer's integrity, and by showing the necessity of interviewing all types of people. Also, the topics to be covered in a series of interviews may be planned to leave the most ego-threatening information to the last in the series.

Another strategy is to use different interviewers to contact respondents who fear the possibility of information being passed among them by the interviewer. This problem is greatest when the community is polarized or fractionalized over issues conceivably related to the topic of the interview. The interviewer's association with members of one group is perceived by members of another as "fraternizing with the enemy." When this polarization is extreme, multiple contacts with each respondent become almost impossible. In this case, one interviewer could specialize in respondents on one side of an issue and another interviewer could deal with the opposite camp.

In contrast to this situation, where the problem is to avoid contamination from one respondent to another or to keep contending parties apart, there is the *group interview* which aims to get the interacting parties together and to stimulate both verbal and nonverbal interaction among them. Here the interviewer is a participant-observer. Although the group interview strategy has been developed mainly for therapeutic purposes, it can also be used for a pure information-gathering or diagnostic functions. Friedman[7] provides an example of the group interview with the families of schoolchildren. The study gives data on 53 families and detailed summaries of four cases showing the dynamics of the relationships among family members as expressed in the interview situation. In this study the aim was to diagnose the possible causes of the student's learning disorders.

Hill[8] shows how the group interview, again with the family, is used in a hospital setting for the diagnosis of health problems. He demonstrates that there are both values and pitfalls to be avoided in the conjoint family interview. Much research remains to be done to explore the conditions under which the group interview may be fruitful for predicting a person's performance in small group situations, for overcoming the memory barrier by using the collective memory of the group, and for other information-gathering functions.

GENERAL TYPES OF RESPONDENTS

In addition to the contrasting types of field situations, another important dimension of strategy is the type of respondent needed for the purposes of the study. Broadly, the types of respondents can be said to correspond, in general, to the kinds of information sought in a study. Here, we are not concerned with personal characteristics of the respondent, but with the general type of information he can offer.

Key informants

The key informant is any person who gives information relevant to any of the strategy problems of a study. In this role, the person does

---

[7] Robert Friedman, "A Structured Family Interview in the Assessment of School Learning Disorders," *Psychology in the Schools,* vol. 6 (1969), pp. 162–67.

[8] William G. Hill, "The Family as a Treatment Unit: Differential Techniques and Procedures," *Social Work,* vol. 11 (1966), pp. 62–68.

not give information directly related to the objectives of the interview. Instead, he helps by supplying information on the local field situation, by assisting in obtaining cooperation, by locating or contacting respondents, and by relaying information during the progress of the study to help meet its objectives. Key informants are particularly necessary in hostile and closed communities.

Special respondents

The special respondent is any person who gives information directly relevant to the objectives of the study and who is selected because he occupies a unique position in the community, group, or institution being studied.

The special respondent is needed because his unique position qualifies him to give special information, either on his own thoughts and actions as he functions in that particular position, or on his observation of others' feelings, thoughts, and actions from his special vantage point.

The special respondent also provides information on the *structural* aspects of the group, institution, or community. Such special respondents would be useful in discovering the difference between the formal and informal organization of an industrial plant, mapping out the channels of political influence in a community, or analyzing the structure of a boys' gang.

A different type of information may be obtained from each special respondent since his unique perspective is his chief contribution to the study.

Representative respondents

The representative respondent, like the special respondent, gives information directly relevant to the objectives of the interview. The representative respondent is chosen because he is *like* other respondents, in that he belongs to a certain category, universe, or population. The representative respondent, as one of a sample of representatives from the same class, contrasts with the special respondent who might be the only member of his special class to be interviewed.

Several important characteristics distinguish the use of special respondents from the use of representative respondents.

a. Representative respondents are worthwhile only when there are enough of them to represent certain variations in the universe or population from which they have been selected.

b. The same questions must be asked all members of the sample.

c. The sample is considered as an *aggregate* of individuals having a range of characteristics similar in variation to the universe. Likewise, the universe is also conceived as an aggregate rather than a *structure* of relationships between individuals.

d. Since the sample is an aggregate, the measurements obtained from individuals are subject to mathematical and statistical operations such as addition and multiplication or to finding a mean, standard deviation, and measures of association.

None of the above characteristics applies to the use of special respondents.

Uses of kinds of respondents

It is important to realize that a single study might require the use of key informants, special, and representative respondents. Furthermore, the same person may be a key informant at one time in the study; later he may be a representative respondent, and even later a special respondent.

To illustrate the use of key informants, special respondents, and representative respondents, let us examine a field study in which all three types are needed. In studying teenagers' conflicts with parents and the relationship of these conflicts to juvenile delinquency, we might begin by contacting key informants, such as the staff of the state juvenile authority, to help select a location for studying the problem. These informants might help find locations with extremely high and low delinquency rates; they might also estimate the extent to which the differences in the official rates reflect actual differences in delinquency rather than in booking systems.

In addition, these key informants could furnish the names of special respondents in the local areas, such as the superintendents of schools, juvenile parole officers, truant officers, and family case workers, who deal directly with known delinquent children. Additional special respondents such as high school counselors, teachers, playground directors, and local police would be able to provide information on many unrecorded delinquencies. Another class of special respondents would be each delinquent's closest friend or the whole gang to which he belongs.

The representative respondents could include a sample of tennagers and their parents from each of the two communities. These teenagers and their parents could supply information on the number and types of conflicts they have experienced. If the two communities were large, with a population of more than 100,000, a one percent sample of teenagers and their parents might easily include some of the special respondents.

It is possible to have a study requiring only special respondents, such as a study of a small community's division-of-labor pattern. At the other extreme, a public opinion poll for predicting election results usually involves only representative respondents. Thus we see that the types of respondent depend upon the purposes of the study and the types of information to be collected.

STEPS IN FIELD STRATEGY

After the problem of the study is clearly formulated and the types of information needed are specified as precisely as possible, the next step is to determine the types of respondents required. With the ideal types of respondents decided upon, it is then necessary to determine the means of locating and contacting them.

Locating and contacting representative and special respondents

If the study calls for a sample of anonymous representative respondents, locating and contacting them may involve merely knocking on the doors of a random sample of an area's dwelling units. If special respondents are needed, there are usually several channels through which they may be identified, located, and contacted. In this case the advantages and disadvantages of one channel must be weighed against those of other channels.

For example, in studying the process of professionalization of occupational therapists, there are several possible channels of contact. The interviewer might obtain the names and addresses of OT's from the national or local association and interview them at their homes. This would avoid seeking the permission of the administration of the hospital where they work. If the study also requires interviewing physical therapists, physicians, nurses, and orderlies working in the same hospital, it would be desirable to obtain the hospital administration's approval so that the names of all of these employees in the local hospital could be acquired. It might also increase the efficiency of the project if some or all of the special respondents could be interviewed at the hospital. This would require additional cooperation from the administration.

After discovering which channels of contact exist and how cooperative each will be, further consideration must be given to the possible effects of each channel of contact upon the respondent's motivation to cooperate.

Securing the cooperation of key informants

If a key informant's permission must be obtained to gain access to several respondents in a closed community or organization, we should try to learn as much as possible about him. The following questions should be answered: Would the study threaten him in any way? What competing time demands might make him reluctant to give access to the respondents? Would this person take an ambivalent position because of conflicting desires or because of an ambivalent picture of the study's purpose or effect? If this person gives his wholehearted permission for the study, what might be the effect of this knowledge upon the respondents?

Some information relevant to these questions might be obtained from written sources if the key informant is a leader or professional person in the community or organization. Company newspapers, college catalogs, local newspaper files, local newspaper reporters, and directories of professional, administrative, business, and occupational groups are all useful sources of information about a person's status and function in a given social setting. Available public documents may yield such facts as the person's full name, his address, correct title and position, phone number, age, race, organizational affiliations, educational background, job history, public activities, and possibly a photograph. Further information might be obtained from other key informants who have contact with the person and can give impressions of his probable attitudes toward the proposed study.

Prepared with this background information, and guarding against prejudices, preconceptions, and sterotypes, the interviewer can approach the person whose approval he desires. The interview with this key informant may accomplish several objectives. It may explain the purpose of the study, the sponsorship, and show how the information is to be used. It may demonstrate how the study can help the key informant, or the interviewer may appeal to an altruistic motive and show precisely how the key informant can help the project. It might also be desirable to show the extent of anonymity involved in the collection and the publication of the information.

The interviewer may also want to ask for advice on such things as the best time and place for interviews. He should also take advantage of every opportunity to show sympathy for any of the problems confronting the key respondent in his decision to cooperate and should probe to clarify the precise nature of the problems instead of trying to discount them as imaginary or inconsequential. This information allows the interviewer to deal more intelligently with the obstacles, and his interest in the key informant gives a sympathetic and responsible impression.

This interview should create an atmosphere encouraging the informant to ask questions and clarify any doubts. It is always good strategy to leave written materials covering the same points as the oral explanation, along with details of where the interviewer and the sponsor might be contacted. In this way, channels of communication remain open.

If there is reason to believe that serious resistance will be offered by the target community, it is often practical to do a small pilot study in a similar community or organization at a distance to obtain perspective and forewarning of some of the potential strategy problems. For example, if a university sociology department wishes to study the problems of public school superintendents in five counties surrounding the university, it would be useful to do a small pilot study in a remote county of the state where a serious strategy error would not damage the final study.

If there is reason to suspect opposition from leaders of a closed community, plans should be made to meet it with constructive counterstrategies. One of the most problematic situations occurs in the study of a closed community in which the power figures are not in sympathy with the study, but do not feel free to publicly refuse cooperation. In this case, covert measures such as keeping the interviewer busy with irrelevant activities, stalling, red tape, and subtle threats to respondents may be used to sabotage the interviewer without directly refusing cooperation. It is well to anticipate, if possible, some of these potential evasions and have countermeasures ready. For example, it is useful to prepare face-saving explanations for the person of influence in case his initial resistance weakens and he wants to avoid the appearance of having acquiesced to pressure. In some cases, it is even necessary to prepare for a hasty retreat if a final rejection seems imminent. If possible, a final "no" should be avoided even at the cost of a temporary retreat.

If permission is refused. If the leaders' formal permission or informal approval is not obtained, there are still several paths toward the next step. At this point it is necessary to deal with several interrelated questions: Is it crucial to study this particular community or organization or can the study be carried on equally well in more friendly territory? Is the leader's power so complete that all channels of contact to the respondent are closed, or is it still possible to contact the respondents as individuals rather than through the group? If the respondents can be contacted as individuals, will the influence of the power figure still prevent their cooperation? These judgments must be made on the basis of information obtained in the local setting.

We must never forget that refusals to cooperate with the formal interviewing of a study may, nevertheless, provide much relevant information. In the discussion of the person's public reasons for noncooperation, real fears and suspicions or some of the powerfully competing time demands will frequently be manifested. In spite of the respondent's adroit mixing of public information and official explanation, the interviewer can find clues to some of the underlying causes of resistance.

In addition, it is possible to obtain relevant factual information while the person is refusing to cooperate. For instance, if an interviewer wished to study conflicts in a small town during desegregation of the public schools, the local mayor would be a good key informant regardless of his attitude toward the study. Even though he would not give confidential information about the performance of the local police force, for example, he would probably be willing to review specific incidents, name parties to the dispute, and give his official interpretation of the events. Regardless of the accuracy of his interpretations, the verifiable facts of time, place, and names would provide leads to other special informants on both sides of the issue.

On rare occasions, it is necessary and effective to challenge the power figure by pointing out that his resistance appears defensive in view of the guaranteed anonymity. In equally rare cases, it can be pointed out (where it is true) as a last resort that the study will have to be carried out with or without his sanction. Of course, in a completely closed community such a statement could not be made.

If permission is given. Plans should be made to maintain cooperation, once it has been obtained, because initial approval, either in an open or closed community, may turn to resistance. For example, people who originally assumed the study to be a survey of public opinion may subsequently feel that "confidential" information is being collected. They may simply be unable to see the relationship between the stated purpose of the study and the specific information gathered, and feeling threatened, they may accuse the interviewer of misrepresenting the nature of the study. This problem must be guarded against early by providing a written explanation which can be referred to later. This explanation may cover the range of information to be collected, or it may allow for more detail to be added from time to time with each interview with the same respondent.

Often, while not objecting to a particular question, the respondent objects to what he believes are certain implications in the relationships between the questions. An example is provided in a study of the social-psychological factors determining the success of rescue operations after a community-wide disaster. The officials of the city were not reluctant to give figures on the number of men and the amount of police, fire, and medical equipment sent to the scene. However, these facts were often viewed differently by the respondents after they had been asked the extent of the disaster, the time when the rescue workers and equipment were needed, and the precise time of their arrival on the scene. Initially, the rescue work was often carried out informally before any of the official organizations (such as the National Guard, Red Cross, Civil Defense, or local police) could mobilize; thus, manpower and equipment in excess of the need were sent, draining the surrounding area of its normal fire, police, and medical personnel. Even though the information was not to be used in judging, praising, or penalizing officials for their performance or for assuming responsibilities outside their jurisdiction, the interview questions were ego-threatening to people who liked to think of themselves as always having things under control.

In this type of situation the ego threat can be reduced by separating the facts so that the ego-threatening relationships are not perceived by the respondent. This may be done by having a series of interviews with the same person. In this way the relevant facts are collected in widely dispersed time, or parts of the picture are collected from different respondents and later assembled into a meaningful whole.

In some cases the initial cooperation of the power figures of a closed community precludes the enthusiastic cooperation of the respondents. This happens if the community is polarized between the superordinates and subordinates. Since the interviewer must have the permission of the leaders to gain access to the community members, the respondents may view the interviewer as a representative of the superordinate group. This difficulty can be ameliorated by the interviewer's frankness in explaining to the respondent that he is not sponsored by the power group but had to gain their permission to do the interviewing. This explanation in itself, truthful and logical as it is, will not necessarily gain the immediate trust of the respondent. The interviewer will have to show by his interest in the respondent's point of view that he is not a spy for the dominant group.

This discussion of possible steps in field strategy has presented a necessarily pessimistic picture, since its aim was to warn of certain problems which might arise and to suggest possible solutions. At each step the worst was assumed by supposing (*a*) that the respondents could not be contacted directly, but were in a closed and potentially hostile community; (*b*) that the situation within a community was complicated and sometimes polarized; (*c*) that it was necessary to persist in the study even though cooperation was refused; and finally (*d*) that even if permission were given, it might turn into resistance unless certain precautions were taken. Fortunately, it is rare to find all of these complications arising in any one field study.

All the possible strategy problems are never encountered in any one study. However, it can never be assumed that any information-gathering project will lack resistance merely for being a good cause in pure or applied human relations. Nor can we assume that all potential respondents will be disarmed and freed from ego-threat by the fact that the social scientist is not going to use information for his personal gain or for penalizing any individual or institution.

Instead of the naively optimistic or the hopelessly pessimistic approach to the strategy problems, a constructively cautious approach will be more useful—preparing for the worst and expecting the best.

Successful strategy involves doing the right things in the correct order and avoiding assumptions about the nature of the field situation without first checking available facts. The researcher must obtain reliable information about the field situation in order to prevent the rise of misperceptions, rumors, and suspicions before he has had an opportunity to explain the study to persons whose cooperation is needed. Unless there is a degree of success at the strategy stage, the interviewer will not have an opportunity to use his skills in interviewing.

So far, the discussion has dealt broadly with strategy by defining strategy in contrast to techniques and tactics, discussing some of the general types of field situations, delineating three type of respondents, and discussing some of the possible steps in field strategy as a decision-making process. This serves as a background for a more detailed treatment of four basic tools of strategy: selecting appropriate respondents, selecting appropriate interviewers, selecting the optimum time and place for the interview, and structuring the interview situation.

DISCUSSION QUESTIONS

1. What is interviewing strategy?
2. Is it possible to not use a strategy in interviewing? Explain.
3. What are some of the most important things we need to know about any subculture to plan a strategy for studying its members?
4. What are three important dimensions which characterize contrasting field conditions? Give an example of how one or more of these dimensions affect the strategy.
5. What are the three general types of respondents and in what way is each valuable?
6. What are some of the problems which may arise at the strategy phase of any study?
7. What general attitude of approach does the writer suggest in planning a field strategy?

9

Selecting appropriate respondents

The type of respondent needed depends mainly upon the type of information sought. The interviewers available and the setting for the interview will also have a bearing; but in discussing the selection of respondents, we will assume that the optimum interviewer and interview situation obtains.

If a special respondent occupies a unique position, then he is irreplaceable. If representative respondents comprise a sample which cannot be altered without damaging its representativeness, then each individual in the sample is irreplaceable. If both types of respondents are irreplaceable, there is no choice in selecting respondents. Then the query becomes, why deal with the *selection* of respondents?

Special respondents are *chosen* in two senses. First, it is necessary to determine which of the many unique positions (role, status, or function) are relevant to the purposes of the study. Second, similar positions are frequently occupied by more than one person. Thus, the special respondent is not a unique individual, but any person occupying a special position in society giving him access to certain observations, actions, and knowledge.

Representative respondents, on the other hand, offer fewer opportunities for purposive selection other than determining whether each is a member of the universe as defined for the study. However, there is an opportunity to maximize the flow of relevant information by "selecting" cases even after the complete sample has been chosen. This is done by deciding which respondents are to be interviewed by which of the interviewers (who are also already selected).

Logically, there are at least four basic criterion questions which must be answered in selecting respondents? Who *has* the relevant information? Of those having the information which are physically and socially *accessible?* Which persons having the information are most *willing* to give it? Which persons having the information are most *able* to give an accurate accounting?

The first two of these questions depend so heavily upon the specific information needed and the specific nature of the field situation that we will deal with them only superficially and then devote the remainder of this section to the last two criterion questions.

WHO HAS THE RELEVANT INFORMATION?

If we are seeking to measure subjective orientations of individuals— such as the attitudes, beliefs, expectations, desires, preferences, or loyalties of a certain population—then obviously everyone in that population has the relevant information. If we want to generalize to that population, we must either interview all or a representative random sample so there is no opportunity to select or reject respondents on any criterion other than being randomly selected from that population.

In contrast to this situation are the many studies which are not interested in the subjective orientations of an aggregate of individuals but in objective facts external to the individual, obtainable from a single person, verifiable through more than one person. Such facts would include objective information about a community, institution, organization, group, or event. For example, all of the following questions seek information of the objective type about Greenville, Ohio:

1. Who is the mayor of Greenville?
2. When will Greenville celebrate its centennial?
3. Who is the Superintendant of Schools in Darke County?
4. What is the property tax rate for public schools?
5. How long must children remain in public school according to Ohio law?
6. Who hires Mexican-American migrant farm labor in Darke County?
7. What are migrant workers paid per day?
8. Is there a Headstart Program for children of migrant workers?
9. Are there literacy classes in the evening for migrant workers?
10. How many attend literacy classes?
11. How is eligibility for food stamps determined?

All of these questions deal with Greenville, and any one of them could be validly answered by one person in Greenville if we found the right respondent. The number of people in Greenville having the information would vary tremendously from one question to another. Thousands of people could answer either question 1 or 2, but perhaps only two or three would know the answer to question 11. Despite the fact that hundreds of families in Greenville may receive food stamps through the local County Welfare Office, it is doubtful whether any of the recipients could be relied upon to know precisely how eligibility is established. The person to ask would be the person in the Welfare Office who processes the applications and makes the decisions on eligibility.

Ideally we should have a systematic scheme for relating general characteristics of respondents to the types of information they are most likely to have. Many descriptive studies relate to this problem, and some attempts at generalization have been made; but the fact that much remains to be done is evident in the apparent conflict between generalizing statements. Most of the literature simply demonstrates that one type of respondent is a better source of certain information than another, without inducing any general statement with appropriate qualifications regarding the type of information in relation to the type of situation. Here we will attempt some tentative generalizations.

High-low status

Often the high status respondents in any organization or community are much better than the lower status person in providing an overall view of the organization or its relationship to other organizations. They are also more likely to be familiar with the legal and financial structure of the organization. They often are more able to report on the past history and future plans of the organization.

Usually lower status persons can be relied upon for the details of daily operation, but they often show reluctance to answer questions of policy. Even among lawyers within a large law firm this tendency was found by Smigel[1], who noted that those lower down in the power structure, and usually younger, were reluctant to discuss policy matters or to make generalizations. They preferred to discuss the technical details, procedures, and routines involved in carrying out the policies. Often the only time the lower status person is articulate about policy is when he feels its pinch and disagrees with it.

If we want an estimate of the subjective state of mind of the rank and file in an organization, it is often more valid to ask even a few of the lower status people than to try to get an overall estimate from the top manager. This has been found in many different organizational settings. For example, Campbell[2] did an experimental study which showed that Navy enlisted men made a more accurate rating of morale among the submarine crews than did the officers.

---

[1] E. O. Smigel, "Interviewing a Legal Elite: The Wall Street Lawyer," *American Journal of Sociology,* vol. 64 (1958), pp. 159–64.

[2] Donald T. Campbell, "The Informant in Quantitative Research," *American Journal of Sociology,* vol. 60 (1955), pp. 339–53.

There are several possible reasons for this lack of awareness by high status people in any organization. First, the etiquette barrier might stop the men from disillusioning the boss who prides himself in keeping high morale. Also, ego-threat to the employee might be strong if the boss does not like to hear any "complaining about low morale." Finally, the boss may tend not to notice any evidence of low morale because he would see it as a personal failure on his part. This same pride in keeping high morale was demonstrated when a manager in a company with over 25,000 employees rejected evidence of low morale provided by a consultant, because management had launched a program five years earlier to develop the atmosphere of "one happy family" among all employees.

Active-passive types

In studies of community structure and process there seems to be considerable evidence that those who are active in community affairs regardless of their position in the social status system are more knowledgeable than the nonparticipants. Of course there are occasional astute observers who rarely directly participate, either because they are outsiders or because they wield indirect power requiring that they remain anonymous. Yet, information regarding the interplay of groups within the community, particularly around public issues, can be obtained better from the community activists. For example, Merton[3] found in his study of community housing that the particularly cooperative respondents were local leaders, who were active participants in organized and informal group life, and who identified strongly with the community.

Just as there are gatekeepers who can provide or deny the interviewer access to certain types of respondents, there are gatekeepers who because they provide certain types of information to the community make particularly good special respondents. Lewin's[4] conception of the gatekeeper was a person who linked the interpersonal communications network within a particular group to the outside world. This may include a link between a very small group like an office staff and the larger organization, or the link between the mayor's commission and the federal government, or between the home office of a U.S. company and its Latin American branches. These gatekeepers have the outside information first and decide what is relevant, when to release

---

[3] Robert K. Merton, "Selected Problems of Field Work in a Planned Community," *American Sociological Review*, vol. 12 (1947), pp. 304–312.

[4] Kurt Lewin, "Group Decisions and Social Change," in *Readings in Social Psychology*, ed. Swanson, Newcomb, and Hartley (New York: Henry Holt, 1952), pp. 459–62.

the information, and may even have suggestions about what should be done about it. These gatekeepers may be either one-way or two-way communicators who also interpret the group to outsiders.

This gatekeeper is the same person that Katz and Lazarsfeld[5] found particularly influential in linking the mass communication media and informal groups. In a sense these gatekeepers act as the on-off switch, even for information in the mass media, by calling the attention of their group to certain content of the newspaper, radio, or television, by interpreting the meaning of the content, or by setting an example of what should be done about the information.

Insider-outsider types

A person may be an outsider in different ways. He may simply be an outsider who never intends to get inside and is therefore useful, not for any insider information, but for his perspective as an outsider. This may mean that the outsider is more objective, or it may mean that he has stereotypes of the in-group or hostility toward them. The latter case is more likely if the outsider belongs to a competing or conflicting group. If the outsider is from another culture, he may be particularly useful in having a different frame of reference for raising useful questions and suggesting alternatives which would never occur to the insiders. On the other hand danger lies in his tendency to misinterpret his observations of the other culture. This is clearly shown by Gorden[6] whose study shows that American Peace Corps Trainees living with Colombian families in Bogotá made consistent errors in conclusions drawn from their observations and conversations in their Colombian homes. For example, the majority of Americans, after living in the Colombian home for several months, mistakenly believed that their host did not expect them to take a bath every day or wrongly concluded that they were not expected to make their own beds. Thus, when the outsider is from a different culture, he may give information which is his false conclusion based upon misinterpretations of his observations.

Just as the outsider has strengths and weaknesses as a potential informant so does the insider. The insider may be better acquainted with the details but his perspective may be too narrow.

A person is not always simply an outsider or an insider. In some cases a person is both, or is a "marginal man." The marginal person may be

---

[5] Elihu Katz and Paul F. Lazarsfeld, *Personal Influence: The Part Played by People in the Flow of Mass Communications* (Glencoe, Ill.: The Free Press, 1955).

[6] Raymond L. Gorden, *Living in Latin America: A Case Study in Cross-Cultural Communication* (Skokie, Ill.: National Textbook Co., 1974).

a *novitiate* coming from outside but being assimilated as a permanent member of the group. The novitiate is more useful in seeing the processes of initiation, socialization, assimilation, and socail control in any group or organization than are the long-time members who have forgotten the pain.

Another type of marginality is the *sojourner.* The sojourner comes with the intention of staying only a short time and therefore does not try to gain complete acceptance in the group nor does he submit completely to its control. The sojourner, as we have noted, can sometimes raise significant questions about what he observes, but often his own answers to these questions may be fallacious.

Another general type of marginal person is the *ex-member.* This is someone who used to be inside and is now outside. The type of information the ex-member has depends upon what his role was when he was an insider, how long he has been outside (since he may forget or his information may be out of date), and the relationship between the ex-member and the group. To clarify this relationship we must know whether the ex-member was rejected by the group (becoming a rejectee, exile, or outcast) or whether he took the initiative (becoming a fugitive, escapee, expatriate, or defector). Although both the expelled and the escaped may have feelings of fear or hostility toward the in-group, there is usually a difference in the type of information they have. If the in-group sees the larger world as threatening its interests, then the escapee may have information considered more dangerous than has the rejectee. Both the rejectee and the escapee are the result of tension and conflict. This is not so with all ex-members.

There is another type of ex-member who does not result from any conflict with the group but simply moves out as a part of the normally expected social process. This includes such persons as the graduate, retired, promoted, pensioned, emeritus, ex-officio, exogamic, expatient, vacationer, post-doctoral, post-juvenile, etc. All of these may have an advantage in having been a member at one time and now having a larger perspective. They may not be so biased against the organization and so willing to provide negative information; they may, however, bias the information positively either because of a romantic nostalgia or a feeling of obligation to protect the group's interest.

A very special type of marginal man is the one who is still in the group but in conflict or disagreement with it to some extent. This is the disaffected person. This type of person has special knowledge of the social control system and how it feels to be subjected to it. Also, since he is still a member, he can continue to be an informant regarding the processes of control, at least until he is considered incorrigible and becomes an outcast.

Mobile-stable types

Some people by virtue of their mobility have a better-than-average overview of the connections between groups or organizations. Such people as taxi-drivers, police, inter-office errand boys, delivery men, and textbook salesmen often have a unique understanding of activity between groups.

A special perspective on a community can often be gained from transients or new residents. In field strategy we often have to locate mobile individuals through agencies which specialize in dealing with them. The most challenging problem often arises in mapping a strategy for locating respondents who have left the organization or community we want to study. This is often difficult, but not impossible.

No systematic treatment has been done of the assets and liabilities of the different types and degrees of mobility in the context of information-gathering problems. We can only suggest that mobile people often have a kind of information rarely attained by stay-at-homes, yet they are often left out of community studies where their knowledge would be of special benefit.

The above classification of respondents into high-low status, active-passive, insider-outsider, and mobile-stable types is a sensitizing frame of reference to use in answering the question: Who *has* the relevant information? These four dimensions help to see where the person fits into the social matrix and make some crude preliminary estimations of his opportunity to acquire the information we seek. There is no guarantee that a person will be *willing* to give information merely because he has it, or that he is *able* to give it at the time of the interview. Let us now turn to the question of which type of respondent is the most willing and able to give relevant information in a valid way.

Who is accessible?

The problem of *accessibility* of respondents is often great. Although a respondent must be accessible if he is to be interviewed, there is a danger that the most easily accessible respondent might not have the other qualifications. In public opinion polls and market research, for example, there is frequent danger of a systematic bias in the selection of respondents when quota sampling is used. For example, the interviewer who must obtain a quota of ten males between 30 and 50 years of age from a certain neighborhood might choose those who are conveniently near the subway station or other artery of transportation. Or he might select those who are most psychologically accessible in that they seem to be middle-class educated people who can "express themselves more clearly." Numerous studies indicate that the opinions of these people differ markedly on many subjects from other socioeconomic classes.

Respondents in the upper socioeconomic class are often difficult to reach. They are highly organized and feel no obligation to respond to the desires of a lower status person. Furthermore, they are suspicious of "con" men or burglars who might be disguised as interviewers, or may fear that information given might be used to their economic disadvantage. In this stratum of society, sponsorship, recommendations, and introductions are extremely important.

It is also difficult to obtain access to lower socioeconomic class respondents under certain conditions. For example, in ethnic-group neighborhoods of urban areas, the interviewer might be suspected of being a bill collector, a salesman, a detective, or truant officer. To complicate matters, some families live in tenement houses or apartments, and the interviewer has no opportunity to speak to the respondent face-to-face before being refused. When someone shouts down the stair well or speaking tube, "Who is it?" the interviewer can only hope that the door does not slam as he shouts back the shortest and most enticing version of his purpose.

Who is willing to give relevant information?

In dealing with this question we will assume that it is known who has the relevant information, and that those who have it are physically and socially accessible. It will also be assumed that the study requires special respondents, but that more than one of each type of special respondent are available.

The question then becomes that of how to select from among the *available* special respondents those that are most *willing* to give relevant information? A more refined version of this question is how to best circumvent the four inhibitors (competing obligations, ego-threat, etiquette, and trauma) which tend to make respondents less willing to give information?

Competing time demands. Often it is possible to reduce the pressure of competing obligations in the interview situation by choosing a lower status person if he can provide the same information as a higher status person. The lower status person will feel more obligated to spend time in the interview.[7] In addition, certain facilitators of communication are more likely to be brought into play in an interview with a lower status

---

[7] Lewis A. Dexter, "Goodwill of Important People: More on the Jeopardy of the Interview," *Public Opinion Quarterly*, vol. 28, no. 4 (Winter 1964), pp. 556–63. Some of the dangers of intruding upon the time and privacy of high status persons are cited here.

respondent. For example, it is more likely to be a release from boring routine, thus appealing to the need for new experience. Also, the lower status person is more likely to feel he is gaining recognition in the experience.

It is possible in some circumstances to reduce the competing time demands by selecting a respondent who has large blocks of unoccupied time. If the same information regarding a teenage gang fight could be obtained either from firemen or drugstore employees who witnessed the event, it would be better to go to the firehouse than the drugstore for an interview. Again, if equal information is possessed by a mother of five children or a retired senior citizen, the latter would feel fewer time pressures.

Interviews with senior citizens have shown that they are often very willing to be interviewed at length if their health permits. Zelan[8] reports on a survey on the use of medical resources by 678 surviving veterans of the Spanish-American War. When the interviewing was done, the youngest were in their late 70s; yet a response rate of 92 percent was achieved. He suggests that anyone needing to study the aged population will find them very willing to talk, providing that they are in reasonably good health and the topic touches them personally.

When interviewing the aged, however, there are some possible disadvantages in using reports of their observations of events and people. For example, Bahs[9] points out, in his study of homeless men, that those who consent to be interviewed are no more likely to be consciously untruthful in replying to questions than are members of any other disadvantaged population. However, because they are aged and some drink excessively, they are somewhat disoriented and tend to be unable to answer questions which have any complexity. Thus, they are very willing, mainly because of a lack of competing time demands and a desire for sympathetic understanding, yet they are unable to answer complex questions or those which might involve chronological confusion or inferential confusion.

Ego threat. The ego threat barrier can sometimes be reduced by the proper selection of respondents. The general principle is to find some person whose ego is not involved in the information sought. There are many kinds of information given much more freely by one person than by another who feels threatened by admitting the truth. The most obvious example is the choice between a respondent who actually perpetrated an act of which he is ashamed and a respondent who saw

    [8] Joseph Zelan, "Interviewing the Aged," *Public Opinion Quarterly,* vol. 33 (1969), pp. 420–24.

    [9] K. C. Bahs and K. C. Houts, "Can You Trust a Homeless Man?" *Public Opinion Quarterly,* vol. 35 (1971), pp. 374–82.

another commit the act, but is neither identified with the perpetrator nor afraid of any reprisals if he gives the information. This is a situation familiar to the legal profession, where the witness for the prosecution has less ego threat than the defendant.

Perhaps more familiar to the social scientist is the situation where one person reports information withheld by another because he does not realize the stigma attached. He is not consciously "tattling," nor acting as a witness against the other, but merely giving a straightforward answer to a question. This is seen in cases where a child or youth tells the straight truth, while the adult, who realizes the implications, tries to alter or completely deny the facts. For example, in a study of teenagers' adjustment problems in school, the child is likely to admit having been suspended from school for three days. In contrast, the middle-class *mother*, who feels that the child's bad behavior is actually due to her own failure, is less likely to be truthful. Also, children are often more free in admitting sibling rivalry than are the parents.

This difference between the frankness of children and adults seems to be just one example of a general principle. The greater the responsibility a person assumes for some deviation from the public norms, the greater the pressure to pretend that the actual behavior conforms with the norms.

Concrete examples will illustrate this principle. The public relations office of a college is more reluctant to admit any conflict between the administration and the faculty over academic freedom than is the student body president. Also, public school superintendents are less likely to admit their school's basic problems in achieving high-quality education than are the young teachers. Similarly, the superintendent of a state mental hospital testified before a state legislature that there was adequate staff to give good care to the patients, an opinion which shocked the nonadministrative staff.

Unfortunately, there is sometimes a dilemma when the person who has the most accurate information will be the least likely to give it because he is most directly connected with the events being studied. This leads to the danger of depending upon more indirect sources of information. In these cases, strategies, tactics, and techniques other than selecting the nonthreatened respondent must be used.

There are circumstances where people in top power positions have valuable inside information that they are unwilling to give until they are ousted from the organization as renegades. Once they are out they no longer are subject to ego threat from the organization and may become very willing to talk. Sjoberg[10] points out that these renegades

---

[10] Gideon Sjoberg, "The Interviewee as a Marginal Man," *Southwest Social Science Quarterly,* vol. 38 (1967), pp. 124–32.

from top power positions are often both very able and willing to give social scientists information, particularly regarding the decision-making processes ordinarily considered secret.

Etiquette. In some cases, it is possible to avoid the etiquette barrier by selecting the appropriate respondent. The problem arises in situations where the interviewer is perceived by the respondent as a person who would be surprised, shocked, or chagrined by candid answers.

The etiquette barrier commonly appears when a person in a responsible position sincerely attempts to evaluate the human relations aspects of his organization by interviewing his own subordinates. If a junior executive in a large firm wants to evaluate a new employee-information program, he would wisely select respondents who do not know him as the designer of the program, since there would be a tendency for the respondents to avoid hurting his feelings by giving any negative impressions. If the information needed calls for representative respondents, this method of eliminating the etiquette barrier is not available. Instead, the *interviewer* must be carefully chosen to avoid selecting anyone who might be perceived by any of the respondents in the sample as having a vested interest in the program to be evaluated. In rare cases, the employees in the sample might fall into two or more distinct types requiring different types of interviewers to minimize the problem.

Often, the etiquette barrier is more effectively minimized if we are free to select the appropriate interviewer, rather than the respondent; but an administrator, or any authority, often finds himself in a position where some knowledge is better than none and must proceed to gather it himself. In such situations, we cannot warn too strongly against the effects of the etiquette barrier. If it is necessary to minimize the etiquette barrier by selecting the best respondent, the interviewer must be intimately acquainted with the norms governing what can be politely communicated from whom to whom. Lack of this knowledge results in serious miscalculations.

Often such knowledge is not possessed at the outset, in which case it becomes part of the strategy phase to discover the relative validity of information coming through certain channels. This can frequently be done in a small pilot study where two or more categories of respondents are asked for the same factual information. The frequency with which the two groups mention events tending to discredit or embarrass the interviewer can be compared. It is also possible to compare written comments from a group of anonymous individuals with oral statements made by the same group to the interviewer. This difference for one category of respondents could be compared with that of another category of respondents.

In general, if a respondent is not inhibited by the etiquette barrier which would usually apply, it is because of one of the following reasons:

a. He does not realize that the information he gives has a negative value in the eyes of the interviewer. Children are often immune to this type of inhibitor for this reason.

b. He might be so in accord with the interviewer's effort to obtain accurate information that he will be candid although being truthful may be painful.

c. He may have a desire to embarrass, belittle, or hurt the interviewer's ego and therefore welcomes the opportunity to elaborate upon all of the details which tend to threaten the interviewer. Although this might be a strain on the interviewer, it often has a cathartic effect, reducing the respondent's hostility toward the interviewer.

d. He may have a relationship with the interviewer which permits such information to flow freely on the particular topic as long as the interviewer's questions are considered genuine, rather than rhetorical, and sincere, rather than designed to obtain a compliment.

Trauma. The trauma barrier is not so rare in interviewing as we might think. Of course it is rarely found in the opinion poll on current public issues or in the practical surveys made in most communities. However, certain interviewers, because of the problems with which they deal, frequently encounter the trauma barrier: these would include the police investigator of homicides and suicides, the coroner who holds inquests, the insurance investigator, the case worker attached to the family relations court, the industrial safety investigator, the minister, the Red Cross disaster worker, and the social scientist investigating such problems as causes of auto accidents, causes of suicide, or adjustments to mental illness in the family.

Often, the problem cannot be circumvented by selecting respondents because the person with the most direct knowledge of the crisis also had the most traumatic experience. But there are occasions when the interviewer can select a respondent with no traumatic experience to supply the relevant information. A police investigator of auto accidents might needs facts such as the time of the accident or the number of passengers in the car which hit a child crossing the street while her mother watched from the curb. In this case, the investigator can choose between interviewing the mother or the two shopkeepers who were eye witnesses.

It should not be assumed that merely because a respondent has had a traumatic experience he will refuse to report it or will stint on detail. This has been shown untrue in interviews with families who have just lost children in a disaster. In these cases it seemed that the respondent's altruism and his needs for meaning, sympathetic understanding, and catharsis were stronger than the urge to repress the memory.

Who is most able to give the information?

Even though two people have the same experiences and are equally willing to report them, there may be a wide variation in the precision or efficiency of their reports. Having had the appropriate experiences does not guarantee the person's ability to report these experiences.

Forgetting. If the interview seeks information on events repeatedly experienced by many people, respondents who have experienced the event most recently can be selected in order to minimize the problem of stimulating the memory. Of course, if the event experienced is a rare one, we may need to wait for it to happen and be ready to interview people immediately while their feelings and images are fresh.

Assume we are studying the changes in family relationships resulting from the arrival of the first child. In an interview one year after the child's birth, it would be difficult to obtain an accurate and detailed picture of these subtle changes. It would be better to obtain from local hospitals a list of patients who have been discharged from the maternity ward long enough to have recovered physically, but who were still establishing their new family routine.

In addition to selecting respondents who have been most recently exposed to the experience, we can select those for whom the event was the most meaningful, problematical, ego-involved, or direct. For example, in studying childhood diseases of primary school children in the Puerto Rican district of New York, the information would be more accurately obtained from the mother than from the father, who feels strongly that raising babies is the mother's complete responsibility.

Chronological confusion. Since chronological confusion is partially a function of a fading memory, any method of selecting respondents which reduces the memory-fading process will also reduce the amount of chronological confusion. There are other safeguards in selecting respondents which can minimize chronological confusion.

First, we might cross-check chronological accuracy by selecting more than one person to give the same information. The two or more respondents selected should have participated in, or observed, the same situation. For some purposes, it may be more revealing to interview those whose observation or participation was completely independent of each other, and for other purposes, it is necessary to select people who interacted in the situation. In either case, the cross-checking of the respondents' stories will alert the interviewer to problems of chronological confusion. It is sometimes effective to have the two or more respondents discuss the event in a group interview. Whether the group interview should precede, follow, or replace individual interviews is decided in the specific setting.

Second, it may be possible to select a person whose role in the situation provides a special perspective for remembering details in chronological order. In an investigation of crowd reactions at an air show where a stunting airplane had crashed into the full grandstand, it was desirable to discover the precise chronology of events immediately preceding the crash. The one person capable of doing this was the master of ceremonies for the show. He was aware of the order in which events had originally been scheduled and the deviations from this order. Also, he could relate the informal, nonscheduled events to the scheduled events, thus establishing a complete chronology.

Inferential confusion. Any selection of respondents which reduces the fading of memory or chronological confusion is helpful in reducing distortion of the facts upon which inferences are to be based. This does not necessarily mean that the inferences made by the respondent will be logically correct.

Most of the solutions to inferential confusion lie in the areas of tactics and techniques; however, we may still reduce the interviewing problems by selecting the respondent who has the best understanding of the types of generalizations to be made, and has no strong prejudices on the topic to bias his logical processes.

Unconscious behavior. The reader will recall that we use "unconscious behavior" to refer only to actions that were automatic at the time they were performed rather than to memories of actions which, although accompanied by a high level of awareness when they were being performed, have been *repressed* into the unconscious because they would constitute a severe ego threat. This aspect of the unconscious has been subsumed under the inhibitor category of ego threat.

If the objective of the interview is to study some segment of human behavior which is experienced at a low level of consciousness, it is often impossible to obtain a valid account in retrospect, even though the behavior was very recent. For example, if we need to know which shoe a person put on first this morning, it is rare to find a person who is sure that his guess is correct later in the day.

It may be impossible to stimulate recall of certain behavior. A different approach is often more valid and practical. Instead of dealing with respondents' past behavior, we can select respondents who are about to undergo certain relevant experiences and will report them, or who can observe others carrying out the behavior in question.

The participant-respondent is asked to participate in the event or situation, observe his own behavior of which he is ordinarily unconscious, and then report it to the interviewer. This approach would be useful for describing such unconscious patterns of behavior as tying one's tie, doing a complicated dance routine, playing a musical instrument, or shaving with a safety razor.

When an observer-respondent is used, he is first given the problem and then sent to observe others' unconscious behavior. The best observer-respondent is one who is interested, unbiased, acute in his observations, and who has access to the situation in which people indulge in the type of unconscious behavior being studied. The observer-respondent is needed only if the interviewer himself does not have access to the situation.

This approach is particularly useful in cases where the act of self-observation might change the pattern of behavior being observed or where self-consciousness might completely invalidate the information.

It would be invalid to ask a mother to observe her own behavior toward her two-year-old son to note how frequently she attempts to avert undesirable behavior of the child by physically removing some object of his attention rather than by first using a verbal command, request, or distraction. The mother, consciously posing this question to herself and observing her own behavior toward the child, might recognize her reliance on the physical method which became a habit before the child learned to speak. In this situation using an older sister as observer-respondent would probably yield more accurate information.

Thus far the problem has been in choosing the respondent to minimize the inhibitors which make him less willing or able to supply relevant information. The respondent was selected with regard to his relationship to both the relevant experiences and to the interviewer. Here, it was assumed that the interviewer-respondent relationship could be manipulated only by the selection of the respondent. In the next section, the assumption will be that the respondent is predetermined. In this situation, the relationship can be manipulated only by selecting from among possible interviewers or by the interviewer selecting the most appropriate role from his repertory.

DISCUSSION QUESTIONS

1. Would the most thought have to be given to the selection of representative respondents for a public opinion poll or to the selection of special respondents for a large-scale community study? Why?

2. What are some of the most important social-psychological forces that tend to make a person *unwilling* to give relevant information but that might be reduced by careful selection of respondents?

3. What are some of the most important social-psychological forces that tend to make a person *unable* to give relevant information but that might be reduced by careful selection of respondents?

4. Give one example of information which one person would be *able* to give but another would not.

5. Give one example of information which one person would be *willing* to give but another would not, despite the fact that both are able to do so.

Laboratory problem 5

Selecting appropriate respondent

This problem requires creative imagination (empathy) in applying principles of communication to this important phase of field strategy. You should imagine interview situations in which one main inhibitor can be either maximized or minimized by the selection of a good type or bad type of respondent, assuming the same interviewer in both cases. You should concentrate on the relationship between the type of information needed, the type of interviewer used, and the type of respondent most likely and least likely to give the needed information.

Give *three* examples of interviews, using the following format for describing each of the three situations. Assume that both respondents have the needed information but one is more willing or able to give it.

- a. The specific *question* to be asked.
- b. The type of *interviewer* used.
- c. The type of respondent *most* likely to give the information.
- d. The type of respondent *least* likely to give the information.
- e. The main *inhibitor* of communication operating between the respondent mentioned under (*d*) and the interviewer.

Here is a sample of one example. Note that there is no need to elaborate with detail.

Example 1

a. *Question:* "What methods are used by building contractors to defraud the client?"

211

b. *Interviewer:* A newspaper reporter.
c. *Best respondent:* Clients who are suing contractors for failure to fulfill the specifications of the contract.
d. *Worst respondent:* Building contractors who have never been involved in any complaints from clients.
e. *Inhibitor:* Ego threat.

Be prepared to defend your example in a class discussion by explaining why you would expect the particular inhibitor to be most important and why you would expect a different respondent to minimize it.

10

Selecting appropriate interviewers

It is fruitful to think of two phases of interviewer selection. First, we look for the most appropriate person for some portion or all of the information-gathering in a particular project. Second, we select a particular person who, from among the possible roles, can play the ones most suitable for specific phases of the project. Let us first examine the process of selecting the person.

SELECTING THE PERSON

The field supervisor, the self-directed research team, and the individual researcher must all be concerned with selecting the most suitable person as interviewer. The field supervisor may find some of the suggestions useful for hiring interviewers for a special project, for selecting from among the continuing staff of interviewers the one best suited for a particular project, or for deciding which ones might be most easily trained for certain types of studies.

When a new interviewing team is being organized, it is important that they be selected for their information-gathering potential. When a study calls for contacting a wide variety of special respondents, it is often more effective to allow each member of the team to specialize in one or two types of special respondents with whom he has the most effective relationship.

The criteria suggested below are useful to sensitize the interviewer to some of his immutable characteristics such as sex, race, and physique, which limit the possible role relationships in his repertory. This in turn restricts types of studies he personally should undertake and suggests the need for collaborators on certain aspects of information gathering.

Some of the suggested criteria will point to areas in which the interviewer must prepare himself before contacting the respondent. Specific knowledge of the interview topic or of the type of respondent and situation in which the respondent is to be contacted fall into this category. In addition, criteria such as the role repertory, attitudes, and situational skills will suggest a long-range program of personal development for the serious student of human behavior.

For this discussion, it will be assumed that skill in interviewing is possessed by all interviewers. Not all possible personal characteristics are considered relevant to selecting interviewers. The criteria will be limited to those having a *direct* bearing upon the problem of maximizing the flow of relevant information between respondent and interviewer. These criteria will be grouped under four headings: overt characteristics, basic personality traits, attitudes, and knowledge. These areas are all interrelated and are significant in that they affect the role repertory as it relates to the interviewing task.

It should be noted that the selection of an appropriate interviewer does not affect as many of the inhibitors as does the selection of an appropriate respondent. This is true because selection of the appropriate interviewer does not affect the respondent's *ability* to give the information, but only his *willingness*. Although there are four inhibitors (competing obligations, ego threat, etiquette, and trauma) which generally reduce the willingness to give information, only two of these, ego threat and etiquette, are clearly influenced by the choice of an interviewer. In addition, it is possible to maximize three of the facilitators of communication (recognition, sympathetic understanding and new experience) by choice of interviewer, quite independent of skill in interviewing techniques and tactics.

It is not enough to accurately assess the qualities of an interviewer; it is also necessary to know how these characteristics will be perceived and evaluated by the potential respondent. During the strategy phase, and within each subsequent interview, we should be alert for clues to the respondent's perceptions of the interviewer. It is often possible for the interviewer to make tactical corrections within an interview which will clarify his role or to correct misperceptions. If not, it is frequently possible to change the strategy of the approach toward future respondents or more effectively match interviewers with respondents.

It should be noted that the relative importance of the interviewer's overt physical characteristics is greater in single-contact than in multiple-contact field situations. These overt characteristics are also more significant in the scheduled than in the nonscheduled interview. The less structured the schedule, the more freedom the interviewer has in expressing basic personality traits.

In discussing the effects of certain characteristics of the interviewer on the flow of relevant information, we are using a shorthand expression for "probable effects in general" or "effects possible under certain conditions," or "tendencies which may or may not be counteracted by certain tactical and technical skills." We must assume intelligent and empathic use of these suggestions which, in specific situations, are to be treated as hypotheses checked by feedback from key informants, by observation of the respondent, and by analysis of the interview results.

Overt characteristics of the interviewer

Such characteristics as sex, age,[1] race,[2] ethnicity, social class,[3] manner of dress, and speech are important. Not only do they create an immediate impression and help determine whether or not the respondent will consent to be interviewed, but they also place certain limits upon the roles which the interviewer may successfully occupy. Many studies on interviewer bias have shown differences in the results when the interviewers vary in these overt characteristics. One of the most systematic studies has been done by Hyman and his associates at the National Opinion Research Center.[4]

In reading and evaluating the many studies done on interviewer bias, we often find apparently contradictory results. Often this is because there is no guiding theory to relate type of interviewer and type of respondent with the type of information to be obtained. Often, studies try to determine the effect, for example, of a "white collar" interviewer versus a "blue collar" interviewer in a random sample survey. The results are likely to be ambiguous since the random sample is composed of both "white" and "blue collar" respondents. Even if the effects were separated according to type of respondent, the effect would be different depending upon whether the topic of the interview were attitudes toward labor unions or preferences for types of shaving cream.

Here, we will try to show how the overt characteristics are meaningful only insofar as they affect the relationship between the interviewer and respondent, which in turn affects the potential barriers to communication.

---

[1] Mark Benney, David Riesman, and Shirley Star, "Age and Sex in the Interview," *American Journal of Sociology*, vol. 62 (September 1956), pp. 143–52.

[2] Aaron Bindman, "Interviewing in the Search for Truth," *Social Quarterly*, vol. 6, no. 3 (Summer 1965), pp. 281–88. This deals with the effects of using Negro versus white interviewers.

[3] Daniel Katz, "Do Interviewers Bias Poll Results?" *Public Opinion Quarterly*, vol. 6 (Summer 1942), pp. 248–68. This classic study compares the results of using "white collar" and working-class interviewers to obtain opinions on war and labor issues.

[4] Herbert Hyman et al., *Interviewing in Social Research* (Chicago: University of Chicago Press, 1954).

Sex. Selecting an interviewer of the proper sex can sometimes reduce the etiquette barrier. For example, male market research interviewers can obtain more spontaneous information about men's shaving habits than female interviewers. Likewise, female interviewers are more successful in obtaining information on feminine hygiene from women. The use of a female interviewer for a market research survey on shaving methods and materials would not be as serious a strategy error as using male interviewers on the feminine hygiene study.

The sex of the interviewer may also operate to increase the facilitators of communication. It would appeal much more to the need for *new experience* to use a male interviewer with respondents in a women's prison or to have an attractive Wac interview soldiers in an isolated garrison post, or to send a male interviewer to an electronics plant where 90 percent of the workers and supervisors are women.

Also, the sex of the interviewer may determine the extent to which the respondent will perceive him as a person capable of giving *sympathetic understanding* to certain problems covered by the interview. A female interviewer would probably be more welcome in interviewing mothers regarding the problems of the housewife. A male interviewer would probably be perceived as more sympathetic in an interview with crane operators about their grievances.

In some cases, the use of a male interviewer appeals to the respondent's need for *recognition.* This was found in several interviews when male respondents expressed surprise that the interviewer was a man instead of a woman as they had expected. They made such comments as, "This must be an important study if they are sending out men to do the job." In this case, a woman, regardless of her qualifications, would have had a disadvantage. Further conversation indicated that the respondent had stereotyped women interviewers as "housewives with a gift of gab, a big curiosity, and time for a part-time job."

In some cases, the sex of the interviewer is important not so much because of the effect it will have upon communication in the interview as upon the probability of even starting the interview. In single-contact interview studies in metropolitan areas, one of the large problems is gaining entrance to the home. For example, it is not rare for the male interviewer in an urban poverty area to notice someone peeking out the window as he comes up the sidewalk; then the radio is silenced and no one answers his knock. This may be because the occupants of the house think he is a bill collector, a truant officer, parole officer, or a salesman. Sometimes in areas which have had recent violent disturbances, whether man-made riots or natural disasters of some type, a male interviewer is mistaken for a newspaper reporter. All of these mistaken identities of the male interviewer usually present problems.

Female interviewers shoud not be used in areas with a high crime rate, particularly at night when male interviewers are most likely to be available. Even though statistics show that most of the major crimes of violence are committed against family members, there is still a greater chance that a woman who is obviously an outsider in the neighborhood will be robbed or harmed in some way. Perhaps most important is the effect of this possibility upon the morale and performance of the female interviewer.

There are rare studies which might require a female interviewer to gain rapport with respondents in this type of area. There are several possible ways to avoid problems under these circumstances. For example, interviewing might be done only during certain hours of the day, interviewers might be sent out in pairs, respondents might be interviewed in another place (perhaps where they work), or having indigenous sponsors vouch for the interviewer might improve safety.

Age. The main social significance of a person's age is that it limits the roles which he can assume and the status he has vis-à-vis another person. In general, an older person has higher status than a younger person when other visible signs are equal and when neither knows the other's function in society. The effects of status difference on communication will be discussed when we focus on the status dimension of the relationship.

Since age offers both possibilities and limits to the role repertory, the individual investigator may examine a typical life cycle of a person of the same sex in his culture and realize that at one time in his life he will be a better interviewer on one set of topics, at another time he will excel on another. A high school student doing a study of family relations might find the etiquette barrier arising in the interview with parents regarding child-rearing problems. Yet the same high school student, with minimal skills in interviewing, could do an excellent job of interviewing students about "problem parents."

Often, it may be necessary to interview people in a very different age bracket because there are few interviewers among the age group being studied and the interest in the specific problem is not widely shared. The interviewer, by skillful tactics and techniques, can often overcome this initial disadvantage. For example, Krause[5] found that as a graduate student, when she interviewed people over 60 years of age on problems of personal adjustment in old age, she had to exercise care to avoid conveying the feeling of superiority because of her higher education. She learned to show by every word and gesture that she appreciated the wisdom they had gained with experience. They were quick to appreciate her sincere respect which they felt was rare in the

---

[5] Luise Krause, "Problems of Interviewing Older People," in M.A. thesis, "Personal Adjustment in Old Age," (Department of Sociology, University of Chicago, 1950).

younger generation. In effect, she had to escape the stereotype of university student and become a personal disciple of the respondent.

Race or ethnicity. Whether or not an interviewer who appears to be of a certain race or ethnic group is an appropriate interviewer depends upon the respondent's perception and evaluation of that group and the role he feels appropriate for the interviewer to assume. Since this affects the status relationship between the interviewer and respondent, there is the possibility of the barriers of ego threat and etiquette inhibiting the flow of certain types of information.

For example, it might be a distinct advantage to be a black in studying nationalistic attitudes of Africans or attitudes of Indian students toward racial discrimination in the United States. On the other hand, in an industrial relations study, a white field worker might find it very difficult to obtain spontaneous information from black workers even after spending months in the plant.[6]

Racial differences between interviewer and respondent not only affect the respondent's attitude toward the interview but also the interviewer's attitudes and stereotypes of the respondent. If the respondent is a member of the minority race, he is quick to sense the stereotyping by the interviewer. He may resent it, conform to it, or both; but in any case, it will affect the flow of information.

There is the additional communication problem caused by differences in the universe of discourse. Racial or ethnic group cultures are quite distinct in some ways from the middle-class white cultures, and this difference impedes communication.

The effect of race of the interviewer and respondent depends, of course, upon the meaning of those particular racial differences within the culture in which the interview is taking place. The problem would be quite different in Hawaii, Brazil, and Arkansas. Only insofar as race is a symbol of role and status will it affect the flow of information in the interview. Whether this effect is positive or negative depends upon the meaning of race, in general, and its significance to the topic of the interview.

An example of clear experimental effects of the race of the interviewer is shown in two studies by Athey[7] in which the white respondents scaled down their expressions regarding nonwhites for both the black and Oriental interviewers in comparison with their remarks to white interviewers.

One of the symptoms of the effect of the interviewer's race is in the

---

[6] Robert K. Bain, "The Researcher's Role: A Case Study," *Human Organization,* vol. 9 (Spring 1950), pp. 23–28.

[7] K. R. Athey, J. E. Coleman, A. P. Reitman, and J. Tang, "Two Experiments Showing the Effect of the Interviewer's Racial Background on Responses to Questionnaires Concerning Racial Issues," *Journal of Applied Psychology* (Spring 1960), pp. 244–46.

respondent's reluctance to elaborate his responses with spontaneous detail. For example, Ledvinka[8] did an experiment in which 75 black job-seekers were each interviewed by a white and a black interviewer in the natural course of his contact with the employment service. On each of six different measures of language elaboration, the respondents elaborated more on their answers to the black interviewers. In a different cultural setting, Alers[9] found that Indian respondents had a poor reaction to the *mestizo* interviewers who came to their village. The basic attitude of the Indian was one of distrust.

We have already warned that no general statements can be made about what characteristics of the interviewer act as inhibitors of communication without also taking into consideration the *triadic* relationship between the interviewer, the respondent, and the topic of the interview in the context of the larger society. To illustrate, Schuman[10] showed that the effect of the race of the interviewer depended upon the particular questions being asked. His study using data from the Detroit Area Project showed that, when northern urban blacks were interviewed, questions dealing with militant protest and hostility to whites showed considerable sensitivity to interviewer effect; but the respondents' reports of racial discrimination, poor living conditions, and personal background showed little distortion due to the race of the interviewer. Similarly, an experiment done by Weller[11] used 3 white and 3 black interviewers to interview 28 black and 27 white respondents who were applicants for job training. All six interviewers were middle-class, college graduates, with the same rating on interviewing skills and with almost identical personality profiles as measured by the Minnesota Multi-phasix Personality Inventory test. On the questions about family relations white interviewers obtained more high quality responses from black respondents than did the black interviewers. However, the race of the interviewer made no difference in the quality of information obtained from the white respondents. Weller feels that this was because the black respondents felt more sure that the white interviewers would not use the information for gossip within the black community, while the white respondents could see no difference in the amount of anonymity afforded by a black versus a white interviewer.

Whether or not communication barriers can be overcome only by

[8] James Ledvinka, "Race of Employment Interviewer and the Language Elaboration of Black Job-Seekers" (Ph.D. dissertation, University of Michigan, 1969).

[9] J. Oscar Alers, "Interviewer Effects on Survey Responses in an Andean Estate," *International Journal of Comparative Sociology*, vol. 11 (1970), pp. 208–19.

[10] Howard Schuman and Jean Converse, "Effects of Black and White Interviewers on Black Responses in 1968," *Public Opinion Quarterly*, vol. 35 (1971), pp. 44–68.

[11] L. Weller and E. Luchterhand, "Interviewer-Respondent Interaction in Negro and White Family Life Research," *Human Organization*, vol. 27 (1968), pp. 50–55.

training interviewers better or by the selection of interviewers depends on the kind of information sought, and the kind of relationship which must be established between interviewer and respondent to obtain this information. In a review of the literature on the helping interview, Banks[12] concludes that more attention needs to be turned to training black interviewers to help blacks rather than doing more studies of the black respondent, hoping to learn how to overcome his distrust and resistance.

The problem of the effects of the race of the interviewer is much more complicated than often assumed by those doing oversimplified or underconceptualized studies of interviewer effects. For example, it should be clear at the outset that the effect of race depends upon the *meaning* which race has to the topic of the interview in the context of the larger society at a given moment in history. First, physical racial differences between interviewer and respondent must be translated into social-psychological relationships such as social distance, status differences, power differences, in-group–out-group relations, or anonymity. Then these relationships must be translated into potential inhibitors or facilitators of communication of a particular kind of information.

For example, a black respondent may feel free to air his complaints about discrimination to the white interviewer who is sponsored by a white mayor clearly interested in eliminating discrimination. The interview becomes a means to recognition or the extrinsic reward of removing discrimination. At a later time the black respondent may not elaborate on discrimination to the white interviewer who is not sponsored by a new black mayor.

The respondent's *definition of the situation* determines whether he would feel more free if the interviewer is like himself or different from himself, whether he prefers anonymity to avoid ego threat, or whether he wants publicity to obtain recognition. As a reflection of these complications Dohrenwend[13] found that under some circumstances there could be an inhibiting effect by either having too much or too little social distance between interviewer and respondent.

At the present state of knowledge of the effect of race on the inhibitors and facilitators of communication in the interview situation, we can only say that—for certain topics under certain conditions—racial differences between interviewer and respondent sometimes has a negative effect on information flow, sometimes it makes no difference, and per-

---

[12] G. P. Banks, "Effects of Race on One to One Helping Interviews," *Social Service Review*, vol. 45 (1971), pp. 137–46.

[13] Barbara S. Dohrenwend et al., "Social Distance and Interviewer Effects," *Public Opinion Quarterly*, vol. 32 (1968), pp. 410–22.

haps more rarely, sometimes it has a positive effect on the information flow. In the practical situation the decision must be made tentatively on the basis of translating what is known about the nature of the questions, the meaning of race in society at that time, and the respondent's probable definition of the situation. Often this tentative decision can be pretested in the field, using interviewers of different races, before going on with the larger study.

Speech. It is common knowledge that the vocabulary, accent, and diction of a speaker are glaring signs ethnicity, status, and role. As such, they affect the flow of information in the interview. In some cases, an accent is sufficient to nullify the effect of obvious racial characteristics. Identical black twins born in England and speaking with a crisp British accent would encounter different reactions in a southern railroad station if one freely demonstrated his accent and wore a turban while the other said nothing to betray his accent.

This is further demonstrated by the experience of a white graduate student studying at the University of Chicago who was doing his master's thesis on a black Muslim cult hostile to white Americans. Upon first contact with the group, the researcher was trying to locate their meeting place in the basement of a vacant building. There he was caught by surprise, frisked, and taken to their leader who explained that the "snooper" was fortunate to have a foreign accent or they would have dealt with him more harshly. Upon discovering that the student was from Baghdad and was a wrestler, they invited him to teach in their "college," which he did for a few months while writing his thesis on the development of the movement.[14]

Dress and grooming. These factors of appearance are symbolic of social status and role as well as of the subculture to which a person belongs. The more superficial the contact with the respondent and the stronger the solidarity of the respondent's "in-group," the more important the effect of dress and grooming. Part of the strategy phase of a field study must sometimes include getting information on the most appropriate way to dress. However, it is usually not possible, practical, or ethical to try to pass oneself off as a full-fledged member of the group being studied. Nor is this usually necessary, although it is often advisable to prevent the interviewer's being falsely perceived as an outsider in a threatening role.

For example, a person studying the activities of teenage gangs in a city's high delinquency area might give the impression that he is a detective by wearing black shoes. Or, if he carries a briefcase, he might be suspected of being a bill collector. Without trying to impersonate

---

[14] This account was given by Hatim Sahib, now returned to Baghdad, in a personal conversation with the author.

the members of the respondent's group, the interviewer must discover how to dress to prevent mistaken identity. In addition, it is possible to reduce the social distance between the interviewer and respondent by dressing more nearly like the respondent without trying to imitate him. A person studying the problems of controlling migrant children from farm areas in an urban neighborhood might do well to dress like the local graduates of the junior college rather than like an Ivy Leaguer.

Physical deviance. There are many settings requiring interviews with persons physically handicapped or otherwise deviant from the normal. Very little research has been done on the effects of using normal versus physically deviant interviewers. An experiment was done by Comer and Piliavin[15] in which handicapped men in wheelchairs and leg braces were interviewed by the same interviewer posing as handicapped (in wheelchair and leg brace) for half of the respondents and as his normal self in the other half of the interviews. The topic of the interview in this case was one which allowed for much elaboration and free-association by the respondent. The questions ranged from "Tell me about yourself," to "What do you think about the importance of sports, religion, money, women, etc., in a person's life?" In those cases where he appeared as his normal self, the interviews were terminated sooner, the respondent showed greater motor inhibitions, smiled less, had less eye contact with the interviewer, and admitted feeling less comfortable during the interview. Since the same interviewer was used none of the differences in response to him could be attributed to any of his personality traits.

To what extent can we generalize to other types of deviants? Should those who interview criminals be criminals? Should only homosexuals interview homosexuals? The general approach to the answer to these questions is the same as to those regarding the effect of race of the interviewer. We must judge each case on its own merits, but the specific facts of the situation must be ultimately translated into the same set of social-psychological variables we have mentioned earlier.

Basic personality traits of the interviewer

An excellent interviewer need not conform to the popular image of a pleasing personality. The sparkling personality is sometimes a valuable asset in making the initial contact or getting in the door, but the same qualities might interfere with communication by stealing attention from the respondent.

---

[15] Ronald J. Comer and Jane A. Piliavin, "The Effects of Physical Deviance upon Face-to-Face Interaction," *Journal of Personality and Social Psychology*, vol. 23 (1972), pp. 33–39.

Basic personality traits are relevant only insofar as they help or hinder the performance of the interview. Three important assets would include flexibility, intelligence, and emotional security. Flexibility allows the interviewer to assume a very active role when it is called for and to assume a more overtly passive role when this will facilitate communication. Intelligence permits the interviewer to clearly appreciate the objectives of the interview, to learn to evaluate critically the information he is receiving, to remember what information has been given, and to probe for greater clarity and completeness. Emotional security frees the interviewer from anxiety about himself and allows him to direct his full attention toward the tasks of maximizing the flow of information and maintaining optimal interpersonal relations.

The absence of flexibility severely limits the interviewer. Some personalities find it impossible to slow down the pace of an interview, allow relatively long silences, and permit the respondent to say what he wishes when he wishes. For this type of person, silence is intolerable; it is a vacuum which must be filled at any cost. He panics when the respondent does not immediately respond in an appropriate manner. This type of interviewer tends to dominate the situation in a way which threatens the respondent's ego. He does not build a permissive and thoughtful mood, and frequently, he unknowingly distorts the information by suggesting answers.

Some interviewers tend to be rigidly passive. This type of person does well as long as the task calls for letting the respondent take the lead, but he can be easily lured into irrelevant bypaths or sociable conversation when this is neither necessary nor desirable. He is reluctant to assume an active role by holding the respondent to the topic, to evaluate critically the information he receives, and to probe for completeness and clarification.

The importance of sufficient intelligence to the tasks of eliciting the information, evaluating it in terms of interview objectives, and probing for clarity and completeness is obvious. This does not imply that any intelligent person will carry out these tasks efficiently at the first attempt. Rather, he must have the basic ability to learn once the task is clear and he has the opportunity to practice.

The interviewer's emotional insecurity could have several detrimental manifestations in the interview. He may display a compulsive urge to dominate, and challenge remarks unnecessarily. In some cases, the challenging response is compulsive and unconscious. The insecure person is often so anxious about himself that (a) he fails to observe the respondent's emotional needs, (b) he communicates his own insecurity to the respondent rather than a positive expectation of cooperation, (c) he may be unable to empathize with the respondent at crucial points in the interview, (*d*) he cannot communicate warmth which leads the respondent to reach for sympathetic understanding and perhaps cathartic communication which might bring relevant information; and (*e*) he is incapable of giving sincere praise to the respondent for his efforts or his performance.

This is not to suggest that anyone having personal insecurities will always manifest them in these detrimental ways, nor does it necessarily indicate that any person who commits any of these errors is a hopeless victim of personal insecurity. As a neophyte interviewer, any conscientious person is likely to be doubtful, self-conscious, and anxious. An experienced interviewer may feel the same way about the first few interviews of a new study. Before one can devote full attention to the respondent's needs, he must take care of his own anxieties which arise in a new situation or with a new study.

Some people show these symptoms of insecurity only in certain types of interviews. Often, the distinguishing factor is the status relationship between the interviewer and the respondent. Some find it very easy to interview people of lower status, but if a respondent tends to assume an equalitarian relationship, the interviewer finds it intolerable. Some find that they cannot interview anyone who is not a peer, while others function most adequately in a subordinate role such as student or seeker of advice.

Ideally, the interviewer should have a flexible personality, free of defense mechanisms which limit his sensitivity to the respondent or his ability to shift roles as the situation requires. If the well-rounded interviewer cannot be found, we should at least recognize the limitations and avoid assignments which demand behavior of which a particular person is not capable.

Much personal insecurity can be controlled to suppress detrimental manifestations. The best prescription is to master some of the basic interviewing techniques, tactics, and skills and to prepare thoroughly for a particular interview by being completely familiar with its purpose, by planning some tentative alternative tactics, and practicing whatever recording techniques are to be used.

Attitudes of the interviewer

Since the positive attitudes intentionally displayed by the interviewer will be discussed later, this section will focus on only those uncontrollable negative attitudes which can be eliminated only by selecting the appropriate interviewer. These attitudes may be negative toward the type of respondent from whom the information must be obtained, toward the topic of the interview, or toward some particular information given by the respondent.

To speak of selecting an interviewer devoid of such negative attitudes does not imply that one must be completely free of such attitudes to be effective. Nor should it be said that training of the interviewer does not help overcome these attitudes, or at least teach how to avoid displaying them so that they affect the interview. Whether we depend upon selection or training depends upon the availability of interviewers, the time available for training, the strength of the negative attitudes, the delicacy of the interview topic, and the degree to which the interview is scheduled.

Here the intent is not to quantify these factors but to give some examples of their symptoms and the direction of their effects. Often a strong attitude toward a certain type of respondent is accompanied by strong stereotypes. The attitude may be toward certain religious, racial, occupational, ethnic, educational, or politicial groups. Leighton[16] found that some research workers in the Japanese relocation centers were unable to lose their stereotypes of Japanese even after living in the center for months. This stereotype acts as a barrier to communication, since it represents a form of insensitivity to individual differences which prevents the interviewer from adjusting his behavior to that of the respondent.

In training social scientists for field work in mental hospitals, high delinquency areas, and foreign cultures, the author has often found fear, suspicion, or a feeling of superiority toward the respondent. Even though these feelings may be controlled to the point of not being manifested to the respondent, nevertheless they may have an effect upon the interview.

The interviewer's attitude may be so strong that is perceived by the respondent and brings ego threat or etiquette into play, inhibiting the response. The attitude toward the respondent may cause the interviewer to use loaded questions in a way which biases responses.

Even if the interviewer suppresses all visible manifestations of his attitude so that it is not perceived by the respondent, there are three important ways in which his attitude still may minimize the flow of relevant information. (1) The interviewer's effort to control his negative attitude may succeed at the price of failing to manifest the positive attitudes of recognition, appreciation, sympathetic understanding, and the expectation of cooperation. Thus, some of the most important facilitators of communication are neglected. (2) The interviewer may attempt to exude a warmth which deceives the respondent, but still fails to empathize with him enough to probe points important to both the respondent and the objectives of the interview. (3) When the com-

---

[16] Alexander Leighton, *The Governing of Men* (Princeton, N.J.: Princeton University Press, 1945).

pletely structured interview prevents the interviewer from using loaded questions, when he is experienced enough to avoid letting his personal attitudes show in the interview, and when the respondent actually gives ample relevant information, there is still the possibility that the interviewer will bias the result in taking notes on the respondent's replies.

An excellent experimentally controlled study done by Fisher[17] shows that the interviewers with strong political attitudes did not accurately record the responses and that the direction of the error was consistent with the direction of the interviewer's political attitudes. This bias in the recording phase of the interview is most likely to occur when the interviewer is attempting to take verbatim notes on responses to broad questions and the respondent is speaking too rapidly to allow the interviewer to actually write everything.

The negative attitude toward the topic of the interview need not be in the form of taking sides in a controversial issue. Just as common is the apologetic attitude which seems to say, "I'm sorry to ask such questions. I'm not sure I have the right to expect you to answer them." This communicates the expectation of failure and may stimulate precisely the anticipated reaction. Such an apologetic attitude would have scuttled studies such as the Kinsey report[18] or Becker's studdy of marijuana users.[19]

Certain types of negative attitudes can be overcome even if they have not been eliminated by the careful selection of interviewers. It has been shown that often interviewers have certain negative expectations about the prospective respondents which are simply not true. It is possible during a short training and orientation period to reduce or eliminate these attitudes. This was shown experimentally by Kumar,[20] who told interviewers in advance whether the respondent was a friendly or a hostile type of person. The interviewers gave an account of each respondent after the interview. These accounts showed that respondents who had been described as hostile appeared to be more hostile than they were, and those described as friendly appeared more friendly than they actually were. This difference can be partly because the interviewer's expectations actually affect the respondent's behavior or affect the interviewer's selective recording or memory of the responses.

---

[17] Herbert Fisher, "Interviewer Bias in the Recording Operation," *International Journal of Opinion and Attitude Research*, vol. 4 (Spring 1950), p. 393.

[18] Alfred C. Kinsey et al., *Sexual Behavior in the Human Male*, chap. 2 (Philadelphia: W. B. Saunders Co., 1948).

[19] Howard S. Becker, "Becoming a Marijuana User," *American Journal of Sociology*, vol. 59 (July 1953 and May 1954).

[20] Usha Kumar, "Client and Counselor Responses to Prior Counseling Expectancies" (Ph.D. dissertation, Ohio State University, 1965).

Some effective ways to overcome an interviewer's false expectations of resistance are to have the interviewer hear tape-recorded interviews of the type he is going to do, talk with interviewers who have had a lot of experience in the type of interview, or have the trainee go with an experienced interviewer to listen and take notes. Depending on the topic, the last of these three ways may have some inhibiting effects.

Special knowledge possessed by the interviewer

Special knowledge refers to specialized information or skills needed by the interviewer in order to gain access to the situation where the respondent can be interviewed, to gain the respect of the respondent, or to understand the topic of the interview. This special knowledge often goes beyond any superficial knowledge or skills which can be gained by the interviewer for the occasion. For example, Howard Becker's study of the jazz musician would not be as thorough and insightful if Becker had not played in dance bands at the time.[21] Again, Hatim Sahib's study of the black Muslim sect was greatly facilitated by his knowledge of the Koran and of Arabic as well as by his skill in wrestling and his ability to teach Iraqi cooking.

Not only does special knowledge act as key to gathering information through sustained contact with the respondents, but it also is needed for certain types of single-contact interviews. For example, in a study of the performance of state police in a local crisis, the interviewer should have considerable knowledge of the usual function, organization, and jurisdiction of the police. To understand their accounts of their activities during the crisis, the interviewer should also be familiar with the local geography and relevant locations such as police headquarters, the radio transmitter, and the highway system.

Regardless of whether he has one or many contacts with the interviewer, the respondent often judges him not on the basis of his skill in interviewing, but on the basis of his knowledge and interest in those subjects in which the respondent is an expert. Where continued contact is needed in a participant-observer field study, the interviewer has an advantage if he can show competence in an area which is understood and respected by the community.

Sometimes it is practical for the interviewer to acquire the special knowledge needed for a specific assignment. At other times, the topic is so technical and complex that it would be more practical to select a person who is already a specialist in the area. For example, to discover some of the problems of coordinating a team of researchers, it would seem advisable to use a social scientist who has had previous experience

---

[21] Howard P. Becker, *The Professional Dance Musician in Chicago* (M.A. thesis, Department of Sociology, University of Chicago, 1949).

in team research. To discover some of the problems of the adjustment of American students in Latin America, the interviewer would need to be familiar with the Latin American culture and the Spanish language.

When doing a study of international organizations, Miles[22] wrote a research note intended for graduate students and others without previous field experience in studying international organizations. In giving suggestions about how to interview, he points out that one important factor is the interviewer's knowledge of the *organizational subculture.* International organizations develop a subculture which is not the same as any one of the nations represented. The knowledge of the organizational structure, the power hierarchy, the universe of discourse, all act as a cultural context needed to determine the meaning of what the researcher sees and hears.

Special knowledge, then, helps the interviewer gain access to the respondent *in situ,* helps him understand the respondent who refers to local detailed information, provides him with the universe of discourse needed, and gives the respondent respect for and confidence in the interviewer. If the interviewer shows that he has not bothered to familiarize himself with needed special knowledge, it may be difficult to persuade the respondent to devote serious time and effort to the project.

When interviewing special respondents, especially those in high status, the interviewer will do well to obtain some advance information on the respondent's personality, life history, and position, particularly as they relate to the topic of the interview.

SELECTING THE APPROPRIATE INTERVIEWER ROLE

Role is probably the most important characteristic of the interviewer. All other characteristics (such as sex, age, race, speech pattern, basic personality traits, knowledge, and attitudes) gain some portion of their significance from the fact that they all create opportunities or limitations for the role behavior of the interviewer.

The nature of role-taking

Selecting the proper role for the interviewer to assume might involve selecting the appropriate interviewer, or the interviewer might need to select from among his role repertory the one or ones most appropriate for the task at hand. Role-taking is distinct from role-play-

---

[22] E. Miles, "The Logistics of Interviewing in International Organizations," *International Organization,* vol. 24 (1970), pp. 361–70.

ing. The former refers to selecting from among a person's actual roles those which are most appropriate to display under the circumstances; the latter refers to taking a role which the person has never assumed in real life or which he is assuming in an artificial situation. Role-playing is done in psychodramas, sociodramas, and ordinary dramatic productions and games. Role-taking is done in everyday life, usually quite unconsciously. The minister in the pulpit does not usually choose to behave in the role of a father or a husband. Within his minister role he may choose to display certain aspects or to withhold them; he may act as a Christian, as a Protestant, as a mentor, or as a chastiser.

Role-taking should not be confused with an unethical form of deceptive play acting, a childish game of cops and robbers, or a romantic cloak-and-dagger operation. In interviewing, role-taking[23] is, a conscious selection, from among the one's actual role repertory, of the role thought most appropriate to display to a particular respondent at the moment. Most of us have no occasion to take an inventory of the roles we play, but if we do so, the number is usually much larger than expected. A man scanning his own experience could find that he has had the following roles from time to time: child, sibling, husband, parent, neighbor, social scientist, consultant, taxpayer, consumer, voter, teacher, student, client, patient, card player, employee, employer, tourist, foreigner, native American, adviser, committee member, writer, musician, photographer, swimmer, subscriber, contributor, translator, insuree, driver, bicyclist, pedestrian, or cook.

Functions of the auxiliary role

All of these roles constitute the role repertory from which one or more may be selected as auxiliaries to the principal role of interviewer. For example, the Fund for the Republic sponsored a study of the state of academic freedom on the campuses of American colleges. Of the sample of 180 colleges, 20 had refused to allow interviewers on campus to interview the social science faculty. One interviewer was assigned to visit some of the 20 reluctant colleges to try to convince the president to change his mind and to interview faculty members and students to discover what, if anything, the college was hiding. Which of his many roles should the interviewer display to which respondents on the college campus? He could, in honesty, present himself as "a representative of the Fund for the Republic," "a consultant hired by Elmo Roper Associates," "a college professor interested in theoretical problems of social conflict," "a sociologist," "a grandson of a Presbyterian minister,"

---

[23] It should be noted that in discussing the role repertory of the interviewer we are concerned with auxiliary roles peripheral to the *central* interviewer role.

"a specialist in interviewing methods"—these roles and many others would be equally true.

Actually, many of these selections from the role repertory proved valuable at certain times with certain respondents. In contacting a sociology professor, it was helpful for the interviewer to mention that he, too, was a sociology professor working as a consultant for the Fund for the Republic. In dealing with the President at one college, it proved an asset for the interviewer to be the grandson of a Presbyterian minister, since the President was a Presbyterian minister himself. In no case did it seem advisable to be presented as "a specialist in interviewing methods," since this would probably cause some ego threat. Even the role of bicyclist was useful in breaking the ice with one professor when the interviewer commented that he, too, rode a bicycle to work if the weather permitted.

The respondent often wants to know "What kind of person is this who is asking the questions?" In a study of family relations, the respondent is relieved to know that the interviewer is not a bachelor but married and the father of two children. Even though this does not necessarily qualify the interviewer to understand the particular respondent's problems, that respondent is less inhibited by the etiquette barrier than if he perceived the interviewer as a bachelor.

A field situation may require the interviewer to actually *function* in an auxiliary role for the duration of the study, rather than merely presenting himself as a person who has a role other than interviewer. The interviewer may choose to function in an auxiliary role in order to gain access to respondents in a certain situation. For example, a researcher studying the professionalization process in a group of occupational therapists might work with several occupational therapists in the hospital in order to discuss their work *in situ.* Or instead of interviewing the "OT" as she works in the hospital, he might have formal interview sessions after working hours in the respondent's home. In the latter case, the interviewer's work in the hospital one or two days per week would have several useful functions. It would acquaint him with the universe of discourse of the hospital setting, clarifying communication in the interview. Furthermore, the interviewer would be more capable of sympathetic understanding. The etiquette barrier would be reduced, since the interviewer now would be considered more of an equal, and this greater equality would usually reduce the ego threat. Also, if the interviewer carefully arranged his working hours so that he actually reduced someone's work load, this might be an effective extrinsic reward to the respondents or their supervisors and make the interviewer's continued presence more welcome.

In general, when taking an auxiliary role, it is advisable to make it clear from the beginning that the main purpose is to study the situation and that the auxiliary role is a way of gaining a more intimate and sympathetic view. Often the key informants in a closed community and prospective respondents are favorably impressed by the interviewer who will take the assignment seriously enough to get his hands dirty in the situation. This is something perceived as a form of recognition and often reduces the respondent's defenses against an "ivory-tower" approach to his problems.

Interviewers have taken jobs as factory workers, custodians, life-guards, hospital orderlies, psychiatric aides, dance band musicians, tax-icab drivers, and have even posed as mental patients or criminals to gain an inside view.

Dimensions of role relationships

Rather than attempting to show the relative values of an almost endless list of specific roles to be taken by interviewers, it is more useful to deal with two salient dimensions of role relationships. The signifi-cance of the interviewer's central role as interviewer and his auxiliary roles lies in the *relationship* generated with the respondent. Two of the most important dimensions of the relationship may be conceived of as the horizontal, or in-group–out-group, relationship and the vertical, or subordinate-superordinate, dimension.

The effect of the interviewer's presenting himself as a physician cannot be predicted unless we know whether the respondent is, for example, another physician or a nurse. The difference is these two pairs can be expressed in terms of relative status. The physician-physician relationship is one of equality. The physician-nurse relationship is one in which the physician is superordinate. To view these same relation-ships in the in-group–out-group dimension would require additional information. For example, the physician-physician pair would be fur-thest toward the in-group end of the continuum if both were members of the American Medical Association, lived in the same town, and con-stituted a clinical team. They would tend to view each other as outsid-ers, however, if one were a physician from the Soviet Union wanting to practice in the United States, or if one had lost his license through malpractice.

In many instances, it may appear that two people have an in-group relationship *because* they are of equal status. Upper-class people may welcome other upper-class people into their homes, but will erect barri-ers to keep lower status people at a distance. On the other hand, there are instances where two people have an out-group relationship because they are of equal status. This is often true in competitive situations where there is conflict between equals. If the chief body designer for X Motor Company were sent to interview the chief body designer of

Y Motor Company, the interviewer would be treated politely perhaps, but would be suspected of spying.

These two basic dimensions of role relationships can either inhibit or facilitate the flow of various types of information.

In-group–out-group relationships. There are advantages and disadvantages to either type of relationship. Which is more desirable depends upon the type of information needed. In some cases, we need information from both vantage points and must use two interviewers to obtain complete results. Since the outsider role is often the easiest for the interviewer to attain, it is valuable to begin by indicating some of its advantages.

Advantages of the outsider role. The outsider has the advantage when he is seeking information on violations of the in-group code. Here, the outsider, not bound by these codes and with no power or desire to enforce them upon the respondent, has an advantage over the insider. The interviewer is not an ego threat to the respondent. Thus, a criminal would more willingly admit to a sociologist than to a member of the underworld that he once squealed on a partner to reduce his own sentence. In another situation, members of a teenage gang admitted to an interviewer that they had never been to a prostitute, but this fact was never admitted to the other members of the gang who would have considered it a sign of inferiority.

This tendency to make one's verbal behavior conform to the perception of the group norms has been experimentally demonstrated in several settings. For example, the writer[24] demonstrated that when the interviewer asked members of a group for their opinions on the Soviet Union, they tended to compromise their private attitudes to conform with what they perceived to be the group norms with respect to the Soviet Union.

Another general circumstance in which the outsider has the advantage is in obtaining information on methods of manipulative control used by those in power to keep subordinates in line. Anthropologists have found that adults of one tribe will give totemic secrets to neighboring tribes, but not to their own children.[25] Similarly, it was found that ministers gave information on how they manipulated their congregations by interpreting and re-interpreting scripture, yet they vehemently denied any such purposive manipulation in a men's club discussion of the minister's role in the church. To give such information to the in-group in which he has status would constitute an ego threat to the minister.

---

[24] Raymond L. Gorden, "Interaction Between Attitude and the Definition of the Situation in the Expression of Opinion," *American Sociological Review,* vol. 17, no. 1 (Spring 1952), pp. 50–58.

[25] Marcel Griaule, "l'enquette Orale en Ethologie," *Revue Philosophique de la France,* vol. 142 (October 1952), pp. 537–53.

The outsider again has the advantage over an insider when the group is looking outward for some type of assistance. This is often experienced by social workers. The outsider in this case has some potential extrinsic reward to offer.

Often, the outsider does not have the disadvantage of facing the etiquette barrier which exists between certain in-group members. For example, a sociologist whom the respondents have never seen before can obtain detailed information of the premarital sex lives of a husband and wife which they have never discussed with one another because it was considered bad taste.

Another valuable function of the outsider role is to evaluate the effectiveness of social-psychological experiments requiring the manipulation or control of the subjects' definition of the situation. The experimenter often tries to set up the experiment to control the participants' perception of the purpose of the experiment, but he does not always know when he has succeeded. Altemeyer[26] tested the relative value of having the experimenter or an outsider interview to find out. He set up the experiment making it obvious that the respondents were not supposed to know the purpose of the experiment. One of the researchers then "leaked" information about the "real purpose." The experimenter and an outsider both did post-experiment interviews. None of the subjects interviewed by the experimenter admitted that they had been given information about the purpose of the experiment, while 50 percent of those interviewed by an outsider admitted that they had been given information. This illustrates the general principle that giving certain types of information to an insider may constitute more of an ego threat or etiquette barrier than giving it to someone from outside.

The outsider may also have a certain advantage in that the respondent's need for new experience can be fulfilled by talking to an outsider. Anthropologists, sociologists, public opinion pollers, and social workers all have moments when they feel that the respondent is more curious about them than they are about the respondent. The respondent may waver between excited curiosity and apprehension. When a later maturity study was done in a deteriorating apartment-house area of Chicago, a charming old lady of 80 years shyly admitted to the interviewer, "I saw you talking to Mrs. Podolsky and I was curious about what you were talking about, but I don't think I would have let you in if you weren't talking to a friend of mine."

Often a respondent will perceive the interview as means of getting recognition. He may not be appreciated in his home, at the office, or in his community. Or it may be that he has already told all his friends,

---

[26] Robert Altemeyer, "Pool Polutions and the Post Experimental Interview," *Journal of Experimental Research in Personality,* vol. 5 (1971), pp. 79–84.

neighbors, and co-workers about certain highlights of his life. In this case, if the interviewer is interested in obtaining a life history the respondent will welcome the chance to have the complete attention of another human being. Such an opportunity to talk about oneself is rare indeed. An insider who already knows certain public facts and perhaps more intimate aspects of the respondent's life has little reason to ask him to "begin at the beginning and tell me everything you feel is significant in your life."

In some circumstances, a strong in-group feeling is developed in a group of people who have suffered together some catastrophe, hardship, or persecution. This common experience is the badge of membership for the in-group. In this case, there is no possibility of an outsider's becoming a full-fledged member of the group unless he too has shared the same experience. If the interviewer has not had the experience, it is sometimes harmful to rapport if he pretends to appreciate the respondent's experience. In this case, the interviewer's approach should be as a sympathetic outsider.

For example, in interviews with respondents who had experienced a community-wide disaster, resentment could be detected in the respondent's manner if the interviewer pretended to fully appreciate the horrors of the experience. It proved a better tactic if the interviewer admitted that he was an outsider striving to catch a glimpse of what it was like to live through a devastating tornado. When a respondent told her listener, "You have no idea how horrible it was. The only way to know is to go through it yourself," the interviewer's best response was that of a sincere and concerned outsider, shown in his reply, "Yes, I've never been through anything like that in my life. I'm sure I can't begin to really grasp what it was like. I can only hope to learn through someone who has lived through such an experience. What would you say kept you going through all this?"

In this kind of situation the interviewer who takes the humble approach has a distinct advantage over the insider, because those who have shared the experience feel little reason to talk about their misfortunes to someone who has been equally unfortunate. The respondent seems to feel that he has more of a right to demand sympathy from the outsider.

In some instances, respondents of an in-group welcome the outsider, hoping that he can fulfill their need for meaning by raising meaningful questions, by clarifying confusion, by settling a controversy, or by sharpening the issue. The outsider is more trusted than the insider, who is suspected of taking sides if the group has been polarized, or who is considered too close to the problem to have the required perspective.

Even in situations where the respondents belong to a closely knit in-group, suspicious toward all outsiders, there are still certain kinds of information which can be obtained by the outsider. He may discover the official line given to the outsider, the extent to which the group is interested in recruiting or proselytizing others, and the in-group's fears and stereotypes of the outside world.

Advantages of the insider role. With all the advantages of the outsider role, there are still many situations when the insider has a distinct advantage. Most of these advantages revolve around situations where the outsider is perceived as an ego threat, where communication with an outsider is restricted by etiquette, or where he is perceived as a person incapable of sympathetic understanding. In some instances, even though the respondent is able and willing to give the relevant information, an outsider is unable to use the jargon fluently enough or is ignorant of the local facts needed to understand what he is told. This last possibility has already been discussed, so let us examine more closely those situations in which communication with the insider involves less ego threat, fewer etiquette restrictions, and a greater satisfaction of the need for sympathetic understanding.

An outsider may constitute an ego threat to the respondent guilty of violations of public norms (laws and mores), who is afraid that such information might be used to damage his reputation. Thus, a person studying social organization in a slum would not have access to much information on underworld activities until he had achieved the status of insider. This might be called a form of in-group defensive secrecy. Thus, Whyte[27] spent months becoming accepted as a friend by the "corner boys" in an Italian-American slum section of a large city before he began to obtain information on certain organized crime activities in the area.

Similarly, studies[28] of Japanese-Americans interned in relocation centers during World War II recorded the difficulties interviewers had becoming accepted as "friends." Some Caucasian researchers never achieved this status. Others succeeded within four or five months. Even the Nisei members of the research team had difficulty avoiding being perceived as "informers" by the camp members although none of the information they received was ever given to the government. Much of the relevant information could not be elicited until the insider role was established.

Another type of information withheld from outsiders might be called trade secrets. These are not withheld for being distasteful, immoral, or illegal, but because they give the possessor advantages in the competi-

---

[27] William F. Whyte, *Street Corner Society: The Social Structure of an Italian Slum* (Chicago: University of Chicago Press, 1943).

[28] Dorothy S. Thomas and R. S. Nishimoto, *The Spoilage* (Berkeley: University of California Press, 1946).

tive struggle. This information must not fall into the hands of a competitor. If the interviewer were perceived as a person who could not conceivably pass on the information to a competitor, the respondent would be less reluctant.

Another disadvantage to the outsider role lies in the etiquette barrier. Even though no ego threat is involved in the outsider's presence, there may be a tendency to treat him as a guest or a "visiting fireman," and the respondent tends to put on his company manners.

Finally, the interviewer from the outside is perceived as a person unlikely to sympathize with the in-group's problems and who has no real interest in the respondents except for what they offer the study. There is a feeling that there is nothing in common upon which to build rapport. Students studying some of the social-psychological aspects of the church meetings in store-front churches report this "feeling of emptiness" between themselves and their respondents. In this case, the respondent correctly senses the lack of any sympathetic understanding on the part of the middle-class college student. Although an interview can be conducted under such conditions, little information on the more subtle feelings, aspirations, and beliefs of the respondent can be obtained, because the answers are not motivated by a desire to share experiences with a sympathetic person. Therefore, responses tend to be short, unspontaneous, and not always relevant.

Establishing the insider role. In spite of the advantages of the outsider role, there are purposes for which the interviewer must have an insider role. How is this role established? There is no simple formula for attaining it with respect to an individual or group, but there are general ways to approach the problem.

The first general way to be accepted as an insider is to participate in the group, institution, or community being studied. The intimacy of the interaction demanded depends upon the nature of the information sought. If the group is very closely knit, the intimacy of participation needed before one is considered "in" is very great. For example, to become an insider in a religious sect actively opposed to existing religious institutions requires more intimate association and active participation than being an insider in a conventional denomination. Joseph Zygmunt[29] found in studying the Jehovah's Witnesses that faithful attendance and participation in the weekly meetings was not enough. He had to spend additional time "witnessing" on street corners and distributing the literature where there was opposition before he was considered really sympathetic.

---

[29] Joseph F. Zygmunt, "The Role and Interrelationship of Symbolic and Structural Processes in the Development of a Sectarian Movement" (Ph.D. dissertation, University of Chicago, 1960).

Religious groups differ not only in their degree of hostility toward the "outside" world but also in the degree to which they are interested in recruiting new members. For example, the Jehovah's Witnesses are both hostile toward conventional religion and actively proselyting for new members. The black Muslim sect mentioned previously is hostile to the white Christian world, but is not interested in trying to convert the enemy. Not hostile to the outside world, the Bruderhoff communities in the United States and England want to explore a new communal way of life and welcome the outsider as long as he participates in their work. The Hutterite communities in the United States and Canada are not at war with the larger world, do not seek recruits, but are withdrawn and generally want to be left alone.

When groups practicing protective secrecy are suspicious of outsiders trying to gain entrance, it is often necessary for the field worker to enter in a subordinate role or not at all. One convenient subordinate role is that of student. By showing a sincere desire to learn from the members of the group something in which they excel and something which distinguishes them, the interviewer can reduce hostility and suspicion by reducing ego threat.

The language of the group can often be learned to gain rapport. This was found true by Whyte in his study of "Cornerville," where he found that learning Italian helped to gain the group's trust. Thomas and Nishimoto also reported that in their study in Japanese relocation centers, the Caucasian interviewers found it useful to learn Japanese, even though they did not become fluent enough to use it in interviews.

This role of student can be adapted to a variety of situations. Bain found that in interviewing workers in industry, the role of student could take the form of asking the respondent to explain his job and the equipment. In interviewing senior citizens, Krause, as a person sensitive to problems of interpersonal relations, found it quite natural to assume the role of a youth seeking insights and perspectives possessed only by her elders.

In addition to the approach of becoming an insider through direct participation, it is often possible to be perceived as an insider through an indirect method of being sponsored or recommended by some trusted person. The degree to which this entrance by sponsorship is successful depends upon how hostile, how closed, and how locally autonomous the group is, and the nature of the information sought. These problems of sponsorship will be dealt with later in this chapter.

Subordinate-superordinate relations. Any two persons having functionally related roles, directly interacting with each other, can be located on a continuum showing that one is superordinate, equal, or subordinate to the other.

In the following pairs having a reciprocal relationship, it can be seen that in each pair there are superordinate-subordinate roles: captor-captive, master-slave, captain-lieutenant, manager-worker, physician-patient, teacher-student. Note that the first three might be called power relations, since they are based upon the use or the threat of force. Even though the subordinate in each case might like to escape his role, he would be forcefully restrained from doing so. The second three might be called dependency relationships. Although the subordinate in each case may break off the relationship he usually endures the subordinate role because it is more beneficial than breaking it off. This attribute alone is not enough to determine the existence of the superordinate-subordinate relationship; it would be possible to have a mutually beneficial relationship where both would suffer equal injury if it were broken. Therefore, to be an unequal relationship, termination must clearly be more injurious to the subordinate.

For the purposes of interviewing, we are interested in this dimension of the interviewer-respondent relationship only insofar as it inhibits or facilitates the flow of relevant information. It is not always clear when the interviewer is in a superordinate, equal, or subordinate role. The reality of the relationship depends not only upon the respondent's perception of the interviewer and upon the interviewer's perception of the respondent, but also upon the degree to which these two perceptions agree.

Upon initial contact between interviewer and respondent, there may be mutually agreeable or clashing perceptions of each other. This relationship develops and fluctuates as they size each other up. For this reason status relations may develop clarity or even reverse directions in the progress of a single interview. This is particularly true when the situation is not clearly defined at the outset and when the interviewer has wide latitude in techniques and tactics.

It is possible to initiate an interview in a superordinate position to gain initial cooperation and then shift to a more equalitarian role to obtain information which would be withheld from superordinates. The initial social distance can be reduced by a skilled interviewer who finds among his role repertory status attributes comparable to those of the respondent or which at least help in conveying to the respondent a nonthreatening image. It is probably easier for the interviewer to move from a superordinate position to an equal or subordinate one than vice versa.

Advantages of the superordinate position. In general, it is easier to make contact, to obtain an appointment, or to begin the interview, if the interviewer is perceived as occupying high status. The obligation to the higher status person tends to reduce the effect of competing time demands. This does not necessarily mean that the interview, once begun, will be successful.

In some cases, the higher status of the interviewer will not only make the initial contact easier but will also facilitate the flow of information, because the interviewer's position symbolizes a moral obligation so strong that refusing to give accurate information would threaten the respondent's self-esteem. The reality of this ego threat depends upon the extent to which the respondent has actually internalized the moral obligation. For example, a child will sometimes lie to a peer, but when confronted with his mother's sternness, will admit the truth.

Sometimes the high status of the interviewer does not have this happy effect because the respondent has not internalized the norm. Or, the ego threat involved in giving a truthful answer would be more painful than the conscience pangs generated by lying. In this type of conflict, the respondent can show great creativity in developing rationalizations for not giving the information. If the ego threat involved is due to the authority position of the interviewer, then the superordinate role is double-edged. This is often the situation where the witness in a trial has taken an oath to tell the truth, but feels threatened if he does.

In some circumstances, the superordinate interviewer has the advantage of appealing to the respondent's need for recognition. The respondent may even hope for some publicity as a result. Of course, this, too, can be double-edged in rare cases where he believes a more sensational tale has a better chance of being published. This was occasionally encountered in interviewing "heroes" in disaster situations. More often, however, the respondent who had been featured as a hero in the local newspaper showed embarrassment over the exaggerations or fiction furnished by an enthusiastic and creative reporter who had found his human interest story for the day.

If the interviewer's higher status is based upon his higher education, his specialized knowledge, or his experiences in a certain area related to the interview topic, the respondent may be motivated by his need for meaning. The father of a delinquent child being interviewed by the social worker, the teenager feeling the first emotional attraction to a member of the opposite sex being interviewed by the high school counselor, or the supervisor who did not receive an expected promotion being interviewed by the personnel department—all might be motivated to talk by a need to orient themselves to the realities and to make sense of the events.

If the interviewer's higher status is of the nonthreatening type, the respondent will be more inclined to show his puzzlement than he would be to equals or lower status people.

Finally, the interviewer in the superordinate position has the advantage of being able to offer extrinsic rewards while the lower status interviewer cannot. The interviewer or sponsor may pay respondents a flat rate per interview "as a symbol of our appreciation of the time and effort you have given us." Other inducements—paying transportation and lodging for the respondents to come to a central point to be interviewed, offering to obtain appointments with influential people, or taking the respondent to lunch—have been beneficial in some instances. Gross and Mason's[30] study of the role of the public school superintendent illustrates this.

Service in some form may also be rendered by the field worker in exchange for information. For example, Oscar Lewis[31] found that to establish good rapport with the people he was studying in the Mexican village, Tepoztlan, it was necessary to help them. Similarly, Albert De Graer[32] found that his role as medical doctor gave him an acceptable reason for intimate contact with both the patients and "doctors" of the Azande tribe in the Belgian Congo. This technique is not only useful when working in exotic cultures but also in our own culture, whether in a factory, hospital, school, or community.

In general, the fact that the researcher is rendering a service to the group or individual he is studying gives a reason for his presence that is much more understandable to many people than the abstract idea of research on human behavior. The service function gives him an opportunity to do more than formal interviewing. It also allows him to be a participant-observer with access to certain situations which might be considered taboo even if he were accepted as a researcher.

In some cases, it is possible for the service to take the form of giving useful information; however, there are some important safeguards which must be observed. First, the information must not have been confidentially obtained from a previous respondent, even if that respondent is anonymous. There is always the danger that the current respondent will be afraid that his information will be passed along. Second, there are many situations in which it is harmful to even give the respondent a statistical summary of the type of data which has been found up to that point in the study. For example, some disaster interviewers tried to reassure a respondent, who felt guilty because he had become so frightened that he could not eat or sleep for two days, by pointing out that "more than 60 percent of the people in other communities studied have shown these same symptoms." This is dangerous for several reasons. In some cases, the respondent may not have been aware that he had been communicating his guilt feelings. Also, he may

---

[30] N. Gross and W. Mason, "Some Methodological Problems of Eight-Hour Interviews," *American Journal of Sociology*, vol. 59, no. 3 (November 1953), pp. 197–204.

[31] Oscar Lewis, *Life in a Mexican Village: Tepoztlan Restudied* (Urbana: University of Illinois Press, 1951), p. v.

[32] Albert De Graer, "L'art de Guerir Chez les Asande," *Congo*, vol. 10, pp. 220–21.

resent being "just another statistic" and want the interviewer to view his case as unique. And from a psychotherapeutic standpoint, the respondent finds it difficult to obtain catharsis if the very basis for his guilt is denied by the interviewer. Finally, there is the danger that giving certain kinds of information will confuse the respondent about the interviewer's role.

Many harmless forms of information can be supplied. For example, an interviewer in a factory may become quite popular during the World Series games by giving the latest report on the scores. Or, an interviewer in an academic institution may pass along some interesting information on new publications and current research projects in the respondent's field.

The effect of extrinsic rewards may often depend upon whether they are of the discriminating or nondiscriminating type. Those discussed previously are nondiscriminating, in that all respondents receive the benefits regardless of their performance in the interview. This type of extrinsic reward is more common in the social science interview in which the interviewer is not in a power position even though he may have high status. The discriminating extrinsic reward is one which is given only to those respondents who have completed the interview successfully according to certain criteria set up by the interviewer. This is often the situation when the social worker is interviewing a respondent; the information obtained may be used to determine eligibility for welfare measures. The personnel interviewer speaking to the job applicant holds out the hope of a job if the respondent is successful according to some criteria which may or may not be known to the respondent. The prison parole officer; the administrator of loans, grants, or fellowships; the manager in charge of promotions; or the physician examining a person to determine eligibility for medical insurance—all these and others interview people to determine whether they are deserving of some reward.

It can readily be seen that the nondiscriminatory extrinsic reward is more clearly an asset to the interviewer than the discriminatory reward. In the latter case, the respondent is highly motivated to pay attention, to comply with requests, and to devote extended periods of time, but there is always the ego threat of possible failure in reaching an admitted objective. To avoid failure, the respondent is tempted to withhold information he feels might be damaging to his case or to exaggerate certain points while distorting others. Whenever it is feasible, information should be collected in situations where no discriminatory rewards are used.

Advantages of equality. The advantages inherent in an equality relationship assume the absence of a competitive or conflicting relationship between equals. Thus, the advantages of equality are gained when there is an in-group relationship between the two. The principal advantage under these conditions is the absence of ego threat.

There is an advantage also in the absence of certain etiquette restrictions. There may never be any relationship completely devoid of etiquette restrictions, but for the purposes of interviewing we are interested in eliminating only those which inhibit the flow of relevant information. Abstractly, we can say that in the equal relationship the quality of the etiquette restrictions is different from that of unequal relationships.

The absence of any power or prestige leverage by the interviewer may make it difficult to obtain the cooperation of an equal unless some bond of friendship, sentiment, or symbiosis is present. The interviewer must depend upon some intrinsic reward to obtain the cooperation. In the equality relationship at its best, it is possible for the respondent to be a true collaborator in a common problem, and once his interest is captured, it can be sustained.

Advantages of subordinate role. The principal advantage in the subordinate role for the interviewer is the absence of any threat to the respondent's ego. If the interviewer demonstrates a high level of competence, he can be respected although in a subordinate role. The respondent who is not pleased by the purpose of the interview, the sponsorship, or some aspect of the strategy is often more apt to express his displeasure to an interviewer "who is just doing a job assigned to him" than to someone in higher status where etiquette might interfere.

Sometimes the respondent gives the information because he feels sorry for the interviewer who has such a "distasteful" job. Or, the respondent may feel no obligation to furnish more than a modicum of information and dismiss the interviewer. Since there is no possibility of applying direct pressure to the respondent, indirect pressure in the form of an appeal to his altruism may be used. To do this successfully, the interviewer must know which values, reference groups, or membership groups might be legitimately identified with the purpose of the interview in the respondent's mind.

The low status interviewer is not in a position to offer any of the discriminatory extrinsic rewards as is the high status interviewer, but he is not completely without resources in offering nondiscriminatory extrinsic rewards. If he is familiar with the type of respondent and the general setting, and if he is sensitive to opportunities to offer small favors in a nondiscriminating way, he may smooth the path of the interview for the single contact or be more sure of appointments for a series of contacts with the same person or organization.

As mentioned previously, the interviewer's auxiliary role might involve a form of participation which is beneficial to the organization or the individual respondent. There are also many types of small services which can be rendered upon a single contact. Helping the respondent bring in the groceries, watching the baby while the respondent puts the groceries away, bringing an armload of wood from the barn into the house, explaining the latest treatment recommended by the Department of Agriculture for a parasitic corn fungus, bringing the newspaper from the foyer to the respondent's third-floor apartment—these types of services, depending upon the setting for the interview, can have a positive effect where the interviewer does not have to worry about losing a superordinate position.

Just as it is possible for the interviewer initiating the interview in the superordinate role to move toward a position of equality as the interview progresses, the subordinate interviewer can also move upward to a position of equality during the interview. The downward shift of the superordinate interviewer is most likely to be accomplished by emphasizing auxiliary roles the interviewer has in common with the respondent. The upward shift of the subordinate interviewer is more often accomplished not by emphasizing auxiliary roles but by performing well in the central role of interviewer.

The central role of the interviewer

Thus far, we have focused the discussion upon the *selection* of the appropriate role for the interviewer, which involves both the selection of the right person to do the interview and the selection of the most appropriate roles from the interviewer's natural role repertory. Since the *selection* process required us to focus upon the background characteristics of the interviewer, the emphasis was upon his auxiliary roles. With the attempt to sensitize the reader to these factors we have perhaps overemphasized the importance of the auxiliary roles and neglected the central foreground factor of the person qua interviewer.

In the final analysis, the auxiliary roles are important only as they impinge upon the central role of interviewer. More directly relevant to the problem of maximizing the flow of relevant information is the way in which the interviewer plays his role of interviewer vis-à-vis a particular respondent. It is often apparent that the respondent has only a very hazy notion of the interviewer's role. This is unavoidable since respondents rarely have extensive practice in their role as a respondent. One exception is the respondent who has undergone treatment by a psychiatrist or clinical psychologist; these respondents are often more secure in a nonscheduled, low topic-control interview, aimed at collecting information on subjective experiences.

The general vagueness of the average respondent's concept of the interviewer's role has advantages and disadvantages. If the concept is vague, the interviewer at least has a clean slate upon which to communicate his expectations of the respondent. If the respondent does have a strong conception of the interviewer's role, often it is a stereotype not appropriate to the particular situation in which he is being interviewed. These incorrect expectations must be detected and corrected by the interviewer.

SUMMARY

We have viewed the process of interviewer selection as having two phases. The first phase is the selection of the person; the second is selecting the most suitable roles a particular person can take vis à vis the respondent. These two phases are functionally related in that the selection of a person determines certain opportunities and limitations for the role-selection phase.

In selecting the person we need to consider his or her overt physical characteristics (sex, age, race, ethnicity, speech pattern, dress and grooming, and physical handicaps), basic personality traits, attitudes (toward the subject of the interview, toward the respondent, and toward his own role as interviewer) and, finally, his or her background of knowledge and experience relevant to the subject matter of the interview, the type of respondent to be interviewed, or the social context in which the interview is to take place.

In selecting the most suitable role for the interviewer, we must not assign new roles for him or her to play but select from among his actual role repertory (such as mother, parent, daughter, taxpayer, church member, voter, consumer, musician, etc.) those which should be emphasized as *auxiliary* to the central role of interviewer. This distinction between role *playing* and role *taking* is essential both in terms of the ethics of avoiding deceit and of the effectiveness of the interviewer.

These auxiliary roles are selected in a way calculated to minimize the inhibitors and maximize the facilitators of communication. Therefore we must consider their effect on the respondent's perception of the interviewer-respondent relationship and his definition of the interview situation. In thinking of the probable effects of certain characteristics of the interviewer on the interviewer-respondent relationship, there are two major dimensions to keep in mind: the in-group–outgroup relationship and the superordinate-subordinate relationship. Each of the combinations of this two-dimensional relationship has its advantages and disadvantages, depending upon the type of information sought in the context of the interview situation and the larger society.

All of the characteristics of the interviewer and his auxiliary roles are relevant only insofar as they affect the performance of his central role as interviewer. All of the effects of the interviewer's characteristics depend upon the meaning they have for the particular respondent in the concrete situation.

The credibility of the interviewer and the predictability of the respondent's definition of the situation can be augmented and supported by selecting the most appropriate scene for the interaction. So within our dramatistic frame of reference, we can say that the interviewer, to convincingly emerge as a real character, must be backed by appropriate props and scenery. Setting the scene is the topic of the next two chapters, which begin with the assumption that the respondents, the interviewers, and their appropriate roles have already been determined.

DISCUSSION QUESTIONS

1. What is the one most important thing to do before selecting interviewers for a particular project?
2. In general why are visible characteristics of the interviewer important?
3. What are some of the most important visible characteristics of interviewers? Explain how they can affect the results?
4. What are some of the most important nonphysical or "invisible" characteristics of the interviewer? How can they affect results?
5. What are the two most important dimensions of the interviewer-respondent relationship? Give an example of how one of these dimensions might affect the results positively? Negatively?

Laboratory problem 6

Selecting appropriate interviewer

This problem requires creative imagination (empathy) in applying principles of communication to this important phase of field strategy. You should imagine interview situations in which one main inhibitor can be either maximized or minimized by the selection of a good type or bad type of interviewer, assuming the same respondent in both cases. You should concentrate on the relationship between the type of information needed, the type of respondent at hand, and the type of interviewer most likely and least likely to give the needed information.

Give three examples of situations, using the following format for describing each of the three situations. Assume that respondent has the needed information but is more willing or able to give it to one interviewer than to the other.

- *a.* The specific *question* to be asked.
- *b.* The type of *respondent.*
- *c.* The type of interviewer *most* likely to obtain the information.
- *d.* The type of interviewer *least* likely to obtain the information.
- *e.* The main inhibitor of communication operating between the respondent and the interviewer described in (d) above.

Below is a sample of one of the three examples. Note that there is no need to elaborate with much detail.

Example 1

a. *Question:* "What do you think of the new open-space middle school pioneered here in Yellow Springs by your Superintendant of Schools?"
b. *Respondent:* Teacher in that school.
c. *Good interviewer:* Teacher from nearby school district.
d. *Bad interviewer:* Member of the Yellow Springs School Board.
e. *Inhibitor:* Etiquette.

Be prepared to defend your example in a class discussion by explaining why you would expect the particular inhibitor to be most important and why you would expect a different interviewer to minimize it.

11

Time and place of the interview

Too frequently the time and place of an interview is not consciously chosen with care because the scene is not considered an important force in determining the quality of the interview. Instead, too often the scene is determined by custom, by the physical or psychological convenience of the interviewer, or by the invalid criterion of dollar cost per interview rather than per item of valid information. The rigid rituals of time and place are seen in such examples as the school principal who always interviews students in his office, in the teacher who always interviews students in front of other students in the classroom, the psychiatrist who has never seen a patient at home, the lawyer who has never interviewed the client at the scene of the issue, or the manager who has never gone to a subordinate's office to talk with him. Perhaps these customary scenes are generally correct, but there are many instances in which consideration of the potential inhibiting effects would call for abrupt departure from the routine.

In discussing the problems of selecting an appropriate time and place for the interview, we will concentrate upon the circumstances that often link the spatial and temporal dimensions of the situation with social-psychological facilitators and inhibitors of communication. No attempt will be made to deal with the relative cost of the different time-space strategies. Most of the experimental studies of the effects of time and space upon both the costs and the validity of the interview have been done in connection with polls and surveys and will be referred to in a separate chapter.

Before dealing with our main concern for the social-psychological meaning of time and place, we will first list the most salient physiological aspects of the situation that can affect the quality of the interview. It is common sense to recognize that the time and place should maximize the respondent's physical comfort as well as the interviewer's, with the temperature, humidity, light, and odors conducive to comfort. Also there should be no visual or auditory distractions that make concentration difficult for the interviewer and respondent. In addition to these physiological aspects, occasionally we must consider physical characteristics such as the spatial relationship between the interviewer and respondent; and if a recording machine is to be used, we should check the location of a functioning electrical outlet, whether there is alternating or direct current, and where the machine and microphone can best be placed. Once these details are known, the more important problem is the social-psychological *meaning* for the respondent of the prospective situation.

There are several interesting and relevant connections between the time-space aspects of a situation and the communication problems which result. These general relationships are pertinent to many interviewing problems.

SOME EFFECTS OF PLACE

Minimizing inhibitors

The selection of an appropriate place for the interview can minimize the competing time demands. This statement may appear to be a contradiction of terms in that it proposes to deal with the *time* dimension by manipulation of the *space* dimension. This is possible only because places contain people, things, and interests that might compete with interview time. Although the aphorism "out of sight, out of mind" is not completely true, there is a tendency in this direction.

To illustrate this, an interviewer studying morale problems of the public school teacher could arrange to interview her in her classroom during a free period, talk with her in the faculty lounge, or interview her at home in the evening. In the first setting, the desk may be stacked with unread English themes or the bulletin board may contain a display a week behind schedule; the blackboard may contain an assignment for which she too must prepare. Although the faculty lounge may be free from these distractions, it may have less privacy than either the classroom or home. In any case, the types of competing time demands activated by each situation are qualitatively and quantitatively different.

The appropriate selection of place can also minimize ego threat. Place is connected with ego threat insofar as it influences the respondent's conception of the role and status of the interviewer and the purposes of the interview, or reminds him of certain values he must uphold or roles which he must perform. In addition, the place may suggest various probabilities of information leaking out to some ego-threatening audience. This suggests that the *place*, like a stage set in a play, provides the context in which the interaction takes place and therefore gives support to each actor's role. The interview setting should be chosen to reinforce the respondent's perception of the interviewer's most appropriate auxiliary role. If inappropriately chosen, the impression of the setting can overpower any attempt of the interviewer to communicate a non-threatening image of himself.

For example, in studying the reasons why high school students choose nursing as a career, the interviewer should not arrange appointments with new recruits in the office of the director of the school of nursing if he wants to avoid identification with the authority of the nursing school. In one study, the interviewer did accept the invitation to use the director's office for the interveiwing. He tried to overcome the handicap by explaining that he was not working for the hospital, but was doing research on his own initiative. Later, it was discovered that several of the girls still did not understand that the interviewer was not on the hospital staff. Some remembered and believed his explanation, but assumed that the interviewer was interested in administration of hospitals or schools of nursing. While some very real reasons for going into nursing were given to the school counselor over a cup of coffee in the cafeteria, they were not mentioned in the more formal interview. For example:

R: Letha and I were talking the other night about her home background and were surprised to find the same things. We are both from strict farm families. In our home town, the Lutheran church does not allow boys and girls to mix in the teenage Sunday School classes. Things are pretty dead in the country and the boys get to run around while the girls just sit at home. The only way you can get away from home is to get married, go away to college, or go into nursing.

I: Why not get a job as a stenographer, waitress, or store clerk?

R: You don't know my dad. He doesn't think waitresses are respectable. And you can't get a job in an office unless you can type well. I went to a school where they don't teach typing, bookkeeping, and that sort of thing. All the girls working in the offices in this town are graduates of the city high schools.

In contrast, in the formal interview situation there was a strong emphasis on such factors as the social usefulness of the nursing profession, the desire to "work with people," and the practical combination of the nursing profession with marriage. Here, the place of the interview considerably affected the information obtained.

Similarly, an interviewer should consider carefully invitations to use the principal's office to interview teenagers on their adjustment problems, the dean's office for interviewing college students, or a management conference room for interviewing employees on their morale problems and perceptions of management. More neutral ground should be used for the interview, if possible.

Of course, if ego threat is to be minimized, it is usually necessary to find a place where privacy is assured. Sometimes the person's home, if there is privacy, provides the greatest security. In other cases, lower status respondents may feel defensive about their economic condition as reflected by the home. This is particularly true of minority groups who are forced to live in slum housing, even though they dress well and drive a late model car. Also, crowded living conditions may make privacy rare in this kind of home except at certain times.

Sometimes there is the problem of achieving the proper balance between privacy and complete isolation. For example, when males are interviewing female respondents, either the respondent or others in the community or organization may become fearful or suspicious of the intimacy that might result.

Considerable ingenuity is often required to find privacy needed for the purposes of the interview. It is very difficult and sometimes impossible to obtain valid information from a subordinate when his superordinates can listen. This obstacle is familiar to the public opinion poller who finds that wives more frequently have "no opinion" on controversial issues when their husbands are present. If it is essential to the results, the need for privacy should be tactfully and firmly explained to the respondent.

Just as the situational setting tends to influence the respondent's perception of the interviewer's role, it also makes the respondent more conscious of one of his own roles than of another. Therefore the ideals, obligations, expectations, and other subjective orientations connected with that role are brought into the foreground of the respondent's consciousness. A respondent who is a father, a businessman, and a deacon of the local church might give different answers to questions from the same interviewer on controversial issues such as local option liquor sales, taxes for schools, or federal aid to religious education, depending on whether he was interviewed at home, in his business office, or in the office of the church. In each setting it is possible that different moral frames of reference gain ascendency in weighing issues. What is considered threatening to the ego depends upon the person's self-concept, which he strives to maintain. It is highly probable that individuals vary considerably in the degree to which their self-concept remains stable and consistent as they move from one role to another. Therefore, whatever flexibility exists will be associated with those changes in setting that highlight different roles.

Many of the same points regarding the connection between the place, role emphasis of interviewer and respondent, and ego threat can be said of the relationship between place, role, and the etiquette barrier which acts as a filter of communication allowing some items to pass and prohibitng others, depending upon the role relationship between the two communicators. Any change in the role of either the interviewer or the respondent will have some effect upon limiting communications. To apply this principle, the interviewer must know how the selection of the place for the interview will affect the respondent's perception of his own and the interviewer's role. In additon, the interviewer needs to be familiar enough with the situation to know which etiquette restrictions are attached to which role combinations.

Although seemingly complex, which it is in theory, in actual practice every mature adult is able to govern his behavior according to many of the subtle requirements of etiquette. The problem becomes acute, however, when an individual in the role of interviewer is required to operate in situations where he is not familiar with the nature of the etiquette restrictions. A vital part of the strategy phase of any study is to become familiar with the restrictions in the new settings.

Simple forgetting and chronological confusion may both be reduced, in some cases, by the selection of an appropriate place. It is important that the place be quiet and private so that the interviewer can establish the appropriate pace and mood for careful recall of events. Without this quiet privacy it is impossible to use some of the techniques and tactics useful for stimulating recall.

Another way of utilizing place to stimulate recall is to effect a return to the scene with certain physical objects prodding the memory. It is sometimes possible to interview the respondent while walking through the actions in their original setting. Where this is impractical, it may be possible to use photographs, maps, tape recordings, and other physical traces of settings and events that relate to the interview.

Often an accurate presentation of the spatial arrangements of the original scene (regardless of whether these are seen in the real setting or in a photograph) will facilitate the untangling of the chronological order and perception of events. This was observed in interviews with building contractors to discover the types of conflicts they had with clients. By either visiting the house he built or by looking at photographs and floor plans, the respondent was stimulated to remember in considerable detail misunderstandings and issues of conflict with the client.

Maximizing facilitators

If the type of information to be obtained requires the establishment of a sympathetic and understanding mood, the place must be quiet and private. In some cases, the location may represent a new and interesting experience for the respondent. Or, the trip to the place of the interview might be an extrinsic reward that attracts respondents. The main value in the location of the interview, however, is the absence of distractions.

SOME EFFECTS OF TIME

Many of the effects of *place* also apply to the selection of a *time* for the interview, in that the relevant characteristics of a particular place change from time to time. Therefore, this aspect of time in relationship to place was assumed as a consideration in selecting the place for the interview.

There is another important aspect of selecting a time for the interview. This is the relationship between the point in time when the interview takes place and the events or experiences about which the interviewer is seeking information. In assessing current opinions and attitudes, this time dimension is not involved. However, in many interviews the time of the interview in relationship to events and experiences determines both the respondent's *ability* and his *willingness* to give relevant information.

The most significant effect of timing is upon the respondent's ability to remember, accurately and completely, avoiding chronological and inferential confusion. To avoid simple forgetting, the interview should take place as soon after the relevant events and experiences as possible. Much psychological research indicates the distorting effects of fading memories. Specific facts, if remembered, may be quantitatively or qualitatively distorted. Complex events may be retained in an essentially correct pattern with nonessential detail omitted; or the whole gestalt of the event may be distorted, thus reversing its significance.

What is forgotten depends not only upon the recency of the experience but also upon how ego-involved it was, whether it was a completed task, whether is was considered a success or a failure, and whether it was routine, dramatic, or traumatic. Regardless of the cause of the forgetting, in general, time is an important factor.

Events are not simply forgotten or clearly remembered. Often the faded memory can be revived by special interviewing techniques and tactics. At the strategy level, information on events more than a month in the past is more efficiently obtained by giving the respondent some advance notice of the interview topic. If the topic of the interview is explained when making an appointment (with or without the suggestion that the respondent might like to think it over), and if this is one or two days in advance, it is often easier to obtain more complete detail in the interview. The advance notice may be given to all respondents at once in the form of individual letters, a public announcement in a newspaper or on a bulletin board, or by radio or any other available public channel. Whether or not the advance notice should be individualized or simply made public depends on the topic of the interview and the nature of the group, community, or institutional setting.

Generally, immediate interviewing will not only reduce the loss of accurate detail, but will also help to avoid chronological confusion, which becomes a major problem in studies of changes in attitudes and beliefs over a relatively long period of time. There is a tendency to forget or repress previous attitudes, beliefs, and expectations. The writer has had occasion to interview the same persons on international relations at six-month intervals. People who at one time vehemently expressed a conviction that war with the Soviet Union was inevitable would deny with equal vigor six months later that they had ever taken such a "defeatist position."

In this case, two interviews six months apart discovered shifts in the respondent's attitude that would not have been revealed by simply asking the respondent, "What is your opinion on the probability of war with the Soviet Union?" and "What was your opinion on this issue six months ago?" The respondent tends to feel that his present position is rational and right and, therefore, the same as it has always been.

Similarly, attempts to discover why a person "chose" to work for his current employer, why he "selected" the college he now attends, or why he "elected" to enter his particular vocation, are all fraught with the danger of chronological confusion. Each in-group, whether it is an industry, college, profession, or community, supplies its members with certain ready-made rationalizations for how and why they came into the group. The virtues of the in-group may be systematically extolled in rhapsodic indoctrination by its myths and ideals, or the individual may develop his own self-congratulatory version of why he made such a wise decision. In either case, it is extremely difficult in retrospect to uncover the original forces accounting for the final decision.

Even though the respondent has selectively forgotten certain things because he desires to forget, we nevertheless classify this in a later interview as an *inability* to give the information. Although originally the memory was repressed, the respondent is being perfectly honest when he says he has simply forgotten since he is not consciously withholding or distorting information. If at the strategy level, we can eliminate the need for extensive retrospection, the technical and tactical problems in the interview will be greatly simplified.

The strategy planner must always keep in mind that sometimes it is either impossible or impractical to depend upon interviewing to obtain information that has been forgotten, and that other sources, such as diaries, public records, personal letters, or other documents should be used, either as a principal source or to supply cues to stimulate the respondent's memory and to guide the interviewer's probing.

There are many other situations in which not only the respondent's ability to remember, but also his willingness, depend upon *when* he is interviewed. Information which could be given freely at one time becomes an ego threat to the respondent at another. When the writer was interviewing college presidents and faculty to discover why the college had refused permission for interviews about academic freedom, he was given an important observation by one of the professors:

> It's a peculiar thing—perhaps if I weren't a social scientist I wouldn't have noticed it—when there was the big dispute on campus about firing Professor X, several faculty members besides myself defended his right to academic freedom. Some of them continued to criticize the administration after the professor's services had been terminated. All of these people except myself have since left, more or less voluntarily. The others who defended Professor X up to the time of his dismissal, but then dropped their objections, are still here. My point is, that of those who are still here, most of them will not admit *now* that the action of the administration was a violation of academic freedom. Yet no new evidence has been admitted to change their original point of view. To me it is quite simple. These people do not want to admit that they would continue to teach in a place which does not have academic freedom because this would be an admission that they are willing to knuckle under; so to save face, they deny that there has been any restriction of academic freedom. Perhaps I am just projecting, but that is the only way I can make sense out of their change in behavior.

If this respondent's assessment of the situation is correct, interviews with the faculty would have been much more fruitful *before* the administration had made the decision to dismiss Professor X. It is now an ego threat to the respondent to admit that X's dismissal was a breach of academic freedom.

Selecting an optimum time for the interview can also increase the respondent's conscious willingness to give the relevant information. One of the simplest ways is to select a time when the respondent has the fewest competing time demands. To do this, the interviewer must be familiar with the daily, weekly, monthly, and seasonal patterns of the respondent.

These patterns vary with the culture, the person's roles in that culture, and personal preferences. The interviewer who sets out to interview students the last week before the semester ends, farmers during harvest season, fishermen leaving in two days for a six-week's voyage, lifeguards on duty, factory "graveyard shift" workers at 11 A.M., housewives at 5:30 P.M., or a fireman immediately after a fire, shows either ignorance or a lack of sympathy with the respondent he is approaching.

The interviewer should not assume that he can guess what the competing time demands will be in a strange situation. Often, the most obvious common sense assumptions are completely wrong. For example, it was assumed that respondents who had experienced a disaster of major proportion (such as the burning of their house, the injury or death of members of the family, the crashing of an airplane into their home) would be reluctant to spend one or two hours in an interview the next day. The assumption seemed sensible, in view of the fact that under these circumstances such respondents would have many new tasks to complete as a result of the disaster.

This assumption is essentially correct *if* the disaster involves only one person, one family, or only a few families in a community. The assumption is completely fallacious, however, in large-scale disasters where the total community is devastated; the community is not yet functioning as an organization, each individual is unable to play his normal roles, and therefore, has few competing time demands. The man whose house has blown away, whose horse and cow have been killed, whose barn and tractor are damaged beyond repair, and whose strawberry patch is covered with heavy debris cannot begin to do anything about his condition. His every move depends upon someone else's making a move. He would like to go to the next town to make arrangements with the insurance adjustor for a new tractor. Ordinarily he would phone, but the telephone lines were destroyed by the tornado; he would drive his car, but it is damaged; although a bus line ordinarily passes the house, the highway is obstructed by fallen utility poles, trees, and high-power lines; he would use his power chain saw to remove some of the trees from the road, but he has no gasoline for the motor and since the electricity is off, there are no pumps working at the local gas station, so he cannot refuel. Thus, he is caught in the paralyzing web of a nonfunctioning community. In his frustration, he is perfectly willing to talk about his troubles and has ample time to do so. Under these conditions, there is no difficulty in obtaining a two- or three-hour interview from the average respondent.

Sometimes an etiquette barrier arises in cases where the interviewer is asking information before it has become public. Etiquette often requires that a hierarchy of people be notified of an event or decision before it becomes public. If the interviewer attempts to obtain the information too soon, his request may be denied. This problem often arises when the interviewer is studying some ongoing community action program *in situ*. If he must continue work in the same community or organization over a long period, repeated requests for advance information could become a serious source of irritation.

In rare cases, the time for the interview may be selected to minimize the inhibiting effects of trauma by providing sympathetic understanding which will lead to catharsis. Immediately after a traumatic experience, the respondent is often willing to talk about it than he will be later. Perhaps this is because the event is vivid in the respondent's mind and he cannot repress it. Since his mind is full of images and internalized conversation about the event, it is no more painful to externalize these thoughts in conversation with the interviewer. Later, when the experience is less fresh and the respondent can cast the thoughts from his mind, he is reluctant to renew the pain by discussing the topic. For example, after a community-wide disaster, interviewers noted a sudden decrease in respondents' willingness to discuss their experiences once the funerals were over. The funeral ceremonies seemed to symbolize the community's return to normal routine.

An interview may be timed to maximize the appeal to the respondent's need for meaning by catching him while he is still undecided, confused, and trying to pin down a future that is in a state of flux. If the purpose of the interview is to study value systems, decision-making processes, role conflicts, or processes of defining situations, then although it might be possible to wait until after the decision has been made before interviewing the respondent, this delay would allow greater memory distortions and deprive the respondent of the opportunity to use the interviewer as a sounding board for his ideas, dilemmas, and ambivalences during his struggle for meaning.

This immediate timing would be fruitful in studying such problems as decisions to marry or divorce, occupational choices, selection of a college, labor turnover, migration, and other major decisions that change a person's life pattern.

Thus far, we have discussed some of the implications of the time of the interview in relation to the individual's pattern of time demands and his experiences to be reported in the interview. Another aspect of the time dimension is selecting the most appropriate *sequence* of interviews with the different respondents.

If a random sample selects representative respondents who are so widely dispersed socially and geographically that they do not communicate with one another, the chronological order for contacting them is usually a matter of convenience and efficient use of the interviewer. But, if there is a possibility of contact between the respondents, so that they might discuss the interview either in prospect or retrospect, the effect of this communication upon the flow of relevant information should be carefully considered in the strategy planning.

Several types of questions should be answered in terms of the specific field situation in which the interviewing is to be done. Should the respondent of higher or lower status be interviewed first? Should the most willing or the most reluctant be interviewed first? Should certain respondents be interviewed first because they will not be available

later? Should those special respondents who can give the broadest picture of the situation be interviewed first?

Ordinarily, it is best to interview the people of higher status first.
Those of lower status may wish to wait to see if those higher up are
going to cooperate by being interviewed. Also, those of higher status
may be insulted if they are the last to be asked for their opinions on
some community issue. This resentment, in extreme cases, might make
it impossible for the interviewer to continue if the offended person has
the power or prestige to blacklist the study.

Where the status of the prospective respondents is equal or irrelevant, it might be desirable to select the most willing respondents first
in order to build a background of experience with the interview topic
and the type of respondent. This experience might be useful in dealing
with reluctant or resistant respondents. Also, the fact that all the others
have cooperated and found it painless and even interesting might exert
some pressure or arouse the curiosity of the reluctant.

In some situations, the interviewer knows in advance that some
segments of the community or the institution will be moving or going
on vacation and should be approached first. Also, certain special respondents might have the type of information which gives a broad view
of the situation helpful in understanding the more specialized experiences of the respondents to follow. Such respondents may also give
information on the relationships between the other respondents or
information about them as individuals.

If there is a possibility of collusion between two or more respondents,
this can sometimes be prevented by interviewing them separately and
simultaneously. This method was used by Burgess and Wallin[1] in gaining information on sexual adjustment in marriage. A husband and wife
were given questionnaires and were interviewed at the same time in
different rooms. Each knew that the other was asked the same questions. This technique was able to elicit private information with great
accuracy, and it provided validity checks.

SUMMARY

We have suggested that all too frequently the time and place of the
interview are determined by rigid ritual, but better results can be
obtained if the time and place are viewed as strategy tools consciously
used to maximize the flow of relevant and valid information. The time
and place can either inhibit or facilitate information flow. There are

---

[1] E. W. Burgess and Paul Wallin, *Engagement and Marriage* (Philadelphia: Lippincott,
1953).

certain physiological inhibitors that must be avoided such as a room which is too hot, too cold, too noisy, or unpleasant smelling, but the more frequently encountered barriers associated with time and place are the social-psychological ones and can be understood only in terms of their *meaning* to the respondent.

The *place* of the interview should be chosen to minimize the inhibitors of communication. For example, competing time demands can be reduced by getting the respondent away from distractions which remind him of his other roles and obligations in life. Ego threat can be reduced by providing privacy as a defense against being overheard or of being seen cooperating with the interviewer; privacy can protect the respondent against being quizzed later by others about the interview. The scene can be chosen to reinforce the credibility of the interviewer's most appropriate auxiliary role, thus reducing ego threat and dissolving the etiquette barrier. Forgetting and chronological confusion can be reduced by interviewing the respondent at the scene of the event being discussed.

The *time* of the interview is important in three different perspectives. The first is in the relationship between the time of the interview and the regular cycles of events in the respondent's life. This perspective is important in choosing a time to minimize competing time demands and in knowing when to catch the respondent in the most opportune place. The second perspective is in the relationship between the time of the interview and the point in time when the event under discussion took place. Often by interviewing people as soon as possible after an event, we can minimize the effects of forgetting and chronological confusion. Also, if the events to be discussed had a strong psychological impact on the respondent, his need for catharsis, for meaning, and for sympathetic understanding will be highest immediately after the event. The third time perspective is in the sequence in which the respondents are to be interviewed. Often it is best to interview high status persons first if their cooperation will insure the cooperation of lower status persons. If status is not as important as a general willingness to be interviewed, then the most willing respondents can be interviewed first so that they will recommend the interview to others. At other times we need to choose the sequence of respondents to give the interviewer an overview of the situation as early as possible, so that he will have the context to understand the more detailed information to come later from other respondents.

Once we have gotten the right interviewer together with the right respondent at the most opportune time and place, we have solved most of the strategy problems. Before the opening question marking the beginning of the technique phase of the interview, there remains the final strategy step of defining the interview situation by the arrangement of physical props and by the interviewer's verbal explanation of the interview. This final bit of strategy is the subject of the next chapter.

DISCUSSION QUESTIONS

1. Is the selection of an appropriate time and place for the interview considered a strategy, technique, or tactic?
2. Explain how the *meaning* of a particular time or place of an interview might affect the respondent's ability or willingness to give relevant information.
3. What else about time or place, besides its meaning, might affect the flow of information from the respondent?
4. Give an example, not furnished by the author, of how the time or place of the interview might inhibit the respondent.

Laboratory problem 7

Strategy problems of time and place

In each problem below specify the most appropriate *time* and *place* for the interview. Consider how the relationships between the interviewer, the respondent, and the information sought might generate inhibitors which could be minimized by the selection of the appropriate time and place for the interview. After you have done this independently, compare your solution with others in the class and discuss why you chose the time and place you did. There may be legitimate differences in solutions depending on the assumptions you make regarding certain unspecified aspects of the situation. The discussion will be valuable in bringing out the different assumptions and showing what additional information might be needed to make the decision.

1. A graduate student from the School of Business Administration wants to interview middle-management people in large industries regarding their problems in bridging the gap between the top policy-making managers and the supervisory personnel. The interview will take from two to three hours.

2. A counselor with the State Vocational Rehabilitation Department is to interview an unwed mother, with a two-year-old child and now on welfare, regarding her possible interest in getting the child into a day-care program and starting a six-month vocational training program during which she will receive an $86.00 monthly incentive allowance.

3. A police officer from the Traffic Division is studying a certain type of accident in order to design a better prevention program.

He needs to interview a woman who witnessed an accident a couple of blocks from her home as she was walking home from the drugstore.

4. A medical interviewer for the U.S. Public Health Service needs to interview General Motors workers who have been treated for venereal disease within the past year. He needs to ask about symptoms to discover whether the treatment was successful and whether there has been any new contact with the disease. All 50 of the follow-up cases work at GMC and live in a nearby community.

12

Structuring the interview situation

DEFINING THE INTERVIEW SITUATION

Here "defining the interview situation" refers to only the final phase of strategy, from the moment the interviewer first contacts the respondent through the opening question of the interview. What the interviewer says and does during this time provides the immediate context of the interview and can greatly affect communication. Decisions must be made in advance relating to eight questions: (*a*) How should I introduce myself? (*b*) How should I explain the purpose of the interview? (*c*) How should I explain the sponsorship of the study? (*d*) Should I explain how and why the respondent was selected? (*e*) Should the respondent be anonymous? If so, how should this be explained? (*f*) *Should any extrinsic reward be mentioned?* (*g*) How should the interview be recorded, and how should the recording technique be explained? (*h*) What are some appropriate alternative wordings for the opening question?

Interviewer's introduction

In presenting oneself to the respondent, what is said is significant mainly in helping the respondent crystallize his perception of the interviewer's role. Therefore, all that has been said regarding selection of the most appropriate role from one's repertory applies to the introduction. In addition, the manner of the introduction will preview the interviewer's degree of aggressiveness, responsiveness, competence, self-assurance, warmth, or objectivity.

Giving one's name to the respondent helps reduce suspicion that might arise if the interviewer remained anonymous. This is true even though the respondent may remain anonymous. This common courtesy personalizes the relationship to some extent. If the respondent is not to remain anonymous to the interviewer, and if his name is known, then the interviewer should use the respondent's name as he presents himself. Generally, the following two phrases would leave considerably different impressions:

"I'm interviewing residents of this community on. . . ."
"Hello, Mrs. Bishop, I'm Mr. Rolph. I'm helping X Organization with a survey of this community on. . . ."

It is often necessary to remind the neophyte interviewer, with his enthusiasm or anxiety to obtain the information, of the desirability of observing such common amenities.

If it is essential that the respondent remain anonymous to the interviewer, the interviewer may nevertheless give his own name and proceed in a way that makes clear that the respondent's name is not needed.

Sponsorship

Often the next phrase of the introduction includes the sponsorship of the study, if it has one. The value of having an organization as a sponsor generally increases in more urban settings and when the interviewer is a stranger to the respondent. In a small village, folk society, or primitive groups, organizational sponsorship is often meaningless. The only meaningful sponsor in this case would be a *person* known to the respondent.

The central strategy problem here is to obtain information on the field situation. Which type of sponsorship and which organization or person will be helpful? Which might be fatal? Again, the significance of sponsorship is its effect upon the respondent's conception of the interviewer's central and auxiliary roles and the effect of this upon the inhibitors and facilitators of communication.

It may be helpful to have both a formal organization and a local person as sponsors. For example:

Mrs. Jones, how do you do! I'm Mrs. Beals from the Association for the Aid of Crippled Children. Reverend Rolf said that you would be a good person to talk to about some of the problems in Yellow Springs.

If the respondent is to remain strictly anonymous, it is still possible to use a personal sponsor in the following manner.

How do you do! I'm Mrs. Beals from the Association for the Aid of Crippled Children. Perhaps you have read in the paper that Reverend Rolf is the Yellow Springs representative for the study now under way here. I would like to talk to you about some of the problems of crippled children in your neighborhood.

In some cases, it is advisable for the interviewer to carry some written credentials including his name and the sponsor's. Respondents will rarely ask, but will be reassured, when identification is routinely shown. Even in cases where the sponsoring organization is unknown to the respondent, he may be favorably impressed by the interviewer's willingness to give information. The credentials may be a lapel button with either an official or an informal look, depending on the nature of the study; or they may be a letter of introduction.

If the interviewer expects to spend several days in the community or organization under conditions where the respondents and potential respondents do not see him every day, it may be advisable to have the credentials reproduced in a form to be left with each respondent, along with a thank you note, so that questions from potential respondents can be answered accurately. This prevents the rise of rumors regarding the identity, sponsorship, or purpose of the interviewer.

Although the optimum sponsorship may be very helpful for getting in the door, it will have to be followed by good interviewing performance to maintain the initial advantages. Since the same sponsorship may not impress all respondents equally, some additional explanations will have to be given.

One of the most difficult situations in which to select sponsorship occurs when studying a group which has polarized for and against an issue related to the topic of the interview. Special care must be taken to find a sponsor perceived as neutral or disinterested. If a disinterested organizational sponsor can be found, it sometimes also helps to find a personal sponsor in each of the opposing camps of the controversy.

Explaining the purpose of the interview

The purpose of the interview should be explained in terms the respondent can understand and in a manner which will account for *all* the types of questions which are going to be asked. If the initial explanation is too narrow or vague, the respondent may not be able to connect certain questions with the stated purpose. His suspicions may be aroused because he feels the interviewer is hiding his "real" purposes. This is particularly likely to happen in a hostile or polarized community.

In order to keep the initial explanation as simple and clear as possible, it may be necessary to plan additional explanations as the interview proceeds, pointing out the relevance of each new line of questioning to the originally stated purpose. In the interests of clarity, the language used should be appropriate to the background of the respondents and free of any technical jargon.

The next problem is to include as many points as possible which will maximize the facilitators and minimize the inhibitors of communication. In the explanation, it is often possible to avoid ego threat while appealing to the need for recognition, sympathetic understanding, new experience, the need for meaning, or some combination of these. For example, if the problem is to discover why one area of a city has much higher delinquency rates than another, and the hypothesis is that social control functions of the family break down when these are not supported by an organized community, we could use the following type of explanation to open an interview with a parent in a high delinquency area:

> You have probably read in the newspaper that Metropolitan Community Studies is interested in the problems of youth in our city. We are talking to parents all over the city to discover if it is more difficult nowadays for parents to bring up children than it used to be when your parents were raising you. What do you think are some of the problems in bringing up children nowadays?

This explanation of purpose is designed to help the interviewer get inside the door. It is short and directly connected to the opening question. It indicates that the study is publicly supported, is a good cause, and is interested in the respondent's practical problems. It appeals, therefore, to the respondent's altruistic impulse, promises sympathetic understanding and possible recognition. Further explanation may be needed and given at transitional points in the interview where the questions in a new topical area are not obviously related to the initial explanation. For example:

> Some people feel that there are different problems for parents living in different parts of the city. Do you feel that there are any problems which you have with children in this neighborhood that parents in other neighborhoods might not have?

The type of explanation needed, the sequence, and the timing of the various vital points depends upon the situation.

Explaining the selection of the respondent

It is not always necessary to explain why and how a particular respondent is selected. Often, the respondent does not question the point, particularly in the more traditional census or opinion poll. But it is especially important to give a clear explanation when interviewing in potentially hostile or polarized territory. In this case, if the *representa-*

tive respondent can be persuaded that he has been chosen in an objective and impartial manner and that he will remain anonymous, ego threat and hostility will be minimized. If he is a *special* respondent, and there not anonymous to the interviewer, it would be helpful to mention that he had been recommended by some person he knows and trusts.

Even in the most friendly territory, the respondent may suggest that the interviewer contact "somebody else who knows more about the problem," or "who has more time." In this case, it is particularly important to explain to the *representative* respondent that he was selected by an impartial sampling procedure and that it is necessary to obtain the point of view of everyone in the original sample, including people who are very busy and do not have time to be experts on the topic at hand. If the person is a *special* respondent, it is usually easier to appeal to his ego by recognizing his unique value to the study. Often, an appeal can be made by pointing out that he was selected because he has, by implication, certain altruistic tendencies. For example, "You have been recommended as a person who has done a lot of volunteer work with youth of the community," or "You have shown an interest in the problems of the senior citizens of Akron," or "You have taken an active interest in the PTA."

There are also ways of explaining the selection of the *representative* respondent that will give him recognition as a member of a particularly interesting or meritorious local group, community, or institution. In a study of the causes of delinquency, the interviewer was collecting information to compare a high delinquency area of a large city with an equal population in a village. Although a random sample of villagers was interviewed, each one was made to feel somewhat unique by the following explanation:

> We are analyzing some of the causes of juvenile delinquency by comparing places with very high delinquency rates with those having a very low delinquency. You can be very helpful to us, since you live in a town with the least delinquency in this part of the state.

The explanation can communicate positive expectations of cooperation by assuming that everyone will cooperate since, thus far, everyone else has. For example:

> We have been able to interview the families in every ninth house in this area and it looks like we will be able to finish today.

This strategy must be used with caution. To avoid being interpreted by the respondent as pressure tactics, careful wording and the appropriate context must be employed. The expectation should be mentioned casually as an interesting sidelight.

Thus we see that even though the respondent is willing to cooperate without an explanation of how and why he was selected, it is often desirable to provide an explanation appealing to altruistic tendencies, giving him recognition, and communicating positive expectations of cooperation. All of these precautions, although not always 100 percent successful, should help to assure optimum interpersonal relations at the outset.

Providing anonymity

It should not be assumed that the respondent, whether special or representative, desires or should be given anonymity. Often, the respondent does not care to be anonymous because this might detract from his recognition. At times, it might be necessary to make clear that the results will be anonymous even though the respondent prefers to tell the world what he has on his mind. This is the case where the respondent sees the interview as a means to some personal gain and colors his report hoping for approval of superordinates or for the discreditation of peers. Under these conditions, his motivation is not to give an objective report but to select, censor, exaggerate, and rationalize, as it best fits his purpose..

There are circumstances where the respondent would prefer to remain anonymous, but should not be granted his wish by the interviewer. This would be the case in studying a controversial issue in a community and attempting to predict who will take what public stand. If the respondent does not feel strongly enough or is not courageous enough to give his point of view to the interviewer, he is less likely to take a public stand later than the person who gives his views in a forthright manner. This principle may be carried further by having the interviewer bring up arguments of the opposition and ask for permission to quote the respondent in his report to some public body or the press.

Thus, we see that the granting or withholding of anonymity is not decided upon the basis of tradition or the respondent's desires, but upon the purpose of the interview. One ethical point must be observed in any case. If the respondent is promised anonymity, that promise should be scrupulously kept; if he is not to be given anonymity, this should be clear to him before the interview begins.

Anonymity is not an all-or-none factor. There are several degrees or types of anonymity which have practical and theoretical implications. The most extreme degree of anonymity consists of the interviewer's being ignorant not only of the identity of the respondent, but also of where he might be contacted again. This would be the case if a sociologist who was studying the underworld had a contact person, who trusted him, bring unapprehended criminals to be interviewed about the practices of the professional criminal.

Another example of this degree of anonymity would be interviewing a random area-sample of the sun bathers on the beach regarding their preferences in bathing suits. Or, people waiting at a railroad station might be interviewed on their opinions of the services to passengers.

This degree of anonymity has a disadvantage in that the same respondent cannot possibly be recontacted if additional information is later needed to complete the picture. There are ways of arranging to recontact the same person while he remains anonymous to the interviewer. The respondent may be identified by an address only, or by a phone number. Also, some "go between" selected and trusted by the respondents might arrange the recontact. In any case, where anonymity is vital to the flow of communication, the respondent must have no doubts of the anonymity. This assurance is always more difficult to provide if the respondent is to be recontacted.

The term *confidential* is often used to refer to a lesser degree of anonymity in which the respondent is known to the interviewer, but not to the client organization. There is still less anonymity when both the interviewer and the sponsor can identify the respondent, but any report either to a select body or the general public keeps the individual anonymous. Still less anonymity is involved when the identity of the respondent is known to professionals in several different agencies. This is often the situation when case study materials collected by a social worker are available to clinical psychologists or juvenile authorities. This sharing of information is often necessary to effect a coordinated approach to the delivery of social services.

Another important dimension of anonymity is the degree of identification of groups versus individuals. In some cases, the respondent is almost as reluctant to have information published about his particular group, organization, or community as he is about himself. This may be because his role in the group is so conspicuous that he too would be identifiable, even though he was not named, or he may simply be so ego-involved in the organization that he feels any threat to its reputation as a personal threat. Here, it is difficult to assure anonymity for the organization if only one such organization is studied. Organizations are easily kept anonymous when many of the same type are studied, and the results reported as either a statistical summary or as case studies which are frankly camouflaged by changing nonessential details and omitting unnecessary identifying materials.

Even though one of the above methods of preserving the respondent's anonymity may be used, there are occasions when a particular respondent is not convinced of the interviewer's sincerity. Sometimes the interviewer's promise is put to a severe test. One respondent may quiz the interviewer for information obtained from another respondent. A management person may ask for some "off the record" information about one of the workers who has been interviewed. In rare cases, the interviewer will be threatened with jail or prosecution for not giving the information. This situation arose in a study of a disaster-stricken community where the chief of police ordered an interviewer to surrender her tape recordings for him to hear. After refusing and explaining that the information was confidential and that the respondents had been promised anonymity, she was threatened with prosecution for "withholding evidence." Of course, such a charge was groundless, since no crime had been committed for which evidence was needed. Probably, the chief was anxious about the possibility of people reporting the shortcomings of the police department during the crisis. Knowing that he was not on firm legal ground, the chief did not attempt to use physical force to obtain the tapes. When the field supervisor explained the situation to the chief, he reluctantly relinquished his claim.

The foregoing discussion on maintaining various degrees of anonymity indicates the need for some serious strategy planning to avoid problems in this area. Closely related to the problems of anonymity in general are the problems that arise regarding tape recording of interviews, which bring up the question of how the interview should be recorded and what explanation of the recording technique should be made to the respondent.

RECORDING THE INTERVIEW

The best method for recording the interview must be decided on the basis of various criteria. For example, the method that obtains the most complete and accurate detail may be chosen, or which affords optimal interpersonal relations, or which makes the analysis of the data most efficient. We assume the most valid criterion is that of obtaining complete and accurate information, regardless of the effects upon the problems of analysis. Information collected efficiently is of questionable value if it is not also valid. Of course, there are degrees of reliability and validity which must be considered in relation to the purpose of the project and weighed against the merits of efficiency.

"Taking notes" may consist of either recording the respondent's statements in his own words, noting important relevant central ideas, classifying the responses by checking some predefined answer categories, or taking "probe notes." Probe notes are specific points jotted down to be elaborated or clarified later, rather than notes taken to record detailed relevant information.

Note-taking on informal interviews

Recording the interview covers many kinds of activities. In the case of informal interviewing (as in anthropological studies), where the respondent does not see the researcher in the formal role of interviewer, the researcher should not take notes of any kind during the interview. It is typical in participant-observation to make notes on one's observations of others and of his own reactions after leaving the scene.

Note-taking on structured interviews

In a more formal interview, the problem of noting the relevant information varies according to the scope of the questions to be asked and the degree to which the answers are structured. Where the scope is broad and the answers left open-ended, there is greater difficulty in recording the answers, unless the breadth and openness are used mainly to facilitate the spontaneous flow of communication and the proportion of relevant information is low and falls into anticipated, clearly recognizable categories. In this case, recording the relevant data can be efficient and does not tend to interfere with with the interviewer's tasks of critically listening and evaluating the information. The interviewer may be simply required to check a box or to circle a number.

Sometimes the response is not clearly codable into the response categories given. In this case, the interviewer should give the response as completely as possible, and in some cases, check the category which seems nearest to fitting the response. This then becomes a coding problem.

In cases where it is advisable to let the respondent know the answer choices, they may be included as part of the question or the choices can be printed on a card to be handed to the respondent, as illustrated in the chapter on interviewing techniques.

Verbatim notes. For some purposes, it is necessary for the interviewer to record the responses "verbatim." In many situations, it is not humanly possible for the interviewer to record the total interview verbatim. When the respondent is highly emotional, ungrammatical, or erratic in his verbal pacing, and yet a complete report is needed, the only solution is to use a tape recorder. The verbatim recording of responses in longhand that is a common practice of many survey-type studies is valid only in the following situations:

a. We need the exact words and phrases used by the respondent.
b. The responses cannot practically be categorized in advance.
c. The scope of the question is narrow enough that the relevant response is short and uncomplicated.

d. The essence of the relevant response can be written without damaging rapport in the interview.

e. The interviewer can complete any missing words immediately after the interview before going on to the next.

f. The interviewer's handwriting is corrected or clarified before going on to the next interview so that the people who code the responses may reliably read them.

Under these conditions, when verbatim notes are needed, the interviewer must carefully discipline himself to avoid paraphrasing or summarizing the respondent's ideas.

One method of obtaining verbatim or other fairly detailed notes without either being distracted from listening to the respondent or using a tape recorder is to use a two-person interviewing team, with one person asking the questions while the other takes notes. In some cases it is useful for the two to exchange roles from time to time. A few of the pros and cons of these "tandem interviews" are discussed by Kincaid and Bright.[1] Although this system has advantages, in that it leaves the interviewer free of note-taking to give full attention to what the respondent is saying and yet avoids the possible objections to a tape recorder, we must carefully evaluate the probable inhibiting effects of the third person in the context of a particular interview situation.

Probe notes. Another type of note-taking is the use of probe notes. In contrast to verbatim notes (which are aimed at storing the information received), the probe notes are taken to remind the interviewer of specific points which should be elaborated or clarified later in the interview. They are similar to verbatim notes in that they include the exact word or phrase used by the respondent rather than a paraphrase or summary. The less the interview is structured by a detailed interview schedule and the more important it is to not interrupt the respondent's association pattern by immediately probing any unclear or incomplete response, the more necessary it is to take probe notes so that the relevant points may be elaborated and clarified later.

Effects of note-taking on rapport. Taking notes in an interview may have several effects. Intense note-taking may distract the interviewer from his task of observing and listening to the respondent. Also, the respondent may feel the interviewer should not neglect him and should show more spontaneous appreciation. When few notes are taken, the respondent may feel that, when the interviewer is writing, something important has been said. In hostile territory, it is usually better to leave note-taking until after the interview if the session is short and the details

---

[1] H. V. Kincaid and M. Bright, "The Tandem Interview: A Trial of the Two-Interviewer Team," *Public Opinion Quarterly*, vol. 21 (Summer 1957), pp. 304–12.

are few. The interviewer can often detect the respondent's positive or negative reaction to the note-taking by the latter's tendency to elaborate at those points where the interviewer is taking notes, to go back and qualify or "correct" those points, or to quickly pass on to a new topic.

In some situations, the poised pencil seems to act as a nonverbal probe to "tell me more about that." Where note-taking seems to have a negative effect, the interviewer can ameliorate some of the effect by devoting his full attention to the respondent and taking as little notice of his own note-taking as possible. The interviewer should never attempt to take notes secretly. If the effect of taking notes is detrimental, then the danger of being caught or even suspected would be much more detrimental. The best approach is to assure the respondent of anonymity and to explain that notes must be taken to insure completeness and accuracy. When he does not accept this idea, it is better to refrain from taking notes.

Tape-recording the interview

The tape recorder is not used in most interviewing, not only because of the cost of tape and recording machines, but also because of the high cost per interview for transcribing and coding the relevant information. If every word of the interview is to be transcribed, it may require from 3 to 12 hours of typing for each hour of recording. This ratio varies with the speed of the speech, clarity, pacing, complexity of vocabulary, and accents of the interviewer or respondent, as well as with the background knowledge and technical skill of the typist.

Despite these disadvantages of economy, particularly for large-scale projects, the tape recorder is an invaluable tool for certain phases of interviewing. Even on those projects which depend mainly on highly structured interview schedules, the tape recorder is an excellent tool in the initial exploratory interviewing and subsequent pretesting of the interview schedule.

The tape recorder is almost indispensable for the teaching and supervising of interviewing. It would seem ludicrous to try to teach painting without seeing the student paint a picture, or to teach swimming without seeing the person in the water, but people are often taught to interview without the advantage of having any experienced person actually hear them interview. Instead, an attempt is often made to learn by reading detailed instructions or basic theoretical ideas, perhaps doing some role-playing, and then going out to learn by doing. Also, the supervisor of the interviewers on a large project may determine the interviewer's skill by noting such objective indices as whether all the questions have been answered, whether verbatim notes are clearly legible, and whether the quota of interviews is completed on schedule. All of these indices do not tell us whether the interviewer unwittingly loads the questions with his tone of voice, whether he interrupts the respondent, whether he probes for more information at appropriate points and whether he correctly codes or records what the respondent has said.

Also, for the person who wants to improve his interviewing independently, the tape recorder is a boon. Without it, he cannot be fully aware of where he accepted inadequate information without probing, where he missed specific opportunities to probe, and where he failed to note important nonverbal cues from the respondent. All of these can be recorded on tape and heard more accurately by the interviewer later when he is free from the strain of listening, recording, and deciding what to say next. Another unique advantage is that precisely the same behavior can be analyzed several times by the same or different people.

In addition to being used as a tool for teaching, supervision, and self-instruction, the tape recorder is sometimes needed for all of the interviews in some types of data-gathering projects. In deciding whether the tape recorder should be used in this way, there are many variables to consider. Objective evidence has been accumulated showing that much of the apprehension about the inhibiting effects of using the tape recorder are valid only under certain limited circumstances. One of the most comprehensive and thoughtful treatments of the pros and cons of using the tape recorder is given by Bucher, Fritz, and Quarantelli.[2] Another article by Engle[3] deals with the advantages of using the tape recorder in consumer research, and Womer and Boyd[4] show the value of the tape recorder in the simultaneous training and selection of an interviewer for a particular field study. These and other more atomistic experimental studies can be subsumed under some general principles to guide our decision as to whether or not we should plan on using a tape recorder on a specific project.

The more complex the information, the less the method should depend upon the interviewer's memory. The more rapid the flow of relevant information, the less we should depend upon taking longhand notes. The more we wish to explore for unanticipated types of responses and the less sure we are of what categories of information are relevant

---

[2] Rue Bucher, Charles E. Fritz, and Enrico L. Quarantelli, "Tape Recorded Interviews in Social Research," *American Sociological Review,* vol. 21, no. 3 (June 1956), pp. 359–64.

[3] J. F. Engle, "Tape Recorders in Consumer Research," *Journal of Marketing,* vol. 26 (April 1962), pp. 73–74.

[4] S. Womer and H. W. Boyd, Jr., "The Use of a Voice Recorder in the Selection and Training of Field Workers," *Public Opinion Quarterly,* vol. 15 (Summer 1951), pp. 358–63.

to the problem, the more we should use a tape recorder, which omits nothing and allows the relevance of the responses to be decided later. The greater the significance of the precise words used and the order in which ideas are expressed, the more necessary it is to use a tape recorder. The less topic control is used, and the less the sequence of topics is controlled, the more important it is for the interviewer to be relieved of verbatim reporting in longhand and allowed to devote more attention to probe notes. The more important it is for the interviewer to devote full attention to the respondent to obtain optimal interpersonal relations, the more important it is to use the tape recorder.[5] However, because of the time consumed in transcribing or coding, the tape recorder should never be used if all relevant data can be validly recorded on the spot by the interviewer. One exception would be the situation where the interviewer tape records in order to improve his technical and tactical skills.

Thus, even though the vast majority of interviews done by both specialized and auxiliary interviewers are not done with a tape recorder, the writer feels that it has a unique function in the exploratory interviewing phase of many large-scale projects, for teaching, supervision, and self-instruction in interviewing, as well as for collecting all of the data on certain types of projects. Thus, it is worthwhile to deal with some of the basic ideas involved in using the tape recorder for any one of these purposes.

When a tape recorder is to be used, here are several precautions that should be taken to facilitate optimal interpersonal relations:

a. The interviewer should become thoroughly familiar with the machine so that he does not feel insecure in its use or devote too much attention to it.
b. The physical setting should be arranged, if possible, so that the tape recorder is out of the respondent's sight.
c. The microphone should be inconspicuous and out of the direct line of sight as the interviewer and respondent face each other.
d. The use of the recording machine should be explained in forthright and matter-of-fact way.
e. Once the interview begins, the interviewer should show no awareness of the tape recorder's presence.

In explaining the use of the tape recorder to the respondent, the interviewer realizes, with experience, that it is rare to find a respondent who will object to its use. It is possible for the interviewer to raise doubts

---

[5] Charlotte H. Wilkie, "A Study of Distortions in Recording Interviews," *Social Work*, vol. 8, no. 3 (July 1963), pp. 31–36. This study shows how distortions in recording seriously limited the worker's understanding of the client's problems.

in the respondent's mind by *asking* for the respondent's permission to use the machine rather than *explaining* why it is used. The interviewer should show by his manner that it is merely routine procedure. Some explanation such as one of the following is usually sufficient:

I am interested in getting all the details of your story in precisely your own words. Since I can't take shorthand and don't want a third person present, the best way is to let this machine do all the work.

or:

We always record the interview so that the information will be accurate. I listen to it and type the relevant material so that the tape can be used over again.

It sometimes breaks the ice to let the respondent hear himself and to assure him that he is right when he says the recording seems to distort his voice.

Transcribing tape-recorded information

The problem of transcribing the information from a tape-recorded interview depends on how much of the total flow must be transcribed, either because it is clearly relevant, near-relevant, or provides a context in which to interpret the relevant. The proportion to be transcribed from the tape could vary from none to 90 percent. It would be none only if coders were to listen to the tape for information clearly falling into relevant categories for which only a frequency count is necessary. If such information occurs rarely, the only way to do a reliability check is to have two coders listen independently to the same tape, record the location on the tape (giving the numbers on the tape meter at that moment), and then check to see if they recorded the same numbers in the same categories.

If the form of the statements, their contexts, or their sequence is important to know, the relevant information must be transcribed regardless of how much or how little there is. Ideally, the interviewer should also be a good typist in the sense that he can type fast and accurately record all relevant information even though there may be misspellings and crossed out words. Let us look at some of the reasons for having the interviewer also do the transcribing.

The transcribing should be done by the same person who did the inter-view. First, if because of field conditions there is some lack of perfect audibility in the tape, the person who did the interview is much less likely to make errors in transcribing. Second, if the interviewer has been careless in those details essential to obtaining a clearly audible recording, he then directly reaps the results of his carelessness. This supplies a strong motivation to get good audibility in subsequent interviews. Third, if there are peculiarities of speech, such as regional, or foreign accents, the interviewer is more likely to be able to understand it. Fourth, it is an excellent training device, since it makes the interviewer acutely aware of his errors in tactics and techniques. Fifth, the interviewer becomes aware of the amount of missing information and is strongly motivated to probe more persistently in subsequent interviews.

The relevant material should first be transcribed in the order it occurred on the tape with no attempt to organize it systematically. Keeping the information in sequence is not only more practical than attempting to code it as we go, but this also preserves the unique context. This practice assumes that the interviewer who is doing the transcribing has a clear grasp of the problem and therefore is capable of selecting the *relevant* information. This assumption is warranted since, as we pointed out previously, unscheduled interviewing cannot be done successfully by anyone who does not thoroughly understand the problem. This selection process sharpens the interviewer's awareness of the problem and makes him acutely aware of any shortcomings in the information he has obtained. As a general rule, unless material is clearly irrelevant, it should be transcribed. It can later be rejected in the coding process.

The transcribed material should then be coded by the interviewer and another person familiar with the problem. As a reliability check, the material should be coded by independent coders who are familiar with the problem. There is a real danger in using the test-retest measure of reliability if this is done only by the original interviewer, because in many cases he tends to read into the material more than is there. If the second coder does not code some material in the same way, it is often because he sees less information in the material than the interviewer does. In this case, the interviewer might become aware that he is judging on the basis of additional information and insights which have not been transcribed from the tape. Often, there is a certain *gestalt* in the total interview which is lost in the transcription, thus possibly making the original interviewer's judgement more accurate. At any rate, the cross-check between the interviewer and the noninterviewer provides a more balanced view and forces the interviewer to support his interpretations with clearer evidence. Often, the interviewer becomes aware that he should include in the transcription significant nonsymbolic cues which influenced his interpretation of the material. This usually increases the agreement between the interviewer and the noninterviewer coding the material.

The interviewers on the project should transcribe and code their first interview as soon as possible so that subsequent interviews will benefit from the experience. This practice is beneficial whether the main purpose of the project is to learn interviewing techniques or whether the main aim is to obtain complete, reliable, and valid information. Having the interviewing, transcribing, and coding all done by the same people improves the quality of the data in situations where nonscheduled interviewing is needed; therefore, the sooner these experiences are combined in one interview, the sooner the next interview will be improved.

Another distinct advantage of alternating interviewing and transcribing is that it provides a more balanced variety of activities throughout the life of the project and saves the interviewer from continuous long hours of tedious transcription and coding of data.

Sometimes the objection is made that having the interviewing, transcribing, and coding done by highly skilled people will make the cost of the operation prohibitive. This argument can be reduced to, "It costs too much to get accurate information so let's spend less and get inaccurate information." We have no choice if we decide that tape-recorded nonscheduled interviews should be used only to get information that could not be obtained just as effectively by a questionnaire or a highly structured interview. Open-ended data cannot be reliably coded by people who do not thoroughly understand the problem. Nor can nonscheduled interviewing be done by people who are merely following mechanical rules. Since it takes a considerable investment of time to familiarize someone with the problem, it is more efficient to use the same people for both the coding and the interviewing. But why shouldn't we use professional typists to transcribe the data? Here the answer is not so clear cut.

There are certain conditions under which it is more efficient to have typists do the transcribing. If the audibility of the tape is extremely clear, if the typists are sufficiently impressed with the importance of accuracy, and if the proportion of relevant data is so high that it is quicker to transcribe the whole interview than to select out the relevant material, then the use of typists may be satisfactory.

We have found the proportion of directly relevant interview material to vary from one to 90 percent. For a number of reasons, the use of typists is probably not economical when, for example, only 40 percent of the information is relevant. They often make errors at crucial points in the interview which can be checked only by having someone familiar with the interview situation listen to the tape and check it against the typescript. Also, the length of time required to type the total interview is sometimes greater than that required for the interviewer, who may not be as good a typist, to select and type 40 percent of the interview. The coding process is cumbersome when there is a large proportion of extraneous material. Also, the amount of inaudible material will be much greater if the interviewers are not responsible for doing their own transcribing.

Poor audibility is one of the main causes of transcribing difficulty! Sometimes one hour of tape-recorded material can be transcribed in as little as three hours if the rate of speech is average and the audibility perfect. However, ten hours might be needed to transcribe one hour of tape with poor audibility.

PLANNING THE OPENING QUESTION

Even though the interview is not scheduled to the extent of providing exact questions or an order for covering subtopics, it is advisable for the interviewer to prepare several opening questions. The importance of the opening question is too great to leave to caprice, yet neither should it be rigidly predetermined.

There are several important and unique functions of the opening question. It may either be broad enough to delineate the entire topic of the interview, or it may select a single point of departure. In either case, it should be clearly connected with the explanation of the interview so that the respondent is immediately aware that the interviewer is pursuing the stated purposes. If possible it should ask for information which is relatively easy for the respondent to give so that there is no chance of ego threat at the outset. The opener may also begin with a point on which the respondent feels particularly qualified to speak, thus appealing to his need for recognition. A well-phrased question might also demonstrate sympathetic understanding of the respondent's problems. Finally, if the interview requires free-flowing and detailed answers rather than simple yes-no responses, it is important that the respondent realize this at the beginning.

In studying the attitudes and problems of the community's senior citizens, an excellent opening question was found to be, "Do you think there is some age at which people should stop working?" A question equally appealing to teenagers in a study of parent-child conflict was, "What are some of the things you feel parents and other adults should know to get along with teenagers?"

It is often desirable to plan opening questions for different categories of representative or special respondents, so that each can begin the interview at a point that concerns him.

In interviews where the main problem is to stimulate the respondent's memory of experiences during a certain period of time, it is useful to begin the interview with a question regarding a point in time prior to the events the interviewer wants reported. This "lead-in" helps establish associations and builds an appropriate mood and pace before dealing with the critical time period. The lead-in portion of the interview may last from 30 seconds to 10 minutes, depending on how far in the past and how detailed the experiences to be reported. The time needed for the lead-in discussion increases when it functions to supply certain background information about the respondent or the event providing a context for the interview.

When approaching each respondent, the interviewer should make it a point to get to the opening question as quickly as possible. The introduction, the explanation of the purpose and sponsorship of the study, the explanation of how the respondent was selected and the extent to which he is anonymous, and any explanation of the recording should be as economical and clear as possible in order to get into the opening question. In some cases, not all of these preliminaries are needed because the respondent understands the situation. At other times, the explanation needed is so long and involved that further explanations of the objectives of the interview, the use of the data, the respondent's anonymity or the recording method might be made as the interview progresses, at points where the context makes it more meaningful.

SUMMARY

Strategy includes the overall planning done before the actual interview is under way. This planning is done carefully on the basis of information gained regarding the field situation, but the strategy plans must be considered tentative and subject to revision on the basis of additional information gained after the interviewing begins.

Three dimensions of the general field situation friendly-hostile, open-closed, and single-multiple contacts) affect the general strategy to be used. These general types of field situations provide a backdrop for making basic decisions.

These basic decisions include the selection of appropriate respondents, of appropriate interviewers and interviewer roles, choosing an appropriate time and place, and structuring the interview situation. All of these decisions are made on the basis of their probable effect upon the respondent's willingness or ability to give the relevant information. All of them are strategy tools which can be used to minimize the inhibitors and to maximize the facilitators of relevant information. All these decisions, and their effect, depends upon their meaning to the respondent.

In selecting appropriate respondents, a distinction must be made between *key informants,* who provide strategy information on how to obtain information, and *respondents,* who provide information directly relevant to the objectives of the interview. Respondents are either *special* respondents, who have specialized types of information which can be obtained only from people in a certain role or status, or *representative* respondents, who are chosen because they share certain characteristics defining a group or category of people.

In selecting respondents, the problem is to determine who has the needed information, who is most able to give it, and who is the most willing to give it. Whether or not the person has the relevant information depends upon his experiences in relation to the purposes of the interview. His ability or willingness to report his experiences depend upon the degree to which the facilitators and inhibitors of communication are present.

Once we know what information is needed, the field situations where it must be sought, the kinds of respondents who possess such information and are most able and willing to report it, the next problem is to decide what type of interviewer is most likely to be able to obtain the information completely, validly, and efficiently. Certain overt characteristics such as sex, age, race, ethnicity, speech patterns, dress, and grooming place limits upon the role repertory of the interviewer by determining the respondent's perception of him. Of these overt characteristics, only dress and grooming are easily changed. The others can be controlled only by selecting the appropriate person as interviewer. The interviewer's basic personality traits are also important insofar as they determine his ability to perform his interviewing task. Since, by definition, these traits cannot be changed to fit the interview situation or the type of respondent, the problem must be solved by selecting the right interviewer for a particular task. Interviewers may also be selected on the basis of certain special knowledge needed and for the presence or absence of certain attitudes. To a certain extent, the relevant knowledge can be acquired for the particular interviewing task and attitudes can be controlled by training, but there are practical limits upon both.

From the point of view of a particular interviewer, his task is to determine which auxiliary role or roles in his own natural role repertory he should present to the respondent or which new auxiliary role he can or should take to facilitate interviewing. The particular role taken by the interviewer is important only insofar as it puts him in a different relationship with the respondent. Role relationships exist along at least two dimensions: the in-group–out-group dimension and the superordinate-subordinate dimension. In appraising the in-group–out-group dimension certain conditions can be specified giving advantages to both ends of the continuum. Similarly, there are advantages and disadvantages in both the superordinate and the subordinate role. The desirability of a particular role relationship depends upon how it affects the respondent's willingness to give relevant information.

The place of the interview provides the opportunity to communicate and, like a stage set, acts as a context for action which brings certain auxiliary roles to the foreground for both the interviewer and the respondent. The respondent's self-perception and his perception of the interviewer has an effect upon the degree to which certain information is inhibited because of ego threat or etiquette. In addition, the setting may minimize competing time demands, stimulate recall, and provide the conditions needed for the interviewer to use his techniques and tactics to full advantage.

The temporal setting of the interview is significant in its relationship to the time of the experiences which the respondent is reporting. When the interviewer asks the question determines to a great extent both the respondent's ability and his willingness to give the information. The selection of an appropriate time can minimize the inhibiting effect of forgetting, ego threat, and competing time demands, as well as maximize the facilitating effect of sympathetic understanding, catharsis, and the respondent's need for meaning.

The final phase of strategy consists of structuring the interview situation before the actual questioning and probing begin. To assure best results, the interviewer must have planned how to introduce himself, how to explain the sponsorship and purpose of the interview, how to explain the selection of the particular respondent, how much anonymity should be promised, how to record the interview, and several possible opening questions. These aspects influence the respondent's views of the interviewer's role and of what information is relevant, as well as his willingness to give relevant information.

Strategy problems have many dimensions. It is impossible to provide a specific solution for each possible problem. Instead, we have pointed to some of the available strategy tools and must leave their application to multitudinous specific situations to the interviewer. The writer's experience in consulting and in training interviewers shows that many of the strategy errors were avoidable in that the interviewer had at his command resources to solve the problems. Failures most frequently resulted from not raising the right questions before leaping into the situation.

Laboratory problem 8

Field strategy in hostile territory

Purpose

This laboratory problem is selected to challenge your creativity in applying concepts and sensitivities to the solution of a real field strategy problem. You should draw upon previous reading, the laboratory problems, and your own personal experiences in designing these armchair strategy plans.

This particular field study was chosen not because it is typical but because it had an unusually large number and variety of strategy problems which had to be solved in a short five-day field operation. It was a field operation in basically hostile territory, since the study was designed to probe deeply into highly sensitive political areas during the witch-hunting days of the Joseph McCarthy era of the late 1950s.

Your problem is to design certain essential aspects in the field strategy of the clean-up phase of this nationwide study[6] in which it was necessary to detect why 20 of the 180 American colleges and universities in the national sample refused to allow interviewers from the Elmo Roper organization to interview faculty members about academic freedom at their institutions.

Procedure

You are to take the role of a consultant-interviewer who was hired by the Fund for the Republic to carry out the clean-up phase on the

---

[6] Paul F. Lazarsfeld and J. W. Thielens, *The Academic Mind* (Glencoe, Ill.: 1958). This book gives the statistical summaries and interpretation of the data collected from the 160 cooperating institutions.

20 reluctant campuses. The field situation is rich with potential strategy problems. You should try to anticipate, avoid, and solve as many of them as possible within the limitations described below.

a.   Carefully read the detailed description of the Academic Freedom Study which follows.
b.   Answer the four essay questions which follow the description, and prepare to discuss your solutions in small groups or in the larger class.
c.   Answer the 14 multiple-choice strategy questions provided by the instructor.
d.   Discuss your answers to the four essay questions with others who have already answered them. Be alert for problems you didn't see or solutions you didn't find, and share your solutions when you think they are as good or better as those of others.
e.   After the instructor has done a summary of the group's responses to the 14 questions, the group can discuss those questions where there was least agreement upon the answers.

Academic freedom study

Purpose: The Fund for the Republic, a foundation to support the study of Constitutional Freedoms in America, was interested in measuring the amount of apprehension developed in institutions of higher learning as a result of the political attacks on academic freedom which had been occuring throughout the nation. Specifically the Fund wanted to discover the nature and amount of curtailment of academic freedom and the amount of fear generated by this repression. Academic freedom was interpreted broadly to include freedom of speech, assembly, and the press for students, teachers, and administrators.

The Fund contracted with Elmo Roper Associates in New York and the National Opinion Research Center in Chicago to send interviewers to 180 colleges and universities in the United States. This constituted a 10 percent random sample of all colleges and universities at that time. The exact nature of the information sought is illustrated by the ten key questions in Exhibit A which were selected from the 28-page questionnaire.

EXHIBIT A

1. Is it your impression that there is greater concern these days than 6 or 7 years ago on the part of the public and groups outside the college over teachers' political opinions and what political matters are taught in the classroom, or not?

2. In the past few years, have you felt that your own academic freedom has been threatened in any way or not? If so, how?

3. Have some colleagues here on campus ever given you advice on how to avoid getting into political trouble at this college?

4. Have you ever wondered that some political opinion you've expressed might affect your job security or promotion at this college?

5. Have you toned down anything you have written lately because you were worried that it might cause too much controversy?

6. I wonder if you would tell me what political groups or organizations interested in public affairs you belong to or make contributions to? Any others?

7. Do you usually express your own personal views on the subjects you teach, or do you usually try to avoid that?

8. Have you ever felt that you were being watched in a classroom?

9. Are there any groups that teachers might belong to that you feel are likely to be attacked as being subversive? Any others?

10. Do you know of any cases of teachers who would have been added to the staff if they hadn't had controversial political views?

Approach to the college administrations

Once the sample of colleges and universities was selected, the presidents of each were contacted by mail to gain their cooperation. The letter is shown in Exhibit B which follows. It was explained that the Fund for the Republic had been set up to do an objective study of the state of the Constitutional Freedoms in America and is, therefore, also interested in freedom of speech on college campuses.

The letter was signed by Paul Lazarsfeld of Columbia University as Director of the study and a sheet was enclosed explaining the purpose of the Fund and giving a complete list of the officers and board of directors (see Exhibit C). It was explained to each president that neither the individuals nor the institutions would be identified in any of the reports. If there was no reply to the letter, it was followed up with a more personal letter. If there was still no response, a telegram request-

EXHIBIT B

ROOM 4601
30 ROCKEFELLER PLAZA
NEW YORK 20, N.Y.

Dear President_____ :

I am writing you about a study we are conducting among a cross section of American colleges and universities. Over the past months and years, many claims and counter claims have been made on the concern about academic freedom that exists among teachers in our colleges and universities. Our aim is an effort to make an assessment of the situation on a nationwide basis.

The study itself will cover a cross section of social science teachers and some administrators at a cross section of accredited academic institutions, and will deal with the presence or absence and the degree of apprehension that exists on the American campus today.

As an educator, you will understand, I feel sure, why we want information in this significant area. In a way, a study like this is a form of "social bookkeeping." It is one effort—by no means the only approach—to find out at this recorded point of time the climate of opinion among social science faculty members and those entrusted with the responsibility of running our colleges and universities. In this sense, we can see some usefulness to historians looking for recorded evidence of this period, as well as for people concerned with assessing the facts in the current situation today. The study is being sponsored by the Fund for the Republic.

We hope to be able to begin interviewing members of your faculty and of your administration within the next few weeks and we would like to work in close contact with you. We are aware, however, of the heavy load you are undoubtedly already carrying and we would be delighted to work with anyone in your administration whom you should want to designate to act for you. On hearing from you, we shall want to get in touch with that person, or with you, regarding the specific details and arrangements for the study.

We shall be deeply grateful for your cooperation

Sincerely yours,
Paul F. Lazarsfeld
Director

EXHIBIT C

THE FUND FOR THE REPUBLIC

The Fund for the Republic was established as an independent corporation by the Ford Foundation, with an appropriation of $15,000,000 "to support activities directed toward the elimination of restrictions of thought, inquiry and expression in the United States, and the development of policies and procedures best adapted to protect these rights."

The Fund, which began operations in early 1953, has no connection with the Ford Foundation today.

The Fund regards its sphere of operation as comprising all questions of civil liberties and racial and religious discrimination in the United States. It takes as its basic charter the Declaration of Independence, the Constitution and the Bill of Rights.

Among the Fund's current and immediate concerns are the problems involved in restrictions and assaults upon academic freedom, the principles of due process and equal protection under the laws, the protection of the rights of minorities, the activities of private groups in censorship, boycotting and blacklisting and the principle of guilt by association and its application in the United States today.

Directors of the Fund:

Paul G. Hoffman, Chairman of the Board of the Fund
Harry S. Ashmore, Executive Editor, Arkansas Gazette
Chester Bowles, Essex, Connecticut
Charles W. Cole, President, Amherst College
Russell L. Dearmont, Attorney, St. Louis
Richard F. Finnegan, Consulting Editor, Chicago Sun-Times
Erwin N. Griswold, Dean, Harvard Law School
Robert M. Hutchins, President, The Fund for the Republic
William H. Joyce, Jr., Chairman of the Board, Joyce Inc., Pasadena
Meyer Kestenbaum, President, Hart, Schaffner & Marx, Chicago
M. Albert Linton, Chairman of the Board, Provident Mutual Life
    Insurance Company, Philadelphia
John Lord O'Brian, Attorney, Coving & Burling, Washington
Jubal R. Parten, President, Woodley Petroleum Co., Houston
Elmo Roper, Marketing Consultant, New York City
Robert E. Sherwood, The Playwrights Company, New York City
George N. Shuster, President, Hunter College
Mrs. Eleanor B. Stevenson, Oberlin, Ohio
James D. Zellerbach, President, Crown Zellerbach Corp., San Francisco

Officers of the Fund:

President: Robert M. Hutchins
Vice President: W. H. Ferry
Secretary: David F. Freeman

The headquarters of the Fund are at 1 East 54th Street, New York 22; Plaza 1–3170

ing a collect reply was sent. As a result of this procedure 160 colleges agreed to cooperate, and the remaining 20 declined for various reasons. The replies of the presidents of 4 of these 20 colleges can be seen in Exhibit D.

Five consultants went to the 20 colleges (each consultant visiting 4) to attempt to obtain the cooperation of the reluctant college presidents. If the president still refused to allow the Roper interviewers to come on campus, the consultant was to discover why the president was refusing, and to obtain accurate information on any specific cases of restrictions of academic freedom which had occurred on campus that the president or others might be trying to hide.

EXHIBIT D

TO: Consultant X
FROM: Louis Harris
RE: Running account of correspondence with 4 nonresponse colleges

College A

On March 16th, President A wrote: "In response to your letter of March 14th I wish to advise that we are not at liberty at this time to join the project of which you speak. Our commitments at this season of the year are such as to preempt the time available to our staff." No further contact.

College B

On March 21st, President B wrote: "We appreciate the honor of being selected by you as one of the colleges drawn for participation in your study of academic freedom. It happens, however, that we are this year engaged in a comprehensive self-study which is commanding the attention of our faculty to such an extent that I believe it unwise to take on an additional project of the type you have in mind. For the remainder of this year the members of our faculty will be carrying an extra load which is so great that we must decline your invitation to participate in your study. Thanks again for the invitation."

University C

No response to original letter of March 14th so we wired President C on March 30, urging him to reply. On March 31 he wired: "In response to your letter and telegram X University will not be able to participate in proposed study."

College D

After two follow-up telegrams, President D wired on April 12th: "Regret state that we shall not be prepared to receive you in April nor before the middle of June even if then." No further contact.

EXHIBIT E

The Fund For the Republic, Inc.
1 East 54th Street
New York 22, N.Y.

———

Plaza 1–3170

To whom it may concern:
   This is to certify that Mr. X is an authorized representative of the Fund for the Republic on special assignment in connection with our study on academic freedom. We will appreciate any cooperation rendered him.

Sincerely yours,
Louis Harris
Co-Director

   If successful in persuading the president to cooperate, the consultant was to call Elmo Roper Associates in New York to have the interviewers proceed in the usual manner. However, the consultant was to continue an informal investigation, off campus if necessary, in case the president changed his mind after the interviewers arrived.

   Each consultant was instructed by the Fund to never begin interviewing on any campus before contacting the president's office so that he could not be accused of snooping without the president's permission.

The strategy problems

   You are the consultant assigned to four colleges in Pennsylvania, Ohio, and Indiana whose replies were given in Exhibit D. You are supplied with a letter "to whom it may concern" from the Fund for the Republic as shown in Exhibit E. You begin your initial contacts in the last week of May.

   On the basis of the information you have in this case, your theory of information gathering, and knowledge of the general nature of academic institutions, give thoughtful answers to the four questions below.

   In answering the questions you should make the following assumptions:

   a. You can stay no more than two days on each campus.
   b. You can systematically interview no more than 10 people in addition to the president on each campus, but others can be contacted on or off campus for specific items of information useful in locating respondents or getting background information.

    c. Most of the presidents will still not give their permission for the full-scale study by the Roper interviewers. Some will try to stop the consultant from talking to any of the faculty.

Part I (*Essay questions*)

1. Make a list of six people, in addition to the president, who you feel would be the most important to interview on each campus. First, describe the *one* most ideal type of respondent; then give a short description of the most relevant characteristics of the other seven. In cases where the relevance of a characteristic is not obvious, explain how it is related to the objectives of the study. List them in the order in which you think it would be best to interview them.

2. Explain in detail how you would go about *identifying, locating,* and *contacting* the most useful respondents on a college campus. Describe the whole process from the time you accept the assignment until the last person is interviewed. Make clear the *sequence* of your moves and indicate all the *sources* of information you would use and how you would use them. This strategy plan should show how you would identify, locate, and contact each of the respondents mentioned in the previous problem and at the same time lead to any other possible respondents which you might not have anticipated.

3. What are some of the strategies which might be attempted by a college president to prevent the interviewer from obtaining the needed information?

4. What type of person would make the ideal interviewer for this study if only one interviewer could be used? Give his personal characteristics and the role and status he should assume while interviewing administrators, faculty, and students.

Part II (*Multiple-choice questions*)

If you are going to do *both* Part I (essay) and Part II (multiple-choice), you should do Part I first and discuss it *before* doing Part II. Then when you approach Part II, you will have to assume a new perspective because you may often feel forced to select the least of the evils in being restricted to the five answer choices. Nevertheless, it will be interesting to compare the "least of the evils" with the solution you might have already proposed in your essay.

The instructor will supply you with the multiple-choice questions.

13

Sample surveys

This chapter deals with the sample survey as one type of field strategy which may provide the context for interviewing as well as other modes of data collection. We will concentrate mainly on the sample survey from the viewpoint of the interviewer and the field supervisor. We will omit the research design phase of the survey by assuming that the purpose of the survey is clear, the specific questions have been formulated, the universe of respondents has been delineated, the statistical treatment of the information has been planned, and arrangements have been made for appropriate data processing. We will deal with sampling design only as it affects the behavior of the interviewer or supervisor and omit the mathematical theory of sampling which is available in standard statistics books.

BASIC TYPES OF SAMPLE SURVEYS

It is desirable to know the basic dimensions that distinguish one type of sample survey from another in order to decide when a sample survey rather than some other strategy should be used and to fit the survey design, when it is needed, to its purposes.

Any study that requires the analysis of only one case *cannot* use a sample survey. The word *case* is used in this context to refer to the element to be analyzed regardless of whether it is a person, a group, an organization, institution, or event. But any study which calls for making statements about an aggregate of many elements belonging to the same category (population, or universe) without studying every case in that category *can* use a sample survey.

Once it is clear that a sample survey is needed, we have the choice of several kinds. First, we must decide whether the sampling element is to be individual people, families, groups, organizations, institutions, events, or processes of change. Second, we can then decide whether the purpose can be best accomplished by a one-shot, cross-sectional survey or a longitudinal sampling at different times. Third, if the time dimension is important, we then must choose among a trend study, a cohort study, and a panel study. Fourth, after these decisions are made we are ready to choose among different sampling strategies. Now let us look at these distinctions one at a time.

Sampling element

The sampling element is the object or events to be analyzed. Too frequently it is assumed that in a survey the sampling element must be an individual. Perhaps this restricted view springs from the assumption that if we *interview* individuals then we are trying to *analyze* individuals. For example, if we want to understand the process of school desegregation in large cities we would have to interview a large number of individuals but the aim is to understand specific cases of an *event* called desegregation. Our element of analysis would be the desegregation event in big-city schools. If we studied only one case, we would not have a sample survey even though many individuals might be interviewed because we would deal only with the key informants who were actually involved in the one decision either to desegregate or not. If, however, we wanted to study many cases of successful and unsuccessful desegregation in order to generalize about the process we would have to take a sample of schools that was representative of all schools of a certain category and compare segregation versus desegregation decisions.

In thinking about the sampling element it is also useful to distinguish between studying static characteristics of any element and studying actions or processes in which it may engage. For example, we can either focus on relatively fixed characteristics of a person such as sex, age, political affiliation, religious background, and race, or we can focus on events or behaviors of that individual, such as how he decides to vote for or against a particular candidate. In the first case we may engage in a spatial sampling of people as physical objects, but in the second situation we must have some way of pinpointing the event in time. Some events, such as births, deaths, marriages, bankruptcies, are already neatly recorded and listed, so that a random sample can be easily drawn. Other events, such as starting to smoke marijuana, having extramarital sexual relations, or deciding to shoplift, are not recorded in any systematic way so that sampling becomes a much more difficult problem.

Cross-sectional versus longitudinal surveys

Once we have specified the sampling elements, we must choose between two general types of sample surveys: the cross-sectional and the longitudinal. The *cross-sectional* survey is used to describe certain properties of the elements at a single point in time. Even though there may be two or more samples or subsamples to allow comparison, the point of the comparison is between two different universes at the *same* point in time. A *longitudinal* survey is one that samples the same universe at two *different* points in time. There are three different varieties of longitudinal surveys: trends, cohorts, and panels.

Trend studies. In *trend* studies the universe is defined as all of those units (persons, groups, institutions, or communities) in a certain category or geographical location at the different points in time they are sampled. For example, trends in Bostonians' attitudes toward divorce could be shown by taking a random sample of the residents of Boston on April 1 of each year. In the trend study the sample will be different people each year because a different sample is taken. Also, the characteristics of the people (age, sex ratio, race, etc.) may differ from sample to sample because of change in the composition of the population of the city from year to year. In this case we do not know whether any change in attitude is due to a general change in U.S. public opinion or to a change in the composition of the city's population unless we also collect information on such demographic variables as age, sex, race, religion, and ethnicity so that we can compare trends among these subsamples.

Cohort studies. A second type of longitudinal survey is the *cohort* study. In the cohort study the universe is defined as a certain age-group. The particular age group chosen for the first survey is followed through time. Thus, if we sample 18-year-olds in 1975, we then take a sample of 19-year-olds one year later. In essence the cohort study follows a certain age group through time, so that the sample is one year older each year. The cohort may be either uniform in age, as in a study beginning with first-graders in the public schools, or varied in age, as in a study of people leaving the Army in 1975. The requirements of a cohort study are fulfilled as long as the successive samples of the same category of people are getting older each year. The point of the cohort study is to focus on changes that take place as a person (or any other sampling element, such as an institution) goes through the life cycle.

Both the trend study and the cohort study preclude any direct analysis of the *causes* for the changes in individuals since different people are in the different samples. For example, if it is found that 50 percent of the 21-year-old college students in 1970 felt it advisable to put the Panama Canal under United Nations' jurisdiction and 90 percent of the 31-year-olds felt this way in 1980, we could not study why certain individuals did change and others did not since there is no way of knowing which people had switched their views. Furthermore, it is possible that the percentage of the sample favorable to United Nations' jurisdiction would be precisely the same in the samples despite the fact that a sizable number shifted from pro to con, because an equal number may have shifted from con to pro. This deficiency is overcome in the panel study.

Panel studies. In the case of the *panel* study the same individuals are studied at successive points in time. Thus, at point B in time the panel can be divided into those who did not change and those who did. Those who did change are further divided by their direction of change. Then additional information about the members of the panel may be used to account for change or lack of change.

There are several limitations to the panel study. It is necessary to select a sample of a given population and faithfully collect all the needed information in repeated interviews of the *same* people. This rules out any secondary analysis of previous studies of other people done by different researchers—which is possible in trend studies and cohort studies. Another limitation lies in the fact that, even though the sample may accurately represent the population at the first point in time, they get a year older each year, thereby omitting any representation of the younger portion of the population. This might be called the *life cycle* effect. Another way in which the panel becomes unrepresentative is in the *education effect* of the repeated interviewing. It has been shown in some studies that the panel members become more sophisticated on the topic of the interview than the population in general because of the thought stimulated by the repeated interviewing. Another difficulty with the panel study is the greater difficulty of analysis, since each individuals' "before" and "after" opinions must be matched and cross-classified into different categories of change or nonchange. However, this objection is invalid since it is a logical necessity in view of the unique aim of the panel study.[1] A final source of decreasing representativeness of the panel is the *attrition* of members.

The life-cycle effects and the attrition effects in the panel study are minimized when the panel is used to explore the causes of short-range changes in the attitudes, knowledge, or opinion of the group. For example, a typical use of the panel study is to discover how people make up their minds to vote for or against a political candidate. In this case the respondent might be interviewed once a month for the last six months preceding the election. However, this short-run use of the panel does not preclude the possible educational effect. The amount of educational

[1] Donald C. Pelz and Frank M. Andrews, "Detecting Causal Priorities in Panel Study Data," *American Sociological Review*, vol. 29 (1964), pp. 836–48.

effect would depend upon the nature of the topic, how specific the interview questions were, the frequency of the interviews, and the relative force of other factors operating to change the respondent's opinion.

Approximating longitudinal surveys

There are several ways in which cross-sectional studies may approximate a longitudinal study without actually interviewing at more than one point in time. All have their strengths and weaknesses. First, the respondent may be simply asked how he feels about a certain topic at this moment and then asked to remember how he would have answered the same question at a previous point in time. This runs the risk of inaccuracy due to the memory barrier. However, it is possible with excellent depth interviewing, using tactics designed to help free the association process of the respondent, to minimize the effect of forgetting. Of course this would increase the cost per interview.

Another method of approximating the longitudinal study is to compare different age groups within the one cross-sectional sample. For example, if we want to know whether attitudes toward premarital sex relations are changing, we could compare the attitudes of the 20 to 29-year-olds with those of the 30 to 39 and the 40 to 49-year-olds. The obvious danger here is that we will confuse a life-cycle change in attitude with a historical trend.

A third way to study processes of change is to analyze the data in one cross-sectional survey according to a *scaling pattern*. For example, if we find that everyone who has done act C has also done acts A and B, and that everyone who has done act B has also done A, then we can assume an ordinal chronological relationship exists: that A must be done before B and B before C. Concretely, this could be applied to discovering the order in which people begin using certain drugs. If, for example, all heroin users had used marijuana, and all marijuana users have smoked tobacco, then we could say that there is an order in which people begin using these drugs. Or in a market research survey, we might find that everyone who owns an electronic oven also owns a freezer, television set, and refrigerator; that all those who own a freezer also have a television set and refrigerator; and that everyone who owns a television set will also have a refrigerator; and some who do not have a television set do have a refrigerator. We would then know that the order in which people acquire major electrical appliances would be as follows: refrigerator, television set, freezer, and electronic oven.

Although this application of scaling to the current pattern does give us a valid description of the chronological order of events, it cannot be interpreted as showing any causal sequence. That is, we cannot say that, because people use marijuana before heroin, this is evidence that the use of marijuana is the cause of the use of heroin. Nor can we validly conclude that since only 5 percent of those who used marijuana ever used heroin the use of marijuana is not one factor in a causal pattern leading to the use of heroin. This would be logically equivalent to saying that only 5 percent of those people exposed to a cold virus actually caught cold and therefore the virus is not a cause of colds. All we can say scientifically is that if X is not always followed by Y then X alone is not the total cause of Y.

All of the one-shot, cross-sectional attempts to study change have weaknesses compared to the longitudinal study. However, for practical purposes the shortcomings are sometimes tolerated, either because the cross-sectional survey is so much less costly than repeating the survey, or because there is not enough time to do repeated surveys into the future so a trend must be established now by reconstructing the past.

BASIC SAMPLING STRATEGIES

Once we understand the differences among basic sampling strategies, we are better able to fit a particular sample design to the type of survey we need to do. Although theoretically all of the basic sample designs could be applied to any survey, regardless of whether the sample element was a person or an institution or whether we needed a cross-sectional or longitudinal study, practically, the problems of identifying sample elements and locating respondents rule out the use of certain sampling strategies in a particular instance.

Simple random sampling

Simple random sampling assumes that we have been able to identify every member element in the universe to be sampled and that each element is represented in some way so that it can be randomly selected. By randomly selected we mean that, each time an element is selected, all of the elements in the universe have an equal chance of being chosen. For example, if we wanted to take a simple random sample of all students at State College, we could take a list of students, number them consecutively, turn to a table of random numbers (which can be found as an appendix in standard texts on survey research methods or statistics), pick an arbitrary starting point and proceed systematically across the page in any predetermined pattern to find the numbers corresponding to those to be taken from the list as the sample. The number needed for a good sample depends upon several factors which will be discussed later.

This simple random sampling method can be applied whether the sampling elements are people, groups, institutions, or geographical areas (such as blocks within a metropolitan area or counties within the United States). However, there are some very real practical limitations. First, you must be able to obtain a complete list of all elements in the universe to be sampled. This is no problem if sampling the patients in a hospital at a given moment or all of the Presbyterian churches in California; in either case there is a list of all units in the universe to be sampled. If we need a sample of all the people in Chicago, San Francisco, New York, or New Orleans, no such ready-made list exists and the cost of making such a list would be prohibitive.

Even in cases where all of the elements in a large universe are already listed (for example, the universe of telephone subscribers in New York, or the people listed in the city directory of Dayton, Ohio), there is the time-consuming task of identifying every member of the universe with a unique serial number so that every time a sample element is selected every element in the universe has an equal chance of being selected. This chore makes simple random sampling inpractical when the universe has millions of elements. There are rare situations in which the universe is large and each unit already has a serial number.

One of the principal advantages of the simple random sample is that you may stop at any point in the selection of the sample with the assurance that the sample is as representative as possible for a sample of that size. A small sample may be drawn and, if it proves to be too small to obtain the amount of accuracy needed, it may be enlarged one element at a time until the needed amount of accuracy is reached. In other types of sampling it is necessary to decide in advance the exact size of sample needed; and during the process of selection the sample does not become truly representative until all sample elements have been drawn. The implications of this will be more clear as we compare simple random sampling with systematic sampling.

Systematic sampling

In systematic sampling we must first decide how many elements we need in the sample, calculate what proportion the sample is of the universe, and then use this proportion as the sampling interval. If the sampling proportion is 10 percent, then the sampling interval is stated as "one out of ten" or every tenth unit. To select every tenth element randomly, all elements of the universe must be arranged in some consistent or systematic order. There are two basic systematic arrangements: chronological order and spatial order. In the first case we are doing a time sample in which we could either take every tenth event in chronological order or we could sample every tenth time unit of a second, minute, hour, day, week, etc.

There are several versions of systematically sampling a spatial order.

If we were to sample every tenth household in a city, we would simply start with one house and move through space in one systematic pattern taking every tenth house in the whole universe. We would not have to identify every dwelling unit in advance but merely identify each separate unit as we went along, skipping nine between each one we took.

Another version of systematic space sampling, not so obviously related to space, is sampling from an alphabetical list or a file of cards. For example, if we take every tenth name in the telephone directory we are sampling ordinal space on each page of the telephone book. In essence it is the spatial arrangement of all of the elements of the universe on a piece of paper which is significant. Whether the people are arranged in spatial sequence on the page according to their height, weight, or alphabetical order is irrelevant. Similarly, in sampling from a card file, then, it would not matter whether cards were arranged alphabetically, by social security number, or in random order.

The advantage of the systematic sample over the simple random sample is obvious. There is no need to identify every unit in the universe with an individual number or name, which in a practical situation is a tremendous savings in time. The basic disadvantage is that we must know in advance the size of sample needed, and we must proceed systematically through the *whole* universe before the sample is representative. For example, selecting 100 names from the telephone directory by taking every 10th name from A through M would not be as representative as taking every 20th name from A through Z. If we did a survey on the assumption that a sample of 100 would be large enough and then found that we needed more cases, we would have to re-design a new sample by taking, for example, every 40th name from A through Z to get an additional sample of 50 cases to increase precision.

The one condition under which the systematic sample is not representative occurs when the sampling interval happens to correspond to some periodicity in the spatial or temporal arrangement of the units in the universe. For example, if in sampling households we are using the sampling interval of 10, and there happens to be 10 houses to the block in the city we are sampling, this could introduce a bias if we began with the corner house. Every house in the sample would be a corner house which might be a second-floor residence above a corner store of some type. The result may be that we have over-represented small-store owners or renters in the sample.

A second type of systematic bias can be introduced by using an interval scale of either time or space when only the ordinal one is appropriate. For example, if in time-sampling programs broadcast by a certain television network, we tuned in every hour at 10 minutes past the hour we would introduce a bias toward the longer programs; obviously any two-hour program would have four times the chance of any half-hour program of being chosen for analysis. In order to get an unbiased sample we could simply select every Nth program in ordinal chronology rather than using some interval scale of time units.

Systematic bias could also be introduced into the space sampling of five file drawers full of mental health case folders. If we pull the cases falling at five-inch intervals, the thicker folders would have a greater chance of being chosen than the thinner folders. This would possibly bias the sample by over-representing the cases that were more complicated or that involved clinical tests, or cases that had simply been with the agency for a longer period of time.

If each case occupies an equal amount of time or space, then the interval scale is superior to the ordinal scale sampling interval. Using an interval scale we avoid counting the number of units in the universe to determine the sample interval needed to get a certain size of sample. We also avoid counting the number of cases in each sampling interval. For example, suppose we wanted to take a sample of 500 cases from the 2,000,000 automobile owners in Los Angeles. If each owner was represented by a card in the file, we would not have to count the number of cards to determine the sampling interval but only measure how many inches of cards are in the file and divide this figure by 500 to obtain the sampling interval in terms of inches. (Thus, if there were 100 cards to the inch those 2,000,000 cards would occupy 20,000 inches of space in the file drawers. Dividing by 500 gives us a sampling interval of 40 inches.) This represents a tremendous savings in time and tedium since you would be measuring off 20,000 inches with your measuring tape rather than counting the two million cards. Even if the total number of cards is known in advance, this would still represent a huge savings in time because a sample of 500 from an universe of 2,000,000 gives a sampling interval of 4,000. Just picture yourself counting out 4,000 cards once (this is a stack over one yard high) and then repeating the process 500 times! More time could be spent in selecting the sample than in collecting the data from the sample.

Multistage sampling

To discuss multistage sampling it is necessary to distinguish between the sampling *unit* and the sampling *element.* So far we have spoken only of sampling *elements* which are the entities to be ultimately studied and compared. The sampling *unit* is the particular entity containing the sampling element at some stage in the sampling process. In the one-stage samples we have discussed to this point, the sampling element and the sampling unit are the same entity, but in multistage sampling they are different. For example, in multistage sampling we might use three stages to arrive at a sample of 500 people from the adult population of Minneapolis. The ultimate sampling element is the adult person, but first we might use the city block as the sampling unit by selecting a random sample of blocks from the universe of city blocks. Then we could use the household as the sampling unit by selecting a random sample of households from those in the randomly selected blocks. Finally we could use the individual as the sampling unit by randomly selecting individual adults from all the adults in the randomly selected houses. Thus in this case the adult person is both the sampling element and the sampling unit in the third stage of sampling.

The multistage sample becomes more advantageous as the universe has a larger number of elements and covers a larger geographical area. If we wanted to select a sample of 5,000 voters to predict a presidential election, it would be impossible to identify each of the millions of registered voters in the thousands of precincts in the United States in order to select a simple random sample or even a systematic sample. Instead, it would be much easier to identify all of the cities and all of the rural counties and take a random sample of each. This would be the first stage of sampling. Then we could identify each city block in each of the sample cities and each enumeration district in the rural counties. These are already mapped and identified by number by the U.S. Census Bureau. We could then take a random sample of city blocks and rural Census Enumeration Districts. Up to this point the sample design is done from maps and Census data without going out into the field. The last two stages must be done in the field, and are usually done by the interviewers.

Each interviewer is given a map showing the location of all the sample blocks or enumeration districts in a certain portion of the city or county. There should also be a blow-up of each block or enumeration district which fills a whole page so that each street is clearly seen. Then the interviewers may begin the *block listing* process.. The interviewer goes to the first sample block, starts at one corner and proceeds around the block, drawing in each residential building along the way. For those buildings which are not single-family dwelling units, the interviewer must indicate the number of dwelling units in the building.

Once all of the dwelling units in the sample blocks are located and identified by address and apartment number, the sample of dwelling units may be selected in one of three ways. *Simple random sampling* could be applied by assigning serial numbers to each dwelling unit. Then using a random numbers table, we could select the appropriate number of dwelling units from the whole pool. *Systematic sampling* could be used by taking every Nth dwelling unit from the total list of dwelling units using whatever sampling interval would obtain the size of sample needed. *Cluster sampling* could be applied by randomly or systematically selecting only one dwelling unit from each block or enumeration district and then taking an additional number immediately adjacent to make a cluster of two, three, four or five. This saves time by not having to select the remaining units in the cluster randomly, and it reduces travel time in reaching the respondents. However, this efficiency of reduced travel time is bought at the price of decreasing the precision of the sample's representativeness. For any given size of sample, precision increases as we reduce the number in each cluster and increase the number of clusters.

If the survey is to be done in a census year or in an area where there has been little change in the number of occupied dwelling units since the last census, we can avoid actually listing all of the units in the block in order to get the sample. By consulting the U.S. Census block publications, we can identify all of the blocks and know the number of dwelling units in each block. When we know in advance the total number of dwelling units in all of the sample blocks and enumeration districts, we need to record only the addresses falling into a systematic sample. For example, if we need a sample of 400 respondents, and there are 40,000 dwellings in our sample of block and enumeration districts, we know that the sampling interval is one out of every hundred dwelling units. Each block lister would walk or drive through the area counting the dwelling units and recording the address of only each 100th unit. This is simple in areas with only single-family dwelling units, but in apartment-house areas we must count the apartments in each building. In this systematic area-sampling process we must have some consistent pattern to follow (around the block and within apartment buildings) in counting to the 100th unit. The details of one method of systematically selecting dwelling units is given by Backstrom and Hursh.[2]

The fourth stage would be the selection of individual respondents living in the sample of dwelling units. This is usually done by the interviewer at the time of the interview. The method for making this selection depends upon the purpose of the survey, and the nature of the universe we are trying to sample. For example, in sampling the whole adult population in a survey of political opinion, we might want the views of all registered voters, or we might be interested only in information from heads of households.

In principle, the procedure is simple. Have some adult in the household give the first names of all members of the household who fall into the universe in which we are interested. If it is heads of household, we ask, "Who is the head of the household?" If it is all persons 18 years old or over, we then ask, "Would you tell me how many

---

[2] Charles H. Backstrom and Gerald D. Hursh, *Survey Research* (Evanston, Ill.: Northwestern University Press, 1963), pp. 38–64.

persons living here are 18 years or over?" Then if there is more than one, "Please give me the first name of each, beginning with the oldest person down to the youngest." Once all members of the universe are listed, then we must have some random way of choosing the one person to be the respondent. If there is only one adult in the household, then there is no problem of selection because this person has already been selected randomly along with the household. If there are two or more, there are several different systems which fulfill the criterion of randomness. One system is illustrated in the respondent selection chart, Figure 13–1.

This respondent selection chart would appear as the first page of every interview schedule. The X's show which person is to be inter-

FIGURE 13–1

RESPONDENT SELECTION CHART
(version A only)

(a) Ask: "How many people 18 years or older live here at the present time?"
Circle this number at the top of the appropriate column and circle the
X in that column.

(b) If there is more than one such person, ask: "Who is the oldest person
living here?"; "Who is the next oldest?"; "Who is next oldest?"; etc.,
until all members of the universe are listed.

(c) The name appearing opposite the circled X is the person you must interview.

First names, oldest to youngest	Number in family				
	1	2	3	4	5
1	X		X		
2		X			
3				X	
4					X
5					

Note: This has the X's filled in one of the five different random patterns running through the set of interview schedules.

viewed, depending on the number of adults in the household. This is accomplished by randomly assigning the X's to columns 2,3,4, and 5. It is sufficient to allow for a maximum of only five adults in a household since larger households are mostly children under 18 years of age. This means that there will be five different versions of the respondent selection chart alternating systematically throughout the series of interviews. The questionnaires would be given serial numbers; and to be sure that respondents were selected randomly, the interviewer would have to use the interview schedules in serial order. If a respondent is not at home, that same interview schedule is assigned to that respondent and used later when calling back. When duplicating 400 copies of the interview schedule, since there are five different versions of the respondent selection page, there would be 80 copies of each version. The five versions would have to be alternated so that they would repeat the series a,b,c,d,e all the way through the 400 copies in serial order. Another technique for selecting the respondent from among the members of the household is given by Backstrom and Hursh.[3]

Stratified sampling

In designing a sample we can increase its accuracy without increasing the size if we stratify the sample into subsamples of different portions of the universe. These portions of the universe must be identified by certain characteristics of the respondents known to be related to (correlated with) the opinions, beliefs, or attitudes we are trying to sample. For example, if we were going to sample opinions on the women's liberation movement, we would want to stratify the universe into subsamples by sex, age, region, and educational level, since, in general, people are more sympathetic to the women's liberation movement if they are female, younger, Northerners, and highly educated. The more we know about the respondents in the universe and how their characteristics correlate with the opinions we are trying to measure, the more effectively we can stratify the sample to gain precision without increasing the number of respondents in the sample. The greater the correlation between the characteristics by which we stratify and the opinions of the respondents, the greater the gain in precision by stratification of the sample.

The problems involved in designing different types of stratified samples and the implications for the field operations are so many and technical that we cannot deal with them here. Because of these complications and costs the stratified sample is usually designed for those national surveys that are done repeatedly, or for longitudinal studies

---

[3] Ibid., pp. 50–59.

where the initial cost of the sample design can be amortized over several surveys.

SURVEY MODE

By survey mode we refer to the four modes of communication used to obtain information from each respondent: the mailed questionnaire, the personally administered questionnaire, the telephone interview, and the face-to-face interview. Although this book's main concern is with face-to-face interviewing, it is fruitful to discuss all four communication modes so that we may rationally choose the most effective for the particular survey at hand.

There are two general criteria for selecting the appropriate mode, *efficiency* of the data-collection process and the *validity* of the data. Validity can be divided into two major dimensions. First is the representativeness of the sample, which depends on having a high completion rate. Second is the completeness and accuracy of the information obtained from those who do respond. This depends on how the communication mode is related to the topic of the interview and how skillfully the mode is used. Unfortunately, these two criteria, efficiency and validity, sometimes conflict. When this is the case, we must always give validity the highest priority since it is useless to efficiently collect invalid data.

This conflict can be seen, for example, in a case where the mailed questionnaire is more economical in *contacting* a sample of respondents, but the completion rate may be so low for a particular survey topic that the sample is no longer representative, or there may be so many omissions of certain answers that it is impossible to correlate responses or to use a cross-tabulation of responses.

The mailed questionnaire

In general the mailed questionnaire survey has certain *advantages* in comparison with the other three modes of communication. First, it is possible to cover a geographically scattered sample very economically since there are no field staff and no travel costs involved. This makes the cost per contact lower than in any other mode of communication. Second, there may be less ego threat because the respondent can be completely anonymous since there is no interviewer to know the respondent. Third, the problems of competing time demands and forgetting may be reduced since there is plenty of time to fit the task into bits of leisure time, and there is time to think the topic over and to recall information. In cases where the sample member is a key informant who has access to objective information, the mailed questionnaire provides more time for him to find the information needed. Fourth, certain segments of the population who are difficult to contact (for example, they may have no telephone or may work the night shift) can be easily reached by mail.

There are many potential *disadvantages* of the mailed questionnaire, depending on the particular topic and circumstances. First, there is no opportunity to personally persuade the respondent to cooperate. This often leads to a high nonresponse rate and a biased sample. Second, there is no way to control the order in which the respondent sees the questions. In some interview topics it is necessary to have the respondent answer the broad questions before seeing the questions with multiple-choice answers, which may suggest answer possibilities prematurely. Third, there is no way to detect whether the respondent actually understands the question or to correct his misinterpretations. For this reason it is more important to provide contexts for questions in the mailed questionnaire than in the other modes of communication. Fourth, there is no opportunity for the interviewer to probe for elaboration or clarification so that the answer is complete and unambiguous in relationship to the objectives of the question. Fifth, there is no opportunity for the interviewer to maximize the facilitators of communication by showing that he expects an answer, by showing sympathetic understanding, or by providing recognition or praise. Sixth, there is usually no opportunity to determine the general characteristics of those who do not reply. Finally, the mailed questionnaire will be ignored by a portion of the population that is functionally illiterate. If we are dealing with a sample of the poor, the mailed questionnaire would be valueless because of the sample-bias that would result.

Despite these limitations the mailed questionnaire has been proven useful under certain conditions. Assuming that the population is literate, the success of the mailed questionnaire depends upon its length and the amount of internal motivation or external social pressure to respond. For example, in filling out an application for a lottery prize or a questionnaire to parents on the preferred hours of the public school, there will be considerable motivation for each person to respond. If in addition the questionnaire is short, and a self-addressed, stamped envelope furnished, the response rate will be high. Furthermore, the effect of sample bias will not be serious since it is safe to assume that those who are vitally interested will respond. External pressure is effective in getting a high response rate in other situations like the income tax form from the Internal Revenue Service, or the questionnaire from the Census Bureau, or a questionnaire from the Selective Service Board. Motivation can also be enhanced by appealing to some altruistic purpose, providing general community recognition, or developing social pressure through the mass media.

Usually, the mailed questionnaire will carry adequate motivation for some respondents and not for others. For those who do not respond to the mailed questionnaire there are other ways of supplementing it. The nonrespondents can be contacted by a second follow-up mailing if a method has been set up to identify the nonrespondents. They can be contacted in a follow-up telephone call asking for their cooperation, or a telephone interview may be substituted if it is short. If all else fails, an interviewer may call on the nonrespondents to personally administer the questionnaire or do an interview.

Studies have shown that the strategy of the initial mailed questionnaire followed by a personal interview is particularly useful in situations where all of the respondents are located in a small area. For example, Gibson and Hawkins[4] report a survey of the Georgia General Assemblymen in which 48 members responded to the mailed questionnaire and an additional 41 were obtained by making a personal call at the Assemblymen's offices. Their analysis indicated that for the topic of this survey (which dealt with the "one man, one vote" concept of representation in the state legislature) they were able to obtain valid information by either the questionnaire or the interview. Therefore, it was valid and more economical to use the questionnaire, for those who would respond, followed by interviews with the remainder. However, it has been shown by many studies that as the questionnaire gets longer and less associated with the respondent's official duties, or less likely to bring any extrinsic rewards, the response rate decreases rapidly.

The personally administered questionnaire

An option having some of the advantages of both the mailed questionnaire and the interview is the personally administered questionnaire. Although it is not as economical in contacting a geographically dispersed sample, there can be a considerable savings in travel time if respondents can be contacted in groups, such as at their place of work, or by having the respondents come to a central location where the questionnaire can be administered to groups. The advantage of anonymity can be retained by not having the respondents' names on the questionnaires and by spacing members of the group so that one respondent cannot see how another answers a question. The personally administered questionnaire loses the advantage of letting the respondent fill it out in his leisure time since it must be done while the field worker waits.

The personally administered questionnaire has several advantages over the mailed questionnaire. The field worker can motivate the re-

---

[4] F. K. Gibson and D. W. Hawkins, "Interviews versus Questionnaires," *American Behavioral Science*, vol. 12 (1968) pp. 9–16.

spondents by giving them a sales pitch before they begin. The order in which the respondents deal with the questions can be controlled by giving them one page to work with at a time and not giving the second page until the first is completed. The administrator can ask the respondents to talk with him about the meaning of the questions. Furthermore, the administrator can ask that each person complete all of the answers before leaving.

Of course the personally administered questionnaire still lacks some of the advantages of the interview since there is no opportunity to probe for elaboration and clarification of the responses. Under some circumstances it is possible to motivate the respondents by having group meetings with all members of the sample to give a sales pitch on the importance of the study and their ability to contribute. The respondents can then be given the questionnaires to work on at their leisure. In this discussion it is often feasible to encourage questions about the meaning of the specific questions. The writer used this method with a sample of college students who were asked to write long essay responses to several broad questions about their evaluation of the work-study program. On the average they spent 3½ hours writing and there was a 100 percent response to the study.

If the questionnaire is short and if the respondents are all located in a small area, such as students in dormitories or office workers in a large business or government agency, it may be an efficient strategy for the interviewer to spend the morning distributing the questionnaires and the afternoon collecting questionnaires and helping people finish them. Of course if the questionnaire is very long, or if it requires supplying information which is not all in the respondent's head, the field worker may have to allow as much as a week before returning.

Telephone or face-to-face

Just as there are two basic modes of questionnaire administration and collection (mail and personal), there are also two basic modes of carrying out an interview. The interview may be done by telephone or in person. It is certainly more economical in terms of cost per interview to do telephone interviews and would certainly be preferable to face-to-face interviews if equally valid information could be obtained this way. Any survey done by face-to-face interview in the respondent's home requires a large amount of travel time and expense. For example, Sudman[5] shows that the amount of the interviewer's time spent in travel varies from 17 percent for social workers to 40 percent for interviewers on probability sample surveys. Travel time is eliminated for

---

[5] Seymour Sudman, "Time Allocation on Survey Interviewing and Other Field Occupations," *Public Opinion Quarterly*, vol. 29 (1965), pp. 638–48.

both the initial contact and any call-backs needed. Not only is there a savings in travel costs but the number of interviewers needed is much smaller. This also substantially reduces the problems of training and supervision.

A second advantage of the telephone interview over the face-to-face one is that the supervisor can control interviewer bias by being present in the interview, monitoring from an extension or just listening to the interviewer's questions. A third advantage is related to efficiency in the elapsed-time factor. In some circumstances it is necessary for practical reasons to quickly and repeatedly measure opinions that rapidly change. For example, in the last few days of certain election campaigns the client (political party) needs to know day-to-day fluctuations. Under these conditions the field strategy using face-to-face interviewing or the mailed questionnaires would be useless.

There are some disadvantages of the telephone interview as compared with the face-to-face interview. First, the telephone interview must be very short, usually less than five minutes. This is in contrast to face-to-face interviews that have lasted up to eight hours in some studies. Second, all of the meaningful visual clues used by the interviewer to assess the respondent's attitudes are missing. This makes it dangerous to use silent probes on the phone since the interviewer does not know whether the respondent is thinking about an answer or has left the phone. Similarly, the respondent cannot see the interviewer's face so does not know whether he is waiting for an answer or whether he waits patiently or impatiently. Third, this lack of visual nonverbal interaction makes it more difficult for the interviewer to motivate the respondent by showing keen interest by facial expression and posture. Nor can the interviewer control the pacing to establish a thoughtful, reminiscent mood. A fourth disadvantage is that certain visual question materials cannot be used. For example, it is impossible to show the respondent a response card with the relevant answer categories on it. Nor can the respondent be asked to sort cards into meaningful categories or to respond to pictorial material as in the Thematic Apperception Test, or to show preferences for different visual stimuli. Finally, the telephone interview may result in a sampling bias because some people do not have a telephone or have an unlisted one. This weakness could be overcome by initially drawing the sample from some list containing people with or without a telephone, doing the telephone interviews first, and then contacting the remainder of the sample in person.

The lack of telephones has been demonstrated in a study by Leuthold and Scheele[6] in 1969 in Central Missouri which revealed that 10 percent of the households did not have a telephone. More important, those

---

[6] D. A. Leuthold and R. Scheele, "Patterns of Bias in Sample Based on Telephone Directories," *Public Opinion Quarterly,* vol. 35 (1971), pp. 249–57.

families with incomes under $8,000 and living in the community for less than five years lacked telephones in 31 percent of the cases. Thus, a sample of the population from a telephone directory would be biased by the systematic exclusion of a large portion of the poor.

In view of the possible reduction in survey costs and the possibility of getting quick results, there is good reason to consider the telephone interview instead of the personal face-to-face interview. Several studies have shown the telephone interview to be a valid and efficient communication mode under the right conditions.[7]

The telephone survey is at its best when there are very few questions. For example, a listenership survey might include only the following questions: "Was the TV set on when the telephone rang?" If YES— "What channel was tuned in?" "What program was on?" "Who was watching?" Similarly, an election survey might ask: "Are you a registered voter?" "Do you intend to vote in the presidential election next month?" If YES—"Who will you vote for?"

This section on survey modes has intended to point out some of the strengths and weaknesses of each mode of communication so that the reader could choose more effectively among the modes or creatively design some combination of modes best suited to the purposes and conditions of the survey.

In the next section on gaining access to the respondent we will assume that we are doing a survey that calls for the face-to-face interview as the major mode of communication.

GAINING ACCESS TO THE RESPONDENT

There is always a possibility that the respondent will refuse an interview. One thing that may be increasing the tendency to refuse an interview is the increased use of the commercial sales pitch disguised as a survey. Typically, this fake survey begins with some questions to discover whether the respondent is in the market for the product being sold and then subtly shifts to questions designed to obligate the respondent to attend a demonstration, to receive a sample, or to buy. This practice has helped to develop a widespread public allergy to surveys, especially in large cities. Biel[8] found in a sample survey of 240 respondents in Chicago that 60 percent had at one time been approached in

[7] For example, see the following three studies:

Henry Assael and J. O. Eastback, Jr., "Better Telephone Surveys Through Centralized Interviewing," *Journal of Advertising Research*, vol. 61 (1966), pp. 2–7.

Irene Janofsky, "Affective Self-Disclosure in Telephone versus Face-to-Face Interview," *Journal of Humanistic Psychology*, vol. 11 (1971), pp. 93–103.

Stephen S. Kegeles et al., "Interviewing a National Sample by Long-Distance Telephone," *Public Opinion Quarterly*, vol. 33 (1969), pp. 412–19.

[8] Alexander Biel, "Abuses of Survey Research Techniques: The Phoney Interview," *Public Opinion Quarterly*, vol. 31 (1967), pp. 298–99.

a phony survey either personally or on the telephone. This sometimes explains why a respondent backs off as soon as the interviewer says the word "survey."

Some supervisors of interviewers who have done little interviewing under the conditions of a particular survey may feel that it is always the interviewer's fault if he gets a refusal. This is far from true, and if the supervisor persists in this unsympathetic view, it will increase the pressures that sometimes result in fabrication of interviews by an interviewer.

Studies have shown that refusal rates vary with the ethnic background of the respondent regardless of who the interviewer is. For example, Snell and Dohrenwend[9] in a study of a sample of 214 respondents in New York found that Irish-Americans had a much higher refusal rate than Jewish, Negro, or Puerto Rican respondents, regardless of ethnic background of the interviewer. Also older people and those who have been in the U.S. a shorter time refused more often.

Perhaps this lower refusal rate of the native Americans is because the survey is beginning to be recognized as a legitimate feature of the American scene. A large minority of the U.S. population has been a respondent at some time in a survey. Hartmann[10] did a sample survey of 1,000 household heads in 1966 which showed that 35 percent of the population had responded to some type of survey. There were 25 percent who responded to a face-to-face interview, 20 percent to a telephone interview, and 12 percent to a mailed questionnaire. The rate was 40 percent among married women 35 to 44 years old and 65 percent if above $15,000 income. While 57 percent of the sample in the Northeast had been surveyed, only 21 percent in the South Atlantic states had the experience.

There is also evidence that the American public is becoming more sophisticated in making distinctions between the disguised sales pitch, the vested-interest commercial surveys, and the survey aimed at promoting the common welfare. For example, Brunner[11] did a survey on pharmaceutical products in which one sample of interviews was sponsored by a private research corporation and the other by the University of Maryland. The first sample had a 33 percent refusal rate and the one sponsored by the University had only a 16 percent refusal rate. There was probably a tendency of the public to assume that any survey by

9 Barbara Snell and Bruce P. Dohrenwend, "Sources of Refusal in Surveys," *Public Opinion Quarterly,* vol. 32 (1968), pp. 74–83.

10 Elizabeth Hartmann, "Public Reaction to Public Opinion Surveying," *Public Opinion Quarterly,* vol. 32 (1968), pp. 295–98.

11 G. A. Brunner and S. J. Carroll, "Effect of Prior Telephone Appointments on Completion Rates and Response Content," *Public Opinion Quarterly,* vol. 31 (1967–68), pp. 652–54.

a commercial firm is more concerned with increasing profits than in improving the product and that a university is more closely identified with the interests of the consumer, taxpayer, and voter.

In trying to reduce the number of refusals a common mistake is made by inexperienced surveyors who first make a telephone call to set up an appointment at a convenient time for the respondent. This strategy has been repeatedly proven ineffective by experimental studies. For example, Brunner,[12] in the same experiment referred to above, showed that the refusal rate among the respondents who were first contacted by phone was much higher than in the cases where the first contact was the personal call. Those contacted by telephone had a refusal rate of 63 percent in contrast to only 33 percent for the face-to-face contacts. In the sample sponsored by the University the rates were 55 percent and 16 percent, respectively.

Other studies have shown that matters are also not improved by first sending a letter instead of making a telephone call. For example, Cartwright and Tucker[13] sent a letter to half of their random sample, explaining that they would like the respondent's cooperation in an anonymous survey of people's health and their use of doctors. The effect of the letter was to *increase* the refusal rate from 22 percent to 34 percent for the middle class, from 15 percent to 64 percent for the working class, from 10 percent to 61 percent for all men, and from 23 percent to 30 percent for all women.

It seems easier for people to refuse when the interviewer is not face-to-face with them at the moment. The difference between the refusal rates with the different modes of initial contact varies not only with the type of respondent as shown above but also with the topic of the interview. If the topic of the interview is viewed as potentially unpleasant by the respondent, he will be more likely to refuse in the absence of any personal influence from the interviewer. The attempt to make an appointment in advance by mail or telephone only increases the refusal problem. Fortunately, there are ways the respondent can be prepared for the survey in advance to reduce the refusal rate.

In general we can say that any advance information received by the respondents should not offer the opportunity to refuse to be interviewed. Instead, information should blanket the total population to be sampled through the news media thus avoiding a direct approach to any individual in the sample. This advance publicity should include: who is sponsoring the study, why it is being done, what potential benefits might arise from it, why it is so important to obtain responses from

---

[12] Ibid., p. 653.

[13] Ann Cartwright and Wyn Tucker, "An Attempt to Reduce the Number of Calls on an Interview Inquiry," *Public Opinion Quarterly*, vol. 31 (1967), pp. 299–302.

10 percent of the members of the sample, how the sample will be selected, how it is anonymous, how the community is receiving recognition from the larger world for its cooperation in the project, and how the results can be obtained by all interested individuals.

In effect we want to indicate general acceptance of the survey in a tone that assumes that the individual respondent will cooperate. At the same time there should not be any advance warning to a particular respondent that he has been selected and will be interviewed on a certain date.

Of course it cannot be assumed by the interviewer that every respondent in the sample has seen the advance publicity. Even when the respondent has not seen it, the interviewers can take advantage of the advance publicity if they each carry a copy of the story showing clearly the name of the newspaper and the date of publication. Also, as Hills[14] points out, his strategy of mailing a reproduction of a local newspaper story on the impending research, with a newspaper photograph of the interviewer, to each member of the sample was one of the major factors contributing to the 98 percent interview completion rate in his survey of participation in local voluntary associations.

The news photo is particularly helpful in communities where people are reluctant to open the door to strangers. There is no reason why this strategy could not be used when there are three or four interviewers. Of course it is most effective if there is only one interviewer who happens to be a relatively prestigious person so that the respondent feels that he gains recognition by being interviewed.

The refusal rate can also be reduced by carefully selecting interviewers whose visible characteristics are most likely to make the respondent want to at least open the door to give them an opportunity to speak. The sex, race, and dress of the interviewer should be matched with the respondent, considering the topic of the interview and where the interview is to take place. The props which the interviewer carries such as a notebook, a clipboard, a zipper case, briefcase, handbag, umbrella or other item should be specified in view of what is known about the local community's cues for identifying various types of people who might come to the door. The problem is to avoid being mistakenly identified as some type of person the respondent does not want to talk to such as a bill collector or salesman.

Finally, the refusal rate can be reduced if the time for the interview is chosen to minimize any competing time demands upon the respondent. The principle is simple to state but its application depends upon considerable knowledge of the particular population to be sampled and

---

[14] Stuart L. Hills, "Increasing the Response Rate for Structured Interviews in Community Research," *American Behavioral Scientist,* vol. 11 (1968), pp. 47–48.

the pattern of demands upon their time. For example, if the population to be sampled is households in the sense that the information needed is facts that can be obtained from any member of the household over 16 years of age, then the time of the day or the day of the week will not be crucial. Whoever is available or has the most time or is most willing can be interviewed. In fact one person could begin the interview and another respondent could finish it. In some cases it might even be a group interview.

In contrast, if the population to be sampled is a specific category of persons, we can accept no substitutes because the information sought is the attitudes, beliefs, preferences, or expectations of each person in the sample. The difficulty in finding a most appropriate time for interviewing such a sample depends upon how homogeneous it is with respect to the pattern of demands upon their time. For example, if the population is unemployed housewives with school-age children, then the best time to interview most of the members of the sample is probably after lunch and before the children come home from school. But if the population includes all persons over 18 years of age in a poll on political beliefs, then we are dealing with a more heterogeneous set of time demands. This population would include members of the labor force who may be divided among three different work shifts. It includes those who work outside the home and those who do not, those with children and those without, those who have to get up to give the baby the 2:00 A.M. feeding, and the elderly who have difficulty sleeping. It includes those who live isolated and lonely lives and those suffering from overactivity in organized social life. Under these conditions it is extremely difficult to know in advance a time of the day or week when most of the respondents in the sample would be available. If there is such a time, it may be so few hours per week that it may be difficult to find enough interviewers interested in interviewing only at these hours to complete such a survey in a feasible length of time.

To find appropriate interview times for such a heterogeneous population, we must abandon the attempt to decide in advance a particular time in common for all members of the sample. Instead, we must either have some relevant advanced information on each member of the sample to pick a most likely time for them, or be content with covering the same geographical territory two or three times to accommodate all of the respondents.

The interviewer must not assume merely because the respondent is home that it is a good time to try to interview him. If the interview is very short, say up to 15 minutes, this may be true; but if it requires an hour and a half, it might be wiser to use the initial contact time to establish a relationship with the respondent and motivate him to give an interview at some other time when not so rushed. If the respondent is not home but some other member of the household is, then the interviewer should use this opportunity to determine the best time to catch the respondent at home and to make a favorable impression on those who are at home. If no one is home, the interviewer can ask neighbors the best time to return.

In sampling some populations it is conceivable that interviewers might spend the whole first day in the field without actually finishing one interview. The time is well spent, however, if interviewers finish the first day with some appointments for that week, some information on the best time for call-backs on those who were not home, and some acquaintances among neighbors, relatives, and friends of his respondents.

For interviewer morale it is important that the interviewers clearly understand that this field activity is an unavoidable and necessary step in getting the job done. The supervisor must be able to provide a realistic picture of the contact strategy and show the interviewers that gaining access to respondents requires as much skill and resourcefulness as the interview itself. With some survey topics making the contacts is the major aspect of the job.

Once the interviewer is face-to-face with a respondent in the sample, there comes a critical moment which depends entirely on the interviewer's power of verbal persuasion. In a small minority of cases the respondent will show some resistance or skepticism and will need to be convinced. At this point the interviewer need not panic; he should realize that most of the forms of resistance have been discovered in previous surveys and certain interviewer responses have been shown effective in the large majority of situations. Also, there are some respondents who would not cooperate regardless of how they were approached. Some of the most typical forms of verbal resistance in sample surveys are succinctly given in a list by Backstrom and Hursh[15], reproduced here in Figure 13–2. Some of the answers might vary slightly in specific surveys, but the forms of resistance are typical of a variety of survey situations.

In this section on gaining access to the respondent in a sample survey, we have shown some of the conditions that should be considered in gaining the respondent's cooperation. This is a critical problem when we need a high rate of return to have a fair amount of precision in representing the whole population on the basis of a sample. We have warned against the mistaken practice of making an initial contact by telephone or letter to obtain permission, or an appointment with the respondent before the interviewer makes his personal appearance on the respondent's doorstep. We have given a few basic suggestions on

---

[15] Charles H. Backstrom and Gerald D. Hursh, *Survey Research,* Evanston, Ill.: Northwestern University Press, 1963, p. 143.

FIGURE 13–2

CHECKLIST 13: STOCK ANSWERS TO RESPONDENTS

WHAT YOU SHOULD SAY . . .

1. IF RESPONDENT ASKS: "Who is doing this survey?"

"This survey is being conducted by the Research Division of Model State University. We are trying to get some idea about what people think about current issues in Model City."

2. IF RESPONDENT PRESSES FOR A BETTER ANSWER ON AUSPICES:

"Well . . . I'm a professional interviewer. The people in charge of this survey are at the Research Division at Model State University. They'd be glad to explain the survey to you. Would you like their phone number so you could call them?" (If "Yes," give trouble number.)

3. IF RESPONDENT WONDERS WHY HE IS BEING INTERVIEWED, OR SUGGESTS INTERVIEWING SOMEONE ELSE:

"You were selected completely *by chance* according to procedures worked out by my office. So *your* opinions are important and interviewing someone else wouldn't be as good."

4. IF RESPONDENT SAYS HE DOESN'T HAVE TIME TO BE INTERVIEWED:

"The questions won't take long. You can go right on with your work and I'll just run through these items." (Begin questioning immediately.)

5. IF RESPONDENT INSISTS HE IS TOO BUSY:

"What would be a better time soon for me to come back? I'll note down an appointment that would be more convenient for you."

6. IF RESPONDENT SAYS HE DOESN'T KNOW ENOUGH TO GIVE GOOD ANSWERS:

"In this survey, it's *not* what you know that counts. Rather, it's what you happen to think about various topics that is important."

7. IF RESPONDENT IS AFRAID TO ANSWER SOME QUESTION OR ASKS: "What are you going to do with these answers?" or "Why do you want to know that?"

"Well . . . many people are being asked these same questions, of course, and what you say is confidential. We are interested in these questions only to see what a *lot* of people in Model City generally are thinking about."

8. IF RESPONDENT RESENTS QUESTIONS THAT TALK DOWN TO HIM:

"The people in my office made up these questions, and we are instructed to read each one just as it is written."

9. IF RESPONDENT IS ANNOYED AND JUST PLAIN REFUSES TO ANSWER A QUESTION:

"Of course, you don't have to answer any question you'd prefer not to. I'm only trying to get your opinion because our study is more accurate that way." Then if respondent still refuses, don't comment, just go on quickly to the next question. Mark the item "Refused."

Source: Backstrom and Hursh, *Survey Research* (1963).

the types of plans, preparations, and approaches designed to reduce the number of refusals, and finally, we have shown that at the last critical moment access may depend upon the interviewer's ability to respond verbally to the various forms of resistance that may be shown by some respondents.

Now we will show how the format of the interview schedule or questionnaire is an important link between the field research team (respondent, the interviewer, and the field supervisor) and the data analysis team.

FORMAT OF THE INTERVIEW SCHEDULE OR QUESTIONNAIRE

The interview schedule in a sample survey is not a simple list of questions; it is a complicated, precision instrument. This section will show the basic functions of the interview schedule and its principal parts as these relate to the sample survey. The interview schedule can be divided into two general functional parts: the face sheet and the body.

Face sheet

Face sheet refers to the initial pages of the schedule which precede the questions dealing with the topic of the interview. There are several important kinds of information on the face sheet, some furnished in advance by the research team and some obtained from the respondent. Some of the items that may be included in the face sheet are described here.

Sample assignment. It is often convenient to identify a particular interview schedule *before* the specific respondent is selected. For example, in multistage sampling the interview schedule can be identified as a particular element in the sample by indicating that the respondent represented by that particular interview schedule is the first in a cluster of three from Block Number 522 in City A.

This sample element identification allows the field supervisor to know which elements of the sample have been assigned to an interviewer and to assign geographically adjacent respondents to the same interviewer. As the completed schedules begin to come in, the field supervisor can record which portions of the sample have been completed and which remain to be done. This identification also assures that the appropriate form of the respondent selection sheet is used in each case. If the interviewers were free to use any interview schedule with any respondent, and thus control which respondent selection chart was used in a particular case, the sample could be seriously biased.

Respondent selection chart. If the sampling method calls for randomly selecting the individual respondent from a household or other group, then the respondent selection chart, discussed earlier, should be included in the face sheet. Since different schedules have different forms of the respondent selection chart, it is important that no substitutions of face sheets be made. For example, if one interview schedule is damaged before it is used, the substituted face sheet should have the same version of respondent selection chart as the original. For this reason it is useful to identify the different selection charts as version A, B, C, etc., on the face sheet. Without this, it is difficult to quickly recognize the different face sheets.

Introductory statement. It is usually helpful to include a suggested introductory statement which the interviewer should use with each respondent. The statement may include the interviewer's name, the organization for whom he works, the organization for whom the survey is being done, the purpose of the survey, the degree of confidentiality or anonymity provided, and how the respondent was selected. Occasionally, some of these elements are omitted or additional ones added. In any case, the interviewer should master the content and meaning so that he may spontaneously give the introductory remarks in a natural manner in his own words.

Respondent identification. In any sample survey it is necessary to have some way of identifying a particular respondent so that the field supervisor will know whether the sampling procedure has been followed and have some way of spot-checking whether the selected respondent has actually been interviewed. The supervisor must also be able to assign a particular respondent to a different interviewer if necessary.

How the selected respondent is to be identified depends on the amount of confidentiality or anonymity which must be provided. If call-backs have to be made by an interviewer other than the one who did the original random selection of the respondent, then it will be necessary to include the street address, apartment number, and some designation such as "husband," "wife," "18-year-old daughter," etc. In some surveys there is no reason for not using the full name, address, and phone number for identification. As long as the names of the individuals in the sample are known to no one except the interviewer and field supervisor, the information is still confidential, since the report to the sponsoring organization or to the public in general does not identify any person in the sample.

Contact record. In obtaining a perfect random sample, it is necessary to locate and interview all members of the sample without any substitutes. For this reason, it is often necessary to try several times to contact some of the hard-to-reach respondents. The contact record allows the interviewer to record all attempts to contact the respondent. He records attempts made when the respondent was not at home. If the respondent was home but must be interviewed later, the appointment time should be recorded. When the appointment is kept, the interviewer must record whether or not the interview was completed or whether a second appointment was made.

If the respondent was not at home on the first call, the interviewer should record when the respondent is usually home according to other members of the household or neighbors, so that he or another interviewer would have a better chance to contact the respondent on the second try.

If the respondent is identified but not contacted on the first try, the interviewer may obtain enough information about the respondent (such as age, sex, race, etc.) to know that it would be advisable to have a different interviewer make the second attempt to reach the respondent in order to have a better match between interviewer and respondent.

Interviewer identification. The face sheet should provide for indicating the name of the interviewer to whom the case was originally assigned and the names of all interviewers making subsequent contacts. It is essential for any interviewer to know what previous contacts the respondent has had with the study. It is also important to the field supervisor, who can obtain the cooperation of the interviewer in filling in missing information and in interpreting handwriting in "verbatim" responses. Also, the supervisor must know who was responsible for selecting, contacting, and interviewing the respondent in order to exercise the quality control essential for a valid survey.

Demographic data. The face sheet should provide for easy recording of certain demographic characteristics of the respondent. Such demographic facts may serve several purposes. If the sample is stratified by demographic characteristics of the respondent, it is necessary to record these characteristics in each case to determine whether the respondent does in fact fall into the intended stratum. Also, such demographic descriptors may be used simply to determine in which subpopulation of the sample the variables measured by the survey are the strongest. For example, if a periodic national survey is used to determine trends in racial attitudes, it may be helpful to know whether prejudice is strongest in males or females, or in older or younger people. This would provide information useful in reaching the right target audience or in designing educational materials for the reduction of prejudice. A third purpose of the demographic data might be to test hypotheses regarding the causes of a particular attitude or opinion measured in the survey. Usually the demographic variable such as age, sex, or level of education is viewed as the independent variable and the attitude, opinion, or knowledge is the dependent variable. For example, we might hypothesize that the respondent's attitude toward fundamentalistic religion on radio programs might be a function of his or her educational level.

Some of the demographic characteristics most useful because of their association with beliefs, opinions, attitudes, and knowledge, and with the channels of communication through which these subjective orientations may be formed or changed, are listed below:

1. Sex	7. Educational level
2. Age	8. Occupation
3. Race	9. Religion
4. Ethnic background	10. Home ownership
5. Marital status	11. Residential mobility
6. Income level	12. Political affiliation

All of these characteristics of individuals tell us something about their probable social environment and their point of view on that environment. Of course, this relationship between individual characteristic and social environment is not simple and absolute.

The answer categories needed for each of these demographic questions vary from the simple male-female sex dichotomy to the most complex classification of occupation. Although many surveys use only the 14 occupational categories used by the U.S. Census Bureau, each of these general categories may include a number of more specific jobs. Using these categories permits the proportion of each occupation in the sample survey to be compared with the proportion in the Census publications. The specific jobs to be included in each category is given in U.S. Census publications and in Backstrom and Hursh.[16]

Case number. The face sheet should provide for a case number, essential for easy identification and location of a particular interview schedule. Once the schedule has been edited for omissions, errors, and ambiguities, it may be desirable to delete the name and/or address of the respondent before passing the case on to the data processors if confidentiality is important. It may also be desirable to retain names and addresses of all members of the sample listed in serial order by case number in the event that some future contact may be needed. This would reduce the number of people on the research team who could link the interview schedule with a particular individual.

Often it is desirable to take the pages of the interview schedule apart so that the keypunch operator can finish with the first page of questions for all cases in the sample before going on to the next page. This is more efficient and accurate than going through one whole interview schedule before going on to the next. In this case it is absolutely essential to put the *case number on every page* before taking the questionnaire apart.

---

[16] Ibid., pp. 99–100.

Otherwise there is no way of getting all of the data belonging to one case back together again.

Body of the interview schedule

The body of the interview schedule includes the actual questions to be asked, the answer categories, the code numbers assigned to each question-and-answer category, instructions to the interviewer regarding asking questions or recording answers, coder's spaces and instructions, and possibly one or more sets of response cards which the interviewer hands to the respondent at certain points in the interview.

Question-answer types. There are four basic types of question-answer formats, depending on the type of information sought. First is the *open-ended* question which has no prefabricated response categories but requires the interviewer to write verbatim the relevant portion of the response in the space provided. Samples of this type and of the others are shown in Figure 13–3.

Second, there is the question with the *nominal scale* answer categories provided in advance. A nominal scale is a set of qualitative (non-quantitative) categories belonging to a single dimension such as sex (male and female), political affiliation (Democrat, Republican, Independent), or marital status (single, married, divorced, separated, widowed).

Third is the *ordinal scale* response format in which the interviewer records quantitative information in the form of ranks rather than some absolute amount. The ordinal-scale item is most commonly used to measure attitudes or to rank preferences or feelings about something. The format of the response usually consists of a five-point scale (for example, strongly agree, agree, neutral, disagree, strongly disagree) in which the point most nearly corresponding to the respondent's feeling is circled.

Fourth, the *interval scale* item calls for information which is quantifiable in terms of absolute values.[17] In measurements of human social behavior most interval scales deal with types of information resulting from enumeration or counting of discrete units, such as years as in age, dollars as in income, or crimes as in crime rate. Interval-scale information may be recorded either by simply writing a number in a blank or by checking a particular class interval in which the number falls. For example, the response to the question, "How old are you?" could be

---

[17] Mathematically, there is an important distinction between interval-scale and ratio-scale data in that the interval scale has equal-sized units throughout the full range of the scale, while the ratio scale has the additional feature of a natural zero point. But this distinction is irrelevant to the format of the interview schedule.

FIGURE 13–3

Examples of Basic Question-Answer Formats

Open-ended question

1. What do you feel are some of the most important qualities to look for in a candidate for mayor in the next election? _____

_____

_____

Nominal-scale question

2. Which of these qualities do you feel is the *most* important in a candidate for mayor in the next election? (HAND CARD TO RESPONDENT) Give me the number of the one most important quality. (CIRCLE APPROPRIATE NUMBER)

1.	Well educated	6.	Democrat
2.	Honest	7.	Experience in city government
3.	Political experience	8.	Interested in this city's problems
4.	Black	9.	Other (WRITE IN)_____
5	Republican		
			_____
		X	No answer

Ordinal-scale question

3. President Jones of State College says the time of political upheaval on American college campuses has passed and will not return in the 1970s!
   Would you agree, disagree, or have no opinion of his statement? Would you say you agree (disagree) *strongly* or just agree (disagree)? (CIRCLE THE APPROPRIATE NUMBER BELOW.)

   1. Strongly agree
   2. Agree
   3. Neutral
   4. Disagree
   5. Strongly disagree
   X No answer

Interval-scale question

4. Which of these categories includes your annual family income? (HAND CARD) Just give me the *letter* in front of the category. (CIRCLE APPROPRIATE *NUMBER* BELOW.)

a.	1	Under $5,000	e.	5	$20,000–$24,000
b.	2	$5,000–$9,000	f.	6	$25,000–$29,000
c.	3	$10,000–$14,000	g.	7	$30,000–$34,000
d.	4	$15,000–$19,000	h.	8	$35,000–or over
				X	No answer
				Y	Don't know

recorded by simply writing in the number 25 or by checking the class interval 25–29. If it is not necessary to record the number of years, it would greatly facilitate the data analysis if the prestructured set of class intervals of age were used instead of merely writing in the number.

Response cards. When the structured response categories are numerous, difficult to understand or to retain in one's memory, it may be advisable to use a response card. This allows the respondent to see all of the choices while making a choice. Also, if the interviewer requests the respondent to choose by simply calling off the appropriate number or letter designating the category, this can help to reduce ego threat, particularly if there is some danger that someone is overhearing the interview.

In question 4 of the examples of basic question-answer formats (Figure 13–3), the response card would have only the letters *a* through *h* designating the categories, because if the interviewer said, "Just give me the *number* of the category," the respondent might feel that he is asking for the number of dollars, but if the categories are designated by letters this ambiguity is eliminated. On the interview schedule, however, both the alphabetical and the numerical designations are used since the numbers are needed by the keypunch operator.

When the answer structure contains more than five or six nominal-scale categories, it is well to use different forms of the response card in which the order of the categories is changed so that the aggregate of responses will not be systematically biased by the respondent's tendency to pay more attention to the first and last items in the list. In this case it is good to reproduce the different forms on different colors of cards in addition to giving them a number identifying each version. The same code letter or number should be used to correspond to a particular response category on all versions of the set of answer categories. This eliminates the need to have different versions of the interview schedule and avoids confusing the keypunch operator by either having different codes for the same response category or by having the same response category located in different positions in the list. The keypunch operator does not need to see the response cards.

Contingency question format. In many surveys the interview schedule contains more questions than are asked of any one respondent because it is often necessary to ask one question before knowing whether other questions apply to the particular respondent. These questions that determine which line of questioning to follow are called *contingency* questions, *filter* questions, or *pivotal* questions. It is important that the format clearly show the alternative routes to follow in the sequence of questions as illustrated in the Contingency Question Format (Figure 13–4).

Note that each question or set of questions that is contingent upon

FIGURE 13–4

Contingency Question Format

C-1 Have you ever heard anything about the Miami Valley Planned Parenthood Association?

1 – Yes
2 – No   ⎤
X – No answer   ⎬— Skip to C-9
Y – Don't know   ⎦

C-2 How did you first hear about it?

1 – On radio
2 – On TV
3 – Newspaper
4 – Friend
5 – Relative
6 – Other: _____
X – Not applicable
Y – Don't know

C-3 Have you ever gotten any services from the program?

1 – Yes
2 – No
X – Not applicable
Y – Don't know

Have you ever gotten . . .
(circle one answer in each row)

C-4 Pelvic exam?	1	2	NA	?
C-5 Sterilization operation?	1	2	NA	?
C-6 Other kind of contraception?	1	2	NA	?
C-7 Abortion?	1	2	NA	?
C-8 Other services?	1	2	NA	?

C-9 Do you know of any organization that will give free birth control information and contraceptive materials?

1 – Yes
2 – No
X – No answer

the answer to the previous question is indented further than the preceding one. This makes it easier for the interviewer to see how far ahead to skip when a series of questions does not apply. For example, if the answer to question C-1 is anything but "yes," then the interviewer jumps ahead to the next question with the same amount of indentation as C-1 which is C-9. The clearer the format, the fewer omissions will be made by the interviewer. Clear formats make it easier for the supervisor to check for omissions. The keypunch operator can punch more efficiently from a clear format.

In the set of answers to those questions which are contingent upon the previous question, it is often wise to include the "not applicable" category so that every column will be punched. Otherwise there would be some confusion as to whether the failure to punch a column corresponding to a particular question was because of the keypunch operator's error or because the question did not apply to a particular respondent.

Schematic sets of questions. When there is a set of questions having identical response categories and related to the same stem question, it is often convenient and efficient to form the set into a *schematic* or tabular form so that the stem of the question does not have to be repeated and the amount of space used for the answer categories can be greatly reduced. This is illustrated by questions C-4 through C-8 in the Contingency Question Format. In the interview specifications, the interviewer should be told that in contingent schematics the column heading "NA" means "not applicable" and that "?" means "don't know."

Some suggestions for good format for interview schedules

Here we will list only some of the most basic characteristics of good format which should be used whenever applicable.

1. Use colored face sheets. In order to distinguish one interview schedule from another or different versions of the same schedule, it is helpful to use different colors of face sheets. If there are different versions of the face sheet (because of the different versions of the respondent selection chart), it might be well to use a different code letter to identify these instead of using different colors.

2. Keep the format consistent. Whatever distinctions in format are used at the beginning of the interview schedule should be consistently kept throughout the whole schedule. For example, if instructions to the interviewer are in capital letters or in boxes, this feature should be maintained throughout the whole schedule.

3. Don't clutter. The telltale mark of the amateur interview schedule or questionnaire is the cluttered, cramped look. Ample space should always be left to write in verbatim answers to open-ended questions, for directions to the interviewer, and for clearly showing the contingency question series. Often the novice is afraid that the questionnaire will look so thick that it will discourage the interviewer or the respondent, so he packs too much on each page. When the respondent discovers how long it takes to get through such a page, it may be more discouraging than watching the more numerous pages of the uncluttered schedule turn over faster. The confusion to the interviewer, supervisor, coder, and keypunch operator caused by the cluttered schedule can be very costly in omitted questions and inefficiency in processing.

4. Have only one question to a line. No two questions should occupy the same line on a page regardless of how short they may be! To avoid confusion and omissions, each successive question must be on a different line with ample space between.

5. Leave space to code open-ended questions. Often open-ended questions are used because the researcher does not know in advance what kind of answer categories would be appropriate from the point of view of the respondent. In this case the open-ended responses can be studied to induce a set of answer categories that fit the data, cover all of the information given, and relate to the purpose of the survey. It is good to have a special blank in the format; for example, a box in front of each open-ended question number, for the coder to enter the appropriate code number after the code has been developed.

6. Assign column numbers to questions. In order to help the coders and keypunch operators, each question should be assigned a number corresponding to the column number on the IBM punch card where that answer is to be punched. This system differs from simply numbering the questions in sequence, for two reasons.

First, there are some types of questions which require more than one column to record the answer. For example, if a three-digit case number must be punched into the IBM card, it would require three columns. If this were the first item on the face sheet, it would look like this:

(C—1–3) Case Number 001.

In this case the keypunch operator would punch the 0 row in column 1, the 0 row in column 2, and the 1 row in column 3.

Second, if the answers to some of the questions on the face sheet are not going to be keypunched, then these items could be assigned letters rather than numbers. Ideally, all of the information not to be punched should be together in a series to make it simpler for the keypunch operator.

It is important to note that if a question has more than one possible answer, as may be the case in any set of nominal-scale categories, then it is necessary to treat each answer category as a separate question and assign a separate column in which the answer "yes," "no," "don't know," and "no answer" can be indicated by punching rows 1, 2, X, or Y, respectively. It is possible to program some electronic data processing so that more than one answer can be coded in the same column, but it is usually desirable to avoid this complication.

7. *Give a row number to each answer category.* If there are twelve or fewer categories in a set of nominal-scale answers, and only one answer is appropriate in each case, the answer can be coded in a single column using codes X, Y, and 0 through 9. If there are more than twelve possible answers, then it would be necessary to reserve more than one column. If two columns are reserved, then up to 99 categories may be used and the answer categories may be numbered accordingly.

The only time an answer category, whether nominal, ordinal, or interval, should not be assigned a row number is when there is no possibility that it would be punched into the IBM card. Sometimes the researcher may forget to assign row numbers to the case number, demographic data, and other face-sheet data needed in the analysis. This error can be costly in time, effort, and frustration.

8. *Use "other" answer category where needed.* Often it is not possible to know all of the possible response categories in advance, so it is advisable to include "other" as the last category on the list, with instructions to write in what this "other" category is in a particular case. Sometimes it is possible and desirable to develop inductively one or more additional substantive categories out of this miscellaneous category.

9. *Use standard nonsubstantive categories.* Wherever appropriate the answer categories should include "no response," "not applicable," and "don't know," so that there will always be some indication that the interviewer did not simply forget to ask the question. If possible the same code such as X, Y, and 0 should be used to indicate these responses. However, the zero cannot be used in cases where it is needed in an interval-scale code. In any case, the designer of the interview schedule should always use these nonsubstantive categories when they are applicable. The "not applicable" category is particularly important to use in a series of contingent questions to indicate that there was no oversight on the part of the interviewer or the keypunch operator.

10. *Avoid check-marking the answer.* Rather than recording the answer by putting a check mark in a blank, it is better to have the interviewer either circle the code number or to put an X in brackets in front of the appropriate answer code. Experience shows that check marks tend to be out of line with the answer categories making it impossible to determine which answer was intended.

11. *Put the case number on every page.* It is often good to give

different portions of the interview schedule to different coders, editors, or keypunch operators, and it sometimes requires more than one IBM card to record all of the answers from one questionnaire. Therefore, there must be some way of matching up the different pages of the questionnaire and the different IBM cards making up the whole case. The most practical way to number the pages, particularly if the questionnaire is long, is to use a serial stamp or a date stamp to save writing by hand.

12. *Start each new IBM card at the top of a page.* If more than one IBM card will be required to keypunch all of the answers to the questions, it is advisable to have the question which starts a new card at the top of a page. In this way one keypunch operator may work with those pages to be recorded on the first deck of cards and another operator may take the subsequent set of pages to fit on the next card. If there is to be more than one IBM card, then it will be necessary to distinguish between the question which belongs in column 1 of the first card from the one that belongs in column 1 of the second card. This can be done simply by numbering the questions for the first card in a series from A-1 to A-80 and those for the second card from B-1 to B-80. (There are only 80 columns to a card.)

This section on the format has shown most of the basic features of the anatomy of the interview schedule and has tried to give some suggestions for clear format. Above all, the aim was to show clearly that the interview schedule, particularly in the sample survey, is much more than a list of questions. It is a highly technical instrument designed as the essential tool for locating, selecting, and identifying the respondents in the sample; for assuring that all of the questions appropriate to a particular respondent are asked and that the answers are completely and accurately recorded; for helping the supervisor make assignments, verify the sampling, edit the interview for omissions or errors, record the progress in initial contacts, call-backs, or completions; and finally, for facilitating the work of the coder, the keypunch operator, and the verifier.

The interview schedule is the instrument which converts the ideas and objectives of the survey into actual field operations. It is the instrument which coordinates the activities of the interviewer, the interviewer supervisor, the coder, keypunch operator, and research director. Experience has shown that the effectiveness of this instrument depends to a large extent upon the design of the format. Poorly designed, it can contribute to incomplete, invalid, and unrepresentative data. The well-designed instrument will not only insure the collection of adequate and valid data, but also will make both the data collection and analysis more efficient.

SUMMARY

This chapter has treated the sample survey as one highly specialized form of field strategy. In a relatively short space we have tried to describe some of the basic types of surveys classified according to whether the unit of analysis is the individual, group, institution, or community, and whether the aim is a cross-sectional study or a longitudinal study. We distinguished between three types of longitudinal studies (the trend study, the cohort analysis, and the panel study) and indicated some of the differences in the purposes, problems, and prospects of each. We discussed three ways of approximating the longitudinal study with an interview at a single point in time.

The strengths and weaknesses of different sample designs have been pointed out, and the most salient steps in applying simple random sampling, systematic sampling, multistage sampling, and stratified sampling were described. The reader interested in the mathematical theory and calculations involved in determining the size of sample needed or in measuring the level of statistical significance should consult standard texts on sampling methodology.

Although this book emphasizes the face-to-face interview, we have discussed the mailed questionnaire and the telephone interview in comparison with the face-to-face interview in the context of the sample survey. The problems of gaining entry to the respondent in the face-to-face interview survey were discussed, and we warned against common pitfalls in contacting respondents, such as trying to make appointments by telephone or mail.

To concretize all of the dimensions of the sample survey, we concentrated on the interview schedule as a technical instrument for coordinating such activities as designing the sample, selecting respondents, contacting respondents, questioning respondents, recording information, supervising field activities, editing interview schedules, coding, and keypunching the data. The interview schedule is the focal record of all of these activities.

Since we were viewing the sample survey as a special type of field strategy, we assumed that all questions had been formulated correctly, their sequence was optimally arranged, and that the interviewer had the skills for communicating the questions, determining the adequacy of the responses, and probing for complete and valid answers. In the next chapters on techniques and tactics we will treat all of these steps as problematical.

DISCUSSION QUESTIONS

1. What is a *sampling element* in a survey? Give examples.
2. What is the difference between a cross-sectional and a longitudinal survey?

3. What are the basic types of longitudinal surveys and how do they differ in *method?*

4. How do the different types of longitudinal surveys differ in the *purpose* for which they can be validly used?

5. How can the purposes of a longitudinal survey be approximately accomplished by a single cross-sectional survey? What are the major limitations of this use of the cross-sectional survey?

6. What are some of the comparative advantages and disadvantages of the simple random sample versus the systematic sample?

7. Under what basic condition is the systematic sample going to be biased?

8. What is the main advantage of the multistage sample over the single stage sample?

9. Under what conditions can we gain an advantage by stratifying the sample?

10. What are some of the relative advantages and disadvantages of the four survey modes: mail questionnaire, personally administered questionnaire, telephone interview, and personal interview?

11. What are some pointers to remember in gaining access to a respondent in a personal interview survey?

12. What are some of the functions of the interview schedule in a sample survey other than supplying questions and answer choices?

13. What are some of the major question-answer types?

14. What are some general suggestions for good format in designing an interview schedule for the sample survey?

SELECTED READINGS

Babbie, Earl R. *Survey Research Methods.* Belmont, Calif.: Wadsworth Publishing Co., 1973.

Part One deals with the scientific context of survey research; *Part Two* gives a good overview of all of the steps in designing a sample survey; *Part Three* details various models for analyzing survey data; and *Part Four* raises the questions of the ethics of applying the results of the survey and its scientific implications.

Backstrom, Charles H., and Hursh, Gerald D. *Survey Research.* Evanston, Ill.: Northwestern University Press, 1963.

Chapter 1 on Planning a Survey, and Chapter 2 on Drawing the Sample, are particularly useful in giving practical details on how to plan and carry out a sample survey. Although the most detailed treatment of sampling mechanics is given for cluster sampling, this includes all of the ingredients for other sampling models.

part four

Techniques in interviewing

14

Verbal forms used by the interviewer

Earlier we defined *techniques* as specific forms of verbal and nonverbal behavior used during the interview, and *tactics* as the way in which specific techniques are varied to meet problems as they arise in the context of a particular interview. Techniques can be classified in isolation from the larger context of the interview, while tactics are the patterns or sequences of questions as they relate to the progress of the interview as a whole. Thus, each question or statement by the interviewer has a technical form in itself and is part of a larger tactical pattern.

Techniques and tactics are functionally intertwined in the dynamics of interviewing, but to simplify the exposition, the two will be separated. In an actual nonscheduled interview, the interviewer must direct his attention toward tactical problems as they arise unpredictably; therefore, the successful interviewer must have mastered a wide range of specific techniques so that their use is automatic before he attempts the more complex task of adjusting the pattern of questioning to the ongoing context of the interview. These techniques include the verbal forms and nonverbal expressions of attitude used by the interviewer. This chapter will focus on the verbal forms and the next will focus on the nonverbal forms and their effects on the inhibitors and facilitators of communication.

Several good experiments clearly demonstrate that disciplined interviewers can consciously control both their verbal and nonverbal behavior to affect the completeness and validity of the information received. Sometimes the verbal behavior is determined by the particular wording of the question and sometimes by more general instuctions to verbally show appreciation for the respondent's efforts. Of course, the nonverbal behavior of the interviewer must be consistent with his verbal behavior. Marquis[1] did a survey of health problems of adults in which interviewers acted according to two different sets of instructions. Each time the respondent reported an illness, the experimental interviewers used a *reinforcing* statement which showed appreciation for the information and interest in the respondent's problem. The experimental interviewers also used a longer introduction to each section of the interview schedule in order to establish a context showing the survey's interest in the respondent. The experimental interviewers also looked at the respondent when talking to him and smiled frequently. The control interviewers omitted all of these verbal and nonverbal techniques and simply asked the questions in a neutral way. The experiment showed that the experimental interviewers obtained 25 percent more reports of symptoms and conditions than did the control interviewers.

In spelling out specific verbal forms and attitudes making up interviewer's kit of techniques, we will also indicate their purposes and probable effects upon the respondent's ability and willingness to give relevant information. The verbal forms and their effects to be discussed here will include (*a*) providing specific *context* for the question, (*b*) selecting the appropriate *vocabulary* in wording the question, (*c*) delimiting the *scope* of the question, (*d*) supplying *answer categories,* and (*e*) *suggesting answers.* All of these verbal forms when appropriately used help the interviewer with his two major tasks of maximizing the flow of relevant information and maintaining optimum interpersonal relations.

CONTEXTS AIMED AT COMMUNICATING THE QUESTION

Every specific question occurs in a context which helps convey its meaning to the respondent. Context is furnished at the strategy level by the respondent's perception of the purpose of the study, the sponsorship, the interviewer's auxiliary roles, and the time and place of the interview. As the next chapter explains, context is also furnished at the tactical level by the sequence of questions and answers in a particular interview. At this point, we are concerned only with the context provided at the technique level by wording a particular question to include the context or by supplying a contextual statement which immediately precedes the question.

Several useful functions can be performed by the provision of an appropriate context with the question. The context may simply clarify

---

[1] Kent H. Marquis, "Effects of Social Reinforcement on Health Reporting in the Household Interview," *Sociometry,* vol. 33 (1970), pp. 203–15.

the meaning of the question; it may increase the respondent's ability to give the relevant information by stimulating his memory, by decreasing the chronological confusion, or by bringing unconscious norms and assumptions to the surface; it may also increase the respondent's willingness to give the information by decreasing ego threat, removing the etiquette barrier, appealing to the need for meaning, or stimulating altruistic motives.

Defining terms. It is often necessary to preface a question with a contextual statement defining crucial terms which might be unclear to the respondent. Ego threat is prevented by giving the definition before the respondent shows that he needs it and without asking whether he understands the term. For example:

There are cases where a man and woman live together as man and wife, set up housekeeping, have children and take care of them, but do not get a marriage license or have a wedding ceremony of any kind. *Do you think children of these common-law marriages should be entitled to the legal rights of inheritance?*

This is better than either asking if the respondent knows what a common law marriage is or assuming that he understands the term.

The same question might have different meanings to different respondents who use different sets of assumptions to interpret the meaning of the question. Garfinkel[2] shows how, in different situations in everyday social interaction, people interpret the actions of others in terms of common sense theories. These theories are composed of assumptions about human behavior, as they know it, which help them to make sense out of what people say and do. He goes further to show that this *context* of unstated assumptions, particularly the cognitive assumptions, changes within a group as a result of the members' past interactions. Each person, therefore, brings to any communication situation a set of assumptions (normative and cognitive) which are derived both from his general cultural background and from the more unique experiential background of the groups of which he is a member. Usually, in the interview situation the respondent and interviewer are establishing a new relationship in which neither knows the unstated assumptions of the other that would bear upon the interpretation of the particular questions to be asked. Under these conditions, if the interviewer does not explicitly furnish a context for interpretation of a question because he unwittingly assumes that there is only one possible context, he is leaving the respondent free to use his own set of assumptions which are unstated and unknown to the interviewer. Thus, not

---

[2] Harold Garfinkel, *Studies in Ethnomethodology* (Englewood Cliffs, N.J.: Prentice-Hall, Inc., 1967).

only is the question different in the minds of these two people, but also the response has a different meaning to each.

Of course, the context for the interview as a whole is partially established by those dimensions of the situation previously treated under the heading of strategy, but at this point we are concerned only with contexts as a verbal technique for more clearly communicating the question.

Studies involving controversial issues on a national and international scale often involve terms not clearly understood by many people. In a random sample of the population such words as "monopoly," "savings," "profit," "free-trade," "mandate," and "right of way" carry only a vague meaning for the majority. In many cases, the respondent will not ask the meaning because he thinks he knows or he is embarrassed to ask.

Providing a time perspective. Often the answer to a question can be completely reversed by a shift in the time perspective. This is particularly true when obtaining facts or opinions on *trends* of any type. For example, in response to the question, "Do you think that the amount of academic freedom on American college campuses has increased, decreased, or stayed about the same?" a respondent's answer might be "increased" or "decreased," depending on the period of time the interviewer has in mind. To bring about a clearer time perspective, the context could be, "Try to remember some of the things happening on this campus five years ago, in 1956, and compare that with the present time. Think of the general psychological atmosphere and its effect upon academic freedom."

If the interviewer has information on some specific events in the local, national, and international scene occurring in 1956 this would be helpful in providing a more vivid time perspective.

Providing a spacial perspective. Just as an answer could be reversed by the time perspective, it could also be reversed by the spacial perspective of the respondent. A citizen's civic improvement organization interested in knowing the public's reaction to its efforts in one section of a large city questioned a random sample of respondents in and near the area where its work was going on, asking, "Do you feel that your neighborhood has got better, worse, or stayed about the same in the last years?" The problem here was that the psychological boundaries of each respondent's neighborhood varied. If the respondent's own psychological boundaries did not coincide with the area the organization had in mind, the answer could be negative since the surrounding area was rapidly deteriorating in its physical and social condition. This was easily remedied by preceding the question with this clarifying context: "Perhaps you are familiar with the area between Wentworth and State streets from 43rd to 57th. Just think of this area and forget for the moment all the areas right around it."

The responses to this question after the context was furnished would be significantly different, particularly for respondents residing near the outside edges of the designated area.

Supplying a social-psychological perspective. A myriad of examples could show that a question in its logical purity, even with clearly defined terms could be answered differently, depending on the circumstances which the respondent has in mind. For example, we could define "bureaucracy" as a pure form of social structure and then attempt to discover people's attitudes and opinions on the desirability of such a form of human organization by asking the question, "Now that we have defined the bureaucracy as we will use it in this discussion, what do you think of it as a general form of organization?"

The answer to this question would vary, depending upon whether the respondent was thinking of the probable effects of such an organization when manned by "those government bureaucrats in Washington" or by "the managers of America's great business enterprises, such as X Motors." The respondent might very well have no opinion on "bureaucracy" in the abstract, and in order to give the question some meaning he would supply his own context if none was supplied by the interviewer.

Supplying criteria for judgment. Closely related to the previous type of context is one which clearly specifies the criteria the respondent is to apply in making a judgment. Of course, in the previous example the respondent might use different criteria in judging a business bureaucracy versus a government bureaucracy, but the interviewer has no way of knowing in advance what the criteria are. The following example is an attempt to focus the respondent's attention on one of many possible criteria for making a judgment.

As you know, there are some counties in this state which have not yet integrated their public schools. Many reasons are given for favoring and opposing the integration, but I am interested in your opinion on the economic efficiency of integration. I am not asking whether you favor or oppose integration. Just assume for the moment that the only problem is one of getting the best education for the most people for the least money from the taxpayer. Do you think integrated schools would be a more efficient or a less efficient use of public funds? (Probes: Why do you say that? Could you explain that a little more?)

It will be difficult to persuade the respondent to use the criterion of efficiency if he is strongly opposed to integration on other grounds. For this reason, it would be necessary to probe carefully as to *why* he feels the integrated system would be more or less efficient.

Supplying needed facts. Many times, the point of an interview is to discover how a person will decide an issue if he has certain relevant facts. Instead of either assuming that he has them or asking him if he is "well informed," the interviewer supplies the salient facts. Thus, he is sure they were taken into consideration insofar as the respondent gives them weight.

For example, in a study of public opinion formation in a small community, the following question was one of those asked of a carefully selected group of opinion leaders:

As you probably read in the *News-Sun,* the Village Council must make a decision at next month's meeting on whether to put in a new gravity-flow sewer system at the cost of $400,000, which will still serve the population 25 years from now, or to put in a new sewer pumping station at the cost of $100,000 but which will have to be enlarged at the cost of $50,000 in five years. With each five-year period, the cost of enlargement would be greater, so that the total cost at the end of 25 years would be about $600,000. Do you personally favor the gravity-flow or the pumping station? (Probes: Why do you favor that? Is there any special reason you favor that? Could you explain that a little further?)

The use which the respondent makes of the supplied facts varies, depending on the additional facts he has, the knowledge he has of the general problem, and the questions he is able to generate in his analysis of the information he has. For example, in the discussion brought out by the probing, one of the better-informed respondents said:

If you look at it from the standpoint of long-run efficiency of service, it is difficult to decide which would cost the taxpayers the most because the total cost of either system depends upon how much money must be borrowed, at what interest rate, for what period of time and, finally, how much inflation or deflation there will be in the local economy during the period for which the money was borrowed. Since I don't know these things, there is no way to make an intelligent choice.

More typical responses were in the direction of the two below, representing both those who favored and those who opposed the gravity-flow sewer.

I think it is best to do what is cheapest in the long run. If it is going to cost the taxpayers $200,000 more within a 25-year period to use pumping stations, I think we should put out a little more money right now by getting the gravity-flow sewer and saving in the long run.

I have heard the argument that it would save us money in the long run to get the gravity-flow sewer, but who is "us"? I may not be here in 25 years or even 10 years. Also, this might be a ghost town by that time and not even need as big a sewer system as we have now. I don't believe in these predictions of the future.

It is clear that both respondents considered the facts but reached opposite conclusions by putting these facts in different perspectives.

Discovering the respondent's own contexts. So far, we have shown how the interviewer may need to provide some context with a particular question in order to define terms, provide a time perspective, give a spacial perspective, locate a particular social-psychological circumstance, supply criteria for judgments, or furnish specific facts to be used in making a judgment. All of these uses of context are aimed at communicating the meaning of the question more precisely to the respondent. Thus, we assume that the interviewer has a particular context in mind which he desired to make clear to the respondent.

There is a contrasting purpose of the interview where the main objective is to discover the respondent's own context which gives meaning to certain words, facts, slogans, or any form of abstraction. In this case, it would *not* be appropriate to furnish the context; special tactics may be needed to discover the respondent's context without appearing to be cryptic or nonsupportive. This problem will be dealt with in the next chapter.

CONTEXTS AIMED AT MOTIVATING THE RESPONDENT

The preceding types of contexts are aimed primarily at communicating to the respondent the precise meaning of the question. Once the respondent clearly grasps the question, it is sometimes also necessary to make him either more *able* or more *willing* to answer fully. The respondent's willingness may be increased by a context which arouses his interest in the topic, acknowledges the respondent's special qualifications, or reduces any ego threat or etiquette barrier. Contexts may also increase the respondent's ability to give relevant information by stimulating his memory, by obviating chronological confusion, and by stimulating unconscious behavior patterns and attitudes.

Arousing the respondent's interest. Often a respondent has a low level of motivation because he fails to see significance in the information he is giving. If it can be done without "loading" the question, supplying contexts from time to time in the interview can help motivate the respondent. For example:

There has been a lot of discussion in Congress recently about free trade. Slogans such as "Trade, not aid to the underdeveloped areas" have been invented. There are two bills before Congress at the moment dealing with the problem. *What does the term "free trade" mean to you?*

This context does more than arouse interest; it provides a perspective suggesting international free trade rather than interstate free trade in the United States. If the international perspective is correct for the purpose of the interview, then this context would not distort the information.

Recognizing the respondent's special qualifications. It is not only useful to remind the respondent of his qualifications at the beginning of the interview when explaining how and why he was selected, but it is also helpful to remind him of his special qualifications at other points in the interview. One way of doing this is to preface a question with a reminder of the respondent's qualifications as is done in the following examples:

You have had much more experience with life than I and can see things in a broader perspective. What advice would you give to young people today to make the "senior citizen" period of their lives more full and happy?

Since you were at one time a member of the gang with the biggest "rep" in East Harlem, could you give me some idea why teenagers join these kinds of gangs?

Within one interview, different aspects of the respondent's qualifications can be mentioned in order to support the respondent's need for recognition.

Reducing ego threat. Questions can be worded to include a face-saving preface to reduce the ego threat. For example, "I know people nowadays do not have time to keep up on everything that is going on in the world, but would you tell me if you have read anything about the Near East crisis?" Several studies of the validity of people's statements regarding current events have demonstrated that they exaggerate the amount of reading they have done and tend to feel guilty about how little they know about current world issues. A preface of this type will reduce the urge to overestimate one's reading and reduce the ego threat involved in an admission of ignorance.

Another approach is to show that "even the Gods have clay feet," and celebrities, too, have failures. This helps place a respondent's possible weaknesses in a nonthreatening perspective. For example:

As you probably know, Winston Churchill, Albert Einstein, and others of that calibre failed in some of their college courses. How many courses have you failed so far?

Depending on the purposes of the interview, the interviewer's knowledge of the respondent, and the general setting of the interview, this principle can be adapted to soften many potentially ego-threatening questions.

Preventing falsification. It often saves a tremendous amount of time and energy to prevent the respondent's committing himself falsely. Once he has taken the false position, he will feel honor-bound to defend it even though he may regret his falsification. Often, an elaborate web of lies has to be built up to preserve consistency with the original lie. It is mainly in detective stories that the culprit breaks down when inconsistencies are discovered in his story. In the interview situation the respondent is not obligated to submit to continual pressure. Neither is a suspicious attitude on the part of the interviewer considered within the bounds of etiquette. Under these conditions prevention is more efficient and less embarrassing.

For example, an employer is interviewing a prospective employee who has been fired from his former job. If the interviewer wants to know something about the respondent's relationship with his former employers, he should let the respondent know that the former employer has informed him the respondent was fired. A straightforward question, after rapport has been built up, would not only save time but would also indicate to the intelligent respondent that the interviewer has no desire to trap him. The interviewer could simply say, "I was told by your former employer that you were fired. They gave me their side of the story, but I would like to hear it from your point of view."

Reducing the etiquette barrier. In the strategy phase, the interviewer-respondent combinations should be selected to avoid role relationships which erect an etiquette barrier. However, there are still situations in which the respondent may identify the interviewer with a role which would damage the flow of information. If the interviewer takes advantage of opportunities to clarify his role as the interview progresses, the probability of the etiquette barrier arising can be reduced. For example, a college professor who was interviewing students regarding their experiences in a new foreign extension of the college conducted a group interview with five students recently returned from abroad. The professor was the designer of the program and this fact was known to most of the students. He assumed that students would be reluctant to criticize the weaknesses of the new program and therefore introduced the discussion as follows:

As you probably know, I was instrumental in designing the original program set up in Guanajuato in 1958. I have had no official connection with it over the past three years and I am somewhat out of touch with what is going on there. I am interested in doing what I can to improve the program at this time. I suspect that in its actual operations the program has certain weaknesses which should be brought out in the open and discussed. That is why I have invited you here today, not to obtain a pollyannaish report of the program, but to get some insight into your personal experiences so that I can see it from the point of view of the students it is supposed to benefit. What are some of the things that should be done to improve the program there in Guanajuato?

Of course, beginning the discussion with a one-paragraph statement aimed at reducing the etiquette barrier is not to be depended upon completely. The group began with some minor criticisms as well as some praise of certain aspects of the program. The interviewer's success in obtaining criticism of the program rested heavily upon his reactions to the group's initial criticisms. When they observed that he did not swell with pride when the program was praised, nor attempt to defend it against their criticisms, they were encouraged to express themselves more candidly. All etiquette barriers were not eliminated by this technique. For example, students interviewing the same groups discovered objections not raised in the discussion with the professor, but these were matters withheld because he was a member of the older generation and not because he was the originator of the program.

We have dealt with several ways in which an appropriate context might reduce the respondent's resistance to giving relevant information. Now we will examine some of the ways to increase his ability to report his experiences.

Stimulating the memory. By reviewing some of the objective facts about a certain situation, the interviewer often can stimulate the respondent's memory of his experiences in that situation. In the following example the interviewer is attempting to reconstruct the pattern of interaction between members of a family when a tornado struck their rural village. He needs to obtain an accurate report of the actions of each person and the extent to which other family members were taken into consideration.

Now after the wind stopped blowing and the house had crashed into the pecan orchard, it was still dark, raining very hard, and someone outside the wreckage was shouting, "Anybody in there?" At that moment did you know where your husband was?

It is not always necessary for the interviewer to know that the respondent was conscious of all the circumstantial facts mentioned, as long as all the facts are accurate and were occurring at the time of the respondent's relevant experiences. In contrast to the example above that describes *events* occurring at the relevant time, the context might focus upon a description of the physical *scene* of the event. In any case, the interviewer should attempt to include those circumstantial facts most salient to the respondent.

Reducing chronological confusion. Often the respondent is less aware of the chronological order of his actions and observations than he is of their relationship to certain salient observations of events not directly related to the objectives of the interview. Even if the respondent does not know the correct order of the irrelevant events, the interviewer who knows their order can use this information to unscramble the respondent's sequence of experiences.

We have been able to clearly establish the order of some events that you might remember from the day of the explosions here in Brighton. First, there was the explosion in the reducing-valve vault under the sidewalk at Twelve Corners, then the gas jets in people's stoves, furnaces, and gas dryers began to make a hissing noise, then the Mellinger house exploded, the next house exploded about 12 minutes later. The first explosion was south of your house, the second was directly west. What were you doing when you heard the first explosion? Where were you when you heard the second explosion?

This technique of preventing chronological confusion is simply an extension of the general principle of using known facts to stimulate recall of additional actions and observations.

Discovering unconscious factors. Of the types of unconscious experience a respondent might have, the one most amenable to verbal techniques is that of the values or norms which govern a person's behavior. Frequently, they cannot be clearly reported because the respondent is not aware of the norm in the abstract, but expresses it in his behavior toward concrete situations. In this case, it is often helpful to use a hypothetical case as the focus for discussion. Several hypothetical cases may be required to delineate the particular norm or pattern of norms in question.

Suppose our problem is to discover the norms governing the relationship between nurses and doctors in a large metropolitan hospital. The interviewer might ask a nurse how the higher status of the doctors is shown in their behavior toward nurses and in their treatment by the hospital administration. The following is one hypothetical case:

Suppose a maternity patient in the hospital is about to give birth to her baby, but the physician in charge of her has not yet arrived. Her labor is in the final phase and the child will be born in a few minutes. This is the patient's fourth child, she is in good health, and her medical history is known to the nurse in charge of her case. Three hours previously, the physician called to say he would arrive at the hospital in four hours which would be in another hour. (1) What would the nurse in charge of her case do? (2) What would the supervising nurse on the maternity ward do? (3) What would the physician probably say if he could be reached by phone and it was explained that the birth was going to take place before he could arrive?

If the interviewer has some hunches of what constitute a violation of the norms in this situation, he might suggest these to obtain the respondent's reaction. Very frequently, we are more aware of specific actions which would constitute a *violation* of a norm than we are of the norm itself. In some problems of this type, the interviewer can simply ask, "What would be the wrong thing for the nurse to do in this situation? or "What could you say for sure the physician would *not* suggest for the nurse to do in this case?"

To stimulate discussion of this hypothetical case, it might be useful to suggest possible actions to obtain a response. For example, "Would the nurse go ahead and deliver the baby herself, if she knows there are no complications in the case?" "Would the supervising nurse ask one of the physicians on the ward who was not busy at the moment to perform the delivery?" "Would the nurse in charge, by previous arrangement with the physician, retard the delivery until the patient's regular physician arrived?"

This extension of the hypothetical case by suggesting possible action solutions must, of course, be constructed so that a full range of action is included, or so that each action or action alternative involves the norms in which the interviewer is interested. Otherwise, we may bias the responses by suggestion or by exclusion of certain relevant alternatives. If the interviewer is not sure of the adequacy of the alternative actions, they could be used only as possible answer choices for the interviewer to check without mentioning any of them to the respondent.

An interesting study in the use of hypothetical cases is reported by Weaver,[3] who wanted to study the norms among Spanish-Americans governing the decision whether to call a *curandero* (folk medicine specialist) or a medical doctor. Instead of asking the question, for example, "When do you usually ask the *curandero* to come?" the respondent was given hypothetical cases of illnesses and asked direct questions about the symptoms, diagnosis, and treatment. In this way the criteria for actions, which were mostly unconscious in the respondent, could be tested by a carefully selected set of hypothetical examples. The hypothetical example as a particular form of context has been shown to be useful not only for teasing out unconscious patterns, but also for avoiding ego threat in situations where, if the respondent were aware of the pattern of his behavior, he would refuse to verbalize it to the interviewer. Under these conditions the interviewer can assume the task of inducing the pattern from the concrete examples, while being careful not to point it out to the respondent. Another value of the hypothetical example is to avoid inferential confusion by not asking the respondent to abstract the rule logically from the specific examples, but by letting the interviewer handle the inference process.

The hypothetical case is often an excellent focus for discussion and will, if well chosen, stimulate salient responses. Good hypotheses cannot be constructed from a swivel chair but must be built upon previous knowledge. Often it is not until the later stages of a study, or at least until after several interviews have been done or some participant-observation used, that relevant hypothetical examples can be produced, since they should contain problematical situations which could really occur.

---

[3] T. Weaver, "Use of Hypothetical Situations in a Study of Spanish-American Illness Referral Systems," *Human Organization,* vol. 29 (1970), pp. 140-54.

SELECTING APPROPRIATE VOCABULARY

Without becoming enmeshed in a multitude of possible examples, let us look at some of the main problems in selecting an appropriate vocabulary for the interview.

a. The words should be clearly understood by the respondent.
b. The words should aid in establishing an optimum role relationship between the interviewer and respondent.
c. In some cases, the question should be worded to include the vocabulary needed by the respondent to give his answer without violating the etiquette of the situation.
d. Emotional words which might unintentionally "load" the question should be avoided.

These apparently simple principles may be very easy or very difficult to put into practice.

The first principle can be thwarted by very subtle differences in the universe of discourse of the interviewer and the respondent. For example, the two questions below obtained quite different responses from rural victims of a tornado:

What were some of the problems which arose during the rescue operations right after the tornado struck?
What sorts of trouble did people have trying to help folks who were hurt or trapped in the wreckage?

The second question obtained a straightforward and spontaneous response relevant to the purposes of the study. The first wording of the question seemed to puzzle some respondents because the word "problems" had a connotation narrower than intended by the interviewer.

The second principle, using a vocabulary that will establish an optimum role relationship between interviewer and respondent, has many manifestations, but it can be viewed in the same two-dimensional system suggested in the previous chapter. The interviewer must recognize that the respondent can quickly classify him as an "insider-outsider" or "subordinate-equal-superordinate" on the basis of his choice of words. For example, in an interview to obtain voters' attitudes toward certain policies of the Department of Agriculture, the interviewer might ask, "What do you think of our policy of allowing farmers to vote on alternative types of farm programs we administer through the Department of Agriculture?" In exploratory, nonscheduled interviews, the interviewer noted that most of the respondents referred to any department of the federal government as "they," rather than "we" as did the interviewer. This prevented the interviewer from being perceived as an "insider" by the farmer. On certain controversial issues, this brought the etiquette barrier into play.

It is often helpful to word the question so that it is clear to the respondent that the interviewer understands the local universe of discourse. This allows the respondent to speak more spontaneously without having to "translate" for the interviewer. Usually, only the more educated or experienced respondent will bother to do this, while the respondent with a narrow range of experience does not realize he has a special jargon. The interviewer can indicate that there is no need to "translate" by using the local jargon in the wording of the question. For example, in an interview with a supervisor in a telephone company, the interviewer said, "I understand, according to one of the CO's, that they expect to install key-pulse dialing when the new rate structure filed with the ICC is approved. When do they expect the ICC to give its decision?" Immediately the respondent was aware that the interviewer understood "CO," "key-pulse dialing," "rate-structure," and "ICC."

There is danger in using the local jargon if the interviewer does not actually understand it or if it puts him in the insider role when it would be more desirable to be an outsider. Often, the outsider role can be retained without forcing the respondent to translate if the interviewer explains that he has learned as much of the jargon as he can for the occasion and will ask for further explanations from time to time. Only a few questions early in the interview will clearly indicate that the interviewer is an outsider.

In some cases, the vocabulary used is crucial in helping the respondent classify the interviewer as an equal or a superordinate. In cases where the interviewer is perceived as a superordinate, the respondent is sometimes reluctant to answer a question because he senses that his vocabulary would be considered vulgar outside his own group, yet he does not know what vocabulary would be considered appropriate by the interviewer. In this case, the interviewer can be careful to supply the vocabulary by his wording of the question so that the meaning is obvious. Then the respondent can use the same vocabulary in answering. For example, in a study of child-rearing practices of mothers in the lower socioeconomic level, the question, "How did you go about toilet training your child?" was ineffective. Instead, it was necessary to use a series of questions to provide the polite vocabulary needed by the respondent. Mothers were asked, "When were you first able to depend on Johnny asking to go to the toilet to have a bowel movement?" and then, "When did he quit wetting himself and going to the toilet instead?" Once these questions were answered, a more detailed discussion of the mother's attempts to toilet-train the child followed rather smoothly, since "bowel movement" had become a common phrase.

It is common sense to avoid using emotionally loaded vocabulary in wording the question. The actual implementation of the principle is not so simple, but depends upon the interviewer's knowing which words have a biasing effect upon the respondent. For example, in a study of communication between North Americans and Latin Americans, the use of the word *gringo* in Mexico to refer to North Americans would have a strongly negative emotional loading. *Gringo* would not have this effect in Colombia where the word *yanqui* is reserved for negative connotations.

There are times when it is appropriate to use emotionally loaded words as long as it is intentional and the direction of the effect is known. This intentional use of the "loaded" question will be discussed later.

DELIMITING THE SCOPE OF THE QUESTION

Questions and probes by the interviewer may vary tremendously in their scope. A question may be so broad that it includes within its confines more than the total objectives of the whole interview, or it may be so narrow in scope that hundreds of minutely specific questions are necessary to cover the same topic. The scope of each question used in an interview is not automatically determined by the objectives or the topic of the interview. People experienced in nonscheduled interviewing realize that it may require twice as many questions to obtain the relevant information from one respondent as from another. In one case, broad questions provide sufficient stimulus for the respondent to cover many specific points within the scope of the general question, while in another the interviewer must specify each bit of information needed.

It is important for an interviewer to become aware of this dimension, called "scope," since most people have an unconscious habit, developed in social conversation, of being unnecessarily restrictive in the scope of their questions. Perhaps it is a way of saving time or of restricting the other person's remarks so that we may express our point of view sooner. Or perhaps the efficient businessman, the incisive lawyer, or the police detective who "get to the point" in mass media portrayals influence our controversial patterns. Regardless of the source, in training interviewers the writer has found that it is usually more difficult for them to ask broad questions than to ask each specific point separately. Frequently, the neophyte interviewer behaves as if his motto were "never use a general question if several specific questions can be used instead." By developing a sensitivity to how apparently small differences in the wording of a question make vast differences in its scope, the interviewer may guide his own behavior in accordance with the objectives of the interview, rather than be guided by unconscious habit.

To illustrate this difference in scope, let us compare three opening questions used by different interviewers in an interview with teenagers to discover some of the educational values of the county fair for city children.

a. Tell me what happened at the Greene County Fair when you were there last Saturday.

b. Tell me what you did at the Greene County Fair when you were there last Saturday.

c. Did you like the horse show at the county fair?

Regardless of which question is the best opener for this type of interview, the vast difference in scope is clear. The first question, by using the term "what happened," leaves the topic open for the respondent to report what he did, what others did, what he saw, what others saw, what he felt or thought about what he did or saw, and what he felt and thought about what others did and saw.

The second question logically restricts the area of discussion as much as 90 percent by asking only what the *respondent did.* This unnecessary restriction of the topic might constitute an ego threat in this case, because the respondent probably was mainly a spectator and could more spontaneously report what he saw than what he did. Also, the impersonality of "what happened" versus "what did you see, do, or think" often makes the respondent less self-conscious.

The third question restricts the conversation to some fraction of one percent of the respondent's impressions of the fair. It also inhibits the spontaneous flow of information, because it prevents the respondent from talking about what, for him, were the most memorable aspects of the fair. It also implies that a simple "yes" or "no" answer is required.

Dimensions of scope

Rather than examining scores of illustrations of differences in scope and discussing their possible effects on the flow of relevant information, we have devised a scheme to show some of the important dimensions of scope. This allows the reader to generate his own examples. The chart (Figure 14–1) delineates five dimensions of scope, represented by the column headings, which apply to all questions. The columns are arranged in the order each dimension usually appears in the sentence structure of a question. Within each column the scope becomes broader as we progress from top to bottom. With some imagination, the reader can construct questions for a hypothetical interview topic, using different breadths of the five dimensions.

To illustrate some questions constructed from different breadths

FIGURE 14-1
Scope of the question

		Dimensions of question			
BREADTH	Interrogative A	Actor (subject) B	Action (verb) C	Relationships (objects) D	Scene E
1	(Request for information) Did . . . ? Was . . . ? Will . . . ? Has . . . ?	(A specific person or thing) "You," "Tom," "your boss," "car," "wind."	(Specific action verb supplied) "Run," "sing," "say," "lift," "drill," "give," "take."	(Both the direct and indirect objects are specified)	(Specific point in time and space specified or implied)
2	(The facts) Who . . . ? When . . . ? Where . . . ? How much . . . ? How many . . . ?	(Unspecified persons or things other than "you") "People," "others," "everyone," "things."		(Only one object is specified)	(A certain event within the scene specified)
3	(Interpretation-explanation) Why . . . ? How . . . ?	(Does not specify "you" or "others") "Anyone?" "Anything?"	(General class of action specified as to overt or covert) "do," "think."	(Only one object is specified)	(A certain limited time period or spatial location)
4	(Request for unspecified information) What . . . ? Tell me about . . .	(No actor category specified)	(No specific action or class of action is specified) "Happened?"	(Neither the direct or indirect object specified)	(No time or place limitation includes the whole scene or topic of the interview)

of each of the five dimensions (see table below), we will assume that the interview topic is a robbery that occurred the week before. Each of the six questions becomes successively broader in scope.

Although many more sentences could be constructed from different combinations of breadths of the five dimensions, it is not possible to construct a meaningful sentence corresponding to every logical combination of breadth. Which combinations are meaningful depends to some extent upon the topic of the interview. In spite of the lack of refinement, this scheme can help sensitize the interviewer to the fact that the scope of a question can be expanded or contracted by gradual degrees, and that the answer to several of the narrower questions could be logically included in the answer to one of the broadest questions on the same topic.

			Dimension			
Breadth	*A*	*B*	*C*	*D*	*E*	*Questions*
1	1	1	1	1	1	"Did you give the gun to Jim in the car before the robbery?"
2	1	1	1	2	1	"Did you give a gun to anyone before the robbery?"
3	2	2	1	2	2	"Who could have provided the gun for the robbery?"
4	3	4	4	4	2	"How did the robbery happen last Thursday night?"
5	4	1	3	4	3	"What were you doing last Thursday night at eight?"
6	4	4	4	4	4	"What happened last Thursday night?"

Consciously or unconsciously the interviewer makes a choice in the nonscheduled interview between (*a*) using broad questions and encouraging the respondent to elaborate to obtain specific details, or (*b*) using many narrow questions to cover the same topic. The tactical problem of shifting from broader to narrower questions or vice versa will be discussed in the next chapter. At this point we will examinee some of the most probable values of broader and narrower questions and indicate some of the limiting circumstances for the use of each.

Values of broad questions.

Broad questions have two general values: first, they must be used to obtain certain types of information which would be distorted by the effect of many specific questions; second, they have certain motivational effects upon the respondent under certain conditions.

Interviews with any or all of the following objectives often require the use of broad questions: (a) discovering the respondent's paths of association regarding a certain topic, situation, or event; (b) discovering the relative importance of various aspects of a topic, situation, or event experienced by the respondent; (c) discovering the frame of reference used by the respondent in observing, analyzing, or acting in a situation; (d) discovering the chronological order of the respondent's experiences in a given situation; (e) discovering the vocabulary used by the respondent in discussing certain aspects of a topic, situation, or event.

In each of these objectives the interviewer must be careful not to impose his own organization upon the topic, but must encourage the respondent to discuss the topic in his own terms. It is practically impossible for the interviewer to divide the topic into many specific questions without imposing his own frame of references, without using a vocabulary he is not yet sure is appropriate, without interrupting the respondent's natural paths of association, and without imposing different perspectives or hierarchies of importance upon the specifics reported.

Broad questions not only help the interviewer to avoid giving rather than receiving information, but also help to increase the respondent's ability and willingness to give relevant information in several ways.

Reducing ego threat. Often certain facts regarding a topic, situation, or event might constitute an ego threat to the respondent if the interviewer calls his attention to the significance of the relationship between these facts. If the interviewer asks for each fact, the respondent may become concerned with how the interviewer is going to evaluate the information. However, if the interviewer does not ask for but is given the facts, the respondent does not know the interviewer attaches any particular significance to them. In rare cases it might be necessary to pose a broad question that focuses on an area only indirectly related to the specific facts needed so that the respondent will not feel threatened by direct questioning on sensitive areas.

Stimulating memory. The objective of the interview may not be to discover the respondent's individual paths of association. Still it is often advisable to allow him to follow his own inclinations in order to assure that he is not forced to give information before he has had an opportunity to recall it. When specifics are asked for before the respondent volunteers them, there is a danger that he will fill the gaps in his memory with his imagination. The respondent may be reporting what he assumes he must have done in view of the logical or moral requirements of the situation; he need not be consciously fabricating.

Giving the respondent recognition. By merely introducing a broad topic of discussion and allowing the respondent to tell his own story, the interviewer implies a respect for the respondent's ability to report relevant material. This lack of restriction also allows the respondent to mention information to his credit even though it may not be directly relevant to the objectives of the study.

Giving sympathetic understanding.   Giving the respondent more freedom to tell his own story in his own way usually implies to him that the interviewer is more interested in him as a unique person than as a source of information. He perceives that the interviewer is "interested in what is important to me" and is encouraged to take advantage of the opportunity. The more that specific, narrow questions are asked, the more likely that the emphasis of the interview will shift away from each respondent's unique concerns.

Encouraging catharsis.   Once an atmosphere of sympathetic understanding is established, the respondent will be encouraged to "get certain problems off his chest" if they are important to him at the moment and are related to the topic of the interview. Of course, whether or not the interviewer should encourage this catharsis depends upon whether the information is relevant, whether the catharsis is helpful or harmful to the optimum relationship between interviewer and respondent, and how efficient the interviewer must be.

Need for meaning.   In some cases, the freedom from the restrictions of specific questions and a generally permissive atmosphere will encourage the respondent to soliloquize. He begins to think out loud and expresses his doubts, fears, and even his decision-making process in forming answers to questions he has. This usually occurs when the interview topic itself or the life situation of the respondent touches upon confusion or crisis. If the interviewer needs to stimulate the respondent's need for meaning by pointing out problems and dilemmas, the broad question does not always allow him to do this.

Values of narrow questions.

As in the case of the broad question, the value of the narrow question depends to a great extent upon the type of information sought and the type of motivation which must be stimulated. In general, if specific facts and opinions are needed rather than more complex structural relationships, a more specific question will be more efficient. For example, if we wish to know a person's age, religion, and marital status and if such information is not ego threatening under the circumstances, then it would be ridiculous to attempt to obtain the information by asking, "Would you please tell me about yourself?" On the other hand, if we wanted to know which were the most salient aspects of a person's self-concept, we would need to know not only his age, religion, and marital status but also many other characteristics, as well as their relative importance and interrelationships in the mind of the respondent. In this case, the broader question would be more appropriate. However, under certain circumstances the narrower question has advantages in motivating the respondent.

Reducing ego threat. There are circumstances where the topic and the respondent are such that broad questions have little meaning to the respondent. He may feel at a loss to begin his report or to organize it into some meaningful whole. This is particularly true when the topic itself is not vital to the respondent or is put in terms that are too abstract. Under these conditions the ego threat is not in the information itself but in the fact that the respondent is embarrassed because he feels he has nothing to say. He is given encouragement and support by the interviewer who dissects the topic into more manageable specifics.

Reducing the etiquette barrier. In some interviews, the respondent is willing to give any information as long as he is sure that it is considered useful or necessary by the interviewer. If the interviewer has a relationship with the respondent that makes him reluctant to report certain information, he will tend to omit it unless the interviewer specifically asks for it.

Stimulating the need for meaning. Often a person's interest in the topic of the interview can be increased by stimulating his need for meaning. This can be done by asking specific questions posing dilemmas, inconsistencies, or problematical relationships. The respondent can often be enticed by the realization that things are not as simple as they might appear at first glance.

Structuring the answer

Questions may include varying degrees of answer structure. The categories of acceptable answers may be explicit or implicit. The respondent may be instructed to choose one or more than one. Answer categories may be mutually exclusive or overlapping. The respondent may be given the choice of either using the answer categories supplied or giving a more detailed answer in his own words. The categories may be qualitative or quantitative.

In general, questions which do not supply the answer categories are called "open-ended" and those that limit the answer choices are called "closed." An example of an open-ended question would be, "What did you see at the County Fair?" An example of a closed question would be, "Which of the following did you see at the county fair: sulky racing, the hog show, the milking machine display, the fruit exhibit?"

The answers to a question need not be either completely open or closed, but may fall in between. Rather than supplying categories, the wording of the question may imply choices, as in these two examples:

"How many times a month, on the average, do you go to church?" and "Do you go to church every week?" The first example implies that the answer should be in terms of times per month. The second implies that either a "yes" or "no" answer is needed. A more completely structured form would be as follows: "How many times, on the average, do you go to church: more than once a week, once a week, two or three times per month, once a month, or less than once a month?"

Of course, none of the above three forms should be used unless preceded by a filter question to determine whether or not the particular respondent did in fact attend some religious body that would be appropriately called a church.

In deciding upon the amount of structuring to use, it is necessary to consider the type of information sought and the effects of the structuring on the respondent's ability and willingness to give the relevant information.

Some of the same information objectives requiring questions with a broader scope also require open-ended questions discovering the respondent's paths of association, frames of reference, and universe of discourse.

If the information can be obtained equally well by either open-ended or closed questions, then the closed question should be used because it increases the efficiency and reliability of the coding and analysis of the data.

In a semischeduled interview in which specific items of information are to be obtained but no wording of the questions or sequence is specified, it is still possible for the interviewer to structure the answers and to record the responses on a multiple-choice code sheet. This eliminates having to convert verbatim notes into code categories. Also, if the correct category for the answer is unclear to the interviewer, he can probe for further clarification.

Structuring answers can have several possible effects upon the facilitators and inhibitors of communication.

Competing time demands. The use of structured answers not only saves time for the interviewers, coders, and analyzers but also for the respondent. If the information is of the type where it is appropriate to structure the answers, the respondent is often happy to see that the interviewer knows exactly what he wants and is businesslike and efficient.

Ego threat. Under some conditions respondents feel threatened by open-ended questions which sound "as if they would require a dissertation to answer." The respondent's insecurity can often be reduced by placing the choices before him.

Etiquette. Often the etiquette barrier can be reduced by supplying specific answer categories which show that the interviewer expects such information. Answer categories can supply the respondent with a vocabulary compatible with the etiquette requirements of the situation. For example: "With which of the following did you have your first complete heterosexual intercourse? (1) With a prostitute? (2) With an intimate acquaintance before marriage? (3) With a girl 'picked up' for the occasion? (4) With your wife before you were engaged? (5) With your wife after engagement and before marriage? (6) With your wife after marriage?" Such a question put in a matter-of-fact tone by a mature interviewer would be more likely to elicit a valid response with less strain on the respondent than would the open-ended form of the same question. If there is no reason why the information must be collected by interviewing, a questionnaire would probably be still more effective in reducing both the ego threat and the etiquette barrier. A compromise between an interview and a questionnaire can be arranged by stating the question orally and then handing the respondent a card with the answers on it and asking him to give the *number* of the correct answer.

Forgetting. Under certain circumstances it is more efficient, valid, and reliable to obtain facts which have faded in the respondent's memory by asking him to choose from among several specific alternatives. It is usually easier to *recognize* the correct answer when it is presented by the interviewer than it is to *recall* it without a suggestion of the possibilities. This is a valid procedure only if the interviewer knows in advance that the suggested choices include the correct answer and that only one answer could be correct. It is also helpful to eliminate as many incorrect answers from the list as possible and to offer possible answers clearly different in their meaning or their sound. For example, students returning for a summer session in Guanajuato, Mexico, were interviewed to determine some of the effects of the cross-cultural experiences. The interviewer wanted to establish where the person stayed during his six weeks there. After learning that it was "some hotel with a Spanish name, but I can't think of it at the moment," he asked:

I: Was it at El Orozco, La Posada de Santa Fe, or El Castillo?
R: Oh, yes, La Posada de Santa Fe, we called it the Posie, or the hotel, because it had such a long name.

Once a memory has faded, it is not always possible for the respondent to recognize the correct answer even though it is included in the choices. A good interviewer can often detect when the respondent is unsure or simply guessing.

When there is no single answer about an objective situation but multiple subjective possibilities, the checklist of answers may coercively suggest invalid answers. For example, when we asked physicians to list as many positive and negative aspects of being a doctor as possible, this open-ended approach elicited no mention of "having to make emergency calls in the middle of the night" as one of the negative aspects. Yet when a checklist was supplied later in the same interview, a significant proportion of them checked this reason.

One way of avoiding the biasing effect of suggestion is to use a list of bi-polar dimensions which suggest both the positive and the negative extremes of each dimension. For example, if we want to discover a person's self-concept, we could provide a list of bi-polar pairs of traits such as secure-insecure, friendly-unfriendly, or we could give a set of hypothetical situations and ask the person to respond in quantitative terms. This direct self-rating has the advantage of stimulating memory by suggesting possible dimensions without loading the answer positively or negatively, but it does not eliminate the ego threat involved in giving oneself a negative rating. The second method of using responses to hypothetical situations does not directly ask the respondent to rate himself nor does it necessarily call to the respondent's attention the fact that dimensions of his personality are being measured. Of course the more educated the respondent, the more he is able to understand that his responses to hypothetical situations may be an indirect way of measuring dimensions of his personality. In this case ego threat may not be so easily circumvented.

An interesting example of a creative structured approach to obtain the respondent's self-concept is reported by Tudor and Holmes[4] who instructed their respondents to introspect about themselves in terms of analogies and opposites. This technique elicited significantly more information about each person in the experimental group than was obtained from the control group whose members were simply asked in an open-ended way to give a description of their self-concept.

Chronological confusion. The interviewer can often help the respondent avoid chronological confusion by supplying a set of events known to be arranged in chronological order and then asking the respondent whether the event in question occurred before or after each event in the list. For example: "Let's see if we can get a little more exact age at which Johnny had the skin allergy. Was it before he could walk, after he could walk but before going to nursery school, or after he was in first grade at Mills School?"

If the events arranged chronologically are also meaningful to the respondent and have some connection with the event to be recalled, this technique may be very helpful to the respondent and save considerable interviewing time.

Thus far, we have indicated some of the conditions under which

---

[4] Thomas G. Tudor and David S. Holmes, "Use of Analogies and Opposites in Helping Interviewees Verbalize Their Self-Concepts," *Journal of Consulting and Clinical Psychology,* vol. 38 (1972), pp. 445–48.

closed questions are particularly useful. The conditions for using open-ended questions are the same as those calling for the use of broad questions and these have already been discussed.

USING LEADING QUESTIONS

The term "leading questions" refers to any question, including its context and answer structure, which is phrased so that it appears to the respondent that the interviewer desires or expects a certain answer; yet the interviewer's expectation could not have been derived solely from what the respondent has already said in the interview.

Forms of leading

A question may be leading because of the *context* in which it appears; this leading context may be of a personal or impersonal type. The following is an example of the personal context.

The President has made several public statements advocating freer trade between nations. Do you think we should eliminate some of the tariff barriers that have been erected against free trade?

The direction of the effect of this loaded context cannot be predicted unless the respondent's attitude toward the President is known. Nevertheless, it is highly probable that changing the context, as in the example below, would obtain a different response from many respondents.

Socialists have historically advocated free trade among nations. Do you think we should eliminate some of the tariff barriers that have been erected against free trade?

In contrast, the impersonal context does not mention the point of view of any individual or group, but brings into play certain facts and logical relationships which tend to influence the answer in one direction. The next question is put into two different contexts tending to bias the response in opposite directions.

In view of the fact that the United States is the richest country in the world do you think that the defense budget should be cut as much as 25 percent? In view of the fact that about 80 percent of the total federal taxes are spent on past, present, and future war expenditures, do you think that the defense budget should be cut as much as 25 percent?

There is little doubt that a random sample poll of the United States, using the two forms of the question, would show significantly different results.

Even when no leading context is provided, the question may be loaded by simply using *emotionally charged* words. For example, compare these two questions:

> How do you feel about blacks moving into this area?
> How do you feel about blacks invading your neighborhood?

Even though in sociology *invading* is not an emotionally charged term, to the respondent *moving into* would appear more neutral.

A third way of loading a question is to structure the answer in a way that restricts the respondent by *omitting a category* most appropriate for him. Compare these two questions:

> What is your religion? Protestant, Catholic, or Jewish?
> What is your religion? Protestant, Catholic, Jewish, agnostic, atheist, or free-thinker?

It is highly probable that the second form would elicit a smaller number of Protestant, Catholic, and Jewish responses.

A fourth way of leading is to make *challenging statements*. The respondent will often change his general point of view expressed in the interview if the interviewer consistently challenges one type of statement and allows the opposite type to go unchallenged. Any of the following would be considered a challenge to some degree: "How do you know that?" "Do you think you could back up that statement with evidence?" "Give me a specific example of that." "That sounds very unusual, I have never heard of such a thing happening. How do you account for that?" "Are you sure that your observations are correct?" "That seems to contradict what you said before."

The effects of such challenges depend upon how sure the respondent is of his rapport, the extent to which he is inclined to show deference to the interviewer, and the tone of voice in which the challenge is made.

Effects of leading questions

In the literature on interviewing there seems to be a preponderance of opinion, usually based upon direct experience in interviewing, that the leading question should be avoided. For example, Cannell and Kahn suggest that "Questions should be phrased so that they contain no suggestion as to the most appropriate response."[5]

Kinsey takes an opposite position at one point in his discussion of interviewing methods used to obtain information on the respondent's sex behavior. He advocates putting the burden of denial on the respondent:

---

[5] Charles F. Cannel and Robert L. Kahn, "The Collection of Data by Interviewing," in Leon Festinger and Daniel Katz, *Research Methods in the Social Sciences* (New York: The Dryden Press, 1953), p. 346.

The interviewer should not make it easy for a subject to deny his participation in any form of sexual activity. It is too easy to say "no" if he is simply asked whether he has engaged in a particular activity. Consequently we always begin by asking when they first engaged in such activity . . . and since it becomes apparent from the form of the question that we would not be surprised if he had had such experience, there seems to be less reason for denying it. It might be thought this approach would bias the answer, but there is no indication that we get false admissions in forms of sexual behavior in which the subject was not actually involved.[6]

Becker, who takes the position that challenging the respondent in an aggressive manner does not necessarily bias the response, points out some of the conditions under which he could obtain more valid information from public school teachers regarding race relations problems in the school. He says that a basic condition for success was

> . . . the professional bond of courtesy which the teacher feels obligated to extend to the interviewer. She felt she must avoid being unpleasant. Such tactics will not prove effective in all situations nor would one want to use them . . . where, for example, your research places you in continuous contact with those being studied, as in a long-term community study, it might be wisest to avoid the possibility of antagonizing informants which lies in this stratagem. . . . Finally . . . the informant must not be of a higher social status than the interviewer because the unspoken etiquette of such a relationship leaves the informant free to be rude through evasiveness and implausibility, free to ignore the demands of the questioner who is stepping out of the confines of his deference role.[7]

None of the authors cited base their conclusions on experimental studies aimed at testing the relative effectiveness of using leading versus nonleading questions. Richardson[8] and Dohrenwend[9] have done experiments which show that the question, "Should leading questions be used?" is not well put, since the answer can be neither "yes" nor "no." Instead, we should try to account for the conditions under which they are successful or unsuccessful. After reviewing much of the literature and his own experiences, the writer suggests that the following factors account for the different effects of leading questions.

It is helpful to distinguish between three types of situations, one in which the leading question helps to obtain more valid information, another in which valid information is obtained in spite of the leading

---

[6] Alfred C. Kinsey et al, "Interviewing," *Sexual Behavior in the Human Male* (Philadelphia: W. B. Saunders Company, 1948).

[7] Howard S. Becker, "A Note on Interviewing Tactics," *Human Organization* (Winter, 1954), pp. 31–32.

[8] Stephan A. Richardson, "The Use of Leading Questions in Non-Schedule Interviews," *Human Organization*, vol. 19, no. 2 (1960), pp. 86–89.

[9] Barbara Snell Dohrenwend and Stephan A. Richardson, "A Use for Leading Questions in Research Interviewing," *Human Organization*, vol. 23 (1964), pp. 76–77.

question, and a third situation where the leading question actually distorts the answer. Here are some of the most important characteristics of the type of situation in which the leading question helps to obtain more valid information:

a.   Respondent has accurate information clearly in mind,
b.   but there is a tendency to withhold it, either because reporting the correct answer would violate the etiquette requirements of the situation, or because the correct answer is potentially ego threatening, since it admits a violation of public ideals of some type.
c.   The respondent either accepts these ideals as valid or assumes that the interviewer does so.
d.   Under the above three conditions the leading question is useful *if* it leads in a direction contrary to the public ideals.[10]

Regardless of whether the bias of the question is toward or away from the correct answer in the case of a particular respondent, such a leading question will be helpful. If the respondent's correct answer happens to be in violation of the public ideals, then the question is biased *toward* the correct answer and the respondent is more likely to admit his deviant experience. This is particularly true when the interviewer's manner shows that he expects the respondent to have had such an experience and that he does not condemn him for it. If the respondent has not had the deviant experience, he is less likely to pretend that he has committed a violation of public ideals. Thus the use of the leading question under these circumstances is based upon the assumption that in general people are less likely to falsely plead guilty than they are to falsely plead not guilty; therefore the bias should be toward guilty.

There are circumstances in which valid information is obtained in spite of the use of leading questions. Here the following conditions are important:

a.   The information is clear in the respondent's mind, free from fading memory, chronological or inferential confusion.
b.   Neither the information to be reported nor the relationship between the interviewer and respondent constitute an ego threat.
c.   There is no etiquette barrier between respondent and interviewer.

To illustrate these circumstances, let us assume that an interviewer is attempting to discover what happened at a meeting attended by the respondent and how he felt about what transpired. Further assume that the meeting lasted one hour, that 15 people attended and that it con-

---

[10] Lois R. Dean, "Interaction, Reported and Observed," *Human Organization* (Fall, 1958), no. 3, p. 36. Demonstrates the tendency of the respondent to falsify his report in the direction of the acceptable norms.

sisted of a short speech and a discussion of the pros and cons of an increase in the public school tax levy. The meeting occurred the night before the interview. Note that all the questions are leading in that they either suggest possible answers or exclude other possible answers, yet none of them cause distortion in the respondent's information.

I: How many people were at the meeting, about 100?

R: Oh no, there were 15 including the speaker; I know them all. There are very few people interested in the public schools, particularly in the summertime.

I: What time did the meeting start, 8 or 8:30?

R: We always start at 7, as we did last night.

I: Did you just have an informal discussion?

R: No, we also had a speaker from Columbus.

I: Was his talk about the usual sort of things which education people have to say about child psychology?

R: The topic was "What can the taxpayer buy for his school tax dollar."

I: Oh, I see. Did you feel that the speaker had little of value to say as is so often true of people speaking on this topic?

R: No, he had quite a bit to say; we selected him because of his analytical objectivity.

I: Do you feel that an excellent speaker of this type will exert a strong influence on improving the public schools?

R: He won't have any strong *direct* influence on the community since he was speaking to only 15 people, but there is a possibility that this will spark some activity among the vitally interested people.

To avoid being led astray by the "harmless" leading question, the interviewer should be reminded that often he will not know in advance that all the necessary conditions are present for rendering the leading question harmless. In some situations the interviewer may know in advance that a certain condition is present, but he often cannot know in advance that other conditions are also present. In any case, it is a good plan to avoid the use of leading questions rather than hope they are of the harmless variety unless the situation calls for their intentional use.

There are types of situations in which leading questions are definitely harmful because they bias the response away from the truth. The following conditions are significant:

a. The respondent does not have the information clearly in mind because of fading memory, chronological or inferential confusion; he is therefore susceptible to suggestions from the interviewer.

b. The information requested is not important to the respondent, and there is little motivation to strive to remember the accurate information.

c. The respondent does not feel free to say "I don't know," because he has an ego-threatening relationship with the interviewer or because the etiquette of the situation requires that he show deference to the interviewer.

d. The question leads in the direction of a false answer.

These conditions typically prevail in settings where the respondents are subordinates in the same community or organization as the interviewer.

For example, Company X, a large corporation, has been carrying on an intensive "educational" program pointing out the virtues of working for Company X—such as its pension plan, job rotation plan, retraining for automation, and family health insurance. In the excerpt below the interviewer is working for the personnel department and is studying the problem of recruiting workers to reduce labor turnover. Four years ago when the respondent came to work for the company, the same interviewer had talked with him. The objective of the present interview is to obtain a complete picture of the factors accounting for why the respondent came to work for Company X. In the course of the interview the following loaded questions obtained these responses:

I-1: We are doing a study of why people come to work for Johnson Electric and why they stay so long. How long have you been working for us?
R-1: About four years, I guess.
I-2: Why did you pick this company to work for?
R-2: Gosh, that was a long time ago. Let me see . . .
I-3: Yes, it was quite a while ago. Who were you working for before you came here?
R-3: For Central Electric.
I-4: Why did you leave there? Didn't you like it?
R-4: No, it wasn't a very pleasant place to work.
I-5: Did they have a pension plan like ours or a job rotation plan, training for automation, family health plan, or that sort of thing?
R-5: No, they didn't have any of those benefits like we do here.
I-6: What did your wife think about your choosing Johnson Electric?
R-6: She was glad I could get the job . . . she likes the family health plan very much, and I like the system of rotating jobs every three months after you have been here a couple of years. It makes things interesting. I learn a lot that way about the company as a whole. I can't understand people who like to hold down one job all the time.
I-7: Did you hear about this company through ads in the paper?
R-7: I spent a lot of time looking at the ads to find a good job.
I-8: Why did you choose to work for Johnson Electric?
R-8: It is a very progressive company. It has a lot of good personnel policies like I mentioned before. For example, I hope I can benefit from the in-service training program so I can be upgraded when we get more automated.

With question 1 the interviewer begins to furnish a biasing context in the phrase "why they stay so long" rather than "why people come and go." Question 2 is loaded with the assumption that the respondent "picked" the present company to work for when actually he might have preferred another but was not accepted. Question 4 suggests an easy way for the respondent to avoid the ego threat of saying that he was fired. Question 5 supplies the answer for questions 6 and 8. In questions 5 and 6 the interviewer does not probe to distinguish between what the respondent and his wife like about Johnson Electric now that he is here and what they knew about it before he applied for the job. Only the latter could have been a reason for coming to Johnson Electric.

Question 7 supplies an answer to what would have been a less biased question: "How did you first hear about Johnson Electric?" After four years the respondent's memory might be vague on how he heard about Johnson Electric and any suggested answer would be tempting. In question 8 the interviewer again assumes that the respondent chose to work at Johnson Electric. Response 8 gives the "company line" answer suggested by the interviewer in question 5 even though response 2 indicates a possible fading of memory.

The overall effect of the leading questions in this situation is to suggest invalid answers which are readily given by the respondent due to the type of communication barriers operating.

The following conditions describe another type of situation in which the leading question has a distorting effect upon the response.

a. The information is clear in the respondent's mind and he is, therefore, *able* to give it accurately.
b. The correct report would constitute an ego threat since it is in violation of public ideals or the apparent wishes of the interviewer.
c. Or, the correct report would violate certain etiquette requirements of the situation.
d. The question is slanted toward the public ideals and, for the respondent, toward a false answer.

These conditions frequently prevail in situations where the interviewer is perceived by the respondent as a superior. The main difference between this situation and the preceding one is that here the ego threat, the etiquette barrier, or the leading must be stronger to distort the response since the respondent has the correct information clearly in mind. He must consciously distort his report to compromise in the situation. In this case, he often produces rationalizations for his falsification such as, "He doesn't really want to know the truth anyway, so why should I give him the benefit of it." "He wouldn't do anything constructive with the information so why give it to him." "He just wants to find out how to get me to work harder; why should I whip myself?" "I don't want to be a stool pigeon!"

By specifying and illustrating some of the relevant conditions determining the positive, neutral, and negative effects of the leading question, we hoped to demonstrate the uselessness of the oversimplified query, "Should leading questions be used?"

An interesting experimental example of the creative use of the leading question is given by Dohrenwend[11] reporting on a study of abortion. When the loaded question was used, 58 percent of the respondents admitted knowing how an abortion was performed, while only 37 percent admitted such knowledge when the unloaded form of the same question was used. Similarly, 51 percent admitted having at least one friend who had an abortion when the loaded form of the question was used, in contrast to only 25 percent when the unloaded form was used.

SUMMARY

This chapter has presented a variety of *verbal* techniques that can be used by the interviewer to minimize the inhibitors and to maximize the facilitators of communication under certain conditions.

Among the verbal forms used as techniques are: providing context with the question, selecting an appropriate wording, defining the scope of the question, structuring the answer, and using leading or nonleading questions. Providing the verbal context with a question is one technique for communicating the question more accurately to the respondent by providing definitions of terms, time perspectives, spatial perspectives, social-psychological contexts, criteria and facts to be used by the respondent in making judgments. In questions where the objective is to discover the respondent's own frames of reference, definitions, criteria and perception of the facts, the interviewer must scrupulously refrain from providing the context.

Verbal context provided with the question may also motivate the respondent by arousing interest in the topic, by giving recognition to the respondent's special qualifications, reducing ego threat, preventing falsification, stimulating memory, reducing chronological confusion, and discovering unconscious subjective orientations of the respondent.

In wording the question itself, the interviewer should try to use a vocabulary which is clearly understood by the respondent, which aids in establishing an optimum relationship, and which does not unintentionally load the question in favor of a particular response.

The scope of a question may vary from the broad type which includes the whole topic of the interview to one which delimits some particular aspect of a particular person's behavior in relation to a particular object at a specific time and place. Broad questions are useful in discovering the respondent's paths of association, hierarchy of values, perspectives,

---

[11] B. S. Dohrenwend, "Experimental Study of Directive Interviewing," *Public Opinion Quarterly*, vol. 34 (1970), pp. 117–25.

universe of discourse, definitions of terms, perceptions of facts, and chronology of personal experiences. Under some conditions, the broad question can reduce the respondent's ego threat, stimulate his memory, give him recognition, provide sympathetic understanding, encourage catharsis, and stimulate the need for meaning. Under other conditions, the narrow question can help reduce ego threat, circumvent the etiquette barrier, and stimulate the respondent's need for meaning.

In structuring the responses, the interviewer should consider the type of information sought as well as the effects upon the respondent's motivation to give such information. The open-ended question is sometimes more useful in discovering unanticipated responses, the respondent's paths of association, his universes of discourse, perspectives, definitions of terms, hierarchy of values, and perceptions of facts. Closed questions are preferred over open ones when equally valid information can be obtained because of the greater efficiency in coding and analyzing the results.

Under certain conditions, the closed question has great motivational value. By speeding up the interviewing process and shortening the interview, the probability of encountering competing time demands is reduced. Providing answer choices reduces the size of the task for the respondent and the ego threat which might be involved when the boundaries of the response are unknown. The structured answer is useful in stimulating the respondent's memory if the correct answer is among the choices. Similarly, choices provided in chronological order may be helpful in reducing the respondent's chronological confusion.

Leading questions are those which tend to indicate that one answer is expected or preferred over another when such expectations or preferences are not based on previous information given by the respondent. The question may be loaded by associating it with a personal or impersonal context having emotional meaning to the respondent. Questions can also be loaded by providing answer categories which stack the cards in favor of a particular response. In extreme cases, the question may be loaded by an accompanying direct challenge.

In some circumstances the leading question seems to obtain more valid answers than a nonleading one. This is true when the respondent has the information clearly in mind, but tends to withhold it because it violates certain public ideals which the respondent either accepts himself or assumes that the interviewer accepts. Under these conditions, if the question leads in the direction contrary to the public ideals, it can often obtain more valid results than the nonleading question. Under other conditions, the leading question seems to have no effect; valid information is obtained in spite of its use. More common, however, are situations in which leading questions distort the response.

This chapter has focused on only the *verbal forms* of interviewer behavior and discussed the possible effects of the verbal techniques both in communicating to the respondent what information is needed and in affecting either inhibitors or facilitators of communication that govern the respondent's ability and willingness to provide complete and relevant information. This is only half of the technique story. The other half is the use of nonverbal techniques to be discussed in the next chapter.

DISCUSSION QUESTIONS

1. In what ways can preceding a question with a contextual statement help in communicating the question?
2. How can contextual statements preceding the question help to motivate the respondent?
3. What are some of the most important problems to be solved or avoided in selecting the appropriate vocabulary for wording the question?
4. What are some of the dimensions of question scope?
5. What are broad-scope questions best for? What are narrow-scope questions good for?
6. What are some of the ways of structuring the answers to questions?
7. How can answer structures inhibit or facilitate communication?
8. Under what conditions are leading questions good or bad?

SELECTED READINGS

The three references below are examples of demonstrations of the use of highly structured verbal forms (leading questions, analogies, and hypothetical cases) to elicit generally hard-to-verbalize information.

Richardson, Stephen A., et al. *Interviewing: Its Forms and Functions.* New York: Basic Books, 1965. Chapter 7, "Expectations and Premises: The So-Called 'Leading Question'," pp. 171–97.

One of the best treatments of the use of the *leading question.* Reviews some of the experiments done on the problem and suggests basic principles.

Tudor, Thomas G., and Holmes, David S. "Use of Analogies and Opposites in Helping Interviewees Verbalize Their Self-Concept," *Journal of Consulting and Clinical Psychology,* vol. 38 (1972), pp. 445–48.

An excellent study demonstrating one application of the general principle of using highly structured stimuli to tease out subtle subjective orientations, in this case the respondent's self-concept.

Weaver, T. "Use of Hypothetical Situations in a Study of Spanish-American Illness Referral Systems," *Human Organization,* vol. 29 (1970), pp. 140–53.

An excellent example of the use of indirect techniques to discover norms, values, expectations, attitudes, or other difficult-to-verbalize subjective orientations. The hypothetical situation gives the respondent the chance to *demonstrate* his norms rather than being asked directly what his norms are.

Laboratory problem 9

Verbal techniques in studying parent-child conflicts

Purpose

The purpose of this laboratory problem is to provide a challenge to creatively link the general purpose, the specific information objectives, and the verbal techniques of an interview. Throughout the whole process you must strive to word the questions so that (*a*) they are *relevant* to the general objectives of the study, (*b*) they clearly *communicate* to the respondent the specific information needed, and (*c*) they *motivate* the respondent to give relevant information as completely and accurately as possible.

Steps in planning

The steps below are not intended to imply a simple, rigid one-way progression since in the actual creative process you may have to move backward and forward several times. However, each of the steps must be taken at least once to complete the process.

1. Specify the objectives. The general purposes of any study must first be converted into specific questions without loosing track of the general purpose. Any problem stated in common sense terms is open to a variety of interpretations. The particular interpretation of the problem should be accurately reflected in the wording of the specific questions.

2. Tentatively word questions. Before finally specifying the particular interpretation of the objectives, brainstorm a lot of tentatively worded questions to get an idea of how the general objective can be broken down into specific questions aimed at various items of information.

3. Anticipate inhibitors and facilitators. Once you see the form and content of the specific questions to be asked, you are in a better position to try to empathize with the respondent to anticipate some potential inhibitors and facilitators.

4. Review the verbal forms. The verbal techniques should be reviewed and selectively applied in wording questions in the light of the potential inhibitors and facilitators.

5. Word the question. In view of the probable effects of the various verbal forms, select the best for the purpose at hand.

Obviously, the five-step process is not infallible and is only as good as the planner's ability to empathize with the potential respondent and to apply the different verbal forms available. In a real study this five-step process produces the tentative rough draft of the interview schedule which must then be field-tested and revised at least once. Also, any weaknesses in the instrument due to its inapplicability to a particular respondent is compensated for by the tactical behavior of the interviewer in adjusting to a particular respondent. However, serious creative work in developing the rough draft saves much floundering in the early stages of the field work.

The study (parent-child conflicts)

Assume that you are to plan an interview to discover the sources of intergenerational conflict in the American culture by interviewing a random sample of high school students regarding the kinds of conflicts they have with their parents. You are interested in all types of conflicts from the most mild to the most violent and want to discover the range of issues involved. You are to explore all conflicts in the year preceding the interview. A comparison of the nature and frequency of the conflicts in different types of communities may render important clues to some of the causes of mental illness and delinquency in teenagers. Assume that the respondent is a 16-year-old high school girl being interviewed by a 22-year-old college student.

The interviewer says, "My name is Linda Johnson. I am helping with a study of family relations sponsored by the U.S. Public Health Department. We want to get the teenager's point of view on family relations and that is why we are talking to hundreds of high school students. Your name was selected randomly for an interview."

Problem 1. What question will open up a free discussion of the types of conflicts the respondent has had with her parents in the past year? This is to be the opening question following the introductory explanation above.

Problem 2. Design a question to discover which kinds of behavior the teenager hides from her parents to avoid open conflict.

Problem 3. Design a question which will also be asked of the parents and will allow you to compare the teenager's point of view with theirs in the area of economic responsibilities and privileges. How you would word the main question? What subsidiary questions are needed? To limit this problem deal with only one type of economic responsibility or privilege, some economic issue over which parents and teenagers are likely to have conflict.

Problem 4. Design a question to discover the respondent's criteria for judging the relative seriousness of conflicts she has had with her parents in the past year. Use one or more questions, whichever is most appropriate.

15

Nonverbal techniques

As we become more educated there is a tendency to overestimate the effect of verbal communication and to underestimate the effect of the nonverbal. Nonverbal communication tends to be nonrational in that the response is direct and immediate, circumventing the conscious deliberative process. Nonverbal messages tend to follow a stimulus-response pattern without any intervening conscious decision-making process we commonly call thinking. For these reasons nonverbal communication is less conscious than verbal communication, but it may be the more powerful force in face-to-face interaction, particularly as a determinant of motivation.

Even though nonverbal communication tends to be less subject to conscious scrutiny, it has been demonstrated by numerous experiments that people can learn to be aware of nonverbal communication, can analyze it, and can experiment with it as a conscious tool if interviewing. Nonverbal cues are essential ingredients in both interviewer-to-respondent and respondent-to-interviewer communication. From the standpoint of the development of skills, the interviewer must learn to be more sensitive to nonverbal cues from his respondent, be more aware of his own nonverbal signals to the respondent, and learn to control the latter as a conscious technical skill.

MODES OF NONVERBAL COMMUNICATION

Most of the nonverbal cues fall under the headings of *proxemics, chronemics, kinesics,* and *paralinguistics.* Proxemic communication is the use of interpersonal space to convey meaning. Chronemic com-

370

munication is the use of time in interpersonal relationships to convey meaning. Kinesic communication is the use of body movement to convey meaning. Paralinguistic communication is the use of volume, pitch, and voice quality to convey meaning. The kinds of meanings most readily conveyed by the nonverbal modes of communication are attitudes, desires, or feelings. In short, nonverbal communication tends to be more affective than cognitive but not exclusively so.

A posture may unconsciously communicate boredom, which is clearly affective, or an American tourist may gesture to the French druggist that he has a headache and the druggest responds cognitively by bringing a bottle of aspirin.

Let us now examine each mode of nonverbal communication as it relates to interviewing.

Proxemics

It is clear that the relationship between interviewer and respondent is both a cause and an effect of proxemic behavior. For example, when an interviewer knocks on a door and someone opens the door, the interviewer may take a short step backward to avoid appearing aggressive and pushy, which might arouse resistance in the respondent. Or the interviewer and respondent, if both are standing, may stand slightly closer together if both are females than if one is male and one is female. When the interviewer and respondent are of the same age, they might stand closer than if there is a large age difference.

It has been shown that if the distance between interviewer and respondent is greater, there is more of a tendency for them to watch each other's eyes for cues to meaning. Goldberg[1] carefully recorded the eye behavior of the respondents when they sat 2½ feet versus 6 feet from the interviewer. At the greater distance the respondents spent much more time looking at the interviewer's eyes.

As shown by Hall,[2] the correct conversational distance varies from one culture to another. In the Middle East you are bathed in your conversation partner's breath; in Latin America equals of the same sex carry on conversation at a much closer distance than do North Americans. When we invade the respondent's boundary line between private space and intimate space, the respondent will feel threatened. If we stay too far away from the respondent in an interview, he will feel that we do not like him, that we do not want to associate with him.

In arranging the interview situation, it is important to position the

[1] G. Goldberg et al., "Visual Behavior and Face-to-Face Distance During Interaction," *Sociometry*, vol. 32 (1969), pp. 43–53.

[2] Edward T. Hall, *The Silent Language* (New York: Doubleday & Co., 1959).

respondent's chair, the interviewer's chair, and the microphone (if used) so that there can be some variation in distance (from two to four feet) to accommodate to different respondents, different sex combinations, and age variations from one interview to the next.

Relatively little experimentation has been done with proxemic communication in the context of the interview, but experienced interviewers agree that sensitivity to the proxemic factor is important. Often, as the subject matter of the interview changes, the interviewer can not changes in the proxemic behavior of the respondent. If he is free to back away, he might do so when the topic is one which is unpleasant or threatens to invade his privacy.

Chronemics

The use of time in interpersonal relationships can convey feelings, attitudes, and desires. For example, if the interviewer or respondent is late in keeping an appointment, this may convey a lack of vital interest in the interview. The order in which members of a given organization are interviewed may carry considerable meaning. However, both of these factors would be classified as a strategy rather than a technique. The most important chronemic *technique* which the interviewer can control is the length of pauses and rate of speech in his own conversation and the length of time he waits after the respondent has finished a sentence before he asks another question. The first technique is called *pacing* and the second is the *silent probe.*

Pacing is one of the principal nonverbal methods of communicating the appropriate mood. The tense interviewer often communicates his anxiety by his rapid-fire rate of speech which in turn increases anxiety in the respondent. To establish the more thoughtful, deliberative mood needed to stimulate free association and recall or to avoid chronological confusion, the interviewer must take the initiative in establishing a more relaxed, deliberate pace, at the technique level, in a setting free from competing time-demands, chosen at the strategy level. It is up to the interviewer to break the vicious circle of mutual reinforcement of anxiety. There is a tendency for one person to unwittingly respond to the other's anxiety with additional signals of anxiety.

The silent probe is such an important technique that we will deal with it in a special section later in this chapter.

Kinesics

Much more research has been done on kinesic communication in the interview than on either proxemic or chronemic communication. Body posture, feet movements, hand movements, facial expressions, and eye movements have all been studied in the kinesics of interviewing. Carmichael[3] experimented with hand movements by having an actor seated behind a curtain so that only his hands were visible. When the viewers were asked to classify the emotions the actor was trying to portray there was substantial agreement between the emotion intended by the actor and that perceived by the viewers.

Even though posture, hands, and feet all communicate, numerous experiments have shown that the communicators tend to focus more attention on the face and are more accurate in their judgments of the others' feelings if they can see the face. For example, Exline[4] demonstrated that a group of viewers responding to head cues only were more accurate in matching photographs to verbal behavior than were respondents to body cues only.

When the viewer is observing the others' head and facial movements, there is evidence that the central focus is usually on the eyes. One of the earliest sociological essays on the human eye as a communication channel was given by Simmel:

> By the glance which reveals the other, one discloses himself. By the same act in which the observer seeks to know the observed, he surrenders himself to be understood . . . the eye cannot take unless at the same time it gives.[5]

This early intuitive observation on human communication has been followed by many experiments on eye-to-eye communication. One of the general findings in many different contexts is that eye behavior communicates the desire to make or to avoid communicative contact. When the person feels shame, he will drop his eyes to avoid the glance of the other not only to avoid seeing the disapproval in the other's eye but to conceal from the other the extent of his own shame and confusion. One specific manifestation of this general principle is the fact that the listener or questioner tends to watch the other's eyes more closely than the respondent or speaker tends to watch the listener. This was demonstrated in an experiment by Exline[6] which showed that individuals in a laboratory situation looked more at the investigator when listening than when speaking to him or her. This experiment also showed

---

[3] L. S. Carmichael et al., "A Study of the Judgment of Manual Expression as Presented in Still and Motion Pictures," *Journal of Social Psychology*, vol. 8 (1937), pp. 115–42.

[4] Ralph Exline, "Body Position, Facial Expression, and Verbal Behavior During Interviews," *Journal of Abnormal and Social Psychology*, vol. 68 (1964), pp. 295–301.

[5] Georg Simmel, "Sociology of the Senses: Visual Interaction," in Robert E. Park and Ernest W. Burgess, *Introduction to the Science of Sociology* (Chicago, Ill.: University of Chicago Press, 1924), p. 358.

[6] R. Exline et al., "Visual Behavior in a Dyad as Affected by Interview Content and Sex of Respondent," *Journal of Personality and Social Psychology*, vol. 1 (1965), pp. 201–9.

that people looked less often at the person with whom they were speaking when personal, rather than more general, matters were being discussed. This seems to suggest that we actively seek nonverbal cues from the other person to understand what he means more than we actively observe to determine whether he understands what we mean.

The fact that the use of chronemic and proxemic communication can be effectively used as a conscious technique by the interviewer has been repeatedly demonstrated experimentally. For example, Matarazzo and Wiens[7] have shown that the respondent can be motivated to give longer, fuller, and more detailed responses resulting in more relevant information when the interviewer makes no change in the verbal forms of the questions but nods his head in approval, makes interested noises like "hmm," "ah," "ah hah," "oh," "wow," and slows down his pace and uses more silent probes. In essence these nonverbal activities reinforce such facilitators of communication as recognition, sympathetic understanding, the need for meaning, and catharsis by establishing and reinforcing a communicative mood.

Paralinguistics

We use the term *paralinguistic* to refer to those aspects of speech that are not verbal or linguistic, yet are much more intimately intertwined with the verbal than are the other nonverbal modes of communication. The paralinguistic factors in speech include volume of voice, (loud or soft), quality of voice (tense, growly, breathy), accent (nuances of pronunciation), and inflectional patterns (intonation or pitch patterns).

One of the basic differences between written and oral communication is that the oral speech give full range to a nonverbal accompaniment. Written communication tries to indicate some of the paralinguistic variables by italicizing words to be stressed, which takes the place of an increase in volume or pitch. Foreign language texts sometimes indicate the intonation pattern of a phrase or sentence in those cases where it is very different from English. A script for a drama might contain parenthetical instructions on how to say a line, but this is usually in terms of the emotion to be communicated rather than specific instructions on tone quality, pitch, or volume. Only the skilled actor can convert the intent of the playwright into the optimum nonverbal rendition. In many cases the nonverbal accompaniment to the dramatic lines is highly stylized and not necessarily like the real thing.

The same sentence can be delivered with several different stress and

---

[7] Joseph Matarazzo and L. Wiens, "Interviewer Influence on Duration of Interviewee Silence," *Journal of Experimental Research in Personality,* vol. 2 (1967), pp. 56-69.

intonation patterns in a way to change the meaning considerably.[8] Using the correct stress pattern can help the interviewer give the intended meaning to a question and give clues to the meaning of the responses. Also, the interviewer can learn to listen for subtle paralinguistic communication which gives clues to the meaning or to the respondent's motivations at the moment. The verbal "yes" can carry the meaning of "maybe" or even "no," depending on the tone of voice and other nonverbal cues. The interviewer must learn to listen for changes in the nonverbal accompaniment and for whether the verbal and nonverbal are harmoniously reinforcing or tend to give conflicting signals, as happens when the respondent is trying to deceive the interviewer.

The fact that the paralinguistic factor alone without any words does carry meaning of its own has been clearly demonstrated in experiments. For example, Davitz[9] had people recite parts of the alphabet to convey feelings of anger, fear, happiness, jealously, love, nervousness, pride, sadness, satisfaction, and sympathy. Tape recordings of these recitations were heard and the listeners were asked to identify which emotion the speaker was demonstrating. For all ten emotions there was a substantial correspondence between the emotion intended and the one identified by the listener. Some emotions, like anger and nervousness, were more reliably identified than others, like pride and jealousy.

The interviewer's bias can be communicated paralinguistically, resulting in biased information from the respondent. This was shown in an experiment by Duncan at al.[10] in which the interviewer changed his voice quality in a way to vary the amount of apprehension felt by the respondent. The amount of bias in the responses was positively correlated with the amount of apprehension produced in the respondent.

In discussing the four modes of nonverbal communication, we have attempted to show only that experimental evidence proves that the nonverbal modes do carry predictable meaning, and that interviewers can learn to use the proxemic, chronemic, kinesic, and paralinguistic communication modes as conscious techniques. There is a gap between the experimental evidence and learning the skills of nonverbal communication. For one reason, the nonverbal communication does not occur in only one of the four modes in a given moment, nor does the

---

[8] For example, see Leo Rosten, *The Joys of Yiddish* (New York: Pocket Books, 1970). Rosten shows several different intonations patterns used with the same simple sentence and their implications for the meaning of a dialogue.

[9] J. R. Davitz and L. Davitz, "The Communication of Feeling by Content-Free Speech," *Journal of Communication*, vol. 9 (1959), pp. 110–17.

[10] Starkey Duncan, Jr., et al., "The Paralanguage of Experimentor Bias," *Sociometry*, vol. 32 (1969), pp. 207–19.

person using the nonverbal communication focus on any one mode or on any one combination, for that matter. Instead, the interviewer learns to focus his attention on certain intentions of communication. Thus, to consciously use nonverbal communication the interviewer does not say to himself "lift your eyebrow" or "widen your eyes"; instead he says "show surprise." Similarly, when listening to the respondent, instead of trying to describe the quality of voice as breathy or high-pitched, the interviewer notes that "the respondent's words say that she is happily married, but her tone of voice expresses pain, so who is she trying to deceive?"

FOCI OF NONVERBAL TECHNIQUES

The interviewer's attention during the interview can be either focused on the means or the ends he is trying to achieve. Generally, the interviewer's focus in nonverbal communication is on the *end result* of sending or receiving certain attitudes (expectations, feelings, desires), because if he tries to think of the specific physical stimuli as the means by which attitudes are communicated while he is engaged in the interview, he will become inhibited like the concert pianist who began to think of the individual muscles involved in obtaining the proper touch on the piano. One notable exception to focusing on the end result is in the use of the silent probe. It has been demonstrated that interviewers can learn to be sensitive to the amount of silence, the quality of the silence, and to inhibit their tendency automatically to fill the silence.

Let us first examine this exceptional means-oriented focus of using the silent probe and then move on to the more typical ends-oriented focus of manifesting or receiving certain attitudes.

Silence as a technique

It might be argued that silence cannot be a technique of interviewing because it consists of doing nothing. Experience and research in social interaction indicate that silence is as meaningful in verbal communication as rests are in a musical score. Research by Gorden[11] and by Matarazzo and Wiens[12] indicates that these is positive correlation between the amount of silence used by an interviewer and the respondent's general level of spontaneity. Hall[13] presents an interesting dis-

---

[11] Raymond L. Gorden, *An Interaction Analysis of the Depth-Interview* (Ph.D. dissertation, University of Chicago, 1954), p. 170.

[12] Joseph D. Matarazzo and Arthur N. Wiens, "Interviewer Effects on Interviewees' Speech and Silence Durations," *Proceedings of the 74th Annual Convention of the American Psychological Association,* 1966.

[13] Edward T. Hall, *The Silent Language* (New York: Doubleday & Co., 1959).

cussion of the cultural differences in the rhythm and pacing of communication and interaction which causes misunderstandings between people from different cultures.

In interviewing, silence not only acts as punctuation but also communicates a mood. The lack of any pauses in the interview often indicates that the interviewer is anxious and insecure. This tends to make the respondent feel the same.

One of the first skills the interviewer must learn is *not to interrupt* the respondent. To interrupt, the interviewer need not begin speaking while the respondent is still talking. Psychologically, an interruption is any audible or visible activity initiated by the interviewer before it is clear that the respondent has finished the thought he is expressing and that he does not intend to continue without direction from the interviewer.

The interviewer can pause for 2 to 20 seconds before asking the next question and yet be interrupting. Ordinarily, if the respondent has completed a sentence with a tone of finality and then looks at the interviewer expectantly, a two-second pause assures that he has finished the comment; but if the respondent stops obviously in the middle of a sentence or is gazing thoughtfully into space, a silence of ten seconds before asking the next question is no guarantee against interruption. For example:

I: How did you know you shouldn't light a cigarette in the area of the plane crash?
R: Well, I just know there was gasoline all over the ground where the crowd had collected and. . . . (15-second silence). . . . Hmm, I guess it was the master of ceremonies of the air show who announced on the public address system that we shouldn't light cigarettes or try to start any of the cars in the parking lot beside the airstrip.

This is typical, in that a respondent often interrupts his own response with a pause while he recalls a more accurate version of the event. In this example, the respondent first assumed that he knew there was gasoline on the ground from his own astute observation, but actually he was reminded by the master of ceremonies who was a veteran United States Air Force ground crewman.

Just as an interruption may occur in spite of a prolonged pause, it is also possible for the interviewer to speak at the same time as the respondent *without* the psychological effect of interrupting. This is the case when the interviewer reacts with "noises" and verbal expressions indicating interest in what the respondent is saying, as in the following expressions: "Uh huh," "hmm," "I see!" Of course, these verbal expressions must be accompanied by the appropriate nonverbal attitudes if they are not to interrupt the flow of information for the respondent.

Besides serving as insurance against interrupting the respondent, silence as an interviewing technique has several other vital functions. It creates a slower pace; this is conducive to a more *thoughtful mood* than could be achieved at a more rapid pace. This mood shows the respondent that the interviewer *expects* him to take time to give thoughtful answers, and it allows time for the respondent to retrace his own paths of association to revive faded images and feelings.

Silence also allows the respondent to *control* the direction of the next step in the conversation. This allows the interviewer to note the order of the respondent's association and the degree to which the respondent is willing to talk without probing. It maximizes the possibility of obtaining relevant information which the interviewer does not anticipate. Often, a silent probe used in an exploratory interview obtains answers to significant questions which the interviewer would never have thought of asking.

If the silence is accompanied by a facial or postural expression of interest and thoughtfulness, it gives the respondent the impression that the interviewer is vitally interested in the story. The opposite practice of interrupting usually gives the respondent the impression that the interviewer is not interested in him or his story.

Too much silence is also possible. The interviewer must develop a sensitivity to the respondent's pace and expectations so that excessive silence will be avoided. The respondent may feel the pressure of expectancy in the silence and yield to it reluctantly by merely repeating what he has already said or by giving a very short statement, as if to say "I've done my part, it's your move." In this case, the interviewer's use of silence has ceased to be a way of creating an informal, permissive, and thoughtful atmosphere and has become a source of embarrassment for the respondent. He may feel that the interviewer is not holding up his end of the conversation. In extreme cases, he may view prolonged silences as a weapon which the interviewer is using to force him into submission, and he may retaliate by trying to outwait the interviewer and beat him at his own game.

The interviewer must develop a sensitivity to the use of silence so that he can adjust appropriately to the pace of a particular respondent and so that he may take the initiative in establishing a more thoughtful mood or in jolting the respondent out of reminiscences not relevant to the objectives of the interview.

Attitudes as foci of nonverbal communication

The interviewer's attitudes, as well as the verbal forms of the question, constitute an essential portion of his technical tools. No amount of clever verbal technique or strategic preparation can compensate for an interviewer's negative attitudes expressed consciously or unconsciously in the interview. On the other hand, strong positive attitudes persistently manifested by the interviewer can both overcome and prevent many a verbal *faux pas*. To a great extent the respondent listens to what the interviewer *means* rather than to what he *says* and the attitudinal accompaniment to the strictly semantic aspects of the interviewer's questions helps to complete the meaning.

As techniques, attitudes differ from the verbal forms of the question in that they may persist beyond one particular question. Also they may be manifested both verbally in statements to the respondent and non-verbally in the tone of voice, gestures, and facial expressions which accompany statements and questions by the interviewer. For this reason we will not be able to illustrate many of the manifestations of attitudes on the printed page.

Attitudes are similar to the verbal forms of the question in that they have an effect both upon the meaning of the question and upon the respondent's motivation (ability and willingness) to answer the question.

Let us proceed by discussing the three major attitudinal foci of nonverbal techniques used by the interviewer. These are the interviewer's attitudes toward (*a*) the general task of interviewing, (*b*) specific items of information given by the respondent, and (*c*) the respondent as a person.

Attitudes toward the interviewing task

Attitudes toward the interviewing task tend to prevail throughout a series of interviews on the same topic; in some cases, an interviewer has certain attitudes toward the interviewing task in general, regardless of the particular topic at hand. In extreme cases, the attitudes may be a function of the interviewer's basic personality pattern.

Regardless of the pervasiveness of the source of the attitudes, we will first look at some of the negative attitudes commonly manifested toward the interviewing task. Negative attitudes often held by interviewers toward the task can be grouped into two types: those that indicate a general lack of *desire* to obtain the relevant information, and those that indicate a basic anxiety over one's *ability* to obtain it.

The interviewer's lack of desire may be based upon his initial lack, or subsequent loss, of interest in the topic of the interview. For example, an interviewer discovering housewife's motivations in buying soap might feel that the problem is inconsequential to the future of mankind and be bored with the procedure. Even in studies of people's behavior in disaster situations, the writer noted a tendency for the interviewers' interest in the problem to decrease once they had done enough interviews to obtain a fairly clear picture of the chronology of events and the variety of reactions to the crisis.

Sometimes the lack of interest in the topic springs from the interviewer's naïve assumption that he knows what the respondent's answer is in advance. This dangerous attitude has been noted in cases where the interviewer is interviewing a friend or acquaintance. The interviewer's lack of interest may lie in the intrinsic nature of the topic or in the formulation of the problem. If the problem was formulated by someone else, the interviewer may have no vital interest in the topic, or he may not agree with or understand the formulation of the problem.

Regardless of the cause of the lack of interest in the interview, there are two results: The interviewer often fails to probe beneath the surface, and accepts incomplete information; also, the respondent often receives the impression that the interviewer is not serious or is incompetent or that the topic is not important. As a result he is not motivated to give complete, thoughtful, and accurate information and may even resent having to devote his time to such unimportant pursuits. The interviewer's boredom can be conveyed to the respondent by his tone of voice, posture, facial expression, and other gestures.

Attitudes reflecting the interviewer's basic anxiety over his ability to obtain the information are found in several common forms. He may feel apologetic for asking the types of questions required by the objectives of the interview. This apologetic attitude is seen in statements selected from two interviews: "You might not want to answer this question but . . . ." "You probably don't see much sense to this question . . ." "I am supposed to ask you if . . ." "Would you mind if I asked you . . ." "This next question is a dilly . . ." "You probably don't remember this but . . ."

This attitude of apology and embarrassment often negatively affects the flow of information. The respondent may feel a lack of the support and recognition he desires. Or sensing the interviewer's embarrassment in asking the question, the respondent may think the answer will shock him. The etiquette barrier then arises. Another possible effect is for the respondent to perceive the interviewer's reluctance as an indication of guilt over some possible hidden purposes of the interview. Thus the respondent may feel some potential ego threat in the situation, which puts him on guard and inhibits the flow of information. Another frequent effect is that the respondent simply tends to fulfill the interviewer's expectations by finding the information very difficult to give. The interviewer's anxiety also manifests itself in a rapid-fire pace which invites superficiality and destroys any chance of building the thoughtful mood needed to recall memories.

The remedy for boredom is often gained with experience. For example, it is the neophyte interviewer who assumes that he knows in advance what the respondent is going to say. With experience he becomes sensitized to clues which should be probed further to bring out the individual respondent's unique point of view. Once this is accomplished, the interviewer can see for himself the difference between the initial, superficial responses and the more complex and fundamental underpinnings which emerge with further exploration.

It is also helpful if the interviewer has a vital stake in the study he is doing. He should understand any practical or theoretical significance of the study and have an appreciation of some of the more subtle methodological problems involved in obtaining complete and valid information. He should have the purpose and specifications of the study so clearly in mind that he is highly sensitive to what is relevant, potentially relevant, and irrelevant to the objectives.

To avoid an attitude of embarrassment or apology, the interviewer should ask himself the following question: "Would I be willing to answer all of these questions if I were approached by an interviewer under the same conditions?"

By "under the same conditions" we do not mean that the interviewer should necessarily be willing to answer the questions if the respondent were to reverse their roles during the interview. Instead, this means that the interviewer should be willing to answer the questions in a study planned to render useful knowledge, in which the sponsorship and purpose of the study were clearly given, and in which the anonymity of the respondent were guaranteed.

If he would not be willing, the interviewer will not be successful in hiding his attitude from respondents. Many field workers, including the writer, feel that such an interviewer has no moral right to ask questions he is not willing to answer himself. Regardless of the moral issue, it has been demonstrated that interviewers' attitudes have an effect upon the degree of candidness of the respondent.

The interviewer must realize in advance that there is likely to be some inconvenience and psychic strain at times for both the interviewer and respondent but that this is necessary to advance applied or theoretical social science. The writer has noted on several occasions that the neophyte interviewer's questions regarding his ethical rights to "ask those questions" typically arise when he is beginning to feel some of the tension involved in overcoming the inhibitors of communication. This tendency to feel that if it is difficult it might be unethical is understandable in terms of psychological mechanisms of guilt, punishment, and rationalization. Nevertheless, it should be avoided by the social scientist.

Now let us examine some of the manifestations and possible effects of the interviewer's *positive* attitudes toward his task. Instead of being bored, apologetic, or embarrassed, the successful interviewer shows that he expects to be successful. He is strongly interested in the topic and assumes responsibility personally for the questions he asks rather than attempting to hide behind the sponsor. He is so "sold" on what he is doing that there is a higher probability of appealing to the respondent's altruism. His competence is a compliment to the respondent who realizes that he is not in the presence of a casual inquirer but an incisive prober with a purpose and a method. Most of these positive attitudes, just as the elimination of the negative ones, grow from the interviewer's instruction and experience.

Attitudes toward the information received

Here, the problem is the interviewer's attitudes toward specific statements made by the respondent rather than toward the interview topic as a whole or toward the questions which must be asked. In general, the interviewer should have a nonjudgmental attitude rather than being shocked by the information received; he should show a lively interest in what the respondent is saying rather than being bored; he should usually maintain an analytical attitude toward the information and the degree to which it fulfills the specifications of the study. He should give praise and recognition to responses which are of a high quality in terms of their detail, completeness, depth, and candidness, regardless of the moral implications of the report.

It is sometimes difficult for the interviewer to avoid showing his personal values when the respondent makes some completely unpredicted statements which catch the interviewer off guard, as illustrated below. In this example a group worker from a settlement house in the slums of a large city is talking to the person indicated in the records as the mother of a boy who has recently committed another delinquency.

I: Hello Mrs. Johnson. I am Mr. Brown from Roger Booth House. I would like to talk with you about John.

R: Come in, Mr. Brown.

I: John spends quite a bit of time at Roger Booth House. We are sorry to hear that he is in trouble and I was wondering if there is anything we can do.

R: That's right nice of you, but I don't think anything can be done now. I have had trouble with him for years. He seems to be just a born renegade. I have done my best but he just can't stay on the beam.

I: How's that?

R: Ever since he was two days old he has been trying to kick over the traces.

I: What does his father think of this?

R: I really can't say. You see, I never met his father.

I: (Making a quick recovery) I see, how old was he when you adopted him?

R: I didn't have to adopt him because I took care of his mother—she was my aunt's sister-in-law. I took care of her since she was nine years old, and I made her promise that when she got married she would give me her first son.

Well, she wasn't married, but John was her first son. In fact, she had him right in this house. This was a much nicer neighborhood then.

The social worker with extensive experience with lower socioeconomic status people of various ethnic backgrounds would not be shocked by the respondent's last statement. However, in this case the interviewer had little experience with people in metropolitan slums and was unable to conceal the fact that he was taken aback by the casual attitude displayed toward middle-class ideals of parenthood and the red tape of adoption procedures. From this point on, the respondent ceased to express herself so candidly and any constructive working relationship was made more difficult.

We could supply many examples in which the interviewer is caught off guard and shows surprise, shock, morbid curiosity, inappropriate amusement, or disapproval of something the respondent has said. The probability of such material entering the conversation depends upon the topic of discussion and the difference in experience, cultural background, and auxiliary roles of the interviewer and respondent. The interviewer must be sensitive to the problem and have wide experience before he can take all the respondent's statements in stride.

It is easier for the interviewer to learn to inhibit the expression of embarrassment, boredom, shock, disapproval, and gullibility in reaction to a respondent's statement than it is to pretend the opposite attitudes when they are not actually felt. However, pretense is not necessary. The most constructive approach is for the interviewer to *learn to express* the following generally productive attitudes.

The nonjudgmental attitude. Generally, the interviewer should not express agreement or disagreement, approval or disapproval of anything the respondent says. He should remember that his goal is to obtain accurate and complete information and that any show of disagreement with the respondent constitutes an ego threat.

The interviewer must learn the fine but important distinction between disapproving of a certain value held by the respondent and rejecting him as a person. At the same time, the interviewer should not assume that the respondent makes this distinction; therefore, it should be expected that any disagreement with the respondent's point of view will be interpreted as a disapproval of him as a person.

It is not suggested that a good interviewer is a chameleonlike character lacking his own values and merely reflecting those of the person he is interviewing. On the contrary, the interviewer, in order to discipline himself so that he will not indulge in unplanned demonstrations of approval or disapproval, must feel secure in his own value position, at least to the point where he does not need to defend it or seek support for his position.

The very values which the interviewer holds and may be working for in the interview can be foiled by his expression of these values during the interview. For example, a person interested in reducing the juvenile delinquency rate thwarts his chance of gaining insight into the social-psychological process by which a child becomes a delinquent by expressing a disapproving attitude toward the delinquent he is interviewing.

The main value of the nonjudgmental attitude is that it frees the respondent from ego threat, taking him off the defensive and allowing him to candidly review his own behavior. There are *rare* occasions when it is appropriate to the objectives of the interview for the interviewer to express approval and disapproval. In learning to interview, however, the nonjudgmental approach is the basic discipline which must be mastered first so that any deviations from it are consciously calculated to meet interview objectives rather than emotional reflexive actions.

Showing an interest in the information. The interviewer's demonstrating or withholding his display of interest in certain aspects of the information is a technique of guiding the focus of the discussion. Also, the general level of interest shown in the information influences the amount of spontaneity shown by the respondent. Here "interest" covers a syndrome of more specific attitudes: a desire to understand how the world looks to the respondent; an appreciation of the things experienced by the respondent; sharing in the respondent's struggle to recall, organize, and express his experiences; appreciating the difficulties involved; and a desire to accurately reflect the respondent's opinions, feelings, and beliefs.

Various aspects of the interviewer's interest in the information can be demonstrated verbally as well as nonverbally. A few examples will illustrate this

R: At that time I had three babies still in diapers and that made it a bit difficult to adjust to the divorce.

I: Three babies all in diapers! How did you manage?

The interviewer who is less sensitive or less appreciative could have merely said, "I see," or "What were some of the problems?" or "How is that?"

The following exchange is taken from an interview with a disaster victim where the objective was to obtain a complete account of the respondent's experiences during the period of crisis.

R: Jim and I were going down highway 67; we didn't see the tornado, but just as we came to one of those banked turns we couldn't make it because the car was off the ground. We were jerked up in the air and I remember seeing a flash as our car hit the high-tension lines. Then we landed bottom side up in a swamp about four feet deep. One more gust of wind came and just flipped the car right side up again.

I: Were you going north or south on highway 67?

After a large number of interviews this interviewer had become insensitive to the experiences of disaster victims. He shows no appreciation for what the respondent is saying. True, this respondent's experiences, although dramatic, are not unusual for people in an area hit by a tornado. But from the point of view of the individual respondent there is little encouragement to elaborate and clarify the details of his experiences. An appropriate responsiveness on the part of the interviewer would have shown that he *expected* more detail at this point, that he *sympathized* with the respondent's traumatic experience, and that he *recognized* the respondent's unique qualifications to report how it feels to fly through the air in a car. All of these facilitators of communication could have been triggered by a natural expression of candid amazement on the part of the interviewer.

Fortunately, the interviewer's temporary lapses into insensitivity were not fatal to the flow of information on this particular topic because of the tremendous need for catharsis which leads most respondents to concentrate their attention on the most devastating portion of their experience. However, the better interviewers seemed to build up "credit" by showing interest in the respondent's account of the impact period of disaster. This credit carried over to the later portion of the interview dealing with information not nearly as important to the respondent himself.

The verbal techniques of showing interest, responsiveness, empathy, sensitivity, appreciation, and recognition are often very simple as long as the nonverbal accompaniment rings true. For example: "That's very interesting to me." "That's exactly what I want to know; could you spell out more of the details?" "That's amazing—how did you do it?" "That's a very unusual experience, to say the least. Now let's see if I have the correct idea." "You must have been really angry by that time!"

All of these expressions of interest in the appropriate context are perfectly natural. For this reason interviewers are sometimes either suspicious of their use or do not think of them as "techniques." We must be careful to avoid the conception of techniques as tricks or insincere play acting. Instead, *techniques consist of increasing one's empathic sensitivity to the respondent's story and a disciplined withholding or expressing of real attitudes.*

There are occasions in some interviews when an undisciplined expression of interest, sympathy, or curiosity by the interviewer, even though sincere, will derail the interview so that the interview is very interesting but the information received is not relevant to the objectives of the interview. Here the over-concern with building rapport reduces the interview to a sociable conversation.

Critical analysis of the information. The nonjudgmental ethical neutrality and the disciplined interest in the respondent's story must be balanced by a third attitudinal stance we will call critical analysis of the information. By "critical" we denote the process of evaluating the adequacy of the information for fulfilling the objectives of the interview.

It is not enough for the interviewer to be vitally concerned with evaluating the adequacy of the information; he must communicate this attitude to the respondent. When this attitude is perceived by the respondent, it helps prevent his temptation to give vague, superficial, incomplete replies which would require an inordinate amount of time to unscramble. The interviewer must prevent the respondent's perceiving him as a simple-minded, superficial, disorganized, or easily misled person.

The interviewer's attitude of critical evaluation is shown in his interest in precise facts, his concern for correct inferences, and his painstaking care in establishing accurate sequences of events when they are relevant. He also demonstrates it in his desire to get beneath clichés or instantaneous conclusions, in his willingness to help the respondent remember, and in his conscientious attempt to correctly reflect the respondent's attitudes. These persistent efforts of the interviewer establish an appropriate mood. In order to help the respondent give the quality of response expected, the interviewer may have to slow down the pace of the interview and establish a thoughtful mood to facilitate memory. He may have to tactfully call the respondent's attention to apparent inconsistencies, contradictions, or omissions in the report.

This critical attitude has two general functions. First, it can be thought of as a balance wheel governing the two previous attitudes of nonjudgment and interst. The interviewer must discipline himself by restricting his interest to those experiences which are relevant to the problem. Similarly, he must restrict his nonjudgmental approach to expressions of approval and disapproval of the respondent or the information given rather than to the completeness, accuracy, or general relevance of the information as measured by the objectives of the interview. The critical attitude reserves expressions of sympathetic understanding for only candid information; it prevents the misplaced expression of appreciation for efforts not up to the capabilities of the respondent.

The second function of the attitude is in its motivation of the respondent. He sees that a high-level performance is expected of him by the interviewer. He sees more potential ego threat in being caught in an attempt to falsify than in a candid report, and this forestalls fabrication. The memory barrier is minimized by impressing the respondent with the importance of an accurate report. Indirectly, the respondent is given recognition since, if he perceives the interviewer as being competent, he is apt to feel that he was respected enough to merit a good interviewer. The appeal to an intelligent respondent's altruism is enhanced because he is more likely to be willing to give his time for a good cause if he feels the cause is in the hands of competent people who will see it through to a successful conclusion. For some respondents a careful interview which insists upon achieving somewhat difficult objectives constitutes a challenging new experience. The interviewer's attempts to get beneath a superficial level often stimulate the respondent's need for meaning by pointing out certain inconsistencies of thinking of which the respondent had not previously been aware.

Now that we have examined some of the manifestations and functions of three general attitudes toward the information received by the interviewer, let us turn to some important aspects of the interviewer's attitude toward the respondent as a person.

Attitudes toward the respondent as a person

It is not possible to make a perfectly clear distinction between the interviewer's attitudes toward the information received and toward the person giving the information because, as has already been pointed out, the interviewer may tend to dislike the respondent if he dislikes many things he says, and the respondent may tend to feel ego threat if the interviewer disagrees with some of his ideas.

For the purposes of this discussion we will use the phrase "attitudes toward the respondent" to refer only to those attitudes toward the respondent that are independent of anything the respondent has said in the interview and that are based upon the interviewer's image of an attitude toward a particular type of respondent. The type of respondent may be distinguished by such characteristics as sex, race, age, personality type, role, social class, and educational background.

There are several specific manifestations of the interviewer's attitudes which hinder communication with one class of respondent. An attitude may range in feeling from a strong dislike, through indifference, to a strong affinity. A negative feeling makes it difficult for the interviewer to empathize with the respondent. The writer has found in the analysis of tape-recorded interviews that interviewers with some experience rarely express a negative attitude toward the respondent in a *direct* manner. Even though they learn to control such direct expressions, there are several indirect ways which betray a lack of interest. An awareness of these indirect manifestations will help an interviewer control his negative attitudes toward a particular category of respondent.

Forgetting previous responses. This is a typical indirect manifestation of a lack of interest in the respondent. In the nonscheduled interview there is always the danger of asking the same or a similar question twice. However, the writer has found that some interviewers, when interviewing certain types of respondents, were more prone to forget what the respondent had already told them even though it was something extremely important to the respondent. For example:

R: I called out "Victor, Victor, Victor". . . as loud as I could yell. The next door neighbor was trying to calm me down, but I just couldn't control myself.

I: What was your husband doing meanwhile? . . . Oh yes, that's right you said he was unconscious all this time.

In this case the interviewer caught his own mistake and softened the blow. Such lapses of memory on the part of the interviewer are readily detected by the respondent when the information he has given is vitally important to him. This is ego threatening to some respondents, and if it happens more than once, it is often interpreted as an indication of the interviewer's lack of sympathetic understanding.

The interviewer can give this unsympathetic impression even when he has not forgotten that he has asked the question and is asking a slightly different question for clarification. There is a danger that the respondent will feel or say, "I told you that once." To prevent this, the interviewer may positively give the respondent recognition by acknowledging the information previously given before probing further. He might say, for example, "You told me that your husband was unconscious after being hit by a board off the barn. What was he doing before that time?"

Neglecting to probe in crucial spots. This neglect communicates a lack of empathy for the respondent. It often pays to probe for elaboration and clarification of ego-involved or emotionalized responses even though the information does not seem to be directly related to the objectives of the interview. Showing an interest in what is important to the respondent is a good rapport-building technique. For example, in an interview to discover some of the factors contributing to the low morale of workers in a steel plant, the conversation was as follows:

I: Are there some supervisors the men find hard to get along with?

R: You have to take a lot of guff off the foreman here. I don't know who he thinks he is—and he has been here only two months.

I: What do you mean by that?

R: Well (with great hostility), the bastard actually violated some of the agreements the union has with the company!

I: Are there any other things that you dislike in the management or supervising system?

The interviewer's last question veers away from one of the respondent's favorite gripes. When the respondent is just beginning to gather momentum and before the interviewer has discovered the actual nature of his complaint, the interviewer rushes on as if he had only a limited amount of time. From the respondent's point of view, this behavior might indicate that the interviewer is not actually interested in his morale problems, and this could discourage the respondent from elaborating on other incidents.

Using a condescending tone. There is a certain saccharine tone heard in tape recordings of interviews where the interviewer is trying to patronize the respondent who is considered in lower status. This tone is often used in an attempt to conceal outright disapproval or complete lack of interest in the respondent as a person. It is rarely successful in convincing the respondent that the interviewer is interested or impressed.

Being rigidly cautious. Although male interviewers rarely use what we called the "saccharine tone," they often become rigidly cautious in the same type of situation. In this case, the interviewer shows little spontaneity, perhaps because he fears betraying his own feelings in an off-guard moment. In some instances we traced this rigidity to the interviewer's feeling that he might lose status in the respondent's eyes by being too informal and spontaneous. This behavior was found in corporation managers while interviewing employees, in sociology students interviewing members of low status ethnic groups, and in social work students interviewing mental patients.

Having shown some common manifestations of the negative attitudes toward the respondent, we now examine some of the ways of manifesting positive attitudes toward the respondent.

Interest in the respondent as a person. Often it is impossible to motivate the respondent by treating him strictly as a means to an end. This is particularly true where the objectives of the interview make heavy demands upon the respondent. Here, the task of the interviewer is to reconcile the apparently conflicting goals of the interviewer who wants to obtain information and the respondent who wants to be understood and considered as a unique individual rather than as a statistic or case. The solution is to show a vital interest in the respondent and his story at those points most relevant to the objectives of the interview. This interest, to be appropriate, must not be an idle curiosity, nor a chummy intimacy, but should be mainly confined to a keen interest in the relevant, unique experiences of the respondent. Such interest is characterized by the desire of the interviewer to see the relevant experiences through the respondent's eyes.

The respondent can be reminded of this attitude not only by its nonverbal manifestations such as the interviewer's paying close attention, responding with facial expressions and tone of voice, but also by such verbal expressions as, "I want *your* side of this story!" "How do you, *personally,* feel about this?" "Tell me what happened to *you* in the tornado." "What is *your* reaction to the rising cost of living?" "Which of these things seem most important to *you?*" "I want to be sure I understand *your* point of view on this issue!"

All of these questions and statements could be worded in an impersonal manner, but with less appeal to the respondent's ego. Personalizing the request for relevant information is one way of showing interest in the respondent as a person without encouraging irrelevant responses.

Interest in the respondent as a person can also be indicated by making statements at appropriate points showing appreciation of the respondent's role, status, or values. This does not mean that the interviewer must agree with the respondent's values. In the following excerpt an interviewer with a Protestant background is interviewing a Catholic woman who has felt the pressures of prejudice from fellow college students.

> *R:* I recall one incident where two girls were talking about how only unintelligent people could be Catholics because they had to accept dogmatic pronouncements no matter how illogical they may be. Then one of them turned to me to see if I didn't agree. I just said, "You can't expect me to agree because I'm a Catholic myself." Were they ever embarrassed! They sputtered out something about they didn't realize I was a Catholic.
>
> *I:* That reminds me of the time I heard a conversation on the bus where one woman said, "How was I to know! She didn't look like a Catholic at all!"
>
> *R:* That's it exactly! They think that Catholics have two heads or something. That's why, in this community, I make a point of being known as an individual *before* I mention what church I belong to. People are less likely to be prejudiced then.

Note that the interviewer did not mention any of his experiences where the same thing had happened in relation to Jews, pacifists, socialists, or any other minority group. It is often a mistake to assume that one minority member sees any similarity between his situation and that of other minorities. And there is always the danger that the comparison will be resented.

Showing appreciation of the respondent's effort. The interviewer should be sensitive to the respondent's need for appreciation and recognition at two points in the interviewing process. First, the interviewer should show that he realizes a particular question places great demands upon the respondent. In doing this, he should not imply that he expects the respondent to fail to meet the demands. If the objectives of the question demand careful searching of one's memory, untangling chronological and inferential confusion, or reporting semiconscious experiences, the interviewer should give some indication that he appreciates the difficulty of the problem. For example, he might say, "This is a difficult question, but I'm quite sure you can give me some good ideas if I just let you think it over for awhile. Let's go back to the time you mentioned when you joined the Black Hawk gang . . . that was about six years ago. Why would you say you joined the gang?"

The second phase of showing appreciation is in praising the respondent for the *effort* he has made and is making. Interviews with respondents regarding their experiences in a nonscheduled interview showed that frequently the respondent himself did not understand why he was having difficulty in reporting some of the relevant information. Furthermore, he was often insecure not knowing whether he was considered successful by the interviewer. In these cases, it is important that the interviewer show his appreciation of the respondent's efforts to give the information.

The interviewer must be sensitive to opportunities to praise the respondent sincerely throughout the interview. The praise need not be lavish nor even direct, but should be given at those points where the respondent has exerted special effort. For example: "That was difficult and you did it very well!" "You seem to understand exactly what I want!" "You have given me an unusual amount of detail on your experiences. This is very valuable information!" "I know it was hard for you to talk about these painful experiences and I appreciate it." "I am grateful for your candid accounts of the conflicts and disagreements you have had with your parents!" "You have done an excellent job in giving me some insight into this problem. Is there anything else you would like to add before we go on to the last topic?" "You have given me a wealth of relevant information!" "You make interviewing very easy!"

It is easy for the interviewer to be so concerned with what information is lacking that he forgets to appreciate what has already been given and the amount of the respondent's effort expended. It encourages the respondent to go beyond the superficial level if he feels that it is expected and appreciated.

SUMMARY

Nonverbal communication is a means for communicating both certain information and attitudes to the respondent and for receiving information about the respondent's attitudes.

Technically there are four basic modes of nonverbal communication: *proxemic* communication is the use of interpersonal space to communicate attitudes, *chronemics* communication is the use of pacing of speech and length of silence in conversation, *kinesic* communication includes any body movements or postures, and *paralinguistic* communication includes all the variations in volume, pitch, and quality of voice.

Although the four modes of nonverbal communication are useful for analytical and experimental purposes, the interviewer must in practice use any natural combinations of these modes in expressing attitudes which facilitate the flow of relevant information. Usually, the interviewer focuses his attention on receiving and sending attitudes rather than upon analyzing the modes by which such attitudes are conveyed. The only specific physical nonverbal activity he needs to be conscious of is the use of silence. He must consciously use the silent probe as a specific nonverbal technique.

In the transmission of attitudes the interviewer must learn to detect subtle manifestations of attitude in the respondent. He must suppress the expression of any detrimental attitudes himself by displacing them with positive attitudes toward the task at hand.

The interviewer must learn to avoid expressing surprise, shock, embarrassment, or disgust in response to any information received. He must strive to maintain a generally nonjudgmental attitude toward information given by the respondent, to maintain a strong interest in the information, and to critically analyze the information in relation to the objectives of the interview. This attitude of critical analysis should be communicated to the respondent in order to prevent carelessness or fabrication in giving responses.

Negative attitudes toward the respondent as a person are frequently shown in the interviewer's errors of omission (such as forgetting a previous response and neglecting to probe in areas important to the respondent), or in his condescending tone of voice or cautious rigidity. These negative manifestations should be displaced by a strong verbal and nonverbal expression of interest in the respondent as a person rather than exclusively as a "case," a "statistic," or "source of information," and by showing appreciation of the respondent's efforts to give relevant information.

Even though the interviewer may unconsciously use some of these essential techniques, their conscious mastery and application will significantly increase his interviewing success.

DISCUSSION QUESTIONS

1. What are the four major modes of nonverbal communication?
2. Compare a telephone interview with a face-to-face interview in terms of the four major modes of nonverbal communication.
3. Which two of the major modes come into play most frequently in the face-to-face interview?
4. What specific kinesic stimuli are most frequently the focus of attention of the listener in the interview situation?
5. Does the speaker or the listener tend to pay the most attention to the other person's kinesic communication?
6. Give an example of experimental proof that the nonverbal "silent language" really communicates.

7. What is the function of the silent probe in interviewing?
8. What are the principal foci of attitudes affecting the inhibitors and facilitators of communication?
9. What can the interviewer do as a technique to counteract any possible negative attitudes he may have toward the point of view divulged by the respondent?
10. What are some of the specific attitudes which must be developed to become a good interviewer?
11. What are some of the specific negative attitudes which must be avoided or counteracted by the successful interviewer?

SELECTED READINGS

The bibliographic items below were selected as examples of studies of four forms of nonverbal communication that can be applied in the interview: Chronemics, Kinesics, Paralinguistics, and Proxemics.

Duncan, Starkey, Jr., et al. "The Paralanguage of Experimentor Bias." *Sociometry*, vol. 32 (1969), pp. 207–19.

A technical experiment demonstrating that intentional *paralinguistic* behavior of the interviewer (voice quality) influenced the respondent in the manner intended.

Exline, Ralph. "Body Position, Facial Expression, and Verbal Behavior During Interviews." *Journal of Abnormal and Social Psychology*, vol. 68 (1964), pp. 295–301.

An experiment demonstrating that the interviewer can make better judgments of the respondent when observing the *kinesic* cues of the head rather than any other parts of the respondent's body.

Goldberg, G., et al. "Visual Behavior and Face-to-Face Distance During Interaction." *Sociometry*, vol. 32 (1969), pp. 43–53.

An experimental demonstration of Hall's *proxemic* principle that at different distances human beings tend to use different sense modes for communication. This experiment shows that when the respondent is seated very close (2½ feet) to the interviewer he feels much less need to make eye contact than when he is seated farther away.

Hall, Edward T. *The Silent Language*. New York: Doubleday & Co., 1959.

Explains and illustrates how *chronemic* and *proxemic* cues have different meanings in different cultures. Particularly relevant are his chapters entitled "Time Talks" and "Space Speaks."

Scheflen, A. E. *Stream and Structure of Communication Behavior*. Bloomington, Ind.: University of Indiana Press, 1969.

For the student wanting to go deeply into the *paralinguistic* forms of communication as they apply to the interview, this book sums up much of Scheflen's work in linguistics as well as paralinguistics and their application to psychiatry.

Laboratory problem 10

Recognizing techniques (vocational choice interview)

Purpose

This laboratory problem provides an opportunity to recognize a variety of techniques as they occur in the context of of the free-flowing initial exploratory interview. More different verbal techniques will be used than you were asked to produce in Laboratory Problem 9.

Also, although there is no way to convey such nonverbal techniques as tone of voice or facial movements on the printed page, you are to detect any interviewer's attitudes that are verbally manifested in what he says or neglects to say. This interview was selected because the particular interviewer does show some of his attitudes verbally.

Procedure

This laboratory problem will require from one to two hours to complete. Below you are given the purpose and setting of the study and the verbatim transcript of the initial exploratory interview. You are to take the following steps:

1. Read the description of the objectives and setting of the interview carefully before reading the verbatim transcript. Try to imagine yourself as the interviewer.

2. As you read the script, classify all of the *interviewer's* verbal behavior that falls into any of the 11 categories in the Analysis Table provided by the instructor. Not all of his behavior falls into these 11 categories, and some of his statements or questions will fall into more than one category.

    a. Each classifiable verbal behavior should be identified by the number on the transcript.

    b. Within any category, the identification numbers should be in *rank order* with commas between, so that your results may be quickly compared with another person's. Example: 2, 5, 6, 9, 19, 33.

    c. Do this in *pencil* so that it can be changed.

    d. Do this independently, without consulting others on your decisions.

3. Now discuss your classifications with a fellow student who has already done it independently and make any changes needed in your classifications as a result of your discussion.

4. Submit your revised Analysis Table to the instructor.

Objectives

The interview aims to explore factors influencing the respondent's choice of a vocation or profession. The following three specific objectives were included in the preliminary definition of informational objectives.

    a. To obtain the respondent's perception of his own education, training, abilities, achievements, interests, values, etc., as they relate to his choice of vocation.

    b. To discover the respondent's perceptions of the demands and rewards of various fields.

    c. To identify the sources of any social pressure, whether through personal contact or the mass media, that influence his vocational choice.

Situational setting

The interviewer, a male graduate student, is interviewing a male undergraduate student. The interview takes place in the graduate student's apartment off campus. The interviewer explained why he wanted to tape-record the interview and met no resistance to the idea. There was some conversation about the interviewer's dog and then the interview begins.

Interview transcript

In the verbatim transcript of the interview the durations of silences are shown in seconds by the numbers in parentheses. You are to classify only the *interviewer's* words identified by *I-0, I-2, I-3,* etc.

    I-0: As you know, we are interested in finding how people select the vocation they go into.

R-0: That should be a fascinating study!

I-1: What I thought we would start out with is some of your earlier thoughts in choosing a field. You can go back as early as you can remember.

R-1: Hmm, that is something! I can't remember a thing before my high-school days!

I-2: Can't you remember earlier than that—just think a moment. When I try, I can remember back to six and seven years old.

R-2: Well, when I was very young, I was interested in the theater. (3)

I-3: I see, how did that happen?

R-3: It has always been more or less the field that I wanted to go into. I started out wanting to be a dancer, and I continued that for two or three years (2) while I was taking lessons, and then I decided to go into the theater.

I-4: How old were you when you first wanted to be a dancer?

R-4: Twelve! (3)

I-5: Can you remember back to the time—way back—when you were interested in other things, anything from wanting to be an Indian to a cowboy? I used to want to be a motorcycle driver.

R-5: I can't remember anything like that (2) of course I suppose I wanted to be a fireman, policeman, cowboy, or something like that when I was younger, but as far as I can remember, I have always been interested in something connected with the theater. I took dancing lessons until I was fourteen.

I-6: So you took dancing lessons until you were fourteen.

R-6: Yeh, well, I moved to Arizona when I was fourteen. They didn't have a good school of the dance, so I started acting. I sort of associated with a children's theater group and became interested in that. But I wasn't there long (3) my parents were getting a divorce, and I moved out with my mother for the proceedings. We lived there over a year. Then I went back to Massachusetts to live with my mother. (3)

I-7: Do you feel that this children's theater group was the main influence leading you toward the theater?

R-7: I don't know about that.

I-8: Why don't you know? Didn't you say that your main interest was really dancing until you were 14?

R-8: Yeh, 13 or 14. (4)

I-9: Did you have any experience with the theater before or during your dancing?

R-9: Yea, we had a tiny group at home, you know, little kids 10 or 11 years old. We'd do little fairy tales, that sort of things. We'd just sort of act them out. But nothing big. (2)

I-10: That was more or less a natural occurrence of growing up, wan't it?

R-10: I'd say that, yeh. We had a girl though that was a junior or senior in high school, and we'd do one or two shows a year, and she'd ask us to do one and be in the show herself, and it'd be the real thing (2) but as far as being really organized, I suppose you could call it a process of growing up.

I-11: Speaking of growing up—where were you from originally?

R-11: I was born in Boston, Massachusetts, but I lived in Williamstown up in the other end of the state. Well, actually my mother still lives there. Both of my parents married again, and my stepfather still lives there. (3)

I-12: You were in Arizona only about a year?

R-12: Only about 15 months, yes. Then we moved back. It was only a temporary move. We were only going to be there 3 months, but stayed longer.

I-13: Ah . . . can you think of any other fields? So you just maintained this interest until you came to college? (2)

R-13: I never really wanted to be anything else. Teaching, but teaching in the theater level. Nothing . . . (3) . . . it is always something connected with the theater.

I-14: How are you at dancing?

R-14: Well, I haven't done much lately, but I was pretty good, or at least that is what I have been told. I've done some. I've taken the modern dance course here, and I suppose with a lot of work I might go somewhere, but I'm not willing to put in the work right now with all my academic work. I wouldn't want to do it for a living.

I-15: Then you don't want to make a career of it?

R-15: Well (2) I did some dancing when I was 13 and 14 in public—it was a lot of fun. This was in Williamstown. All my friends came to see me, and I got quite a charge out of it. I did a little of everything then, tap, modern, ballet, and even folk dancing of a rather complicated kind.

I-16: I see. What do you think is the best for you, dancing or theater?

R-16: Well, that depends on what aspect of the theater you want to talk about. In fact, dancing is part of the theater, and there are many facets even to the acting area of theater. For example, directing, stage management, business management, choreography, singing, teaching and . . . well all kinds of things. I don't know which is the most practical. (5) Do you think it might be a good thing for someone who isn't terrifically talented as an actor to go into teaching dramatics? (4)

I-17: Well—you know the old saying, "If you can't do it yourself, teach someone else to do it, and if you can't teach it, then teach others to teach."

R-17: Well, I love acting, and I'll admit that I'm not any Olivier, but nowadays you have to be either a genius or have a lot of what Hollywood is looking for . . . sex appeal. (2)

I-18: The main reason that you don't feel acting is for you is that you sort of feel that you're—well not by my standards, but by the standards of the theater—you are mediocre.

R-18: Well . . . I . . .

I-19: Well, I hate to use that word . . .

R-19: I think probably with training I could . . . I mean I, I've had plenty of experience. I've had any number of stock company work and things, but it would take a lot of training, but I don't have quite the right bark to be (2) you know—a *great* actor, and I'm not a he-man so I could never become another Burt Lancaster.

I-20: Or a Marlon Brando.

R-20: Yeah, you either have to be really good in your art or you have to be really bad Hollywood. There are very few really good actors in Hollywood except for people who go out to do *one* film . . . (2) . . . but people like Burt Lancaster and that sort of thing all build on their sex appeal . . . Marlon Brando too.

I-21: Well, he does pretty good things no matter how he's cast.

R-21: Yeh, he's sort of a natural.

I-22: He's got talent as well as sex appeal.

R-22: Well, talking along these lines, I saw an old movie when I was up in Akron a while back. Ray Milland, now I thought Ray Milland could do a decent job in . . . oh, I saw him in "Time Out for Murder" with Hitchcock, now he was entertaining in that film. I mean not a great dynamic or great stirring emotional actor, but pleasant as an Englishman, dignified, refined. I just hate to see somebody cast like that (2) and it tears your heart out to see somebody who really loves the theater, it makes me ill . . . don't you think so?

I-23: Yeh, that's very true. I think they should keep Broadway actors out of movies. They can't be expected to do well at both media.

R-23: To see somebody of ability . . . Well, I'm off the subject. (2)

I-24: Do you feel that your parents influenced your decision?

R-24: No, that's one nice thing about my mother and father both. They never tried to tell me "You ought to be an actor or a dancer when you grow up." Children should have a mind of their own!

I-25: What does your father do?

R-25: He teaches business administration at Harvard Business School.

I-26: And what about your mother. Did she ever have any aspirations to the stage which were interrupted by getting married? I know that sort of thing is not at all unusual.

R-26: Well, before she got married she was a bank teller at a bank.

I-27: Did she go to college?

R-27: She went three years to a college in Boston—Erskine. It's no longer in session. She never finished school.

I-28: And what was her interest there?

R-28: I really don't know. She doesn't talk about it very much, and I never asked her. I don't know.

I-29: Do you think your parents' backgrounds might have influenced your choice of field?

R-29: Well, both my parents are very (2) or have, have a lot of background in, a creative arts background. Art was a minimum, but music especially. They both liked music very much, and I do know that I do like music because I heard it ever since I was yea-high. You know, listening to it all the time whenever they had it on, good music . . . so I like good music.

I-30: Did your parents enjoy theater too?

R-30: Oh yes—doesn't everyone in Boston? Or I should say every *educated* person.

I-31: I guess that's right. Do you have any brothers or sisters?

R-31: Yes, one younger brother and some stepbrothers and sisters.

I-32: What does your younger brother intend to do?

R-32: Well, as far as I know he wants to follow in my father's footsteps in economics, that's the last thing I heard. (2) He is sort of a "papa's boy" and is easily influenced by father.

I-33: I see—he doesn't really have a strong will of his own.

R-33: I guess that's it.

I-34: When you were living at home after your parents were divorced, where did you live, with your father or your mother?

R-34: With my mother.

part five

Tactics of interviewing

16

Advance planning of tactics

Tactics of interviewing are dealt with in three chapters. This chapter focuses on those tactical sequences that can be developed, planned, and frozen into the interview schedule. The next chapter on probing and the following one on dealing with resistance in the respondent focus on those tactical maneuvers that cannot be planned in advance but must be selected in response to a particular respondent's behavior. The planning of tactics is a creative art, and the parry and thrust of probing and meeting resistance after the interview begins is a performing art.

Tactics in interviewing consists of choosing the appropriate order for the interviewer's statements, questions, and probes. While the interviewer's techniques can be classified according to the form of the verbal or nonverbal behavior at a given point without any reference to what came before or after, it is not possible to view any particular behavior as a tactic without seeing it in a chronological context. We must know what came before and what we expect to come after as well as how it fits into the larger aims of the total interview. Thus, what might be a perfectly good question or probe at one point in the interview may be threatening at another point. Also, the meaning of a question at one point in the interview depends upon the questions and answers which preceded it.

Tactical patterns may be planned in advance and rigidly followed, tentatively planned and loosely followed, or left completely to the discretion of the interviewer after he is engaged in the ongoing give-and-take of a particular interview. At one extreme the typical opinion survey may have all of the tactical patterns built into the interview schedule and may strictly forbid any deviation in question form or sequence by the interviewer. At the other extreme an administrator may spend a large portion of his time asking questions to obtain information from other members of his organization, yet he may never prepare an interview schedule with a fixed order of questions. Instead, he would have a clear idea of the information needed and begin an informal discussion in which he probes important points as they emerge.

The portion of the tactical decisions that can be legitimately frozen into the interview schedule depends on the type of information sought, the setting of the interview, and the amount of information needed. If many interviews are to be done on the same topic, much of the tactical pattern can be developed in exploratory interviews. Developing sensitivity to the chronological patterning is essential for anyone who wants to do exploratory interviewing more effectively, or who wants to be able to do tactical planning and interview schedule construction for others.

Assuming that the interviewer knows precisely what bits of information are needed, there are several areas in which he may do advance planning of tactics. However, all of these plans must be considered as tentative in the nonscheduled interview and may be changed with field testing. The interviewer must decide how many subtopics there actually are in his broad topic. He should decide which one to begin with and perhaps work out pivot questions to determine whether subsequent subtopics are relevant to the particular respondent. He might devise lead-in questions which are designed to psychologically prepare the respondent for questions which will follow but which do not intend to directly obtain information relevant to the purposes of the interview. When getting chronological material from the respondent, the interviewer must decide whether to begin the discussion precisely at that point in time relevant to the objectives of the interview or to go back further and do a lead-in designed to help the respondent reconstruct the scene and the situation immediately preceding the relevant period of time. Once the order of topics and the means of getting from one subtopic to another are decided, tentative plans must be made for developing the discussion within each subtopic area. Here the interviewer must decide on all possible alternative wordings of questions, on how contexts can be provided when needed, on alternative sequences of questions; and above all, he must select some clear way of recording what has and has not been covered in the progress of the interview. The latter will be a problem particularly when the interviewer does not follow a fixed sequence of specific questions.

In addition to deciding what subtopics are needed, possible orders of these subtopics, and methods of expanding each of these subtopics to cover all of the specific information needed, the interviewer must also prepare to meet certain infrequent crises which require special treatment. For example, we might find a question which unexpectedly constitutes an ego threat to the respondent. What do we do? Or what do we do if the respondent simply says, "I'm sorry, I'm too busy now to be interviewed"? What do we do if he says, "Ask someone else who knows something about this topic; I don't know anything about it"? Or if he says he does not want to have his voice tape-recorded, or he stops in the middle of the interview to ask, "Why are you taking notes?" If he responds to a question by saying he does not remember or does not know, are we to take this literally? If, in response to a question, he uses the Yankee system of asking you the question, what tactics should be used? Or what if we merely suspect that the respondent is resisting, that he is not giving all the information he has and is withholding something? What can we do to test a hypothesis of this kind?

This chapter deals with these problems of arranging topics and subtopics, pivot questions, lead-in questions, and transitions; developing each topic to cover the specifications of the interview; meeting resistance by the respondent, and testing whether or not he is actually resisting. To a certain extent, successful use of tactics depends upon basic skills which have been developed, but perhaps to a larger extent it depends upon an awareness of what kinds of tactical problems might arise and planning some possible ways of meeting these problems. Once we know how to make these plans, all that remains is to practice planning for a wide variety of interviews so that required basic skills can be developed.

ARRANGING TOPICS AND SUBTOPICS WITHIN AN INTERVIEW

It is possible to have an interview so simple in its objectives that there are no topics or subtopics. The simplest possible interview might contain only one question:

"As you know, _____ and _____ are running for President of the United States. For whom do you intend to vote?" At the other extreme, an interview's objectives might include the opinions of the respondent on several public issues, certain personality traits that he might have, some of his social background characteristics, such as religion, social class, political views, the amount of influence he has on others, and his position in the community. The number of topics or subtopics perceived within such a complex interview depends upon the degree of relationships between the various objectives and the level of abstraction used to hold the topics within the common frame of reference. For example, a respondent's opinion on three topics such as antivivisection, the United States' role in the United Nations, and parent-child relations in the United States might be conceived as three separate, nonrelated topics. However, if the objectives of the interview include discovering the respondent's personality characteristics and relating them to his opinions on selected public issues, then these three topics become merely three selected public issues and are subtopics more related to each other than to a battery of questions regarding the respondent's personality traits. This example illustrates that what might be a whole interview in one case is a topic within an interview in another case; it could also be a subtopic within a topic of another interview. Regardless of how finely we slice the total subject matter of the interview into topics, we are faced with the problem of deciding how the specific questions must be grouped into topics or subtopics and what their chronological order will be.

Chronological order of topics and subtopics

Although it is impossible to provide specific rules for determining the chronological order of subtopics within an interview, it is possible to indicate some of the most important questions that must be considered when determining the order of topics. However, these questions can be answered specifically only within the context of a particular interview problem. Too frequently, the interviewer tends to arrange the order in a purely logical fashion in order to simplify the coding and analysis of the data, or to arrange questions in a sequence that seems natural to him. Although both of these criteria are important, the criterion which has precedence over either of these is the effect upon the respondent's willingness and ability to give the relevant information. If the order which maximizes the flow of valid, relevant information is also the logical order which will minimize the problems of analyzing the data, this is fortunate. But it is not always the case.

Let us look at some examples in which the order of topics has an effect upon the flow of information.

Ego threat. Frequently one sequence of topics is more ego-threatening than an alternate sequence of the same topics. If we wish to discover the relationship between a person's premarital sex behavior and his subsequent marital adjustment, the interview obviously contains a minimum of two separate topics. In this case, we might have to do several exploratory interviews to determine which of these topics seems to threaten the respondent the least. Is he more likely to withhold the details of his premarital sex behavior after discussing his marital adjustment, or vice versa?

To give another example, suppose we want to discover the relationship between the respondent's opinion on foreign aid and his religious participation. Foreign aid is an opinion topic, while his religious participation (such as what his church affiliation is, how many times a year he attends, whether he participates in action projects sponsored by the church) is not. In this case, it is highly probable that the interview should first discuss the respondent's opinions on foreign aid before reminding him of his religious connections. If the procedure were reversed, there would probably be a greater tendency for the respondent to present his opinions on foreign aid as being more harmonious with his professed religious principles.

In other instances the respondent's ego is threatened by the fact that the sequence of topics is structured in a logical fashion that makes him aware that his arguments are not logical, and contain some threatening inconsistencies. For example, an interview might contain five subtopics represented by the following questions:

1. Do you believe that the United States has sufficient military power to destroy the Soviet Union's industrial civilization?
2. Do you think that the Soviet Union has enough military power to destroy the United States industrial civilization?
3. Do you think that either the Soviet Union or the United States has an efficient system of defense which would prevent the other from destroying its industrial civilization in the event of an all-out atomic war?
4. Do you think that the Soviet Union feels that the present military power of the United States is sufficient to crush her industrial civilization in the event of an all-out atomic war?
5. Do you feel that the United States should continue to put an increasing proportion of her national wealth into agumenting her military power?

It is highly probable that the respondent who feels that the United States should continue increasing its military power would feel threatened in stating this opinion if the question were preceded by the other four as suggested above. It is possible that such a respondent would find himself in the position of saying that the purpose of armaments and military power from the point of view of the United States is to deter the Soviet Union from attacking. He may also feel that we have enough military power to destroy the Soviet Union's industrial civilization and that the Soviets believe that we have such power. Furthermore, he may feel that there is no way for either the Soviet Union or the United States to defend themselves against an all-out atomic attack of the other. In view of these premises, he might find it quite difficult to justify his feeling that we should continue to increase the military power of the United States.

Stimulating the memory. It is often possible for the sequence of topics to have an effect upon the respondent's recall of relevant detail, and subsequently upon the possibility of chronological or inferential confusion clouding his reports.

There are several remedies for this. For example, the respondent might be asked to give the most easily recalled facts first. These may be more easily recalled because they happened more recently or because they were more ego-involved for the respondent. In an interview to determine the relationship between student adjustment to a field of study and the factors which influenced him to pursue this field, it might be preferable to begin by discussing his adjustment to the field in which he is presently engaged. After this has been developed sufficiently, an abrupt transition could be made to the question of how he decided to enter the field. (Reasons for using either abrupt or smooth transitions from one topic to another will be discussed later in the chapter.)

In this case, it is clear that discussing the person's adjustment in his field of endeavor is inevitably going to bring about certain associations with how he got into the field and how things actually were in the field compared to his expectations. When shifting to the second topic of how he decided to go into the field, every effort must be made by the interviewer to help the respondent overcome chronological confusion by distinguishing between his reasons for preferring the field now that he is in it and his initial reasons which involved preliminary perceptions and expectations.

It is also possible to minimize the problem of inferential confusion in an interview having two distinctly different kinds of topics, one which asks the person for specific factual details about certain events or a certain period of time and another topic which asks the person for his judgments, opinions, or overall perspectives on these events or period of time. In this case, it is highly probable that a more accurate account of the person's overall feelings and views can be obtained if we first develop the detailed facts of the events. In this way, the respondent is allowed to review in detail with the help of the interviewer the specific factual events which have to be considered in order to make a valid overall judgment of the situation.

Maximizing facilitators. If we wish to get off to a good start in the interview and build rapport, it is often helpful to begin with a particular subtopic that maximizes the amount of recognition to be given to the respondent or which gives him a chance to obtain sympathetic understanding or catharsis, or to begin with a topic that stimulates his need for meaning and raises questions that arouse his interest.

In some complex interviews, there may be three or four topics that would have great natural interest for the respondent and another three or four that would be quite boring or inconsequential for him. Sometimes it is helpful to alternate between one type of topic and the other.

Varying the sequence of topics with the respondent. In some cases, it is quite clear that one sequence of topics is better for maximizing the flow of information and maintaining optimum interpersonal relations than another, and that this optimum sequence would be the same for all respondents. In other cases, it may be apparent that the optimum sequence varies from respondent to respondent, depending upon the nature of each respondent's particular relationship to the topic or his particular experience. It may be necessary to do exploratory interviews to know whether we can use a fixed sequence of topics or whether we should allow it to vary to fit the needs of a particular respondent.

There are several ways in which the interviewer can allow the respondent to select his own sequence. The first way is simply to begin the interview with a broad question covering all the topics and subtopics and then allow the respondent to begin where he chooses. Once he finishes the subtopic with which he began, the same general question or another one slightly narrowed may be asked, allowing him to pursue any of the remaining subtopics. For example, in interviewing disaster victims, we needed to know what the person actually *observed* during the crisis period, what he *did* during the crisis period both to protect himself and to help others, what he thought about what was going on, and numerous subtopics covering the later phase of relief and rehabilitation which may have lasted for days or weeks. The subtopics of the crisis period could be introduced by the general question, "Tell me what happened to you in the storm." The subtopics related to the relief and rehabilitation period could be introduced by the broad question, "Tell me about some of the relief work that went on after the storm was all over."

Another means of giving the respondent the choice of topic sequence is to simply announce at the beginning that you are going to cover three or four topics and give the respondent his choice as to where he should begin, as in this example:

Metropolitan Studies is interested in your opinion on three issues which are being discussed on the local scene. The first is the antivivisection issue; the second is the issue of metropolitan government; and the third is the juvenile delinquency wave. With which of these would you like to begin?

A third general tactic for allowing the respondent to discuss topics in his own sequence is to use a pivot question to introduce a new topic area. This method is discussed in detail in the following section.

Introducing each topic

Once we have decided whether or not we can predetermine the order of topics and if so how, we need to consider how each new topic or subtopic can best be introduced.

Using lead-in questions. A lead-in question is one that is not directly relevant to the objectives of the interview but which has the function of effectively leading the respondent to a relevant question area in a way that prepares him to give more accurate and valid information. In some cases, where none of the questions seems to be of any great interest to the respondent, it is helpful to ask a preliminary question that is interesting to him and also related to the topics which follow. This we might call the interest lead-in question.

Sometimes if the respondent is not psychologically prepared for a question the answer will be inaccurate and unreliable. For example, Haberman[1] found that without any lead-in questions the answer to the simple question, "What was the last grade in school you completed?" disagreed about 38 percent of the time with the answers given by the same people three years later. He suggested using three lead-in questions to prepare the respondent for the fourth:

1. "Did you have a chance to get as much education as you wanted?"
2. "How old were you when you were last in school?"
3. "What was the name of the last school you attended?"
4. "What was the last grade in school you completed?"

In this case the lead-in questions help to stimulate the respondent's memory, give him a face-saving chance to say he did not have a chance to get as much education as he wanted, and perhaps suggest that the interviewer could possibly check with the school that the respondent names. In any case, the lead-ins improve the reliability of the answers.

Another type of lead-in question is the chronological lead-in. This is a question regarding a point or period in time which precedes the period relevant to the objectives of the interview. This type of warm-up question gives the respondent a chance to get in a reminiscent mood which stimulates recall of a particular period of time. It also prevents chronological confusion by having the respondent looking forward in his mind to a bit of the past rather than looking back at it from the perspective of the present. For example, if we are interested in an employee's view of management's handling of an educational meeting for the employees, it might be well to introduce the topic with a question such as, "When did you first know there was going to be a special meeting for the employees?" This question might be followed by other lead-in questions such as, "Where was the meeting held?" "Who did you go to the meeting with?" These questions all establish a specific, concrete feeling of the past and lead the respondent up to the point of evaluating the meeting itself.

Another function of the lead-in question is to establish an appropriate atmosphere by allowing the interviewer to display the proper attitudes toward the respondent and toward a subject matter closely related to

---

[1] P. W. Haberman and J. Sheinberg, *Public Opinion Quarterly*, vol. 30 (1966), pp. 295–301.

the relevant information. For example, if the purpose of the interview is to discover problems North American students have adjusting to their Colombian host families, the interview with the Colombian *señora* could begin with a lead-in question or lead-in topic about problems *other señoras* have had with their North American guests.

All types of lead-in questions (or statements that imply a question) share one characteristic. The information sought by the lead-in question is not going to be used in the analysis of the data because it is not directly relevant to the objectives of the interview.

Using pivot questions. A pivot question acts as a turning point in the line of questioning by determining which of two or more possible new topics would apply to the particular respondent. The pivot question is sometimes called a "contingency question," particularly when used in a questionnaire. Whenever we introduce a new topic for discussion in an interview, we usually make certain assumptions regarding the appropriateness of the new line of questioning. We assume that the respondent has had the appropriate experiences (*a*) to understand the question and (*b*) to have some relevant information. The pivot question is an attempt to test these assumptions before proceeding with the next topic.

We cannot always anticipate the need for pivot questions in advance simply because we are not aware of the assumptions we are making regarding the experiences of the respondent. It is often necessary, therefore, to do some exploratory nonscheduled interviews to determine the type and location of needed pivot questions. In this phase, the interviewer, instead of using predetermined pivot questions, must be constantly alert for unanticipated pivot *responses* which indicate a need for a change in the line of questioning.

For example, in the study of academic freedom mentioned previously, it was assumed that restrictions of academic freedom would center about controversial issues in economics and politics, particularly as they related to Communism. It was discovered that in a small minority of colleges, political issues had neither arisen nor been repressed. Instead, the main issues involved conflicts between fundamentalistic religious beliefs and the findings of the biological and social sciences. A professor might be threatened with dismissal if he insisted upon discussing Darwin's theory of evolution in a biology course. Only in interviewing a professor at such a college did it become apparent that the study of academic freedom had been based upon the assumption that such controversies between science and religion were no longer live issues on college campuses.

Similarly, in interviewing respondents living in disaster-stricken communities, the interviewer would often assume that because the respondent was a resident of the community he would be able to give information on the disaster's effects on the community. In some cases, this was proved incorrect because (*a*) the respondent was out of town the day the disaster struck, (*b*) he was immediately rendered unconscious before he was aware of any approaching crisis, or (*c*) he completely withdrew from the situation and made no attempt to discover what had happened or to help any one. The respondent was usually willing to give information regarding (*a*) or (*b*) but would sometimes attempt to prevent the interviewer from discovering (*c*). In this situation, much confusion could be avoided if the interviewer would ask, "Where were you when the storm stuck Judsonia?" If the respondent had been in Judsonia at the time, another pivot question could follow: "Were you injured in any way?" If the respondent had been in Judsonia and was not injured, then a series of questions on his participation in the immediate rescue operations became relevant. The interviewer might have these specific pivot questions in mind and obtain the answers without directly asking each question. In any case, it was helpful for the interviewer to know whether he was talking to a rescuer or to one of the rescued.

Although a small number of exploratory interviews might discover all of the pivot questions that are needed, it is often impossible or impractical to do the amount of exploratory interviews needed in order to completely eliminate any surprises regarding the assumptions made. Therefore, in any interview that is complicated by several topics and subtopics, the interviewer will need to be alert for clues indicating that some lines of questioning are not applicable to a particular respondent. The preplanning of pivot questions is even less feasible when interviewing only one or two persons from each category of special respondents.

Providing transitions. Once we have decided upon the order of topics or subtopics and have located the points where pivot questions can determine the appropriateness of a new topic or subtopic, our next problem is to determine whether it is necessary to provide specific material to act as a bridge from one topic to another. There are at least three reasons for providing a special transition:

a. It may be needed to show the respondent the relationship between the old and the new topic in order to help him maximize any advantages in the particular sequence of topics.

b. It may relate the new topic to the basic objectives of the interview so that the respondent may not become confused or suspicious that the "real purpose" of the interview was not stated in the original explanation.

c. It may be needed to emphasize a change in frame of reference, perspective, or mood so that the respondent will not carry over an inappropriate context from a previous topic.

Let us give an example of transitions fulfilling each of these three functions.

In a study of the effects of foreign travel, we included the following five topics, in the order indicated:

1. The respondent's specific experiences abroad within the past two years.
2. The effects of these experiences in *changing* his views of the foreign country.
3. The effects of these experiences in *changing* his views of his own country.
4. Courses taken in college that influenced the meaningfulness of the foreign experience.
5. Certain personality traits that might affect the respondent's adjustment to the foreign culture.

In the first few exploratory interviews it was discovered that the respondent usually did not make the correct connection between topics 1 and 2. His tendency was often to merely talk about interesting experiences he had abroad under the first topic and then forget to make any connection between these experiences and specific *changes* in his views of the foreign country. It was found helpful to provide the following transition:

> You have told me about many of your experiences abroad which you found outstanding. Now that you have had a chance to think about your experiences in Germany, let us move on to a more difficult topic. I would like to know how any of these experiences you have mentioned, or any others you might recall, changed your views on Germany, the German people, or their culture. It is sometimes helpful to think of those things which surprised you because they were not what you expected or those which seemed to give you a more positive or negative feeling toward the country. Which of your experiences seemed to change your views on Germany?

Even with this transition aimed at making a connection between specific experiences and changes in beliefs or attitudes, there was still a tendency for the respondent to begin discussing his current views on the foreign country without stating whether these were new views gained by his recent experience or whether they were old views held before going abroad. The interviewer had to be constantly alert to establish which views represented *changes* and which specific experiences were associated with these changes. Needless to say, the respondent often found it difficult to link a particular change to a particular experience. In any case, providing the transition made it easier for the respondent to see the second topic in its proper perspective and reduced the number of times the interviewer had to redirect the respondent toward the objectives of the interview.

The second function of the transition as described in (b) above can also be illustrated with this same interview. Most interviewers discovered in the first exploratory interview that a transition was needed between topics 4 and 5. Since the first four topics had all obviously dealt with effects of foreign travel, specific questions under the fifth topic seemed out of place to the respondent. For example, questions like the following needed some transition:

> In a group discussion do you usually tend to be one of the listeners or one who does much of the talking?
>
> Do you enjoy making introductions at a party when you discover that some of the people aren't acquainted with each other?

Without some special attention to topic transition, these questions may seem so out of context to the respondent that he becomes suspicious that the whole interview "is really an indirect attempt to psychoanalyze me." As one respondent put it, "I thought you said you were interested in the effects of foreign experience, but now it looks like you forgot to bring your couch along." This suspicion can be avoided by a transitional statement such as the one that follows:

> It is claimed by some people interested in this problem that the same foreign experience would have very different effects upon two people with different basic personality traits. I am going to ask you ten simple, straightforward questions about the type of person you think you are.

This transitional statement proved helpful in allaying suspicion about the relevance of the final ten questions and also signaled to the respondent that the questions were not intended to be deep or devious.

The third function of the transitional statement described in (c) above is perhaps the most frequent. When two consecutive topics involve different but related frames of reference which might become confused in the respondent's mind, it is necessary to make a complete break between the two topics so that the old frame of reference is not unconsciously retained in the new topic. For example, in a study of factors influencing college students' choice of a vocation, college seniors were interviewed to determine: (a) the occupational field they had chosen and the extent to which they were sure of their choice; (b) their conception of the ideal way of making a living; and (c) the compromises with reality students made in selecting an occupation. In the exploratory interviews it was discovered that the respondents found it difficult to shift from the realistic frame of reference in the first topic (a) to the "ideal" frame of reference called for by the second topic (b). There was a tendency for the students not to want anything obviously beyond their reach. In some cases, it might have been a bit ego-threatening to be reminded of the differences between one's realistic plans and one's ideal. The following transitional statement, however, helped encourage the respondent to relinquish his realism and to more enthusiastically discuss the idealistic conceptions called for in the second topic.

You have given me a clear idea of what you want to do vocationally after you graduate, and I get the feeling that you are very realistic and clear in your plans. Now I would like you to just let yourself go, throw realism to the winds and talk about what you see as the *ideal* way of making a living. By ideal, I simply mean that you are to consider only what you would *enjoy* doing for a livng. Assume that there would be no question of your having the ability or talent needed, no problems in obtaining the necessary training, the job paid well and had high status in the world. The only taint of reality which I want you to retain is in limiting yourself to choosing some type of job which really exists. So take your pick, what type of job would you enjoy most, assuming that you could obtain such a job and were capable of holding it?

This preliminary statement helped the respondent make a transition into the mood needed to encourage such unrealistic talk. Once the respondent caught the spirit and realized that the interviewer was not going to judge him for his lack of realism, it was not difficult for him to relinquish the realism of the previous topic. After the second topic was carefully explored, the respondent was brought back to reality by being asked what real limitations prevented him from aspiring to his ideal job.

In the above examples we have emphasized those situations where special care must be taken in making a transition either to maintain a connection between two topics, to show the relevance of a new topic, or to abruptly sever the connection between one topic and the next to prevent carrying over an inappropriate frame of reference. In some cases, however, the flow of the topics is such that no particular care must be taken in making the transitions, because all of the topics obviously fall within the interview objectives, the relationship of each topic is obvious to the respondent, and each topic happily provides an appropriate background or frame of reference for the subsequent one. This lack of any need for special transitional statements is sometimes referred to as the "smooth" or the "natural" transition that can be achieved by merely arranging the topics in the correct order.

Preparing an interview guide

To clarify the meaning of "interview guide," let us compare it with two related instruments, the interview schedule and the questionnaire. Theoretically, the *questionnaire* has built-in all of the techniques and tactics of gathering the relevant information, so that nothing is left for the interviewer to do. The questionnaire may be either mailed to the respondent or handed to him in person, and it is supposed to be completely sufficient in specifying what information is relevant and in motivating the respondent to write in the information.

An *interview schedule*, as the questionnaire, specifies the questions to be asked, fixes their wording, supplies contexts where the need is anticipated, and determines the degree of answer structure to be supplied by the interviewer. Here, the interviewer is still necessary. He is needed from time to time (1) to clarify the intent of the question, (2) to probe for any clarification or elaboration of the responses so as to meet the objectives of the interview, and (3) to motivate the respondent by demonstrating appropriate attitudes toward the interviewing task, the information received, or the respondent himself.

An *interview guide* is used in the nonscheduled interview. In contrast to the interview schedule, which emphasizes the *means* of obtaining information, the interview guide emphasizes the *goals* of the interview in terms of the topics to be explored and the criteria of a relevant and adequate response. The interview guide is like the interview schedule in that it provides the framework for recording the responses or for keeping a running inventory of which objectives have been met and which ones have not. Thus the interview guide provides the interviewer with a conceptual map of the areas to be covered and a convenient way of recording the progress of the interview.

In actual practice, plans made by the interviewer may fall at some point between the interview guide, which provides only the *goals*, and the interview schedule, which provides the *complete means* to the objectives of the interview. To give a typical example, an interview guide might contain not only the list of topics to be covered but also a tentative sequence for covering them, alternative wordings of some specific questions, notes indicating where contexts and transitions should be supplied, and possible sequences of detailed questions within topics which may or may not be needed in each interview.

It is advisable, even in an apparently simple interview topic, to prepare an interview guide before approaching the first respondent. This is fruitful even though it may be necessary to change the guide or to structure it in greater detail as a result of experience. In some cases, it is possible and desirable for the interviewer to memorize the interview guide. In other cases, the guide might be memorized except for an answer sheet upon which the respondent's open-ended answers are coded during the interview.

Thus far, we have examined some of the tactical problems in determining the optimum sequence of topics within an interview and of introducing new topics with lead-ins, pivot questions, and transitional statements. Let us now examine the tactical problems of guiding and motivating the respondent toward the objectives of a particular topic.

Here we will spell out some of the basic question patterns which can be used to develop a topic.

GENERAL PATTERNS OF QUESTIONS FOR DEVELOPING A TOPIC

It is usually not sufficient for the interviewer simply to have an interview guide listing the general objectives and subtopics of an interview, and then to ask only one question per topic. The interviewer must be constantly alert to guide the respondent toward the objectives of each topic by supplying any additional statements or questions to obtain further clarification or elaboration needed to meet the objectives of the interview. These additional questions, which are not specified in advance for all respondents but which the interviewer sees are needed to obtain more exact information, are usually referred to as "probes."

In this section we will deal with some of the basic patterns of questions that can often be employed in developing a topic to minimize the necessity for probing, and in the next section we will discuss several patterns of probing, showing their strengths and weaknesses.

The two general patterns of questions to be dealt with here are the "funnel sequence" and the "inverted funnel sequence." Each is useful under certain specified conditions that may usually be determined in advance of a particular interview. Both of these sequences are patterns of question-scope described as a technique in the preceding chapter.

The funnel sequence

In the funnel sequence each successive question has a narrower *scope* than the previous one and is either included within or related to the previous question. This type of sequence may characterize the whole interview as a unit, but it is more likely to occur within particular topics or subtopics of the interview.

For example, if we were interested in discovering how people's views of social problems are related to the magazines they read, we might want to know what sorts of things the respondent thinks of as social problems, the relative seriousness of each, the amount of information he has on the subject, the sources of his information, and whether certain magazines have influenced his thinking on the problem. If we were to ask the following questions, the sequence given below would be a funnel sequence.

1. What do you think are some of the most important social problems in the world today, and why?
2. Of all the problems you have just mentioned, which one do you think is the most important one to solve?

3. Where have you gotten most of your information about problem X?

4. Do you read *U.S. News and World Report?*

The above example might be more accurately described as two funnel sequences, since the scope of question 2 is clearly within that of question 1, and the scope of question 4 falls within question 3, but it is not clear that the scope of question 3 falls within that of question 2.

There are several situations in which the funnel sequence will avoid tactical problems and minimize the need for probing. We will discuss the four most important ones.

a. When the objective of the interview is to obtain a detailed description of an event or situation and when the respondent is motivated to give a spontaneous account of his experiences in that situation, then introducing the topic with the broadest question will often eliminate the need for asking myriad, detailed questions.

Under the above conditions it is more efficient if we can avoid asking every detailed question; also, it is often more conducive to good interpersonal relations, since the interviewer interrupts the respondent less and is apparently interested in whatever is important to the respondent. Of course, there is always the danger of the broad question allowing the respondent to roam too far afield, but the alert interviewer can prevent this with fewer interruptions than if he had to ask every minute question.

For example, if we wish to know hundreds of details regarding a person's experience when his town was struck by a tornado, we could either begin by asking detailed questions such as, "Were you home when the tornado struck?" "Did you see the black funnel approaching before it struck?" "What did it do to your house?" "Are you married?" "Do you have any children?" "Were any of your immediate family injured?" "Were you injured?" "Did anyone help you after the tornado passed?" "Did you help anyone else?" "Were you able to take anyone to the hospital?" This approach would be much less efficient and much less likely to give the respondent an opportunity for recognition, sympathetic understanding, and catharsis, or to fulfill his need for meaning than if the interviewer had simply asked, "What happened to you in the storm?" This question is not only broad, it puts the spotlight on the respondent's experiences and allows him to tell his own story in his own way. It shows that the interviewer is interested in the respondent and his experiences rather than in countless details.

b. Under the conditions specified in (*a*) above, the funnel approach helps the respondent to recall details more efficiently, since he is allowed to report them by following his own paths of association.

By giving the respondent greater freedom at the beginning, it is not necessary to interrupt his train of thought constantly to ask hundreds of specific details in an order which might be meaningless or disorganized from the respondent's point of view.

c. By asking the broadest questions first, the interviewer can avoid imposing a perspective or frame of reference upon the discussion before obtaining the respondent's perspective.

Once the respondent's perspective is discovered, the specific questions can be asked within this framework. Then the detailed questions could be worded to conform to the respondent's universe of discourse. Or it could be used where the broader question would allow the respondent to show the sequence in which he had certain experiences; the more detailed questions would then deal with each experience in order.

d. When the objectives of the interview are both to *discover* unanticipated responses and to *measure* the frequency of responses to certain anticipated categories, then the discovery function achieved by the broader question should be pursued first.

For example, we might wish to discover the variety of reasons people have for wanting to go abroad, regardless of where they would like to go. If we also wanted to measure the relative frequency of people's preferences for Mexico, Germany, and France as a place to go, then the questions should be dealt with in that order. In this case, the funnel would consist in the sequence of the two objectives or subtopics, rather than in a sequence of specific questions. The first objective would probably have to be pursued with many questions and probes before moving on to the second which could be achieved with one well-worded question.

The inverted funnel sequence

Under the heading, "Scope of the question," the preceding chapter discussed the conditions under which the narrow question is preferable to the broad question. That discussion considered only the isolated question. Here we will restrict the discussion to cases where a *pattern* of narrower questions followed by broader ones should be used. The phrase "inverted funnel" is borrowed from Kahn and Cannell.[2]

There are at least two kinds of situations in which detailed questions should be followed by broader questions:

---

[2] Robert L. Kahn and Charles F. Cannell, *The Dynamics of Interviewing* (New York: John Wiley & Sons, 1957), p. 160.

a. When the topic of the interview is one which does not strongly motivate the respondent to speak spontaneously, either because the relevant experiences are not important to him or not recent enough to be vivid in his memory, it is often helpful to begin with the narrower questions and reserve the broader ones until later.

It seems that the more specific questions are easier to answer than the more general ones when the respondent does not have strong positive motivation to speak on the topic. Often a respondent's feeling of inadequacy can be dispelled if he starts successfully with the simpler tasks and receives praise.

This inverted funnel often motivates the respondent to take an interest in the topic if the initial, specific questions stimulate his need for meaning. This form of intellectual seduction is most successful when the specific questions can be readily answered but where the answers themselves are either contradictory, inconsistent, or unsatisfactory to the respondent for some reason. The logic of his answers may violate his value system. These initial disturbances of his mental equilibrium may rouse the respondent from his complacency and stimulate him to respond more wholeheartedly to braoder and more profound questions.

The second situation calling for the inverted funnel deals with the problem of avoiding inferential confusion.

b. If the objective of the interview is to obtain a generalization in the form of a judgment regarding some concrete situation, and if the facts of the situation are unknown to the interviewer but are known to the respondent, then the narrower questions aimed at establishing specific facts should precede the request for an overall judgment.

Two kinds of situations require the inverted funnel tactic to avoid inferential confusion. The first, mentioned by Kahn and Cannell, is the case where the respondent has no strong feeling regarding the topic or does not have a previously formulated judgment of the type sought in the interview. The interviewer's task is to help the respondent formulate a generalization by making inferences from specific facts.

In the second type of case, the respondent may have very definite feelings on the topic and a previously formulated judgment based upon prejudice rather than the facts of the case. Here, the interviewer aims at preventing the respondent from stating his prejudicial judgment before reviewing the facts of the case. Once the respondent has stated his position to the interviewer, any attempt to change it constitutes an ego threat. By first reviewing the facts in detail, the respondent is allowed an opportunity to change his position without appearing to have been influenced by the interviewer.

The latter type of problem was encountered in attempts to obtain a respondent's judgment regarding the effectiveness of the rescue operations during a disaster. There was a prejudice that became strongly fixed two or three days after a major disaster that made people say that the rescue operations were carried out with miraculous speed and effectiveness. This was particularly true in communities where no organized agency involving outsiders was participating in the rescue operation. In this case, it was better to deal with the specifics first, later asking for the generalization:

1. How many people were killed in the tornado?
2. How many do you suppose were injured so seriously that they had to go to the hospital?
3. Was there a need for blood transfusions at the hospital the next morning?
4. How do you think that most of the people died (electrocution, internal injuries, brain concussions, bleeding, asphyxia, or what other cause)?
5. How long was it before most of the injured got to the hospital?
6. Did you see anyone administer first aid by giving artificial respiration or stopping bleeding? Who was it?
7. Did you have an opportunity to give any first aid yourself? If so, what kind?
8. In general, how well do you think the first aid and rescue operations were carried out?

If this eighth question were asked first, the respondent had a tendency to base the generalization on wishful thinking. He was glad to be alive, and began to feel that it was miraculous that only 50 people were killed in a town of 3,000 where 90 percent of the buildings had been demolished. With this context in mind, his response was that the first aid and rescue operation was something close to a miracle.

However, if the general question were preceded by the seven more specific questions, the respondent's account of the rescue operation would show that people were dug out of the rubble, and the seriously injured laid in rows beside the road waiting for it to be cleared so a truck or ambulance could get through. Once a victim was lined up for the ambulance, the rescuers would go back to dig someone else out. It was rainy and cold; there was often a lapse of one or two hours before a person could be taken to the hospital, and in the meantime the respondent had neither seen nor heard of anyone stopping bleeding or giving other first aid. When this picture began to emerge, the respondent became acutely aware that many people must have bled to death or died of shock while lying in the rain.

In this case, the inverted funnel sequence had the effect of making the respondent able to give a more realistic assessment of the situation, but the ego threat involved in the awful conclusion based upon the evidence the respondent himself had given would often reduce his willingness to verbalize what he had on his mind and subject him to an unnecessary shock. In this case, since the objective was not to have the respondent himself assess the factual evidence, the evidence given by the respondent could be assessed by the interviewer and the last general question omitted. In order to further protect the respondent's ego and avoid a possible breakdown in the rapport, the first five questions in the series could be asked of the hospital officials who would not blame themselves for not having given artificial respiration or having stopped bleeding in the few minutes after the disaster struck. This example illustrates how a specific tactical pattern may be technically effective, but in certain situations have an unfortunate side effect when tested in the field.

We have shown some of the conditions under which the use of the funnel, or the inverted funnel, pattern can solve certain tactical problems. Regardless of the way the relative scope of questions is arranged in the interview, there still remains a certain amount of probing to be done to adequately meet the objectives.

SUMMARY

In this chapter we have been concerned with the type of tactics that can be preplanned to some extent, depending upon the nature of the topic, the extent to which the researcher has clarified his objectives, the amount of exploratory field testing that has been done, and the strategic setting of the interviewing.

In many thoroughgoing studies using depth interviews an excellent interview schedule is developed over a period of time by beginning with the most unstructured, exploratory interviewing and then gradually structuring the interview schedule as the information objectives become more precise and the potential facilitators and inhibitors are defined. In the beginning of this developmental process the tactics are not preplanned, while in the final phase of exploration the interview guide is refined and structured into an interview schedule with most of the tactics planned in advance.

This advance chronological structuring of the interview schedule involves selecting the most appropriate order of topics and subtopics so that ego threat will be avoided, the memory stimulated, and facilitators maximized. Once the sequence of topics is determined, then we must determine where we need lead-in questions, pivot questions, and transitional statements. Within any subtopic we also should be alert to the relative value of a funnel sequence beginning with broad-scope questions and becoming progressively narrower, versus the inverted funnel which begins with the most specific and then ends with the most general, or broad-scope, questions.

This chapter has concentrated on the types of tactical patterns which can be built into the interview schedule and the general process by which the pattern is determined. Yet there is another phase of tactics that cannot and should not be structured in advance. This is the interviewer's probing to obtain complete and valid information in response to a particular question. This is a necessary phase in the development of even the most structured interview, and it may be the *major* tactic in interviews that cannot be structured in advance. In these situations the interviewer's probing skills are tested to the utmost. This important tactical probing is the focus of the next chapter.

DISCUSSION QUESTIONS

1. How does the chronological arrangement of topics, subtopics, and questions in the interview potentially affect the results? Give an example.
2. What is a *lead-in* question and what are some of its most important functions?
3. What is a *pivot* question? What other names does it have?
4. What are some of the most important functions of *transition* statements?
5. What is the difference between the *interview guide* and the *interview schedule?*
6. What is a *funnel sequence,* and what is its most important function in the interview?
7. What is an *inverted funnel* sequence, and what is its most important function in the interview?
8. Under what circumstances are *tactics* the least prestructured?

17

Probing to meet informational objectives

A probe can be defined as a form of verbal or nonverbal behavior used by the interviewer when the respondent's reply to the question is not relevant, clear, and complete. The interviewer does not know in advance whether a probe will be needed or what form of probe will be most appropriate. For this reason probing requires thinking on one's feet to keep the respondent moving toward the objectives of the interview.

PROBING VERSUS OTHER TACTICS

Probing is not the only tactic for obtaining needed elaboration or clarification of relevant information. The general idea of building rapport by minimizing the inhibitors and maximizing the facilitators of conversation is assumed as a general background or atmosphere for the interview. But building rapport, making the respondent feel good, or getting the respondent to talk spontaneously is not a guarantee of relevant information. Nor is the giving of relevant information a guarantee that the information will be complete and clear. Probing is a way to motivate the respondent and steer him toward giving relevant, complete, and clear responses to meet the objectives of the interview.

Some interviewers use other tactics, such as sharing with the respondent their own ideas and experiences in the area being discussed to encourage the respondent to give a full and candid report. Others use the tactic of reflecting the respondent's words and feelings at those points that need elaboration and clarification. Experiments comparing the effectiveness of *probing, revealing,* and *reflecting* show that probing is the most effective, valid, and reliable tactic for this purpose.

Vonderacek[1] did an experiment in which interviewers used probing, reflecting, and revealing as tactics for motivating respondents to reveal personal information about themselves. Probing was the most productive tactic. Although there was a tendency for some respondents to engage in more self-disclosure than others, all gave more relevant information when the probing tactic was used.

Earlier we noted that one important attitude the interviewer must develop is critical listening in the sense that he must listen to the response to determine whether what the respondent is saying is relevant, complete, and unambiguous. If responses are not adequate in all of these ways, the interviewer must decide what he will do about it.

The neophyte interviewer will often ask relevant questions and dutifully record the respondent's reply, but his most common weakness is in not realizing that the response is inadequate for the purposes of the interview. The interviewer may move from question to question with mechanical precision, ignorant of his failure; or he may realize the inadequacy of the answer but, not knowing how to probe, he may either rush on in panic or attempt to elicit further information in a way that suggests responses and obtains biased information.

To avoid the meager results of the innocent, ritualistic plodding or of the panicky flight through the interview, the interviewer must not only be intimately acquainted with the specific objectives of the interview but also must be able to use skillfully a variety of probing tools when the occasion demands.

In the fixed-schedule interview, probing is usually restricted to those attempts of the interviewer to obtain a more relevant, complete, or clear answer to the immediately preceding question.

To illustrate probing within the scheduled interview the example in Figure 17–1 shows the relationship between the objective of a question, the actual wording of the question, probing instructions, and some inadequate responses that would require probing to meet the objectives.

An examination of this small sample of inadequate responses shows that it is impossible to specify the exact probes to meet every possible form of inadequate answer. Instead, the interviewer must have the objectives clearly in mind, carefully listen to evaluate the relevance and adequacy of the response, then probe to help the respondent provide more relevant information without restricting, distorting, or suggesting answers.

---

[1] Fred Vonderacek, "The Manipulation of Self-Disclosure in an Experimental Interview Situation," *Journal of Psychology,* vol. 72 (1969), pp. 55–59.

FIGURE 17-1

Objectives (specified in the instructions to the interviewer)

Since the shooting of Senator Robert F. Kennedy there have been various attempts to legislate restrictions on the sale and possession of firearms to private citizens. We want to know how people now feel on this topic six months after the assassination, without being reminded by the interviewer of the use of guns to assassinate public figures. We are interested in discovering *what* the respondent thinks *should* be done in this controversial area. We are not interested in what he thinks *others* want to have done, nor in *why* he feels something should be done, nor in *how* he thinks it could be done.

The question (the seventh question in the interview schedule)

7. WHAT DO YOU THINK SHOULD BE DONE, IF ANYTHING, TO REGULATE THE SALE OF GUNS AND RIFLES AND OTHER FIREARMS TO PRIVATE CITIZENS?

Possible probing instructions (immediately following the question)

a. Probe (for what respondent thinks should be done)
b. Probe if needed
   What do *you*, personally, think should be done?
   Should anything be done or not?
   What, for example, should be done?
   Should anything else be done?

Some inadequate responses which need to be probed

a. I really think it is time to do something about it!
b. There has been a lot of talk about that lately.
c. I agree, something should be done quickly!
d. I hope something will be done but I doubt if it can.
e. The gun manufacturers aren't going to like any change.
f. The NRA (National Rifle Association) would object.
g. I personally feel the federal government should do something.
h. I haven't the foggiest notion what can be done.

TOPIC CONTROL

When the objectives are more exploratory and the schedule less fixed, the interviewer has a broader responsibility in probing.[2] In this case he is free to decide whether he should probe to clarify the response to a particular question before going on to the next or to take a probe note at the time and wait until later to probe to avoid inhibiting the

---

[2] Barbara Snell Dohrenwend and Stephen A. Richardson, "Directiveness and Non-Directiveness in Research Interviewing: A Reformulation of the Problem," *Psychological Bulletin*, vol. 63, no. 5 (1963), pp. 475–85. This is a useful step forward in the conceptualization of the idea of directiveness in interviewing.

respondent's momentum or interrupting his chain of associations. In the less structured interview, then, the probe may concern the immediately preceding response or any of the preceding responses. The following situation is one in which the interview is not scheduled. It illustrates the need for a wider range of probing tools. This full range of probing we call "topic control."

A lawyer is questioning in his office a possible witness to an accident in which his client has been involved. He is trying to reconstruct the scene and assess the evidence for guilt.[3]

I: I need your help in getting a clearer picture of the accident. Could you tell me in your own words what happened? (1)

R: Well, actually I didn't see much. (3) I just came out of Kronsky's pool hall when I heard some brakes screeching, and the cars plowed into each other at the corner.

At this point the interviewer can do a variety of things. The choices are endless, and the progress of the interview will depend upon the alternative chosen by the interviewer at this point. Among the many possible forms of probes are the following:

I: *a.* Whose fault was it?
  b. Where is Kronsky's exactly?
  c. Just what did you see of the accident?
  d. Tell me a little more about it.
  e. Pause for three or four seconds

Here, the range of probes varies. The most topic control is (*a*) where the focus of the discussion is shifted from "what happened" to "whose fault it was." This probe also demands a *specific* answer to what might be a highly complex question. The lowest degree of topic control is (*e*), which is a "silent probe." The success of this silence depends upon whether the respondent is actually intending to continue his story without waiting for a specific question and upon the interviewer's ability to show an interested, expectant attitude. It should be noted that the silent probe, if successful, allows the respondent to continue in the same trend of thought, to elaborate some previous response in greater detail, or to change the topic completely.

Probe (*b*) does not shift the focus outside the scope of the previous response, but narrows it to a specific detail, the location of Kronsky's pool hall. Probe (*c*) controls the topic less than (*b*) because it refers to the general area the respondent is already talking about and allows him to select the particular details he wants to mention. Probe (*d*) exercises even less topic control than (*c*) because it does not narrow the boundaries of the discussion to what the respondent *saw;* thus, probe (*d*) would

---

[3] The numbers in parentheses indicate the number of seconds of silence.

allow him to continue his story, regardless of whether it dealt with what he had or had not seen, felt, heard, or inferred.

The examples of the opinion-poll interviewer and the lawyer illustrate how the variety of probing tactics the interviewer is allowed to use is greater as the interview is less structured by a fixed schedule. Of the seven types of topic control defined below, the first four can be used in both fixed-schedule and unscheduled interviews; the remaining three can be used only in less structured interviews.

Types of topic control

At this point we are not yet concerned with which of the possible probes would be the most productive, but are merely illustrating what is meant by degrees of topic control. In order to be able to discuss this aspect of interviewing technique, we list the following categories of topic control ranked in order of the degree of control with (1) representing the least control. This rank order usually, but not always, holds true since it sometimes depends upon the *context* in which the probe occurs. The interviewer should learn to recognize and to manage his own tendency to control either too strongly or weakly.

1. *Silent probe.* The silent probe is a very useful technique which will allow the respondent to proceed in whatever direction is most interesting and meaningful to him. In a sense, it is the most neutral of all possible probes because it neither designates the area of the discussion nor structures the answer in any way. The interviewer must learn to distinguish between the "permissive pause," which is often very productive and the "embarrassing silence," which can be damaging to rapport.

2. *Encouragement.* This category includes all remarks, nonverbal noises, and gestures which indicate that the interviewer accepts what has been said and wishes the respondent to continue speaking without in any way specifying *what* the respondent should talk about. This includes such things as: "uh huh," "really," "I see," "hmmm," "is that so!" a nod of the head, or an expectant facial expression.

3. *Immediate elaboration.* The interviewer may go beyond encouraging the respondent to continue speaking by indicating that he would like the respondent to elaborate upon the topic at hand, whatever that topic may be. A request for elaboration may take several forms. First, elaboration might imply a need for continuing the "story" or finishing the trend of thought. This would include such probes as, ". . . and then?" "Then what happened?" "What happened next?" Note that the interviewer is not asking for anything specific. Second, the elaboration might not imply a "moving on" with the story, but merely requests the respondent to say more about the topic at hand. For example: "Tell me more." "Tell me more about that." "Would you like to tell me a little more about that?" "What else could you say about that?" "Is there anything you would like to add?" "Could you spell that out a little more?" "Would you please elaborate on that?"

4. *Immediate clarification.* The clarification probe not only asks for more information on the topic under discussion, but it also specifies the kind of additional information that is needed. A request for clarification may take many specific forms of two general types. First, the interviewer might request that the respondent give a more detailed *sequence* of events, beginning at a certain point in the action described in the immediately preceding response. For example: "What happened right after you opened the door?" "Where were you just before the lights went out?" "What happened that night after you got home?" Second, the interviewer might probe for more detailed information on some specific aspect, rather than some particular period of time. This would include such probes as: "*When* did that happen?" "*How* did you find out about that?" "How did you *feel* when you saw the building collapse?" "*Why* do you suppose they did that?"

5. *Retrospective elaboration.* In this type of probe, the interviewer indicates a general interest in a topic that has been mentioned by the respondent some time previous to the immediately preceding response, but he does not specify *what* he wants to know about that topic. For example: "A while ago you said that your mother didn't want you to go out with girls when you were 15 years old. Could you tell me more about that?" "Let's go back to the point where you had the argument with your high school chemistry teacher; tell me more about that." Note that the form of these probes is in essence the same as those under (3) above. The difference is that the topic referred to is *not* contained in the immediately preceding response but was further back in the interview.

6. *Retrospective clarification.* This type of probe specifies what additional information is needed as in type (4) above. The difference is that the area to be clarified was not contained in the immediately preceding response. Here, the topic is changed to one which has been mentioned by the respondent before the immediately preceding response, and the interviewer specifies what he wants to know about this topic. For example: "You told me how you looked out the window and saw this big black funnel and realized it was a tornado; what was the first thing you *did* when you saw the funnel?" "What did you say to your mother that first time she waited up for you and you got in late?" Note that here clarification has the same meaning as in type (4) above, but the *retrospective* clarification refers the respondent to a *previous* topic of discussion.

7. *Mutation.*[4] This type of probe introduces a new topic that cannot be construed to be an elaboration or clarification of any preceding response. The interviewer takes the initiative in introducing the new topic, rather than waiting for the respondent to lead into it naturally. Sometimes the interviewer softens the abruptness of the transition by bridging it with some specific topic which has already been discussed or by showing how the new topic fits into the overall purpose of the interview. For example: "So far, you have given me a very good picutre of how you and the rest of your family got along during the disaster, but I need to know something about what other people in the community were doing meanwhile; could you help me with that?"

---

[4] This term was borrowed from Merton and is used in the same general way as in Robert K. Merton, "The Focused Interview," *American Journal of Sociology,* vol. 51 (May 1946).

The author's analysis of many interviews done by beginners shows the two most "natural" types of topic control are types (4) and (7). The other five types are relatively rare in the neophyte's interviews but are used more frequently once he becomes aware of their value. Usually the beginning interviewer is simply not aware of the wide range of topic control which is possible and so cannot consider the value of the various possibilities.

Using topic control

We cannot assume that the interviewer must always exercise strong topic control to attain the objectives of the interview efficiently. In some types of interviews, strong topic control may lower the respondent's motivation; it may also degenerate the interview into a "battle of wits" or into a rigid question-answer session in which the respondent plays a passive role; or it may prevent the interviewer's obtaining the respondent's own frame of reference on the topic, or tend to bias the response by suggesting certain contexts or answer categories.

In other interviews, it may be appropriate to exercise strong topic control because a low level of respondent motivation is already present, or because the respondent's task is simply to give a few salient facts such as his name, address, and occupation. Or the topic may be such that if the respondent were given great freedom he would tend to give much irrelevant information.

It must be remembered that even though low topic control may be useful in building rapport, it also may fail to obtain all the relevant information. In some cases, low topic control may make the respondent feel insecure because he is not sure what information is wanted. This insecurity can grow into hostility when the respondent feels that the interviewer has no clear objectives and is merely wasting time in chit-chat. As we consider some of the values and dangers of each type of topic control, it will become apparent that most interviews call for a wide range of topic control.

Values of the silent probe. The silent probe, rarely used by the beginner, has several legitimate functions. Since it exercises absolutely no topic control, it allows the respondent to follow his own path of associations. This is useful when discovering associations is a purpose of the interview, or when the respondent needs to refresh his memory by telling the story his own way. The liberal use of silence also helps to establish a slower pace and a more thoughtful mood. Then, too, the only sure way to know that we are not interrupting the respondent is to use a silent probe before trying a verbal probe. Using the silent probe also gives the interviewer time to think of the most appropriate verbal probe (which is often not needed because the silent probe itself is successful).

Of course, there is a danger in using too much silence at the wrong point in the interview. For example, if the respondent has nothing he is eager to say, does not know exactly what the interviewer expects, and feels a need for some support and direction from the interviewer, then the pregnant pause becomes an embarrassing silence.

Values of neutral probes. The term "neutral probe" refers to two types of topic control, the encouragement probe and the elaboration probe. Both are neutral in the sense that their wording does not tell the respondent what information is desired. They merely imply that the interviewer understands and accepts what has been said, and that he wants to hear more.

When the respondent actually has more information to give, the neutral probe has several advantages. Like the silent probe, the neutral verbal probes give the respondent freedom in following his own paths of association. The neutral probes also imply a strong interest in what the respondent is saying. Unlike the silent probe, they give the interviewer more opportunity to communicate positive attitudes through the tone of voice used. The interviewer can give the respondent recognition, show sympathetic understanding, and allow the respondent to obtain catharsis when the need is there.

Perhaps the most important value of neutral probes is realized when they are used to follow up a broad question. When the broad-scope question is more appropriate than a series of narrow and specific questions, we need some way of motivating the respondent to continue speaking on the broad topic without having to suggest specific subquestions. As explained earlier, the value of the broad question lies (*a*) in its ability to obtain specific bits of information without pointing out any ego-threatening relationships between them, and (*b*) in allowing the respondent to provide his own context, frame of reference, or perspective on these specifics without a barrage of detailed questions interrupting his trend of thought. The interviewer needs a tactic which motivates the respondent to elaborate further but does not control the path he takes. This is the unique value of the neutral probe.

Another important tactical function of the neutral probe is to give the interviewer time to formulate a more specific probe which is appropriate. Often, tactical errors are made when the interviewer is caught by surprise and blurts out some specific question that is inappropriate. A great deal of concentration is demanded of the interviewer; he must show an interest in the respondent as a person, listen carefully to what is being said at the moment, evaluate the relevance of the information, and constantly reformulate probes that might be needed in case the respondent stops talking. Needless to say, there are times when the respondent stops talking at an inopportune moment when the interviewer is not clear on what to probe. In this case, the ability to use a spontaneous neutral probe that fits the context of the interview is a great boon. It relieves the interviewer of the fear that he may be caught unprepared and inadvertently bias the response or damage rapport. Of course, the interviewer's nonverbal communication must not indicate that he is caught unprepared or is using a time-stalling tactic. This tactic should not be used so frequently that topic control becomes weak when it should be strong. In most cases, even if the neutral probe does not succeed in eliciting the desired information, neither does it interrupt the respondent's trend of thought. Furthermore, it allows the interviewer time to organize his own thoughts. This function of the neutral probe can only be fully appreciated by those with experience in nonscheduled interviewing.

Of the two types of neutral probes (encouragement and elaboration), it will be noted that elaboration probes exert more topic control than encouragement probes. The former must at least indicate to the respondent whether he is expected to "move on" with the story or to elaborate the current theme, while the encouragement probe merely indicates that the respondent should keep talking. It is possible, however, that neither one of these neutral probes will furnish the respondent with the guidance and support he needs. The interviewer must be sensitive to the respondent's reaction to low topic control and not allow him to develop a feeling of insecurity or hostility toward the interviewer.

In general, making encouraging noises and facial expressions gives support to the respondent and spurs him on to give a more complete and detailed account. Matarazzo[5] did an interesting experiment in which all conditions of the interviews were the same except that during the second of three 15-minute periods in each interview the interviewer said "hmm" "uh huh" all the time the respondent was talking. The results showed a 31 percent increase in the average duration of the respondent's utterances.

It should be recognized that when encouragement takes the form of praising the respondent for a specific response by saying, "Good!" for example, we are exerting considerable topic control regardless of whether or not the respondent feels that these comments influence his answers. We should distinguish between encouragement by showing an interest in the respondent's efforts and in whatever he may say and showing interest by praising specific comments of the respondent which may bias the results as shown in an experiment by Hildum and Brown.[6]

---

[5] Joseph Matarazzo, "Interviewer Mm-Humm and Interviewee Speech Duration," *Psychotherapy: Therapy, Research and Practice*, vol. 1 (1964), pp. 109–14.

[6] D. C. Hildum and R. W. Brown, "Verbal Reinforcement and Interviewer Bias," *Journal of Abnormal and Social Psychology*, vol. 52 (July 1956), pp. 100–111.

Elaboration versus clarification. It is obvious that the clarification probe exerts more topic control than the elaboration probe because the latter merely indicates that the respondent should continue on the current theme while the former singles out some particular aspect of the previous response for clarification.

The elaboration probe is most useful in cases where the objective of the interview is to obtain detailed descriptions of objective situations or of subjective reactions and orientations. It is also helpful where the respondent is willing and able to elaborate without undue strain or without resorting to fabrication in order to fill the vacuum. Under these conditions the elaboration probe has two distinct advantages over the clarification probe: (*a*) it allows the interviewer to obtain specific details he might never think to ask for, and (*b*) it often elicits the answer to several detailed questions without the interviewer's having to ask them. Clarification probes, both immediate and retrospective, will be needed after the elaboration probes reach a point where they are not producing much relevant information.

There are conditions where the clarification probes should be used without first trying elaboration probes. If the objectives of the interview call for only a few isolated facts, not related in the respondent's mind to a particular topic, period of time, or event, then the tactic of using specific questions followed by clarification probes where needed is more efficient and less threatening to the respondent's ego.

Immediate versus retrospective probes. The distinction between an *immediate* and a *retrospective* elaboration or clarification might seem arbitrary in that the immediate probe is related to the immediately preceding response while the retrospective probe is related to *any* of the responses before the immediately preceding one. Even though the range of choice in formulating retrospective probes is much greater than it is with immediate probes, in actual practice the distinction between the two seems to be more important than differences within either category. From the respondent's point of view, any probe regarding the current theme exerts less topic control than reverting to some previously mentioned topic. This, in turn, exerts less topic control than a mutation—changing the subject to some new topic not yet mentioned by the respondent.

An important tactical decision must be made repeatedly. Should each elaboration or clarification be obtained immediately, before the respondent can move on to other topics? Or should it be delayed until the respondent's momentum wanes or the topic has been covered as completely as possible with the use of only silent and encouraging probes? When the interviewer decides to wait until later to return to the theme at hand, he is exchanging less topic control early in the interview for more topic control later.

The question then becomes, when should the interviewer postpone his probing until later in the interview and when should he probe immediately for elaboration or clarification? In making this tactical judgment the interviewer should probably postpone the probe until later, if

1. the objectives of the interview call for a wealth of detail, including some "unanticipated" information which the interviewer would not think to ask for specifically;
2. topics, subtopics, or questions are so interrelated that there are opportunities for the respondent to give several needed specifics in response to subsequent general questions;
3. the topic is one in which the respondent can be motivated to talk fairly spontaneously in response to broad questions; or
4. there is a danger that too many interruptions for needed clarifications might inhibit the respondent's spontaneity, as is often the case early in an interview.

Conditions 1 and 2 depend mainly upon the nature of the problem and are, therefore, more constant throughout the whole interview. Conditions 3 and 4 tend to fluctuate from moment to moment and therefore require the interviewer to vary the amount of topic control he uses.

Whether using an immediate or a retrospective probe, the following precautions should be observed:

1. Do not interrupt the respondent in order to probe; wait until you are sure he has finished his current thought. If you intend to use an immediate elaboration probe, it might be well to first use a silent probe in case it will accomplish the same purpose.
2. Be careful that your probe doesn't give the impression that you have failed to hear something the respondent has said.
3. Use the respondent's own words whenever possible in referring to something he has said.

The following illustrates the difference between a good and a bad probe for immediate clarification.

Example of good clarification probe:[7]

R: In general, I got along fine with both of my parents. We lived out in the country and I went to high school on the bus, so none of the kids came to my house. Of course, we had a little skirmish now and then, but basically I liked my parents and they liked me, even when I was a wild teenager.

I: I see. (3) Tell me a little about some of the skirmishes you had now and then. What were they about?

---

[7] The numbers in parentheses indicate the number of seconds of silence.

R: Well, there weren't too many of them. (3) I remember one when I wanted to use the car to go to a basketball game and Dad wanted to go to a Grange meeting. We finally compromised and he took me to the game and I went home with someone else so he could go to the Grange meeting.

Example of bad clarification probe:

R: By the time I was a senior in high school I guess I gave my folks a rough time now and then. I don't know who I thought I was kidding, because I always came out second best and usually cut off my nose to spite my face.

I: Why do you suppose you usually lost the battle?

R: I wouldn't say I lost the battle because there wasn't really any open fight. I was just stubborn and wouldn't do things just because I thought my folks wanted me to.

Although using the right tactic does not always guarantee complete success, these two excerpts are typical of the tactics and the results obtained by two different interviewers working on the same study of parent-child conflict in families with teenage children. Note that both interviewers are trying to obtain more specific description of some concrete conflict situation. The first interviewer actually has two probes in one in that he first gives an encouraging "I see" followed by a three-second silent probe. He then makes it clear that he has been listening and is interested by using the respondent's own key word, "skirmishes," in phrasing the probe. In return, the respondent gives some detail regarding a concrete instance of conflict with his father.

The second interviewer has precisely the same problem as the first, in that the previous response was general, vague, and unclear. However, his attempt to clarify is unsuccessful for several possible reasons. First, he interrupts the respondent to ask the question (since he allowed no silence before probing); second, he does not use the respondent's own words in phrasing the probe. Instead of asking, "How did you give your folks a rough time?" he attempts to paraphrase what he thinks is the central ideal of the response. This paraphrase is perceived as inaccurate by the respondent who, instead of giving any concrete information, defensively denies that there was a "battle."

The interviewer must take particular care to prevent giving the impression that he has not heard or remembered pertinent information when using retrospective probes. It is also probably more important to use the words of the respondent so that he can immediately recognize the exact point the interviewer is probing. Sometimes it is helpful to preface the retrospective probe with a contextual statement which provides a clearer orientation to the past point being probed and which gives the respondent recognition for information already given on the particular point. For example:

I: Very good! Now let's go back to the point where you had the first disagreement with your parents over dating. You mentioned that you wanted to take this girl to the strawberry festival and your mother objected. Tell me a little more about that situation.

This is infinitely better than the following probe which indicates a certain degree of insensitivity to the problem from the respondent's point of view:

I: Now tell me something about any disagreements you had with your parents over dating!

This probe does not show the respondent that the interviewer heard, remembered, and appreciated information already given, nor does it provide a concrete "handle" for the respondent's memory to grasp.

The recapitulation probe. The recapitulation probe is a special form of the retrospective elaboration probe which takes the respondent back to the *beginning* of the time period covered by the interview. This return to the beginning of the story is a tactic which has many advantages when used correctly under appropriate conditions.

The recapitulation probe is subject to all the same conditions and precautions as any retrospective probe, plus one additional condition. The topic must be one which the respondent tends to elaborate as a chronologically organized story. There are many types of topics in which the respondent tends to relate events in chronological order, particularly when encouraged by the interviewer to do so. A person's life history or any aspect of it such as his marital relations, his car-buying habits, his experiences in a crisis, his account of an accident he has witnessed, his views of the changes in the social structure of his community, or his political behavior—all may be elicited in story form.

The following three examples of recapitulation probes are taken respectively from interviews on human behavior in disasters, car-buying motivations, and development of delinquency behavior. After each of these interviews had been under way from 20 to 45 minutes, these recapitulation probes proved particularly useful:

You said that the sky turned sort of yellow-green and you looked out the kitchen window and saw this black funnel coming toward you. Can you tell me more about that moment?

You mentioned that the first time you drove a car was when you learned to drive a jeep in the army in Colorado. You said it gave you a good feeling. Tell me more about how you felt about driving the jeep.

Now the first time you remember ever "lifting" anything was when you were about 11 years old and used to steal candy bars and pocket knives from Schmidt's Drugstore. Could you tell me more about the gang of kids you ran around with then?

Where there is a tendency for the respondent to relate his experiences in story form, he will usually add new detail to the story the second time through. In order to help the respondent cover the whole time period again, it is usually necessary for the interviewer to follow the recapitulation probe with a series of silent probes and neutral probes designed to keep the respondent moving forward in his story. Thus, if the respondent has once covered the relevant period of time but omitted 30 needed details, the interviewer could either ask 30 specific questions or use one recapitulation tactic which might obtain 15 to 25 of the needed details.

This natural tendency of the respondent to give further elaboration in the second telling of the story gives several important advantages to the recapitulation probe. It is often an efficient method of obtaining information since it reduces the number of interruptions of the respondent's thoughts and cuts down on the number of detailed probes needed. This also encourages spontaneity and aids the respondent's memory by giving him freedom to associate events in his own way.

Another advantage is that this tactic provides an indirect way of obtaining material where a direct question would constitute an ego threat. For example, if the interviewer were to ask directly, "Did you remember to take the children with you when you ran from the burning building?" and if the respondent had been so panicky that he ran out without them, the ego threat might cause him to falsify the report by simply answering "Yes." If the interviewer, instead, has the respondent give a detailed chronological account beginning with, "What happened when you first realized that the apartment was on fire?" and then follows with recapitulation probes, it may be obvious that the respondent did not actually think about his children until he saw a neighbor woman leading them out of the burning building.

The recapitulation probe is also an effective exploratory tactic which will maximize unanticipated responses by eliciting relevant information which the interviewer would never think to ask for.

A final and obvious advantage of the recapitulation probe is in obtaining a chronological picture of the respondent's covert or overt behavior. A series of recapitulation probes will often provide a cross-check on the chronological order of specific events.

The reflective probe. We use the term "reflective" in slightly broader sense than defined by Rogers,[8] who emphasizes the reflection of the respondent's *feelings.* Here, a reflective probe is any attempt by the interviewer to elicit additional information by repeating the respondent's implicit or explicit statement without including a direct question.

---

[8] Carl R. Rogers, "The Non-Directive Method as a Technique for Social Research," *American Journal of Sociology,* vol. 51 (1945), p. 143.

In the following excerpt, the first, the third, and the last probes are all reflective.

R: The main reason I came to Antioch College was because of the combination of high academic standards and the work program. It appealed to me a lot.

I: It appealed to you a lot?

R: That's right.

I: Could you tell me a little more exactly why it had this appeal for you?

R: I don't know—it was just that the place sounded less stuffy and straitlaced than a lot of places, with just as good an academic program.

I: You don't like places that are stuffy and straitlaced?

R: You can say that again. A lot of places spend most of their time trying to work out a way of controlling the students, assuming that they are completely incapable of self-control. They have a housemother in every dorm, require class attendance becauses classes are so dull that no one would come if there wasn't a cut system, and they require chaperones at every party . . . that sort of thing.

I: Why do you suppose Antioch has less supervision by the administration?

R: Well it is part of the educational philosophy, and it would be ridiculous to send students all over the United States on jobs—New York, Los Angeles, Cabbage Key, and even Paris—where they are on their own and trusted to act like adults with no one to tell them when to go to bed, what to eat, and how to behave with the opposite sex, and then to treat them like children when they get back to compus.

I: Let me see if I have grasped the whole picture—you like a school with high academic standards, but which is not too straitlaced and operates on the assumption that college students can exercise self-control if they are not treated like children. These are the things you like about Antioch?

R: That hits it on the head. People go away to college because they want a chance to grow, to be autonomous as an adult should. I think this is a vital part of a liberal education.

Note that there is considerable variation in the form and function of the three reflective probes. Within our definition there are three subtypes of reflective probes which can be distinguished:

a. the *echo* probe, which simply repeats certain words from the previous response,
b. the *interpretive* probe, which does not literally repeat the respondent's words but attempts to reflect the meaning or feeling behind the words in the previous response, and
c. the *summary* probe, which might combine selected elements from a long previous response or from several previous responses.

It is possible to combine types (*b*) and (*c*) in the same probe as the interviewer has done in his last comments above. His first remark, "It appealed to you a lot?" is an example of the echo probe and his comment, "You don't like places that are stuffy and straitlaced?" is an example of an interpretive probe where the interpretation is limited to explicitly stating implied feelings.

Under what conditions is each type of reflective probe likely to be useful in achieving the objectives of an interview? In our experience we have found the simple echo probe to be relatively useless if the interviewer repeats the immediately preceding phrase which happens to have little emotional content for the respondent. The most typical response is, "That's right," "Yes," "Uh huh," "That's what I said," or something to that effect. If the interviewer repeatedly uses the echo probe with purely factual details that happen to occur at the end of a response, the respondent may feel that the interviewer is not listening closely or that he is being very mechanical. Regardless of whether the echo is in the form of a statement or whether it is given an upward inflection to imply a request for elaboration or clarification, the result is about the same. However, if the echoed phrase contains material of great emotional implications for the respondent, it is enough to start him elaborating the topic, probably because the respondent feels that the interviewer is aware of the importance of the particular phrase.

Similarly, when the reflective probe is one which interprets what is meant by a statement or what feeling is implied by the statement, the respondent feels that the interviewer is interested in what is being said, and responds empathically to the feelings behind what is being said. It is more important to note that the attitude expressed by the interviewer in interpreting the respondent's feelings must be nonjudgmental or sympathetic. If the tone is even slightly accusing or rejecting, it would be better if the feelings were left unreflected.

There are times when the *correct* interpretation and reflection of the respondent's feelings may damage rapport. This is true when the feeling is socially unacceptable (for example, hating one's mother) and the respondent is not yet ready to accept this feeling as his own. His repression of the feeling is complete enough to hide the feeling from himself, and he sincerely believes that the interviewer either has not been listening carefully or is projecting some of his own distorted ideas.

There is also always a danger that the interviewer may incorrectly reflect the respondent's words or implied feelings. This danger is probably greater in the interpretive-summary probe where the number of opportunities to make an error is greater. Richardson[9] found in one experiment that only one out of 43 times did the respondent correct the interviewer who made an incorrect summary of what had been said. These uncorrected, distorted summaries lead to inaccurate information and, in some cases, a lowered rapport with the respondent, who feels that the interviewer does not understand what is being said.

There are other conditions under which the distorted summary would stimulate a voluminous and spontaneous response that would

---

[9] Stephen A. Richardson, "Training in Field Relations Skills," *Journal of Social Issues,* vol. 8, no. 3 (1952).

clarify and enrich the information obtained. On rare occasions, we have found that a summary intentionally distorted to convey an incorrect picture which is less socially acceptable than the respondent's actual behavior may lead the respondent to elaborate upon his actual behavior to correct the interviewer's "misunderstanding." The conditions of success are very similar to those described in the earlier discussion of leading questions.

Mutations. Although a "mutation" is certainly a type and degree of topic control, it cannot properly be called a probe, since it is actually a general question introducing a new topic not yet discussed in the interview.

If a series of topics in an interview are interrelated in the respondent's mind, it is often possible for the interviewer to avoid using mutations to introduce the next topic or subtopic by allowing the respondent to take the lead in moving into the new topic. Whether or not such a smooth transition is desirable has already been discussed earlier in this chapter under the topic of transitions.

In general, the neophyte interviewer tends to use mutations too soon, before exhausting the relevant information on the current topic. Frequently, the beginner actually interrupts the respondent, who is still giving information relevant to the current topic, and rushes on to the next topic only to discover, when analyzing the interview data, that the first topic had been sketchily discussed.

It is helpful for the interviewer to get in the habit of asking himself whether the current topic is covered adequately before going on to a new one. Sometimes, if the current topic is complex, several precautions can be taken to avoid leaving it prematurely. First, the interviewer can obtain time to check his interview guide and his probe notes (which are described in the next section) by simply saying to the respondent, "Excuse me for a moment while I check to see if you have given me all the information I need. Meanwhile you might think of something else you would like to add on this topic before we move on." Or, if the interviewer is sure that all of the anticipated information has been obtained and he wants to give the respondent one more chance to give some relevant but anticipated type of information, he can simply give a summary of what the respondent has said and ask if there is anything he would like to change, revise, or add. Before going on to a mutation, the interviewer should always use a silent probe to be sure the respondent has nothing more to add.

There is one situation where it is appropriate to change the topic of discussion before exhausting the current one. This would be advisable when for some reason the respondent needs to be jolted out of some undesirable rut in the current topic by leaving it temporarily. For example, the respondent may have become defensive about the topic or may be fabricating information in an attempt to be consistent with a previous, incorrect statement or to meet what he thinks are the etiquette requirements or the interviewer's expectations. If the interviewer suspects this, it may be useful to act as though the topic has been covered satisfactorily and go on to some unrelated topic. Later, after he has had an opportunity to establish a more sympathetic atmosphere and to show his interest in critically analyzing the information, the interviewer can then approach the old topic from a new angle so that the respondent will not revert to his defensive mood.

TAKING PROBE NOTES

Taking notes in an interview has two general functions. First, note taking is a method of storing relevant information; and second, the notes are a tactical aid to remind the interviewer which areas have been adequately covered, what points need further elaboration or clarification, and what words the respondent used in talking about points that need further probing. We refer to notes serving the second purpose as "probe notes."

The distinction becomes clear in a nonscheduled interview in which the whole conversation is tape-recorded. Obviously, notes are not needed to store the information, since it is on the tape in complete and accurate form. Nevertheless, the experienced interviewer takes probe notes if the interview is complex enough to warrant the use of a tape recorder. The less scheduled the interview, the less topic control used, and the more complex the interview, the greater the need for probe notes.

Assuming that the nature of the interview calls for taking probe notes, there are several points of techniques to be observed if the notes are to be of maximum value:

1. The notes should not be voluminous, but should include only key words or phrases to remind the interviewer of what the respondent has said.

2. These key phrases should be in the respondent's own words so that if the interviewer wishes to probe, he can use the respondent's own words.

3. The key phrases may either be written as a continuous story in the order given by the respondent, or may be recorded under appropriate categories provided by the interview guide. In this case, the guide should provide ample space for notes under each category.

4. If certain ideas need further elaboration or clarification, the interviewer can underline or circle the key phrase as a reminder.

5. As these points are elaborated and clarified, with or without prob-

ing, the key phrases which had been underlined can be crossed out to indicate that a probe is no longer needed.

6. If the interview is not tape-recorded and the notes must, therefore, also act as a means of storing the information, it is helpful to take triple-spaced notes. The extra space allows the interviewer to fill in omitted words and phrases immediately after the interview.

This system of note taking can be expanded, contracted, or modified, depending upon the complexity of the interview, the degree to which the interviewer is familiar with its objectives, and the amount of topic control called for.

Even when a tape recorder is used, the interviewer often finds it useful to make notes of all the main relevant ideas rather than trying to note only the points that need probing. There are two reasons for this. First, the interviewer is not always immediately aware that a particular idea needs probing; it may become problematical later when it apparently conflicts with subsequent information. Second, it is often easier to record all relevant key phrases than to decide which ones to omit or include.

Considerable experience is required before an interviewer can gauge the appropriate amount of note taking in various types of interviews and before he prevents its distracting him from listening carefully to the respondent. The skill lies in selecting only key phrases and words. In training interviewers, the author has found that the use of probe notes in tape-recorded interviews vastly decreases the amount of missing or ambiguous information in the nonscheduled interview.

SUMMARY

By knowing many forms of probes ranging in topic control from the silent probe through the mutation, the interviewer has a better chance of steering the respondent toward relevant, complete, and clear answers to the questions without damaging rapport or doing too much violence to the respondent's natural thought processes. The probe forms for the skilled interviewer are a set of fine tools used to deftly tease out relevant information without contaminating it by subtle suggestion or restriction. Each of the seven forms has its time and place for use.

We discussed the special strengths and weaknesses of each of the degrees of topic control and gave several examples of probes falling into each level of topic control. The silent probe and the two types of neutral verbal probes are useful when minimal topic control is needed to avoid restricting the respondent, to allow him to free-associate, and to encourage him to build momentum and spontaneity. The immediate elaboration and clarification probes can be used when there is no danger of blocking the respondent's momentum, and the response to the current question can be brought up to specifications before moving on. If there is danger of damaging the spontaneity, the interviewer can refrain from probing immediately to complete the respondent's story, and wait until later, and use retrospective probes referring back to points which need to be clarified or elaborated.

Since retroactive probes may have to wait a long time, the interviewer must take probe notes as the interview progresses even if it is being tape-recorded. Then, when the respondent has covered all the high spots, the interviewer can lead him back over the territory to have him elaborate and clarify certain points indicated in the probe notes.

All of this treatment of probing assumes that the respondent has not used any particular tactics of his own to resist the interviewer's probing. In the next chaper we will describe some tactics the interviewer can use to counter typical tactics of resistance sometimes used by the respondent.

DISCUSSION QUESTIONS

1. What is a probe? How does it differ from a question?
2. When probing, reflecting, and revealing have been compared as tactics for getting more relevant information, which usually works best?
3. In which type of interview is there the most need for probing? The least?
4. What are some of the special values of the silent probe?
5. What is an encouragement probe? Is there any evidence that it is effective?
6. When is an elaboration probe more useful than a clarification probe?
7. When is an immediate probe more useful than a retrospective probe?
8. What is the special value of a recapitulation probe?
9. Do you need to take probe notes if the interview is being tape-recorded? Why, or why not?

SELECTED READINGS

The two references below have some of the most thorough treatments of probing to meet the objectives of the interview. Both overlap considerably with the concepts given in this book but use somewhat different language and give different types of examples.

Kahn, Robert L., and Cannell, Charles F. *The Dynamics of Interviewing: Theory, Tactics and Cases.* New York: John Wiley & Sons, 1957.

The most relevant portion is in Chapter 8, "Probing to Meet Objectives," that deals with clues to formulating good probe questions and tactics for handling inadequate responses. A variety of examples are given from medical, employment, and other types of interviews.

Richardson, Stephen A., et al. *Interviewing: Its Forms and Functions.* New York: Basic Books, 1965.

The most concentrated treatment of probing is in the section in Chapter 11, "Achieving Response Quality through the Question-Answer Process," in which the criteria of validity, relevance, specificity, clarity, and coverage are used to determine whether probing is needed. The problems of recognizing inadequate responses and probing are related to three types of interviews: the limited response, the free response, and the defensive response.

Laboratory problem 11

Recognizing forms of probing (vocational choice)

Purpose

This problem provides an opportunity to clarify the *meaning* of the different probe forms and to *recognize* them as they occur in the context of a real interview. It will also help you solidify the difference between *techniques* which can be classified without reference to the larger context of the interview and *tactics* which involve the context. This is done by having you apply the tactical analysis to the same interview you analyzed for techniques earlier.

Procedure

The following procedure, including the discussion, should take from one to two hours' time.

1. *Review* the meaning of the seven degrees of topic control described in this chapter.

2. *Read* the same vocational choice interview you analyzed for techniques in Laboratory Problem 10 at the end of Chapter 15. This time concentrate on the forms of probing.

3. *Classify* the interviewer's probes, using the *Analysis Table* provided by your instructor. Do this independently and refer to the definitions in this chapter if necessary. Do this in *pencil* and enter the probe numbers in serial order, separated by commas (for example 2,7,8,15,23, etc.) within each category to facilitate the comparison of Analysis Tables.

4. *Compare* your classifications with another person's, also done independently, and *discuss* any differences in classification.

5. *Revise* your classifications in those cases where you are convinced by the discussion that your original classification was incorrect.

6. *Submit* your revised *Analysis Table* to the instructor.

Note: You may not be able to arrive at perfect agreement in your classifications because of the ambiguity of some of the interviewer's behavior.

18

Dealing with symptoms
of resistance

The phrase *symptoms of resistance* has been used advisedly rather than "resistance" to alert us to the fact that we cannot assume that certain overt verbal phrases always indicate actual resistance by the respondent. The phrase, "I don't remember," may simply be a statement of fact rather than an attempt to evade the interviewer's question. Or it may mean "I don't remember very much at the moment" or "Let's talk about it a bit and see if I can recall some more."

In general the tactical danger lies in the tendency of an inexperienced interviewer to respond to the symptom of possible resistance in a way which converts the possibility into reality, by activating ego threat, failing to help the respondent's recall process, and converting the interview into a battle of "I can't" versus "Yes, you can!"

In describing some of the typical symptoms of resistance by the respondent and in offering suggestions for countering them, we make no promise that the countertactic will always be effective. No experimental studies have been done of a large enough number of these countertactics to show clearly what accounts for their success for failure. The countertactics are offered as possible solutions when nothing obviously better occurs to the interviewer in the situation. Each symptom of resistance will be discussed in the order in which it is most likely to occur in the interview.

SPECIFIC COUNTERTACTICS

"I'm too busy now!"

In situations where the interviewer contacts the respondent without a previous appointment, there is the possibility that the respondent will be too busy at the moment to cooperate or he will use this excuse when the real source of his resistance may be lethargy, ego threat, or dislike of talking to strangers.

The tactics that are possible at this point depend, among other things, on whether (a) the respondent must be included in a sample or whether a substitution can be made, and (b) whether it is possible for the interviewer to return at another time.

In some cases, the interviewer suspects the respondent is making an excuse, but it is necessary to interview this particular respondent. If it is possible for the interviewer to return, the following tactic may be effective in avoiding a return trip.

I: How do you do? I am Mr. Gregg. I'm helping with a study of the community which is being done by Metropolitan Studies, Inc. You have probably read in the Dayton Daily Times about how this study is going to help plan improvements in traffic, parking, and shopping problems.

R: I think I have heard something about it, but right now I am too busy to talk about it.

I: I see. I realize that you didn't expect me at this time. Since it is so important to talk to a wide sample of people, I will be willing to come back at any time you say—this week or next week, it doesn't matter.

R: Well, I don't know—let's see . . .

I: The interview doesn't take much time, we just want to know something about your shopping habits, where your children go to school, and that sort of thing.

R: Both of my children go to high school, and I don't even go downtown to shop any more since the new shopping center went in.

I: You have already answered two of the things I wanted to know. There are just a few more questions like that.

R: Well, if it won't take long, you might as well come in and let's get it over with and you won't have to come back.

I: Thank you very much.

When this tactic is used, the person who is really too busy but would be willing to talk will usually not hesitate to make an appointment. If the respondent actually has the time at the moment, but is hoping to turn the interviewer away, he realizes that this will not work since the interviewer will return again. Also, in this case, once the respondent knew the nature of the questions, she felt less threatened and decided to "get it over with."

In some cases, the interviewer has overcome resistance at this point by explaining how short the interview is, the importance of the project, that the respondent need not stop his work while answering the questions, that Mrs. X (a friend of the respondent's) warned that she would probably be very busy, but she would be able to give the needed information, or that it is very important to get the opinions of busy people rather than the leisure class.

Often, such a situation can be prevented if the interviewer is able to launch immediately into an initial question which rouses the respondent's interest, appeals to his ego, and shows that the interview is not difficult. This can sometimes be done even before a full explanation of the purpose of the study is given. The explanation can be given in installments where it is directly relevant to the information requested.

In rare cases in which the respondent is very fearful of the interview, he may make an appointment and then be out when the interviewer returns. This evasive tactic was found several times in a study of marital success,[1] when making appointments with a few of the people who felt that their marriage had been a failure and did not want the interviewer to discover it. In these cases, the interviewer learned to arrive for an appointment about 15 minutes early. In some instances, he encountered the couple leaving their apartment house 10 minutes before the appointment time.

When the respondent feels the pressure of competing time demands, persuading him to submit to the interview is sometimes of little value. He may feel tense and apprehensive throughout the interview if he is neglecting his own work. In these cases, the interviewer might suggest that he return to finish the interview at another time.

"I don't know anything about that!"

The interviewer who meets this phrase from the respondent just as he has finished his explanation of the purpose of the interview, or has asked the first question, may become a bit panicky. For example:

I: How do you do? I am Mrs. Karen. I am working with the Community Service in doing a study of people's opinions on antivivisection. Do you know what antivivisection means?

R: Oh yes, it has something to do with cutting animals that are alive. But I don't know a thing about it. Why don't you talk to my next-door neighbor? Her husband works at the drugstore and he knows all about that sort of thing. I just couldn't help you a bit.

I: But it's not necessary to know all about it. I just want to find out what people do know.

R: That's easy! I know nothing.

I: Oh, I'm sure you have something to say. You have probably seen it mentioned lately in the paper because there has been a big controversy over it.

R: I said I knew nothing about the subject . . . I think you should interview someone else. (slams door)

Compare the interviewer's performance above with the episode which follows:

---

[1] E. W. Burgess and Paul Wallin, *Engagement and Marriage* (Philadelphia: Lippincott, 1953).

I: How do you do? I'm Mrs. Gerhardt. I am working with the Community Service in doing a study of people's opinions on antivivisection. Do you know what antivivisection means?

R: Yes, vaguely. It deals with operating on live animals, but I don't know any more about it than that.

I: I see. Why do you suppose this is done?

R: I don't know. I suppose it is done to give medical students practice so that they won't have to practice on people.

I: Is there any other reason that anyone might operate on a live animal?

R: Well, of course, veterinarians operate on dogs when they are sick or to keep them from having puppies.

The contrast between these two episodes demonstrates a basic principle which emerged from experience with a wide variety of interviews: the interviewer should avoid challenging the respondent or even persuading him to cooperate. In a sense, the first interviewer is almost demanding a declaration of surrender from the respondent before he will formally launch the interview. The second interviewer simply accepts the idea that the respondent knows very little about the topic, but proceeds immediately with a relevant question without formally declaring the interview started and without seemingly trying to persuade the respondent to surrender.

If possible, the interviewer should focus the attention immediately on the respondent as in the following example:

I: How do you do? I am Mr. Black with the National Opinion Research Center. We are doing a study of how people manage in disasters in order to be of some help in planning for future disasters during either peace or war.

R: Well, I can't help you none because I wasn't even in Judsonia when the tornado struck.

I: I see. Where were you at the time?

R: I was all the way over in Searcy when I saw the big clouds over Judsonia way.

I: What did you think it was when you saw the clouds?

R: I was afraid to my bones that it was a twister. And I knowed that some of my family was here and I didn't know what was happening to them.

I: Then what did you do?

R: I got in the pickup truck and high-tailed it for home as fast as I could git. It seemed like a hundred miles because I was in a hurry and the road was full of all kinds of trees, telephone poles, and everything. I had to go off the road several times, but still couldn't get through with a car. I had to walk the last mile and a half. I just couldn't believe my eyes. With all the houses and the water tower blown away, I could hardly find the way to my house, or I should say the place where my house used to be . . .

As it was, the respondent was well on the way without having formally consented to the interview. The interviewer was able to put the spotlight on the respondent by asking, "Where were *you* at the time?" Instead of this, the interviewer could have gone into a long explanation of why he had to obtain a random sample, what a random sample was, and why the respondents who were not in the town at the moment the storm struck still had useful information. All of this would be more time-consuming and more likely to cause resistance in the respondent.

In the type of study where there is no need for a random sample and where we want to locate key respondents who can give an objective report of specific facts and events, we often should not attempt to persuade a reluctant respondent to cooperate by being interviewed. Instead the interviewer should ask him for advice on who might have the kind of information he is seeking.

"I don't want to be on tape!"

On rare occasions, respondents will consent to being interviewed but will object to having the interview tape-recorded. If after an explanation the respondent still objects, the interviewer's next move depends upon whether a tape recording is essential or merely convenient, and whether the respondent also objects to the interviewer's taking notes. If the former is not essential and the latter is permissible, then written notes are the solution.

It is sometimes helpful for the interviewer to clarify the nature of the respondent's objections so that they can be met. The interviewer can simply ask, "Would you mind telling me why you would prefer not to have the interview tape-recorded?" This question followed by some appropriate probes put in a sympathetic spirit has elicited responses such as the following:

a. I have heard some of these tape-recorded interviews with newspaper reporters on TV newscasts and they sound silly!

b. I don't want everybody hearing what I have to say. I don't mind telling you, but I don't know who else might hear it!

c. My voice sounds bad and I don't see any reason to preserve it for posterity.

d. I might say something that is not correct, or that I don't really mean, and there it is on the record forever.

The first response, if it is the genuine reason for the objection, can easily be overcome by explaining the difference between the purpose of the interviewer and of a news reporter. The second response and its variations can be dealt with by giving any of the following explanations when they are true: that no one but the interviewer will hear the tape; that the tape will be used over again after relevant information is taken off; that the transcribing will be done by people who are far away and do not know anyone interviewed in the study; that no exact quotes will be used; or that if quotes are used, the respondents will not be identified.

The third response can sometimes be overcome by reassuring the respondent that the tape does not sound like the real person since it is not high-fidelity. Or the interviewer might demonstrate how he sounds on the recorder, then ask the respondent whether he thinks it sounds like the real thing. The interviewer might record the response to this question and play it back to show the respondent that having one's voice recorded is not a painful experience. If the respondent's initial resistance seems to be giving way to his curiosity, the interviewer might propose that they try recording the first two or three minutes, and then if it still seems to cause "stage-fright" it can be turned off.

The last response is closely related to the first two, but is more concerned with the apparent permanence of the responses when recorded or with the fact that the tape records precisely what the respondent says rather than what he really means. It could also indicate a fear that the interviewer might pressure the respondent into saying something he does not mean, or not give time for the respondent to carefully consider or to correct his own responses. In this case, several tactics have been found useful. The interviewer can suggest that the tape recorder be used and that if at the end of the interview the respondent still feels the tape recording does not represent his views accurately he can either have the recording erased on the spot or suggest any corrections or additions after listening to it. In such a case, the respondent usually discovers in the progress of the interview that the interviewer is genuinely concerned with helping him express his views as accurately as possible without high pressure tactics, and he loses any desire to eliminate the tape recording.

In this type of situation the interviewer might need to check any possible inhibiting effects of the presence of the tape recorder by using an informal post-interview which is explained later.

"Why are you taking notes?"

Even though the need for note taking might have been explained at the outset of the interview, sometimes the respondent seems to become suddenly aware of the fact that the interviewer is taking notes. He may ask directly why notes are being taken, or he may merely show nonverbally or indirectly that he is concerned. His concern may be only with the interviewer's recording a particular statement or with note taking in general. If the interview is being tape-recorded, he might merely be curious about what the interviewer chooses to write down and what he omits.

The sensitive interviewer who detects the respondent's concern can discover what is bothering him and give the appropriate explanation. Often, the respondent is satisfied by the interviewer's offer to show him the notes. This offer should not be made if the interviewer cannot follow through without endangering rapport. If the notes are in the respondent's own words and do not involve any interpretation or evaluation, there is little danger in showing them. Any suggestions the respondent might have should be accepted gracefully. Interviewers have discovered repeatedly that the main problem lies in being sensitive to symptoms of the need for an explanation of the note taking. Once the explanation is given, the respondent is usually satisfied.

"I don't remember, I don't know!"

Often after the interview is well under way, the immediate response to a specific question is "I don't know" or "I don't remember." Usually, this is not a form of resistance by the respondent but merely expression of modesty, tentativeness, or cautiousness with which many people preface an answer. Systematic analysis of tape-recorded interviews has shown that only rarely does the respondent literally mean that he does not know. It would be safer in many cases to translate this as "give me a moment to think." Apparently, the most successful tactic in this situation is to allow a moment's silence and show by your expression that you are assuming that the respondent is thinking. If this does not bring results, the interviewer can say something to the effect, "I realize that the question might be difficult to answer without some careful thought." Also, the interviewer can supply some cues in an attempt to aid the respondent's memory.

All of this will be unsuccessful if (a) the respondent never had the information, (b) it is deeply repressed or completely forgotten, or (c) if the respondent has the information but does not want to give it because of ego threat, trauma, or etiquette. In the latter two situations, it is well to avoid directly pressing for the information and wait for recapitulation probes to either stimulate recall or allow time for a more permissive relationship to be built up.

There are two general types of questions that will often obtain the "I don't know" response because the respondent feels that he cannot give a precise enough answer. One of these types is the question dealing with the future such as, "Is your daughter going to college next year?" or "Do you think that prices will be higher or lower six months from now?" If the objective of the interview is to obtain the respondent's best estimate, then the interviewer will have to encourage the respondent to do the best he can. If the respondent says "I don't know," the interviewer can say, "Well, of course, nobody knows for sure, but the way it looks now, what do you think?" Another type is the question which asks for some factual or quantitative information such as, "About how many hours per week do you watch television?" To encourage the respondent, the interviewer can say, for example, "I don't have to know exactly. What is your best guess?"

In some cases, "I don't know" represents a case of incipient resistance. Here it is better to avoid pressing for an answer and to merely accept the response at face value while continuing the discussion. For example, a Colombian interviewer is speaking to a Colombian housewife about the North American student who lived in her home for six months:

I: Was your North American guest the tidy type or not?

R: I don't know.

I: I see . . . you just didn't have an opportunity to observe!

R: Well, not exactly . . . I just don't know how to put it. Because I noticed a lot of things about her behavior in my house, but they are not consistent!

I: What do you mean by "not consistent"?

R: She was very neat in the way she dressed, but she always left the bathroom a mess in the morning. Also, she would make her bed very well, but would leave her shoes and slippers on the floor. She never put her books and papers away, but left them on the desk in her room.

In this case, the interviewer skillfully led the respondent into giving the answer without the dangers involved in not accepting the response by saying, for example, "Surely, you had some impression of her since she lived in your house for six months!"

"What do you think about that?"

There are several reasons why the respondent might ask the interviewer this question after the interview has been in progress for some time. He might have already expressed his own opinion on the matter and feel uneasy about expressing himself so freely without knowing the interviewer's opinion. This is most likely to happen when discussing controversial issues. At other times, the question merely represents the natural desire to seek some responsiveness from the interviewer. It is also possible that the respondent is simply curious about the interviewer's position on the subject.

The basic problem is to find a way to satisfy the respondent so he will not feel rejected or feel that the interviewer is secretive, and yet avoid offering information which will inhibit or bias subsequent responses. If the respondent's question is in response to a straightforward fact question from the interviewer, and if it is clear that the respondent does not know the answer, the only danger in answering is that it might change the respondent's frame of reference. This is undesirable when the objectives of the interview include discovering the frame of reference used by the respondent. There is also the danger that the respondent might feel inferior or that he is being "tested" by someone who already knows all the answers.

In many circumstances it would be better for the interviewer to say something like, "I'm not sure about that, but even if I knew I'm not allowed to give my opinions. It is your opinion that counts." Or he could say, "I'm not allowed to try to influence you by giving my opinions. My job is to understand and respect your opinion." If the respondents in the study are not in communication with each other, if the interviewer has already used statements similar to those above more than once in the interview, and if there seems to be a danger of the rapport breaking down because of the interviewer's refusal to reciprocate, then the interviewer could say, "I'm not trying to keep any secret from you, but I'm not allowed to say anything to influence your answers. But I will be very glad to answer any questions you have as soon as I get your opinions. I would enjoy that."

There are times when it is in the best tactic for the interviewer to tell the respondent how he feels about the issue being discussed. However, this should be done only if (a) the interviewer is sure of the respondent's point of view on a particular issue, (b) if the interviewer agrees with some aspect of the respondent's point of view, (c) if the respondent exhibits a need for some support from the interviewer, and (d) if the interviewer agrees spontaneously and naturally. There is always the danger that the interviewer might miscalculate the respondent's point of view and thus unintentionally disagree with the respondent. This tactic should be used only when there is no danger that one respondent will communicate the interviewer's point of view to a future respondent. This condition often exists in studies of a random sample of people in a large metropolitan area.

"What do you mean by that?"

When the respondent asks this question in response to the interviewer's question, it may be a symptom of mild resistance in which the respondent is attempting to shift the attention from himself to the interviewer. It may also be a way for the respondent to stall for time while he thinks of the answer or finds a way to avoid giving the answer. Perhaps the most common meaning is simply that the respondent is not sure what the interviewer's question means.

Regardless of the meaning behind the question, the interviewer must treat it as a simple request for clarification. The problem is to communicate the meaning of the question without suggesting an answer and without changing the meaning so that different representative respondents are asked different questions.

If the object of the interview is to discover the respondent's frame of reference for interpreting the question, the interviewer must avoid providing an interpretation. One tactic often used is to say that the question should be answered according to what it means to him and then repeat the question in exactly the same words.

This tactic is of little value if the purpose of the question is to communicate a particular frame of reference for its interpretation, but the respondent does not understand it. In this situation it is sometimes helpful for the interviewer to ask, "Could you tell me what it is about the question that you are not sure about?" Often the respondent will then say, "I don't know whether you mean X or Y." If the clarification of these alternatives does not interfere with the purposes of the interview, the interviewer can say, "I mean X in this case." Or, the respondent may point to a specific phrase which is not clear to him in the context of the question. In this case, the question may be reworded or a more complete context provided so that the respondent understands how the information is to be related to other parts of the discussion. For example:

I: What attracted you to your present location in Ohio?

R: What do you mean, to the neighborhood where we live, or the plant where my husband works, or the school where the kids go?

I: That's right—you live here in Wright View and your husband works in Dayton, and the kids go to school in Fairborn. Take the whole situation; what did you hear about it while you were still in Harlan County that made you decide to leave Kentucky and come to Ohio?

R: That's easy! It was the job. My husband had some friends working in Dayton and they promised they could get him a steady job, and that's something he didn't have in Kentucky. He had worked only 5½ months last year and the pay was bad. We had a little patch of land for vegetables and raised chickens or we wouldn't have kept body and soul together.

It was fortunate that the respondent did not understand the first question above since it did not supply the clear context needed to be sure the respondent would answer the question in terms of what she knew about the Ohio situation *before* coming from Kentucky. It would have been easy for her to list a lot of specific things she liked about the neighborhood, the city of Dayton, her husband's work, and the children's school. Most of these would be irrelevant to the question of why the family left Kentucky and came to Ohio, since the details would have been learned *after* living in Ohio.

Sometimes the respondent does not understand a particular word in the question. In this case, the interviewer must be careful to reword the question so that it carries the original meaning. In the following excerpt, a representative of the Z Telephone Company is interviewing a subscriber regarding his attitude toward the service he is receiving and toward a possible rate increase. The interviewer rewords the question to avoid the word "subscriber":

I: How do you feel most subscribers feel about the kind of service they get from Z Telephone?

R: What's that got to do with telephones?

I: I should have said, how do you think most of the people who have telephones feel about the kind of service they get from Z Telephone?

R: As far as I know they have no kicks about it, and it is improving all the time.

The interviewer had assumed that the subscriber would be familiar with the word in connection with the telephone company since much of the literature included with the monthly bills had a salutation to the "subscriber."

It is often useful to give examples to clarify a question. Although they often save time and make the respondent feel secure, there is a danger that the illustrations might suggest an answer to the respondent or unintentionally narrow the scope of the question to the area suggested by the specific example. The following is a flagrant instance of such a biasing effect:

I: How do the officers show unnecessary superiority over the men?

R: What do you mean?

I: Well, for example, officers not introducing anyone but officers to girls at a public dance, or officers not going to a certain dance hall because too many enlisted men come.

R: Yes, that's right. They do just that!

It is sometimes safer to either give examples of what is *not* intended by the question or to supply the full range of abstract categories of behavior which would be considered relevant to the question. The following example combines both:

I: How do the officers show unnecessary superiority over the men?

R: I'm not sure what you mean!

I: I assume that for purely military reasons there must be difference in rank and authority to keep order under battle conditions. I wouldn't call that *unnecessary* display of superiority, but in other areas of peacetime military ritual, religious functions, social and recreational situations, housing arrangements for families, and that sort of thing.

R: Oh, I see. Let me think . . . in the social area there are a lot of distinctions which I feel are unnecessary.

I: Uh huh. Can you think of a specific case?

Regardless of the particular tactic used to clarify the meaning of a question, the interviewer should be alert to judge by the response whether the revised question has carried the intended meaning to the respondent. Sometimes several attempts at clarification are necessary before the respondent accurately grasps the question. This problem usually arises more frequently in the early exploratory stages of interviewing on a particular topic where many of the same questions are asked of different types of special respondents to obtain their differences in perspective. In this case a particular question may be very clear to one type of respondent and unclear to another.

The interviewer must also be alert for symptoms of the respondent's misunderstanding when the respondent himself is not aware of his confusion and, therefore, does not ask for a clarification.

Again, we would like to caution that our suggestions for dealing with active resistance by the respondent do not specify all the conditions for their success. However, sharing our experiences will sensitize an interviewer to the problem of resistance and show some of the tactics that have been successful for us and other interviewers in this situation.

Dealing with falsification

Falsification by the respondent is usually a symptom of ego threat or the etiquette barrier. Much potential falsification can be *prevented* if certain precautions are taken. First, if there is a possibility that the respondent may lie to hide certain facts that the interviewer already knows, it is often good to let the respondent know immediately that the interviewer has the information and makes no judgment concerning it. This often avoids the embarrassing situation where the respondent is forced to spin out an increasingly complicated fiction in order to be consistent with certain falsifications laid down early in the interview.

A second preventative tactic is useful when the interviewer has information the respondent would be tempted to hide, but rapport would be damaged if the respondent realized this. In this case, the interviewer needs to obtain a "voluntary" admission from the respondent. If this information is the subject for the remainder of the interview, then the admission must be obtained early in the interview. This is a point where the leading question strongly loaded in the direction of the least socially acceptable answer is often useful. This was the tactic used by Kinsey, as discussed earlier.

A third general preventative tactic is to leave those questions judged in advance to be potentially ego-threatening until the latter part of the interview so that the interviewer will have more time to build up the nonjudgmental atmosphere.

In spite of precautions aimed at preventing falsification, there are instances when the respondent still fabricates his report. This is particularly likely when the interviewer was unable to predict the potential ego threat in a question. For example, the apparently innocuous question, "Where were you when the tornado struck your house?" did not ordinarily constitute an ego threat, but in the following excerpt the interviewer correctly suspects that it does. He wisely *retreats* from the point before the respondent makes a point of denying his actual whereabouts.

I: Where were you when the tornado struck your house? Were you home?
R: No.
I: What time do you get off work at the box factory?
R: Four-thirty. (The respondent begins to appear very uneasy for the first time in the interview.)
I: How did you find out that the tornado struck your house?

Here the interviewer's natural tendency was to ask, "Where were you between 4:30 when you got off work and 6:30 when the storm struck your house?" Instead he guessed by the respondent's reaction that he did not want to divulge where he was during that two-hour period. The interviewer tactfully skipped the topic and an hour later in the interview the respondent volunteered that he had stopped by the Oasis Tavern for a drink with some of the boys. The tavern was demolished by the same tornado that struck the respondent's home and injured his wife and child. The respondent's need for catharsis led him to admit his guilt feelings for having been flirting with "one of the girls that hangs out at the tavern" when he should have been home helping his wife and child during the storm.

In rare cases, the interviewer may directly *challenge* the respondent he suspects of lying. For example, he might say, "I'm amazed that such a thing could happen! I think you are trying to kid me." or "You don't have to give that old line because I don't expect it." or "I find that very difficult to believe; it doesn't jibe with the rest of the picture." or "This is not consistent with what you said earlier; which is correct?"

These are very strong tactics and always carry the potential of completely inhibiting the flow of information. For this reason, such tactics should be used only as a last resort and, if possible, postponed until all of the other relevant information has been gathered. Also, the attitude with which the interviewer "challenges" the respondent is important. It can be done without hostility or condescension but in a spirit of equality as if to say, "You don't have to hide things from me; we both know better." Further, the direct challenge can be followed by a qualifying phrase such as, "If what you say is literally true, then you will have to explain to me how it fits in with the fact that . . ."

If all of the usually appropriate techniques and tactics are tried and the respondent still persists in fabricating, then the interviewer usually has nothing to lose by challenging the respondent as a last resort. The one danger is that even though the challenge is successful the respondent might become hostile and retaliate by contacting potential respondents to warn them of the "third degree" tactics used by the interviewer. This possibility can be minimized by following the formal portion of the interview with a short, informal post-interview.

THE INFORMAL POST-INTERVIEW

The informal post-interview is a "chat" which takes place after the interview is formally closed and that is not defined as part of the interview by the respondent.

The informal post-interview has two tactical functions. First, it can be used as an ego-building period designed to leave the respondent in a good mood so that he will not spread negative attitudes to potential respondents. In addition to giving sincere praise to the respondent at crucial points throughout the interview, it is sometimes especially important to spend a few minutes after the formal information-gathering is finished to build up the respondent's ego and give him a chance to express any anxieties about his performance and to regain his composure. This is particularly important where the nature of the subject matter and the objectives of the interview lead the respondent to give information which is difficult to recall, ego threatening, or traumatic. Even though the interview may have been very successful in the amount and quality of the information obtained, it may leave the respondent disturbed. If the nature of the study calls for many interviews in the same community where one respondent knows and communicates with another, it becomes crucially important not to leave a respondent with an unpleasant feeling about the interview. He might prevent others from cooperating by referring to the "third degree" or to "psychoanalysis," and similar comments. Five minutes added to the regular formal interview for ego-building may be well invested.

A second function of the informal post-interview is to detect any possible inhibiting effects of certain aspects of the formal portion of the interview. There are times when the interviewer feels that the respondent generally has been withholding information throughout the interview. For some reason, the interviewer senses a lack of the proper spontaneity. His hunch might be correct, or it might simply be a characteristic of the respondent's personality or his lack of information on the subject of the interview. If the respondent has actually resisted, some of the reasons could be verified in an informal post-interview. For example, the respondent might be uneasy about the interviewer's using a tape recorder or his taking notes. He might feel that even though the interviewer himself is to be trusted, the sponsor is not worthy. Or the formality of the situation might give him the impression that he is going "on record" even though he has been told that his responses will be kept anonymous. However, if the respondent feels threatened by the interviewer himself for any reason, the informal post-interview will show no better results.

The informal post-interview takes place after the interview is formally closed. The end of the formal interview can be indicated in a variety of ways. If it is being tape-recorded, turning off the recorder marks the end; if the interviewer is taking notes, he ceases to do so. The interviewer might bring the interview to a formal close by saying, "Now the last question I have to ask is . . ." or he can thank the respondent for his cooperation and launch into an informal conversation.

Launching into the informal post-interview can usually be done with little effort. For example, the casual remark, "Are you glad that's over?" will often start the respondent talking about his reactions to the interview. Sometimes the respondent will ask questions about the purpose of the interview, the nature of the study, or whether he can see its results. This offers a springboard for the interviewer to branch off into exploration of the respondent's feeling about the interview itself. In some cases, the interviewer may have to ask a direct question such as, "Did you enjoy it in general?" "What were some of the things that made it difficult in spots?" "Do you have some suggestions on how I could make it easier for people I will interview from now on?" "What do you think might stop some people from giving information of this type?" "Do you think everyone would be willing to give me this information?" "If some people were a little reluctant or cautious, why do you think this might be?"

Interviewers who have experimented with the informal post-interview in a variety of situations agree that there is usually nothing to be lost except a few minutes of time, and often much to be gained. Some report, for example, that what they had interpreted to be a fear of the tape recorder was actually nothing but personal peculiarity of the respondent, still apparent after the tape recorder was turned off. In other cases, the respondent would confess that he had fabricated certain portions of the interview because of his perception of the possible audience. In the words of one respondent, "I didn't want to insult anybody, particularly when they had done their best and their intentions were good." Sometimes the interviewer trying this tactic was shocked to find that much of his introductory explanation of the purposes, sponsorship, and anonymity of the interview had been quickly forgotten by the respondent.

The interviewer may actually try to obtain some of the information that was not forthcoming in the formal interview, or he may only attempt to evaluate the respondent's attitude toward the interview in order to estimate the completeness and validity of the information given. If he discovers that the respondent has withheld vital information, he may attempt to relieve the respondent's suspicions or fears, leaving the door open for another interview under better conditions.

SUMMARY

In using specific countertactics to meet the respondent's symptoms of resistance, the interviewer should not automatically assume that these symptoms signal some insurmountable barrier. Instead, he should merely move ahead gently without contradicting the respondent's claims that he has no time for an interview, that he does not know anything about the topic, or that he has forgotten the relevant information. The success of specific verbal countertactics of the interviewer depends to a great extent upon their nonverbal accompaniment. If the interviewer shows fear, expectation of failure, or hostility toward the respondent, he will probably increase the respondent's resistance.

If specific countertactics leave doubt as to the respondent's full cooperation, there remains one final tactic: the informal post-interview. Here the skilled interviewer can often elicit clues to the respondent's attitude toward the formal interview to help judge its validity, and in some cases, he can obtain missing information.

In these last five chapters we have divided the tools of interviewing into techniques and tactics. We have shown that the specific techniques of particular questions and probes may or may not succeed, depending on how they are synchronized into patterns (tactics), some preplanned and others spontaneous. A conceptual knowledge of the tools is no guarantee of successful interviewing any more than buying a set of carving tools will make a sculptor. The additional ingredient needed is skill. The next chapter gives a framework for planning, executing, and analyzing one's own interviews in a way that will improve basic skills in using a variety of tools and that will avoid ossifying one's old habit patterns.

DISCUSSION QUESTIONS

1. What are some of the common verbal symptoms of possible resistance by the respondent?
2. What are some types of common reactions by inexperienced interviewers to these verbal symptoms, which tend to increase the resistance?
3. What is the best way to deal with falsification by the respondent?
4. When should the informal post-interview be used?
5. What should the interviewer try to accomplish in the informal post-interview?

part six

Developing skills in interviewing

19

Focal skills in interviewing

Earlier we said the planning of an interview is a *creative* art and its execution is a *performing* art. This chapter will concentrate on the skills needed for the performing art. In our fascination with the give and take of the drama and our admiration for an expert performer, we must not lose sight of the fact that underlying the apparent uniqueness of each interview encounter is a general cycle of repeated activity requiring a few basic skills which can be learned by thoughtful practice.

INTERVIEWING PERFORMANCE CYCLE

As shown in Figure 19–1, the performance cycle can begin with the interviewer asking a particular question or probe, which is communicated by both verbal and nonverbal cues to designate the information needed and to motivate the respondent. Since the respondent is not an automaton, he will first interpret the "true meaning" of the question and the intent of the interviewer, then determine whether he has any relevant information or not. If he has none, he may either simply say so, or may try to meet the interviewer's expectations by saying something irrelevant or by fabricating apparently relevant information. If the respondent feels that he does have information relevant to the question, he may give it freely, withhold parts of it, or withhold it all by giving a smoke screen of irrelevant information or by inventing seemingly relevant information. Which he does depends on the facilitators and inhibitors operating in the interview situation. The respondent, both verbally and nonverbally, conveys relevant, irrelevant, or fabricated information to the interviewer. Then the interviewer must

FIGURE 19–1

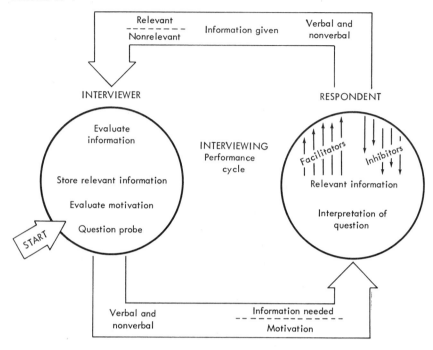

evaluate the information received, separating the relevant from the irrelevant and the valid from the invalid. He stores (notes, records, etc.) the relevant, valid information. Then after estimating the respondent's ability and willingness to give relevant information, he formulates a probe or goes on to the next question.

THE FOCAL SKILLS

Assuming that the interviewer has asked a well-worded question, all of the activities which follow involve skills that can be subsumed under three main headings: (*a*) accurately receiving information, (*b*) critically evaluating the information received, and (*c*) regulating one's own behavior at the verbal and nonverbal level in selecting and delivering the next question or probe.

Accurately receiving information

The task of accurately receiving information can be broken down into several specific skills. It involves (*a*) accurately *hearing* what the respondent has said, (*b*) *observing* the respondent's nonsymbolic behavior, and (*c*) *remembering* information received. Let us examine each skill separately to see why it is important and to note some of the factors which interfere with its accurate performance.

Accurately hearing the respondent. It is important to hear accurately what the respondent has said even though every word is being recorded on tape. The interviewer must hear to be able to probe for elaboration or clarification. Also, if the interviewer shows that he has not accurately heard the respondent, it is likely to damage *rapport* or bias future questions and responses.

In discussing tape-recorded interviews with the interviewers themselves, the writer discovered several common conditions that interfere with an accurate perception of the respondent's words. Certain reasons were given repeatedly for situations in which the interviewer had overlooked a significant comment by the respondent that needed to be probed for further elaboration and clarification.

Often the interviewer was too absorbed in the process of *taking notes* to concentrate fully on the respondent's statements. This can be overcome by limiting the amount of writing to key phrases and not looking at the paper, by using a tape recorder to reduce the amount of notetaking needed, and simply by practicing.

Another distraction was a certain amount of *anxiety* in the interviewer, who worried over what and how to probe or over the interpersonal relations in the interview. Inexperienced interviewers would sometimes report that their minds "went blank" because of insecurity, anxiety, or tension.

A third frequently reported cause for inaccurate perception was the *loss of interest* either in the topic of the interview or in the respondent as a person. This source of inaccuracy was increasingly frequent as the interviewer had done more interviews on the same topic. The interviewer would begin with a natural curiosity which was soon satisfied, and he would neglect to probe relevant clues because he had not realized what the respondent was saying.

A fourth cause closely related to the boredom factor is simple *fatigue.* The result of fatigue has been quantitatively observed by the author while supervising the work of interviewers in the field. For example, in a field study where 30 interviewers worked for 12 days doing approximately 600 tape-recorded interviews one to two hours in length, it was discovered that the second interview of each day was always shorter than the first one by approximately five written pages. The first interview averaged almost 30 pages, and the second only 25 pages. The effect of the combination of fatigue and boredom could be seen in the fact that the length of the first interview of each day became shorter over the 12-day period.[1]

---

[1] Raymond L. Gorden, "An Interaction Analysis of the Depth-Interview" (Ph.D. dissertation, Department of Sociology, University of Chicago, 1954), p. 122.

A fifth common cause of inaccurate perception of information lies in the interviewer's *expectations* of what the respondent is going to say and his interpretation of the meaning of the response in accord with these expectations. Instead of probing to obtain a more precise clarification, the interviewer merely assumes that the respondent means what the interviewer expected him to say.[2]

This difficulty arises when the interviewer has done several interviews on the same topic and begins to anticipate what all respondents or certain types of respondents are going to say. When the response is vague, the interviewer projects his expectations into his interpretation of the response. This difficulty often arises when the interviewer is a friend or acquaintance of the respondent or when the respondent is a stranger strongly stereotyped by the interviewer. In the first case, the interviewer assumes that he knows how his friend feels because "he feels the same way I do; that's why we are friends." In the second case, an expectation that the respondent will behave "true to type" is so strong that it blinds the interviewer to any responses that do not fit.

A sixth cause of failure to hear the respondent correctly can be distractions in the interview setting. The room temperature may be uncomfortable or the air stuffy. There may be noise or disturbing visual stimuli. Of course, the distraction is greater if it involves persons with some relationship with the interviewer or respondent. It requires diplomacy to remove a wandering visitor from the interview, particularly if that person ordinarily has access to the space being used, as in the case of the interrupting child in the home or the fellow worker in the office. All of these can distract the interviewer as well as the respondent from the central task and should be considered in the selection of a time and place for the interview.

Language barriers can also interfere with hearing the respondent. The barrier may be only a local accent, or the interviewer or the respondent may be using a second language that they understand fairly well, but which at times causes them to lose some of the subtleties of the conversation. This problem can be dealt with at the strategy level in selecting bilingual interviewers, or at the tactical level by asking the respondent to speak more slowly or to repeat. Of course, if the objectives of the interview require a spontaneous flow of associations from the respondent, the language barriers must be removed by linguistic matching of interviewer and respondent.

Accurately observing the respondent. It is important to observe the nonverbal accompaniment to the flow of verbal information both to

---

[2] H. L. Smith and Herbert Hyman, "The Biasing Effects of Interviewer Expectations on Survey Results," *Public Opinion Quarterly*, vol. 14 (Fall 1950), pp. 491–506. This experiment shows that the interviewers often recorded the answer they expected rather than the answer actually given.

interpret the meaning of the words and to assess the possible effect on inhibitors and facilitators of communication.

It has been demonstrated that trained observers can agree on the attitude of the respondent in an interview with a high level of reliability. Furthermore, this does not depend upon agreement between the observers on specific "operational" clues to each attitude. Oldfield[3] shows that the observers could agree on the respondent's attitude even though they did not use the same clues. Some would listen to the respondent's tone of voice, others would watch his hands, others would take special note of the respondent's posture, and so on.

Studies have shown how body motion is an indicator of a person's attitudes, and Birdwhistle[4] has shown how observation of the eye and hand movements of the respondent can be used by the interviewer.

Some of the common types of nonverbal behavior noted by interviewers are laughing or giggling nervously, using the "formal tone" as if speaking to an audience, looking about apprehensively as if someone might be listening, trailing off into a whisper or mumble, losing flexibility in pitch or pace, watching the tape recorder or the note-taking, halting abruptly in the middle of sentences, sighing, fidgeting, fingernail biting, doodling with a pencil, perspiring, grinding teeth, refusing to look at the interviewer, or playing with a handkerchief or other object.

All of the conditions which were previously mentioned as interfering with the interviewer's ability to accurately hear what the respondent is saying also interfere with his observation of what the respondent is doing. There is an additional factor which interferes with observing the nonsymbolic behavior of the respondent which can be called *over-rapport*. In this case, the interviewer is so spontaneously responsive to the respondent's nonverbal behavior that he reacts to it without consciously observing it. The interviewer must retain a higher degree of detachment and objectivity than he would when chatting with his friends, otherwise the respondent will control the situation. The problem for the interviewer is to make conscious the observation upon which his reaction depends.

Remembering what the respondent has said. Skill in remembering information received is particularly important in the nonscheduled interview for at least three reasons. It is necessary if the interviewer is to probe for clarification and elaboration where needed. It allows the interviewer to see inconsistencies and contradictions even though they

---

[3] R. C. Oldfield, "The Display and Perception of Attitudes," *The Psychology of the Interview* (London: Methuen, 1947).

[4] R. Birdwhistle, "Body Motion Research and Interviewing," *Human Organization* (Spring 1952), p. 37.

occur at widely separated points. In studies involving repeated interviewing of the same person over a long period of time, it becomes increasingly important to recognize inconsistencies, contradictions and changes in point of view. It is important that the interviewer does not arouse resentment in the respondent by showing that he has forgotten information received.

Of course, the skillful use of probe notes will be a great aid in remembering what has been said. However, if the interviewer is to give the necessary attention to the respondent, he must often take very sketchy notes, giving cues to the interviewer's recall but not substituting for it. The more acute the interviewer's memory, the fewer notes he must take, the more skillfully he can use them, and the less his note-taking will interfere with his other functions.

All of the same factors that interfere with the interviewer's ability to listen accurately to the respondent also interfere with his ability to remember what the respondent has said. There are some additional factors which interviewers report. First, if the interviewer is unfamiliar with the topic of the interview and all its specific objectives, he has difficulty remembering parts of the responses that are relatively meaningless to him.

Another common complaint is that when two interviews are done in rapid succession, there is sometimes a tendency for the interviewer to confuse information given in the first interview with information given in the second. The same confusion also applies to questions asked. The best solution for this is skillful use of probe notes.

Another source of memory distortion not reported by interviewers but demonstrated experimentally by Fisher[5] is the tendency for the interviewer to remember statements that agree with his own point of view and to forget those that disagree. This principle applies to relatively inexperienced interviewers asking questions on a controversial issue.

Assuming that the interviewer has accurately received the information due to his careful listening to the verbal message, his thoughtful observation of its nonverbal accompaniment, his clear memory of the past responses, and his accurate recording of the key phrases, then his next task is critically evaluating the information received.

Critically evaluating the information

The nonscheduled interviewer must be able to do an instantaneous evaluation of information received. He must be able to keep a running

---

[5] Herbert Fisher, "Interviewer Bias in the Recording Operation," *International Journal of Opinion and Attitude Research*, vol. 4 (1950), p. 393.

inventory of the relevance and adequacy of the information with respect to the objectives of the interviewer and with respect to the state of the interpersonal relations between interviewer and respondent. Without this constant vigilance there is little hope that the interviewer will be able to use his array of techniques and tactics successfully.

The interviewer's critical evaluation of the information depends upon two kinds of skills: (*a*) his ability to recognize information that is relevant or irrelevant, adequate or inadequate in terms of the objectives of the interview, and (*b*) his ability to evaluate empathically the presence of potential inhibitors and facilitators of communication.

The first skill, assuming that the conditions for accurate reception of information prevail, depends upon the interviewer's familiarity with the objectives of the interview. This familiarity must be intimate and precise; otherwise the interviewer may obtain large quantities of information applicable to the general topic of the interview but only vaguely related to its specific objectives.

The second skill, assuming that the conditions for accurate reception of information prevail, depends upon the interviewer's ability to empathize with the particular respondent. Many of the conditions for successful empathy are determined at the strategy level in selecting the particular combination of interviewer and respondent. Insofar as we are concerned with increasing the interviewer's skill in empathizing with the respondent, we must concentrate on creating conditions allowing the interviewer to utilize fully his empathic potential.

Appropriately regulating the interviewer's behavior

Once the interviewer has accurately received the information and has critically evaluated it, he must then move from the diagnostic phase into the action phase. At this point he must regulate his own behavior in a manner appropriate to the objectives of the interview and the present state of interpersonal relations.

Before the interviewer can be successful in appropriately regulating his own behavior to fit the needs of the situation, he must have sufficient facility in using the full range of techniques and tactics so that he does not feel uneasy, stiff, or mechanical. If the interviewer does not feel natural, there is a strong possibility that he may sound insincere to the respondent.

In order to regulate his own behavior, the interviewer must also learn to *observe himself* much more objectively than he would in ordinary circumstances. Most interviewers find it more difficult to be constantly aware of their own nonverbal behavior than of their verbal techniques or tactics. An interviewer can be totally unaware of the fact that he sounds bored, unsympathetic, anxious, rushed, flippant, condescending, or unsure of himself. The pacing, tone of voice, posture and other nonverbal cues can sometimes neutralize the positive effects of good verbal techniques and tactics. It is quite common for a neophyte interviewer who is anxious about the situation to report sincerely that all of his respondents seem to be uneasy and unspontaneous. This may be either because he unwittingly communicates his own anxiety to the respondent, or because his own feelings are so strong that he projects them into his observation and interpretation of the respondent's behavior.

The interviewer must have the *self-discipline* actually to *do* what the situation calls for without wandering from the course. The lack of this self-discipline shows very quickly when the interviewer is fatigued. He will find himself rationalizing that he need not probe any further; he may escape into a sociable chat on the pretext of building rapport; he may be distracted by the temptation to pursue therapeutic bypaths; or he may succumb to morbid curiosity or his desire to be a detective. Methods for increasing skill in the use of techniques and tactics, for improving one's self-observation and self-discipline are suggested in the following section.

A PROCEDURE FOR IMPROVING INTERVIEWING SKILLS

Improving one's performance skills depends upon more than simply putting in time interviewing. The effect of the practice depends upon the degree of self-consciousness with which it is done. This, in turn, depends as much upon what the interviewer does *before* and *after* the interview as during it. Therefore, this description of the learning procedure begins with preparation for the interview and ends with the analysis of the results. In a study by Parker[6] 26 enrollees in a nine-month counseling and guidance institute constructed a list of the problems in learning to interview and indicated what they thought had been most helpful in overcoming these problems. It was clear that actual practice interviewing and the analysis of this practice were reported as making the greatest contribution to the solution of the problems.

Experiments have also shown that although practice and analysis can quickly improve performance skills, the same skills deteriorate with disuse or with the lack of critical self-analysis. For example, a study by Wolleat[7] showed that although interviewing performance was im-

---

[6] Aileen Parker and Clinton Meeks, "Problems in Learning to Interview," *Counselor Education and Supervision*, vol. 7 (1967), pp. 54–59.

[7] Patricia L. Wolleat, "An Investigation of Changes in Interviewing Effectiveness of Student Counselors Associated with Enrollment in a Combined Didactic-Experimental-Practical Core Course" (Ph.D. dissertation, Department of Education, University of Minnesota, 1971).

proved by one course in counseling interviewing, eight months later with no intervening practice all of the gains had been lost. This suggests that one must keep in shape for interviewing in the same way a violinist must practice or chess player must keep playing. This does not mean that the person who had a skill and lost it will require the same amount of time to revitalize it as was necessary to develop the skill the first time.

Preparing for the interview

Becoming familiar with the objectives. There is no possibility of success in a nonscheduled interview unless the interviewer is intimately familiar with the objectives of the study. Only if the objectives are thoroughly understood can the interviewer reduce them to specific questions to be asked, anticipate and plan for potential inhibitors and facilitators of communication, have criteria for critically evaluating information, and know what points need further probing to meet specifications.

This preparatory step of becoming familiar with the objectives contributes in several ways to skillful performance in the interview.

a. The interviewer can receive information more accurately because he can concentrate his attention on making distinctions relevant to the objectives of the interview.
b. Familiarity with its complexities often increases his interest in the problem. This increased interest contributes to a more skillful performance of all the tasks in the interview.
c. A thorough understanding of the interview objectives supplies the criteria for critical evaluation of the information and guides the interviewer in his probing.
d. This increased intellectual appreciation of the interview goals reduces the danger of *over-rapport* that interferes with objective observation of the respondent and oneself in the interview.
e. This understanding facilitates note-taking by allowing a faster and more accurate selection of relevant material.

Regardless of whether the objectives of the interview have been determined by the interviewer himself or have been assigned to him by someone else, the interviewer must so sensitize himself to the specifications that the interview becomes "his problem." This is perhaps more difficult when the problem is assigned to the interviewer.

In studying and analyzing the objectives of the interview, there are several questions that the interviewer should ask himself. First, he should ask: What is the central purpose of the interview? The purpose can be viewed in terms of the central focus of the *information* and in terms of the actual *purpose* for which the information is to be used. If the purpose of the information is to test theory, then the interviewer must be intimately familiar with the theory he is testing. If the purpose is to gather information as a basis for social action, the interviewer should know to what extent the alternative actions are predetermined and to what extent the purpose of the interview is to discover categories of possible action perceived by the respondents. If the alternatives are predetermined, then the interviewer should be familiar with what the alternatives are and their relationship to the specific objectives of the interview.

Second, he should ask: What categories and subcategories of information are needed to fulfill the central purpose of the interview? How are the categories defined? Do these definitions articulate with the central purpose of the interview? Can the categories be broken down into subcategories for increased clarity or to assist the respondent in more completely covering the topic? What specific questions are needed to obtain information relevant to each category? How are the categories and subcategories of information related? What level of abstractness or concreteness is required by the objectives?

Third, the interviewer should try to anticipate the potential range of relevant responses and even some of the apparently related but irrelevant responses. How abstract or concrete must the answer be to fulfill the purposes of the interview?

Interviewers often fail to appreciate the meaning of the need for *concrete examples.* To be truly concrete, an example of an object, event, or situation must be located in a *unique time and place,* and therefore involve a unique scene, objects, actors, and plots.

Potential dangers in being familiar with the objectives. In discussing the need for the interviewer to be intimately familiar with the objectives of the interview, we have neglected to point out that there are potential, but not inescapable, dangers in having knowledge of the theoretical or practical objectives of a study.

Knowledge of the hypotheses being tested or of the social-action implication of the findings may tend to bias the interviewer's behavior in gross or subtle ways which distort the responses themselves or the interviewer's interpretation or recording of the responses. One of the best general collection of studies of experimenter effects is presented by Rosenthal.[8] He reports many experimental studies of the effects of the sciences. We have already mentioned the classical study by Rice[9], in which he had 12 skilled interviewers talk individually with a sample

---

[8] Robert Rosenthal, *Experimenter Effects in Behavioral Research* (New York: Appleton-Century-Crofts, 1966).

[9] Stuart A. Rice, "Contagious Bias in the Interview: A Methodological Note," *American Journal of Sociology,* vol. 35 (1929), pp. 420–23.

of 2,000 applicants for charity. The interviewers were to diagnose the cause of their dependency status. One of the interviewers, who was a staunch prohibitionist, found three times as many persons blaming alcohol as did another interviewer with socialist views who, in contrast, found many more responses blaming industrial factors. Rice interpreted these results to mean that the *responses* had actually been different. But more recent studies would suggest that much of the bias was in the interpretation and recording of the responses. Since the interviews were not tape-recorded, there is no way of testing the truth of these alternative hypotheses.

Just as the respondent tends to give answers that he feels the interviewer wants or expects, so may the interviewer tend to produce results which he thinks the study director, the theory, the hypotheses, or the sponsoring organization may desire. One of the many experiments reported by Hyman[10] shows that under some circumstances the interviewer will consciously fabricate answers to questions they never asked and force ambiguous answers into the categories supplied by the interview schedule when they obviously do not fit. In this experimental study, "planted" respondents carefully rehearsed answers especially designed to be ambiguous, equivocal or contradictory in order not to fit the categories provided.

More subtle effects, not involving intentional fabrication, were demonstrated by Wyatt and Campbell[11] in an experimental study of the effects of the interviewer's expectations on a survey regarding the 1948 presidential election. They found that the interviewers who expected more of the respondents to have discussed the campaign with others tended to obtain responses that bore out this expectancy.

Several different solutions have been practiced to prevent the interviewer's knowledge of the purposes of the study from biasing the results.

Using highly structured interview schedules. This is perhaps the most commonly used method in large-scale opinion and attitude surveys. It is assumed that by not allowing the interviewer any freedom of selection of techniques and tactics we will at least standardize the questions so that they will not be unwittingly loaded to bias the responses in any systematic way. This is true to a great extent, but has three clear limitations. First, it does not control all of the *paralinguistic* communication which can bias the response by either changing the meaning of the question or by showing the interviewer's attitude to-

---

[10] Herbert H. Hyman et al., *Interviewing in Social Research* (Chicago: University of Chicago Press, 1954).

[11] D. F. Wyatt and D. T. Campbell, "A Study of Interviewer Bias as Related to Interviewers' Expectations and Own Opinions," *International Journal of Opinion and Attitude Research*, vol. 4 (1950), pp. 77–83.

ward the question. Second, the procedure does not eliminate the problem but merely shifts the responsibility for its solution from the interviewer to the person designing the interview schedule. This may be an improvement, however, if it shifts the responsibility to a more highly trained and qualified person. But in those cases where the interview objectives cannot be attained with a highly structured interview schedule, the responsibility must be shifted back to the interviewer. Third, even though by controlling and standardizing the stimulus question we can avoid biasing the actual response, this does not prevent misinterpretation or inaccurate recording of the response even when the answer categories are prestructured. As we have seen, this is particularly true when the responses are vague, ambiguous, or contradictory.

Using a tape recorder. The tape recorder may be used to train the interviewer by allowing him to hear his own verbal and nonverbal techniques and detect possible biasing effects. The recorder is also invaluable in allowing more than one person to hear precisely the same interview and to interpret, record, and categorize the responses to do a test of the reliability of the data.

Reducing the interviewer's presence. The interviewer can in some instances be entirely removed from the scene by using a mailed questionnaire instead of an interview. A partial removal of the interviewer is achieved by tape recording questions which have been tested and standardized in advance to avoid any bias in wording or tone of voice. Also, all of the possible bias of the visual cues is automatically eliminated since the interviewer is now invisible. Both of these methods have their legitimate application, but cannot be used where the respondent needs active help in interpreting the question or where he must be motivated to supply a relevant and valid answer. The warmth of the human contact has been shown experimentally to be a strong motivational factor in many kinds of performances of subjects in experiments as well as respondents in interviews. For example, Ware, Kowal, and Baker[12] found that, regardless of the various conditions of environmental stimulation occurring during the signal detection task, those subjects who had been contacted by warmer acting experimenters detected signals significantly better than those who had been contacted by the cooler acting experimenters. Also, the experiment by Reece and Whitman[13] shows the same motivational effect of the warm experimenter and has the added advantages of clearly and operationally defining warm versus

[12] J. R. Ware, B. Kowal, and R. A. Baker, "The Role of Experimenter Attitude and Contingent Reinforcement in a Vigilance Task" (Unpublished paper, U.S. Army Armor Human Research Unit, Fort Knox, Kentucky, 1963).

[13] M. M. Reece and R. N. Whitman, "Expressive Movements, Warmth and Verbal Reinforcement," *Journal of Abnormal and Social Psychology*, vol. 64 (1962), pp. 234–36.

cool behavior. In the "warm" behavior, the experimenter leaned toward the subject, looked directly at him, smiled, and kept his hands still. In the "cool" behavior, the experimenter leaned away from the subject, looked around the room, did not smile, and was drumming his fingers.

Counterbalancing the bias. It is actually possible under certain conditions to obtain the same result from one study where all of the interviewers are unbiased and another study in which half of the interviewers are biased in one direction and half in the other. If we do not know the direction or strength of the bias of any of the interviewers, it is sometimes proposed that we simply select several interviewers at random who in turn select a large sample of respondents at random. In this way it might be assumed that we not only cancel out the biases of the interviewers but also of the combination of interviewer and respondent. However, this is not necessarily the happy result of opposing biases. In their analysis of an opinion survey, Stember and Hyman[14] demonstrated that interviewers holding the more popular opinion tended to report data that inflated the number of respondents with the same opinion as their own. But the interviewers holding the less popular opinion did not simply inflate the opposite answer, but inflated the "don't know" category instead. In this case, rather than cancelling out the distortion by one interviewer's bias counteracting the other's, the error was cumulative. This strongly suggests that it is much more desirable to correct error at its source than to depend upon statistical randomization or purposive selection of interviewers with opposing biases.

All of the above solutions to the possible biasing effects of the interviewer's knowledge about, and attitude toward, the purposes of the study, place external restraints upon the interviewer or depend upon counterbalancing the error after it occurs. Both solutions work under limited conditions, but become less appropriate (*a*) when the major purpose of the interview is discovery, (*b*) when there is no highly structured interview schedule, (*c*) when more flexibility is needed to communicate the question to different kinds of respondents and (*d*) when more interviewer activity is needed to motivate the respondent to give relevant and valid information.

Under these conditions, the only solution is to select and train interviewers to know when active flexibility must be exercised and how to use the freedom to motivate the respondent to give valid information rather than to bias his response. The interviewer must learn to replace external restraints by internal ones which allow more creative activity.

Anticipating potential inhibitors and facilitators. In attempting to an-

---

[14] C. H. Stember and H. H. Hyman, "How Interviewer Effects Operate Through Question Form," *International Journal of Opinion and Attitude Research*, vol. 3 (1949), pp. 493–512.

ticipate potential inhibitors and facilitators of communication, the interviewer should keep in mind that the inhibitor or facilitator is *potentially* present, depending on the type of information the prospective respondent has to give. Whether or not the potentiality becomes actuality depends upon the nature of the interviewer-respondent relationship as seen by the respondent in the larger context of the interview situation.

Unfortunately, the interviewer does not know in advance the type of information the prospective respondent has to give; therefore in anticipating potential inhibitors he must consider the possible range of answers to the specific questions he intends to ask. If some of the possible answers to the question would tend to be inhibited by the respondent, then the question should be treated as a potential communication inhibitor, and appropriate strategy, techniques, and tactics should be used to minimize the inhibiting effect.

Each topic, subtopic, and question that is planned in advance of the first interview should be earmarked to show which main inhibitor or facilitator might be involved. Subsequent experiences might prove these anticipations incorrect in some instances. Nevertheless, the attempt to anticipate will be generally useful and contribute to a more skillful performance.

Planning the strategy of the approach. Now that the interviewer is clear on the precise objectives of the interview and has considered some of the potential inhibitors and facilitators of communication, he is ready to consider the means of obtaining the information. Usually, it is well to consider the strategy problems first. If we assume that the problem is within the interviewer's ability and role repertory, the next strategy decisions are selecting the appropriate role for the interviewer, choosing a respondent most willing and able to give the required information, setting an appropriate time and place for the interview and, finally, deciding how to structure the interview situation.

Structuring the interview situation includes introducing oneself to the respondent, explaining the sponsorship of the study, explaining the purpose of the interview, explaining how the respondent has been selected, providing anonymity, and planning the method of recording the interview. All of these facets of the situation are relevant only insofar as they relate to the respondent's ability or willingness to give relevant information. Usually, it is a good rule to say that if a problem can be anticipated and solved at the strategy level this should be done, rather than depending upon techniques and tactics. Usually enough problems will remain which can be solved only on the spot, in the interview situation.

Preparing an interview guide. The interview guide has two basic functions. It not only helps guide the interviewer through the interview but also furnishes a method of recording what has been covered. To provide a method of recording, the guide may include a list of specific topics, subtopics, specific questions or categories of answers that may be checked off after they have been covered adequately. Or, the guide might provide space under each topic or subtopic for probe notes to remind the interviewer of what should be clarified or elaborated to meet the specifications of that topic. In some cases when a tape recorder is not used, enough space is provided under each topic to take notes on all the relevant information received. Various combinations of these three formats can be used.

The interview guide, particularly before the first interview has been done, should be viewed as a flexible aid rather than a fixed outline that prevents the interviewer from using any technique or tactic that might prove to be appropriate on the spur of the moment. The degree to which specific techniques and tactics can be planned in advance depends upon the nature of the subject matter and the number of interviews that have gone into the reformulation of the interview guide.

In preparing the interview guide, the interviewer must translate the objectives of the interview into (a) subtopics, (b) questions which need to be answered that may or may not have to be asked directly, (c) possible probes to use, and (d) in some cases, categories of relevant answers that might be expected. Wording of questions should be planned carefully considering the vocabulary, context, scope, answer structure, and the possibility of using intentionally leading questions. The usual two criteria should be used in selecting among various possible techniques: (a) their relevance to the information objectives of the interview, and (b) their probable effect upon minimizing potential inhibitors and maximizing potential facilitators of relevant information.

In addition to planning the verbal techniques that to some extent can be built into the interview guide, the interviewer should also do an introspective analysis of his own attitude toward the topic of the interview, toward the interviewing task, and toward the type of respondent to be interviewed. In this way he may be able to anticipate certain points at which he must exert special effort to withhold expression of negative attitudes and to express positive attitudes.

Once the objectives of the interview have been reduced to specific subtopics and questions, tentative plans can be made for the sequence in which subtopics will be discussed; how they will be introduced; what transitions or pivot questions might be needed; where funnel, or inverted funnel, sequences might be needed to develop a topic; how much topic control to use in probing each topic; and how any symptoms of resistance in the respondent might be treated.

The preplanned strategy, techniques, and tactics suggested above may not be followed in every detail during the interview; nevertheless, careful preplanning will help the interviewer to improve his interviewing skill. In the first place, it makes the interviewer aware of the differences between what he expects and what actually happens in the interview and lays the foundation for the post-interview analysis where he attempts to account for these discrepancies. And second, since much of the preplanning is successful, it reduces the amount of confusion in the interview, allowing the interviewer to concentrate on the types of tactical problems which cannot be anticipated.

Of course, the process of becoming familiar with the objectives and anticipating potential inhibitors and facilitators is necessary before any of the preplanning can be done. Both are also necessary for skillful probing in the interview.

Doing the interview for self-improvement

Pretesting the situation. Regardless of how much experience an interviewer might have, he should always pretest the specific interview situation associated with a series of interviews on a new topic. This is particularly vital for the person aiming to improve his skills. By "pretesting the situation" we mean that the interviewer should become accustomed to the concrete details of the setting and the instruments to be used in the interview before doing the first interview. This would include such things as becoming familiar with the place where the interview is to be done, insofar as possible making the physical arrangements conducive to communication, becoming familiar with the use of the tape recorder in the specific setting, practicing taking probe notes and using the interview guide in the particular physical setting, and perhaps role-playing some practice introductions by which the situation is structured for the respondent.

Without these precautions it is improbable that even the best plans and sophisticated theory could be skillfully implemented because of some unanticipated, ridiculously obvious practical problem. The following are typical examples of such practical problems found by interviewers: there may be too much noise in the area, the room may be so small that it soon becomes stuffy, there may not be the right type of electrical outlet for the tape recorder, the interviewer may not know how to operate the particular tape-recording machine that is available, the machine may be out of order, there may be no available surface for writing probe notes. Most of these problems can be avoided by pretesting the situation and arriving in advance of the interview to check the setting and equipment. There is nothing more embarrassing for the interviewer than to find that neither he nor the respondent has a pencil or that some simple mechanical error in the use of the tape recorder has resulted in a blank tape. Familiarity with the interview setting eases the interviewer's mind and makes it easier for him to concentrate on the task of helping the respondent relax.

Using a tape recorder. In order to make the most of each interview for the purpose of improving basic skills, the interview should be electronically recorded. This is particularly important in learning nonscheduled interviewing because it frees the interviewer from the burden of trying to record all of the relevant details and allows him to devote more attention to the respondent and to regulating his own techniques and tactics. Since he is able to use tactics and techniques more self-consciously he is more likely to learn from the experience. In addition, the tape recording allows the interviewer to relive the experience by listening to it later when he is freer to observe his own and the respondent's behavior.

Using the interview guide. An interview guide is usually a necessity when the interview is even slightly complex, when the interviewer has not had experience with many interviews on the same topic, and particularly when the interviewer is attempting to improve his interviewing skills. Since the guide is a reminder of the specific interview objectives, it should alert the interviewer to any inadequacies of information *during* the interview in time to test various techniques and tactics for obtaining the information vis-à-vis the respondent.

Taking probe notes. The taking of probe notes in conjunction with the use of an interview guide helps the interviewer keep a running account of what has been covered. Probe notes also provide vital clues to what needs to be probed further and supplies some of the vocabulary to be used in probing. This, in turn, makes the interviewer more secure and less likely to panic, which frees his energies for tactical problems. This increased attention to the important problems during the interview maximizes the learning value of the experience. Taking probe notes during the interview also lays the basis for a more meaningful post-interview analysis.

Focusing on the basic tasks. Once all the preplanning is done, the situation has been pretested, and the objective procedures of using a tape recorder, taking probe notes, and using an interview guide are previewed, the problem during the interview is to *concentrate* on a few major tasks.

He should constantly be asking himself: What is the respondent saying? What portion of it is relevant? Is it adequate or does it need clarification or elaboration? What question or probe should be used next to meet the objectives of the interview? What are the verbal and nonverbal clues to the state of the interpersonal relations between the respondent and myself? How might these affect the informational objectives of the interview?

In sensitizing himself to the respondent's nonverbal behavior, it is often helpful for the interviewer to concentrate his attention on *changes* in the nonverbal communication, whether these be changes in tempo, tone of voice, posture, hand movements, facial expression, eye movements, or forcefulness of speech. It is important to focus upon changes in the respondent's behavior rather than attempting a direct comparison of one respondent's manner with another's because of general personality and cultural differences between respondents. For example, we cannot always assume that a deliberate, measured pacing with frequent pauses indicates that the respondent is being cautious about the information he is divulging. If the person's normal speech pattern is rapid and fluent and at some point becomes halting and monotonous, the interviewer should note this change and in the context of the total situation judge whether anything can or should be done about the tension which is indicated.

Analysis of the interview for self-improvement

The interviewer can improve his skill more rapidly in a series of interviews if he carefully analyzes each one *before* attempting another in the series. The interviewer must not be so disappointed with the results of his first attempt in an interview series that he is sure that he can improve without bothering to analyze his experience. It is tempting to assume that it was mainly the respondent's peculiarities which were to blame for the inadequacies in the information and believe that the next interview is destined to be better. Or, the interviewer may be extremely lucky in one interview and not realize how much of the relevant information was obtained *despite* rather than because of the methods he used. If this is the case he may be shocked by the difficulties encountered in later interviews.

In order to make solid progress in interviewing skills the interviewer must resist any tendency to abandon impatiently a calm analysis of each interview in favor of rushing into feverish activity of "learning by doing."

The analysis of the results of each interview should be translated into improved plans for the next interview. In doing this it is important for the interviewer to avoid assuming that any technique or tactic which did not succeed in one interview should be abandoned in future interviews. It might simply be that the particular respondent did not actually have the information or that certain inhibitors of communication were operating because of the role relationship between interviewer and respondent. In either case, the specific techniques or tactic should not be blamed.

Let us now examine some of the specific steps in analyzing the results of an interview as a means to improving skills.

Analysis of strategy.   In view of his experience in the first interview of a series, the interviewer is often aware of some improvements which can be made in his selection of and approach to the respondent. The interviewer should make a checklist of all the strategy problems that might be involved and then indicate which ones were dealt with in the strategy plans, which of these were apparently adequate in actual practice, and which problems had not been anticipated. It is also probable that some of the strategy plans were not actually needed. Any suggested improvements in strategy can be incorporated in the plans for approaching the next respondent.

Analysis of nonverbal responses.   Before becoming involved in the detailed analysis of the information obtained or the methods used to obtain the information, it is often helpful for the interviewer to listen to the tape-recorded interview to note the nonverbal responses. At this time the interviewer is freer to concentrate fully on the respondent since he does not have to take probe notes or plan the next question. Of course, the tape does not preserve the visual nonverbal responses but it is helpful in showing changes in tone of voice, pacing, pitch, hesitations, nervous giggling, self-interruptions, and interruptions by the respondent. As was previously suggested, it is best to concentrate upon *changes* in the quality of the nonverbal communication.

When such changes are noted, the interviewer can raise the question of whether any of the inhibitors or facilitators of communication which he had anticipated might underlie the fluctuations in the nonverbal communication. If the interviewer is able to diagnose any difficulty, he can plan to meet it better in future interviews on the same topic. The interviewer should ask himself whether he had noticed all of the nonverbal messages while actually doing the interview. If some were not noted, perhaps the interviewer can discover why. If the respondent's nonverbal behavior shows symptoms of either inability or unwillingness to give information, then the interviewer should note what he either did or neglected to do about it.

Analysis of adequacy of information.   By listening to the tape a second time the interviewer can analyze the information obtained. This should be done by using either the interview guide or a special coding system to categorize all of the information that is relevant to the objectives of the interview.[15]

This content analysis can be more meaningful if done by both the interviewer and another person. If two people independently analyze the results and then discuss any disagreements they have, both will

---

[15] Lester Guest, "A New Training Method for Opinion Interviewers," *Public Opinion Quarterly,* vol. 18 (Fall 1954), pp. 287–99. The author shows that the interviewer's error was reduced more when coding (interview analysis) was included in the training program than when practice interviews were included.

increase their sensitivity to inadequate responses and the need for probing to obtain clear and complete information. Disagreements between the interviewer and the other coder about the relevance of a particular item of information are often due to the tendency of the interviewer to assume hopefully that the respondent meant more than he said. Another possibility is that one of the coders or both do not understand the precise specifications of the information sought.

Any time there is a disagreement between coders as to the meaning, relevance, or completeness of the information, they should discuss what type of probe would have helped to clarify any ambiguity or to supply any incomplete information. It might also be necessary to discuss the criteria of relevance by clarifying the definitions of the categories of information. Either type of discussion will clarify the objectives and sensitize the interviewer to means of reaching these objectives.

Of course there will be many occasions when both coders agree that certain information which was accepted as relevant and adequate during the interview breaks down under cold analysis into a meaningless confusion. In this case, it becomes clear that the interviewer either neglected to pursue the objectives or was unsuccessful in his attempt. It has been found that in the early stages of learning nonscheduled interviewing, most interviewers do not obtain all the relevant information. Either they lack a precise understanding of the objectives of the interview or they fail to recognize the inadequacy of the information until they begin to analyze the results. A novice rarely tries to probe persistently for clarification and elaboration to discover whether the respondent is unable or unwilling to give the information.

Once the interviewer has become acutely aware of the adequacies and inadequacies of the information, he is in a better position to analyze the techniques and tactics he used.

Analysis of techniques and tactics. By listening to the tape-recording a third time, the interviewer can hear the techniques and tactics he used. He should become aware of how much of the specific information was obtained by careful questioning, how much was obtained without any special effort, how much was missed because of his failure to probe, and how much was missed in spite of his attempts to probe.

The interviewer should critically examine his every probe and question and decide whether there might have been a more appropriate one at that point. In doing this, the interviewer must consider the type of information sought and the potential inhibitors and facilitators to be dealt with. He should be sensitive to any failure to communicate the question clearly and the need to reword it, provide contexts, or change its scope. He might also discover misused leading questions or neglected opportunities for using leading questions advantageously.

In listening to the tape the interviewer should try to evaluate his own attitudes as demonstrated in the interview. Does he manifest positive attitudes toward the interviewing task? Does he show a nonjudgmental attitude toward the information he receives? Does he evince a vital interest in the information and indicate that he does not accept everything uncritically? Does he show positive attitudes toward the respondent as a person? Are there opportunities where the respondent could be praised for his effort or performance? Does the interviewer give such praise? Does the interviewer sound afraid, unsure, or confused? All of these questions can be answered by listening carefully to both the verbal and nonverbal behavior of the interviewer.

There are some symptoms of confusion and tension which the interviewer should learn to detect in himself. Three of these symptoms found most frequently are (a) the tendency to reword questions for no defensible reason, (b) the tendency to use multiple questions, and (c) the tendency to mechanically use the echo probe. Let us examine some typical examples.

Rewording the question. The frequent recurrence of this form of verbal behavior often indicates that the interviewer is tense and fears that the respondent will not understand the question. Sometimes it indicates that the interviewer has a low opinion of the respondent's ability. Even though this is not true, there is the danger of the respondent's so interpreting the behavior. The general compulsion to reword questions must not be confused with the occasional self-correction or clarification. The following are typical examples of compulsive rewording.

I: When was the first time you ever owned or drove a car? When did you become an owner or learn to drive any type of automobile?

I: Have you had any disagreements with your parents in the last year? Have you had any squabbles, arguments, or verbal battles with them recently? Either one of them?

Regardless of the interviewer's reason for rewording the question, a failure to pause between each successive rewording tends to give the impression that the interviewer is impatient and wants to accelerate the pace of the interview.

Multiple questions. A related habit shared by many neophyte nonscheduled interviewers is the tendency to add one question to another before the respondent has an opportunity to answer the first. For example:

I: What is your general philosophy of raising children? Do you feel that modern psychology is of any value or not? Would you be more in agreement with psychoanalytic approaches or not?

This example is typical in that multiple questions are often in the form of a funnel sequence becoming increasingly specific without allowing the respondent to answer them in turn. This defeats the purpose of a funnel sequence and gives the respondent the impression that the interviewer is impatient or confused.

Sometimes such behavior is prompted by the fear that the respondent will not be able or willing to answer the broader question. Usually such a fear is groundless and is actually a projection of the interviewer's general insecurity in the situation.

Echo probes. The reader will recall that the echo probe is generally the least fruitful of the three types of reflective probes. It is usually effective only if the words which are echoed happen to be emotionally charged for the respondent. When this is not true, as in the example below, the echo probe is useless.

> *R:* When I heard the first explosion, I thought it was the city blasting for the new water main. But then when I heard a bigger explosion next door I knew something had gone wrong. I think that was about 12:30 when I heard the second blast!
>
> *I:* About 12:30?

Generally, such a probe merely elicits a "that's right" from the respondent. If the same type of echo probe is used too frequently, it may give the respondent the impression that the interviewer does not hear well or is not paying attention. For some interviewers the echo probe is unconsciously developed as a stopgap measure in cases where they do not know what else to do.

It is often worthwhile to pay special attention to the use of silence as it affects the general pace and mood of the interview. The interviewer should note the extent to which he adjusts to the respondent's pace or vice versa. He should check whether the pacing is monotonous and mechanical or flexible and meaningful in the context of the interview, and he should look for interruptions of the respondent, whether intentional or not.

In critically listening to his own tactics, the interviewer should first be aware of any deviations from the tactical preplanning and ask whether the deviation was intentional and whether it was an improvement over the original plans. Was the original arrangement of topics and subtopics followed? Were there some questions which should have been introduced by lead-in questions, pivot questions, or transitional statements? If so, what should they have been? When was the funnel, or inverted funnel, sequence of questions used? When should it have been used?

The interviewer should listen carefully to his on-the-spot probing to detect tendencies to under-control or over-control. Awareness of one's natural tendency in probing can help the interviewer become more flexible and use a wider range of topic control when it is appropriate. Although the basic skills in which we are interested are associated with the phases of the interviewer's activity *during* an interview, the general procedure for learning these skills emphasizes the learner's activity *before* and *after* the interview. The ultimate goals are to receive information from the respondent more accurately, evaluate this information more critically, and to exert more control over one's own behavior during the interview. However, these goals can be reached more rapidly by thoughtful preparation and by careful analysis after each interview before rushing on to the next.

SUMMARY

Despite the many purposes and settings of the interview, there are common basic interviewer tasks in the *interviewing performance cycle*. The tasks performed in this repeating cycle call for three general categories of skills: (*a*) accurately receiving information, which depends upon skills in listening, observing and remembering, (*b*) critically evaluating the information received, which depends on skill in retaining the objectives clearly in mind and constantly assessing the gap between information received and that needed to fulfill the objectives, and (*c*) appropriately regulating one's own verbal and nonverbal behavior to direct the respondent toward needed information and to motivate him to give needed information.

The development of interviewing skills depends upon a three-phase process. First, we must *plan* the interview, at least tentatively. Second, we *do* the interview, being sensitive to any need to deviate from the plan. Third, we must *analyze* the results both in terms of the amount of relevant information obtained and the strategies, techniques, and tactics used by the interviewer. To complete the cycle the results of the analysis phase must be fed into the planning of the next interview. Without the planning and analysis phases, practice will only tend to harden certain habit patterns.

Before going on to actually plan, do, and analyze your own interview there are two more laboratory problems, one at the end of this chapter and the first laboratory problem of the next chapter, which will help bridge some of the remaining gaps in connecting concepts with behavior in the interview. Enjoy the vicarious experience of the armchair critic while you can, because after these next two problems you will be launched into a stage performance for self-teaching.

DISCUSSION QUESTIONS

1. What are the principal phases of the Interviewing Performance Cycle?

2. What are some of the main skills involved in accurately receiving information from the respondent?

3. What are some of the causes of the interviewer's failure to accurately receive information from the respondent?

4. Is it more difficult to critically evaluate the information given by the respondent in a scheduled or a nonscheduled interview? Why?

5. What are some of the forms of the interviewer's own nonverbal behavior he can become aware of by listening to his tape-recorded interviews?

6. In order to improve our interviewing skills, what must we do besides more interviewing?

7. What are the major things to be done in preparing to do an interview?

8. What are the main points the interviewer should focus on while doing the interview?

9. What are some of the main aspects of analyzing one's own interviews for learning skills?

Laboratory problem 12

An interview critique (car-buyer motivation study)

Purpose

In the preceding laboratory problems on techniques and tactics, you were asked only to *identify* each type as it occurred in the interview script. You did not have to *listen* to an ongoing interview, or to *record* relevant information, or to take *probe* notes, or to critically *evaluate* the interviewer's techniques and tactics. All of these opportunities are provided in this laboratory problem.

The verbatim transcription of this motivation research interview has been carefully selected despite its vintage because it illustrates many of the problems of obtaining another person's point of view through interviewing. Since it is the initial exploratory interview in the study, there is much room for improvement

Procedure

Your instructor may want to assign all four phases of the problem or only two or three. If more than one phase is to be done, they must be done in the order indicated.

Phase 1: Taking probe notes on live interview

1. Read the purpose of the interview as described below.
2. Two people may role-play the interview from the script or the instructor may make a tape-recording of the role-played interview. You will listen carefully and note words and phrases that are relevant even though in some cases the information is not

complete or clear. The point here is to indicate those responses which should be probed further.

3. Discuss why certain points need to be probed in view of the objectives of the interview.

Phase 2: Coding relevant content

4. If you have not done Phase 1, carefully read the purpose of the interview as described below.

5. Study the Content Analysis Sheet provided by the instructor to review the categories of relevant information.

6. Read the interview script, taking notes in the appropriate cells of the Content Analysis Sheet by entering only words and phrases identified by the number of the response as shown in the script.

7. Compare your Content Analysis Sheet with another one done independently. Discuss the differences in your entries.

Phase 3: Critique of interviewer's techniques and tactics

8. Read the script a second time *stopping* at each of the 20 interviewer's probes having the serial number in parentheses. Do <u>not</u> judge a probe by its immediate effect or anything which comes after, but view it in the context of what has gone on before it. Indicate on the *Diagnosis-Treatment Sheet* supplied by the instructor:

   a. What is wrong, if anything, with the interviewer's probe or question, and

   b. What the interviewer should have said instead. If in a particular instance there is no room for improvement, say so.

Phase 4: Multiple-choice problems

9. Answer the 20 multiple-choice problems while referring to the interview script in the Textbook. The instructor will furnish the problems and a special Answer Sheet.

10. Submit your answers to the instructor who will summarize the group's responses as a basis for discussion.

Phase 5: Comparison and discussion

The instructor will supply you with materials for comparing your Critique and/or Multiple-Choice Problem answers with the suggestions furnished by the author.

The interview

Purpose. This is the first interview in a series of exploratory interviews aimed at discovering why the sales of Brand X automobiles had dropped off 50 percent the previous year. The interviewer had expected to do five or six exploratory interviews to develop a more detailed interview schedule which would be used with a larger sample of car buyers; but he had sharpened the problem and planned the approach to some extent before this first interview. Generally, the interviewer wanted to know why the respondent bought his Brand X car which he currently owns and how these motivations compare with the reasons for buying previous cars and with his ideas about buying any future car. The relevant information would fall into three basic categories.

a. Rational values: such as efficiency, price, safety factors, gasoline economy, mechanical dependability, parking efficiency, etc. These could only be fulfilled by possible changes in the product.

b. Nonrational values: such as feeling of youth, power, social status, aesthetic appeal, feeling of escape, etc. These could be fulfilled by suggestive advertising copy.

c. Social pressures: such as pressures by friends, relatives, work associates and others with whom the buyer interacted. Only those influences which ran counter to the buyer's own private desires are to be considered pressure. This information could be used to suggest different channels of advertising or sales influence.

Strategy and tactics. The interviewer planned to first select current owners of Brand X cars and focus mainly on the person's values and pressures that influenced him *at the time* he purchased his Brand X. In addition he wanted to use a chronological approach to the respondent's car-buying history beginning from the first car he owned. This would put the Brand X buying situation in a more meaningful context by allowing some logical cross-checks upon the buyer's own statements of motivation. For example, if he said that he bought Brand X for a reason that is different from or conflicts with the reasons given for buying other cars in the past or his expected reasons for buying a particular brand in the future, then the interviewer would have to probe to check whether the respondent is confused, or fabricating, or whether his motivations are changing through time. If it could be established that motives typically change as a person goes through the life-cycle, this would be useful information.

As a guide in this exploratory set of interviews, the interviewer devised the "Guide for Probe-Notes or Content Analysis," reprinted here as Exhibit A, which could be used in two ways. During the interview it reminded the interviewer of the areas to be covered as represented by the column headings. He filled in the row headings according to which brands of cars the respondent had bought previously. After the interview was completed, since it was tape-recorded, the interviewer

EXHIBIT A

Guide for Probe–Notes or Content Analysis (car buyer motivation study)			
Cars driven	Rational values	Nonrational values	Social pressure
Chevy Jeep Ambulance			
Kaiser (1947)			
Kaiser (1949)			
Brand X			
Future cars			
Changes in motivation			

listened to it and did a content analysis of the relevant information on a second copy of the same form. This allowed a quick comparison of the information from one respondent with that given by another.

INTERVIEW SCRIPT: Car-Buyer Motivation Research

I-1: What I'd like to have you tell me is, can you remember when you first bought or drove a car? Tell me something about . . .

R-1: Well, when I first drove a car, it was a jeep in the army.

I-2: Oh, uh huh.

R-2: And (2) I'll have to go back before that, I drove a 1934 Chevy that belonged to a high school friend of mine and he gave me a free driving lesson in that and then next I drove in the army I drove this jeep I got into the motor pool in the army and drove a jeep for a while that was my next driving experience (2) Then also while I was in service I was . . . it was necessary for me to drive other vehicles, including an ambulance across the Alps in a blizzard one time. So (3) then when I got out of the service I bought my own car. I bought a '47 Kaiser, the first Kaiser that came out. (2)   (STOP 1)

(I-3): That was your own car that you bought after you got out of the army?

R-3: That was my own first car. And (2) let's see my wife and I uh bought that and then we traded that in for a '49 (3) as soon as we could. (2)

I-4: '49 Kaiser?

R-4: '49 Kaiser and then we got divorced and she took the car with her and I was without a car for a couple of years (3) Is this what you want, you want the history of my automobile owning?   (STOP 2)

(I-5): Well, we might as well proceed along that line up to the present.

R-5: Right up to the present. Then I felt the need for an automobile, but I couldn't afford one until I moved from Park Forest into Chicago. Of course there was a great span of time in here. By this time I was divorced and living with my parents and my parents moved away. So I was out in Park Forest and I needed a car out there but I couldn't afford one so I moved into Chicago, sold the furniture and all that stuff and that gave me a little cash ahead and I started working at this motor club and then I needed a car definitely, I needed one in my work so I shopped around, and (2) my idea was to get (3) a postwar or rather . . . yeah a postwar car that (2) would be initially reasonable to purchase and would still be dependable and in shopping around I saw this '47 Brand X and (3) . . . well, because it's a Brand X it didn't cost me much, I bought it in '51, (2) I bought it in '52 and it cost me $400 (4) . . . And so that way I at that time it was a (4) fairly late model car for me so and the initial outlay was very small so I got into a car that I could use for my business.   (STOP 3)

(I-6): That's very good. Now I'd like to go back little bit. Can you remember, putting yourself back in time, can you remember how you felt about some of your earliest experiences with a car like when you shared the Chevy with or when your high school buddy gave you the lesson in driving or in the jeep in the army. Can you remember how you felt about this?

R-6: Well, I remember this (3) that I was very pleased that my high school buddy had a car and of course that gave us an opportunity to get around a little bit and I was tickled pink that he would let me drive now and then, or rather give me a lesson because I wasn't capable of driving and of course that was a brand new experience, a feeling of importance being able to drive a car. That's about what my feelings were then as I remember now. And in service (2) driving a jeep was quite a big thing, I mean (4) to learn . . . the jeep was very new and it was an exciting thing to think that you would be permitted to drive it (2) and I remember the first driving lesson I had I think was up the side of a mountain. It scared the living hell out of me. That's an emotion I definitely remember. (Interrupting)

I-7: Where was this?

R-7: In Colorado, Camp Carson, Colorado

I-8: Oh unhuh! (2)

R-8: They showed us how to put it in four-wheel drive and so on (4) . . . And run it up the side of this mountain (2) . . . I guess, thrill and excitement again was the idea, in that case. And, (2) well from then on I just kinda became, I felt I could drive and drive capably, and it became a normal chore driving.

I-9: I see

R-9: What else, is that about what you want? (STOP 4)

(I-10): Yes that's fine I'm just trying to get a general background here and then pretty soon maybe I'll find something I want to go a little deeper into.

R-10: Can you shut it off for just a moment I've got to put the waffle on.

Tape-recorder is off for a few minutes while waffles are put on.

I-11: You say there was a lot of publicity for what the jeep could do! (Referring to respondent's remark while putting on the waffles.)

R-11: Yeh, it got a good deal of promotion you know secret weapon of the American army and all that, and as a result (3) to be able to drive one was a special thrill. (2) (STOP 5)

(I-12): How would you compare the experience of driving a jeep with your later experience when you got the Kaiser?

R-12: Well . . . (9) the thrill of ownership I think can be described, can accurately describe (3) owning the Kaiser. It was the first car I ever had (2) . . . that really belonged to me. The thrill of driving was over, you know, the thrill of being able to maneuver a car was over (2) and how to own one on your own (3) and to have the feeling of importance you get with owning a $2500 piece of equipment.

I-13: You bought this new, the '47?

R-13: Yes (Uh huh) and that was part of it too, of course at that time it was a very abnormal market you know you couldn't get cars easily, (2) and if you did or if you could find one you felt was in good condition that you'd like to buy, it was $200 or $300 under the table and all that stuff (2) so we, this Kaiser was available as a demonstrator and we got some of the price knocked off of it, and we were real thrilled that (2) we could that we'd found a car that was within our price range and also a new one (2) uh, my wife and my father were skeptical about it, but I felt that this was the thing, this was the car for us, that we could afford the money and so on, and it was initially my decision that we bought it (2) which we regretted later on because the first Kaiser wasn't too much of an automobile in comparison with the other makes (2). (STOP 6)

(I-14): Well, forgetting about the fact that you were disappointed later on can you remember some of the things that made you use the phrase, "this is the car for me" can you remember why you'd say that? (2)

R-14: I think it was purely an emotional thing, Ray, I really do. I think the whole idea, (3), I'd suddenly found (4) a car that was available. (3) Now of course you realize I was quite young then . . . I was still (4) I think I was 24 years old and it was I think primarily an emotional thing that decided it the car was shiny and it seemed to be reasonable far more reasonable than anything else we could buy with the market the way it was then (2) and just being thrilled to think we could have it that is was available decided my mind. It wouldn't today, (3) I mean I realize that when you spend that amount of money you're making a real decision but at that time it was purely emotional. (3)   (STOP 7)

(*I-15*): Would you say that a Kaiser had any different significance for you than some other car? I mean, after all other cars are shiny too.

R-15: Probably if I'd seen any other car and it had been in the price range that we were ready to pay (2) and you put the two together, I probably would have taken (3) . . . now wait, that does bring up, that does bring something to mind. (6) . . . I don't know, ah (2) I think there was an appeal there for this new automobile manufacturer I think I felt like I'd like to give him a break. (Pauses to put dishes on table.) Not many people owned Kaisers, and I felt if I could be one of them, now what do you call that (2) that's wanting to be different I suppose.

I-16: Distinctive.

R-16: Unhuh, I think that was a great part of the appeal in that case. Now put it up against another car, a Buick or Pontiac or an Olds, (2), I may have been less emotional about it and made a hard-headed decision that it's better to get into a well established brand of automobile rather than a Kaiser however, that being distinctive still had a very strong appeal.

I-17: Well, you said your father was skeptical of this (R: Here's cream if you want it. I: No, thanks) R: yes. I: what was the basis of his skepticism?

R-17: That it's a brand new make of automobile. You're going to put $2,000 into an automobile that (2) you don't know how long it's going to hold out, it's a brand new car on the market; wait a couple of years before you buy one you're a fool (3).

I-18: Well, in a sense you

R-18: (Interrupting) that was his objection   (STOP 8)

(*I-19*): (Interrupting) Unhuh, in a sense you would say that your motivation for doing it was quite the opposite point of view, because it was new this was one, at least it didn't deter you because it was a new manufacture you sort of . . .

R-19: No, as a matter of fact that has appeal to me (5)

I-20: Oh, now you've mentioned this idea, that buying a Kaiser is something distinctive not everybody has one.

R-20: Unhuh

I-21: Well, is there any other kind of a car which might fulfill this same function if it were equal in other respects? (2)

R-21: At that time or do you mean today?

I-22: Either at that time or today.

R-22: I don't think so, available on the market at that time. Today yes, foreign cars on the market (5) And I think that my next car will be a British Consul or a Hillman Minx or (3) some car like that, small economical to run, and incidentally well maybe not incidentally it may be above all, it's different. (2)   (STOP 9)

(*I-23*): Now what do you mean?

R-23: I'll repeat that. At first it's small, easy to park, economical to run and so on and incidentally is also distinctive it may be above all it's distinctive, and secondly, however . . . no I can't say that . . . these buying factors I think will be about equal that I have a car that is easy to run. It's important that I have a car that's easy to park in small spaces because I'm going around the city constantly and I just might buy a Rambler too, or a . . . maybe one of the Nash Metropolitans because they're small, easy to run but probably because of this other thing, this being distinctive I think I'd like to have a British Consul or a Hillman Minx (4)   (STOP 10)

(I-24): As you look back as you've gone through time in this area, would you say that your general attitude toward cars, towards the ownership and driving of cars, that you've gone through any process of change?

R-24: Oh yes, like anything (3) . . . maturing I think and feeling or rather understanding the value of a dollar bill changed my ideas about buying a car personally (2) in working for the Motor Club I am in a position to see the people that buy automobiles, how they buy them and where they buy them and so on, and personally I cannot understand or agree with people that buy a new car year after year when they can't afford it. And I've seen so many people like that (2). They're a thousand dollars behind on their . . . or rather they still owe a thousand dollars on their '53 car and they're shopping for a '54. They've gotta get out of the old one and into a new one and still they don't have the television set paid for. Why they ever bought a television set in the first place, when they were extended so far on the car, and they need new furniture they need new rugs they're not putting any money away, but still they're shopping for a '54 automobile. So far from that I do not feel that it's necessary for me to have a new car every year or even every two or three years. I'll run this one until I feel that it's in a mechanical shape where it's going to be more expensive to fix it than to get a new one or some other logical reason for getting out of it not because I feel . . . now I think that perhaps I'm different from the regular car buying public in this respect (2) because I do not feel any urge now to get into shiny things and drive around flashy, I would like to be distinctive, yes, but I'm not going to get a *new* Hillman and I'm not going to get a *new* Consul. I'll get a *used* one . . . (3) so those are ways that my attitudes have changed about.

I-25: (interrupting) that's very interesting

R-25: (continuing) buying cars in the years since I bought my first one

I-26: Sort of a growing realism with regard to expense and the longer range outlook on this.

R-26: unhuh (2)   (STOP 11)

(I-27): Now would you say that you're still able to get (4) . . . well let's put it this way, how does pleasure fit in, now you were talking mostly about the economics of it. How does the pleasure element and satisfactions, other deeper satisfactions fit in? Has that changed in any way?

R-27: Pleasure?

I-28: Yeh, connected with ownership and driving a car (3)

R-28: Well, the pleasure to me now I could call convenience, and that's what it is, being able to step out of doors get into the car and go where I want to at any time . . . And other than *that* pleasure I . . . I can't think of any. I will add this (2) I would like to get a convertible the next car I buy . . . I've never owned one and I think that maybe I could add to the element of pleasure by getting one.   (STOP 12)

(I-29): Could you tell me a little more about this, I mean . . .

R-29: Well, (12) . . . uh . . . this perhaps too is, (4) I don't know, I just feel that I could probably have more fun. I could just take the top down in summer and buzz around I may find as I say never having owned one, that it's going to be a hell of a bother. It may be colder, it's gonna leak and do things that a hard top doesn't do, but I'm willing to try it; I just think it would be fun having a convertible, and if I find that this is so, the next one the following one I get won't be a convertible. I haven't tried it yet, so I think I'll try to get one. (2)   (STOP 13)

(I-30): Could you . . . is there any, could you give me an idea by giving sort of a picture of a . . . what you could consider an ideal situation which you're using this car in the way in which it would give you the most pleasure . . .

R-30: Yes I think

I-31: (continuing) by virtue of the fact that it's a convertible?

R-31: Yes, I think weekend trips, maybe going off to Michigan or something with the top down and with a girl friend. I think it would be more fun . . . because (4) on a lovely sunny day just to drive along with the top down and the breeze blowing over you and you'd be able to see the landscape and so on, completely unrestricted view. And just the idea of an open car rather than a closed car. (2) I think there's an association there with pleasure.   (STOP 14)

(I-32): Could you a . . . is there anything you can put your finger on there about the difference between open and closed? Can you describe any feeling or imagery this gives you?

R-32: uh, yeh, I think there's kind of a carefree feeling, about sitting in an open car . . . ah, (2) ah (2) you can push on the pedal, that is push on the accelerator and off you go. You're breathing fresh air and you feel like you could stretch out your arm above you, and all is open and you can just fly if you want to; and I think the difference is feeling of confinement in a closed car. I don't think you get that carefree, happy gayness that you can have in a convertible. If this helps you I don't know, it's difficult to explain.

I-33: Well, you're doing very well (4) so any vague, no matter how vague an idea you may have it may be difficult to express, but it's very significant to us.

R-33: I think that's about it. I think it's probably a feeling of youth and freedom and associations like that. (4)   (STOP 15)

(I-34): That's very interesting, I think you've expressed it very well (3) now with your Brand X which is the car you have now, (3) let's see . . . you told me a little bit about how you came to buy it, but could you elaborate on it a little bit. Was there anybody around trying to influence you like your father or father-in law? Anybody in this case? Did you buy it new?

R-34: (interrupting) By golly I wanted to buy a Packard convertible for $900 and it was a lovely car, it was in excellent condition and it had electric windows you know was just it was a '49. And I asked my dad to lend me $600, my stepfather the same one as it was before (3) and he refused. (2) So then I had to get something much cheaper, so I shopped around, and I felt that if I got an older, or rather if I got an off-brand car, and I'd buy a big car I'd be able to get into a later model for $400 than if I got into a, if I bought a late car of a well-known brand, they're much more in demand.

I-35: Oh, in other words the resale value was lower on the Brand X for the same year and for that size of a car.

R-35: unhuh. The bigger a car is the less in demand it will be on a used car market and of course then when it's an off brand, well, then it'll be less in demand. And so I saw this Brand X, the biggest one they made in '47 and it just seemed to get the bill perfectly. And it was in good condition too when I bought it and so that's what made up my mind.   (STOP 16)

(I-36): Was there anything else you'd say which entered into this besides the economic factor, so far you've been stressing the fact that you could get it cheaply, is there any other psychological factor involved do you think? Any satisfaction you might get out of this particular car? (3)

R-36: Well, it was well appointed, that . . . that . . . that's one reason that . . . I probably decided, well this is probably the car I'm going to buy I mean I decided this is probably the car I am going to buy and I looked it over, I mean this is what I want, this fits in all ways it seems up to now. Of course if I found out the back seat was all burned out I wouldn't buy it, but otherwise it fit. So I looked at it and it seemed well appointed. It had all the equipment in it that makes owning a car a little more fun.   (STOP 17)

(I-37): Like what?

R-37: Radio and a heater and (3) this one had an automatic drive too but it didn't work, but it was in there and I hoped that maybe I could get it fixed up some day . . . (2) but it was well appointed and it had dividing (2) arm rest in the rear seat and the upholstery was clean and nice colors good fabrics (3) so that pleased me too and that helped make up my mind about buying it. (3)

I-38: You think if you . . . let's see if just the strictly economic factors, and you got an equally good buy say in a Mercury for example, how would this comparison impress you?

R-38: I think that I probably would have bought the Mercury . . . all things being equal, mileage and tires and all, (2) because I realize that (3) now did you say Mercury because you feel it's the same size of automobile or because you feel it's a, or for what other reasons.   (STOP 18)

(I-39): Well, the Mercury I feel is comparable in some ways

I-40: (continuing) I just don't know enough about different models of the Brand X for example there's such a wide, wide range in different models to know what's comparable.

R-40: Well, Mercury of course has a better resale value and it seems like a somewhat smaller car because the wheelbase on this thing that I'm driving is very big, very big so I think that I would have bought the Mercury for these reasons . . .

I-41: You think . . . which do you think is the more distinctive car, the Mercury or the Brand X? . . . in the same sense as you used it in reference to the Kaiser for example . . .

R-41: today or at that time   (STOP 19)

(I-42): at that time. (4)

R-42: I think the Brand X is the most distinctive car because it was the homeliest car in the streets in 1947 (both laugh) it had this wide gaping grill and still had the prewar dies, and it was like a box and stood way up high, and

I still think it had the homeliest lines of any car on the street so for that reason I think it was distinctive. (Laugh together)   (STOP 20)

(*I-43*): I see. Did this sort of enter in, was this a negative factor in your decision, this homeliness?

R-43: No, not at all. My idea was to get (3) a good car reasonable, and with that I didn't care much how it looked and I (3) that's the reason I bought it. I think today (2) that I'm somewhat changed. I think I'd like a little better-looking automobile. If I put myself today in that same situation I may not have selected the Brand X I'd shop some more.

20

Two data-gathering problems

The laboratory problem at the end of the previous chapter provided the first opportunity to evaluate the interviewer's behavior in terms of both techniques and tactics. But there was no opportunity to criticize the overall *strategy* or to judge the accuracy of the interviewer's *coding* of the respondent's answers into structured answer categories. The first laboratory problem in this chapter adds both of these problems and retains all the problems of techniques and tactics. The second laboratory problem in this chapter will provide an opportunity to plan, do, and analyze a series of three of your own interviews in order to apply some of the procedures for developing interview skills suggested in the last chapter. It would probably be helpful to review your experiences with laboratory problems 9, 10, and 11 before attacking the two problems in this chapter.

Laboratory problem 13

The layman's conception of science

Purpose

In addition to adding more simultaneous dimensions to evaluate, this problem will show how a proposed study sometimes develops from discussions of social issues. It is most important that you keep the purposes of the study in mind in your critique and in your alternative plan for improving the relevance, validity, and completeness of the data. The experiences provided by this problem will help lay the groundwork for the series of do-it-yourself interviews that come next.

Formulation of the study

A group of physical, biological, and social scientists were discussing the attitudes of laymen toward science. There was general agreement that college freshmen had a blind faith in the physical sciences and a highly skeptical attitude toward the application of scientific method to the study of human behavior even though they were equally ignorant of both fields. For example, as one physicist put it,

> When I show the freshman a model of a molecule or a diagram of an atom, he hasn't the slightest doubt of their existence, even though he has never seen either. But if I discuss such concepts as the subconscious mind, he shows great skepticism. Yet if I were called upon to give a classroom demonstration showing direct evidence of the existence of either an atom or the subconscious mind, I think the latter would be easier. It would require no more than a demonstration of post-hypnotic suggestion. I suppose this is because no one has constructed a physical model of the

subconscious mind as a pedagogical device to help the freshman focus his attention.

There was an agreement among scientists in all three fields that the accumulation of systematic scientific generalizations had proceeded further in the physical and biological sciences than in the social sciences but that the layman was not aware of the progress which had been made in the social sciences and was more skeptical of the fruitfulness of the social sciences than of the physical or biological sciences.

After some discussion the following chain of hunches was constructed to provide a very tentative explanation of the phenomenon of the differential awareness of physical and social sciences.

First, the layman's conception of science is mainly composed of the *products* of science, and he is mostly aware of the practical products as opposed to the theoretical products such as a principle, law, hypothesis or theory.

Second, the type of practical products he is most aware of are those which are frequently mentioned in the mass media of communication such as TV, radio, newspapers, movies, and magazines. Here the word "science" is most frequently heard in an advertisement of some consumer product or in connection with national interests.

Third, since the products of the social sciences (for example, unidimensional attitude scales, I.Q. tests, random sample surveys, sociometric analysis, and so on) are rarely saleable to individual consumers on a mass basis, they are rarely mentioned in advertising. Neither is this type of product as adaptable to visual presentation as are physical gadgets. Even biological processes such as a headache or a stomachache must be represented on TV as a series of mechanical gadgets operating within the human body.

Fourth, the omnipresence of physical science and the absence of social science products in the context of mass media leads the layman to assume that physical science is more potent than it is and that social science is less potent than it is. Perhaps this lack of faith in social sciences is accompanied by the layman's fear that social sciences aim to reduce human behavior to a mechanical formula and, therefore, human freedom to zero. This fear flows quite naturally from applying the imagery of physical sciences to the social sciences. The "reasoning" would be somewhat as follows: "The more that is known about the laws of physics, the more man makes a slave of the physical world; therefore, the more that is known about the laws of human behavior, the more man will make a slave of himself."

Fifth, this combination of lack of faith in the possibility of developing social sciences and the fear that they might become too developed constitutes a barrier to the progress of the social sciences at a time when

they are most sorely needed to solve many of the social problems resulting from the advance of physical science and technology and to seek
ways of resolving international conflicts without resort to war before
man destroys himself with his new physical and biological inventions.

In order to try to bring this armchair speculation to an empirical test,
the scope of the problem was considerably narrowed to conduct a
small-scale pilot study of a small segment of laymen and to test a few
crude hypotheses. On the basis of this pilot a follow-up study could be
done with more precision and larger numbers of people. The small
segment of laymen chosen for study was all the freshmen at one small
liberal arts college.

The hypotheses do not cover all the points in the speculation mentioned above but were considered some of the most easily tested points
of departure. The hypotheses were:

1. Most freshmen tend to think of "science" as strictly physical to
the exclusion of biological and social sciences.

2. Most freshmen are more concerned with the practical results or
applications of sciences and have very little awareness of the methods
by which they are attained or with the aims of pure theoretical science.

3. Those freshmen who show some awareness of and interest in the
means used by the scientists to solve their problems will be more aware
of specific techniques and instruments which can be easily represented
visually than with general scientific methods as applied in all fields.

4. Most of the freshmen's knowledge of the results of science will
be the type which is supplied by the mass media of communication,
particularly in advertising consumer products and headline news items.

5. Freshmen will have little awareness of inventions or discoveries
in the biological or social fields.

6. Most freshmen will have a definition, often unconscious, of inventions and discoveries that prevents them from including biological and
social inventions.

7. Most freshmen will assume that the physical sciences can accomplish feats that physical scientists themselves feel impossible according
to their own theory, and they will assume that the social sciences cannot
perform feats that have already been accomplished.

This last hypothesis was considered of crucial importance because
it distinguishes between a simple lack of awareness of social sciences
due to their lesser accomplishments and a form of prejudice against the
latest immigrant into the scientific world.

Objectives of the study

1. *First information objective.* To discover the qualitative variety of
those images and feelings about science in general and about social

science in particular that either help or hinder the freshman's advocacy of the social sciences.

2. *Second information objective.* To quantitatively test the seven specific hypotheses given above.

3. *Methodological objective.* To efficiently use the remaining six weeks of the academic quarter to explore, develop, and test valid strategies and instruments for collecting data on both of the information objectives in a larger survey of a national sample of college freshmen.

Since it was an exploratory study, it was important to proceed in such a way as to discover aspects of science that were important to the respondent even though not included in the seven specific hypotheses. For example, in connection with the second hypothesis there might have been other aspects of science with which freshmen were concerned other than practical results, theoretical aims, and method or techniques. Also, in the third hypothesis, for example, it would be desirable to discover what additional possible sources of influence affect the respondent's image of science.

Analysis to be made

You should write an analysis of the methods described below using the following outline:

I. *Critique.* (Succinctly describe what is wrong in each area.)
   1. Strategy.
   2. Interview schedule.
   3. Tactics of the interviewer (see script below.)
   4. Accuracy of coding of answers.

II. *Alternative plan.*
   1. Strategy plan.
   2. Interview schedule or guide. (Assume this is for the first interview.)
   (Show the order of the topics.)
   (Include questions for first information objective.)
   (Show which hypothesis each question is related to.)
   (Include examples of probes at appropriate points.)

The study

Methods used. At this college all of the freshmen live two to a room in college dormitories. The freshmen are not mixed with older students but have their own dormitories. All freshmen were taking a general education course in social sciences, biological sciences, physical sciences, and English. The college is coeducational, private, and non-denominational. It has a general liberal arts program.

The study was done under the auspices of social science departments who reached all freshmen by making the following announcement in the four introductory social science classes during the ninth week of the 12-week spring quarter.

As you all know, there is a growing concern with improving science programs throughout the country. The upgrading of training and of the quality of people recruited is a concern of the physical, social, and biological fields. We are beginning a study of some of the important aspects of the problem. We need your cooperation. You will be contacted by student interviewers from the psychology and sociology departments beginning next Monday.

We are telling you about this now for two reasons: first, so that you will understand the general nature of the problem and, second, you will have some time to think about it between now and then so that you will be able to give more relevant information in a short time to the interviewer.

The interviewer will talk with you about your ideas of science, where you got these ideas, your definitions of invention, what you perceive to be scientific method, and differences in your perception of the physical, biological, and social sciences. They are not interested so much in any specific knowledge but only in your general ideas and opinions. The interview will not take much of your time, perhaps only half an hour, and you will find it an interesting experience. We will appreciate your help.

This explanation was given on Thursday, and the interviewers began interviewing the freshmen in the dormitory rooms on the following Monday. The approach used by the interviewer was as follows:

I am John Jacobs. I am working on the study of attitudes toward science which was announced in class last Thursday. I have just nine questions I would like to ask. Do you have any questions you would like to ask before we begin? (Here the interviewer was instructed to answer any questions the respondent might have to ease his mind before proceeding. Usually there were no questions, and the interviewer went ahead with the first question.)

The interview schedule is presented in the following section. In the questions with structured answers, the interviewer merely checked the most appropriate response, or if the respondent had an answer not provided for by the categories, the interviewer would write it in. In the open-ended questions (8 and 9), the interviewer was instructed to write everything the respondent said. If the respondent spoke too rapidly, the interviewer was to take sketchy notes and fill them in immediately after the interview. The interviewer was instructed to follow the order of the interview schedule shown.

INTERVIEW SCHEDULE

Freshman's name ————

Major field ————

(if chosen)

1. When you hear the word, "science," which do you think of? (*Hand the respondent the card with the following categories.*)

   a. ____ The physical sciences only.

    b. ____ Physical and biological sciences.

    c. ____ Physical, biological, and social sciences.

    d. ____ Biological and social sciences only.

    e. ____ Biological sciences only.

    f. ____ Social sciences only.

2. When you think of science, which aspect comes to your mind mainly? *(Hand the respondent the card with the following categories.)*

    a. ____ A general method of solving problems of cause and effect.

    b. ____ Specific techniques used in a certain field of science.

    c. ____ Practical results or applications of science.

    d. ____ Theoretical aims or results of science.

    e. ____ Something else (if so, what?).

3. Where do you get most of your ideas about science? *(Do not give answer categories to respondent, but classify his responses by checking all the sources he mentions.)*

    a. ____ From a course in high school.

    b. ____ From courses now being taken in college.

    c. ____ From family.

    d. ____ From friends.

    e. ____ From TV, radio, movies, newspapers, or magazines.

    f. ____ From own independent study of scientific books.

    g. ____ From other source (if so, what?).

4. Now you have mentioned getting ideas from_____. Which of these has had the most influence for you?

5. Most of us have some degree of blind faith in something. Would you say that you tended to have the most blind faith in which of the following:

    a. ____ The ability of physical science to solve physical problems.

    b. ____ The ability of social sciences to solve social problems.

    c. ____ The ability of biological sciences to solve biological problems.

    d. ____ None of these.

6. Which of the following ideas do you think should be included in a definition of a "scientific discovery"? *(Hand respondent the card.)*

    a. ____ Can be something found accidentally.

    b. ____ Must be intentionally sought.

    c. ____ Must have theoretical importance.

    d. ____ Must have practical importance (immediate application).

    e. ____ Can be a physical (nonliving) tangible object.

    f. ____ Can be a living object.

    g. ____ Can be a principle, law, or theory.

    h. ____ Can include social phenomena.

    i. ____ Other_____

7. Which of the following ideas do you think should be included in the definition of invention? (invention as a noun.) *(Hand card to respondent.)*

    a. ____ Must be a result of intentional human effort.

b. ____ Must solve some human problem
c. ____ Must be of practical value.
d. ____ Must be a physical object of some kind.
e. ____ Can include a living object.
f. ____ Can include a process by which a result is achieved.
g. ____ Other____

8. I will give you one minute to name as many results of science as you can. By results I mean discoveries or inventions.

9. What sort of picture comes into your mind when you think of a scientist? (Areas to be covered in probing: What is he doing? Location of work. Type of problem he is working on. For whom is he working? What kind of person is he? How is he dressed? What does he do when he is not working? What kind of social life does he have?)

A SAMPLE INTERVIEW[1]

I-1: Hello, I'm Jerry Levi. I am working on the study of attitudes toward science which was explained in class last Thursday. I have been assigned to interview everybody in this dorm. I would like to ask you about nine questions. Do you have any questions you would like to ask me before we start?

R-1: Yes, what's the first question on this test? (smiling)

I-2: Good (smiling back), here it is. When you hear the word "science" which of these do you think of? *(Hands card to respondent.)*

R-2: Hmmm, let's see. Well, I think of all of them. Then the answer would be *c.* Who would only think of social sciences!

I-3: When you think of science, which aspect comes to your mind mainly? *(Hands respondent the card.)*

R-3: I'd say that all of these would be included.

I-4: Which would be the main one?

R-4: Well, of course everyone is interested in results, but you can't get any results unless you know the methods and techniques. Detailed techniques are interesting, even the cyclotron is a technique, but the broadest, (3) and I'd say the most important, aspects would be the general method because it is something that is applied in all fields of science.

I-5: I see, that's a good way of putting it. Where do you get most of your ideas about science?

R-5: You see, I've always been interested in science. I think my high school chemistry teacher was the first one to make science interesting for me. And of course now I'm taking the course called the Physical Science World-Picture. I find that very interesting. It is a lot different from the high school course.

I-6: Any other sources of ideas about science?

R-6: I have done some reading on my own because I am interested in it. I have even read some science fiction just for kicks.

I-7: Anything else?

R-7: No, that's all I can think of.

---

[1] The numbers in parentheses indicate the number of seconds of silence.

I-8: Now you mentioned that your ideas came from the high school chemistry course, your college course called the Physical Science World-Picture, and your own independent reading of books. Which one of these sources do you feel had the most influence on your general idea of science and the feeling you have toward it?

R-8: I think that it depends mostly on my own reading. After all I have been in college only six months and I have been reading on my own since before that.

I-9: Most of us have some degree of blind faith in certain things. In which one of the following would you tend to have the most blind faith? The ability of physical science to solve physical problems, the ability of the biological sciences to solve biological problems, the ability of the social sciences to solve social problems, or none of these?

R-9: I'd say, "none of these," if you are talking about *blind* faith, because that's one thing a scientist should not have is blind faith. He has to have faith in human intelligence, but that is well-founded on the past history of man's successful efforts to solve all kinds of problems. Physics, for example, has demonstrated that it can get results to fulfill anything man is capable of imagining. I'd go so far as to say that I have faith in the physical sciences, but I wouldn't call it blind. Yes, I'd say I have *blind* faith in none of these!

I-10: Which of the following ideas do you think should be included in a definition of a scientific discovery? *(Hands card to respondent.)*

R-10: It doesn't have to be found intentionally. A lot of discoveries were accidental. Wasn't the way of curing rubber discovered accidentally? Many times a scientist is looking for one thing, but finds another. I'd call it a discovery if it had either theoretical or practical use. In either case it is of some value to man. Also it can be a tangible object, either living or nonliving, or some principle or law. It would also have to include any practical or theoretical finding about social phenomena. I can't think of anything else that should be included.

I-11: That's fine. Now which of the following ideas do you think should be included in the definition of invention? Here we are using "invention" as a noun. *(Hands card to respondent.)*

R-11: That's right—the invention is a result of intentional human effort. You just can't make inventions accidentally like you can discoveries. And it must solve some sort of human problem—using the term broadly—you know, building a better mouse trap and all that. A mouse trap is an invention that solves a problem. Practical value—well, yes. If it solves a problem, it's practical. Yes, I suppose an invention is always a physical object. It cannot be a living object because then it it is not man-made. No, the process is not the invention, but the product of the process might be an invention. Also an invention is something that people usually patent and sell.

I-12: I will give you just one minute to name as many results of science as you can. I'll tell you when to start and when your minute is up. By "results of science" I mean any discoveries or inventions you can think of. All right, start now.

R-12: Airplane, penicillin, radio, cotton gin, telephone, internal combustion engine, atomic energy, television, polio vaccine, sputnik, ICBM, transistor, vacuum tube, electric light bulb, electricity, washing machine (4).

I-13:   Your time's up. That was very good.

R-13:   Gosh, I got stuck and couldn't think of another thing. I'll probably think of a million things later.

I-14:   What sort of picture comes to your mind when you think of a scientist?

R-14:   A scientist . . . the easiest thing to conjure up is a man in a white coat over a gurgling retort or watching the dials on some electronic machine.

I-15:   What kind of problem is he working on?

R-15:   I don't know . . . he is trying to invent some sort of wonder drug or working with radioactive isotopes. There is a lot going on in that field now—trying to use atomic physics in combating cancer. Or maybe he would be figuring a way to simplify the new breeder reactor; you know that's the machine which allows one atomic fuel to be converted into another type of atomic fuel. It sounds like it defies the law of conservation and energy.

I-16:   Where is he working?

R-16:   In some laboratory—gosh, I don't know!

I-17:   Well, who is he working for?

R-17:   I don't know exactly. He might be working for the government or some big industry or some university. It depends on the project.

I-18:   I see. Now tell me a little about what kind of person he is.

R-18:   First of all he is devoted to science. He lives to make discoveries. He has learned to discipline himself so that he is not distracted by the routine events that most of us spend so much time with. Sort of like Madame Curie. You know, that's funny, sometimes when you say scientist, I think of a bald-headed neatly shaven man in a white coat. Other times I think of a man with sloppy long hair and an old wrinkled sweatshirt like Einstein. I guess that is the philosopher or mathematician. The man with the technical know-how is neat.

I-19:   What kind of social life does the scientist have?

R-19:   Social life? He has no social life—except when they have a party to celebrate some accomplishment. He has just a small circle of trusted friends who don't make too many demands on him. They have a simple life with little or no publicity unless he makes a breakthrough on some problem.

ANSWERS RECORDED

The answers the interviewer recorded on his code sheet for the first seven questions, which have structured answers, are as follows: (1) *c,* (2) *a,* (3) *a, b, f,* (4) *f,* (5) *d,* (6) *a, e, g, h,* (7) *a, b, c.*

Laboratory problem 14

Images and feelings on the American way of life

Purpose

The central purpose of this problem is to give you an opportunity to put into practice the general procedure for learning interviewing skills through planning, doing, and analyzing your own interview. The topic and specifications of the interview you are to do have been chosen because they demand a wide range of skills, yet all of the problems are soluble to some degree even in the first attempt.

To provide ample opportunity for improving through critical experience, this assignment is to do a *series of three interviews* on the same topic. To apply the procedure for development of skills, each of the three interviews will be carefully planned in advance, performed, and analyzed before going on to plan the next interview. If possible all three interviews should be tape-recorded. If only two of the three can be recorded, it should be the last two. In any case the last one must be tape-recorded.

Objectives

The objectives can be divided into the informational objectives specifying the type of information to be collected and the methodological objectives in terms of the development of the strategies, techniques, and tactics expected at the end of the series of three interviews.

Informational objectives. There are four dimensions of the meaning of "The American Way of Life" which must be explored:

a. What is The American way of life in the mind of the respondent? What are the most salient *ideas* and *images* associated with the term?

b. What about the American way of life is *changing* for the better? For worse?

c. What are the *sources* of the respondent's most salient ideas, images, or feelings?

d. What is the *feeling tone,* attitude, or value attached to the most salient ideas or images? What is good or bad about the American way of life?

Methodological objectives. You are to use the three interviews to develop strategy, tactics, and techniques for achieving the informational objectives. Your final report after the third interview will contain your latest revision of the methods.

Form of your final report

Your final report should be written after analyzing the results of your third interview and should include the following parts in sequence. The estimated number of pages (typed double-space) for each part is given in parentheses. If you try to be concise, the total report should have fewer than ten pages.

1. Revised strategy plan. (1 page) Describe the strategy you would use if you were to do more interviews. How does it differ from what you had done before?

2. Revised guide or schedule. (3 pages) Revise the interview guide or schedule used in your third interview to improve it as much as you can on the basis of your experience to this point.

3. Coded information. (2 pages) Code *all* of the relevant information *verbatim* in some organized manner from your third interview only.

4. Revised hypotheses. (½ page) State your revised hypotheses which are *post hoc* answers to the four topical questions of the interview. Show what you would expect the answers to these four questions to be if you were to do a hundred more interviews. If any different categories of data would be needed than those used in part 3 above, show how they would differ.

5. Experience report. (2 pages) Show what you learned by doing the series of three interviews. What were the main problems encountered? What surprised you about the project? What would you need to work on most in the future to develop skills in interview planning and performance?

Procedures

This is not a laboratory project assignment to be done in a couple of hours but a field assignment requiring from 10 to 14 days elapsed time and from 20 to 35 hours work time, depending on the circumstances, how thoroughly each step is done, and how the group works together. The extent to which each of the steps below shall be done independently and how much in group discussion in or out of the regular group sessions will be determined by the instructor.

1. Review and refine objectives. Look at the four dimensions of the meaning of "The American Way of Life" as given above and think of different possible interpretations of the kind of information required by each dimension. For example, in probing for the most salient images and ideas associated with "the American way of life," should the interviewer define the phrase for the respondent at the onset or only if the respondent asks for a definition; or should the interviewer insist that the respondent use his own definition by giving whatever he associates with the verbal phrase?

2. Develop hypotheses. By hypothesis we mean a tentative answer, on the basis of theory or an intuitive hunch, to each of the four topical questions. For example, for dimension a a hypothesis would be a tentative answer (in advance of the interview) to the question: What are the most salient ideas and images the respondents in general will associate with "the American way of life"? The hypothetical answer may be given at any level of abstraction, depending on what you feel to be the most appropriate. For example, a very concrete answer might be that the most salient image will be the American flag or the Statue of Liberty. In contrast, it could be a very abstract; for example, "Most respondents will associate images of physical objects rather than social institutions," or "Most respondents will associate individual rights and freedoms more frequently than obligations or duties."

In any case you should *not* restrict your interview to testing your hypothesis but always leave it open enough to allow for a full range of unanticipated responses in addition to testing your hypotheses. After each interview you should revise your hypotheses in light of the information collected.

3. Prepare interview guide or schedule. Plan an interview guide or schedule to perform both functions: (*a*) to *explore* for better hypotheses, and (*b*) to *test* the hypothesis. Remember, for exploration and discovery you must use broad-scope questions and have a lot of neutral probes on hand to keep the conversation going. Both for the exploratory function and testing the hypotheses you must be careful that you do not suggest answers by the wording of a question, by the structuring of the answers, by the chronological order of questions, or by verbal or nonverbal statements. Put this in a form you will actually use in the interview!

4. Anticipate main inhibitors and facilitators. In view of the general types of questions represented by the four subtopics of the interview, and in view of some of the possible answers as expressed in your hypotheses, try to anticipate some of the *potential* inhibitors and facilitators in the situation. Keep these in mind for your next steps of planning your strategy, techniques, and tactics.

5. Plan the strategy. You will have to accept as a given the fact that *you* are to be the interviewer and that someone in your organization (college, university, plant, agency, office, etc.) is to be the respondent. You are to decide within the limitations of the local situation *who* to interview, *when,* and *where,* and what you will say or do to locate the respondent, to get his cooperation, and to define the interview situation. This should be done keeping in mind the specific objectives of the interview, the nature of the situation, and the potential inhibitors and facilitators. Some of the important facts about the nature of the situation are that you will be doing three interviews, others will also be interviewing on the same topic, and you must proceed in an ethical manner.

6. Do the interview. The interviews should be *tape-recorded* in a place where there is privacy and quiet. Do not forget to pretest the situation so that you can be sure to obtain a clearly audible recording. Even though you use a tape recorder you should also take *probe notes* as an aid to pursuing the informational objectives.

7. Type relevant content. Listen to your tape-recording, keeping in mind your informational objectives, and type (if possible) the words, phrases, or sentences constituting the relevant data. In cases where the meaning of the response is not clear, out of context, supply the context in parentheses. For example, often the response is meaningless without seeing the question or probe that prompted it. Do not try to rearrange the order of the relevant information; type it in the order it appears on the tape. Only a portion of the information will be relevant. Don't try to get perfect copy—strike over or x-out errors and barge on ahead. Make a carbon copy, and type double-spaced lines.

8. Code relevant content. Construct a code sheet for your interview showing the categories of information needed to test your specific hypotheses related to topics *a* (images or ideas), *b* (changes), and *c* (sources). Topic *d* (feeling tone) will be considered as a separate dimension applicable to all of the three preceding topics. For example, assume that your hypothesis for topic *a,* on images and ideas, is that *more abstract ideas than concrete images will be given.* Then your code would look like this:

a–1 abstract idea (Ex. freedom, individualism, idealistic)
a–2 concrete image (Ex. Statue of Liberty, traffic jam, smog.)
a–X other (Any idea or image not classifiable in the two hypothesized categories either because an additional category was needed or the meaning is not clearly abstract or concrete.)

Note that the "a" indicates that the information deals with topic *a* and the numbers 1 and 2 indicate hypothesized categories of responses to topic *a*, and the X indicates information which is relevant to topic *a* but does not fall into the categories.

After you build a code for the first three topics, each relevant image, idea, change, or source can be cross-classified according to whether the feeling toward the particular item of information is positive, negative, or neutral. The content of one interview could be represented, then, on a coding sheet as shown in Figure 20–1.

FIGURE 20–1

| Code | TOPICS | FEELING TONE | | |
		Positive (+)	Neutral (?)	Negative (−)
a-1	Abstract			
a-2	Concrete			
a-x	Other			
b-1				
b-2				
b-3				
b-4				
b-x	Other			
c-1				
c-2				
c-3				
c-x	Other			

After you have constructed your code sheet (make duplicate if you are going to have a coding partner also code your interview), go through one copy of the *typed relevant data,* and code each element of information which is relevant. Remember that relevant data includes all data which fall into a category needed to test a hypothesis or into the X category under each topic, indicating that it is relevant to the topic but not specifically to your hypothesis about that topic. Each bit of relevant data must be designated with a *serial number,* followed by the code (the *topic letter* and the *answer-category number*) in parentheses, followed by the feeling-tone symbol, all written immediately above the under-lined words (see Figure 20–2).

Once the transcription of relevant data has been coded as in the example above, it can be summarized by merely putting the *serial numbers* in the appropriate cells in the code sheet. It will be noted that, on the feeling-tone dimension, the coder assumed that he could classify smog and pollution as negative, but was not sure that any of the others was clearly positive or negative in the mind of the respondent, and he had failed to probe the feeling dimension. Sometimes the feeling tone

FIGURE 20–2

I think of smog and pollution as well as the Star–Spangled Banner and apple pie. The Washington Monument, the Statue of Liberty or the Empire State Building is what most

people would think of. But (what distinguishes

America from most countries) is amount and

type of residential and personal mobility.

is clear from the context or tone of voice, but in other cases it is necessary for the interviewer to probe. Otherwise he is merely indicating his own rather than the respondent's evaluation of the particular idea or image.

The attempt to code such material from the first interview will alert the interviewer to the need to probe for feeling tone, using something like the following:

When you mentioned personal mobility just now, was that a good or bad aspect of the American way of life?

or

Would you classify personal mobility as a good, neutral or bad part of the American way of life?

The interviewer might avoid having to probe every image or idea for its position on the feeling dimension by asking broad questions such as "What are some of the best things about the American Way of Life?" "What are some of the worst things about the American Way of Life?" or "What are some of the most typical things of the American Way of Life? Which of these are good and which are bad?"

9. Criticize strategies, techniques, and tactics. Your self-critique should keep in mind the informational objectives of the interview as you ask yourself the following questions:

Accurately receiving information

   a. Did you hear all of the relevant points during the interview or did you notice some of the information for the first time when you listened to the tape-recording?

  b. Did you observe anything about the respondent's nonverbal reactions to the interview? If so, what?

  c. Did you have any trouble remembering the relevant things the respondent said during the interview, so that you could know what had been covered and what had not?

Critically evaluating the information

  a. What about the informational objectives, if anything, do you need to clarify before you go on to the next interview?

  b. Where in the interview did you fail to probe when you should? Why do you suppose this was?

  c. Did your probe notes indicate many points that needed further clarification or elaboration?

Controlling techniques and tactics

  a. Did you have a plan regarding where to use broad-scope questions versus narrow-scope questions?

  b. Had you planned several potential broad-scope questions to cover the same topic area in case the first one was not fruitful?

  c. How often did you use low-topic-control encouragement probes?

  d. How often did you use a silent probe and how often did you interrupt the respondent?

  e. Did you ever directly praise the respondent for his efforts during the interview?

  f. What should you do differently next time in strategy, techniques, or tactics? Consider a few of the most important possibilities.

10. Revise strategy, techniques, and tactics.   On the basis of your analysis of relevant content in step 8 and your analysis of your strategy, tactics, and techniques in step 9, revise only the methods you feel most clearly need to be changed. After the first interview it may be necessary to make only minor changes, or it may be advisable to change the whole plan radically, depending upon the amount of work, insight, and luck involved in your preplanning of the first interview. After two interviews the plan for the third may take a clearer shape.

Steps 1 through 10 are done three times, once in connection with each interview, and do not require you to write any formal report. The five parts to your formal report have been specified earlier and can be done only after the completion of the third interview.

If you proceed in a creative, sensitive, and disciplined manner without undue rush, you will develop an invaluable pattern of self-instruction you can use in the future to review and improve your skill and insight into the total interview process, including clarifying the objectives, designing the interview strategy, constructing the interview guide, doing the interview, and finally analyzing the relevant data and criticizing the field methods used. This is the creative process which is the major portion of any small-scale, high quality research; and it is the crucial preliminary phase in large-scale projects using a number of interviewers who are given a field-developed and pretested interview schedule and strategy instructions.

By following the basic formula of planning, doing, and analyzing, you will discover that much depends upon preplanning and post-analysis as well as upon an alert, sensitive impromptu performance in the interview. Through this three-phase cycle of learning activity you will improve your ability to transform the informational objectives, the conceptual model of facilitators and inhibitors, the tools of strategy, techniques, and tactics into specific behaviors of the interviewer. Only when this creative and insightful connection is made can we expect results in terms of information that is more relevant, more valid, and more complete. Good luck in your field venture!

Epilogue

After dealing with the complexities of interviewing methods and the procedures for learning to interview, it is time to reaffirm the essential spirit and purpose of this book and renew its perspectives. We will specify some of the book's underlying assumptions, review the high points of interviewing methdology, and make some general observations about the subjective experience of learning to interview.

AIMS AND ASSUMPTIONS

The direct empirical study of human behavior includes interviewing, empathy, participation, and observation. Each of these approaches could be dealt with at length separately, but interviewing involves certain aspects of the other three general methods.

Interviewing, unlike any of the basic methods in the physical sciences, depends upon an empathic relationship between the observer and the observed. There is nothing to be gained by lamenting or ignoring the fact that there are dangers of mis-empathizing or over-empathizing, since empathy is a necessary element in human communication.

On the contrary, one of the advantages the social sciences have over the physical sciences is the fact that under certain conditions the human observer may successfully empathize with the object of his observation. The study of human behavior not only depends upon but also helps to develop empathy. Thus, we assume a complementary rather than an antithetical relationship between empathy as a common human characteristic and social science as a specialized, abstract, objective analysis of human behavior. Qualitatively valid observations must always precede any quantitative observation or analysis. This complementary relationship is further emphasized in the fact that the application of the results of any social science study depends upon an empathic relationship between the social engineer and the people in the community where the results are to be applied.

Thus, the whole social science enterprise may be viewed as a systematic extension of the range and quality of human empathy. The ability of man to invent and build the social structures needed to support cooperation over ever widening circles, from familial and tribal to national and international, depends upon this progressive extension of empathy.

The foregoing assumptions may at first glance seem to have little connection with learning to interview. Actually, these ideas regarding the relationship between human empathy, social science, and the general welfare of society have been some of the silent assumptions underlying this particular approach to interviewing. Instead of perceiving empathy and objectivity as antithetical, we see the problem as being one of developing an "informed empathy" that gives the observer of human phenomena an advantage over, for example, the psychologist studying the motivation of rats.

The successful application of the theoretical framework of inhibitors and facilitators of communication rests upon the interviewer's ability to empathize in the planning, execution, and analysis phases of the interviewing enterprise. This is not to say that we blindly trust empathy but that, since we cannot avoid using it, we must try to use its positive aspects and avoid its pitfalls. Methods of analyzing both the interviewing process and the resulting data can help correct empathic error.

The writer has been considering interviewing as including the total process of planning, executing, and analyzing the interview, rather than taking the narrower view that interviewing properly includes only that portion of the process which is performed vis-à-vis the respondent.

This perspective does not conceal the vital interdependence between the strategy planning and the methods used by the interviewer when he faces the respondent. If the strategy is designed without benefit of exploratory participation, observation, or interviewing in the field, there is the grave danger that the conceptualization of the problem may be inappropriate, the questions may be beside the point, or the contexts, wording, and sequence of questions may all work to inhibit rather than facilitate communication. Only in rare cases can the skilled interviewer completely overcome the initial disadvantages of a poorly planned strategy or an ill-conceived interview guide.

The selection from among the many tools of strategy, techniques, and tactics is the essence of the creative process of interviewing, and like all creative processes it is not a fixed mechanical sequence. For this reason no set of "do's" or "don'ts" can realistically be offered as a guide to successful interviewing. Instead, we can learn to use tools, concepts, and principles.

REVIEW OF CONCEPTS AND TOOLS

Interviewing as maximizing communication

The basic tasks of the interviewer include accurately communicating the question to the respondent; maximizing the respondent's ability and willingness to answer the question; listening actively to determine what is relevant; and probing to increase the validity, clarity, and completeness of the responses. All of the strategies, techniques, and tactics of interviewing must contribute in some way to accomplishing these central tasks.

The interviewer must proceed in a way that will maximize the flow of relevant information while maintaining optimum interpersonal relations with the respondent. The flow of relevant information depends on the interviewer's maximizing the facilitators of communication and minimizing the inhibitors. The writer has found the inhibitors and facilitators of communication to be a practical sensitizing framework for people who plan, do, or evaluate interviewing. The eight inhibitors (competing time demands, ego threat, etiquette, trauma, forgetting, chronological confusion, inferential confusion, and unconscious behavior) and eight facilitators (fulfilling expectations, giving recognition, providing altruistic appeals, supplying sympathetic understanding, giving new experiences, fulfilling the need for meaning, facilitating catharsis, and supplying extrinsic rewards) of communication are not proposed as an elegant theoretical model fitting neatly within one discipline. The variables are related to several disciplines bearing upon human behavior. Two values of this eclectic frame of reference are that each concept clearly represents a real factor found in face-to-face communication situations; also, each concept is relatable to basic theory and empirical findings in the social sciences.

We have not undertaken a systematic presentation of the evidence from empirical studies or of the basic theories of the social sciences, in order to keep closer to the task of learning to interview. However, we have pointed out some results of experiments dealing specifically with interviewing.

To use this sensitizing framework effectively, we conceive of the inhibitors as potential forces that are activated only under certain circumstances. Thus, it is not necessary to know that the potential has been activated in the specific case at hand, nor do we have to be sure that the remedies (in terms of certain strategies, tactics, or techniques) are actually needed before we apply them. Generally, a preventative approach can be used without damage to the communication process.

Similarly, it is not necessary for the interviewer to wait until it is clear that certain facilitators are needed before applying them. Nor can he expect magical stimulus-response reactions to his attempts to maximize the facilitators in a particular interview. What we can expect is that statistically we will be much more successful in establishing a fruitful relationship with the respondent if we make the effort to nourish these facilitating social-psychological forces.

Strategies of interviewing

Strategy includes all those decisions regarding the approach and setting made before a particular interview is under way. Initially, someone must decide whether interviewing is the most valid and efficient way to obtain the information needed. Sometimes it is a grave error to assume that interviewing should be used instead of public records, census data, diaries, letters, or essays written by the respondents for the occasion. Only after it is clear that interviewing is needed must we then decide who should be interviewed, who should do the interviewing, what would be the most appropriate role to be used by the interviewer, when and where the interview should be done, how to define the interview situation for the respondent, and how to record the interview.

All of this planning should be considered tentative, to be modified after the first field experiences. To be fruitful, the strategy planning must begin with the broadest view of the total situation. There is a danger of beginning a field study with a bundle of restrictive assumptions, often unconscious, regarding the range of strategies to be considered. Often, these assumptions are built upon previous experience, direct or vicarious, with strategies for collecting data in a particular situation. Even the professional researcher may be caught in the net of habit and try to solve a new problem with only old formulas. For example, a person accustomed to doing public opinion polls or census-type surveys may unintentionally cripple a study of the local community power structure by assuming that all of the respondents should be randomly selected. This strategy of selecting respondents would make it impossible to trace the informal chain of command or to cross-check the account of one witness with that of another person participating in the same situation.

One American accustomed to studying pre-literate people in exotic cultures assumed that, in order to study the role conflicts experienced by Latin American professional women, he must first have a series of informal visits with each potential respondent in order to build up rapport before doing any formal interviewing. This was soon seen as a waste of valuable time for both the interviewer and the respondent who might say during the first visit, "I'm fascinated with your study of the roles of professional women. Are you going to use nondirective interviewing or do you have a questionnaire?"

Some of the basic dimensions of the field situation that determine or limit appropriate strategies are whether the interviewer is operating (*a*) in friendly or hostile territory, (*b*) in open or closed communities, and (*c*) whether he is making single or multiple contacts with each respondent.

Once we are aware of the actual and potential field situation in which a study has to operate in view of the type of information to be sought, we can then decide what types of key informants, special respondents, or representative respondents are needed and in what order they should be approached. Once we know the different types of respondents needed, we can then deal with the selection of the most appropriate interviewers.

In selecting the interviewers we must try to assess the probable effects of the individual's overt characteristics (such as age, sex, race, accent, mode of dress and grooming) upon the inhibitors and facilitators of communication in view of the information sought and the characteristics of the respondent.

Also, we must consider which roles the interviewer is capable of assuming and which would be most appropriate under the specific circumstances. General dimensions of role relationships, such as the in-group–out-group or the subordinate-superordinate, have demonstrable effects on the types of information which will be communicated in the interview situation. Always the interviewer has the central role of interviewer. This role may be clearly defined to him, but it may be vague to the respondent. In this case, the interviewer's auxiliary role assumes more importance, and he must choose carefully the ones he wishes to bring to the foreground of the interview situation.

Once the plot (the interview purpose) is clearly specified and the actors (the respondents and interviewers) are chosen, then we can consider the scene (time, place, and definition of the situation) in which the "minidrama" called the interview will take place. Time and place are not to be considered as physical aspects relevant only to the logistical efficiency and convenience of the field study; they must be evaluated in terms of their symbolic value in the communication of the particular information needed. Thus, time and space must be seen in relationship to both the nature of the information sought and to the interaction between interviewer and respondent.

Important aspects of the scene other than time and place include the psychological props which establish a certain definition of the situation for both interviewer and respondent. The way the interviewer is introduced, the way the sponsorship, purpose of the interview, and selection of the respondent are explained, and the method of recording all bear upon the potential communication of a particular type of information.

Once the interviewer has begun with his opening question, much has already been done to influence the outcome of the interview. Yet much of the outcome still depends upon the skillful use of techniques and tactics during the interview.

Techniques in interviewing

Techniques are specific forms of verbal and nonverbal behavior used during the interview to communicate a particular question and motivate the respondent to answer it. Silence is an important interviewing technique. Its successful use depends upon the interviewer's sensitivity to the respondent's behavior and upon the interviewer's ability to control his own impulses to a degree not customary in ordinary sociable conversation.

There is a tendency for interviewers to be unaware of the need to supply a context for the interpretation of questions. Often, it is necessary to do some exploratory interviewing to detect several possible interpretations of a question by the respondents. These varying interpretations may surprise the interviewer who has carefully used clear and unambiguous wording. Differences in interpretation may spring from different subculture backgrounds of the respondents, multiple frames of reference possessed by a particular respondent, or changes in frames of reference due to recent personal experiences or current public events. Often, the interview schedule can avoid having overcomplicated questions by providing an introductory context, meaningful to a range of respondents, which will help them all arrive at the interpretation intended by the interviewer.

These verbal contexts may help to clarify and standardize the meaning of a question by defining terms, providing the appropriate time perspective, building a special perspective, furnishing criteria for judgment, or supplying needed facts. In addition to clarifying the meaning of the question, a verbal context may motivate the respondent to give the answer; it may arouse interest, give recognition to the respondent for his special qualifications, help prevent falsification, reduce the etiquette barrier, stimulate memory, reduce chronological confusion, or help the respondent probe his own unconscious experience.

Assuming that the essential meaning of a particular question can be clearly communicated, the interviewer designing the questions must decide the extent to which the scope of the question should be made broad or narrow, the extent to which the answer should be left open or structured, and finally whether or not a leading question should be used to suggest a particular answer. All of the different combinations of question scope and answer structures have a valid use. Each type is likely to obtain accurate and complete information under certain conditions. Each form of question must be evaluated in terms of the probable effect upon the flow of specific types of information under certain interviewing conditions.

Techniques also include the nonverbal expression of attitudes. These attitudes are as essential in their effect as are the verbal techniques; yet they cannot be mechanically structured or turned on and off at will. The interviewer who thinks that he can produce the appropriate attitude on cue probably is merely deceiving himself, but he is likely to be less successful in deceiving the respondent.

How then can we use expressions of attitude as a technique? In some cases, we must select interviewers who already have the needed positive attitudes toward the interviewing task in general, toward the specific kinds of information sought, and toward the type of respondent to be interviewed.

An interviewer can avoid the expression of negative attitudes by concentrating on the positive attitudes which he already has. Also, many of the needed positive attitudes are strengthened with actual practice in interviewing a variety of people on many subjects.

The most important attitude needed in many types of interview is a nonjudgmental attitude toward the respondent as a type of person and toward any behavior which he reports. This is not a mere attitudinal vacuum; it consists of showing interest in the information, appreciation for the respondent's efforts in giving it, interest in the respondent as a person, and critical assessment of the relevance of the information.

All this does not mean that the interviewer must have no values or beliefs contrary to those of the respondent. He does not need to be a sociopsychological chameleon, but he must perceive that in his role as interviewer his task is to see the world through the eyes of the respondent, not to approve or disapprove of what he sees. In his role as citizen he is free to judge whether or not the purposes of the particular proposed study are in agreement with his own values. If they are not, he should not participate in the study. Maintaining an operational distinction between his role as interviewer and as citizen is one of the disciplines a successful interviewer must learn.

We may describe techniques in a particular interview in terms of the verbal forms of each specific question and its underlying nonverbal attitudinal accompaniment. However, a new dimension of interviewing must be introduced to take into consideration how these discrete questions are interconnected in the ongoing flow of the interview as a whole.

Interviewing tactics

Tactics are those *sequential patterns* of techniques which facilitate the flow of relevant information and which maintain optimum interpersonal relations. Part of this sequential dimension can be built into the interview schedule in advance, but some aspects may have to be improvised in the give-and-take of the interview.

Building tactics into the interview schedule. Several dimensions of tactics may be tentatively planned in advance for the first trial interview. Some of the sequential patterns may be revised on the basis of the pretest interviews. The pretesting may also show that other sequences have to be left for the interviewer to determine in each interview. A tentative initial plan should specify the sequence of topics and the sequence of questions within each topic.

After the tentative order of the topics is decided, we can think in terms of the types of contexts needed to launch the first topic, to connect one topic with another, or to determine which topics or questions are pertinent for a particular respondent. The use of lead-in questions, pivot questions, and transitional contexts varies greatly from one general subject matter to another and from the very simple interviews to the very complex ones.

Even though it is often possible to freeze the sequence of topics and the questions within a topic on the basis of careful pretesting, we cannot predict the precise probes needed to obtain a relevant response.

Probing to meet the objectives of a topic. Even though the interviewer gives an appropriate introduction or transition to a topic and asks a well-worded question, there is often a need to probe to obtain further clarification or elaboration of the response. Generally, probing is needed more frequently with open-ended questions of broad scope, but it is also needed to clarify the response to a question that has a completely structured answer in order to be sure that the coding of the response is valid and reliable.

Usually, the interviewer probes to complete and clarify the response to one question before going on to another. This is not always the best way to maximize the flow of relevant information. Sometimes it is better to wait until the respondent spontaneously covers several questions and begins to lose momentum before interrupting with a probe of any kind.

Seven types of probes represent varying degrees of topic control: silent probe, encouragement, immediate elaboration, immediate clarification, retrospective elaboration, retrospective clarification, and mutation. Each of these types has unique values under different conditions. The interviewer must learn to use the full range of topic control rather than following the habits acquired in sociable conversation. Only after mastering the mechanics of the full range of probe types, can the interviewer begin to develop a sense of when each is appropriate. For example, the interviewer who is unaware of the possibilities of the silent probe, the encouragement probe, or the recapitulation probe will never find an occasion to use them.

Not only does the interviewer have to be constantly alert for the need to probe, but he must also have an emergency kit of tactical tools to deal with a respondent's possible resistance to giving relevant information.

Dealing with symptoms of resistance. We cannot know in advance when the respondent is going to resist the efforts of the interviewer by saying, "I'm too busy now," "I don't know anything about that," "I can't remember," or "What do *you* think about that?" If the interviewer is unprepared for such respondent action, he may become flustered, damage the rapport in his efforts to respond, or be thrown into a state of panic. We have discussed some of the general ways of dealing with these potential hindrances which can induce panic in the inexperienced.

The informal post-interview. The informal post-interview is that sociable chat between interviewer and respondent which takes place after the formal interview is over. The end of the formal interview can be signaled by a verbal statement, by putting away notebook and pencil, by turning off the tape recorder, or any of several other ways. In this post-interview period the situation is redefined and the relationship between interviewer and respondent is changed.

There are two basic functions of the post-interview period. First, it may provide an opportunity to build the respondent's morale and confidence so that he will have a better feeling toward the interviewer as a person and toward the study which he is doing. This is particularly important in field studies where one disgruntled respondent might infect potential respondents with a negative attitude toward being interviewed. Second, it gives the interviewer an opportunity to detect any change in behavior that would indicate that some aspect of the formal interview had been inhibiting the respondent. In this case, it might be possible to glean some of the missing information during the informal period, to re-interview the respondent at a later date under different conditions, or to change the strategy, tactics, and techniques in future interviews.

Developing skills in interviewing

There is a considerable distance between having an intellectual understanding of interviewing and being able to do excellent interviewing. For this reason we have suggested a three-phase procedure for improving interviewing skills which includes thoughtful planning, self-conscious interviewing, and critical evaluation of the performance. We have given a demonstration example of this procedure to launch a self-directed program of improving interviewing. Even those interviewers with years of experience find this self-improvement procedure not only effective in improving skills but also in rejuvenating their interest in the whole interviewing process.

SUBJECTIVE ASPECTS OF LEARNING TO INTERVIEW

In training interviewers with widely differing backgrounds, the writer has encountered many subjective reactions to learning to interview. Often these are curiously parallel to the culture shock felt when one must change his linguistic and other habit patterns to adjust to a new way of life. Of course, this jolt is not so keenly felt when we simply read *about* an exotic culture or *about* interviewing. The experience is more profound when we must learn to *act* in a new way, when old habit patterns are no longer appropriate under the new circumstances, when we have an opportunity to see ourselves in a new perspective. In the cross-cultural experience, this new perspective is attained when we are able to communicate with the foreigner well enough to understand that his perception of us does not agree with our own image of ourselves. In learning to interview we can more quickly attain this new perspective by hearing ourselves interviewing on tape.

The shock of self-recognition can be both depressing and refreshing at different phases of the learning process. The writer has observed a tendency for an initial euphoria to develop as the person plays with some of the new concepts, sees a broader horizon before him, and accepts the challenge to expand his repertoire of basic skills. Then comes a phase in which the learner's morale may drop as he increases his awareness of the complexities of the task, of the type and amount of skill needed, and of some of his own shortcomings in controlling his own behavior in accordance with his intellectual understanding of the problem.

In this curiously contradictory situation his self-esteem as an interviewer may drop as his actual performance is making dramatic improvement. For example, in cases where the learner does a tape-recorded interview at the beginning and at the end of a training period and is asked to discuss each interview with the instructor immediately after each recording session, there is a clear tendency for the learner to be much more critical of his performance in the post-test interview than he was of his pretest interview earlier. Yet, the post-test interview is usually far superior to the pretest. The remedy for this drop in morale was simple and dramatic. When the learner was allowed to hear a portion of both his pretest and post-test in the same session, he was impressed and often surprised by his substantial improvement. Often, however, in order to demonstrate his increased awareness of the problems and solutions in interviewing, he would use the more modest approach of remarking about how gullible or insensitive he was in the pretest, rather than directly saying how perceptive and sensitive he was in the post-test.

The learner must avoid allowing his desirably increased appreciation of the tasks of interviewing and his greater ability to criticize his own behavior to dampen his appreciation of the progress he has made or his faith in continued improvement.

Also, to avoid being overwhelmed by the intellectual complexity of the interviewing task, the reader should remember that, although we have illustrated many interviewing problems in a relatively short space, only a small proportion of them would normally occur in any series of interviews in a particular field study. The sheer number of strategies, techniques, and tactics need not lead to despair since only a few of them may be legitimately used in any one study. Furthermore, it is not necessary to retain the whole inventory of interviewing tools in one's mind since most of these decisions are made in the planning and evaluation stage in which we can use references. Although some of these interviewing tools may be rarely used, it is important to be familiar with them because we cannot predict when the situation will arise in which they are sorely needed.

The areas which the interviewer must master as his own are the performance skills of listening, manifesting positive attitudes, critically evaluating the information received, probing for elaboration and clarification of the responses, taking notes, and dealing with symptoms of resistance in the respondent. This is enough for anyone to concentrate on at one time!

One way the neophyte can convert his early euphoria into depression is to jump into a practice interview unprepared and expect inspiration to guide him to success. This is not to say an interviewer should never go into an interview unprepared; it might help jolt him out of his old habits and leave him free to experiment. It is more likely, however, to show him the need for advance planning.

In the early stages of learning to interview, it is best to avoid attempting long and highly complex interviews with many topics and subtopics. The basic skills can be developed just as well in a short, simple interview. Fatigue and confusion do not enhance the learning value of the experience for the beginner. He can build endurance later.

The person learning to interview should not select a friend or acquaintance as the respondent. This creates a confusion of roles in which both the interviewer and the respondent may be tense, confused, or amused by the sudden change in his friend's behavior. This creates an artificial relationship incompatible with both friendship and interviewing. For the initial experience, it is easier and more fruitful to interview a stranger, but he should be someone in the same social class and subculture as the interviewer to avoid possible communication problems that could unnecessarily complicate the interview.

It is sometimes essential to morale for the interviewer to realize that the best of strategies, techniques, and tactics will sometimes be relatively unproductive for reasons that are not his fault. For example, the respondent may simply not have the relevant information. In this case, good interviewing may appear to be unproductive since no useful information is obtained. Actually, this is a positive rather than a negative outcome since the insensitive interviewer with a "bull in the china shop" approach might obtain a large quantity of fiction worse than useless. Also, a respondent who has relevant information may be fatigued, irritable, or sick. Sometimes the physical environment may be uncomfortable or lack privacy. It is even possible in rare cases that a personal characteristic of the interviewer may have some special meaning to the respondent who simply "can't talk to that type of person." These idiosyncratic circumstances do not arise often and should not be allowed to lower the interviewer's morale. The experienced interviewer will quickly diagnose such an interview situation as impossible and simply find a graceful way out.

The intelligent interviewer realizes that interviewing can never be a magical process by which the "truth, the whole truth, and nothing but the truth" can be efficiently extracted from any respondent. All of the present-day knowledge combined with the most intelligent and skillful application will not completely avoid some distortion or incompleteness in the information obtained from some respondents. But when we consider the contrast between the conditions and methods that can be used in much social science interviewing with the conditions and methods of communication between a prosecuting lawyer and a hostile witness, between an employer and potential employee, or between an applicant for admission to a university and the admission officer of that university, we see that many serious decisions are based upon information received under conditions not nearly so favorable to obtaining truth as can usually be attained in the social science interview.

If the reader will consider the ideas in this book as something to act upon, to verify and modify in active interviewing practice, the rewards will be much greater than if he views the book merely as a collection of theoretical concepts seasoned with interesting illustrative cases. It is hoped that this book will not be accepted on faith as gospel nor rejected because some of the ideas do not form an elegant theoretical or literary model that pleases the esthetic senses.

The book should be accepted for what it is. It is the writer's sincere attempt to organize his insights, based upon his own and others' experiences in interviewing and upon ideas assimilated from systematic studies of the interviewing process, into a meaningful progression of conceptual and experiential steps. The writer has attempted to share his discoveries in a way designed to launch the interviewer into a period of self-sustained development rather than to limit his potential growth by presenting a set of rules on interviewing. Insofar as the writer has been able to share this voyage of discovery, the reader will have a broader grasp of the nature of the interviewing task, an expanded repertory of interviewing tools, and crescent insight into the appropriate use of these tools in a variety of interviewing settings. The continued development of interviewing skills will depend upon practice that combines thoughtful planning and disciplined interviewing with a critical evaluation of one's own performance and of the concepts presented here.

Appendixes

Appendix A

Sharing the consultants' experiences

This appendix is intentionally not mentioned in the text to avoid alerting the reader to the fact that the answers to the four strategy questions in Laboratory Problem 8, on the academic freedom study, are contained here. If the reader intends to do the laboratory problem (at the end of Chapter 12), he should do so *before* reading this appendix. First, is a general sociocultural context giving some background assumptions from which the suggested answers to the four strategy questions flow. Second, are the suggested answers to the questions. It is not expected that the reader's answers should approach the amount of detail in these suggested answers which have benefited from the shared experiences of two of the consulting interviewers on the project. These answers are not presented as the only possible solutions but to open up a wider range of possibilities in the reader's mind. The comparison between the reader's own answers and those suggested here should provide a better understanding of the problems of planning strategy for use in potentially hostile territory.

Sociocultural context of the study

Before presenting answers to the four strategy questions, we will give some of the salient relationships between the information sought, the college subculture and the larger society. Since, by definition, a violation of academic freedom is conflict between a faculty member and those who have the power to force him to conform, some faculty member must know about every instance of such a conflict. The probability of the professor having *direct* experience in a conflict would vary

531

with (*a*) the field in which he teaches, (*b*) his personal background, and (*c*) the extracurricular activities in which he participates on and off campus. Let us discuss these characteristics one at a time.

Those teaching in a field which deals with subjects which are controversial in the particular college community are more likely to experience restriction of their freedom. Issues are controversial either because the *evidence* is ambiguous or the *values* are conflicting. Values are in conflict when there is some social change going on and one group's values lag behind those of another. If members of these two groups are brought together, there is likely to be conflict. If one group is represented by a faculty member and the other by the administration, there is likely to be restrictions on academic freedom.

When two individuals disagree, the one who is in the subordinate power position is considered to be the nonconformist; therefore, the nature of nonconformity in a closed society like a college campus depends upon the value position of those in the superordinate power position. The way in which nonconformists get into the academic community depends upon the relationship between the academic institution and the larger society. If the college is more conservative than the larger society, as would be the case in a small college administered and supported by a fundamentalistic denominational church, it is almost forced to admit "heretics" in the fields of philosophy, history, economics, sociology, political science, anthropology, archaeology, and psychology because (*a*) if they want to be fully accredited, they must have a certain proportion of Ph.D.'s on the faculty, and (*b*) it is usually not possible to obtain the Ph.D. degree in these subjects from a university controlled by the same fundamentalistic denomination. Under these conditions the nonconformity will be in the form of religious "heresy" or "iconoclasm" and is often an instance of the conflict between science and religion. If the college is more liberal than the larger society and is secular in orientation, the nonconformity will more likely be in the form of opposition to certain values or policies of government or business which represent the beliefs of the majority or a vocal reactionary minority.

In the first type of college a biology professor who taught the theory of evolution, an archaeologist who disagreed with the fundamentalist's conception of the origin and age of the earth, an anthropologist who does not agree that men are born with a conscience which tells them what is right and what is wrong, a sociologist who uses the church as an example of cultural lag, or a psychologist who said masturbation is not harmful would all be subjected to administrative pressure.

In the second type of college the biologist and archaeologist are not likely to become targets for suppression, while the sociologist, anthropologist, and social psychologist are all still likely candidates along with political scientists and economists. Thus, in selecting the teaching field as a specific characteristic of the respondent most likely to have direct experience with restriction of academic freedom, we must keep in mind the type of college we are studying.

The personal background of the person teaching in a "sensitive" field also changes the probability of his being involved in a controversy. For example, the following characteristics would often be relevant: having a degree from a liberal university or one which differs considerably from the college where he is now teaching, being young and not teaching at the present college for over ten years, belonging to organizations which are at variance with the values of the administration (these might include such things as the ACLU, NAACP, AAUP, Socialist Party, Unitarian Church, etc.).

The extracurricular activities in which the faculty member participates might be related to some of the outside affiliations mentioned above, or they might consist of certain administrative duties or committee work. Such sensitive spots would include being on the administrative committee which deals with such problems as faculty tenure, promotions, hiring and firing, or being the official representative for the American Association of University Professor which is concerned with the protection of academic freedom, or serving as the adviser to the college newspaper or other publications involving public relations. The professor in the latter position might or might not be in agreement with the policies he is supposed to enforce, but in either case he will be less likely to want to talk about academic freedom if he is involved in repressing freedom of speech in any channel.

In general we can say that the faculty members who would be most willing to give the information they have would be those who (a) are identified with the repressed rather than the repressors and (b) are not fearful of any retaliation if they talk. The lack of fear of retaliation may exist in any particular case because the person intends to leave at the end of the year and has another job, or because he came as a one-year visiting professor, or because the administration has already meted out all the punishment it can in his case, or as happens in rare cases, he has the protection of someone in higher power than his immediate superior who would be interested in retaliating, or because he has complete faith that the information he gives will be kept anonymous.

An ideal faculty respondent would be one who has had his academic freedom restricted and is being asked to leave and who has signed a contract with another institution for the next year. Another ideal respondent would be one who has been punished to the full extent of the administrative power but has not been fired. He is likely to be a nucleus of discontent on the campus and have knowledge of any other cases of restriction of academic freedom. Those who have not had any restrictions placed on their behavior and who want to stay and gain promotions will be less likely to tell about any cases they are familiar with because they either agree that the action was just and do not consider it to be undue restriction, or they feel it was unjust and do not want to admit that they are willing to compromise with such an institution and so tend to look for rationalizations and optimistic interpretations of the event.

It is highly improbable that the administrators are unfamiliar with any case of restrictions of academic freedom on a college campus, particularly if the college is small. The main problem is to find one who recognizes a violation of academic freedom when he sees a specific case of it, and who does not rationalize the situation or have guilt feelings which make any admission of restriction of academic freedom a threat to his ego, and who is not afraid that a frank admission might bring retaliation from someone in a higher power position. Due to these considerations it is more probable that only an administrator who is being fired because he does not agree with policies of restriction of academic freedom or who is leaving voluntarily because of his disagreement with the policies would be willing to tell more than has already become public knowledge.

Sources of information. Useful information can be obtained from any administrator who is familiar with the policies as they have been operating. This information might be of several types:

a. Public information. If some controversy has already become public knowledge locally or otherwise, the administrator will be afraid to withhold it for two reasons. First, he would not want the interviewer to get the information from another source after he had denied such information existed. Second, he would like to give his own interpretation of the facts and "correct" any wrong impressions which might be obtained from any other sources. This official information source is helpful to the interviewer because it saves time in obtaining a list of at least the publicly known controversies which can then be explored by interviewing the people who had been involved on various sides of the issue.

b. Value orientations. A very important type of information is usually given by the administrator whether he intends to or not. This is his value orientation, which in turn strongly influences his definition of the situation, including his definition of academic freedom. It is usually found that the term "academic freedom," like freedom in general, has a positive value connotation on nearly all college campuses; but its meaning, particularly in actual practice, varies tremendously. In one college it may mean the professor's freedom from dictatorship as long as nothing is said which disagrees with the views of parents, administrators, alumni, and the church. In another it means that the professor has the right to explain all sides of an issue, to take a definite stand on a controversial issue as long as he is sincere in doing so regardless of whose toes might be stepped on in the process. Thus on one campus academic freedom does not include the right of the geology professor to disagree with the sponsoring church's official statement of the actual age of the earth, while at a state university in a state with strong dairy interests it does not include the right of an organic chemist to publicly compare the food value of oleomargarine with butter. Attached to the value orientations with respect to academic freedom will usually be found a set of psychological rationalizations for any action which the administration has been forced to take by power groups off campus. Rationalization is necessary for the administrator who, like all human beings, wants to preserve his feeling of self-esteem and, therefore, cannot admit that he has been coerced into taking an action he does not believe in.

c. Degree of fear. In cases where certain restrictions of academic freedom due to off-campus pressures have not become public knowledge, the administrators often are not proud of their actions and feel a considerable ego threat in being discovered. In these situations the interviewer may obtain no information of type (*a*) above but will be able to detect and roughly measure the degree of fear the administrator has of having his actions discovered by some segment of the larger community which would not approve. If the administrator reports that there is absolute academic freedom on the campus yet does not want to cooperate with the study, the interviewer should hypothesize that something is being hidden from public view.

In trying to determine the amount of fear connected with the survey, it is necessary for the interviewer to use a strategy which (*a*) will not be considered intentionally coercive by the administrator, (*b*) will distinguish between legitimate reasons for not cooperating and flimsy excuses, (*c*) will allow a crude form of measurement, and (*d*) will not jeopardize or compromise the interviewer's right or ability to interview other respondents. An attempt to meet these objectives simultaneously was made by using the strategy illustrated by the exchange between the interviewer and the president of College D shown later in this appendix.

In locating students who have direct knowledge of restriction of academic freedom, we should keep in mind that students can give relevant information in two areas. First is the area of restrictions placed upon the teaching faculty as they see it in the classroom situation. Second are the restrictions placed on students in the classroom and in the activities of various student organizations and extracurricular activities on the campus.

Therefore, we would look for students who had taken courses in the fields where academic freedom is most likely to be repressed on the particular campus and who are in certain organizations such as National Association for the Advancement of Colored People, Americans for Democratic Action, Fellowship of Reconciliation, Young Progressives of America, World Federalists, American Association for the United Nations, Hillel Foundation, Unitarian Fellowship, War Resister's League, Young Socialists, or any group which is controversial or representing a minority group on that particular campus.

In addition there are certain integral functions of student life regulated by the administration where certain students hold key positions with access to information on campus events and with exposure to any pressures which exist to regulate the free flow of this information. This would include the student body president, the editor of the college paper, the head of the debate society, the president of the Pan-Hellenic Council, etc.

Suggested answers to questions

Question 1. *Make a list of the six people, in addition to the president, who, ideally, should be interviewed (in the order in which it would be best to interview them). Give a short description of their most relevant characteristics. In cases where the relevance of a characteristic is not obvious, explain how it is related to the objectives of the study.*

1. Sociology professor. Ideally this professor should be young, have his Ph.D. very recently from a university noted for its protection of academic freedom (also his B.A. or M.A. should have been acquired from a similar type of institution), and he should have no aspirations to remain at the college beyond the current academic year. His background should be as different as possible from that of the administration. This person, if not directly involved in a controversy, will be able to give a picture of the campus politics and will understand and believe the promise of anonymity given by the interviewer.

2. Resigning or fired professor. A professor who has been forced to resign over an academic freedom issue, who is contesting the case but who has already signed a contract for the next year with a more liberal college. This person can give a blow-by-blow account of what has happened to him and, since he has openly contested the action, he will probably have become a rallying point for others who are either fellow-sufferers or admirers. He would be a good source of information on the types of issues which are controversial on the campus, the types of tactics used by the repressors of academic freedom, and the rationalizations used to excuse their actions.

3. Social-action professor. This professor ideally should be young, have been at the college for one or two years, but not interested in staying unless he can be successful in promoting certain unpopular ideas, and be actively participating in certain faculty extracurricular organizations such as the American Association of University Professors, the American Civil Liberties Union, or the Teacher's Union. His social action orientation might be manifested in activities in political organizations which are unpopular on campus. He might also be the official or unofficial sponsor of certain unpopular student organizations.

4. *Unpopular professor.* This professor may be unpopular with either the students, the administration, or the off-campus community. He should be one who is not being fired because he has tenure or knows how to stay within the bounds necessary to retain his job, or has some protection from certain factions on or off campus which would cause a great deal of unfavorable publicity for the college if he were fired. In this case perhaps the college is merely quietly punishing him by simply not giving him an advance in rank or salary.

5. *Detached dean of the faculty.* The dean will have access to relevant information and would be more willing to give information if he came from another institution which had more academic freedom than the present one, if he has no aspirations to stay or to become president, or if he is planning to leave the next year. In any event, he is usually willing to give information on cases which are already public knowledge, and he might have more time to supply details not mentioned by the president.

6. *Public relations director.* The person performing this function may or may not have this title. He might be the "assistant to the president," director of the news bureau, etc. He will be concerned with the relations between the college and certain relevant sections of the larger community such as the local community, the alumni, the donors, the taxpayers, prospective students, etc. In his concern over presenting a desirable picture of the college to the outside world, he will be highly sensitive to any events on campus which would tend to cause difficulty if known outside. Ideally, he should be a person with a strong professional orientation rather than a strong allegiance to the local institution. If he intends to move out of the present job and has qualifications to make more money elsewhere, or if he is familiar with the ethics of preserving strict anonymity of the respondent in social studies of this type, he will be more willing to give the relevant information.

7. *Representative of off-campus pressure group.* Sometimes a particular administrative officer, who may be high or low in the on-campus hierarchy, considers himself the "watch dog" for certain outside interests who may be distrustful of intellectuals or who are concerned with suppressing certain types of ideas which often obtain a hearing on college campuses, such as pacifism, socialism, world government, racial

equality, communism, liberal religion, etc. Thus, such organizations as the American Legion, Daughters of the American Revolution, "Americanism" committees of various types, and church groups might become involved in controversies over academic freedom through one of their members in the college administration. This person could give the conservative or reactionary point of view on the controversial issues involved and would be highly sensitive to any incidents which might be called to his attention.

8. Student newspaper editor. This should be the incumbent editor for the past year rather than the incoming editor. He is in a position to know the kinds of things which are repressed, who represses them, the reasons given, and any changes which might have occurred during his occupancy of the position.

9. Nonconformist student-action leader. Such a respondent could include the current or past leader of the "most radical" organizations on the campus or a representative of a category of students on campus who are deviants from the official line, such as a woman who smokes on a campus where it is forbidden, or one who plays cards or dances when it is officially forbidden, or a socialist, a pacifist, etc., on a campus where such activities are officially unpopular. Such a person would have the needed information and would be in need of some catharsis of sympathetic understanding.

10. Student majoring in a controversial subject. This should be one who has been on campus at least two years and knows some of the differences in professors' and students' behaviors and reputations. Preferably this would be a transfer student from another college who is now graduating.

Question 2. *Explain in detail how you would go about* identifying, locating, *and* contacting *the most useful respondents on a college campus. Describe the whole process from the time you accept the assignment until the last person is interviewed. Make clear the* sequence *of your moves and indicate all the* sources *of information you would use and how you would use them. This strategy plan should show how you would identify, locate, and contact each of the six respondents mentioned in the previous problem and at the same time lead to any other possible respondents you might not have anticipated.*

Our suggested strategy plan which we will spell out in detail is based upon certain general assumptions which underlie and guide the general approach.

a. The interviewer must be prepared for the worst possible reception on the campus. This means that the interviewer should prepare a strategy which would obtain the maximum amount of information in case the president exerts his full power and prestige in preventing access to information.

b. Therefore, the interviewer should get as much information as he can at a distance which will not alert the president or others interested in withholding information and which does not violate any legal or moral obligation to the president. This is a necessary precaution since the president and others can exert influence to prevent others from cooperating in giving information. In case the administration is going to be hostile, there should be as little forewarning as possible, and this should come only after the cooperation of the administration is needed.

c. Although the interviewer prepares for the worst, he should show that he expects the best by acting as though he assumes that people will cooperate and that there is no threat involved in the study. He should offer face-saving devices making it easier for anyone who has previously refused to cooperate to change his mind.

d. The fact that both the individual respondents and the institutions will be kept anonymous should be made clear by word and deed at every step of the strategy.

e. An overall strategy plan should be conceived in as great detail as possible, but at the same time should be considered as tentative and to be modified at any point where new relevant information is assimilated or when unexpected opportunities or obstacles are encountered.

The larger strategy

We will divide the strategy into four time-space phases: (1) that used before arriving in the local community containing the college, (2) that used in the local community before going on-campus, (3) that used on-campus, and (4) that used off-campus in case the interviewer is ordered to leave the campus by the president.

1. Before arriving in the local setting. Obtain as much information as possible about the college and the local community in which it resides *before* going into the local situation. This would include such sources as the college catalog, other publications from the college, standard library volumes describing objective characteristics of colleges and universities in the U.S., etc. Here the interviewer is playing his role as ordinary citizen having access to certain public information about an institution.

This information can be useful for many purposes. For example, it may help acquaint the interviewer with the universe of discourse peculiar to the institution, or it may give clues to the prevalent values officially espoused by the administration, or it will supply a general background or history which will help in understanding the relationship of the college to the larger society, or it will supply names of key individuals and certain background information about them which will help in building *rapport* or in evaluating their desirability as a respond-ent. It can also familiarize the interviewer with the formal structure of the organization and the time table of yearly and weekly activities which will determine the accessibility of the respondents or their will-ingness to talk. Often useful information can be obtained showing the general relationships between the college and the larger community such as whether the students are mostly local or not, whether there is cooperation with the larger community on such projects as adult educa-tion, artistic and dramatic events, sports, etc.

2. After arriving in the local setting. Again the interviewer should exploit his role as a citizen in getting both official and unofficial views on the college. Informal contacts with the hotel manager, the bellboy, the taxi driver, the barber, or the waitress might be used to get some of the flavor of the relationships between the college and the local community.

Later, more formal contacts could be made with the editor of the local newspaper, a local high school teacher, or minister. Such people who have lived in the community for several years have access to public information as well as certain private information and rumors. This group should be "neutral" in that they are not directly involved in any campus controversies and would not feel obligated to warn either the pro or anti people that they are being "investigated."

People representing certain organizations which could be safely as-sumed to be pro–academic freedom in the local setting, such as the American Civil Liberties Union representative, the American Associa-tion for the United Nations, the League of Women Voters, American Association of University Women, or B'nai Brith, could then be con-tacted.

Finally, representatives of any organizations which, on the basis of the information obtained thus far, can be assumed to be anti–academic freedom can be interviewed. To allay any suspicion, it should be made clear that official contact will be made with the college as soon as possible. It is helpful if the interviewer can arrive in town Saturday in order to have time to obtain all the needed off-campus information before seeing the president on Monday.

Local, written sources of information such as the telephone book, a map of the town and college campus, or a city directory may also be helpful in becoming oriented to the situation.

All these off-campus sources could be used in order to obtain public information about specific incidents on the campus, to identify relevant individuals or groups on the campus, to improve the interviewer's uni-verse of discourse and insight into the attitudes involved, and the de-gree to which the campus is open or closed to the public in general. This last bit of information helps the interviewer understand what campus facilities and people he has access to as an ordinary citizen without having to announce any special purpose or being perceived as a "snooper."

3. On campus. The interviewer should first exploit all those sources of information which are customarily open to the public at large without any formalities or without being asked to identify himself. For example, in the library there could be an older or newer edition of the catalog than could be found elsewhere. Yearbooks contain the names and photographs of possible respondents who would be very useful; the student directory, faculty directory, a map of the campus, and current and back copies of the school newspaper or other publications might be useful.

Bulletin boards give up-to-date information on activities, organizations, people, issues which might be directly relevant to the study or at least indicative of a general atmosphere on campus. The cafeteria, coffee shop, or dining room on campus provide places to strike up an informal conversation with students. The bookstore might have maps or directories of students or faculty which were not available elsewhere.

So far all the information has been collected "incognito" but possibly not without attracting some attention; therefore, the first official contact with the president's office should be made in a few hours after arriving on campus. If by this point in the strategy plan it seems highly probable that the president will not receive the interviewer gracefully, an attempt could be made to obtain some more time on the campus without "going behind the president's back" and yet without giving him an opportunity to request the interviewer to leave. This can sometimes be accomplished by making it clear to the president's receptionist or secretary that there is no great urgency in seeing the president but that you represent the Fund for the Republic, will be in town two more days, and would like to have an appointment to talk with him some time that day if possible. Often it will be two to four hours before the president is able to see the interviewer.

In the meantime the interviewer must work rapidly in case the president is likely to deny him access to the campus. This time can be used to lay the groundwork for interviewing faculty and students whether the presidential blessing is obtained or not. In the latter case all interviewing will have to be done off-campus.

The interviewer should locate the offices and home addresses of any key respondents not yet located, talk to some of them, explaining the nature of the study and the sponsor and the fact that he has an appointment with the president to obtain his approval for sending Roper interviewers on campus to interview some of the social science faculty. In explaining the study to the faculty, the president, and the students, the following points should be carefully included:

a. A sample of 180 colleges and universities has been selected for the study.
b. Already 160 out of these have been studied.
c. Those who have not yet cooperated probably have not understood that it is not a time-consuming process, since it would take only an hour for each of a small proportion of the faculty. Or perhaps some other point such as anonymity, purpose of the study, etc., has not been understood.
d. The fact that both the individuals and the institutions will be anonymous and the findings will be in the form of statistical summaries for certain types of institutions. For example, all small, private, nondenominational colleges would be one type, or all large, state-supported institutions would be another type.
e. Now is the time to shed some calm, intellectual light on the subject of academic freedom by getting some quantitative, factual information rather than merely emotional statements of accusation and denial.

Information indirectly related to the main purpose of the study could be obtained from key faculty immediately in their offices. Such information as their prediction of the president's reaction to the request and the reasons for this reaction will be very useful in preparing to meet the president and might also lead to an informal conversation directly related to the purpose of the study. Also, the particular faculty member's attitude can be assessed, and if it is cooperative, he might be asked for suggestions as to people who could give relevant information on either or both sides of any issues on campus. In addition, an appointment for a formal interview in the faculty member's home might be made for any time after the appointment with the president.

Information helpful in approaching students (such as their predominant political, religious, and socioeconomic backgrounds) may be obtained from a faculty member. The names and locations of key informants among the student body might be obtained or verified against previous sources.

Almost any student can give such relevant information as the exact location of the most popular off-campus student hangout and the time of day or night what kinds of people are there. This might be a very vital piece of information in case the president forbids the interviewer to talk to students on a campus where all students live in dormitories. Key students could be encouraged to volunteer any relevant information without a formal systematic interview in which the interviewer takes notes in the presence of the respondent.

If the interview with the president is successful to the extent that he gives permission for the original full-scale study, the interviewer still should keep appointments with faculty and students as well as any other administrators, with the explanation that the study to be done by the Roper interviewer involves many specific formal questions to be directed at the social science faculty only and that he wishes to obtain a broader impressionistic perspective by including various viewpoints.

If the president will not give permission for the full-scale study, then the interviewer should make it clear that he accepts the president's veto and proceed along a series of propositions arranged in order from the most to the least threatening. This tactic can achieve two things. First, it will help the interviewer to discover what he can do with the president's approval. Second, it can obtain a crude measurement of how afraid the president is of being exposed and through which channels. In this discussion the interviewer should be careful to avoid asking the president's permission to interview anyone *off-campus* because he has no legal or moral right to make such a decision in a democracy; and, since the interviewer plans to meet people off-campus regardless of the president's attitude, there is little to be gained by allowing the president to state a position only to be flagrantly violated by the interviewer.

The following example of a conversation between the interviewer and a college president illustrates the strategy of gauging the respondent's sensitivity to investigation.

I: Now that we have discussed more thoroughly the nature and purpose of the study, what do you think of inviting the Roper interviewer to come on campus?

R: It sounds all right to me, but I couldn't act on this unilaterally. I would first have to persuade the administrative committee which doesn't meet right away. If you would have the New York office send some more written material and give me a list of the names of the faculty in the sample, I could try to get their cooperation if the administrative committee approved.

I: How soon do you think you could get the administrative committee together?

R: It would be a couple of weeks anyway. They don't usually meet but once in two months, and they just met last week.

I: Since the spring semester ends tomorrow and commencement is Saturday, there would be little value in this because all the data from the 180 colleges will be needed before next fall. I assume most of the faculty will be gone during the summer since you don't have a summer session. I appreciate your efforts, but I think it is impossible under these conditions to do the full-scale interviewing study.

R: Well, I'm sorry but that is the best I can do.

I: I appreciate it. Instead of the original plan perhaps I could just talk to one or two of your social science staff while I am here without taking time to get any more than an impressionistic perspective rather than any detailed interview.

R: I'm afraid that would be impossible right now since this is examination week and the faculty will be very rushed until commencement.

I: I see. I'm sorry I couldn't come sooner, but I didn't realize in time that your semester ended earlier than most colleges. In that case I could make appointments with them now to talk to them after commencement. Saturday afternoon would give me plenty of time since this would be nothing elaborate and they will have finished all examinations.

R: I'm sure that would not be very practical since they all scatter to the four winds immediately after the commencement exercise. Some of them have their bags packed and their cars waiting and don't even go home after the commencement exercise. There is nothing to hold them in this small town, and they are glad to get away. Those that don't leave will be the ones who are just too exhausted and need a week's rest before they leave.

I: I could contact them and see which ones are still at home on Monday and see if they feel up to a short interview and not say that you suggested it. Or I could say that you suggested that I not disturb them until after they had an opportunity to catch up.

R: I'd rather you did not do that. (In a firm tone and rising from his seat).

I: Since the interview seems impossible, perhaps I could arrange with each one to send a questionnaire to their summer address.

R: I would approve of that if you just give me a list of the faculty in your sample and send me the appropriate number of copies and I will forward them to the summer addresses.

I: This has never been done in this way before, but since this is an emergency, I will ask the New York office if they will do this. If they will, you will receive the materials within the week. Will you still be here?

R: As far as I know now I will be.

I: Very well, While I am here, I would like to talk to some students who are active in campus affairs. Could you recommend any or simply allow me to find some on my own?

R: As I said, this is examination week, and they are all very busy cramming. You know how that was when you were a student.

I: That's right. I suppose that is a universal trait of students. I noticed on the examination schedule on the bulletin board that for seniors the exams were over yesterday so they have no more examinations before commencement on Saturday. Perhaps they would like to help me.

R: The seniors have a lot of things to do in preparing for commencement. That is why their exams have to be finished two days early. Usually their parents are here and staying in town or at some motel to be with their son or daughter until graduation.

I: I see. The customs are very different from campus to campus. In that case, perhaps I could talk to some of the seniors today to see which ones will be available before Saturday in case some of the parents don't arrive until tomorrow.

R: You amaze me! I'm sure you are a capable and well-meaning person. Don't you find it distasteful to have to make a living in this manner, going into places where you are not wanted? Certainly there must be something a man of your training could do which is more pleasant!

I: I'm sorry—I didn't realize that I simply wasn't wanted on campus although I realized that it would cause some inconvenience.

R: You have been very insistent. I don't know anything about the Fund for the Republic nor Mr. Lazarsfeld who signed the original letter to me. That's why at the beginning of this discussion I suggested that you have the New York office send some more written material so that I would have something to show to the administrative committee. I have never seen such pressure applied to me on anything before. After that letter I told them there would be no time for such a study on this campus. Then they sent a telegram to pressure me some more. Now you arrive without even writing me a letter that you are coming.

I: I'm sorry, but when I was first given the list of colleges who had not yet been studied, I looked at their catalogs and discovered yours had the earliest closing date. In fact I had that information only yesterday and had to plan my itinerary to go about 1,000 miles out of my way to some here first. There would not have been time to get an airmail letter to you and wait for your answer . . . You are right about my being a bit insistent. There are two main reasons for this. First, since we want a reliable quantitative description of American colleges and universities in general, we must obtain as complete a sample as possible. Also, I want to be sure I have done everything I can so that any particular type of institution will be prevented from appearing to contain a larger proportion of noncooperating colleges than others. For this reason it is helpful for me to get some information even though it is now impossible for us to do the original type of study.

R: Frankly, I don't need you to tell me that my staff is overworked, underpaid, and half sick. I know this . . . and they are sticking loyally by the cause. For example, I have a public relations man who was offered $3,000 more at another institution, but he is determined to see the job through. Some of my staff are sick, and we can't replace them. We don't have enough money to pay what new faculty want. Our constituents pay taxes to keep up the big state universities which already have millions and are our competitors for students and faculty. Yet the parents of our students have to pay additional money for a college education after paying taxes to send someone else's children to school. This is a form of forced self-destruction. Meanwhile, the faculty at Columbia University have time to write me letters and send telegrams and you are flying around the country on foundation money . . . Another thing . . . we are coming up for reevaluation for accrediatation by the American Association of Colleges and Universities. And I have so much paper work to do that I haven't had any lunch yet. Now if you don't mind I would like to go to lunch while I still can.

I: I will take up no more of your time . . . and I hope that we may meet again under more pleasant circumstances.

4. If ordered off campus. If the president refuses his blessing on either the full-scale study or on the interviewer's talks with administrators, faculty, or students on campus, the interviewer should continue his contacts with students and faculty off-campus. Those faculty members who seemed the most sympathetic to the study in the preliminary contacts should be contacted first. They should not be given the false impression that the president approves of your interview with them nor that the president specifically disapproves since he was never given this opportunity. The following statement would be good:

I was unable to obtain the president's blessing for sending out the Roper interviewers, nor would he approve of interviewing anyone but himself on the campus. (Give president's reason). I did not ask whether he approved of faculty members who were willing to speak to me in their own homes. I assumed he would not want to be put in the position of deciding on a question of this type over which he has no official legal jurisdiction or moral right in a democratic society. It would be like asking 'Do you grant your faculty the right to speak to anyone they wish to invite into their homes, or should they ask your permission first?'

At this point the respondent should be further reassured that the interviewer did not indicate that he intended to interview faculty in their homes, and that he in no case will tell anyone whom he has interviewed unless that person wants to have it mentioned.

This strategy was proven to be necessary in some of the cases and was very effective where it was necessary. It is precisely in those cases where the president was most insistent that the interviewer "go home" that it was most necessary to continue the investigation to discover what was being hidden from view. Also in these same cases the faculties needed to obtain sympathetic understanding, catharsis, recognition and to satisfy their need for meaning in what appeared an unjust, contradictory, and hostile world.

In approaching the students off-campus, I used almost the same explanation as given to the faculty. However, in both cases the reason which the president gave for his refusal was given as accurately as possible regardless of whether the interviewer believed it to be a rationalization or not. This provided a face-saving device for the president and also for the respondent who could say, for example, "Well, in general, he is right; the faculty are pretty busy now, and he wouldn't want to be put in the position of asking them to do more overtime work than they are already, but it just happens that I'm not too busy today and am very interested in the topic, so it will be no chore for me."

We have shown a strategy plan founded on the assumption that the interviewer must be prepared for the worst possible reception and that this plan can always be modified if the reception is more cordial. The pessimistic preparedness is necessary because beginning with the optimistic assumption that all will be sweetness and cooperation would leave the interviewer open to a surprise attack which would leave him speechless and deny him the information he came to obtain. The main barrier to communication to be expected in that type of field situation is *ego threat*, which in some cases is so acute that the faculty and/or administration will use a clever strategy to attempt to foil the interviewer. In these cases the interviewer has two main forces on his side: first, is his foresight in planning strategy, and second, is the fact that no one wishes to openly challenge academic freedom as a value or to admit that they are fearful of being investigated because they do not have academic freedom. Under these conditions the institution's strategy of evasion seldom includes an outright admission that they fear an "investigation." This brings us to the next question.

Question 3. *What strategy might be attempted by the president to prevent the interviewer from obtaining the needed information?*

Our answer to this question is based on the strategies actually used by some of the presidents of the 20 "reluctant" colleges.

Polite refusal. The president pretends to be sorry that he cannot cooperate but gives some reason beyond his own control. For example, "I'm sorry we didn't understand the exact nature of the study because not enough information was given in the letter we received. If we had known, we would have been honored to participate in the study. However, it would be impossible on such short notice because we cannot take on this added demand on the faculty's time."

False acceptance. To throw the interviewer off the trail without any argument or unpleasantness, the president appears to accept the interviewer's proposition realizing that due to conditions of which he hopes the interviewer is unaware it will be impossible to carry out the study. For example, "Now that we understand the purposes of this study, I think that the faculty would be happy to participate in it. Why don't you go right ahead." He does not mention that the faculty are all leaving the next day and are not in their offices at the present time.

Indirect threat to respondents. "I think I agree that this is a worthwhile study so to expedite matters, if you will just give me a list of the faculty members who have been selected in the sample, I will contact them to get their cooperation." In one case this type of offer of cooperation was followed by calls to the faculty warning them they should be careful what they say and that they would be perfectly within their legal rights to refuse the interview. In another case the president called the faculty member immediately in the presence of the interviewer and asked him to come over right away because someone wanted to know if there was any academic freedom on the campus. The president told the faculty member and the interviewer to "just use my secretary's office since you are both right here. She won't be back for at least 15 minutes." The whole interview had to take place within earshot of the president which made it useless as a source of reliable information. In both of these strategies the president ignored the explanation that the respondents were to remain anonymous.

The "red tape" barrier. There is an endless variety of possibilities for placing organizational obstacles in the path of the interviewer which the president can use without taking the responsibility for directly refusing the interviewer's request. For example, as one president put it, "I'm sorry we didn't have enough information to act before. You realize this is just one of hundreds of requests we have for giving information for various studies. If you will just have the New York office write me a letter stating all the things you have just told me, I will have something to show the Board of Trustees at the next meeting. I will do what I can, but I can't promise they will consent."

The "Bear-leading" approach. There are two basic principles upon which this approach depends. First, the administrator can keep the interviewer busy with activities which are difficult to politely refuse, which seem to promise some leads to relevant information, but which actually avoid the issue, while consuming as much of the interviewer's limited time as possible. Second, the interviewer can be lead directly to discussions of academic freedom, but in each case the respondent has been selected by the administration to give the proper point of view. Often the president will turn the interviewer over to his assistant whose main function is public relations and is best qualified to bear-lead the interviewer.

The rumor barrier. In this strategy the president may or may not directly refuse to cooperate with the interviewer, but after the interviewer has left his office, the president may launch strategically placed rumors which will define the interviewer as a highly undesirable and threatening outsider. The image which will do this best depends upon the value system on the campus. To be most effective the rumor must picture the interviewer as threatening to students, faculty, and administration alike. For example, in one case the rumor was that this "snooper does not have proper identification and might very well be from a rival college trying to obtain damaging information to prevent the college from attaining full accreditation with the regional accrediting organization." Or in some cases it would be equally effective to intimate that the interviewer might be from a "communist-front organization."

Righteous indignation. This strategy relies on a blustering emotional outburst giving the impression that the administrator has been personally insulted rather than the more correct impression that he is afraid of any investigation. For example, in one case when the interviewer mentioned that he had studied the college catalog in the library before the appointment with the president, the latter seized upon this opportunity to righteously accuse the interviewer of "snooping," in spite of the fact that the library was open to the public and certainly the college catalog contains nothing but public information. He said, "I don't care what your purpose is. It is obvious from your snooping methods that you are up to no good. It is a personal insult to me for you to be investigating our campus before you have the good manners and common consideration of coming to the president's office and making your presence known. Therefore, I forbid you to continue this investigation which is completely unwarranted. Not even the FBI could get away with a thing like that!"

The head-on attack. This strategy was never used by itself since it constitutes an attack on academic freedom itself. But the following example actually occurred. When the president saw the interviewer's reaction was one of interest in the president's own views, he softened the attack and retreated to the "red tape" strategy described above. "I don't want to be plagued with any such study. All this bellyaching about academic freedom doesn't interest me. It is just a slogan to either cover up incompetence or subversion, and I'm not interested in either. It takes all the time I have to keep this institution financially above water. There would be no academic life of any kind, let alone academic freedom, which is of dubious value, without the money!"

These strategies probably do not exhaust the possibilities at the disposal of the president, but they represent those actually used. They sometimes were combined when the first attempt to outmaneuver the interviewer failed. This can be seen in the preceding example of "gauging the respondent's sensitivity to investigation." These examples of avoidance strategies plus the chronicle of specific problems encountered on one college campus (Appendix B) indicate that the interviewer's overall strategic principle of "preparing for the worst while hoping for the best" is necessary when entering the field. Some of the most salient features of the field conditions were:

a. The information had to be gathered quickly to be of any value.

b. Cases of repression or violation of academic freedom could not be uncovered without threatening the administrator's ego even though no legal threat was involved.

c. Since the investigator had no legal power to demand the president's cooperation and since no publicity was to be given to a particular institution or its personnel, the president could refuse.

d. Since his social status was higher than that of the interviewer, the president felt no social pressure to *explain* in detail why he could not cooperate or to assume an added burden for himself or his staff.

Under these conditions the president had nothing to motivate him to cooperate except his general habit of being cooperative and very little to prevent his refusing except his desire to avoid appearing to be opposed to academic freedom.

Question 4. *What type of person would make the ideal interviewer for this study if only one interviewer could be used? Give his personal characteristics and the role and status he should assume while interviewing administrators, faculty, and students.*

Personal characteristics. The interviewer should have experience in "one-shot" field studies where information must be gathered rapidly with no opportunity to build up personal relationships with respondents or to interview them the second time. He should have experience in devising strategy in potential conflict situations. He should be flexible in his interviewing approach in order to adapt to college presidents or freshmen. He should be thoroughly familiar with the organization, vocabulary, and problems of academic institutions and should have a vital interest in academic freedom but enough training in social sciences to avoid a moralistic condemnation of the people who are subjected to the pressures causing them to suppress academic freedom. He should be from outside the college he is studying and the community in which the college is located, and should have a generally warm and nonthreatening personality.

All of these qualifications could be found some professors of sociology, psychology, anthropology, or political science who had the proper experience in interviewing techniques and field strategy and who, preferably, are from another state.

Role and status in the interview. In talking to the president it would be best to explain that the interviewer is a consultant hired by the Fund for the Republic for one job only and not mention that he is also a professor in social sciences at another college or university. In speaking to faculty members it could be mentioned that although at the moment he is doing consulting work, he has had a number of years experience teaching. If the respondent wants to know at what college, the interviewer may say that he has been requested not to identify himself with any particular college in order not to influence the respondent's replies. In talking to people in the same field the interviewer might identify the exact field of his training in order to build rapport. In talking to the students his former role as college professor should not be mentioned.

Appendix B

One strategy account

The following excerpts from the interviewer's notes on his field strategy illustrate some of the errors, wrong guesses, blind alleys, and lucky breaks which necessitate a change in strategy. This account deals with the problems encountered on a campus where the president showed *extreme* resistance to the interviewer. We shall call the institution College D.

"When I received the telephone call from Elmo Roper and Associates asking whether I could work for ten days contacting the 'reluctant' colleges, it was already May 20. By the time I had made arrangements for someone to assume my lecturing duties and had made a preliminary study of the four colleges assigned to me and had made transportation arrangements, it was May 23.

"While planning the order of my visits, it became apparent after studying the catalogs of the colleges that the sequence of visits could not follow the simple logic of geographical location to minimize travel but that the college farthest away must be visited first, since the last day of final examinations at College D was May 25; therefore, College A was the fourth campus I visited even though it was the closest. If I. had not noted the closing dates and assumed that they were all in the first week of June or later, I would have missed the opportunity to speak to faculty in 50 percent of those on my list.

"Although ideally it would be desirable to spend at least three full days on each campus, only eleven days remained before the last of the colleges closed for the summer. These eleven days included one weekend, during which direct contact with respondents would be limited, and time for traveling over 1,000 miles, only 300 of which could be done by air. The most time spent on any one campus under these conditions would be about two days.

"Before leaving my own campus I was able to gather considerable information about College D from their catalog which would be helpful in planning strategy and becoming familiar with its organization, its general value system, and some aspects of its unique universe of discourse. For example, I discovered that it was a college sponsored by a Protestant church which was a fundamentalistic denomination, and that the governing body of the institution must, according to the charter, be selected from the membership of the church and contain a majority of ministers. Chapel attendance was required of all students. This immediately gave me a clue that not only the social science faculty might feel restrictions on academic freedom but also the faculty in biology, geology, archaeology, or philosophy if the latter were not someone who had his training in religion.

"Also possible conflicts between the academic standards and certain religious and economic considerations could be explored by reading the catalog. For example, a careful scrutiny of the listing of course offerings indicated that there was either an attempt to give the impression that many more courses were listed than could be offered simultaneously by such a small faculty, or that the faculty was greatly overloaded. Brumbaugh's *American Colleges and Universities* showed that the college had a very small endowment for the size of its student body and that the tuition for the students was quite low. Thus the probable necessity for low faculty salaries, difficulty in keeping good faculty, and attempts by the administration to keep faculty by appealing to their 'loyalty' to their school. There might also be attempts to help the newer members of the teaching staff to lower their level of aspiration as far as academic standards are concerned so that they could carry the heavy load and not have guilt feelings about not doing a good job. The administration would probably be hypersensitive to the alumni's attitude toward the college since their donations were sorely needed.

"Also I hypothesized that the college would fear the prospects of being re-evaluated by the regional college accrediting association since the proportion of faculty members with higher degrees was dangerously low. Evidence of the probable conscious attempt to pad the listed faculty with Ph.D.'s could be seen in such things as the fact that the head of a department would typically have a B.A. from College D, and yet there would be other names in the department with Ph.D.'s attached who on closer scrutiny would be found to teach only a one-semester course every three years and happened to be a relative of some member of the administration. This hypothesis that the President of College D would fear the prospect of losing accreditation was later clearly borne out in the interview with him.

"Another indication of the probable conflict between secular and sacred values on the campus was the fact that all sociology courses were taught by the head of the German Department, and the course descriptions in the catalog showed that "Christian sociology" was taught. It would probably be very difficult to find a Ph.D. in sociology who would teach 'Christian sociology' particularly if limited to fundamentalistic-Protestant-Christian sociology.

"Immediately after arriving in Bear Falls I talked with the local newspaper reporter who covered all the news on College D and its relationship to the town. Although the campus was only six blocks from the center of town, there was very little interaction between 'town and gown.' This particular offshoot distinguished itself from the main body of the denomination by a special covenant with God. The idea that someone might accuse the college of being infiltrated with communists or that the faculty should take a "loyalty oath" would be greeted with humor if anyone were to raise it. The town was predominantly Democratic and becoming more so with the influx of new industry. The college was described as:

> Much too conservative to be Republican. In fact they are too conservative to vote until the Christian Amendment is put into the U.S. Constitution. The only kind of issue between the college and the town was mainly in the mind of the college administration. That was about three years ago when a bunch of the men students climbed a ladder into one of the girls dorms on campus. The college called the police from town and had them all taken to the police station, but at least half of the people in town thought the whole thing was funny.

This type of information led [me] to suspect that such things as politics, communism, and academic freedom would not be an issue, but that the 'sins of the younger generation' would be the basis for conflict on the campus. The reporter also explained that the big on-campus issues were how to keep the men from smoking, how to keep campus plays censored to omit stage kisses, and how to prevent the students from playing cards and dancing. He also pointed out that the students were not all members of the church, which caused some submerged unrest because some students were more liberal on certain issues than many of the faculty and all of the administration. Luckily the reporter supplied me with a map of the town including a detailed map of the campus which, however, did not label six of seven buildings. He wished me luck in my venture and I headed for the campus.

"Since I felt that the President's welcome might not be too cordial, I first went directly to the library which the reporter assured me I could use unnoticed. There I found the new catalog for the next academic year and compared it with the one for the current year, hoping to find some names of present faculty not intending to return. I was delighted to find three such names. I then looked at the current *College Annual* for the photographs of these three people as well as of the president, his assistant, the dean of the faculty, the student body president, and the editor of the student newspaper. In addition to the three faculty who were not listed in the next year's catalog, I found three others whose vitae sounded as if they might be out of place in College D. One had a recent Ph.D. in philosophy from Columbia and the other had a recent M.A. in education from the University of Chicago. At that moment I thought I had five good prospects, but actually as it turned out, only one was a good prospect and my efforts to contact her were foiled by the administration.

"From the library I went out to look for a coffee shop, bookstore, or other place where students might have some leisure time to talk. I spotted a coffee shop across campus and started in that direction. On the way I met a student and asked him where the social science building was or where the faculty offices were of people teaching sociology. His cordial attitude dampened slightly and he said that I could inquire at the public relations office which was in 'Old Main.' I had not quite decided what to make of this when I met another student and asked "Are you a senior?" and he proudly replied "Yes, I am!" Then I asked the question about the location of offices again and was given the same answer. Another try with a third student convinced me that I had run head-on into the current policy for the treatment of strangers on campus. After this I wondered whether there was any value in trying to talk with students about anything, but I headed doggedly for the coffee shop. I ordered a cup of coffee, sat at the counter, and had the good luck to have the President of the Student Senate sit beside me. I explained that I was looking over the campus and having a cup of coffee before going in to see President Jones. Since the student seemed outgoing and friendly, we chatted, cautiously at first, about the campus; and I was able to get some information which proved very valuable. For example, I discovered to my surprise that many of the students lived off campus in private homes which were approved by the college. I also found that I could buy a student directory complete with off-campus addresses at the bookstore. By simply asking him if in his four years at College D he had courses from certain teachers who would, like himself, not be back on campus next year, it was discovered that two of the three were over 65 and were retiring officially since they had been ill for some time. The third one was a young woman instructor in dramatics 'who had gotten a raw deal' because the President had decided to fire her last November but did not tell her this until after the spring play on May 10 because he was afraid she might quit on the spot without producing the last three plays of the season. Since I had assumed that I could talk to her directly, I did not press him for any details of the case. This student also told me that the recent Ph.D. from Columbia was a person who had taught at College D for 18 years, was 56 years old, and was a relative of one of the older members of the Board of Trustees. 'What's more,' he added, 'you'd never recognize her from her picture in the annual which was taken at least 20 years ago.' My five possible propsects were reduced to one, but the fifth promised to be a good place to make the initial contact with the faculty since it was definitely established that she was leaving.

"If I had known then what I know now, I would have tried to contact the young dramatics instructor, Miss Baldwin, before seeing the president. I knew that I could get her home address from the faculty directory and preferred to interview her off-campus so assumed that I could reach her later.

"I also looked at all the bulletin boards to see what types of clubs, organizations, meetings, speakers, etc., were to be found. There were no political organizations of any type nor any of the usual social action or study groups or debate societies to be seen.

"When I went into the president's office and asked the secretary for an appointment to see the president, she explained that he was so busy I would have to come in next week; then I explained that I was in town for only two days. She went into his office and came out saying he would see me in 25 minutes. I thanked her and said I would get a cup of coffee and be back in 20 minutes. I had not counted on having an appointment so soon and managed to talk to only one more student at the coffee shop before seeing the president.

"From the student I learned about the local campus issues of smoking, dancing, and playing cards, and that Miss Baldwin not only did not have a telephone but lived in the Dean's house where there was no private entrance. I learned the Dean's name and address but had not more time before returning to the president's office. My interview with the president indicated that he was very fearful of any 'unwarranted investigation' sponsored by people connected with 'those tax-supported atheistic institutions.' He had resented the 'intrusion' from the time he received the first letter from Paul Lazarsfeld. The end result was that I promised to leave campus and not return. After trying to soothe the president's temper, I left feeling that he felt satisfied and victorious and that our paths would not cross again; but I was wrong.

"I went to the corner drugstore immediately and called the campus asking for Miss Baldwin. The switchboard operator wanted to know who wanted to talk to her. Since this question was unexpected, the best thing I could think of off-hand that was both true and nonthreatening was that I had come into Bear Falls on my way from Bigtown where Miss Baldwin went to graduate school and hoped to talk to her before I had to leave the next day. There was some whispered conversation on the other end, and then the line was disconnected. I tried to call back immediately but could get no answer.

"Then I went to the home where the student editor of the college newspaper lived and was able to talk to her quite freely for over an hour and a half about the control of the content of the newspaper to hide issues on the campus, and about Miss Baldwin who was being fired because she wore slacks while building stage sets and was also accused of not carefully supervising the changing of costumes backstage. In addition, she allowed stage kisses and was dating a Korean War veteran who was a student her own age. She also told me that Miss Baldwin was always on campus at this time of the day and would be leaving in about 15 minutes driving a yellow Plymouth. I went back to campus immediately and waited on the side street near the only entrance and exit to the parking lot. I noticed a female come out the back door to Old Main and walk toward the parking lot. I could recognize her as Miss Baldwin from her picture in the Annual. I called to her, probably somewhat timidly, but she did not hear. I waited for over 30 minutes at the entrance to the parking lot, but she never came out. It was now five o'clock and people began to emerge from Old Main and go toward the parking lot. Since I did not care to meet the president at this location, even though I was off campus, I left.

"I stopped in the drugstore and called one of the faculty, Mrs. Frances Horn, at her home which was in another town about ten miles away. She said she would be happy to talk with me. I did not mention the president's attitude toward the study, only that I had seen him that day. She told me which bus to take and I went immediately to her home. When I arrived at her apartment, it was almost 90 seconds before she answered the door. When I entered, there was another woman there of about the same age (50 years) who was looking furtively about the room while I was talking to Mrs. Horn who had asked me to sit down but had not yet seated herself. My feeling that they expected something to happen was confirmed when the phone rang. Mrs. Horn answered it and said it was for me. It then seemed highly probable that Mrs. Horn had called the president immediately before I entered since he was on his way home from college while I was on my way to Mrs. Horn's apartment and could not be called much sooner. She probably told him I was arriving and he called back immediately. There is no other way I can see that he could have been so psychic as to my whereabouts and timed his call so precisely.

"In the conversation with President Jones on the telephone, he admitted that I was within my legal rights and that he was also within his when he let the faculty know his attitude toward the study. When I tried to reassure him as to the nature of the study, he expressed concern over the types of questions being asked. When I proposed to postpone this interview until after I had shown him the questions, he declined, saying that it would make him much happier if I would just omit College D from the study entirely. He accused me of trying to drive a wedge between him and his faculty by giving them the impression that he approved of this 'intrusion.' When I explained that I had been careful not to give this impression, he quickly reversed his tactics and said that I was trying to drive a wedge between him and his faculty by giving them the impression that he was trying to infringe on their rights to give their views or by giving the impression that the president had something to hide. He summed up his point of view by saying that he would be happier if I would just leave town. I promised that I would not attempt to interview any more faculty since I felt the present atmosphere not conducive to the most candid expression of the faculty's views.

"The next day I talked again with the local newspaper reporter who happened to see me at the hotel. Of course I did not give him any of the details but said I was able to obtain some additional information all of which fell into line with the point of view he had given me and thanked him.

"This college frustrated me more than any of the others where I was able at least to talk to some faculty members with or without the president's blessing. Nevertheless I was able to obtain information from the three students, the president, and the reporter which was consistent regarding the issues which put the faculty in jeopardy on the campus."

Appendix C

Highlights of information collected

The highlights from the four colleges given below clearly demonstrate that even under the hostile conditions encountered by the interviewer it was possible to (*a*) discover what each institution was trying to hide by refusing access to the Roper interviewers, and (*b*) to show that the issues causing the disputes were so different from those anticipated by the planners of the study that it would have been a waste of time to send out the Roper team with the highly structured interview schedule.

College A. A large institution supported by private funds, city taxes, and state taxes had fired a philosophy professor because some of his teachings were considered anti-church by the local clergy who had organized local city power groups to bring pressure upon the university. Others in the Department of Sociology felt threatened for having used the church as an example of "culture lag." Neither of these situations were admitted by the administration.

College B. A small private denominational college had fired a biology professor for insisting on teaching the theory of evolution and for pointing out that the earth is millions of years old, in contradiction to the denomination's interpretation of the Book of Genesis. Another professor was blamed for the "revolt" of students who, in protest against compulsory chapel attendance, loaded all of the hymnals onto a freight train headed for Chicago. The administration freely admitted these two incidents, which had been made public in the local newspaper, but staunchly defended their "right to preserve the integrity of the institution."

College C. Another small private denominational college had just fired one psychology professor for saying that people were not born with a conscience and that masturbation was not harmful. Also, a sociology professor was being fired for supporting the psychologist's view of the human conscience and for using the church as a case study in institutional power and cultural lag.

College D. Another small private denominational college was firing a young woman who was the drama instructor, because she allowed stage kisses in the plays, did not closely supervise the backstage changing of costumes to avoid "indecent exposure," wore slacks when working on stage sets, and dated a student her age who was a Korean War veteran. In addition, a history professor was in difficulty because he had refused to require every student in his U.S. History course to memorize the denomination's "Christian Amendment to the Constitution."

Bibliography

Aaron, Daniel. "The Treachery of Recollection: The Inner and Outer History," in R. H. Bremner, *Essays on History and Literature.* Columbus: Ohio State University Press, 1966.

Abelsar, Herbert. "A Role-Rehearsal Technique for Exploratory Interviewing." *Public Opinion Quarterly,* vol. 30, no. 2 (1966), pp. 302–5.

Abrams, Mark. "Possibilities and Problems of Group Interviewing." *Public Opinion Quarterly,* vol. 13 (1949), pp. 502–6.

Adams, J. S. *Interviewing Procedures: A Manual for Survey Interviews.* Chapel Hill: University of North Carolina Press, 1958.

Adams, Richard N. *Human Organization Research.* Homewood, Ill.: Dorsey Press, 1960.

Alderfer, Clayton. "Comparison of Questionnaire Responses with and without Preceding Interviews." *Journal of Applied Psychology,* vol. 52 (1968), pp. 335–40.

Allport, Gordon W. *The Use of Personal Documents in Psychological Science.* New York: Social Science Research Council, 1942.

Altemeyer, Robert. "Pool Pollutions and the Post Experimental Interview." *Journal of Experimental Research in Personality,* vol. 5 (1971), pp. 79–84.

Anderson, Nels. *The Hobo: The Sociology of the Homeless Man.* Chicago: University of Chicago Press, 1923.

Armstrong, Fred G. *An Experimental Study of a Structured Interview for Determining Vocational Interests.* Thesis, Temple University, 1957. University of Michigan Microfilm 746.

Assel, Henry, and Eastback, J. O., Jr. "Better Telephone Surveys through Centralized Interviewing." *Journal of Advertising Research,* vol. 71 (1966), pp. 2–7.

560

Athey, K. R.; Coleman, J. E.; Reitman, A. P.; and Tang, J.   "Two Experiments Showing the Effect of the Interviewer's Racial Background on Responses to Questionnaires Concerning Racial Issues." *Journal of Applied Psychology,* Spring 1960, pp. 244–46.

Axelrod, Morris, and Cannell, Charles F.   "A Research Note on an Attempt to Predict Interviewer Effectiveness." *Public Opinion Quarterly,* vol. 234 (Winter 1959), pp. 571–76.

Babbie, Earl R.   *Survey Research Methods.* Belmont, Calif.: Wadsworth Publishing Co., 1973.

Babchuk, Nicholas, and Gordon, C. Wayne.   "The Child as a Prototype of the Naïve Informant in the Interview Situation." *American Sociological Review,* vol. 23, no. 2 (April 1958), pp. 196–98.

Back, Kurt W., and Stycos, J. Mayone.   *The Survey under Unusual Conditions: Methodological Facets of the Jamaica Human Fertility Investigation.* Society for Applied Anthropology, Monograph No. 1 (1959).

Backstrom, Charles H., and Hursh, Gerald D.   *Survey Research.* Evanston, Ill.: Northwestern University Press, 1963.

Bailer, Barbara A.   "Recent Research in Re-interview Procedures." *Journal of the American Statistical Association,* vol. 63 (1968), p. 321.

Bain, Robert K.   "The Researcher's Role: A Case Study." *Human Organization,* vol. 9 (Spring 1950), pp. 23–28.

Balinsky, Benjamin.   *The Executive Interview: A Bridge to People.* New York: Harper & Row, 1959.

Balinsky, Benjamin, and Dispenzierei, A.   "An Evaluation of the Lecture and Role Playing Methods in the Development of Interviewing Skills." *Personnel Guidance Journal,* vol. 39 (1961), pp. 583–85.

Ball, John C.   "The Reliability and Validity of Interview Data Obtained from Fifty-nine Narcotic Drug Addicts." *American Journal of Sociology,* vol. 72 (1967), pp. 650–54.

Banaka, William H.   *Training in Depth Interview.* New York: Harper & Row, 1971.

Banks, G. P.   "Effects of Race on One to One Helping Interviews." *Social Service Review,* vol. 45 (1971), pp. 137–46.

Basset, Glenn A.   *Practical Interviewing, A Handbook for Managers.* New York: American Management Association, 1965.

Becker, Howard S.   "Problems of Inference and Proof in Participant Observation. *American Sociological Review,* vol. 23 (December 1958), pp. 652–60.

———.   "A Note on Interviewing Tactics." *Human Organization* (Winter, 1954), pp. 31–32.

———.   "Becoming a Marijuana User." *American Journal of Sociology,* vol. 59 (July 1953–May 1954), pp. 235–42.

———.   "The Professional Dance Musician in Chicago." Thesis, University of Chicago, 1949.

Becker, Howard S., et al. (eds.).   *Institutions and the Person.* Chicago: Aldine Publishing Co., 1968.

Belson, William, and Bell, C. R. *A Bibliography of Papers Bearing on the Adequacy of Techniques Used in Survey Research.* London: Oakwood Press, 1960.

Benjamin, Alfred. *The Helping Interview.* Boston: Houghton-Mifflin, 1969.

Benney, M.; Riesman, D.; and Star, S. A. "Age and Sex in the Interview." *American Journal of Sociology,* vol. 62 (September 1956), pp. 143–52.

Benson, L. "Studies in Secret Ballot Technique." *Public Opinion Quarterly,* vol. 5 (1941), p. 79.

Berdie, Ralph. "Psychological Processes in Interviewing." *Journal of Social Psychology,* vol. 43 (August 1943), pp. 3–31.

Berelson, Bernard. "The Verbal Report," *Human Behavior: An Inventory of Scientific Findings.* New York: Harcourt, Brace and World, 1964, pp. 29–33.

Berent, Paul. "The Depth Interview." *Journal of Advertising Research,* vol 6, no. 2 (June 1966), pp. 32–39.

Bermosk, Loretta L., and Mordan, Mary I. *Interviewing in Nursing.* New York: Macmillan Co., 1964.

Berreman, Gerald D. *Hindus of the Himalayas.* Berkeley, Calif.: University of California Press, 1963.

Berry, Fred C., Jr. "A Study of the Accuracy in Local News Storeis of Three Dailies." *Journalism Quarterly,* vol. 44 (1967), pp. 482–90.

Bersoff, Donald, and Grieger, Russell. "An Interview Model for the Psychosituational Assessment of Children's Behavior." *American Journal of Orthopsychiatry,* vol. 41 (1971), pp. 483–93.

Bessie, J. "The Effect of Praise on Respondent's Answers in a Public Opinion Poll." *American Psychologist,* vol. 13 (1950), p. 629.

Beveridge, Wilbert E. *Problem Solving Interviews.* London: Allen and Unwin, 1968.

Bevis, J. C. "Interviewing with Tape Recorder." *Public Opinion Quarterly,* vol. 13 (Winter 1949), pp. 629–34.

Biel, Alexander. "Abuses of Survey Research Techniques: The Phoney Interview." *Public Opinion Quarterly,* vol. 31 (1967), pp. 298–99.

Bindman, Aaron. "Interviewing in the Search for Truth." *Social Quarterly,* vol. 6, no. 3 (Summer 1965), pp. 281–88.

Bingham, W. V. D.; Moore, B. V.; and Gustad, J. W. *How to Interview.* 4th ed. New York: Harper & Bros., 1959.

Birdwhistle, R. "Body Motions Research and Interviewing." *Human Organization* (Spring 1952), p. 37.

Blanc, H. "Multilingual Interviewing in Israel." *American Journal of Sociology,* vol. 62 (September 1956), pp. 205–9.

Blankenship, A. "The Effect of the Interviewer upon Response in a Public Opinion Poll." *Journal of Consulting Psychology,* vol. 4 (1940), p. 134.

Blau, Peter M. *Exchange and Power in Social Life.* New York: John Wiley & Sons, 1964.

Blum, Fred H. "Getting Individuals to Give Information to the Outsider." *Journal of Social Issues,* vol. 8 (1952), p. 35.

Blumer, Herbert. "Collective Behavior," in *An Outline of the Principles of Sociology*, ed. Robert S. Park. New York: Barnes & Noble, 1946.

Bonilla, Frank, and Glazer, Myron. "Note on Methodology. Field Work in a Hostile Environment: A Chapter in the Sociology of Social Research in Chile," Appendix A in *Student Politics in Chile*. New York: Basic Books, 1970.

Booker, H. S., and David, S. T. "Differences in Results Obtained by Experienced and Inexperienced Interviewers." *Journal of the Royal Statistical Society*, vol. 115, pt. 2 (1952), pp. 232–57.

Boyd, H. W., Jr., and Westfall, R. "Interviewers as a Source of Error in Surveys." *Journal of Marketing*, vol. 19 (April 1955), pp. 311–24.

Brunner, G. A., and Carroll, S. J. Effect of Prior Telephone Appointments on Completion Rates and Response Content." *Public Opinion Quarterly*, vol. 31 (1967–68), pp. 652–54.

Bryan, James H. "Apprenticeship in Prostitution." *Social Problems*, vol. 12 (1965), pp. 287–97.

Bucher, Rue; Fritz, Charles E.; and Quarantelli, E. L. "Tape Recorded Interviews in Social Research." *American Sociological Review*, vol. 21, no. 3 (June 1956).

Burdock, E. I., and Hardesty, A. S. *Structured Clinical Interview Manual*. New York: Springer-Verlag, 1969.

Burgess, E. W., and Wallin, Paul. *Engagement and Marriage*. Philadelphia: J. B. Lippincott Co., 1953.

Cady, H. M. "On the Psychology of Testimony." *American Journal of Psychology*, vol. 35 (1924), pp. 110–12.

Cahalan, D.; Tamulonis, V.; and Verner, H. W. "Interviewer Bias Involved in Certain Types of Opinion Survey Questions." *International Journal of Opinion and Attitude Research*, vol. 1 (March 1947), pp. 63–77.

Campbell, Donald T. "The Informant in Quantitative Research." *American Journal of Sociology*, vol. 60 (1955), pp. 339–53.

Cannell, C. F., and Axelrod, M. "The Respondent Reports on the Interview." *American Journal of Sociology*, vol. 62 (September 1956), pp. 177–81.

Cannell, C. F., and R. L. Kahn. "Interviewing," in *The Handbook of Social Psychology*, 2d ed., vol. 2., ed. G. Lindzey and E. Aronson. Reading, Mass.: Addison-Wesley Publishing Co., 1968, pp. 526–95.

Cantril, Hadley. "Experiments in the Wording of Questions." *Public Opinion Quarterly*, vol. 4 (1940), p. 330.

———. *The Psychology of Social Movements*. New York: John Wiley & Sons, 1941, pp. 53–77.

Caplow, T. "The Dynamics of Information Interviewing." *American Journal of Sociology*, vol. 62 (September 1956), pp. 165–71.

Carmichael, L. S., et al. "A Study of the Judgment of Manual Expression as Presented in Still and Motion Pictures." *Journal of Social Psychology*, vol. 8 (1937), pp. 115–42.

Cartwright, Ann, and Tucker, Wyn. "An Attempt to Reduce the Number of

Calls on an Interview Inquiry." *Public Opinion Quarterly,* vol. 31 (1967), pp. 299–302.

Chandler, Margaret. "An Evaluation of the Group Interview." *Human Organization,* vol. 13, no. 2 (Summer 1954), pp. 26–28.

Clark, John P., and Tifft, Larry L. "Polygraph and Interview Validation of Self-Reported Deviant Behavior." *American Sociological Review,* vol. 31 (1966), pp. 516–23.

Clive, Victor B. "Ability to Judge Personality Assessed with a Stress Interview and Sound Film Technique." *Journal of Abnormal and Social Psychology,* vol. 50, no. 2 (March 1955), pp. 183–87.

Colcord, Joanna C. "A Study of the Techniques of the Social Case Work Interview," *Social Forces,* vol. 7 (1929), pp. 519–27.

Comer, Ronald J., and Piliavin, Jane A. "The Effects of Physical Deviance upon Face-to-Face Interaction." *Journal of Personality and Social Psychology,* vol. 23 (1972), pp. 33–39.

Corey, S. "Professed Attitudes and Actual Behavior." *Journal of Educational Psychology,* vol. 28 (1937), p. 271.

Crespi, L. P. "The Interview Effect in Polling." *Public Opinion Quarterly,* vol. 12 (Spring 1948), pp. 99–111.

Crutchfield, R. S., and Gordon, D. A. "Variations in Respondents' Interpretations of an Opinion-Poll Question." *International Journal of Opinion and Attitude Research,* vol. 1 (September 1947), pp. 1–12.

Dakin, Ralph E., and Tennant, Donald. "Consistency of Response by Event-Recall Intervals and Characteristics of Respondents." *Sociological Quarterly,* vol. 9 (1968), pp. 73–84.

Davies, Martin. "Interviewing Techniques," *New Society,* vol. 3 (1964).

Davis, John D. *The Interview as Arena.* Standford, Calif.: Stanford University Press, 1971.

Davitz, J. R., and Davitz, L. "The Communication of Feeling by Content-Free Speech." *Journal of Communication,* vol. 9 (1959), pp. 110–17.

Dean, J. "Participant Observation and Interviewing," in *An Introduction to Social Research,* ed. J. T. Doby. Harrisburg, Pa.: The Stackpole Co., 1954.

Dean, Lois R. "Interaction, Reported and Observed." *Human Organization,* vol. 3 (Fall 1958), p. 36.

DeFleur, Lois B. "On Polygraph and Interview Validation." *American Sociological Review,* vol. 32 (1967), pp. 114–15.

De Graer, Albert. "L'art de Guerir Chez les Asande." *Congo,* vol. 10, pt. 1, pp. 220–21.

Denzin, Norman K. (ed.). *Sociological Methods: A Sourcebook.* Chicago: Aldine Publishing Co., 1970.

Deschin, C. S. "Research Interviewing in Sensitive Subject Areas: III. Some Further Applications and Suggested Principles." *Social Work,* vol. 8, no. 2 (1963), pp. 14–18.

Dexter, Lewis A. *Elite and Specialized Interviewing.* Evanston, Ill.: Northwestern University Press, 1970.

————. Good Will of Important People: More on the Jeopardy of the Interview." *Public Opinion Quarterly,* vol. 28, no. 4 (Winter 1964), pp. 556–63.

————. "Role Relationships and Conception of Neutrality in Interviewing." *American Journal of Sociology,* vol. 62 (September 1956), pp. 153–57.

Dohrenwend, Barbara S. "Experimental Study of Directive Interviewing." *Public Opinion Quarterly,* vol. 34 (1970), pp. 117–25.

Dohrenwend, Barbara S., et al. "Social Distance and Interviewer Effects." *Public Opinion Quarterly,* vol. 32 (1968), pp. 410–22.

Dohrenwend, Barbara Snell, and Richardson, S. A. "Directiveness and Nondirectiveness in Research Interviewing: A Reformulation of the Problem." *Psychology Bulletin,* vol. 63, no. 5 (1965), pp. 475–85.

————. "A Use for Leading Questions in Research Interviewing." *Human Organization,* vol. 23 (1964), pp. 76–77.

————. "Analysis of the Interviewer's Behavior." *Human Organization,* vol. 15 (Summer 1956), pp. 29–32.

Dorner, K. "Interview and Exploration." *der Newvenarzt,* vol. 37, no. 1 (1966), pp. 18–25.

Dotson, Floyd. "Intensive Interviewing in Community Research." *Journal of Educational Sociology,* vol. 27, no. 5 (January 1954), pp. 225–30.

Drake, Frances. *Manual of Employment Interviewing.* New York: American Management Association, 1946.

Duncan, Starkey, Jr., et al. "The Paralanguage of Experimentor Bias." *Sociometry,* vol. 32 (1969), pp. 207–19.

Durbin, J., and Stuart, A. "Differences in Response Rates of Experienced and Inexperienced Interviewers." *Journal of the Royal Statistical Society,* vol. 114, part 2 (1951), pp. 163–95.

Dvorak, B. J.; Fox, F. C.; and Meigh, C. "Tests for Field Survey Interviewers." *Journal of Marketing,* vol. 16 (January 1952), pp. 301–6.

Edsall, R. L. "Getting 'Not-at-Homes' to Interview Themselves." *Journal of Marketing,* vol. 23 (October 1958), pp. 184–85.

Ekman, Paul. "Body Position, Facial Expression, and Verbal Behavior during Interviews." *Journal of Abnormal and Social Psychology,* vol. 68, no. 3 (1964), pp. 295–301.

Elkind, David. "Piaget's Semi-clinical Interview and the Study of Spontaneous Religion." *Journal for the Scientific Study of Religions* (1965).

Engel, J. F. "Tape Recorders in Consumer Research." *Journal of Marketing,* vol. 26 (April 1962), pp. 73–74.

Fearing, F. "The Appraisal Interview," in *Studies in Personality,* ed. Q. MacNemar and M. Merrill. New York: McGraw-Hill Book Co., 1942.

Fein, Edith. "Inner-City Interviewing: Some Perspectives." *Public Opinion Quarterly.* vol. 34 (1970–71), pp. 625–29.

Feldman, Jacob J.; Hyman, Herbert; and Hart, C. W.   "A Field Study of Interviewer Effects on the Quality of Survey Data." *Public Opinion Quarterly* (Winter 1951–1952).

Fenlason, Anne; Beals, G.; and Abrahamson, A.   *Essentials in Interviewing.* rev. ed. New York: Harper & Row, 1962.

Ferber, Robert.   "On the Reliability of Responses Secured in Sample Surveys." *Journal of the American Statistical Association,* vol. 50 (September 1955), pp. 788–811.

Ferber, Robert, and Wales, H. G.   "Detection and Correction of Interviewer Bias." *Public Opinion Quarterly,* vol. 16 (Spring 1952), pp. 107–27.

Festinger, Leon.   *A Theory of Cognitive Dissonance.* Evanston, Ill.: Row-Peterson, 1957.

Festinger, Leon, and Katz, Daniel.   *Research Methods in the Social Sciences.* New York: Dryden Press, 1953.

Festinger, Leon, et al.   *When Prophecy Fails.* New York: Harper & Row, 1956.

Field, Joan B.   "The Effect of Praise in a Public Opinion Poll." *Public Opinion Quarterly,* vol. 19 (1955), pp. 85–90.

Fields, Harold.   "An Analysis of the Use of the Group Oral Interview." *Personnel,* vol. 27, no. 6 (1951), pp. 480–86.

Finesinger, Jacob E.   "Psychiatric Interviewing." *American Journal of Orthopsychiatry,* vol. 105, no. 3 (September 1948), pp. 197–204.

Fink, Raymond.   "The Retrospective Question." *Public Opinion Quarterly,* vol. 24, no. 1 (Spring 1960), pp. 143–48.

Fisher, Herbert.   "Interviewer Bias in the Recording Operation." *International Journal of Opinion and Attitude Research,* vol. 4 (1950), p. 393.

Franzen, R., and Williams, R. J.   "A Method for Measuring Error Due to Variance among Interviewers." *Public Opinion Quarterly,* vol. 20 (Fall 1956), pp. 587–92.

Freeman, G. L., et al.   "The Stress Interview." *Journal of Abnormal and Social Psychology,* vol. 37 (1942), pp. 427–47.

Frenkel-Brunswik, E.   "Dynamic and Cognitive Categorization of Qualitative Material." *Journal of Psychology,* vol. 25 (1948), pp. 261–77.

Freud, Anna.   *Introduction to the Technique of Child Analysis.* New York: Nervous and Mental Disease Publishing Co., 1928.

Froelich, Robert, and Bishop, F. M.   *Medical Interviewing.* St. Louis, Mosby, 1969.

Gans, Herbert.   *The Levittowners.* New York: Pantheon, 1967.

Garber, C. W., Jr.   "Play Techniques for Interviewing on Durable Goods." *Public Opinion Quarterly,* vol. 15 (Spring, 1951), pp. 139–40.

Gardner, Burleigh B., and Whyte, William F.   "Methods for the Study of Human Relations in Industry." *American Sociological Review,* vol. 11 (1946), p. 509.

Garfinkel, Harold.   *Studies In Ethnomethodology.* Englewood Cliffs, N.J.: Prentice-Hall, 1967.

———. "Studies of the Routine Grounds of Everyday Activities." *Social Problems*, vol. 11, no. 2 (Winter 1964), pp. 225–50.

Garrett, A. *Interviewing: Its Principles and Methods.* Family Welfare Association of America, 1942.

Gaylin, Willard. *In the Service of Their Country: War Resisters in Prison.* New York: Viking Press, 1970.

Geismar, Ludwig L., and La Sorte, Michael A. "Research Interviewing with Low-Income Families." *Social Work*, vol. 8, no. 2 (April 1963), pp. 10–13.

Giallombardo, Rose. "Interviewing in the Prison Community." *Journal of Criminal Law, Criminology and Police Science*, vol. 57 (1966), pp. 318–24.

Gibson, F. K., and Hawkins, D. W. "Interviews versus Questionnaires." *American Behavioral Science*, vol. 12 (1968) pp. 9–16.

Gill, Merton N.; Newman, Richard; and Redlich, Frederick. *The Initial Interview in Psychiatric Practice.* New York: International Universities Press, 1954.

Glazer, Myron. *The Research Adventure: Promise and Problems of Field Work.* New York: Random House, 1972.

Goffman, Erving. *The Presentation of Self in Everyday Life.* Edinburgh: University of Edinburgh Social Science Center, 1956.

Gold, Martin. "Undetected Delinquency Behavior." *Journal of Research on Crime and Delinquency*, vol. 3 (1966), pp. 27–46.

Goldberg, G., et al. "Visual Behavior and Face-to-Face Distance During Interaction. *Sociometry*, vol. 32 (1969), pp. 43–53.

Goldman, Alfred E. "The Group Depth Interview." *Journal of Marketing*, vol. 26, no. 3 (July 1962), pp. 61–68.

Gorden, Raymond L. *Living in Latin America: A Case Study in Cross-Cultural Communication.* Skokie, Ill., National Textbook Co., 1974.

———. "An Interaction Analysis of the Depth Interview." Thesis, University of Chicago, 1954.

———. "Interaction Between Attitude and the Definition of the Situation in the Expression of Opinion." *American Sociological Review*, vol. 17, no. 1 (1952), pp. 50–58.

Gottschalk, Louis, et al. *The Use of Personal Documents in History, Anthropology and Sociology.* New York: Social Science Research Council, 1947.

Grey, David. "Interviewing at the (Supreme) Court." *Public Opinion Quarterly*, vol. 31 (1967), pp. 285–89.

Griaule, Marcel. "L'enquette Orale en Ethologie." *Revue Philosophique de la France*, vol. 142 (October 1952), pp. 537–53.

Gross, N., and Mason, W. "Some Methodological Problems of Eight-Hour Interviews." *American Journal of Sociology*, vol. 59, no. 3 (November 1953), pp. 197–204.

Guest, Lester. "A New Training Method for Opinion Interviewers." *Public Opinion Quarterly*, vol. 18 (Fall 1954), pp. 287–99.

Guest, Lester, and Nuckols, R. "A Laboratory Experiment in Recording in

Public Opinion Interviewing." *International Journal of Opinion and Attitude Research*, vol. 4 (Fall 1950), pp. 336–52.

Gusfield, Joseph R. "Field Work Reciprocities in Studying a Social Movement." *Human Organization*, vol. 14, no. 3 (Fall 1955), pp. 29–33.

Guttman, Louis. "A Theory of Intergroup Beliefs and Action." *American Sociological Review*, vol. 24 (June 1959), pp. 318–28.

Haberman, Paul W., and Sheinbergh, Jill. "Education Reported in Interviews: An Aspect of Survey Content Error." *Public Opinion Quarterly*, vol. 30, no. 2 (Summer 1966), pp. 259–301.

Hall, Edward T. *The Silent Language.* New York: Doubleday Co., 1959.

Hammond, Phillip E. (ed.). *Sociologists at Work: Essays on the Craft of Social Research.* New York: Basic Books, 1964.

Hamovitch, Maurice B. "Research Interviewing in Terminal Illness." *Social Work*, vol. 8, no. 2 (April 1963), pp. 4–9.

Hannerz, Ulf. *Soulside: Inquiries into Ghetto Culture and Community.* New York: Columbia University Press, 1969.

Hanson, Robert H., and Marks, Eli S. "Influence of the Interviewer on the Accuracy of Survey Results." *Journal of the American Statistical Association*, vol. 53 (September 1958), pp. 635–55.

Hare, Paul A. "Interview Responses: Personality or Conformity?" *Public Opinion Quarterly*, vol. 24, no. 4 (Winter 1960), pp. 679–85.

Hare, Paul A., and Davie, James S. "The Group Interview." *Sociology and Social Research*, vol. 29, no. 2 (November-December 1954), pp. 81–87.

Hariton, Theodore. *Interview! The Executive Guide to Selecting the Right Personnel.* New York: Hastings House Publishers, 1971.

Harral, Stewart. *Keys to Successful Interviewing.* Norman: University of Oklahoma Press, 1954.

Hart, Clyde. "Bias in Interviewing." *American Philosophical Society Proceedings*, vol. 92, no. 5 (1948), p. 399.

Hartmann, Elizabeth. "Public Reaction to Public Opinion Surveying." *Public Opinion Quarterly*, vol. 32 (1968), pp. 295–98.

Heath, Clark W. "An Interview Method for Obtaining Personal Histories." *New England Journal of Medicine*, vol. 234 (1946), pp. 251–57.

Heyns, Roger W., and Lippitt, Ronald. "Systematic Observation Techniques," in *Handbook of Social Psychology*, ed. Gardner Lindzey. vol. 1. Reading, Mass.: Addison-Wesley Publishing Co., 1954.

Hildum, D. C., and Brown, R. W. "Verbal Reinforcement and Interviewer Bias." *Journal of Abnormal and Social Psychology*, vol. 52 (July 1956), pp. 100–111.

Hill, William G. "The Family as a Treatment Unit: Differential Techniques and Procedures." *Social Work*, vol. 11 (1966), pp. 62–68.

Hills, Stuart L. "Increasing the Response Rate for Structured Interviews in Community Research." *American Behavioral Scientist*, vol. 11 (1968), pp. 47–48.

Homans, George C.   *Social Behavior: Its Elementary Forms.* New York: Harcourt, Brace and World, 1961.

Hyman, Herbert H.   "Do They Tell the Truth?" *Public Opinion Quarterly,* vol. 8 (1944), pp. 557–59.

Hughes, Helen McGill (ed.).   *The Fantastic Lodge: The Autobiography of a Drug Addict.* Greenwich, Conn.: Fawcett Publications, 1971.

Humphreys, Laud.   *Tearoom Trade.* Chicago: Aldine Publishing Co., 1970.

Hyman, Herbert H., et al.   *Interviewing in Social Research.* Chicago: University of Chicago Press, 1954.

Irwin, John.   *The Felon.* Englewood Cliffs, N.J.: Prentice-Hall, 1970.

Jacobson, Harold K.   "Deriving Data from Delegates to International Assemblies: A Research Note." *International Organization,* vol. 21 (1967), pp. 592–613.

Janes, Robert W.   "A Note on Phases of the Community Role of the Participant-Observer." *American Sociological Review,* vol. 26, no. 3 (June 1961), pp. 446–50.

Janofsky, Irene.   "Affective Self-Disclosure in Telephone versus Face-to-Face Interview." *Journal of Humanistic Psychology,* vol. 2 (1971), pp. 93–103.

Jonsson, Erland.   "On the Formulation of Questions in Medico-Hygienic Interview Investigations." *Acta Sociologica,* 1963, pp. 193–202.

Josephson, Eric.   "Resistance to Community Surveys." *Social Problems,* vol. 18 (1970), pp. 117–29.

Kahn, Robert L., and Cannell, Charles F.   *The Dynamics of Interviewing.* New York: John Wiley & Sons, 1957.

Kastenbaum, R., and Sherwood, S.   *VIRO: A New Scale for Assessing the Interview Behavior of Elderly People.* Proceedings of the 20th Annual Meeting of the Gerontological Society, 1967.

Katz, Daniel.   "Do Interviewers Bias Poll Results?" *Public Opinion Quarterly,* vol. 6 (Summer 1942), pp. 248–68.

Katz, Elihu, and Lazarsfeld, Paul F.   *Personal Influence: The Part Played by People in the Flow of Mass Communications.* Glencoe, Ill.: The Free Press, 1955.

Kegeles, Stephen S., et al.   "Interviewing a National Sample by Long Distance Telephone." *Public Opinion Quarterly,* vol. 33 (1969), pp. 412–19.

Kemsley, W. F. F.   "Interviewer Variability and a Budget Survey." *Applied Statistics,* vol. 9, no. 2 (June 1960), pp. 122–28.

Kephart, Newell C.   *The Employment Interview in Industry.* New York: McGraw-Hill Book Co., 1952.

Keys, Ancel.   *Human Starvation.* Minneapolis: University of Minnesota Press, 1950.

Kincaid, H. V., and Bright, M.   "Interviewing the Business Elite." *American Journal of Sociology,* vol. 63 (November 1957), pp. 304–11.

————.   "The Tandem Interview: A Trial of the Two-Interviewer Team." *Public Opinion Quarterly,* vol. 21 (Summer 1957), pp. 304–12.

Kinsey, Alfred C., et al. "Interviewing," *Sexual Behavior in the Human Male.* Philadelphia: W. B. Saunders Co., 1948.

Kish, Leslie. "Studies of Interviewer Variance for Attitudinal Variables." *Journal of the American Statistical Association,* vol. 57 (March 1962), pp. 92–115.

Klare, G. "Understandability and Indefinite Answers." *International Journal of Opinion and Attitude Research,* vol. 4 (1950), p. 91.

Kloetzle, W. C., et al. "Guide for Interviewing the Minister and Selected Key Members of the Congregation of the Urban Church Effectiveness Study." *Social Compass,* vol. 9 (1962), pp. 387–402.

Krause, Luise. *Personal Adjustment in Old Age.* Thesis, University of Chicago, 1950.

Krugman, Herbert E. "Interviewing Ex-Communists in the United States." *Public Opinion Quarterly,* vol. 20, no. 2 (Summer 1956), pp. 473–77.

Langdon, Grace. *Teacher-Parent Interviews.* New York: Prentice-Hall, 1954.

Lasswell, Harold. "The Contribution of Freud's Insight Interview to the Social Sciences." *American Journal of Sociology,* vol. 45 (1939), p. 375.

Lazarsfeld, Paul. "The Controversy over Detailed Interviews—an Offer for Negotiation." *Public Opinion Quarterly,* vol. 8 (Spring 1944).

Lazarsfeld, Paul F., and Thielens, J. W. *The Academic Mind.* Glencoe, Ill.: 1958.

Leighton, Alexander. *The Governing of Men.* Princeton: Princeton University Press, 1945.

Lennings, Mary J. "Explorations of the Personalistic Approach in Interviews with Mexican Entrants to the United States." *Civilizations,* vol. 14, no. 4 (1964), pp. 289–313.

Lenski, Gerhard E., and Leggett, John C. "Caste, Class and Deference in the Research Interview." *American Journal of Sociology,* vol. 65 (1960), pp. 463–67.

Lerner, Daniel. "Interviewing Frenchmen." *American Journal of Sociology,* vol. 62, no. 2 (September 1956), pp. 184–87.

Leuthold, D. A., and Scheele, R. "Patterns of Bias in Sample Based on Telephone Directories." *Public Opinion Quarterly,* vol. 35 (1971), pp. 249–57.

Lewin, Kurt. "Group Decisions and Social Change," in *Readings in Social Psychology,* ed. Swanson, Newcomb, and Hartley. New York: Henry Holt, 1952.

Lewis, Oscar. *Life in a Mexican Village: Tepoztlan Restudied.* Urbana: University of Illinois Press, 1951.

Liebow, Elliot. *Tally's Corner.* Boston: Little, Brown & Co., 1967.

Lindzey, Gardner. "A Note on Interviewer Bias." *Journal of Applied Psychology,* vol. 35 (June 1951), pp. 182–84.

Litwak, Eugene. "A Classification of Biased Questions." *American Journal of Sociology,* vol. 62, no. 2 (September 1956), pp. 182–88.

Maas, James B. "Patterned Scaled Expectation Interview: Reliability Studies on a New Technique." *Journal of Applied Psychology,* vol. 49, no. 6 (1963), pp. 413–33.

Maccoby, Eleanor E., and Maccoby, Nathan. "The Interview: A Tool of Social Science," in *Handbook of Social Psychology*, vol. 1, ed. Gardner Lindzey. Reading, Mass.: Addison-Wesley Publishing Co., 1954.

Maier, Norman R. F. *The Appraisal Interview: Objectives, Methods and Skills.* New York: John Wiley & Sons, 1958.

Maier, Norman R. F.; Hoffman, L. Richard; and Lansky, Leonard M. "Human Relations Training as Manifested in an Interview Situation." *Personnel Psychology*, vol. 13 (1960), pp. 11–30.

Manniche, E., and Hayes, D. P. "Respondent Anonymity and Data Matching." *Public Opinion Quarterly*, vol. 21 (Fall 1957), pp. 384–88.

Marquis, Kent H. "Effects of Social Reinforcement on Health Reporting in the Household Interview." *Sociometry*, vol. 33 (1970), pp. 203–15.

Matarazzo, Joseph. "Interviewer Mm-Humm and Interviewee Speech Duration." *Psychotherapy: Therapy, Research and Practice*, vol. 1 (1964), pp. 109–14.

Matarazzo, Joseph, and Wiens, L. "Interviewer Influence on Duration of Interviewee Silence." *Journal of Experimental Research in Personality*, vol. 2 (1967), pp. 56–69.

Matarazzo, Joseph D., and Wiens, Arthur N. "Interviewer Effects on Interviewee's Speech and Silence Durations." *Proceedings of the 74th Annual Convention of the American Psychological Association* (1966).

Mauldin, W. P., and Marks, E. S. "Problems of Response in Enumerative Surveys." *American Sociological Review*, vol. 15 (October 1950), pp. 649–57.

McGinnis, Robert. "Scaling Interview Data." *American Sociological Review*, vol. 18 (October 1953).

Menzel, H., and Katz, E. "Social Relations and Innovation in the Medical Profession: The Epidemiology of a New Drug." *Public Opinion Quarterly*, vol. 19 (1956), pp. 337–52.

Merton, Robert K. *The Focused Interview: A Manual of Problems and Procedures.* New York: The Free Press, 1956.

———. "Selected Problems of Field Work in a Planned Community." *American Sociological Review*, vol. 12 (1947), pp. 304–12.

Miles, E. "The Logistics of Interviewing in International Organizations." *International Organization*, vol. 24 (1970), pp. 361–70.

Milford, Nancy. "The Golden Dreams of Zelda Fitzgerald." *Harper's Magazine*, January 1969, pp. 46–53.

Milgram, Stanley. "The Lost Letter Technique," *Psychology Today*. vol. 3 (1969), pp. 30–33.

Miller, S. M. "The Participant-Observer and 'Over-Rapport.'" *American Sociological Review*, vol. 17 (1952), pp. 97–99.

Mills, C. Wright. "Situated Action and the Vocabulary of Motives." *American Sociological Review*, vol. 6 (December 1940), pp. 904–13.

Moore, B. V. "The Interview in Industrial Research." *Social Forces*, vol. 7 (1929), pp. 445–52.

Moore, Mary Rowena. *The Effects of Two Interviewing Techniques on Aca-*

demic Achievement and Certain Non-intellectual Factors Affecting Academic Success. Thesis, Indiana University, 1958. University of Michigan Microfilm 1916.

Moos, Rudolf H., and Porter, Langley. "The Retention and Generalization of Operant Conditioning Effects in an Interview Situation." *Journal of Abnormal and Social Psychology,* vol. 66, no. 1 (January 1963), pp. 52–58.

Morrison, Denton E. "A Boxing System for Interview Schedules." *American Sociological Review,* vol. 23, no. 1 (February 1958), pp. 83–84.

Moscovici, S. "Attitudes and Opinions." *Annual Review of Psychology,* vol. 14 (1963), pp. 231–60.

Murray, Henry A. "Dyadic Creations," in Warren G. Bennis et al., *Interpersonal Dynamics.* Homewood, Ill.: Dorsey Press, 1964, pp. 638–46.

Muscio, B. "On the Influence of the Form of a Question." *British Journal of Psychology,* vol. 8, pp. 351–89.

Namias, Jean. "Measuring Variation in Interviewer Performance." *Journal of Advertising Research,* vol. 6, no. 1 (March 1966), pp. 8–12.

National Opinion Research Center. *Interviewing for NORC.* Denver, 1947.

Newstetter, W. I. "Social Psychological Problems in Relation to Social Work Practice and Theory," in *Emerging Problems in Social Psychology, Series III,* ed. Muzafer Sherif and M. O. Wilson, Norman, Okla.: The University Book Exchange, 1957.

Oldfield, R. C. "The Display and Perception of Attitudes," in *The Psychology of the Interview.* London: Methuen, 1947.

Orlans, Harold. *Contracting for Knowledge.* San Francisco: Jossey-Bass Publishers, 1973.

Parker, Aileen, and Meeks, Clinton. "Problems in Learning to Interview." *Counselor Education and Supervision,* vol. 7 (1967), pp. 54–59.

Parker, C. A.; Wright, E. W.; and Clark, S. G. "Questions Concerning the Interview as a Research Technique." *Journal of Educational Research,* vol. 51 (November 1957), pp. 215–21.

Parsons, Talcott, and Bales, Robert F. *Family, Socialization and Interaction Process.* New York: The Free Press, 1955.

Paul, B. D. "Interview Techniques and Field Relationships," in *Anthropology Today,* ed. A. L. Kroeber. Chicago: The University of Chicago Press, 1953.

Payne, S. L. *The Art of Asking Questions.* Princeton: Princeton University Press, 1951.

Pelz, Donald C., and Andrews, Frank M. "Detecting Causal Priorities in Panel Study Data." *American Sociological Review,* vol. 29 (1964), pp. 836–48.

Phillips, Bernard S. *Social Research, Strategy and Tactics.* New York: Macmillan Co., 1966.

Podell, Lawrence. "An Interviewing Problem in Values Research." *Sociology and Social Research,* vol. 41, no. 2 (November-December 1956), pp. 121–26.

Polansky, Norman A. *Ego Psychology and Communication: A Theory for the Interview.* New York: Atherton Press, 1971.

Redl, Fritz. "Strategy and Techniques of the Life Space Interview." *American Journal of Orthopsychiatry,* vol. 29, no. 1 (January 1959).

Reece, M. M., and Whitman, R. N. "Expressive Movements, Warmth and Verbal Reinforcements." *Journal of Abnormal and Social Psychology,* vol. 64 (1962), pp. 234–36.

Reiss, Albert J., Jr. "Stuff and Nonsense About Social Surveys and Observations," in *Institutions and the Person,* ed. Howard S. Becker et al. Chicago: Aldine Publishing Co., 1968.

Rice, Stuart A. "Contagious Bias in the Interview: A Methodological Note." *American Journal of Sociology,* vol. 35 (1929), pp. 420–23.

Rich, J. *Interviewing Children and Adolescents.* New York: Macmillan Co., 1968.

———. "Training in Field Relations Skills." *Journal of Social Issues,* vol. 8, no. 3 (1953).

Richardson, Stephen A. "The Use of Leading Questions in Non-schedule Interviews." *Human Organization,* vol. 19, no. 2 (1960), pp. 86–89.

Richardson, Stephen A., et al. *Interviewing: Its Forms and Functions.* New York: Basic Books, 1965.

Richardson, Stephen A.; Dohrenwend, Barbara Snell; and Klein, David. *Interviewing, Its Forms and Functions.* New York: Basic Books, 1965.

Riesman, David. "Orbits of Tolerance, Interviewer, and Elites." *Public Opinion Quarterly,* vol. 20, no. 1 (Spring 1956), pp. 49–73.

Riesman, David, and Benney, Mark. "Asking and Answering." *Journal of Business,* vol. 29 (October 1956), pp. 225–36.

Riesman, David, and Glazer, Nathan. "An Experiment in the Interpretation of an Interview." *International Journal of Opinion and Attitude Research,* vol. 4 (Winter, 1950–51), pp. 515–40; vol. 5 (Spring 1951), pp. 53–78.

Roethlisberger, F. J., and Dickson, W. J. "Interviewing Methods," in *Management and the Worker.* Cambridge, Mass.: Harvard University Press, 1946.

Rogers, Carl R. "The Characteristics of a Helping Relationship," *On Becoming a Person.* Boston: Houghton Mifflin, 1961.

———. "The Non-Directive Method as a Technique for Social Research." *American Journal of Sociology,* vol. 51 (1945), p. 143.

Rogers, Carl R., and Roethlisberger, F. J. "Barriers and Gateways to Communication." *Harvard Business Review,* vol. 30, no. 4 (July-August 1952), pp. 46–52.

Rose, Arnold. *Human Behavior and Social Processes.* Boston: Houghton Mifflin, 1962.

———. "Interviewing to Test for Validity and Reliability." *International Journal of Opinion and Attitude Research,* vol. I (1947), p. 100.

———. "A Researcher Note on Experimentation in Interviewing." *American Journal of Sociology,* vol. 51 (1945), pp. 143–44.

Rosenthal, Robert. *Experimenter Effects in Behavioral Research.* New York: Appleton-Century-Crofts, 1966.

Rosten, Leo. *The Joys of Yiddish.* New York: Pocket Books, 1970.

Roth, Julius. "Hired Hand Research." *American Sociologist,* vol. 1 (August 1966), pp. 190–96.

————. *Timetables: Structuring the Passage of Time in Hospital Treatment and Other Careers.* Indianapolis: The Bobbs-Merrill Company, 1963.

Roy, Donald F. "The Role of the Researchers in the Study of a Social Conflict." *Human Organization,* vol. 24 (1965), pp. 262–71.

Ruch, F. L. "Effects of Repeated Interviewing on the Respondent's Answers." *Journal of Consulting Psychology,* vol. 5 (July-August 1941), pp. 179–82.

Salzinger, K., and Pisoni, Stephanie. "Reinforcement of Verbal Affect Responses of Normal Subjects during an Interview." *Journal of Abnormal and Social Psychology,* vol. 60 (1960), pp. 127–30.

Sapir, Edward. "The Unconscious Patterning of Behavior in Society," in *The Unconscious: A Symposium,* ed. E. S. Dummer. New York: A. A. Knopf, 1927.

Schatzman, Leonard, and Strauss, Anselm. "Social Class and Mode of Communication." *American Journal of Sociology,* vol. 60, no. 4 (1955), pp. 329–38.

Scheflen, A. E. *Stream and Structure of Communication Behavior.* Bloomington, Ind.: University of Indiana Press, 1969.

Schuman, H., and Converse, J. M. "Effect of Black and White Interviewers on Black Responses in 1968." *Public Opinion Quarterly,* vol. 35 (1971), pp. 44–68.

Schutz, Alfred. *Collected Papers,* ed. Maurice Natanson. The Hague, Netherlands: Martinus Nijhoff, 1962.

Schwab, P. P. "Why Interview? A Critique." *Personnel Journal,* vol. 48 (1969), pp. 126–29.

Schwartz, Morris S., and Schwartz, Charlotte Green. "Problems in Participant Observation." *American Journal of Sociology* (January 1955), pp. 343–53.

Scott, Marvin B., and Stanford, Lyman M. "Accounts." *American Sociological Review,* vol. 33, no. 1 (February 1968), pp. 46–62.

Scott, William A. "The Avoidance of Threatening Material in Imaginative Behavior." *Journal of Abnormal and Social Psychology,* vol. 52 (1956), pp. 338–46.

Sears, Robert R. "Comparison of Interviews with Questionnaires for Measuring Mothers' Attitudes towards Sex and Aggression." *Journal of Personality and Social Psychology,* vol. 2, no. 1 (July 1965), pp. 37–44.

Sewell, William H. "Field Techniques in Social Psychological Study in a Rural Community." *American Sociological Review,* vol. 14 (1949), pp. 718–26.

Shapiro, S., and Eberhart, J. "Interviewer Differences in an Intensive Survey." *International Journal of Opinion and Attitude Research,* vol. 1, no. 2 (1947), p. 1.

Shaw, Clifford R. *Brothers in Crime.* Chicago: University of Chicago Press, 1938.

Sheatsley, P. B. "An Analysis of Interviewer Characteristics and Their Relationship to Performance." *International Journal of Opinion and Attitude Research*, vol. 4 (Winter 1950–51), pp. 473–98; vol. 5 (Spring 1951), pp. 79–94; vol. 5 (Summer 1951), pp. 101–220.

————. "Closed Questions Are Sometimes More Valid than Open End." *Public Opinion Quarterly*, vol. 12 (1948), p. 12.

Sherwood, Hugh C. *The Journalistic Interview*. New York: Harper & Row, 1969.

Shoulksmith, G. *Assessment through Interviewing*. Oxford: Pergamon Press, 1968.

Sidney, Elizabeth, and Brown, Margaret. *The Skills of Interviewing*. London: Tavistock Publishing Co., 1961.

Simmel, Georg. "Sociology of the Senses: Visual Interaction," in Robert E. Park and Ernest W. Burgess, *Introduction to the Science of Sociology*. Chicago, Ill.: University of Chicago Press, 1924.

Sjoberg, Gideon (ed.). *Ethics, Politics and Social Research*. Cambridge, Mass.: Schenkman Publishing Co., 1971.

Sjoberg, Gideon. "The Interviewer as a Marginal Man," *The Southwest Social Science Quarterly*, vol. 38 (September 1957), pp. 125–32.

Smigel, E. O. "Interviewing a Legal Elite: The Wall Street Lawyer." *American Journal of Sociology*, vol. 64 (September 1958), pp. 159–64.

Smith, H. L., and Hyman, Herbert. "The Biasing Effect of Interviewer Expectations on Survey Results." *Public Opinion Quarterly*, vol. 14 (Fall 1950), pp. 491–506.

Snell, Barbara, and Dohrenwend, Bruce P. "Sources of Refusal in Surveys." *Public Opinion Quarterly*, vol. 32 (1968), pp. 74–83.

Star, Shirley A. "Obtaining Household Opinions from a Single Respondent." *Public Opinion Quarterly*, vol. 17 (Fall 1953), pp. 386–91.

Steinkamp, Stanley. "Some Characteristics of Effective Interviewers." *Journal of Applied Psychology*, vol. 50 (1966), pp. 487–92.

Steinmetz, Lawrence L. *Interviewing Skills for Supervisory Personnel*. Reading, Mass.: Addison-Wesley Publishing Co., 1971.

Stember, C. H., and Hyman, H. H. "How Interviewer Effects Operate Through Question Form." *International Journal of Opinion and Attitude Research*, vol. 3 (1949), pp. 493–512.

Stember, Herbert. "Which Respondents Are Reliable?" *International Journal of Opinion and Attitude Research*, vol. 5 (Winter 1951–52), pp. 475–79.

Stember, Herbert, and Hyman, Herbert. "Interviewer Effects in the Classification of Responses." *Public Opinion Quarterly*, vol. 13 (Winter 1949), pp. 669–82.

Stephan, F. F. "Public Relations and Research Interviewing." *Public Opinion Quarterly*, vol. 28 (1964), p. 118.

Stock, J. S., and Hochstim, J. R. "A Method of Measuring Interviewer Variability." *Public Opinion Quarterly*, vol. 15 (Summer 1951), pp. 322–34.

Stycos, J. M. "Interviewer Training in Another Culture." *Public Opinion Quarterly,* vol. 16 (Summer 1952), pp. 236–46.

Sudman, Seymour. "Time Allocation in Survey Interviewing and in Other Field Occupations." *Public Opinion Quarterly.* vol. 29 (1965), pp. 638–48.

Sullivan, Harry S. *The Psychiatric Interview.* New York: W. W. Norton and Co., Inc., 1954.

Sutherland, E. H. *The Professional Thief.* Chicago: University of Chicago Press, 1937.

Symonds, P. M., and Dietrich, D. H. "The Effect of Variations in the Time Interval between an Interview and Its Recording." *Journal of Abnormal and Social Psychology,* vol. 36 (1941), pp. 346–53.

Taietz, Philip. "Conflicting Group Norms and the Third Person in the Interview." *American Journal of Sociology,* vol. 68, no. 1 (July 1962), pp. 97–104.

Thomas, Dorothy S., and Nishimoto, R. S. *The Spoilage.* Berkeley: University of California Press, 1946.

Thumin, F. J. "Watch for Those Unseen Variables." *Journal of Marketing,* vol. 26 (July 1962), pp. 58–60.

Toman, W. "Pause Analysis as a Short Interviewing Technique." *Journal of Consulting Psychology,* vol. 17, no. 1 (1953), pp. 1–7.

Tudor, Thomas G., and Holmes, David S. "Use of Analogies and Opposites in Helping Interviewees Verbalize Their Self-Concepts." *Journal of Consulting and Clinical Psychology,* vol. 38 (1972), pp. 445–48.

Turner, David. *Employment Interviewer.* New York: Arco Publishing Co., 1968.

Vaughn, C. L., and Reynolds, W. A. "Reliability of Personal Interview Data." *Journal of Applied Psychology,* vol. 35 (February 1951), pp. 61–63.

Vidich, A., and Bensman, J. "The Validity of Field Data." *Human Organization,* vol. 13, no. 1 (Spring 1954), pp. 20–27.

Vidich, A., and Shapiro, A. "Comparison of Participant Observation and Survey Data." *American Sociological Review,* vol. 20, no. 1 (February 1955), pp. 28–33.

Volkart, Edmund H. (ed.). *Social Behavior and Personality.* New York: Social Science Research Council, 1951.

Vonderacek, Fred. "The Manipulation of Self-Disclosure in an Experimental Interview Situation." *Journal of Psychology,* vol. 72 (1969), pp. 55–59.

von Hoffman, Nicholas; Horowitz, Irving L.; and Rainwater, Lee. "Sociological Snoopers and Journalistic Moralizers: An Exchange." *Transaction,* May 1970, pp. 4–8.

Wales, Hugh G., and Ferber, Robert. *A Basic Bibliography on Marketing Research.* 2d ed. Chicago: American Marketing Association, 1963.

Wallen, R. "Ego Involvement as a Determinant of Selective Forgetting." *Journal of Abnormal and Social Psychology,* vol. 37 (1942), pp. 20–39.

Wallin, Paul. "An Appraisal of Some Methodological Aspects of the Kinsey Report." *American Sociological Review,* vol. 14 (1949), pp. 197–210.

Walsh, Bruce W.   "Validity of Self-Report." *Journal of Counseling Psychology,* vol. 14, no. 1 (1967), pp. 18–23.

Ware, Caroline F.   *Greenwich Village 1920 to 1930.* Boston: Houghton Mifflin Co., 1935.

Ware, J. R.; Kowal, B.; and Baker, R. A.   "The Role of Experimenter Attitude and Contingent Reinforcement in a Vigilance Task." Unpublished paper, U.S. Army Armor Human Research Unit, Fort Knox, Kentucky, 1963.

Warner, William Lloyd, and Lunt, P. S.   "Field Techniques," in *Social Life of a Modern Community.* New Haven: Yale University Press, 1941.

Wax, M., and Shapiro, L. J.   "Repeated Interviewing." *American Journal of Sociology,* vol. 62 (September 1956), pp. 215–17.

Weaver, T.   "Use of Hypothetical Situations in a Study of Spanish American Illness Referral Systems." *Human Organization,* vol. 29 (1970), pp. 140–54.

Webb, Eugene J.; Campbell, Donald T.; Swartz, Richard D.; and Sechrest, Lee.   *Unobtrusive Measures: Nonreactive Research in the Social Sciences.* Chicago: Rand McNally, 1966.

Weinland, James D., and Gross, Margaret V.   *Personnel Interviewing.* New York: The Ronald Press Co., 1952.

Weiss, Carol H.   "Validity of Welfare Mothers' Interview Responses." *Public Opinion Quarterly,* vol. 32 (1968–69), pp. 622–33.

Weiss, D. J., and Davis, R. V.   "An Objective Validation of Factual Interview Data." *Journal of Applied Psychology,* vol. 44 (December 1960), pp. 381–85.

Whyte, William F.   "Interviewing for Organizational Research." *Human Organization,* vol. 12, no. 3 (Summer 1953), pp. 15–22.

———.   *Street Corner Society: The Social Structure of an Italian Slum.* Chicago: University of Chicago Press, 1943.

Wilkie, Charlotte H.   "A Study of Distortions in Recording Interviews." *Social Work,* vol. 8, no. 3 (July 1963), pp. 31–36.

Willingham, W. W., and Jones, M. B.   "On the Identification of Halo through Analysis of Variance." *Educational and Psychological Measurement,* vol. 18 (Summer 1958), pp. 403–7.

Wilson, Elmo C., and Armstrong, Lincoln.   "Interviewers and Interviewing in India." *International Social Science Journal,* vol. 15, no. 1 (1963), pp. 48–58.

Wiseman, Jacqueline P.   *Stations of the Lost,* Englewood Cliffs, N.J.: Prentice-Hall, 1970.

Womer, S., and Boyd, H. W., Jr.   "The Use of a Voice Recorder in the Selection and Training of Field Workers." *Public Opinion Quarterly,* vol. 15 (Summer 1951), pp. 358–63.

Wyatt, D. F., and Campbell, D. T.   "A Study of Interviewer Bias as Related to Interviewers' Expectations and Own Opinions." *International Journal of Opinion and Attitude Research,* vol. 4 (1950), pp. 77–83.

Young, Pauline V.   *Interviewing in Social Work.* New York: McGraw-Hill Book Co., 1935.

Zelan, J.   "Interviewing the Aged." *Public Opinion Quarterly,* vol. 33 (1969), pp. 420–24.

Zygmunt, Joseph F.   "The Role and Interrelationship of Symbolic and Structural Processes in the Development of a Sectarian Movement." Thesis, University of Chicago, 1960.

Index

Index

A

Aaron, Daniel, 115
Adams, J. S., 59
Alderfer, Clayton, 184
Alers, J. Oscar, 219
Allport, Gordon W., 34, 56
Altemeyer, Robert, 233
Altruism, as facilitator of communication, 126–27
Anonymity, 268–69
    and ethics, 158
    and field strategy, 268
Answers
    critically evaluating, 468–69
    structuring of, 353
Anticipating inhibitors and facilitators, 475–76
Assael, Henry, 309
Athey, K. R., 218
Attitudes
    negative
        cautious rigidity, 389
        condescending tone, 389
        forgetting previous responses, 388
        neglecting to probe, 388
    positive
        appreciation of respondent's efforts, 390
        critical analysis of response, 386
        interest in information received, 384
        nonjudgmental attitude, 383
    toward information received, 382
    toward interviewing task, 379

Attitudes—Cont.
    toward the respondent, 387
    and selection of interviewers, 224

B

Babbie, Earl R., 154, 329
Backstrom, Charles H., 301, 329
Bailar, Barbara A., 8
Bain, Robert K., 110, 218
Banks, G. P., 220
Barriers to communication; see Communication, inhibitors of
Becker, Howard S., 226–27, 359
Benjamin, Alfred, 81
Benney, Mark, 215
Bermosk, Loretta, 59, 81
Berreman, Gerald D., 154, 162
Berry, Fred C., 8
Bershoff, Donald, 21
Bias
    counterbalancing, 475
    and ethics, 147–49
    and leading questions, 358–64
    in recording responses, 226
    and validity of conclusions, 10–11
Biel, Alexander, 309
Bindman, Aaron, 215
Birdwhistle, R., 467
Blau, Peter M., 134
Blumer, Herbert, 119
Body motion; see Nonverbal communication
Bonilla, Frank, 166
Broad questions, values of, 350
Brunner, G. A., 310

581

Brymer, Richard A., 157
Bucher, Rue, 274
Burdock, E. I., 81
Burgess, E. W., 447

C

Cain, Leonard, 147
Campbell, D. T., 10
Cannell, Charles F., 81, 358
Cantril, Hadley, 131
Carmichael, L. S., 373
Cartwright, Ann, 311
Catharsis, as facilitator of communication, 129–30
Challenging the respondent, 457
Chronological confusion, as inhibitor of communication, 116–17
Chronological patterns; see Tactics
Clarification probe
    immediate, 427
    retrospective, 427
Clark, John P., 88
Coding, 511–13
Cognitive dissonance, 131
Comer, Ronald J., 222
Communication
    cognitive substructure, 96
    connotative versus denotative, 94–95
    facilitators of
        altruism, 126–27
        catharsis, 129–30
        detecting, 70
        expectations, 123–24
        extrinsic rewards, 133–34
        need for meaning, 131–32
        new experience, 128–29
        recognition, 125–26
        sympathetic understanding, 127–28
    inhibitors of, 104–5
        chronological confusion, 116–17
        competing time demands, 107
        detecting, 70
        ego threat, 108–11
        etiquette, 112–13
        forgetting, 115–16
        inferential confusion, 117–18
        trauma, 114–15
        unconscious behavior, 119
    nonverbal; see Nonverbal communication
    universe of discourse, 92–93
    verbal; see Techniques, verbal forms
Competing time demands, as inhibitor, 107
Confidentiality, 269
Contacting respondents, 202
Contacts, multiple, 184
Content analysis of interview, 511–13

Contexts, to
    arouse interest, 339
    communicate the question, 334
    define terms, 335
    discover unconscious factors, 343
    prevent falsification, 340
    provide spacial perspective, 336
    provide time perspective, 336
    reduce chronological confusion, 342
    reduce ego threat, 340
    reduce etiquette barrier, 341
    stimulate memory, 342
    supply criteria of judgment, 337
    supply facts, 337–38
    supply recognition, 339
    supply social-psychological perspective, 337
Contextual model, 85
Conversation, compared with interviewing, 50
Crutchfield, R. S., 95

D

Daniels, Arlene K., 164
Davis, John D., 59
Davitz, J. R., 375
Dean, Lois R., 360
Definition of the situation, 86, 220, 263
De Fleur, Lois B., 8
De Graer, Albert, 240
Denzin, Norman K., 40, 56
Dexter, Lewis A., 59, 81
Dohrenwend, Barbara Snell, 220, 359, 364
Duncan, Starkey, 375, 393

E

Ego threat, as inhibitor to communication, 108–11
Elkind, David, 20
Empathy
    defined, 41
    validity of, 41–43
    values and limitations of, 44–49
Engle, J. F., 274
Ethics of interviewing
    and anonymity, 158
    as conflicting loyalties, 142
    defined, 138
    and intentional bias, 147–49
    and interviewer responsibility, 149
    and suppression of findings, 142–43
Evaluation of information received, 468–69
Exline, Ralph, 373, 393
Expectations, as facilitator of communication, 123–24
Extrinsic rewards, as facilitator of communication, 133–34

F

Facial expression; see Nonverbal communication
Facilitators, anticipating, 475–76
Facilitators of communication; see Communication, facilitators of
Falsification
  dealing with, 456–58
  prevention of, 456
Fatigue
  of interviewer, 150–51
  of respondent, 185
Fein, Edith, 178
Fenlason, Anne, 59, 81
Festinger, Leon, 36, 56, 131, 165
Field, Joan B., 126
Field situations
  friendly versus hostile, 181–83
  open versus closed, 182–83
  polarized, 182
  single versus multiple contacts, 184–86
  types of, 181
Field strategy, steps in, 190
Filter (pivot) questions, 409
Fisher, Herbert, 226, 468
Forgetting, as inhibitor to communication, 115–16
Friedman, Robert, 187
Friendly territory, 181–83
Froelich, Robert, 59

G

Gans, Herbert, 36
Garfinkel, Harold, 96, 335
Gaylin, Williard, 145, 178
Giallombardo, Rose, 178
Gibson, F. K., 306
Glazer, Myron, 144, 160, 162
Gold, Martin, 20
Goldberg, G., 371, 393
Gorden, Raymond L., 150, 167, 232, 465
Gottschalk, Louis, 34, 56
Grey, David, 20
Griaule, Marcel, 232
Gross, N., 185, 240
Guest, Lester, 481
Guttman, Louis, 9

H

Haberman, P. W., 408
Hall, Edward T., 371, 393
Hannerz, Ulf, 36
Hariton, Theodore, 81
Hartmann, Elizabeth, 310
Heyns, Roger W., 3
Hildum, D. C., 430
Hill, William G., 187
Hills, Stuart, 312
Homans, George C., 126

Hostile territory, 181–83
Hughes, Helen McGill, 35, 56
Humphreys, Laud, 37, 159
Hyman, Herbert, 215, 473

I

Identification; see Empathy
Inferential confusion as inhibitor to communication, 117–18
Informal interviews, 271
Informal post-interview, 458
Informants, key; see Respondents, types of
Inhibitors, anticipating, 475–76
Inhibitors of communication; see Communication, inhibitors of
Interruption defined, 376
Interview(s)
  combined with questionnaire, 78–79
  compared with questionnaire, 75–76
  informal, 271
  objectives, becoming familiar with, 471
  objectives, discovery
    categories, to define, 67–68
    inhibitors and facilitators, to detect, 70–71
    problem, to focus, 67
    range of response, to determine, 68
    sequence of questions, to determine, 68–69
    special informants, to locate, 66
    special vocabularies, to detect, 70
  objectives, explanation of, 265
  objectives, measurement, 72–74
  schedule, 74
  schedule, examples of, 503–4
  scheduled, 62–65
  situation
    anonymity, providing, 268–69
    introductions, 263
    place, 249
    respondent selection, explaining the, 266–67
    sponsorship, 264–65
    structuring the, 263
    time, 253
  styles and objectives, 58–66
Interview guide, 74–75
  defined, 414
  preparation of, 413, 476–78
Interviewer(s)
  age of, 217
  anxiety, 483–84
  attitudes of, 224
  auxiliary role of, 229
  bias caused by, 215–27
  central role of, 231
  dress and grooming of, 221
  ethical responsibilities, 149
  ethnicity of, 218

Interviewer(s)—*Cont.*
  fatigue in, 150–51
  overt characteristics of, 215
  personality traits of, 222
  physical deviance, 222
  race of, 218
  responsibility
    to larger society, 142
    to research organization, 149
    to respondent, 153
  roles, 228, 237
  selection of, 213
  sex of, 216
  special knowledge, 227
  speech characteristics, 221
  tasks of, 91
Interviewing
  compared with conversation, 50
  compared with other data gathering, 33–37
  employees, 14, 17, 22, 24
  errors, 12
  exploratory; *see* Interview, objectives, discovery
  homosexuals, 159–60
  objectives of, 66, 90–91
  patients, 18–19
  performance cycle, 463–64
  practice, 478–80
  subjective aspect of, 525–27
  trends in, 3–4
  validity in; *see* Validity
Interviewing on
  academic freedom, 284
  American way of life, 508
  army training of recruits, 164–65
  auto accident, 16
  car-buyer motivation, 487
  crime, 19–20
  cross-cultural communication, 166–67
  delinquency, 13
  disasters, 342
  health records, 15
  layman's conception of science, 499
  parent-child conflicts, 367
  personnel turnover, 17
  prison life (war resisters), 145, 178
  vocational choice, 394, 443
Introducing interviewer, 263

J

Jacobson, Harold K., 20
Janofsky, Irene, 309
Jonsson, Erland, 20
Josephson, Eric, 178

K

Kahn, Robert L., 417, 441
Kastenbaum, R., 59

Katz, Daniel, 215
Kegeles, Stephen, 309
Key informants
  defined, 187
  securing cooperation of, 190–91
Keys, Ancel, 156
Kincaid, H. V., 272
Kinsey, Alfred C., 226, 359
Kloetzle, W. C., 20
Krause, Luise, 217
Kumar, Usha, 226

L

Langdon, Grace, 59, 82
Lansberger, Henry A., 146
Lead-in questions, 407
Leading questions, 357–64
  defined, 357
  effects of, 358–64
  forms of, 357–58
  values of, 360
Learning to interview
  by analyzing own interview, 480–85
  practice, 478–80
  subjective aspect of, 525–28
Ledvinka, James, 219
Leighton, Alexander, 225
Length of the interview and fatigue, 185
Leuthold, D. A., 308
Lewis, Oscar, 162, 240
Lie detector, 8, 88
Liebow, Elliot, 36
Listening to respondent, 464–65
Locating respondents, 190

M

Marquis, Kent, 334
Matarazzo, Joseph D., 374, 430
Measurement objectives, in interviewing, 72–73
Memory; *see* Forgetting, as inhibitor to communication
Merton, Robert K., 82
Milford, Nancy, 20
Miles, E., 228
Milgram, Stanley, 38
Mills, C. Wright, 95
Mood and pacing, 378
Moore, B. V., 16, 115
Motivating the respondent; *see* Communication, facilitators of
Multiple question, 483
Mutation probe, 427, 438

N

Narrow questions, values of, 352
National Opinion Research Center, 58

Need for meaning
    and cognitive dissonance, 131
    as facilitator of communication, 131–32
Neutral probe, 429
New experience, as facilitator of communi-
    cation, 128–29
Nonscheduled interview, 62–65
Nonverbal communication, 96–100,
    370–76
    chronemics, 372
    kinesics, 372–73
    modes of, 370–76
    paralinguistics, 374
    proxemics, 371
    silence, 376
Note-taking
    effects of, 272
    in informal interviews, 271
    probe notes, 272, 439
    in structured interviews, 271
    verbatim, 271

O

Objectives, becoming familiar with, 471
Observation of respondent, 466–67
Oldfield, R. C., 467
Opening question, 279
Orlans, Harold, 174

P

Paralinguistic communication, 374
Parker, Aileen, 470
Parsons, Talcott, 126
Participant-observation, 36–38
Pelz, Donald, 294
Personal documents, 34
Persuasion, 51–52
Pilisuk, Marc, 148
Pivot (filter) questions, 409
Paying respondents; see Extrinsic rewards,
    as facilitator of communication
Place of interview
    in maximizing facilitators, 252–53
    in minimizing inhibitors, 249–51
Planning the interview, 471
    strategy, 476
    techniques, 413, 476–78
Polansky, Norman A., 58, 108
Post-interview, 458–60
Probe, types of
    challenge, 457
    clarification, 427
    echo, 436, 484
    elaboration, 426
    elaboration versus clarification, 431
    encouragement, 426
    immediate versus retrospective, 431
    interpretive, 436
    mutation, 427, 438

Probe—Cont.
    neutral, 429
    recapitulation, 434
    reflective, 435
    silent, 426–28
    summary, 436
Probe notes
    defined, 272
    function of, 439
    how to take, 439, 479
    sample guide for, 490
Probing
    versus other tactics, 422
    topic control, 424
Purpose of the interview
    explaining to respondent, 265
    familiarizing oneself with, 471

Q

Questionnaire
    combined with interview, 78
    versus the interview, 75–77
Questionnaire format
    body, 320
    contingency questions, 322–23
    face sheet, 316
    general suggestions, 324–28
    question types, 320
    response cards, 322
    schematic questions, 324
Questions
    broad, value of, 350
    contexts, 334–44
    lead-in, 407
    leading, 357–64
        effects of, 358
        forms of, 357
    multiple, 483
    narrow, value of, 352
    opening, 279
    pivot (filter), 409
    rewording of, 483
    scope of, 347
    sequence of, 68–9, 415–18
    transitions between, 410–11
    vocabulary used, 345

R

Random sample of respondents, 296
Rapport; see Empathy
Recognition, as facilitator of communica-
    tion, 125–26
Recording; see Note-taking; Probe notes;
    and Tape recorder
Reece, M., 474
Reflective probe, 435
Refusals, 192–93, 310
Reiss, Albert J., 37
Reliability, 5–6

Remembering responses, 467–68
Resistance by respondent, 445–58
Respondents
    accessibility of, 202
    active-passive, 199
    insider-outsider, 200
    locating and contacting, 190
    mobile-stabile, 202
    selection of, 196
    selection of, explaining, 266–67
    status of, 198
    types of, 187
        key informants, 188, 190–91
        representative, 188
        special, 188
Response categories, 67–68
Responses
    critical evaluation of, 481
    range of, 68
    structuring of, 353
Rewording question, 483
Rice, Stuart A., 472
Rich, J., 59
Richardson, Stephan A., 359, 366, 437, 442
Ritual in conversation, 53–54
Rogers, Carl, 435
Role of interviewer, 228
    auxiliary roles, 229
    dimensions of, 231
        ingroup-outgroup, 232
        insider-outsider, 232, 236
        subordinate-superordinate, 237
    as strategy, 213
Role-taking, nature of, 228
Rosenthal, Robert, 472
Rosten, Leo, 375
Roth, Julius, 150
Roy, Donald F., 89

S

Sampling element, 292
Sampling strategies, 296
    block listing, 300
    multistage, 299
    respondent selection chart, 302
    simple random, 296
    stratified, 303
    systematic, 297
Sapir, Edward, 119
Schatzman, Leonard, 69
Scheduled interview
    contrasted with nonscheduled, 62–65
    highly structured, 503–4
Scheflen, A. E., 393
Schuman, Howard, 219
Schutz, Alfred, 115
Schwab, P. P., 9
Scope of the question, 347–48
Scott, Marvin B., 112

Scott, William A., 108
Selecting respondents, 196
Selecting respondents, explaining, 266
Sequence of questions, 68–69
    funnel, 415
    inverted funnel, 417
Sequence of respondents, 257
Sequence of subtopics, 403
Shaw, Clifford R., 127
Sherwood, Hugh C., 59, 82
Shuman, H., 87
Silence
    defined as a technique, 376
    effects of, 378
Silent probe
    as minimum topic control, 426
    values of, 428
Simmel, Georg, 373
Sjoberg, Gideon, 174
Skills
    basic to interviewing, 464–70
    procedure for learning, 470
Smith, H. L., 466
Snell, Barbara, 310
Social exchange theory, 134
Sponsorship, 264–65
Steinkamp, Stanley, 8
Steinmetz, L., 59, 82
Stember, C. H., 475
Strategy; see also, Field situations and Sampling strategies
    analysis of own, 481
    assumptions underlying, 180
    defined, 177
    place of interview, 249–53
    planning, 476
    reviewed, 519
    time, 253–58
Strauss, Anselm, 69
Style
    interviewing, dimensions of, 60–66
    scheduled versus nonscheduled, 62–65
    standardized versus nonstandardized, 61
Sudman, Seymour, 307
Surveys (sample)
    gaining access to respondent, 309
    mailed questionnaire, 304
    modes of, 304
    personally administered questionnaire, 306
    publicity, 312
    refusal rate, 310
        and forms of resistance, 315
        and interviewer characteristics, 312
        and time of interview, 312–13
    telephone versus face-to-face, 307
    types of, 291
        cohort studies, 293
        longitudinal, 293–95

Surveys (sample)—*Cont.*
  types of—*Cont.*
    panel studies, 294
    trend studies, 293
Sutherland, E. H., 126
Sympathetic understanding, as facilitator
    of communication, 127–28

T

Tactics
  advance planning of, 401
  analysis of own, 482–85
  anonymity, 268–69
  defined, 401
  funnel sequence, 415–17
  inverted funnel sequence, 417–20
  lead-in questions, 407
  meeting falsification, 456–58
  meeting resistance, 445–58
  order of topics, 403
  pivot question, 409
  post-interview, 458–60
  probing, 422; *see also,* Probe, types of
  reviewed, 523–24
  transitions, 410–11
Taking notes; *see* Note-taking *and* Probe
    notes
Tape recorder
  effects of, 273
  as learning device, 474–79
  transcribing, 276–78
Tape recording, transcribing time of,
    278–79
Techniques
  analysis of own, 482–85
  defined, 333
  error in, 483
  nonverbal forms, 370–98
    attitude
      critical analysis, 386
      toward information, 382
      nonjudgmental, 383
      toward respondent, 387
      toward task, 379
    silence, 376
  reviewed, 521–22
  verbal forms
    challenging respondent, 457
    contexts to communicate the question,
      334–39
    contexts to motivate the respondent,
      339–45
    leading questions, 357–64.
    scope, 347
    selecting vocabulary, 345
    structure of answer, 353
    versus tactics, 333

Thomas, Dorothy S., 235
Time, effects on interview, 253–58
Topic control, types of; *see* Probe, types of
Topic sequence, 403
  adjusting to the respondent, 406–7
  effects of, 404
  introducing new, 407
Transcribing
  procedure for, 267–78
  time required for, 278–79
Transitions between topics, 410–11
Trauma
  as inhibitor to communication, 114–15
  and time, 256–57
Triadic relationship, 87
Triangulation, 40
Tudor, Thomas G., 356, 366
Turner, David, 59

U

Unconscious behavior, as inhibitor to com-
    munication, 119
Universe of discourse, 92–93
  as a special vocabulary, 78
  and wording the question, 345
Unobtrusive measures, 38

V

Validity
  and barriers to communication; *see*
    Communication, inhibitors of
  and interviewing, 6–12
  tests of, 7–10
van den Berghe, Pierre L., 139
Vaughan, Ted R., 140
Verbal forms, as technique, 333
Verbatim notes, 271
Vocabulary in the question, 345
Volkart, Edmund H., 127
Vonderacek, Fred, 423

W

Ware, J. R., 474
Weaver, T., 344, 366
Webb, Eugene J., 38, 57
Weiss, Carol H., 8
Weller, L., 219
Whyte, William F., 55, 235
Wilkie, Charlotte H., 275
Wolleat, Patricia, 470
Womer, S., 274
Wyatt, D. F., 473

Z

Zelan, J., 20
Zygmunt, Joseph F., 236

This book is set in 10 and 9 point Caledonia, leaded 2 points. Part numbers and chapter numbers are 16 and 30 point Gael italic. Part titles are 16 point Gael and chapter titles are 16 point Gael italic. The size of the type page is 27 × 45½ picas.